Computational Biology

Computational Biology

Editor: Daniel McGuire

www.callistoreference.com

Callisto Reference,
118-35 Queens Blvd., Suite 400,
Forest Hills, NY 11375, USA

Visit us on the World Wide Web at:
www.callistoreference.com

ISBN: 978-1-63239-806-2 (Hardback)

Cataloging-in-publication Data

Computational biology / edited by Daniel McGuire.
    p. cm.
Includes bibliographical references and index.
ISBN 978-1-63239-806-2
1. Computational biology. 2. Genetics--Data processing. 3. Bioinformatics. 4. Genomics. I. McGuire, Daniel.
QH324.2 .C66 2017
572.8--dc23

Table of Contents

Permissions

List of Contributors

Index

Preface

In order to study the biological, behavioral and the social systems, the development and application of data analytical and theoretical methods of mathematics modeling and computational simulations are used. This field of study is called computational biology. It is considered to be an important element for analyzing informatics processes of various biological systems. This book is a valuable compilation of topics, ranging from the basic to the most complex advancements in the field of computational biology. From theories to research to practical applications, case studies related to all contemporary topics of relevance to this field have been included in this book. It aims to provide an elaborate understanding of the field. Those in search of information to further their knowledge will be greatly assisted by this book. It will serve as a resource guide for researchers, experts, academicians and students engaged in the field of computational biology at various levels.

Every book is a source of knowledge and this one is no exception. The idea that led to the conceptualization of this book was the fact that the world is advancing rapidly; which makes it crucial to document the progress in every field. I am aware that a lot of data is already available, yet, there is a lot more to learn. Hence, I accepted the responsibility of editing this book and contributing my knowledge to the community.

While editing this book, I had multiple visions for it. Then I finally narrowed down to make every chapter a sole standing text explaining a particular topic, so that they can be used independently. However, the umbrella subject sinews them into a common theme. This makes the book a unique platform of knowledge.

I would like to give the major credit of this book to the experts from every corner of the world, who took the time to share their expertise with us. Also, I owe the completion of this book to the never-ending support of my family, who supported me throughout the project.

Editor

Ensemble-Based Network Aggregation Improves the Accuracy of Gene Network Reconstruction

Rui Zhong[1][9], **Jeffrey D. Allen**[1,2][9], **Guanghua Xiao**[1], **Yang Xie**[1,2]*

1 Quantitative Biomedical Research Center, Department of Clinical Sciences, University of Texas Southwestern Medical Center, Dallas, Texas, United States of America,
2 Harold C. Simmons Comprehensive Cancer Center, University of Texas Southwestern Medical Center, Dallas, Texas, United States of America

Abstract

Reverse engineering approaches to constructing gene regulatory networks (GRNs) based on genome-wide mRNA expression data have led to significant biological findings, such as the discovery of novel drug targets. However, the reliability of the reconstructed GRNs needs to be improved. Here, we propose an ensemble-based network aggregation approach to improving the accuracy of network topologies constructed from mRNA expression data. To evaluate the performances of different approaches, we created dozens of simulated networks from combinations of gene-set sizes and sample sizes and also tested our methods on three *Escherichia coli* datasets. We demonstrate that the ensemble-based network aggregation approach can be used to effectively integrate GRNs constructed from different studies – producing more accurate networks. We also apply this approach to building a network from epithelial mesenchymal transition (EMT) signature microarray data and identify hub genes that might be potential drug targets. The R code used to perform all of the analyses is available in an R package entitled "ENA", accessible on CRAN (http://cran.r-project.org/web/packages/ENA/).

Editor: Alberto de la Fuente, Leibniz-Institute for Farm Animal Biology (FBN), Germany

Funding: This work was supported by NIH grants 5R01CA152301 and 1R01CA172211, and Cancer Prevention Research Institute of Texas award RP101251. The funders had no role in study design, data collection and analysis, decision to publish, or preparation of the manuscript.

Competing Interests: The authors have declared that no competing interests exist.

* Email: Yang.Xie@utsouthwestern.edu

[9] These authors contributed equally to this work.

Introduction

With the advent of high-throughput technologies such as microarrays, next generation sequencing, and other state-of-the-art techniques, huge datasets have been generated in a variety of contexts (*e.g.*, cancer and aging) in order to identify novel biomarkers and drug targets [1]. However, the utility and interpretation of those collected data remains challenging and needs to be improved. Recently, reconstructions of gene regulatory networks (GRNs) from high-throughput data have been widely used to identify novel drug targets or therapeutic compounds [1–4]. GRNs provide new information regarding gene-gene interactions and how they work in networks to regulate cellular functions, allowing for a systematic understanding of the molecular and cellular mechanisms underlying specific biological functions and processes [5–10]. For GRNs in particular, genes that have many interactions with other genes (called "hub genes") are likely to be "drivers" of disease status, based on their GRN regulatory roles. An analysis of hub genes is thus a promising approach for identifying key tumorigenic genes for both basic and clinical research [11–15].

Although accurate reconstruction of GRNs has proven valuable to a myriad of areas throughout biomedical research, the method remains only moderately satisfactory [7–10]. Researchers have previously used approaches such as Bayesian Network- [16,17], Correlation- [18], and Partial-Correlation-based approaches [19,20], all of which have demonstrated various strengths and weaknesses under different biological/simulation settings, with no one method excelling under all conditions [21]. Additionally, leveraging gene expression data from multiple datasets to construct gene networks is often difficult, due to discrepancies in microarray platform selection as well as in normalization and data processing techniques [22–24]. In this study, we propose an Ensemble-based Network Aggregation (ENA) approach to integrate gene networks derived from different methods and datasets, to improve the accuracy of network inference.

For the construction of our ENA, we used a non-parametric, inverse-rank-product method to combine networks reconstructed from the same set of genes. The rank-product method, introduced by Breitling et al [21,25,26], is effective for detecting differentially expressed genes in microarray studies. Because the rank-product method is both powerful and computationally efficient, it has now been extended for use in other fields, such as RNAi screening [27] and proteomics [28]. Additionally, this method can be directly related to linear rank statistics [29]. In this study, we show three ways to leverage this approach to generate ensemble-based networks: 1) samples in a dataset can be "bootstrapped" to reconstruct multiple networks out of a single original dataset using a single reconstruction method, which can then be aggregated into a more accurate and reproducible network; 2) networks produced by various reconstruction methods can be aggregated into a single network that is more accurate than the network provided by any individual method; and 3) networks reconstructed from different studies that contain the same genes can be combined into a single, more accurate network, despite differences in platforms or normalization techniques. Because this approach requires few resources, it can be applied efficiently to dozens or hundreds of networks reconstructed on the same set of genes. We show here that this approach has the ability to improve the accuracy of GRN reconstruction in all three of the above-described applications, based on simulated gene expression data as well as on *Escherichia coli* (*E. coli*) datasets [30–33].

An important application of network reconstruction is to identify hub genes in a network that might be biologically and pharmaceutically interesting. When we applied ENA to microarray data that was previously used to delineate an epithelial-mesenchymal transition (EMT) signature [34], we built a network for the identification of hub genes that had been experimentally validated to be EMT-relevant, thus representing potential drug targets. Though our demonstration is focused on microarray data for consistency purposes, ENA should be easily implemented in the analysis pipeline of next-generation sequencing (NGS) data, such as RNA-Seq. Cutting-edge technology enables the simultaneous measurement of millions of cellular data points and sheds light on a brand-new pattern in drug discovery, where medication is viewed in the context of pathways and networks rather than individual proteins or genes [1]. In the near future, in combination with patient-specific genomic profile and drug-target interaction knowledge, GRNs could be used to facilitate both the prediction and treatment of personalized therapy [2].

Materials and Methods

Overview of the inverse-rank-product network aggregation approach

Reconstructed gene networks are often returned as a weighted undirected graph $G = (N, \Omega)$, where G is a reconstructed graph, $N = \{1, ..., n\}$ is the set of vertices (genes) in the graph, and $\Omega = [\omega_{ij}]_{i,j \in N}$ is referred to as the adjacency matrix, in which ω_{ij} represents the confidence score of the interaction between genes i and j. A larger (absolute) value of ω_{ij} indicates a stronger interaction or higher confidence in the edge between genes i and j, while $\omega_{ij} = 0$ indicates no interaction or conditional independence between genes i and j. Some techniques, such as Sparse PArtial Correlation Estimation (SPACE) [19], return a sparse matrix in which many of the possible interactions are 0; other techniques return complete graphs in which all edges are assigned non-zero weightings. Additionally, the distribution of ω_i can vary drastically among reconstruction techniques. For this reason, aggregating networks that were reconstructed using different techniques or different datasets is challenging. However, the rank-based method offers a non-parametric approach that does not depend on the actual distribution of scores of edges derived from different methods [35]. In this study, we used a rank-product method to combine networks to overcome the problem of different distributions observed in this approach.

Specifically, suppose $G = \{G^k\}$ is a set of networks constructed on the same set of genes N, where $k = \{1, ..., K\}$ is the index of a particular network. For each single network $G^k = (N, \Omega^k)$, we calculate r_{ij}^k, the rank of ω_{ij}^k for $\{i, j \in N$ and $i < j\}$. Since the adjacency matrix Ω of an undirected graph is symmetric, we only need to calculate the rank of the $N * (N-1)/2$ elements in ω_{ij}, constituting the lower triangle (i<j) of Ω. In this study, we assign the lower rank to the higher confidence interaction. For example, the interaction with the highest confidence will have rank 1. This operation is performed on each individual graph G^k independently. After the rank of r_{ij}^k has been computed for each network G^k, we calculate the rank of a particular edge between genes i and j in the aggregated network by taking the product of the ranks of

the same edge across all networks in G, according to: $\tilde{r}_{ij} = \prod_{k=1}^{K} r_{ij}^k$. This function is iterated over all possible edges to construct the aggregated network $\tilde{G} = (N, \tilde{r}_{ij})$, in which the confidence scores of the edges in the new network are based on the aforementioned rank-product calculation.

This algorithm can be efficiently applied to large networks with many reconstructed networks in G. The complexity of the algorithm is that $O(K \cdot |N| \log(|N|))$, as $\frac{|N|^2 - |N|}{2} = O(N^2)$ elements must be sorted for each network in G^k.

Three applications of our ENA approach

The initial application was to leverage the rank-product method to "bootstrap" samples. Each time, we constructed the gene network using a randomly selected subset of the available samples. By repeating this process B times, we created a set G consisting of B graphs, each reconstructed using only randomly selected bootstrap samples in the dataset. For example, here is the procedure to generate the bootstrapping network from a microarray dataset designated MD:

$$MD \xrightarrow{Bootstrap} \begin{cases} MD^1 \to G^1 = \{N, \Omega^1\} \to r_{ij}^1 \text{ (for } 1 \le i < j \le n) \searrow \\ \vdots \qquad \vdots \qquad \vdots \qquad \to \text{RankProduct} \to \tilde{G} \\ MD^B \to G^B = \{N, \Omega^B\} \to r_{ij}^B \text{ (for } 1 \le i < j \le n) \nearrow \end{cases}$$

Of course, this bootstrapping procedure inflates the computational complexity of GRN reconstruction by several orders of magnitude, as GRNs must be reconstructed B times rather than just once. Because each graph in G can be reconstructed independently, it is possible to take advantage of the "parallelizability" of these simulations by utilizing multiple cores or computers, as we discuss below. Note also that the complexity of GRN reconstruction does scale on the order of samples included, so that each permuted GRN can be constructed slightly more quickly than a single global GRN. For the reconstruction techniques employed in this study, however, the performance did not vary greatly based on the number of samples included.

The second application of the rank-product network merging method was to reconstruct an aggregated GRN, based on the output of multiple different reconstruction techniques. We have observed that reconstruction techniques perform differently based on different simulation settings [21], with no one method outperforming the others on all metrics. Thus, we were interested to see whether or not merging these GRNs would improve performance. In this application, the set of graphs G consist of one graph per network reconstruction technique employed. In our analysis, we leveraged GeneNet [20], Weighted Correlation Network Analysis (WGCNA) [18], and SPACE, creating a set of three graphs which could then be aggregated. GeneNet and SPACE are partial-correlation-based inference algorithms. GeneNet uses the Moore-Penrose pseudoinverse [36] and bootstrapping to estimate the concentration matrix. The SPACE algorithm creates a regression problem when trying to estimate the concentration matrix and then optimizes the results with a symmetric constraint and an L1 penalization, while WGCNA is a correlation-based approach that can identify sub-networks using hierarchical clustering. Conceptually, the aggregated graph should place higher confidence on those edges that consistently rank highly across the three methods and lower confidence on those edges that ranked highly in only one graph. The following procedure is used to derive the ensemble network, based on M different methods within the same dataset MD:

$$MD \begin{cases} \xrightarrow{\text{method1}} G^1 = \{N, \Omega^1\} \rightarrow r_{ij}^1 \text{ (for } 1 \le i < j \le n) \searrow \\ \vdots \qquad \vdots \qquad \vdots \qquad \rightarrow \text{RankProduct} \rightarrow \tilde{G} \\ \xrightarrow{\text{method}M} G^M = \{N, \Omega^M\} \rightarrow r_{ij}^M \text{ (for } 1 \le i < j \le n) \nearrow \end{cases}$$

The final application evaluated in this study was in the merging of networks constructed from different datasets. Historically, gene expression datasets have been collected from various sites on different microarray platforms with different procedures for tissue collection, which creates incompatibilities and difficulties when performing analyses on data from different datasets simultaneously. Because the rank-product method makes no assumptions about the distribution of the data at any point, we employ it to combine GRNs produced from different datasets, yielding a single aggregated GRN which aims to capture the consistencies in network topology from the GRNs produced on different datasets. We thus derive the aggregated network from datasets MD^1, MD^2.... MD^D as follows:

$$\begin{array}{ccccc} MD^1 & \rightarrow & G^1 = \{N, \Omega^1\} & \rightarrow & r_{ij}^1 \text{ (for } 1 \le i < j \le n) \searrow \\ \vdots & & \vdots & & \vdots \qquad \rightarrow \text{RankProduct} \rightarrow \tilde{G} \\ MD^D & \rightarrow & G^D = \{N, \Omega^D\} & \rightarrow & r_{ij}^D \text{ (for } 1 \le i < j \le n) \nearrow \end{array}$$

Software

The code used to bootstrap samples and aggregate the resultant networks was written in the R programming language. We created an R Package entitled "ENA" and made it available on CRAN (http://cran.r-project.org/web/packages/ENA/index.html), from which the compiled binaries, as well as all original source code, are also available for download.

Because of the parallelization opportunities in this algorithm, we ensured that our software would be able to distribute the bootstrapping process across multiple cores and multiple nodes using MPI [37]. Thus, if 150 CPU cores were available simultaneously, a bootstrapping of 150 samples could run in approximately the same amount of wall-clock time as a single reconstruction using all the samples. The ENA package includes robust documentation and (optionally) leverages the RMPI package to allow for parallel execution of the bootstrapping simulations, where such a computational infrastructure is available.

Additionally, we leveraged the Git revision control system via GitHub (http://github.com) to control not only the R code developed for the ENA package, but also all code, reports, and data used in the aforementioned simulations and reconstruction techniques; all of this code is freely available at https://github.com/QBRC/ENA-Research. All the data analysis code used to generate the results in this study was compiled into a single report and can be reproduced easily using the knitr R package [38,39]. Due to the computational complexity involved in reconstructing this quantity of gene regulatory networks, the execution may take some time to analyze larger networks if the process is not distributed across a large computing cluster.

Reproducibility

Our analysis code and results were structured in reproducible reports, which are publicly available at https://github.com/ QBRC/ENA-Research. The results in this study can be regenerated by a simple mouse click to make everything transparent to researchers.

Results

Simulation

We first tested the ENA methods on a wide array of simulated datasets. We simulated the gene expression datasets based on previously observed protein-protein interaction networks [40,41] from the human protein reference database (HPRD), while the expression data were simulated from conditional normal distributions [42]. We extracted five different network sizes in an approximately scale-free topology: 17 genes with 20 connections, 44 genes with 57 connections, 83 genes with 114 connections, 231 genes with 311 connections, or 612 genes with 911 connections by varying the number of publications required for each connection. For example, if we required each connection to be supported by at least 7 publications (the most reliable connections), it resulted in a very small network with 17 connections; while if we required each connection to be supported by at least 3 publications, it led to a very large network with 911 connections. For each network size, we simulated datasets with differing numbers of samples (microarrays): 20, 50, 100, 200, 500, and 1,000. Finally, we varied the noise by setting the standard deviation of the expression values to 0.25, 0.5, 1.0, or 1.5. In total, we generated 120 datasets to cover all possible arrangements of the above variables.

To test the effect of integrating networks derived from different datasets, we generated three different datasets of 200 samples each from the 231-gene networks with noise values (standard deviation of the distribution of gene expression) of 0.25, 1, and 2. We used the methods described above to reconstruct three networks (one from each dataset) and then aggregated those networks. For comparison, we also combined all three datasets into a single dataset containing these 600 samples and then reconstructed a single network from this larger dataset.

The performance of methods in this setting can be represented by a Receiver Operating Characteristic (ROC) Curve, which plots the True Positive Rate against the False Positive Rate, demonstrating the performance of the method at all relevant edge confidence score thresholds. The performance of a method can be quantified by calculating the Area Under the ROC Curve (AUC). The greater the AUC, the better the performance of the method represented. A perfect reconstruction would have an AUC of 1, while a random guess would obtain an AUC of 0.5. An alternative approach to evaluating gene regulatory network reconstruction is the Area Under the Precision Recall curve (AUPR). In a precision recall curve, recall (also known as sensitivity) is plotted against precision (positive predictive value).

ENA of bootstrapping samples

We found that bootstrapping samples can increase the accuracy of network inference. In our study, we randomly selected 70% of all samples and rebuilt networks and repeated the abovementioned process more than 100 times for each dataset to get the bootstrapping results. For example, the networks reconstructed from the dataset on the 231-gene network with a noise value of 0.25 can be compared to demonstrate variations in performance (Figures 1 and 2).

Figure 1 (left) shows that by bootstrapping samples using the SPACE algorithm, the AUC of the reconstructed network can improve from 0.748 to 0.816. In order to evaluate the precision of ENA, we also plotted the Precision-Recall Curve (Figure 1, right); the area under the precision-recall curve improved from 0.249 to

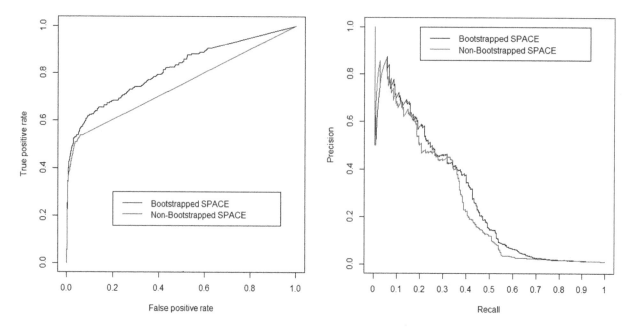

Figure 1. Receiver Operating Characteristic (ROC) curves and the Precision Recall Curve both demonstrate the performance of the SPACE algorithm on the 231-gene network with 20 samples and a noise value of 0.25 when performing a single iteration (*i.e.*, "non-bootstrapped") or bootstrapping the dataset using the Ensemble Network Aggregation approach. In this case, the Area Under the ROC Curve (AUC) of the non-bootstrapped SPACE method was 0.748, while that of the bootstrapped SPACE method was 0.816. The Area Under the Precision-Recall (AUPR) curve also improves from 0.249 (SPACE) to 0.273 (bootstrapping).

0.273. Figure 2 shows the degree of AUC improvement with each iteration of bootstrapping in SPACE, WGCNA and GeneNet with sample sizes of 20, 50 and 100 (left, middle and right panels). As shown in this figure, the bootstrapping method increases the performance of SPACE substantially, improves GeneNet slightly (when the number of microarrays is small), but does not noticeably improve the performance of WGCNA. The AUC improvements for different sample sizes and different network sizes are plotted in Figures S1–S4 in File S1. From these figures, we can see that SPACE benefits from bootstrapping in 80% of all simulated networks and in 89% of "large" network simulations. Figure 3 shows the average performance increase achieved by bootstrapping SPACE on different network sizes. The improvement increases as the network size increases. Based on this evidence, we suggest employing the bootstrapping approach when using the SPACE algorithm, but not when using the others evaluated in this study.

ENA of different methods

Aside from optimizing individual reconstruction techniques, we found that combining different network reconstruction techniques that were executed on the same dataset also has the power to significantly improve the accuracy of the reconstructed networks. Using the dataset from the 83-gene network with 200 samples and a noise value of 0.25, we evaluated the comparative performance of each reconstruction technique, as well as that of the aggregated network. Figure 4 shows that the aggregated network outperformed all of the individual constituent reconstruction techniques.

We also observed this trend to hold true across most of the datasets (Figure S5 and Figure S6 in File S1) that we tested: the aggregated method typically outperformed any single reconstruction technique. This is especially beneficial in scenarios in which the top-performing individual network reconstruction technique

may vary based on the context, *e.g.*, some methods perform well on larger networks, while others excel in datasets containing few samples. Thus, to have an aggregation technique that consistently outperforms or matches the best performing individual method eliminates the need to choose a single reconstruction technique based on the context.

In addition, we compared our method with the method used in Marbach et al. The result (Figure S8 in File S1) indicates the proposed ENA method performs better in the simulation settings.

ENA of different datasets

Finally, we found the ENA approach to work very well when attempting to integrate various datasets, especially among heterogeneous datasets containing different distributions of expression data. After generating three datasets from the 231-gene network, each with 200 samples and noise values of 0.25, 1, and 2, we reconstructed each network using bootstrapped SPACE, GeneNet, and WGCNA, and then aggregated the resultant networks into a single network for each of the three datasets. We then used the ENA approach to consolidate these three networks into a single network representing the underlying network behind the three distinct datasets. We also compared this approach to the alternative of simply merging all three datasets into a single 600-sample dataset and using the same approach to reconstruct a single network. As shown in Figure 5, the proposed ENA approach outperformed the alternative approach of simply combining the expression data into a single dataset. Reconstructing on each dataset independently produced AUCs of 0.96, 0.96, and 0.89 from noise values of 0.25, 1, and 2, respectively. "Naïvely" merging the datasets by combining them into one large dataset yielded an AUC of 0.96. The network aggregation approach, however, yielded the best performance, with an AUC of 0.98.

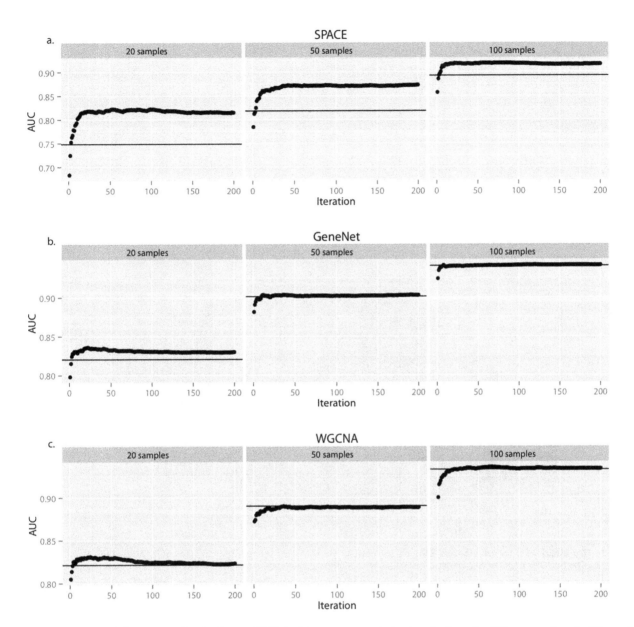

Figure 2. Comparison of the Area Under the Curves (AUCs) of the re-constructed networks from the 231-gene network with a noise value of 0.25 and different sample sizes (20, 50 or 100) for SPACE (a.), GeneNet (b.), and WGCNA (c.). In these plots, the y-axis shows the performance of the reconstructed network, measured by the AUCs; a horizontal line is drawn to represent the AUC of the non-bootstrapped reconstruction (a single reconstruction using all available samples). The x-axis represents the number of iterations in the bootstrapping process. Points below the horizontal line represent a loss in accuracy of the reconstructed networks, and points above the horizontal line represent a gain of AUC (*i.e.*, an increase in model performance).

Evaluating ENA approach in *E. coli* datasets

We then tested the ENA approach on three *Escherichia coli* (*E. coli*) datasets: 1) the Many Microbe Microarrays Database ("M3D") [30] containing 907 microarrays measured under 466 experimental conditions using Affymetrix GeneChip *E. coli* Genome arrays; 2) the second dataset ("Str") of expression data from laboratory evolution of *E. coli* on lactate or glycerol (GSE33147) [31], which contains 96 microarrays measured under laboratory adaptive evolution experiments using Affymetrix E. coli Antisense Genome Arrays; and 3) the third dataset [32,33] ("BC") containing 217 arrays measuring the transcriptional response of *E. coli* to different perturbations and stresses, such as drug treatments, UV treatments and heat shock. The RegulonDB database [43,44],

which contains the largest and best-known information on transcriptional regulation in *E. coli*, was thus used as a "gold standard" to evaluate the accuracy of the variously constructed networks.

We were able to obtain similarly positive results by employing these approaches on the *E. coli* data (Figure 6). Bootstrapping and aggregating the three methods on each dataset independently produced AUCs of 0.574, 0.616, and 0.599 for the BC, Str, and MD3 datasets respectively. By merging the three networks produced on each dataset using ENA, we were able to produce a network with an AUC of 0.655, larger than the AUC of any network produced by any of the datasets independently. Because the performance of ENA in the real dataset was evaluated based on our current biological knowledge, which may only be a partial

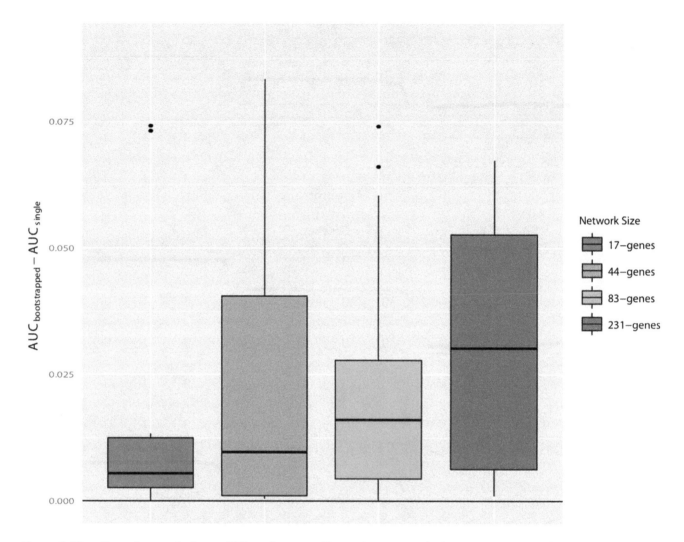

Figure 3. The effect of network size on ENA performance. The y-axis represents the improvement in AUC of the bootstrapped SPACE networks vs. the non-bootstrapped SPACE networks. Different bars represent different sizes of networks in the simulation study.

truth, the overall network reconstruction accuracy observed in the real dataset was much lower than those in the simulated datasets, where the full truth was known. On the other hand, simulated data might also partially reflect the true situation by simplifying aspects of an over-complicated biological process. However, the ENA approach consistently improved the network reconstruction accuracy in both simulated and real datasets.

Network reconstruction via ENA to identify potential drug targets

Network reconstruction of gene expression data helps identify hub genes that might be novel drug targets because of their role in engaging multiple molecules, a process that has been used to identify gene sets predictive of benefit for adjuvant chemotherapy in non-small-cell lung cancer [13]. Here we applied ENA to a dataset consisting of 76 genes from 54 non-small-cell lung cancer (NSCLC) cell lines that were previously identified to comprise an epithelial-mesenchymal transition (EMT) "signature" for NSCLC [34]. This signature consisted of genes whose expressions were either positively or negatively correlated with at least 1 of 4 putative EMT markers, including E-cadherin (*CDH1*), vimentin

(*VIM*), N-cadherin (*CDH2*) and/or fibronectin 1 (*FN1*), and followed a bimodal distribution pattern across the cell lines [34].

Overall, we attempted to identify hub genes clinically interesting for NSCLC treatment. We thus employed multiple methods to build GRN networks and combined them via ENA. As shown in Figure 7, we identified three major nodes. Of these, *ZEB1*, which had the highest degree in the resulting ENA network, is a well-known EMT activator and tumor promoter that represses stemness-inhibiting microRNAs [45] and mediates the loss of E-cadherin expression to allow cell detachment [46]. *MARVELD3* is known as a tight junction molecule and has been shown to be downregulated during Snail-induced EMT [47]. Finally, *EPHA1*, the first member of the erythropoietin-producing hepatocellular (Eph) family of receptor tyrosine kinases, was recently shown to potentially play a role in carcinogenesis and the progression of several cancer types [48]. *EPHA1* is also frequently mutated in NSCLC patients, along with other known "driver" mutations [49].

Discussion

The ability to aggregate networks using the rank-product merging approach has proven to be a valuable contribution in

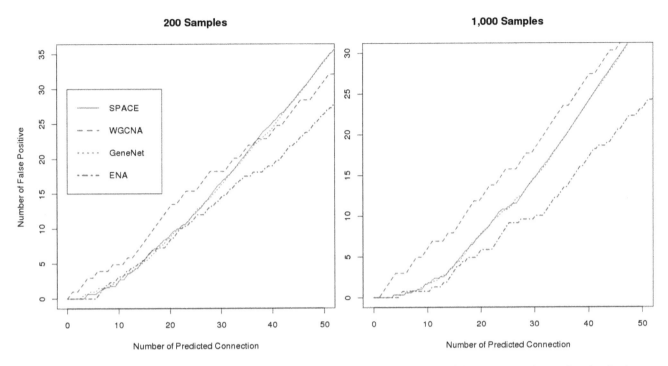

200 Samples   **1,000 Samples**

Figure 4. The performance in aggregating different methods. A comparison of the accuracy of the reconstructed networks using the datasets containing 200 samples (left) and 1,000 samples (right) from the 83-gene network with a noise value of 0.25. As can be seen here, the ensemble network aggregation approach performs better than any of the other individual techniques on these two networks.

reconstructing gene regulatory networks – and likely in other fields, as well. By bootstrapping a single dataset using a single approach such as SPACE, we were able to significantly improve the performance of the algorithm. By aggregating the networks produced by different reconstruction techniques on a single dataset, we were able to consistently match or outperform the

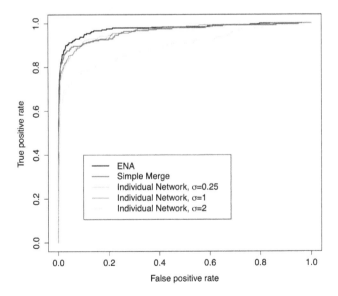

Figure 5. The ROC curves of different approaches to reconstruct the gene network based on three simulated datasets. The ENA approach outperformed the alternative approach of simply combining the expression into a single dataset and individual network with increasing noise of 0.25, 1, and 2. AUCs of all five approaches are 0.98, 0.96, 0.96, 0.96, and 0.89 respectively.

best-performing technique for that dataset, regardless of fluctuations in the performance of any one algorithm. By aggregating networks constructed independently on different datasets capturing similar biological environments, we were able to reconstruct the network more accurately than would be possible using any one dataset alone. So far, the study of integration of gene regulatory networks has been continuously advancing. Both Marbach D. et al. 2012 [50] and Hase T. et al. 2013 [51] have devised methods for integrating gene regulatory networks. The former is based on integration through rescoring gene-gene interaction according to average ranks across multiple methods, while the latter is focused on combining the confidence of each gene-gene interaction by multiple algorithms through leveraging the diversity of the different techniques. ENA is able to integrate networks from multiple algorithms. In addition, ENA performs bootstrapping within single dataset and also takes advantage of integrating multiple datasets to improve the performance. In this study, we showed that when integrating bootstrapped samples, different algorithms and data sets could achieve the best performance (Figure 6).

It is likely that SPACE was the only method to show consistent and significant improvement from bootstrapping because the SPACE algorithm models gene regulation using linear regression; as a result, the network construction problem is converted to a straightforward variable selection problem. In SPACE, the variable selection problem is solved by sparse regression techniques with a symmetric constraint. By solving all the regression models simultaneously, SPACE attempts to accrue the globally optimized results. However, due to the instability in variable selection [52] caused by collinearity in the data, the networks constructed by SPACE are sensitive to sampling. A small change in the samples selected may lead to a relatively large

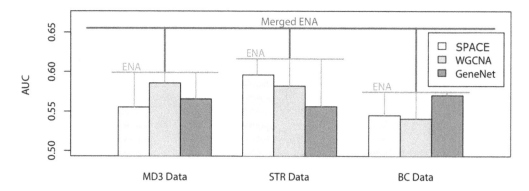

Figure 6. The AUCs of the generated networks when executed on the E. coli datasets. Note that the aggregating ENA networks from SPACE, WGCNA and GeneNet increase the accuracy within each individual dataset, and aggregating results from three datasets further increases the accuracy beyond that of any one dataset.

change in the network structure. As a result, the networks constructed from bootstrapping samples are relatively "independent", which leads to greater accuracy in the aggregated network.

As a sample application, we applied our approach to an EMT signature data set, successfully building a gene regulatory network and identifying hub genes with interesting therapeutic and

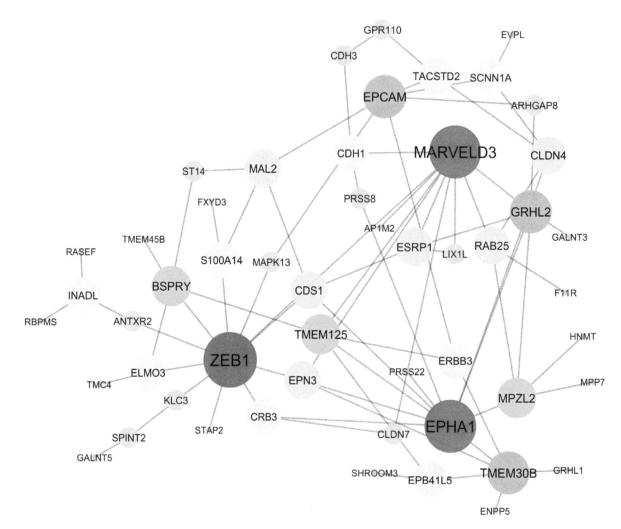

Figure 7. Network reconstruction (based on a previous epithelial-to-mesenchymal transition gene signature) [34] via ENA identifies potential drug targets for non-small-cell lung cancer (NSCLC). Microarray data from 54 NSCLC cell lines were analyzed using four different methods and the results integrated via ENA. Identified hub genes *ZEB1*, *MARVELD3* and *EPHA1* have interesting clinical implications as novel drug targets. Node color and size are proportional to the degree of connectivity (*i.e.*, the number of edges connecting each node).

pharmacological implications (Figure 7). Our discovery has also been experimentally validated in previous literature. Ingenuity Pathway Analysis (IPA) (http://www.ingenuity.com/products/ipa) is a pathway and network database based on curated literatures. When we used IPA to analyze our data, ZEB1 was identified as a hub gene, which confirmed our discovery using the ENA approach. Additionally, predicted interactions such as the CDH1–CDH3 interaction and the CLDN4-GRHL2 interaction were also confirmed (Figure S7 in File S1). While here we showed results only from microarray data analyses, ENA can also be conveniently applied to next-generation sequencing techniques such as RNA-Seq. Thus, combining individualized genomic profiles with the reconstruction of gene regulatory networks might facilitate personalized therapy (possibly using "hub genes" as therapeutic targets).

To make ENA implementation user-friendly for the biological research community, we provide a publically available R package to allow others to use these techniques on their own datasets. By leveraging the MPI framework, we were able to run the bootstrapping process in parallel across many cores and nodes, drastically reducing the amount of time it takes to run such analyses. We include in this package a function that can permute random networks and perform ENA in order to better estimate the significance of any particular connection observed in a network.

This function can be used to reduce a continuous, complete graph to an unweighted graph that includes only statistically significant edges.

Finally, we went to great lengths to ensure that all of our analysis would be as reproducible as possible by collating our analysis code into reproducible reports – most of which can be regenerated at the click of a button – and making all of these freely available online at https://github.com/QBRC/ENA-Research. We feel that this transparency is an important but uncommon step in the scientific process and hope that other researchers may begin incorporating such practices into their own investigations to foster more open, collaborative research.

Author Contributions

Conceived and designed the experiments: JA RZ GX YX. Performed the experiments: RZ JA GX YX. Analyzed the data: RZ JA GX YX. Contributed reagents/materials/analysis tools: JA RZ GX YX. Wrote the paper: RZ JA GX YX.

References

1. Sun X, Vilar S, Tatonetti NP (2013) High-throughput methods for combinatorial drug discovery. Sci Transl Med 5: 205rv201.
2. Rix U, Colinge J, Blatt K, Gridling M, Remsing Rix LL, et al. (2013) A Target-Disease Network Model of Second-Generation BCR-ABL Inhibitor Action in Ph+ ALL. PLoS One 8: e77155.
3. Zhao H, Jin G, Cui K, Ren D, Liu T, et al. (2013) Novel modeling of cancer cell signaling pathways enables systematic drug repositioning for distinct breast cancer metastases. Cancer Res 73: 6149–6163.
4. Wang XS, Simon R (2013) Identification of potential synthetic lethal genes to p53 using a computational biology approach. Bmc Medical Genomics 6.
5. Friedman N (2004) Inferring cellular networks using probabilistic graphical models. Science 303: 799–805.
6. Ihmels J, Friedlander G, Bergmann S, Sarig O, Ziv Y, et al. (2002) Revealing modular organization in the yeast transcriptional network. Nature Genetics 31: 370–377.
7. Lee I, Date SV, Adai AT, Marcotte EM (2004) A probabilistic functional network of yeast genes. Science 306: 1555–1558.
8. Sachs K, Perez O, Pe'er D, Lauffenburger DA, Nolan GP (2005) Causal protein-signaling networks derived from multiparameter single-cell data. Science 308: 523–529.
9. Segal E, Shapira M, Regev A, Pe'er D, Botstein D, et al. (2003) Module networks: identifying regulatory modules and their condition-specific regulators from gene expression data. Nat Genet 34: 166–176.
10. Stuart JM, Segal E, Koller D, Kim SK (2003) A gene-coexpression network for global discovery of conserved genetic modules. Science 302: 249–255.
11. Kendall SD, Linardic CM, Adam SJ, Counter CM (2005) A network of genetic events sufficient to convert normal human cells to a tumorigenic state. Cancer Research 65: 9824–9828.
12. Mani KM, Lefebvre C, Wang K, Lim WK, Basso K, et al. (2008) A systems biology approach to prediction of oncogenes and molecular perturbation targets in B-cell lymphomas. Molecular Systems Biology 4.
13. Tang H, Xiao G, Behrens C, Schiller J, Allen J, et al. (2013) A 12-gene set predicts survival benefits from adjuvant chemotherapy in non-small cell lung cancer patients. Clin Cancer Res 19: 1577–1586.
14. Nibbe RK, Koyuturk M, Chance MR (2010) An Integrative -omics Approach to Identify Functional Sub-Networks in Human Colorectal Cancer. Plos Computational Biology 6.
15. Slavov N, Dawson KA (2009) Correlation signature of the macroscopic states of the gene regulatory network in cancer. Proceedings of the National Academy of Sciences of the United States of America 106: 4079–4084.
16. Friedman N, Linial M, Nachman I, Pe'er D (2000) Using Bayesian networks to analyze expression data. J Comput Biol 7: 601–620.
17. Liang F (2009) Learning Bayesian Networks for Gene Expression Data. In: Dey D, Ghosh S, Mallick B, editors. Bayesian Modeling in Bioinformatics: Chapman & Hall/CRC Biostatistics Series.
18. Langfelder P, Horvath S (2008) WGCNA: an R package for weighted correlation network analysis. BMC Bioinformatics 9: 559–559.
19. Peng J, Wang P, Zhou N, Zhu J (2009) Partial Correlation Estimation by Joint Sparse Regression Models. J Am Stat Assoc 104: 735–746.
20. Schäfer J, Strimmer K (2005) An empirical Bayes approach to inferring large-scale gene association networks. Bioinformatics 21: 754–764.
21. Allen JD, Xie Y, Chen M, Girard L, Xiao G (2012) Comparing statistical methods for constructing large scale gene networks. PLoS One 7: e29348.
22. Allen JD, Wang S, Chen M, Girard L, Minna JD, et al. (2012) Probe mapping across multiple microarray platforms. Brief Bioinform 13: 547–554.
23. Liu J, Huang J, Ma S (2013) Incorporating network structure in integrative analysis of cancer prognosis data. Genet Epidemiol 37: 173–183.
24. Ma S, Huang J, Song X (2011) Integrative analysis and variable selection with multiple high-dimensional data sets. Biostatistics 12: 763–775.
25. Breitling R, Armengaud P, Amtmann A, Herzyk P (2004) Rank products: a simple, yet powerful, new method to detect differentially regulated genes in replicated microarray experiments. FEBS Lett 573: 83–92.
26. Breitling R, Herzyk P (2005) Rank-based methods as a non-parametric alternative of the T-statistic for the analysis of biological microarray data. J Bioinform Comput Biol 3: 1171–1189.
27. Birmingham A, Selfors LM, Forster T, Wrobel D, Kennedy CJ, et al. (2009) Statistical methods for analysis of high-throughput RNA interference screens. Nat Methods 6: 569–575.
28. Wiederhold E, Gandhi T, Permentier HP, Breitling R, Poolman B, et al. (2009) The yeast vacuolar membrane proteome. Mol Cell Proteomics 8: 380–392.
29. Koziol JA (2010) Comments on the rank product method for analyzing replicated experiments. FEBS Lett 584: 941–944.
30. Faith JJ, Driscoll ME, Fusaro VA, Cosgrove EJ, Hayete B, et al. (2008) Many Microbe Microarrays Database: uniformly normalized Affymetrix compendia with structured experimental metadata. Nucleic Acids Res 36: 866–870.
31. Fong SS, Joyce AR, Palsson BØ (2005) Parallel adaptive evolution cultures of Escherichia coli lead to convergent growth phenotypes with different gene expression states. Genome Res 15: 1365–1372.
32. Sangurdekar DP, Srienc F, Khodursky AB (2006) A classification based framework for quantitative description of large-scale microarray data. Genome Biol 7.
33. Xiao G, Wang X, Khodursky AB (2011) Modeling Three-Dimensional Chromosome Structures Using Gene Expression Data. J Am Stat Assoc 106: 61–72.
34. Byers LA, Diao L, Wang J, Saintigny P, Girard L, et al. (2013) An epithelial-mesenchymal transition gene signature predicts resistance to EGFR and PI3K inhibitors and identifies Axl as a therapeutic target for overcoming EGFR inhibitor resistance. Clin Cancer Res 19: 279–290.
35. Lim J, Lee S, Choi H (2006) Information loss from censoring in rank-based procedures. Statistics & Probability Letters 76: 1705–1713.
36. Penrose R (1954) A Generalized Inverse for Matrices; 1954. pp. 406–413.
37. Gabriel E, Fagg GE, Bosilca G, Angskun T, Dongarra JJ, et al. (2004) Open MPI: Goals, Concept, and Design of a Next Generation MPI Implementation. Proceedings, 11th European PVM/MPI Users' Group Meeting. Budapest, Hungary. pp. 97–104.
38. Xie Y (2013) knitr: A Comprehensive Tool for Reproducible Research in R. In: Stodden V, Leisch F, Peng D, editors. Implementing Reproducible Computational Research: Chapman and Hall/CRC.

39. Xie Y (2013) Dynamic Documents with R and knitr: Chapman and Hall/CRC.

40. Mishra GR, Suresh M, Kumaran K, Kannabiran N, Suresh S, et al. (2006) Human protein reference database—2006 update. Nucleic Acids Res 34: 411–414.

41. Peri S, Navarro JD, Kristiansen TZ, Amanchy R, Surendranath V, et al. (2004) Human protein reference database as a discovery resource for proteomics. Nucleic Acids Research 32: D497–D501.

42. Pan W, Lin J, Le CT (2002) How many replicates of arrays are required to detect gene expression changes in microarray experiments? A mixture model approach. Genome Biol 3.

43. Gama-Castro S, Salgado H, Peralta-Gil M, Santos-Zavaleta A, Muñiz-Rascado L, et al. (2011) RegulonDB version 7.0: transcriptional regulation of Escherichia coli K-12 integrated within genetic sensory response units (Gensor Units). Nucleic Acids Res 39: 98–9105.

44. Salgado H, Martinez-Flores I, Lopez-Fuentes A, Garcia-Sotelo JS, Porron-Sotelo L, et al. (2012) Extracting regulatory networks of Escherichia coli from RegulonDB. Methods Mol Biol 804: 179–195.

45. Wellner U, Schubert J, Burk UC, Schmalhofer O, Zhu F, et al. (2009) The EMT-activator ZEB1 promotes tumorigenicity by repressing stemness-inhibiting microRNAs. Nat Cell Biol 11: 1487–1495.

46. Schmalhofer O, Brabletz S, Brabletz T (2009) E-cadherin, beta-catenin, and ZEB1 in malignant progression of cancer. Cancer Metastasis Rev 28: 151–166.

47. Kojima T, Sawada N (2012) Regulation of tight junctions in human normal pancreatic duct epithelial cells and cancer cells. Ann N Y Acad Sci 1257: 85–92.

48. Peng L, Wang H, Dong Y, Ma J, Wen J, et al. (2013) Increased expression of EphA1 protein in prostate cancers correlates with high Gleason score. Int J Clin Exp Pathol 6: 1854–1860.

49. Maki-Nevala S, Kaur Sarhadi V, Tuononen K, Lagstrom S, Ellonen P, et al. (2013) Mutated Ephrin Receptor Genes in Non-Small Cell Lung Carcinoma and Their Occurrence with Driver Mutations-Targeted Resequencing Study on Formalin-Fixed, Paraffin-Embedded Tumor Material of 81 Patients. Genes Chromosomes Cancer.

50. Marbach D, Costello JC, Kuffner R, Vega NM, Prill RJ, et al. (2012) Wisdom of crowds for robust gene network inference. Nat Methods 9: 796–804.

51. Hase T, Ghosh S, Yamanaka R, Kitano H (2013) Harnessing diversity towards the reconstructing of large scale gene regulatory networks. PLoS Comput Biol 9: e1003361.

52. Breiman L (1996) Heuristics of Instability and Stabilization in Model Selection. The Annals of Statistics 24: 2350–2383.

2

Exome-Wide Somatic Microsatellite Variation Is Altered in Cells with DNA Repair Deficiencies

Zalman Vaksman[1]**, Natalie C. Fonville**[1]**, Hongseok Tae**[1¤]**, Harold R. Garner**[1,2*]

1 Virginia Bioinformatics Institute, Virginia Tech, Blacksburg, Virginia, 24061, United States of America, **2** Genomeon LLC, Floyd, Virginia, 24091, United States of America

Abstract

Microsatellites (MST), tandem repeats of 1–6 nucleotide motifs, are mutational hot-spots with a bias for insertions and deletions (INDELs) rather than single nucleotide polymorphisms (SNPs). The majority of MST instability studies are limited to a small number of loci, the Bethesda markers, which are only informative for a subset of colorectal cancers. In this paper we evaluate non-haplotype alleles present within next-gen sequencing data to evaluate somatic MST variation (SMV) within DNA repair proficient and DNA repair defective cell lines. We confirm that alleles present within next-gen data that do not contribute to the haplotype can be reliably quantified and utilized to evaluate the SMV without requiring comparisons of matched samples. We observed that SMV patterns found in DNA repair proficient cell lines without DNA repair defects, MCF10A, HEK293 and PD20 RV:D2, had consistent patterns among samples. Further, we were able to confirm that changes in SMV patterns in cell lines lacking functional BRCA2, FANCD2 and mismatch repair were consistent with the different pathways perturbed. Using this new exome sequencing analysis approach we show that DNA instability can be identified in a sample and that patterns of instability vary depending on the impaired DNA repair mechanism, and that genes harboring minor alleles are strongly associated with cancer pathways. The MST Minor Allele Caller used for this study is available at https://github.com/zalmanv/MST_minor_allele_caller.

Editor: Michael Shing-Yan Huen, The University of Hong Kong, Hong Kong

Funding: This work was funded by the Virginia Bioinformatics Institute Medical Informatics Systems Division director's funds, Virginia Bioinformatics Institute Genomics Research Lab Small Grant (CLF-1172), high performance computing was supported by a grant from the National Science Foundation (OCI-1124123) and NSF S-STEM grant (DUE-0850198). This work was supported by these 4 funds. The first two funds were internal university funds (Virginia Tech), and the latter two were from the National Science Foundation (NSF). None had a role in the study design, data collection and analysis, decision to publish, or preparation of the manuscript. These funds supported portions of author salaries and benefits, computer costs, laboratory supplies, sequencing services, publication costs, and overhead (indirect expenses to the university).

Competing Interests: HT currently works at Caris Life Sciences; the work for this paper was done when he was employed at Virginia Tech and is in no way connected to his current employment. Harold Garner is owner and founder of Genomeon, however Genomeon was not involved in funding or directing this work.

* Email: garner@vbi.vt.edu

¤ Current address: Bioinformatics group, Caris Life Sciences, Phoenix, Arizona, 85040, United States of America.

Introduction

Microsatellites (MSTs) are regions of repetitive DNA at which 1–6 nucleotides are tandemly repeated; and are present ubiquitously throughout the genome, both in gene and intergenic regions. Observations of somatic variation in MSTs have demonstrated that MST mutation rates are between 10 and 1000 time higher than that of surrounding DNA [1,2], rendering microsatellites mutational "hot-spots" [3,4]. The increased mutational rate of MSTs is thought to be primarily due DNA polymerase slippage and mis-alignment of the slipped structure due to local homology [5–7]. This difference in primary mutational mechanism suggests that, unlike non-repetitive DNA whose mutational spectrum is primarily SNPs, microsatellites are more prone to INDELs [4,7,8]. Specifically MSTs are prone to INDELs that are 'in-phase' or result in expansion or contraction by complete repeat units. For example, a dimer microsatellite will typically expand or contract by 2N nucleotides while a trimer will expand or contract by 3N [1].

MSTs are found in and around a significant number of coding and promoter regions and specific microsatellite variations have been linked to over 40 disorders, such as the CAG microsatellite whose expansion is associated with Huntington's disease and the CGG repeat whose expansion is associated with Fragile X [1,9]. In addition, a more general increase in MST instability has been associated with colon cancer, which, if detected, results in better prognosis and can influence treatment [10,11]. Currently, MST instability is clinically defined based on the results of a kit that tests somatic variation of 18–21 "susceptible" loci (PowerPlex 21, Promega). Although the test has been shown to be effective for identifying MST unstable colon cancer [12], it is significantly less effective for most other disorders including other cancers [13–15]. The ability to capture and discern variation patterns exome-wide would provide a more accurate and useful clinical data for a broader range of disorders. In recent reports next-gen sequencing has been used to uncover MST instability in intestinal and endometrial cancers by observing genotype changes in MSTs between tumor and healthy tissue [14,15].

The goal of this research was to identify patterns of somatic variation in MSTs as a possible marker for genomic instability. We hypothesize that the variable nature of MSTs and the quantification of minor allele content makes them ideal candidates for in-depth next-gen analysis and that somatic variation of microsatellite loci can be quantified using high-depth sequencing. A broadening of the definition of MST instability to include changes in somatic variability and using an exome/genome-wide approach may enable a more accurate diagnosis of patients then what is currently provided by PowerPlex 21.

Somatic variability, novel genomic polymorphisms that arise within a cell population not found in the progenitors, plays a critical role in cellular reprogramming leading to the development and progression of cancer [16]. Suppression of mutations is essential for genomic stability, therefore cells have evolved multiple mechanisms to repair damaged or unpaired nucleotides [17,18]. Currently the only established DNA repair defect that that has been directly linked to MST instability is mismatch repair (MMR). MMR impairments have been shown to increase somatic variation at MSTs in both cell lines and tumors [19–21]. Although the role other DNA repair mechanisms such as inter-strand crosslink repair (as seen in Fanconi anemia genes) and homologous recombination (HR) play in MST instability is less clear, both are important for genomic and chromosomal stability (reviewed by [22,23]).

In this study we first show that we can robustly detect signatures of MST mutation bias and somatic variation occurring in cell lines in next-gen data including a high frequency of in-phase INDELs. We are then able to construct a pattern of somatic MST variation (SMV) by using DNA repair proficient cell lines. Our results indicate that ~5% of microsatellite loci show somatic variation, i.e. have at least one additional non-haplotype allele present. Finally, we are able to differentiate between cell lines with known defects in various DNA repair mechanisms (mismatch repair, DNA crosslink repair, homologous recombination), which correlate with an altered distribution of loci with non-haplotype alleles. These findings suggest that signatures that distinctly define specific defective DNA repair mechanisms can be gleaned from next-gen sequencing data and that this information has the potential to be utilized for detection of individuals with altered levels of somatic variation that are at increased risk of disease or the evaluation of patient's tumor that may yield clinically actionable information.

Methods

Cells, DNA prep and sequencing

HEK (human embryonic kidney) and MCF10A (immortalized breast epithelial) and HEK293 (human embryonic kidney) cells were obtained from ATCC. PD20 and PD20 RV:D2 (FANCD2 and FANCD2 retrovirally corrected) cell lines were obtained from the Fanconi Anemia Foundation (Eugene OR). Sequencing data for Capan-1 cells was previously published by Barber and coworkers [12].

PD20, PD20 RV:D2 and HEK293 cells were grown at 37°C with 5% CO_2, in DMEM supplemented with 10% FBS (Invitrogen) and 1X pen/strep (Invitrogen) to 80% confluence. MCF10A cells were grown to confluence in DMEM/F12 medium (Invitrogen, Carlsbad, CA), supplemented with 5% horse serum (Invitrogen), antibiotics- 1X Pen/Strep (Invitrogen), 20 ng/mL EGF (Peprotech, Rocky Hill, NJ), 0.5 mg/mL hydrocortisone (Sigma), 100 ng/mL cholera toxin (Sigma), and 10 μg/mL insulin (Sigma) at 37°C with 5% CO_2. All cell lines were collected by trypsinazation and prepared for DNA extraction. DNA was extracted using the Qiagen DNAeasy kit (Qiagen) as per manufacturers instructions.

Since PD20 RV:D2 were derived from PD20 cells by retroviral insertion of the corrected FANCD2 gene we confirmed the maintenance of the corrected version using the sequencing data. Further, a comparison of growth-curves showed an order of magnitude more cells 48 hours after exposure to the DNA interstrand cross-linker Cisplatin, confirming a partial rescue phenotype.

Sequencing and analysis pipeline

Exome paired-end libraries were prepared using the Agilent (Chicago, IL) SureSelectXT Human All Exon V4 capture library. 2×100 bp reads were obtained using an Illumina (San Diego, CA) HiSeq 2500 instrument in Rapid Run mode on a HiSeq Rapid v1 flowcell. Indexed reads were de-multiplexed with CASAVA v1.8.2.

Paired-end sequencing reads were trimmed using fastX_Toolkit and aligned to HG19/GRCh37 human reference genome (http://www.genome.ucsc.edu) using BWA-mem. The output was then sorted, indexed and PCR duplicates were removed using SAMTOOLS [24]. Bam files were then locally realigned and target loci marked using GATK IndelRealigner and TargetIntervals. MST alleles were retrieved and analyzed using software described in the next section.

Microsatellite minor-allele software

A catalogue of MST loci was generated from the HG19/GRCh37 reference genome using Tandem Repeats Finder [25] (with the following parameters: 2.7.7.80.10.18.6). The list was filtered to remove any loci that were shorter than 8 nucleotides, had less than 3 copies of a given motif unit or were below 85% sequence purity. Duplicated loci were identified based on sequence purity and sequence length and were removed.

MSTs were analyzed using a custom MST minor-allele caller based on GenoTan and ReviSTER software [26,27], which were developed by this group to improve MST haplotype predictions (https://github.com/zalmanv/MST_minor_allele_caller). The minor-allele caller extracts marked MSTs from bam files using SAMTOOLs. MST loci are called based on predicted alignments and an adjustable length flanking sequence (this study used either 5 or 7 nucleotide sequence). Reads with low base call scores (below a base score of 28) for nucleotides within the repeats and those with mapping quality score below 10% were eliminated. Alleles are initially called only when two or more reads, verified in both directions of a paired-end run, have the same sequence. All alleles for a given locus are binned with the number of supporting paired-end reads. The final number of alleles is computed based on a user specified minimal requirement of substantiating reads (for this study the minimum number of substantiating reads is either 2 or 3 reads per allele). If more than one allele per locus was found, zygosity and the sequence length difference from the most common allele were recorded. Heterozygotic loci were called using the following criteria as described and confirmed in the GenoTan and ReviSTER manuscripts [26,27]: 1) it is the second most common allele, 2) The number of confirming reads is greater than 25% of the total reads for the locus or greater than 50% of the depth for the most common allele, if the total is below 25% of the total depth.

In addition to MST loci, we also generated a somatic variability profile for non-MST loci. To make the data comparable we randomly selected 3 million loci, each consisting of 15 nucleotides segments, from the HG19 genome. We then filtered out any loci that intersected with our MST and were left with over 2 million loci. The same pipeline as for MSTs was used to generate the data for non-MST loci. This data yielded information on the number of loci with minor alleles and type of mutation (SNPs and INDELs).

Sequence validation and allele calls validated by independent Sanger sequencing method

The MST minor-allele caller we use in this paper is a modified version of a published and experimentally verified code, however to further validate the multi-allele capability of the modified code 30 loci, including 17 showing multiple alleles, were verified using Sanger sequencing. Figure S1A in file S1 shows the data from the minor-allele caller output at one of these loci, chr10:72639137-72639161, at which we would predict at least 3 alleles to be present in this sample (MCF10A) with lengths of 21, 23, and 25 nucleotides. Sanger sequencing confirmed that multiple alleles were present, with the alleles being greater than 21 nucleotides long (figure S1B in file S1). Of the 30 loci 28 loci verified the genotype and 14 of 17 loci with minor alleles also had visible minor alleles by Sanger sequencing.

Modeling error rates to establish rules that differentiate errors from high confidence minor alleles

Two methods were used to generate models of NGS runs for chromosomes 17 and 21; 1) Wgsim (https://github.com/lh3/wgsim) a commonly used paired-end read generator and 2) in-house designed generator. Both methods were set to have a per nucleotide error rate between 0.5% and 5%. The major difference between the two methods was that wgsim was used to obtain modeling data with fairly similar coverage (read depth) across the reference chromosome while the lab-designed algorithm allowed for a more variable coverage as is observed in a typical next-gen sequencing run. The generated fastq files were run through the same pipeline as actual real sequencing data. The accuracy of the pipeline was analyzed by the verification of the predicted alignment. Predicted error rates ranged between 1.3% and 1.9%, with the majority of errors due to misalignments.

Results

We modified a previously published and verified MST genotyper [26] to enumerate all possible alleles present within next-gen data, as opposed to only capturing the most common (haplotype) alleles. We first characterized the error which may cause false positive allele calls via a parametric sensitivity study conducted on in-silico generated data, and showed that our measure can then be used to accurately quantify minor alleles and thus be used to distinguish between mutational mechanisms that are exhibited in different cell lines. To accomplish this, we establish a baseline SMV profile from DNA repair proficient cell lines, and compared this to what is seen in cell lines with various DNA repair defects.

Characterizing the effect of sequencing error on minority allele calling

This analysis evaluates each MST locus to establish the one or two alleles that define the genotype, then it robustly calls additional non-haplotype or 'minor' alleles that are present at lower frequency within next-gen data. However, the accuracy of such minority allele calls can be significantly affected by sequencing errors found within the raw reads that map to each locus. To minimize the number of false positive 'alleles', we first established the minimal number of reads necessary for confirming

an allele in the presence of typical next-gen errors. It has been established by a number of studies that 3 reads mapped to a loci is sufficient to properly call major alleles [28–30]. To corroborate this, we created an in-silico sequencing data set for chromosomes 21 and 17, with randomly generated errors ranging from 0.5% to 5% which mimicked next-gen sequencing data in both the error types that were created and read coverage per locus (results depicted in figure 1).

We first determined the parameters required to optimize the measurement of the fraction of loci without minor alleles in sequencing data with the above-mentioned error rates. Alignment and zygosity calling accuracy is displayed in table S1 in file S1. The sequencing data generator produced between 8 and 10.5 million reads that contained over 58,000 targeted MSTs. Over 98.5% of the reads mapped correctly with an accuracy of over 99.8% in coding regions (regions captured by exome sequencing). The accuracy of zygosity calls was over 99.98% for all error rates. Next we varied the minimum number of reads covering a locus required to call an allele. Changing the threshold from 2 confirming reads (figure 1A) to 3 confirming reads (figure 1B) statistically and significantly decreased the fraction of loci with more alleles than the haplotype number (1 if homozygotic or 2 if heterozygotic). Using a threshold of 2 confirming reads per allele, the fraction of loci without minor alleles identified (due to sequencing errors being interpreted as alleles) was 19–62% for simulated data sets with error rates ranging between 5%–0.5% respectively (figure 1A), indicating that requiring only 2 reads to identify an allele leads to a high level of false alleles. By increasing the threshold to 3 confirming reads the percent of loci without minor alleles increases to 73%–99% for the same data set (figure 1B). By increasing to 4 confirming reads per allele we further increase the number of loci without minor alleles 87%–99% (figure S2A in file S1). However, at error rates close to the actual HiSeq rates (of ~1%), we only saw a modest increase in the number of loci without minor alleles, a change from 97% (3 reads per allele) to 99% (4 reads per allele). This is in contrast to an increase from 61% with 2 reads per allele to 97% with 3 confirming reads per allele.

We next examined how sequencing error might affect the number of alleles present in our data. To do this we used modeling data with error rates similar to the actual HiSeq error rate (1%) and 2.5% error (figure 2), and determined the average read depth per locus with increasing alleles. For the in-silico generated data, we found a linear increase in the total read depth as the number of alleles increased (using 2–4 confirming reads per allele) up to 8 alleles (figures 2 and Figure S2 in File S1). A comparison of these results to actual sequencing data from our cell lines (discussed in more detail later) shows that when 3 or more reads are required to confirm an allele, the number of alleles called for a given read depth is greater than what would be expected from error, even at a rate of 2.5% which is substantially more than the observed next-gen error rate of 1% (figure 2B and Figure S2B in File S1), i.e. more alleles are called at a lower read depth in the actual data than would be present due to error. Based on these results, requiring a minimum of 3 reads covering a locus to confirm an allele minimizes the number of 'false' alleles being identified due to sequencing error.

Polymerase slippage vs. nucleotide misincorperation

Another potential source of error in calling alleles from sequencing data is amplification errors induced during the library preparation process [31]. These errors would likely be present at higher frequency than errors generated during sequencing [31,32]; therefore cannot be minimized by solely increasing the minimum

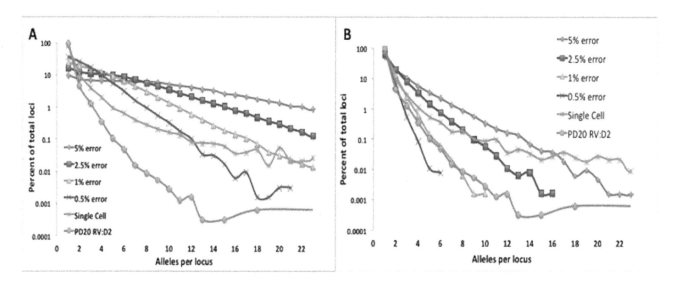

Figure 1. Effects of sequencing error and the minimum number of reads required to call an allele on the number of alleles called in sequencing data. Modeling data with different error frequencies (0.5%–5%) showed an increase in loci with multiple alleles as error increased when both 2 (A) and 3 (B) reads were minimally required to call an allele. In contrast, standard exome sequencing data from DNA repair proficient cells (PD20 RV:D2 cells) and exome sequencing after whole genome amplification from a single cell were insensitive to the cut-off used.

read coverage (as above). Somatic mutation of MSTs is primarily associated with polymerase slippage [33,34], which is thought to cause the characteristic INDEL bias [31,35,36]. In contrast, nucleotide mis-incorporation errors during *in-vitro* amplification would be predicted to lead primarily to SNPs in sequencing data [37]. Both of the mentioned DNA synthesis methods would lead to an increase in the number of loci with non-haplotype alleles, however with a predicted variation pattern that is distinctly different. To differentiate between the two predicted SMV patterns including minority alleles, and to assess the influence of nucleotide mis-incorporation/amplification error on our results, we compared a standard exome sequence from cells which are proficient for DNA repair (described later) that did not undergo whole genome amplification (WGA) with data from the sequencing of a single cell [38] which would be expected to have no somatic variation within the sample, but has necessarily undergone WGA to generate the quantity of DNA necessary for sequencing. Therefore, for the WGA sample, presumably all non-haplotype alleles present are due to amplification error. As expected, genome amplification increases the number of loci with non-haplotype alleles (figure 1) to 11.3% and 7% of the total with a threshold of 2 and 3 reads, respectively. The DNA repair proficient cells, which did not undergo extensive amplification, were only decreased by 1.7%, from 7% to 5.3%, by altering the minimum read cutoff. From this it can be concluded that neither errors during library prep nor during the sequencing run account for more than 4 percent of the total non-haplotype alleles detected.

Approximately 85% of mutations found within microsatellite loci in the WGA single-cell data were SNPs, which is expected as a consequence of polymerase errors during amplification. These results were comparable to those predicted by our model, which showed that ~88% of the total minor alleles were composed of alleles carrying SNPs rather than INDELs (Figure 3). In contrast, SNPs account for only 36% (±3.4%) of the total minor alleles in DNA repair proficient cell lines. In addition, although for all the DNA repair proficient cell lines the most common MST motifs with minor alleles observed were mono-nucleotide repeats found within 56%–66% of loci, loci containing tri-nucleotide motifs

accounted for over 55% of the total loci with minor alleles in the WGA data (table S2 in file S1). These results further support the hypothesis that this approach can differentiate between distinct MST mutational profiles: INDELs, particularly at mono-nucleotide runs predominantly reflect DNA repair proficient biological SMV whereas SNPs in MSTs, particularly at tri-nucleotide motif containing loci are predominantly amplification-induced errors or potentially due to altered DNA maintenance capacity. This is further supported by a similar study that has found that the majority of MSTs that are variable within the normal population (individuals sequenced as part of the 1,000 Genomes Project) are predominantly INDELs at mono-nucleotide runs [30].

MST vs non-MST regions

MSTs are considered to be more susceptible to mutations than the surrounding non-repetitive DNA regions [3,14,39]. Because of this, one could expect that non-MST regions would have less somatic variability (non-MST equivalent of SMV) than MST regions. In order to perform a fair comparison with the MST data, 2 million segments consisting of 15 nucleotides each were randomly selected throughout the genome. The same analysis as was performed on loci containing MSTs was also applied to these non-MST regions. It was found that for these non-MST loci the average fraction of loci that were homozygotic was 98.9% with a standard deviation of 0.2, while only 96.7% of the MST containing loci was homozygotic. Even more significant, only 2% (standard deviation of 0.2) of the non-MST loci (homozygotic and heterozygotic) had minor alleles, while 5.1% of the MST loci harbored minor alleles (table 1). Further, a comparison of SNP and INDEL distributions indicated that, unlike MST regions where INDEL variations prevail (64%), SNPs account for the majority (96.9%) of the differences in minor alleles at non-MST loci (table 2). Taken together, these results confirm that, consistent with the literature, MSTs are more susceptible to mutation [2–4,34].

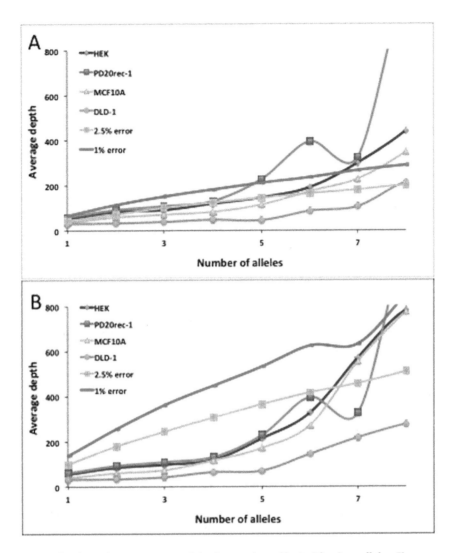

Figure 2. Variation in average depth per locus cannot explain the number of loci with minor alleles. The average read depth at loci with increasing numbers of alleles using A) 2 and B) 3 confirming reads per allele for in-silico generated data using 1% and 2.5% induced error rate for 4 different cell lines.

Reproducibility within a cell line

The objective of this study is to characterize the pattern of SMV from DNA repair proficient cells and then compare to cell populations in which DNA repair is compromised. SMV changes associated with disease will likely be subtle and require highly reproducible control data. To test the reproducibility of SMV measurements within a cell line, two biological replicate cultures of PD20 RV:D2 (PD20 RV:D2-1 and PD20 RV:D2-2) cells were grown separately and sequenced. PD20 RV:D2 are fibroblasts derived from an individual with Fanconi Anemia subgroup D2, retroviraly complimented with a functional copy of FANCD2 [40]. Using a minimum read depth cutoff of 15 to genotype a given loci, we successfully called over 280 K and 250 K loci (at an average depth of 52 and 45 reads per locus) for PD20 RV:D2-1 and 2 respectively. Both samples showed a similar SNP to INDEL ratio, with INDELs making up over ~67% of the minor alleles (table 2). A genotype analysis showed that approximately 96.8% of called loci were homozygous while heterozygosity was observed in ~3.2% of the loci called (table 1). Comparison of those loci that were called in both samples shows that haplotype discordance (i.e. homo- or heterozygotic using standard genotyping) was 1.1%

(table 3), of which 92% were due the fraction of reads supporting a second allele being below the haplotype threshold (see method) and was therefore counted as a minor allele instead of a second haplotype allele, as is the convention in established genotype callers. Only 173 discordant loci were due to sequence differences between the two samples.

For the purpose of this study SMV is defined by the presence of variant MST alleles that are supported by a minimum of 3 confirming reads but do not contribute to haplotype. An analysis of variant MST alleles found a total of 5.4% and 5.3% of MST loci in the PD20 RV:D2-1 and 2 samples, respectively, had 1 or more minor alleles (table 1). The concordance of loci without minor alleles in either sample is 93.9% while 3.4% of loci have at least one minor allele in both samples. By concordance we mean a locus has minor alleles or the same haplotype in multiple samples. Conversely, discordance, where a locus in only one of the compared samples had minor alleles, was 2.7% (table 3). To confirm the significance of these values, we calculated the probabilities of concordance and discordance based on a cohort of randomly selected loci (5.4% and 5.3% of a total samples), which was <0.25% concordant, and compared with our results.

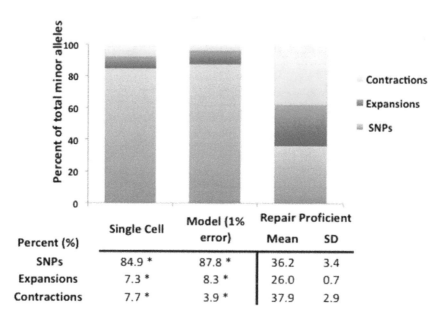

Figure 3. DNA repair proficient cells vary significantly from the *in-silico* modeling and single cell sequencing analysis with respect to SNPs and INDELs. The percent of SNPs, expansion and contractions for single cell sequencing and the *in-silico* model as well as the mean and standard deviation for the control cell lines. * significant difference p<0.01.

Using a Pearson's goodness of fit X^2, we verified that the concordant loci are not randomly distributed (p<0.0001). To determine within cell line reproducibility we compared the percent of loci having minor alleles by chromosome as a whole and binned into a million base regions. A linear regression model comparing the percent of loci with minor alleles for each chromosome (as depicted in figure S3 in file S1) shows a significant correlation ($R^2 = 0.85$ and p<0.001) between two independently cultured samples (Figure 4A). Similarly, a comparison of the binned chromosome also shows a significant correlation ($R^2 = 0.60$ and p<0.001, figure 4B). Visualization of the distribution of fraction of MST loci showing somatic variation in a representative chromosome (chr1), depicted in figure 5, indicates specific chromosomal regions that may harbor SMV "hot-spots". An evaluation of MST loci in translated (exon) regions found over 820 genes containing MSTs with a minimum of 2 minor alleles in both PD20 RV:D2 samples, with some of genes found within segments of chromosome 1 with increased SMV depicted in figure 5 (a complete list of exonal MSTs with the minor alleles called, for all cell lines discussed in this paper are available in File S2).

Taken together these results support our hypothesis that this method truly reflects SMV rather than error generated during sequencing and that the results are highly reproducible. The data further suggests that within an individual or cell line, specific genomic regions may contain MSTs that are more susceptible to somatic variability.

Reproducibility between cell lines

To begin to establish a SMV baseline for DNA repair proficient cells, we compared the haplotype, minor allele and SNP/INDEL distributions for two DNA repair proficient cell lines and the PD20 RV:D2 cells discussed above. MCF10A cells are immortalized breast epithelial cells derived from a healthy human female and HEK293 cells are a human embryonic kidney cell line derived from a healthy male fetus. Sequencing produced over 45 million reads with over 170 K microsatellite loci called at an average depth of 42 reads per locus for HEK293 cells and over 190 K

microsatellite loci called at an average depth of 39 reads per locus for MCF10A cells. Considering major alleles only, 96.4% and 97.0% of all MST loci, respectively, are homozygotic (table 1). The average fraction of loci with minor alleles for all three cell lines was 5.1% with a standard deviation of 0.4%. Although MCF10A cells had fewer loci with minor alleles than the PD20 RV:D2 and HEK293 cells (4.5% compared with 5.3% and 5.4% respectively, table 1), and showed a difference in the fraction of secondary alleles with SNPs compare to INDELS (table 2), MCF10A was not considered an outlier (using Grubb's test for outliers). When we compared the haplotype and minor allele concordance between two non-related cell lines, MCF10A and PD20 RV:D2, we found that 3.8% of loci have different genotypes with only 60% due to haplotype differences. For those loci with minor alleles, discordance is 4.0% and concordance is only 2.0%, the result is significantly above what would be anticipated by chance with Pearson's X^2 (i.e. <0.3%,). Interestingly, a full factorial comparison of the fraction of loci with minor alleles for each chromosome (as depicted in figure S4 in file S1), using a linear regression model, found a non-significant correlation ($R^2 = 0.061$ and p<0.23, figure 4C). However, a correlation using the 1 million base bins is significant with an R^2 value of 0.33 and a p<0.0001 (figure 4D), supporting the concept that certain regions contain minor allele susceptibility hot spots. These results demonstrate substantial reproducibility between unrelated independently grown DNA repair proficient cell lines even when the samples are derived from different tissues of origin. These results also suggest that a baseline profile of SMV can be established for DNA repair proficient cells to compare to cell lines with DNA repair defects.

SMV in cells with compromised DNA repair capacity

Thus far we have established that (1) three DNA repair proficient cell lines show similar SMV with low variability both within and between cell lines and that (2) we can differentiate between different SMV trends based on the ratio of INDELs to SNPs. However, the larger goal of this study is to compare SMV

Table 1. Exome sequencing data indicates that MST and non-MST haplotype and somatic polymorphism are reproducible in DNA repair proficient cell lines.

Percent (%)	Microsatellite loci				Repair Proficient		Non-Microsatellite loci				Repair Proficient	
	PD20 RV:D2-1	PD20 RV:D2-2	MCF10A	HEK293	Mean	SD	PD20 RV:D2-1	PD20 RV:D2-2	MCF10A	HEK293	Mean	SD
Homo-zyg	96.8	96.8	96.4	97.0	96.7	0.3	99.0	99.0	98.6	99.1	98.9	0.2
Hetero-zyg	3.2	3.2	3.6	3.0	3.3	0.3	1.0	1.0	1.4	0.9	1.1	0.2
Multi-alleles	5.4	5.3	4.5	5.3	5.1	0.4	1.7	2.0	2.1	2.1	2.0	0.2

Table 2. MST and non-MST containing loci from exome sequencing of DNA repair proficient cells, but not from sequencing of a single cell after whole genome amplification, show the expected high ratio of INDELs (expansions and contractions) to SNPs.

Percent (%)	Microsatellite loci				Repair Proficient		Non-microsatellite loci				Repair Proficient	
	PD20 RV:D2-1	PD20 RV:D2-2	MCF10A	HEK293	Mean	SD	PD20 RV:D2-1	PD20 RV:D2-2	MCF10A	HEK293	Mean	SD
SNPs	33.6	32.7	41.4	36.9	36.2	3.4	96.9	96.6	96.8	97.2	96.9	0.2
Expansions	26.2	27.0	25.3	25.5	26.0	0.7	1.3	1.6	1.6	1.4	1.5	0.1
Contractions	40.3	40.3	33.3	37.5	37.9	2.9	1.8	1.8	1.6	1.3	1.6	0.2

Table 3. Percent concordance/discordance of haplotype and loci with minor alleles for cell lines.

	Genotype	More then haplotype alleles		Haplotype Allele number
	Discordance	Concordance	Discordance	Concordance
PD20 RV:D2-1 & -2	1.06	3.43	2.69	93.88
PD20rec-1 & PD20	1.15	2.50	3.07	94.43
PD20rec-1 & MCF10A	3.79	1.99	3.95	94.10
PD20rec-1 & Capan-1	2.68	1.92	12.68	85.40
MCF10A & Capan-1	2.19	1.24	13.62	85.10

patterns between cell lines representative of healthy individuals and those that may have altered DNA repair capacity. To test this, we evaluated 3 cell lines commonly used to study DNA repair and stability. DLD-1 cells are MST instability (MSI) high colon cancer cell line, impaired in Mismatch repair (MMR), selected as positive controls for this study [41]. Capan-1 cells were sequenced previously [12] and are a BRCA2- cell line that can propagate in culture. PD20 cells are from a FANCD2(-) cell line from which the PD20 RV:D2 cells were derived [40]. Both the Capan-1 cells and the PD20 cells have mutations in genes that are involved in

normal DNA repair (homologous recombination and interstrand crosslink repair, respectively).

For DLD-1 and PD20 cells, the number of loci that passed filters ranged between 185 K and 260 K with an average depth of between of 56 and 62 reads per locus respectively. Only 124 K loci were called for Capan-1 cells, with an average depth of 71 reads per locus. To capture MST differences between the DNA repair proficient and DNA repair defective cell lines we first evaluated haplotypes and the presence of minor alleles for each cell line. Both DLD-1 and Capan-1 cells significantly differ with respect to

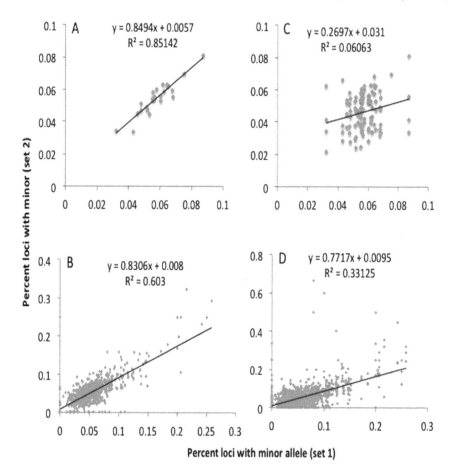

Figure 4. A regression analysis indicates a significant within and between cell line correlation in the fraction of loci with one or more minor alleles. Full factorial plots of the fraction of loci with minor alleles by chromosome, regression line and correlation coefficient for A) PD20 RV:D2-1 and 2 C) PD20 RV:D2-1, 2, MCF10A and HEK293. Also full factorial plots of the fraction of loci with minor alleles for the corresponding 1 million base segments of all the chromosomes, a regression line and the correlation coefficient for B) PD20 RV:D2-1 and 2 D) PD20 RV:D2-1, 2, MCF10A and HEK293.

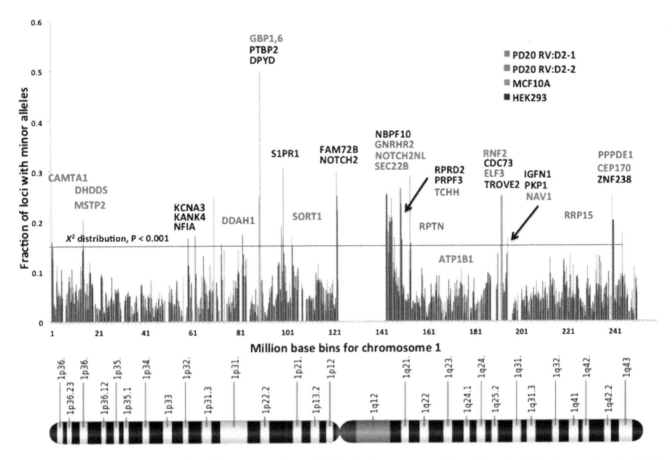

Figure 5. The distribution of MST loci showing somatic variability for chromosome 1 binned into 1 million base regions in PD20 and the derived PD20 RV:D2 cell line. The horizontal line demarcates outlier segments, based on a X^2 distribution. All genes shown were found to contain exonal MSTs that with at least 2 minor alleles in both PD20 RV:D2 samples and were found in regions that exceeded the demarcated level. Genes shown in red were found to contain exonal MSTs with at least 2 minor alleles in all 4 DNA repair proficient cell line samples and those shown in blue were found in 3 of the 4 samples. The chromosome image shown at the bottom was obtained from http://en.wikipedia.org/wiki/Chromosome_1 _(human).

haplotype distribution from DNA repair proficient cells (table 4). Capan-1 cells showed a significant decrease in heterozygotic loci, 2.1% compare to 3.3% for DNA repair proficient, which was anticipated due to the known trend for loss of heterozygosity in these cells as reported in the literature due to gene conversion in the absence of BRCA2 [42,43]. In contrast, there was an increase (5.5%) in hetereozygotic loci in DLD-1 cells, which can potentially be attributed to increased mutation due to the MMR defects responsible for the MSI in DLD-1 cells. Surprisingly, haplotype distribution analysis at non-MST loci shows that DLD-1 cells, but not Capan-1 differ significantly from DNA repair proficient (1.8% compared to 1.2% for DLD-1 and Capan-1 respectively). This was unexpected because neither mutation mechanism (homologous recombination nor MMR) would necessarily be restricted to MST vs non-MST regions. A comparison of SNPs and INDELs in the DNA repair impaired cell lines showed Capan-1 cells significantly differed from the DNA repair proficient mean in the fraction of SNPs, with 47% and 91% for MST and non-MST loci respectively (table 5). Conversely, DLD-1 and PD20 cells were not found to be different from DNA repair proficient cell lines. For the DNA repair proficient cells the mean fraction of loci with minor alleles was 5.1% with a SD of 0.4%. Capan-1 cells showed again, a greater susceptibility to mutation with a significant increase (6.2%) in the number of loci with minor alleles (table 4). In contrast, PD20 and DLD-1 cells both show a significant

decrease in loci with minor alleles, 3.1% and 3.2% respectively. This was surprising, particularly because the PD20 cells showed a decrease with respect to their corrected cell line PD20 RV:D2. Concordance of loci with minor alleles between the two related cell lines, PD20 and PD20 RV:D2, was 2.5% while discordance was 3.1%, which was significantly above chance (Pearson's X^2). However, it was greater than the concordance between PD20 RV:D2 and MCF10A, which is to be expected since PD20 and PD20 RV:D2 are related strains (Table 3).

Because Capan-1 cells displayed the highest disparity in mutation rate from DNA repair proficient cell lines, including changes in SNP:INDEL ratios, we decided to check the concordance of genotype and minor allele containing loci between them and PD20 RV:D2s (table 3). Genotype concordance for the loci that were found in both samples, was over 97.3%, even higher than when we compared PD20 RV:D2 with MCF10As. When comparing the loci with minor alleles ~2% of the total had minor alleles in both samples (were concordant) however 12% were found to have minor alleles in only one samples, meaning discordance (table 3). Although this is strikingly different, for the PD20 RV:D2 cells to MCF10A comparison, the concordance rate is still significantly greater than expected by chance. Very similar results were obtained when Capan-1 cells were compared to MCF10A cells. These results offer additional support the

Table 4. Haplotype distribution and somatic polymorphism rate differ in DNA repair defective cell lines compared to DNA repair proficient cell lines.

| | Microsatellite loci | | | | | Non-microsatellite loci | | | | |
| | Repair Proficient | | Repair impaired cell lines | | | Repair Proficient | | Repair impaired cell lines | | |
Percent (%)	Mean	SD	PD20	DLD-1	Capan-1	Mean	SD	PD20	DLD-1	Capan-1
Homo-zyg	96.7	0.3	97.2 [#]	94.5 [#]	97.9 [#]	98.9	0.2	98.8	98.2 [#]	99.2
Hetero-zyg	3.3	0.3	2.8	5.5 [#]	2.1 [#]	1.1	0.2	1.2	1.8 [#]	0.8
Multi-alleles	5.1	0.4	3.1 [#]	3.2 [#]	6.2 [#]	2.0	0.2	1.2 [#]	1.2 [#]	3.7 [#]

[#] significantly different p<0.01 - z-test.

Table 5. SNP and INDEL fractions differ in DNA repair defective cell lines compared to DNA repair proficient cells.

| | Microsatellite loci | | | | | Non-microsatellite loci | | | | |
| | Repair Proficient | | Repair impaired cell lines | | | Repair Proficient | | Repair impaired cell lines | | |
Percent (%)	Mean	SD	DP20	DLD-1	Capan-1	Mean	SD	PD20	DLD-1	Capan-1
SNPs	36.2	3.4	35.7	36.9	47.6 [#]	96.9	0.2	95.4 [#]	94.9 [#]	90.8 [#]
Expansions	26.0	0.7	26.3	29.7	21.2 [#]	1.5	0.1	2.1 [#]	2.2 [#]	2.8 [#]
Contractions	37.9	2.9	38.0	33.3	31.2	1.6	0.2	2.5 [#]	2.9 [#]	6.4 [#]

[#] significantly different p<0.01 - z-test.

hypothesis that some MST loci are more susceptible to mutations than others.

For DLD-1 cells, the increase in heterozygotic loci coupled with the significant reduction in the number of minor alleles is counterintuitive. This suggests the possibility of a proliferation of a small number of subpopulations. If our hypothesis is correct we would anticipate two things to occur: 1) an increase the average depth of reads that define the second allele and 2) an increase in the read depth supporting minor alleles without an increase in the number. To test our hypothesis we first compared the fraction of total reads covering the second allele regardless of haplotype and reads covering only minor alleles. As depicted in figure 6, DLD-1 cells show greater than a 4% increase with respect to the DNA repair proficient average in the fractional coverage of the second allele and more than 8% increase (figure 6A and B) for the percent coverage supporting minor alleles. Both were statistically significant. Neither Capan-1 nor PD20 were found to be different from the DNA repair proficient group for either of these parameters. These results suggest a population bottleneck where only a small number of distinct subpopulations are the predominant contributors of the reads captured by the sequencer.

SMV in exons

MSTs are present ubiquitously throughout the genome and are found in over 16% of exons [1]. Although MST expansions or contractions in promoter and interexonal regions can affect transcription, mutations in exons are the most frequently implicated in downstream effects, consistent with exons being under significant selective pressure. An analysis of heterozygotic loci found that exons had significantly less heterozygotic loci, a reduction of over 1.2% compared to untranslated regions (2.4% and 3.8% respectively, figure 7A). However the difference in the fraction of loci with minor alleles in exons and untranslated regions was not significant (5.1% and 5.6%, figure 7B). In the previous sections we showed that DLD-1 cells, a strain defective in MMR, was found, unexpectedly, to have a significant reduction in the number of MST loci with minor alleles and an increase in heterozygotic loci. Based on this comparison it appears that the results are due to the increased difference between translated and untranslated regions. As shown in figure 8A, the fraction of MST loci with minor alleles in exons is 1.1% (compared to 4.7% in untranslated regions) while the fraction of loci that are heterozygotic is 1.7%, compared to 7.9% in untranslated regions

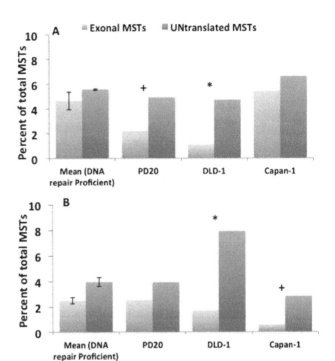

Figure 7. A comparison of the percent of heterozygotic loci and loci exhibiting SMV in exons and untranslated genomic regions in DNA repair proficient and impaired cell lines. A) The percent of MST loci that for which minor alleles were found and B) percent of heterozygotic MST loci, in exons and untranslated regions. Depicted in both figures are the means for the DNA repair proficient cell lines and the individual percentage for PD20, DLD-1 and capan-1 cell lines. (+) p<0.05 as compared to DNA proficient cells and (*) p<0.001 as compared to DNA proficient cells in measurement of the difference between exons and untranslated regions.

(figure 8B). These results further support hypothesis that DLD-1 cells have undergone a population bottleneck.

To determine the potential genetic implications of minor allele hot spots, we focused on the analysis of genes affected, specifically we inspected genes containing MST loci found in exons that with 2 or more alleles that did not contribute to the haplotype (minor alleles). This data is provided in a spreadsheet (file S2). The

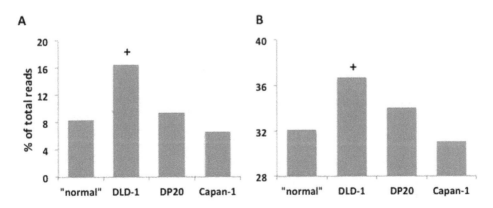

Figure 6. An increase in the fraction of reads substantiating the second alleles if present, and all minor alleles. The average fraction of reads representing A) all minor alleles (only for loci with minor alleles) and B) the second allele in both heterozygotic and homozygotic loci that have at least one minor allele, for DLD-1, PD20 and Capan-1 cells were compared to the average of the DNA repair proficient cell lines. The (+) denotes a significant difference from DNA repair proficient (p<0.01) with z-test.

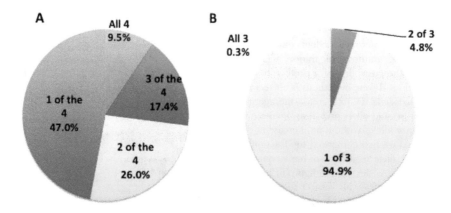

Figure 8. The distribution of genes that show SMV in DNA repair deficient cell lines appears random while those in the DNA repair proficient cell lines show significant similarity. The percent of genes with MSTs that with MSTs that have a minimum of 2 minor alleles in A) DNA repair proficient cell lines and B) DNA repair deficient cell lines that are found in all the or some of the sequenced samples. In figure B) the genes that are present in all three DNA repair deficient cell lines is 0.3% and the slice of the pie chart is not visible due to the small percentage.

spreadsheet lists the MST loci (based on the HG19 genome), gene name, cell genotype, total number of alleles, variants called and other pertinent information. Of the 2603 genes whose exons harbor minor allele containing loci found in at least one of the 4 DNA repair proficient samples sequenced 47% were found to have 2 or more minor alleles in more then one sample and 9.5% were found in all 4 samples (figure 7A). A Genome Ontology (GO) analysis of the 247 genes harboring MSTs with multiple minor alleles in all 4 samples found only a borderline (p<0.01, we use a lower p then 0.05 to compensate for the number of comparisons) significant enrichment of GOTERM categories that included transcription factors, regulators, repressors and DNA binding genes. In addition, there was no significant enrichment for any KEGG pathway categories or cataloged disorders. Conversely, of the ~1100 minor allele harboring genes found in the DNA repair impaired cell lines, only 3 (0.27%) were found in all three cell lines while 95% are in only 1 of the three cell lines (figure 7B), which suggests this concordance pattern was primarily random. Further, no genes with multiallelic MSTs were found in all of the sequenced samples and only 18 were found in 6 of the 7 cell line samples. A KEGG pathway enrichment analysis of the minor allele harboring genes found in the DNA repair impaired cell lines suggests a pattern associated with various cancer pathways. Significant KEGG terms enriched were general cancer, colorectal cancer, myeloma, cervical cancer and cell adhesion (with p<0.001). Together, these results support the hypothesis that specific MST loci in repair proficient cells are more susceptible to somatic mutations but the genes associated with them are not associated with any specific categorized pathway. In contrast, for cells that have impairments in DNA repair pathways, somatic mutations in MSTs appear in higher frequency in loci that are specific to the DNA repair deficiency, and these mutations are implicated in disease, specifically cancer.

Discussion

Somatic mutation can lead to subpopulations of cells carrying mutated alleles. These are examined in cancers, as tumors can be considered to contain subpopulations of cells, i.e. the tissues are not gnomically homogenous [44,45]. Tumors usually carry an allele or set of alleles that confirm their abnormal growth. These alleles, when detected in the tumor but not parent cells, can be the basis for important clinical treatment decisions [11,38,45]. In cell

populations with increased somatic mutation rates, like those with altered DNA repair capacity, there may be a concordant increase in subpopulation diversity. As a subpopulation propagates the mutations become more abundant, which becomes detectable in next-gen sequencing data [31,32]. A major assumption of our analysis is that an increase in the number of alleles detected in next-gen sequencing data is reflective of an increase in cell subpopulations or somatic mutation present in the sequenced sample. In this paper we evaluate allele frequencies at MSTs in various cell populations as a quantifiable indicator of variation.

The data presented here evaluate both the standard genotype and minor alleles that are present in next-gen data to establish a baseline for SMV in DNA repair proficient cells and compare this to cells with altered DNA repair capacity. The focus on cell lines with known etiologies is to establish the viability and robustness of our approach. The results show the utility in identifying the consequences of DNA repair impairments on genomic stability. There are several major objectives/findings from this analysis including (1) complimenting genomic analysis away of matched DNA samples with in-sample quantification of variation, (2) demonstrating that DNA repair proficient cells and those with different defects in DNA repair can have different SMV profiles that may be potential markers for these defects and (3) a quantitative measure of the fraction of loci that exhibit minor alleles may be reflective of subpopulations of cells with different genomic content, potentially those cells that may contribute to tumor formation. MST instability is important in the prognosis and selection of treatment for various cancers, and better, more accurate identification methods are always being sought [10,11].

These data demonstrate that the SNP:INDEL ratio at MSTs can be used to distinguish between different in-vivo mutational mechanisms and PCR amplified genomes. Both the WGA single cell sample and the Capan-1 cell line showed an increase in SNPs compared to INDELs at MST loci, however the fractions differed greatly. This is consistent with what was expected from both nucleotide mis-incorporation errors by polymerases (WGA single cell sample) and defects in DNA repair (Capan-1). Neither DLD-1 nor PD20 cells, which are defective in MMR and interstrand cross-link repair, respectively, had a significant alteration of the ratio of SNPs:INDELs at MST loci.

Capan-1 cells displayed a reduction of heterozygotic loci as compared to DNA repair proficient cell lines. This was expected since Capan-1 cells are a BRCA2- cells (impaired in homologous recombination) and have been shown to exhibit a loss of heterozygocity [43]. However, our analysis also indicates a significant increase in the fraction of loci with minor alleles. This could be due to two reasons: 1) Capan-1 cells are a hypotriploid with over 35 structural rearrangements (www.path.cam.ac.uk/%7epawefish/index.html) and with multiple chromosomal regions having more than three copies [46,47]. The minor alleles in Capan-1 cells can therefore be part of the genotype rather than somatic variation. Conversely, 2) Capan-1 cells have been reported to have an extremely high rate of INDELs and SNPs, significantly higher than expected from the hyperploidy [12]. The results shown here could be due to increased mutation rate shown with this cell line [12] and further support general genomic instability in Capan-1 cells.

Unexpectedly, although DLD-1 cells are a MST unstable cell line, they did not display either of our predicted markers for increase in MST mutation rate: 1) an increase in the number of minor alleles, as was seen with Capan-1 cells, or 2) a decrease in the number heterozygotic loci and the number of minor alleles, as we found in Capan-1 and PD20 cells (table 5). Conversely, DLD-1 cells showed both a significant increase in the number of heterozygotic loci and a reduction in the fraction of loci with more than two alleles. Further, they displayed a great reduction in both the fraction of loci with minor alleles and heterozygotic loci in exons (conserved chromosomal regions). We hypothesize that this is the result of defective MMR leading to an increase in mutations that have become fixed in the population. Alternatively, this may have resulted from a bottleneck in the growth of the cell population. If this was the case, the increase in heterozygotic loci allele may be a product of a limited set of surviving cell subpopulations. If a subpopulation with an un-repaired mutation, reached a sufficient proportion of the population due to the bottleneck it would generate sufficient reads for the locus to be mistakenly called heterozygotic. This point is reinforced by the significant increase in the portion of the total number of reads covering the second allele while the fraction of loci with minor alleles and the number of minor alleles per locus are decreased. This is important to note because it suggests that we can not only distinguish between different mutational mechanisms using the minor alleles in next-gen sequencing, but may also be able to identify cells that have experienced a growth-limiting condition as we expand this work in the future.

The work presented here is a proof-of concept of an approach to assess somatic variation in MSTs using next-gen sequencing. Using this analysis we were able to establish a SMV profile in DNA repair proficient cell lines which we can use to compare to cells with potential or known alterations in DNA repair capacity to begin to evaluate exome or whole genome sequenced samples without requiring a matched genomic sample as baseline. Based on the results presented here this approach can be used to ascertain both scientifically and clinically relevant information.

Scientifically, even with known mutations the consequences on the genome as a whole is still relatively unknown. Clinically, somatic variation is a measure of genomic stability and this approach might be used as an addition to current MST instability criteria.

Supporting Information

File S1 Contains the following files: **Figure S1.** Sanger sequencing confirms the prediction of the at least 3 different alleles, in a locus found to have minor alleles in nextGen data. A) The output produced by our caller (locus is shown in the first 5 columns in line 1) predict 3 different length alleles using a minimum of 2 reads to confirm an allele. The major allele is 23 nts with 2 minor alleles, 25 and 21 nts long. B) The sequencing chromatogram. The black arrows are showing the start point of different alleles. **Figure S2.** Effects of sequencing error and the minimum number of reads required to call an allele on of the number of alleles called in sequencing data. (A) Modeling data with different error frequencies (0.5%–5%) showed an increase in loci with multiple alleles as error increased when 4 reads were minimally required to call an allele. (B) The average read depth at loci with increasing numbers of alleles using 4 confirming reads per allele for in-silico generated data using 1% and 2.5% error rate and 4 different cell lines. **Figure S3.** The distribution of MST loci showing somatic variability by chromosome for both PD20 RV:D2 samples. **Figure S4.** The distribution of MST loci showing somatic variability by chromosome, for both PD20 RV:D2, MCF10A and HEK293 cell lines. **Table S1.** In-silico model mapping and genotyping accuracy. **Table S2.** The total minor alleles sorted by MST motif length indicate that single cell exome amplification alters the distributions observed in DNA repair proficient cell lines.

Acknowledgments

We thank the system administrators in the VBI computational core (Michael Snow, Dominik Borkowski, David Bynum, Douglas McMaster, and Vedavyas Duggirala) for technical support. We also acknowledge members of the VBI Genomics Research Lab (Saikumar Karyala, Jennifer Jenrette, Megan Friar, and Kris Lee) for the library prep, and sequencing of genomic and Sanger validation samples.

Author Contributions

Conceived and designed the experiments: ZV HRG. Performed the experiments: ZV NCF. Analyzed the data: ZV NCF HRG. Contributed reagents/materials/analysis tools: ZV HT. Wrote the paper: ZV HRG. Wrote the software: ZV HT.

References

1. Gemayel R, Vinces MD, Legendre M, Verstrepen KJ (2010) Variable tandem repeats accelerate evolution of coding and regulatory sequences. Annu Rev Genet 44: 445–477.

2. Fonville NC, Ward RM, Mittelman D (2011) Stress-induced modulators of repeat instability and genome evolution. J Mol Microbiol Biotechnol 21: 36–44.

3. Bagshaw AT, Pitt JP, Gemmell NJ (2008) High frequency of microsatellites in S. cerevisiae meiotic recombination hotspots. BMC Genomics 9: 49.

4. Payseur BA, Jing P, Haasl RJ (2011) A genomic portrait of human microsatellite variation. Mol Biol Evol 28: 303–312.

5. Delagoutte E, Goellner GM, Guo J, Baldacci G, McMurray CT (2008) Single-stranded DNA-binding protein in vitro eliminates the orientation-dependent impediment to polymerase passage on CAG/CTG repeats. J Biol Chem 283: 13341–13356.

6. Hile SE, Eckert KA (2008) DNA polymerase kappa produces interrupted mutations and displays polar pausing within mononucleotide microsatellite sequences. Nucleic Acids Res 36: 688–696.

7. Ananda G, Walsh E, Jacob KD, Krasilnikova M, Eckert KA, et al. (2013) Distinct mutational behaviors differentiate short tandem repeats from microsatellites in the human genome. Genome Biol Evol 5: 606–620.

8. Leclercq S, Rivals E, Jarne P (2010) DNA slippage occurs at microsatellite loci without minimal threshold length in humans: a comparative genomic approach. Genome Biol Evol 2: 325–335.

9. Budworth H, McMurray CT (2013) Bidirectional transcription of trinucleotide repeats: roles for excision repair. DNA Repair (Amst) 12: 672–684.

10. Xiao H, Yoon YS, Hong SM, Roh SA, Cho DH, et al. (2013) Poorly differentiated colorectal cancers: correlation of microsatellite instability with clinicopathologic features and survival. Am J Clin Pathol 140: 341–347.

11. Hong SP, Min BS, Kim TI, Cheon JH, Kim NK, et al. (2012) The differential impact of microsatellite instability as a marker of prognosis and tumour response between colon cancer and rectal cancer. Eur J Cancer 48: 1235–1243.

12. Barber LJ, Rosa Rosa JM, Kozarewa I, Fenwick K, Assiotis I, et al. (2011) Comprehensive genomic analysis of a BRCA2 deficient human pancreatic cancer. PLoS One 6: e21639.

13. Lacroix-Triki M, Lambros MB, Geyer FC, Suarez PH, Reis-Filho JS, et al. (2010) Absence of microsatellite instability in mucinous carcinomas of the breast. Int J Clin Exp Pathol 4: 22–31.

14. Yoon K, Lee S, Han TS, Moon SY, Yun SM, et al. (2013) Comprehensive genome- and transcriptome-wide analyses of mutations associated with microsatellite instability in Korean gastric cancers. Genome Res 23: 1109–1117.

15. Kim TM, Laird PW, Park PJ (2013) The landscape of microsatellite instability in colorectal and endometrial cancer genomes. Cell 155: 858–868.

16. Poduri A, Evrony GD, Cai X, Walsh CA (2013) Somatic mutation, genomic variation, and neurological disease. Science 341: 1237758.

17. Harris RS, Kong Q, Maizels N (1999) Somatic hypermutation and the three R's: repair, replication and recombination. Mutat Res 436: 157–178.

18. Kunz C, Saito Y, Schar P (2009) DNA Repair in mammalian cells: Mismatched repair: variations on a theme. Cell Mol Life Sci 66: 1021–1038.

19. Baptiste BA, Ananda G, Strubczewski N, Lutzkanin A, Khoo SJ, et al. (2013) Mature microsatellites: mechanisms underlying dinucleotide microsatellite mutational biases in human cells. G3 (Bethesda) 3: 451–463.

20. Shah SN, Hile SE, Eckert KA (2010) Defective mismatch repair, microsatellite mutation bias, and variability in clinical cancer phenotypes. Cancer Res 70: 431–435.

21. Eckert KA, Mowery A, Hile SE (2002) Misalignment-mediated DNA polymerase beta mutations: comparison of microsatellite and frame-shift error rates using a forward mutation assay. Biochemistry 41: 10490–10498.

22. Roy R, Chun J, Powell SN (2012) BRCA1 and BRCA2: different roles in a common pathway of genome protection. Nat Rev Cancer 12: 68–78.

23. Kottemann MC, Smogorzewska A (2013) Fanconi anaemia and the repair of Watson and Crick DNA crosslinks. Nature 493: 356–363.

24. Li H, Handsaker B, Wysoker A, Fennell T, Ruan J, et al. (2009) The Sequence Alignment/Map format and SAMtools. Bioinformatics 25: 2078–2079.

25. Benson G (1999) Tandem repeats finder: a program to analyze DNA sequences. Nucleic Acids Res 27: 573–580.

26. Tae H, Kim DY, McCormick J, Settlage RE, Garner HR (2013) Discretized Gaussian mixture for genotyping of microsatellite loci containing homopolymer runs. Bioinformatics.

27. Tae H, McMahon KW, Settlage RE, Bavarva JH, Garner HR (2013) ReviSTER: an automated pipeline to revise misaligned reads to simple tandem repeats. Bioinformatics 29: 1734–1741.

28. McIver LJ, McCormick JF, Martin A, Fondon JW 3rd, Garner HR (2013) Population-scale analysis of human microsatellites reveals novel sources of exonic variation. Gene 516: 328–334.

29. McIver LJ NCF, Karunasena E, Garner HR (Submitted) Microsatellite genotyping reveals a signature in breast cancer exomes. Breast Cancer Research and Treatment.

30. Fonville NC LJM, Vaksman Z, Garner HR (Submitted) Microsatellites in the exome are predominantly single-allelic and invariant. Genome Biology.

31. Schmitt MW, Kennedy SR, Salk JJ, Fox EJ, Hiatt JB, et al. (2012) Detection of ultra-rare mutations by next-generation sequencing. Proc Natl Acad Sci U S A 109: 14508–14513.

32. Gundry M, Vijg J (2012) Direct mutation analysis by high-throughput sequencing: from germline to low-abundant, somatic variants. Mutat Res 729: 1–15.

33. Kruglyak S, Durrett RT, Schug MD, Aquadro CF (1998) Equilibrium distributions of microsatellite repeat length resulting from a balance between slippage events and point mutations. Proc Natl Acad Sci U S A 95: 10774–10778.

34. Jarne P, Lagoda PJ (1996) Microsatellites, from molecules to populations and back. Trends Ecol Evol 11: 424–429.

35. Kanagawa T (2003) Bias and artifacts in multitemplate polymerase chain reactions (PCR). J Biosci Bioeng 96: 317–323.

36. Meyerhans A, Vartanian JP, Wain-Hobson S (1990) DNA recombination during PCR. Nucleic Acids Res 18: 1687–1691.

37. Brodin J, Mild M, Hedskog C, Sherwood E, Leitner T, et al. (2013) PCR-induced transitions are the major source of error in cleaned ultra-deep pyrosequencing data. PLoS One 8: e70388.

38. Hou Y, Song L, Zhu P, Zhang B, Tao Y, et al. (2012) Single-cell exome sequencing and monoclonal evolution of a JAK2-negative myeloproliferative neoplasm. Cell 148: 873–885.

39. Mestrovic N, Castagnone-Sereno P, Plohl M (2006) Interplay of selective pressure and stochastic events directs evolution of the MEL172 satellite DNA library in root-knot nematodes. Mol Biol Evol 23: 2316–2325.

40. Ohashi A, Zdzienicka MZ, Chen J, Couch FJ (2005) Fanconi anemia complementation group D2 (FANCD2) functions independently of BRCA2- and RAD51-associated homologous recombination in response to DNA damage. J Biol Chem 280: 14877–14883.

41. Chen TR, Hay RJ, Macy ML (1983) Intercellular karyotypic similarity in near-diploid cell lines of human tumor origins. Cancer Genet Cytogenet 10: 351–362.

42. Holt JT, Toole WP, Patel VR, Hwang H, Brown ET (2008) Restoration of CAPAN-1 cells with functional BRCA2 provides insight into the DNA repair activity of individuals who are heterozygous for BRCA2 mutations. Cancer Genet Cytogenet 186: 85–94.

43. Butz J, Wickstrom E, Edwards J (2003) Characterization of mutations and loss of heterozygosity of p53 and K-ras2 in pancreatic cancer cell lines by immobilized polymerase chain reaction. BMC Biotechnol 3: 11.

44. Tang DG (2012) Understanding cancer stem cell heterogeneity and plasticity. Cell Res 22: 457–472.

45. Schor SL (1995) Fibroblast subpopulations as accelerators of tumor progression: the role of migration stimulating factor. EXS 74: 273–296.

46. Sirivatanauksorn V, Sirivatanauksorn Y, Gorman PA, Davidson JM, Sheer D, et al. (2001) Non-random chromosomal rearrangements in pancreatic cancer cell lines identified by spectral karyotyping. Int J Cancer 91: 350–358.

47. Grigorova M, Staines JM, Ozdag H, Caldas C, Edwards PA (2004) Possible causes of chromosome instability: comparison of chromosomal abnormalities in cancer cell lines with mutations in BRCA1, BRCA2, CHK2 and BUB1. Cytogenet Genome Res 104: 333–340.

3

Multiple Thyrotropin β-Subunit and Thyrotropin Receptor-Related Genes Arose during Vertebrate Evolution

Gersende Maugars[1], Sylvie Dufour[1], Joëlle Cohen-Tannoudji[2], Bruno Quérat[2]*

1 Muséum National d'Histoire Naturelle, Sorbonne Universités, Biology of Aquatic Organisms and Ecosystems (BOREA), Paris, France, Université Pierre et Marie Curie, Paris, France, Université Caen Basse Normandie, Caen, France, Unité Mixte de Recherche (UMR) 7208 Centre National de la Recherche Scientifique (CNRS), Paris, France, Institut de Recherche pour le Développement (IRD) 207, Paris, France, 2 Université Paris Diderot, Sorbonne Paris Cité, Biologie Fonctionnelle et Adaptative (BFA), Paris, France, UMR CNRS 8251, Paris, France, INSERM U1133 Physiologie de l'axe gonadotrope, Paris, France

Abstract

Thyroid-stimulating hormone (TSH) is composed of a specific β subunit and an α subunit that is shared with the two pituitary gonadotropins. The three β subunits derive from a common ancestral gene through two genome duplications (1R and 2R) that took place before the radiation of vertebrates. Analysis of genomic data from phylogenetically relevant species allowed us to identify an additional *Tshβ* subunit-related gene that was generated through 2R. This gene, named *Tshβ2*, present in cartilaginous fish, little skate and elephant shark, and in early lobe-finned fish, coelacanth and lungfish, was lost in ray-finned fish and tetrapods. The absence of a second type of TSH receptor (*Tshr*) gene in these species suggests that both TSHs act through the same receptor. A novel *Tshβ* sister gene, named *Tshβ3*, was generated through the third genomic duplication (3R) that occurred early in the teleost lineage. *Tshβ3* is present in most teleost groups but was lostin tedraodontiforms. The 3R also generated a second *Tshr*, named *Tshrb*. Interestingly, the new *Tshrb* was translocated from its original chromosomic position after the emergence of eels and was then maintained in its new position. *Tshrb* was lost in tetraodontiforms and in ostariophysians including zebrafish although the latter species have two TSHs, suggesting that TSHRb may be dispensable. The tissue distribution of duplicated *Tshβs* and *Tshrs* was studied in the European eel. The endocrine thyrotropic function in the eel would be essentially mediated by the classical *Tshβ* and *Tshra*, which are mainly expressed in the pituitary and thyroid, respectively. *Tshβ3* and *Tshrb* showed a similar distribution pattern in the brain, pituitary, ovary and adipose tissue, suggesting a possible paracrine/autocrine mode of action in these non-thyroidal tissues. Further studies will be needed to determine the binding specificity of the two receptors and how these two TSH systems are interrelated.

Editor: Marc Robinson-Rechavi, University of Lausanne, Switzerland

Funding: The authors have no funding or support to report.

Competing Interests: The authors have declared that no competing interests exist.

* Email: bruno.querat@univ-paris-diderot.fr

Introduction

Thyroid-Stimulating Hormone (TSH) is a pituitary glycoprotein hormone responsible for the activation of the thyroid gland, playing a key role in the control of development and metabolism in mammals and other vertebrates [1]. TSH is also responsible for triggering specific developmental processes such as larval metamorphosis in amphibians [2,3], as well as larval and secondary metamorphoses in some teleost species [4–8]. In addition, TSH may participate in the modulation of various functions for example in the immune or reproductive systems, *via* pleiotropic effects and multiple target tissues of thyroid hormones [9–12].

The vertebrate pituitary glycoprotein hormones, TSH and the two gonadotropins, luteinizing hormone (LH) and follicle-stimulating hormone (FSH) are heterodimers composed of a common α subunit, and a β subunit that confers hormonal specificity [13]. It has recently been demonstrated [14] that the three glycoprotein

hormone β (GPHβ) subunits were generated by successive duplications starting from an ancestral glycoprotein hormone β subunit gene (*ancGphβ*) through two rounds of genomic duplications (1R and 2R) that occurred early in the evolution of vertebrates [15]. During 1R the original *ancGphβ* duplicated into two paralogous genes, one of which became the evolutionary precursor of the gonadotropin β subunit genes (*preGthβ*) and the other, the precursor of the *Tshβ* subunit gene (*preTshβ*). *Lhβ* and *Fshβ* were generated next by the duplication of *preGthβ* during 2R. *Tshβ* derived from *preTshβ* but the presence of a 2R-derived *Tshβ* subunit sister gene has never been demonstrated [14]. Analysis of the glycoprotein hormone related gene repertoire of the elephant shark (*Callorhinchus milii*) interestingly revealed the presence of two copies of *Tshβ* subunit related genes. Whether they resulted from a specific, local duplication of the *Tshβ* gene or from the conservation in cartilaginous fish of the *Tshβ* subunit sister gene derived from the 2R, could not be determined at that time [14].

The scenario appears rather similar in extant teleosts [16] despite the specific genomic duplication (3R) that took place in this lineage [17]. A $Tsh\beta$ sister gene was however identified in some teleost genomes, that was shown to be derived from the 3R [14,18].

The glycoprotein hormones exert their action by interacting with specific and evolutionarily related G protein-coupled receptors. The glycoprotein hormone receptors (GPHR) are characterized by a large extracellular hormone-binding domain composed of a leucine rich domain connected to a seven-transmembrane domain by a hinge region [19]. If a second TSH related hormone is present in some species, it seems logical to assume that it acts through a novel receptor, as suggested by the recent characterization of a second TSHR-like gene in some teleost species [20,21]. However, it was not clearly demonstrated whether this second TSHR was generated at the 3R or by a specific duplication early in the teleost lineage.

Whether additional $Tsh\beta$ subunit genes and $Tshr$ genes were derived from 2R and 3R were questions we addressed in this study. We took advantage of the recently released genomic data from several species that have a phylogenetically relevant position among vertebrates: two representatives of cartilaginous fish (chondrichthyes), a group that preceded the divergence of ray-finned fish (actinopterygies) and lobe-finned fish (sarcopterygies), the elephant shark, an holocephalan for which a new version of the genomic assembly was recently released [22] and the little skate (*Leucoraja erinacea*), an elasmobranch; the spotted gar (*Lepisosteus oculatus*) a ray-finned fish representative that took root before the teleost radiation and the 3R [23] and the coelacanth (*Latimeria chalumnae*), a lobe-finned fish that appeared just prior to lungfish [24], the lungfish group being the sister group of tetrapods [25]. The genomes of a number of teleost fish species including the eels (*Anguilla anguilla* and *A. japonica*), representatives of the basal group of Elopomorphs [26–29] also recently released, were searched for the 3R generated $Tsh\beta$ related subunit and for a $Tshr$ related gene. The tissue distribution of the two $Tsh\beta$ and the two Tsh receptors was analysed in the European eel.

Materials and Methods

All aspects of animal care and experimentation were in accordance with the Ethic committee of the Museum National d'Histoire Naturelle and approved by the Institutional Animal Care and Use Committee of the Animal Protection and Health, Veterinary Services Direction, Paris, France.

Identification of vertebrate $Tsh\beta$ and $Tshr$ sequences

Blast analyses [30] were performed on-line using protein as query (tBlastn) on NCBI (http://blast.ncbi.nlm.nih.gov/Blast.cgi), Ensembl (http://www.ensembl.org/Multi/blastview), DDBJ (http://blast.ddbj.nig.ac.jp/), as well as on web sites for little skate (Skatebase: http://skatebase.org/skateBLAST and elephant shark (http://esharkgenome.imcb.a-star.edu.sg/blast/). Eel sequences were identified from European and Japanese eel genomes available on the website Eel Genome of ZF-Genomics (http://www.zfgenomics.org/sub/eel) in addition to the assembly available in NCBI, using the CLC BIO software (Qiagen, Denmark).

Protein sequences were predicted from retrieved genomic or Expressed Sequence Tag (EST) sequences by using consensus splice donor and acceptor site and by sequence identity comparison with related $Tsh\beta$ or $Tshr$ genes (Table S1 and Table S2).

The signal peptide cleavage site was determined using SignalP (http://www.cbs.dtu.dk/services/SignalP/). Receptor transmembrane domains were predicted using TOPCONS (http://topcons.cbr.su.se/).

Phylogenetic and syntenic analyses

Alignments were fitted manually using Se-AL editor (http://tree.bio.ed.ac.uk/software/seal/). The phylogenetic reconstructions were performed on-line by using a maximum likelihood method with PhyMyL 3.0 software [31] on the website file (http://www.phylogeny.fr/) with HKY85 as substitution model for TSHβ-related nucleotide sequences and WAG for TSHR-related amino-acid sequences and default settings for the other parameters. The robustness of the reconstruction was estimated by the aLRT score and/or by bootstrapping over 500 replicates. Nucleotide sequences of the entire coding region (including signal peptide) were used for $Tsh\beta$ subunits with truncation in the 3' end of the longest sequences. The amino acid sequences were used for the TSHR tree reconstruction.

Mapping the genomic neighborhoods of $Tsh\beta$ and $Tshr$ genes were performed with region overview on Ensembl, NCBI and EBI genome browsers and for the Elephant shark genome on the specific Ensembl website (http://ensembl.fugu-sg.org/index.html).

Flanking genes of duplicated $Tsh\beta$ and $Tshr$ were identified and annotated in the eel from the eel genome databases, using CLC BIO software.

Tissue distribution of $Tsh\beta$ and $Tshr$ transcripts in the eel

Tissue distribution analysis was performed on RNA samples previously prepared from female silver migrating eels caught in the River Loire, France [32]. Total RNA extracted from pituitary, thyroid follicles, olfactory bulb, mesencephalon and diencephalon, telencephalon, cerebellum, medulla oblongata, eyes, liver, intestine, muscle, adipose tissue, gills, and ovary were used. Reverse transcription was performed as previously described [32].

Primers for quantitative real-time PCR (qPCR) for European eel $Tsh\beta$ (Table S3) were previously reported [32]. Eel specific primer sets for $Tsh\beta3$, $Tshra$ and $Tshrb$ were designed using Primer3 [33,34] spanning intron sequences. The specificity of the primer sets was controlled by sequencing PCR product. Moreover, in each case, we checked that the isolated cDNAs of one of the duplicated genes could not be amplified by the primer set corresponding to the other duplicated gene.

Messenger RNA was quantified on LightCycler using the LightCycler FastStart Master plus Sybr green I kit (Roche, Mannhein, Germany) as recommended by the manufacturer. The final primer concentration used was 500 nM. Each sample was run in duplicate using a 1/5 cDNA dilution. The PCR conditions were 95°C for 10 min followed by 50 cycles at 95°C for 5 sec, 60°C for 10 sec and 72°C for 10 sec. The specificity of amplified product was checked by melting curve analysis after the amplification reactions. Relative transcript abundance was calculated from standard curves prepared from pituitaries and thyroid follicles cDNA using LightCycler software. Transcript levels were normalized using total tissue RNA content as previously described in [35].

Results and Discussion

A 2R-generated $Tsh\beta$ subunit related gene conserved in cartilaginous and in basal lobe-finned fish

Two related $Tsh\beta$ subunit genes were characterized from the coelacanth genome (Fig. 1A). One of them was in the same genomic region as the known "classical" vertebrate $Tsh\beta$ subunit

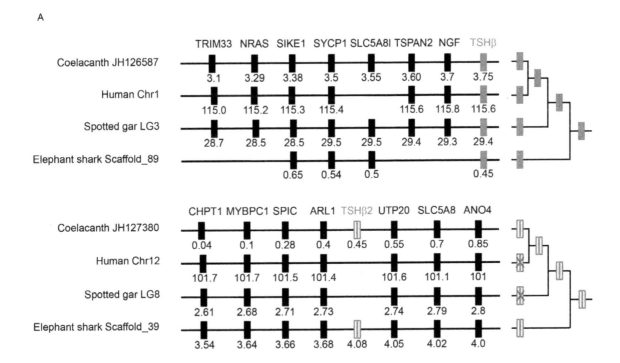

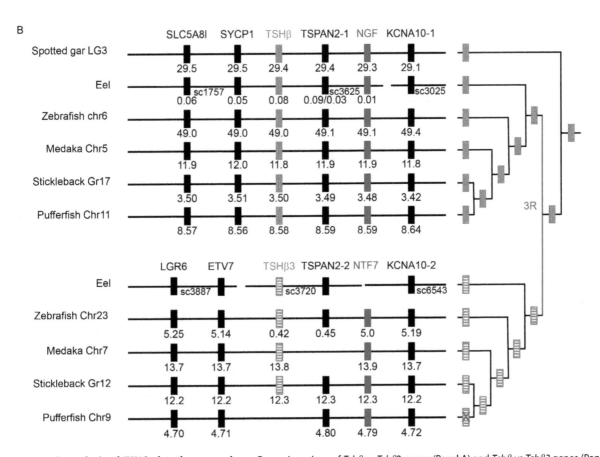

Figure 1. Syntenic analysis of *TSHβ* related gene regions. Genomic regions of *Tshβ* vs *Tshβ2* genes (Panel A) and *Tshβ* vs *Tshβ3* genes (Panel B) were analysed in representative species (chromosome number or linkage group references are attached to the species name) by using the region overview on the Ensembl genome browser or by blast analysis on the eel draft genome (see Fig. S2A for details). The phylogenetic relationships

between the representative species are summarized on the right panel. The 3R symbolizes the teleost-specific genome duplication. Genes are named according to the Ensembl nomenclature (Table S4). Gene positions are given (in Mega base) below the symbolized genes.

gene. A second gene was located on a genomic fragment that encodes several genes among which three (*Mycbpc1*, *Spic* and *Ano4*) were demonstrated to belong to the fourth paralogous group of genes derived from the duplicated *ancGphβ* genomic region (see additional file 9 in [14]). This fourth glycoprotein hormone β subunit gene then clearly represents the *Tshβ* sister gene derived from the 2R and was named *Tshβ2*.

The genes for the two *Tshβ* subunit cDNAs (HQ174785 and HQ174784) previously characterized in elephant shark from a pituitary library [14] were present and complete in the new version of the genome, on scaffold_89 and scaffold_39, respectively. The former was flanked by genes belonging to the "classical" *Tshβ* subunit paralogous gene set (Fig. 1A). This was the one unfortunately named *Tshβ2* when first characterized [14]. The other *Tshβ* subunit gene on scaffold_39 was co-syntenic with genes located in the same genomic region as the coelacanth *Tshβ2* (Fig. 1A). The hypothesis formulated at the time that one of these genes may be the *Tshβ* sister gene issued from the 2R is thus confirmed.

The skate genome is not fully assembled yet and most of the genes of interest were fragmented into as many contigs as coding exons. The first and second exons of the *Tshβ* subunit related gene were identified and tentatively linked (Fig. 2).

Only one *Tshβ* subunit gene was found in the spotted gar genome. It was located on the same genomic region as the classical *Tshβ* subunit gene (Fig. 1A).

A 3R-generated *Tshβ* subunit-related gene conserved in most teleosts

The classical *Tshβ* and a second *Tshβ* subunit in teleosts were confirmed in a number of representatives from basal elopomorphs like the eel to the acanthomorphs (stickleback, tilapia, tuna, sablefish) through ostariophysian species (Mexican tetra, zebrafish) (Fig. 2, Fig. S1 and Table S1). The first exon of a second *Tshβ* was also identified in the Atlantic salmon (*Salmo salar*) (Fig. S1, Table S1) suggesting that salmonids also have this second form of TSH. This was not the case in tetraodon and fugu species where only the classical and already characterized *Tshβ* subunit genes could be found in the complete genome. Synteny analysis shows that the additional *Tshβ* subunit is located in a conserved genomic region (Fig. 1B), close to the 3R issued duplicated form of *Ngf*, *Ntf7* [36]. This additional Tshβ gene was named *Tshβ3* with reference to the 3R.

Tshβ subunit sequences part into three monophyletic groups

Tshβ subunit sequences of vertebrate representatives were aligned for a phylogenetic analysis. As expected from the synteny analysis, a monophyletic group emerged that clusters the coelacanth *Tshβ2* together with the elephant shark *Tshβ*-related subunit HQ174784 (Fig. 3), the protein deduced from the assembled *Tshβ* exons from the skate and the known *Tshβ* from the Australian lungfish [37]. The robustness of the monophyletic group that constitutes a sister group to all other *Tshβ* subunits was strongly supported by a bootstrap value of 93% in 500 replicates. These *Tshβ* genes were named *Tshβ2*. The other coelacanth and elephant shark *Tshβ* genes were included into the "classical" *Tshβ* cluster at positions compatible with their phylogenetic relationships

Although two *Tshβ* related genes were identified in elephant shark, only one was tentatively characterized in the skate. It branches out with the coelacanth *Tshβ2*. The classical *Tshβ* subunit sequence was not found. One possibility is that only one *Tshβ* subunit was conserved in skate or in holocephals. More likely, however, since *Ngf* was also absent from the genomic data, the entire locus may have been missed in the sequencing process.

Teleost *Tshβ* sequences were divided into two monophyletic groups. This is in agreement with the syntenic analysis and supports the hypothesis that they result from the third genomic duplication (3R) that took place early in the radiation of teleosts. The *Tshβ3* sequence branch length from this phylogenetic tree was 1.6 longer in average (Fig. S4) than for the classical *Tshβ* sequences indicating that they evolved more rapidly.

The spotted gar belongs to a group that emerged before the radiation of teleosts and its specific genome duplication. It logically lacks the *Tshβ3* gene. It also lacks the *Tshβ2* gene although the genomic region, where it should be located, is well conserved (Fig. 1A) discarding a possible problem with the sequencing data. It then seems that the *Tshβ2* gene was lost at least twice, in the lobe-finned fish lineage before the radiation of tetrapods and early in the ray-finned fish lineage. It must be of significance that teleosts specifically retained the newly generated *Tshβ3* gene when they lost the other 3R-generated *Gphβ* gene duplicates [38].

TSHβ2 and TSHβ3 sequences present specific signatures

Both TSHβ2 and TSHβ3 retained most structural features shared by all types of glycoprotein hormone β subunits like the cysteine residues and many other amino acids that are conserved in position (Fig. 2) indicating that these sequences are subject to functional constraints. It is then most likely that they are able to associate to an α subunit and form an active heterodimer. TSHβ2 and TSHβ3 are predicted to be cleaved from the signal peptide at roughly the same position as in the classical TSHβ, one or two amino acids before the first conserved cysteine residue (Fig. 2). Sequence alignment indicates that five amino acid positions are well conserved in the TSHβ2 group that are different to or variable in the classical TSHβ subunit sequences. Two are located within the first exon and 3 within the second. The amino acid composition from the two associated skate exonic sequences are well in agreement with their assembly into a unique gene belonging to the *Tshβ2* group. TSHβ2 and TSHβ subunits share the two additional amino acid residues between the cysteines 5 (the last encoded by the 1st exon) and 6 (20 amino acids apart) as compared to LHβ and FSHβ subunits [39]. By comparison, in the tunicate ciona GPB5, like in the gonadotropin β subunits, the homologous cysteine residues are 18 amino acids apart [40,41]. Given tunicates are the closest relatives to vertebrates [42] and since *ancGphβ* was generated by a duplication of *Gpb5* just prior to the emergence of vertebrates[14], it is likely in the ancGPHβ subunit precursor, the cysteines were also 18 amino acids apart. Thus, the *preTshβ* evolutionary precursor likely acquired these two codon insertions at the time of the 1R. It can be inferred from the aligned sequences that the insertion/deletion event was not generated at the splice site (Fig. 2). In the coelacanth TSHβ sequences however, the splice site is shifted twelve nucleotides towards the 3' end.

TSHβ3 sequences display particular signatures (Fig. 2 and Fig. S1). The most significant is that TSHβ3-type subunits harbor two potential N-linked glycosylation sites. The glycosylation pattern of

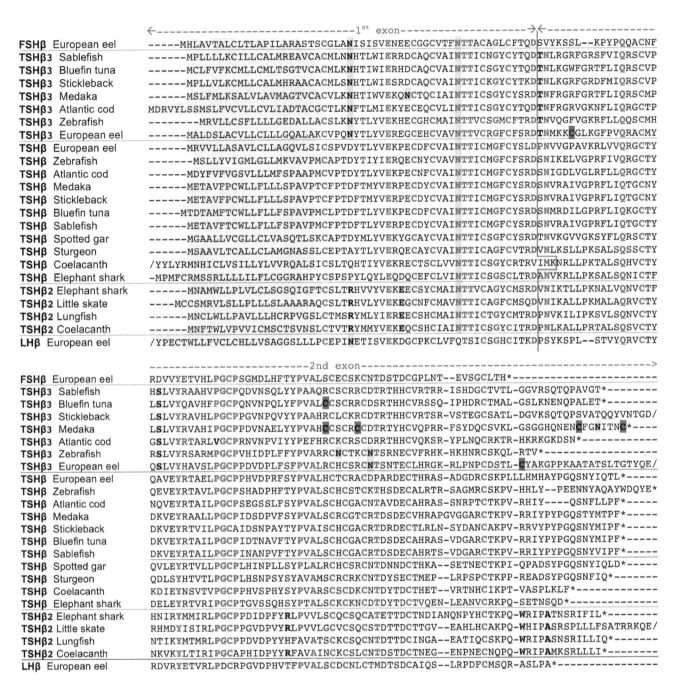

Figure 2. TSHβ-related sequence alignment. Amino acid sequence alignment of representatives of the three groups of TSHβ subunits. Eel LHβ and FSHβ sequences are given for comparison. The predicted signal peptide is highlighted in blue. The exon splicing site is indicated by the red vertical bar. Overall conserved amino acids are in bold red. Specific positions in TSHβ2 or -β3 sequences relative to TSHβ are highlighted in yellow. Potential glycosylation sites are highlighted in green. Additional, non-conserved cysteine residues are highlighted in red. Sequences might be truncated in the signal peptide or the carboxy-terminal end for convenience. Full-length sequences are presented in Fig. S1 and references are given in Table S1.

vertebrate glycoprotein hormone β subunits is usually well conserved with two sites in FSHβ and most likely in the ancestral β subunit, whereas LHβ have kept one site (the one towards the N-terminal), and TSHβ the other. The *Tshβ* subunit precursor gene that was duplicated during the 3R encoded a subunit with only one glycosylation site found, at the second position, as for all classical TSHβ subunits. The additional site was then *de novo* created by mutation of a well-conserved aspartic acid (D) to an asparagine (N) at the first position, two amino acids upstream of a conserved threonine. Since glycosylation sites are more likely to be created by generating a serine or threonine residue downstream of an existing asparagine [43], there may be some kind of structural constraints for this glycosylation site to be re-created precisely at this position. Similar constraints should have applied for human LHβ subunit, also characterized by a glycosylation site that is, conversely, switched from the first position to the second, TSH-type position. Other scattered potential glycosylation sites are observed in some TSHβ3 sequences (Fig. 2). Another feature of

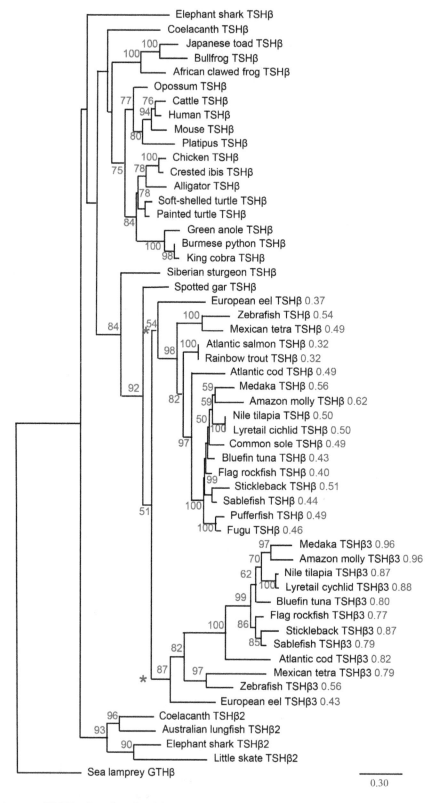

Figure 3. Phylogenetic tree of TSHβ related nucleotide sequences. Phylogram of maximum likelihood relationships between *Tshβ* coding sequences of representative species. The bootstrap values over 500 replicates (in %) are given next to each node in red (only the values above 50% are given). Cumulated distance values (from the node marked with a blue asterisk) are given in blue next to the species name for comparison of the estimated relative rate of evolution of teleost TSHβ and TSHβ3 sequences (see Fig. S4 for the regression curve). *Tshβ* gene references are given in Table S1.

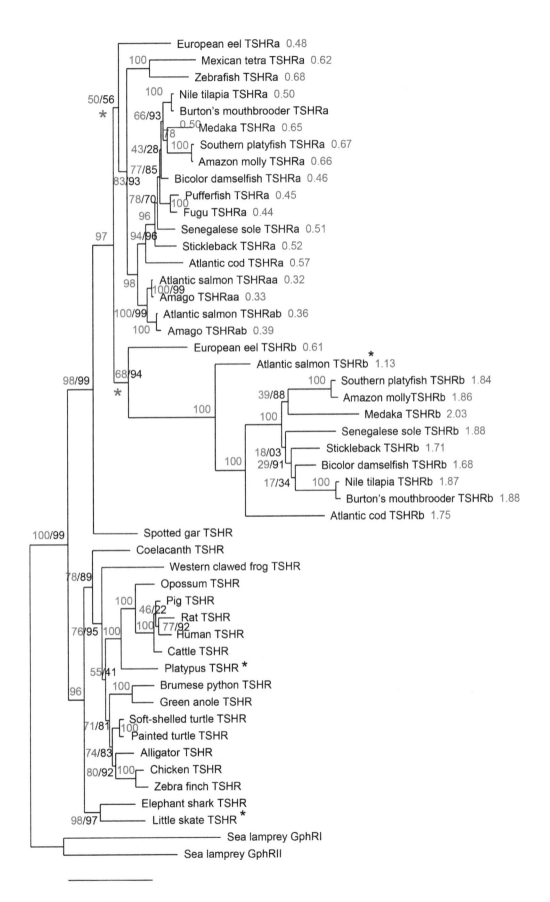

0.7

Figure 4. Phylogenetic tree of TSHR-related amino acid sequences. Phylogram of maximum likelihood relationships between TSHR amino acid sequences of representative species. The bootstrap values (in %) are given next to each node in red and the SH-like aLRT scores are given in black (when different from the boostrap value). Cumulated distance values (from the node marked with a blue asterisk) are given in blue next to the species name for comparison of the estimated relative rate of evolution of teleost TSHRa and TSHRb sequences (see Fig. S4 for the regression curve). *Tshr* gene references are given in Table S2. Black asterisks indicate partial sequences.

these TSHβ3 sequences is the presence of additional cysteine residues, up to maximum of four in the medaka sequence. Whether these cysteine residues are involved in generating intra- or inter-subunit disulfide bonds remains to be determined.

A single receptor for TSH and TSH2 in cartilaginous fish and basal lobe-finned fish

Only one receptor gene was identified in the coelacanth and elephant shark genomes, although they have two TSHβ subunits. It is thus likely that the additional TSH2 made up of TSHβ2 and the common α subunit, would act through binding to the same TSH receptor, as the classical TSH. Such a redundancy might have led to the loss of the second TSH in tetrapods and in ray-finned fish. The lungfish *Tshβ2* subunit cDNA [37] as well as the two *Tshβ* cDNAs from the elephant shark [14] were cloned from pituitary libraries. In situ hybridization studies will be needed to determine whether they are produced by the same cells.

Examination of tissue distribution could also reveal whether they are expressed in non-pituitary tissues.

One or two potential receptors for TSH and TSH3 in teleosts

Two TSH receptor sequences were identified in most teleost groups (Fig. S3). Phylogenetic analysis (Fig. 4) showed that teleost TSHR are divided into two monophyletic groups, each one with one eel TSHR-type branching at a basal position. In contrast, only one TSHR was found in the spotted gar, confirming that the duplication of *Tshr* occurred early in the teleost radiation [20,21]. Synteny analysis revealed that one of the teleost duplicated receptors is conserved in the same chromosomal region as before the duplication event (Fig. 5). This is the *Tshra*-type receptor as previously named [21]. The eel *Tshrb* is maintained in a similar genomic region as *Tshra*, in agreement with it resulting from the 3R (strict double conserved synteny). In contrast, in more derived

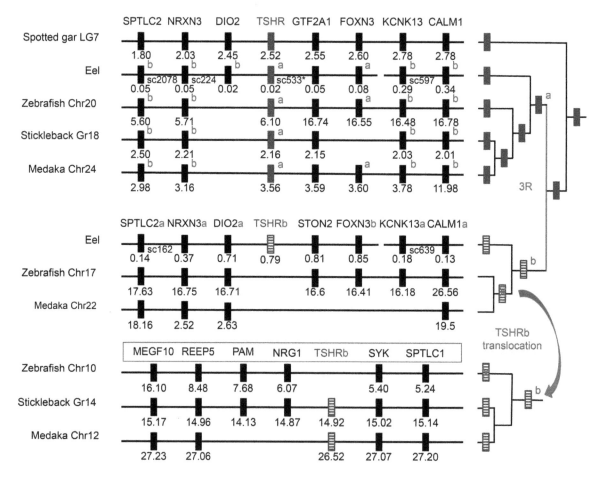

Figure 5. Syntenic analysis of TSHR-related genomic region. Genomic region flanking *Tshr*-related genes were analysed in representative species (chromosome number is attached to the species name) by using the region overview on the Ensembl genome browser or by blast analysis on the eel assembled genome (see Fig. S2B for details). The phylogenetic relationships between the represented species are summarized on the right panel. *Tshrb* was translocated sometime between the emergence of eel and stickleback lineages. Genes are named according to the Ensembl nomenclature (Table S4). Gene positions are given (in Mega base) below the symbolized genes.

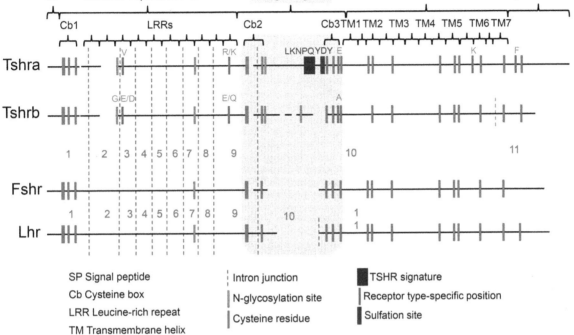

Figure 6. Schematic representation of TSHRa and TSHRb sequence features. Representation of the two types of teleost TSHR. LHR and FSHR are given for comparison. The exons splicing sites are indicated by a red dotted vertical bar. Both TSHR have conserved the typical architecture of the glycoprotein hormone receptor composed of a long extracellular domain comprising, from N- to C-terminal, a signal peptide (SP); a leucine-rich domain formed by successive leucine-rich repeat (LRR); a hinge region (in pink); a seven-transmembrane domain composed of seven helical regions (TM) connected by intracellular and extracellular loops alternatively and a cytosolic tail. Cysteine boxes at the N-terminal of the leucine rich domain and flanking the hinge are indicated (cb). Cysteine residues are in red, N-glycosylation sites in green. TSH-specific motif is in brown and sulfation site (YDY) in purple. Specific amino acids are labelled in blue.

teleost species such as cod, medaka and stickleback, *Tshrb* was found in a new genomic region (Fig. 5 and Table S4). This indicates that *Tshrb* was translocated some time after the emergence of Elopomorphs to another environment where its new location was stabilised. This change in the genomic environment of the *Tshrb* gene may alter the control of its expression, notably through epigenetic modifications and thus its response to environmental factors [44,45].

Like vertebrate *Tshr*, teleost *Tshra* is encoded by 10 exons. Nine of them encode the leucine-rich repeat (LRR) domain and, the large 10th exon encodes the transmembrane domain together with the carboxy-terminal cytosolic tail (Fig 6 and Fig. S3). This structure is conserved in eel *Tshrb*. In contrast, the domains encoded by the 10th exon appeared to be split into two exons in *Tshrb* from more derived teleosts (Fig. S3). Furthermore, the intracellular domain which usually exhibits signalization and internalization properties appeared to be shorter in TSHRb in these teleosts. However, alternative or additional exons could have been missed in our tentative sequencepredictions. Cloning of full length *Tshrb* cDNA in these teleost species could validate shortening of the cytosolic tail.

In Atlantic salmon, three *Tshr* sequences could be reconstructed from genomic data (Table S2). Phylogenetic analysis (Fig. 4) shows that two of them branch out together with the two characterized Amago receptors [46] and are of the a-type as previously shown [21]. These two a-type receptor genes likely result from the

salmonid-specific genome tetraploidization event (4R) [47]. A third, partial Atlantic salmon *Tshr* sequence identified here appears to be of the b-type indicating that salmonids are likely to have both types of TSHR.

A single *Tshr* (*Tshra*) is present in the genome of tetraodontiformes (e.g. fugu, pufferfish). The loss of the duplicated *Tshrb* in this teleost group is in agreement with the fact that they possess only one TSH. In contrast, *Tshrb* was also absent in ostariophysians (zebrafish, Mexican tetra), while they possess two potential TSHs. This indicates at least two independent losses of *Tshrb* during the radiation of teleosts. As with coelacanth or elephant shark TSH and TSH2, ostariophysian TSH and TSH3 might act through a unique TSHR receptor.

TSHRa and -b sequences present specific signatures

The TSHR sequence alignment showed high conservation features throughout the vertebrate evolution (Fig 6, Fig. S3). As compared with FSHR and LHR sequences, both TSHR types present a specific long hinge region, delimited by two conserved cysteine boxes (cb2 and cb3) connecting the extracellular domain to the transmembrane domain. The fact that most of these TSHR structural features were maintained in TSHRb indicates that it is subjected to similar functional constraints.

In both types of TSHR, two potential glycosylation sites were conserved, one close to the LRR2 region (N88 of the alignment in Fig. S3) and the other at the end of LRR6 (N210), the latter being

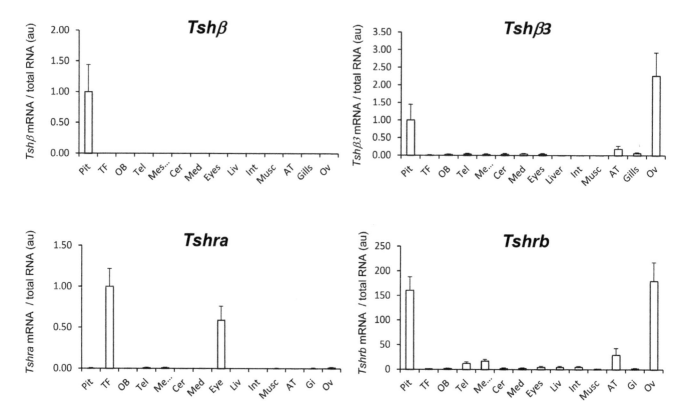

Figure 7. Tissue distribution profile of *Tshβ*, *Tshβ3*, *Tshra* **and** *Tshrb* **mRNA in the eel.** Tissue distribution was analysed by RT-qPCR on RNA extracted from various tissues in the immature female European eel. Owing to the different nature of the tissues, transcript levels were normalized using total tissue RNA content: pituitary (Pit), thyroid follicles (TF), olfactory bulb (OB), mes-/diencephalon (Mes/), telencephalon (Tel), cerebellum (Cer), medulla oblongata (Med), eyes, liver, intestine (Int), muscle (Musc), adipose tissue (AT), gills, and ovary (Ov). Transcript levels of *Tshβ* subunit and of *Tshr* were normalized to the level in the pituitary and in the thyroid follicles, respectively and are expressed as arbitrary units. Results are represented as mean values ± SEM (n = 8).

common to all glycoprotein hormone receptor types. The N-glycosylation site at the end of the cysteine box 2 (N324) was also conserved in both types of TSHR (except for the medaka TSHRb). The N-glycosylation site found in tetrapod sequences at the end of the LRR5 (N188) is conserved in lobe-finned fish and cartilaginous fish but is absent in ray-finned fish. Except in the eel, teleost TSHRb have additional potential N-glycosylation sites within the hinge region. They also differ from all other TSHR by lacking a conserved negative charge at position 262 at the start of the LRR9. A low amino acid conservation was observed within the hinge region for the TSHRb compared with the other TSHR (Fig. S3). In addition, one key cysteine of the cysteine-box 3 that was demonstrated to be involved in the disulfide bonding that gives its conformation to the hinge region is lost in cod. The THSRb hinge region lacks the common TSHR signature LKNPQ. The highly conserved tyrosine sulfation motif site [Y-(DE)-Y] within the hinge region involved in hormone recognition and signal transduction [48] that is still present in the eel is not conserved in more derived teleosts. In addition, the conserved glutamic acid (E) at position 446, which is a key determinant for the activation of the receptor [49], was switched to an alanine. Whether these differences in structure impact on binding specificity and on the signaling pathway will have to be determined.

TSHRb diverged at many points after the emergence of the eel as reflected by longer phylogenetic branch lengths (3.1 times that of TSHRa; cf Fig. 4 and Fig. S4), demonstrating an accelerated rate of evolution. Such a change in evolution rate is likely related to the duplication event with one gene keeping its original features

(the type-a receptor) allowing the other to acquire new specificities in spatial or temporal control of its expression and in binding characteristics of its encoded protein [15,50]. Studies of functionality of the duplicated TSH and TSHR should be addressed in the future by developing recombinant hormone and receptors for various teleost species. Such investigations are required to characterize the binding selectivity of the two TSHR and to determine whether they activate the same signaling pathway.

A dual TSH system in the European eel

The tissue distribution analysis by qPCR of the two duplicated *Tshβ* transcripts in the immature female eel showed that the classical *Tshβ* subunit was exclusively expressed in the pituitary (Fig. 7). A low expression of *Tshβ3* could also be detected in the pituitary. Further *in situ* hybridization studies will be needed to pin-point if both duplicated *Tshβ* are expressed by the same pituitary cells. In addition, *Tshβ3* was highly expressed in the ovary and was detected in adipose tissue, gills, brain structures and eye. This is the first report of a comparative tissue distribution of the two *Tshβ* subunits in teleosts. It clearly shows that the two β subunits have a differential tissue expression, which may represent one of the evolutionary drives leading to the conservation of the duplicated hormone. In stickleback, *Tshβ* and *Tshβ3* expression was compared only in the pituitary where both are expressed but *Tshβ3* showed differential transcriptional regulation according to the ecotype [18]. Unlike in the eel, the classical *Tshβ* subunit was shown to be expressed not only in the pituitary but also in the gonads of the fathead minnow [51] and the grouper [52]. EST

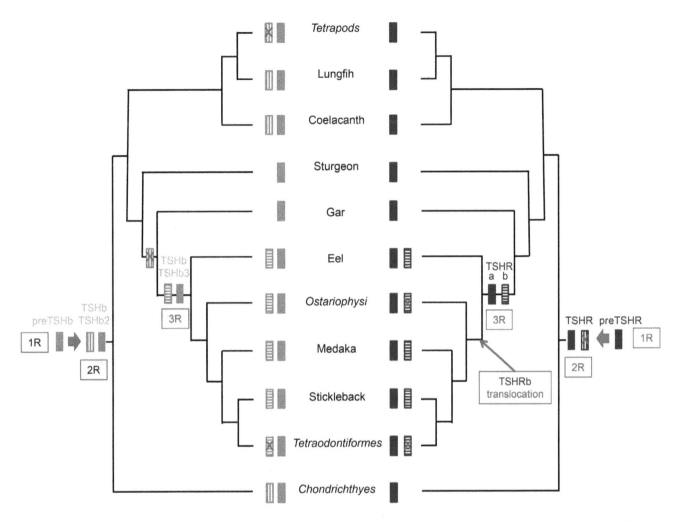

Figure 8. *Tshβ* and *Tshr* **gene evolution.** *Tshβ* and *Tshβ2* (left panel) were generated by duplication of a *preTshβ* gene through the 2R before the emergence of Gnathostomes. *Tshβ2* was lost (red crossed box) in tetrapods and in ray-finned fish before the emergence of the gar. *Tshβ3* was generated in teleosts by duplication of *Tshβ* through the 3R. Most teleost groups have kept *Tshβ3*. Only one *Tshr* (right panel) is found in vertebrates except in teleosts where a second gene was generated through the 3R. It was translocated to a new genomic environment after the emergence of the eel. Several groups of teleosts have lost this second *Tshr*.

data mining indicates that *Tshβ* transcripts are expressed in the brain of several teleost species (zebrafish - EH470445.1 and goldfish - DY231942; tilapia - GR616157.1; medaka - DK0206541) unlike the eel. In particular, *Tshβ* transcripts are found in the *saccus vasculosus*, at the base of the hypothalamus in salmon and may be involved as a photoperiodic signal transducer [53]. It is too early to draw conclusions about the absence of significant expression of the classical TSH in other tissues than the pituitary in the eel. Whether it is linked to its basal phylogenetic position relative to the duplication event, the physiological stage of the silver eel, or species specificity in the respective functions of the two TSHs will have to be further explored.

Tshβ3 was identified among transcripts isolated from liver in the adult Antarctic toothfish (FE210400.1) and from the ovary in the yellow perch (GO658547.1) indicating that the expression of this gene in these species as well as in the eel, is not restricted to the pituitary gland.

In the eel, as with the two *Tshβ* subunits, the duplicated *Tshr* showed a differential tissue distribution pattern. The thyroid follicles showed a high expression of *Tshra* while a low level of *Tshrb* transcript could be detected (Fig.7). This suggests that Tshra would mediate the classically described thyrotropic endocrine

function of TSH. This is in agreement with the conserved synteny and sequence of teleost *Tshra* as compared with tetrapod *Tshr*. Together with the major expression of the classical *Tshβ* in the eel pituitary, this allowed us to infer that endocrine control of thyroid function via the classic TSH produced by the pituitary and classic TSHR expressed by the thyroid, is conserved through vertebrate evolution. Both *Tshra* and *Tshrb* are expressed in eel non-thyroid tissues with specific distribution. *Tshra* is expressed in the eye while *Tshrb* is mainly expressed in the pituitary and ovary and also detected in different parts of the brain and adipose tissue as well as some other peripheral tissues (Fig. 7). The similarity of expression profiles between *Tshβ3* and *Tshrb* makes it very tempting to speculate that TSHβ3 might act as a paracrine or autocrine factor of TSHRb.

Non-thyroidal expression was reported for TSHRa in other teleosts, notably in the gonads in catfish [54,55] and fathead minnow [51], two ostariophysian species that, in contrast to the eel, might possess only this type of receptor. *Tshra* was also found in the gonad of striped bass [56] and European sea bass [57], species which may possess both receptors, according to their phylogenetic position among teleosts. The only available information about the tissue distribution of the b-type receptor is restricted to the truncated transcript of *Tshrb* in the sole, that showed similar expression patterns as classical *Tshra* [20]. It will be interesting to investigate what effect the translocation of *Tshrb* from one genomic region to another has had on control of its expression.

In mammals, in addition to the thyroid follicles, TSHR expression has been described in several tissues notably anterior pituitary, hypothalamus, ovary, testis, skin, immune cells and adipose tissue [58–61] but the specific roles in these non-thyroid tissues are not fully known. As compared to the mammalian single TSHR, the tissue distribution of the duplicated eel TSHR highlights a clear sub functionalization, with TSHRa involved in the thyroid control and TSHRb in various non-thyroidal functions.

Conclusion

The present study revealed that two TSHs would have arisen from the second global genome duplication (2R) in early vertebrates (Fig. 8), concurrently with the two gonadotropins LH and FSH [14]. The duplicated *Tshβ2* has been conserved in cartilaginous fish and in early lobe-finned fish, but would have been lost both in tetrapods and in early ray-finned fish. This loss of the second *Tshβ* may be related to the redundancy of two TSH, acting via a unique receptor, since the putative duplicated TSH receptor issued from the 2R would have been lost early in the vertebrate evolution (Fig. 8). A second chance for a TSH system doubling occurred in teleosts when a novel global genome duplication (3R) occurred in the lineage. Both duplicated *Tshβ/Tshβ3* and duplicated *Tshra/Tshrb* are found in various extant teleosts, while *Tshβ3* and *Tshrb* may have been lost in some teleost groups. The eel provides a remarkable example of conservation of a duplicated TSH/TSHR system. The endocrine thyrotropic function in the eel would be essentially mediated by the classical TSH and TSHR, which are mainly expressed in the pituitary and thyroid, respectively. The comparison of the distribution pattern of the duplicated *Tshβ3* and the duplicated *Tshrb* shows a striking similarity that could confer a possible autocrine/paracrine role for this couple in several non-thyroidal tissues in the eel. However, the higher evolutionary rate observed in teleosts for the duplicated *Tshβ3* and *Tshrb* suggests that their functions may not be fully stabilized yet. These advances in the evolutionary scenario of TSH and TSHR in vertebrates open new research avenues concerning the functional relationships between the two duplicated TSH and TSHR. Until now little is known about the TSH-TSHR system except in tetrapods. The structural characteristics of duplicated

TSHβ in teleost have been well conserved suggesting it might be functional. Further investigations on ligand properties and receptor selectivity and activity are required to evaluate the biological importance of the duplication of the system TSH-TSHR and to infer evolutionary drives that contributed to the maintenance of the duplicated ligand –receptor system.

Supporting Information

Figure S1 **TSHβ subunit-related sequences alignment.**

Figure S2 **Reconstructed eel genomic regions flanking TSHβ (A) and TSHR (B) genes.**

Figure S3 **TSHR-related sequence alignment.**

Figure S4 **Relative evolution rates between TSHβ and TSHβ3 and between TSHR-a and -b sequences.**

Table S1 **Database references for TSHβ subunit-related sequences.**

Table S2 **Database references for TSHR-related sequences.**

Table S3 **European eel primer sets for quantitative real-time PCR.**

Table S4 **Database references for the genes in TSHβ and TSHR genomic regions.**

Acknowledgments

The authors are grateful to Dr M. Familari, University of Melbourne, for English corrections.

Author Contributions

Conceived and designed the experiments: GM BQ. Performed the experiments: GM BQ. Analyzed the data: GM SD JCT BQ. Contributed reagents/materials/analysis tools: GM SD BQ. Wrote the paper: GM SD JCT BQ.

References

1. Yen PM (2001) Physiological and molecular basis of thyroid hormone action. Physiol Rev 81: 1097–1142.
2. Tata JR (1997) Hormonal signaling and amphibian metamorphosis. Adv Dev Biol 7: 37–274.
3. Denver RJ (2013) Neuroendocrinology of amphibian metamorphosis. Curr Top Dev Biol 103: 195–227.
4. Inui Y Miwa S (1985) Thyroid hormone induces metamorphosis of flounder larvae. Gen Comp Endocrinol 60: 450–454.
5. de Jesus EGT, Toledo JD, Simpas MS (1998) Thyroid hormones promote early metamorphosis in grouper (Epinephelus coioides) larvae. Gen Comp Endocrinol 112: 10–16.
6. Manchado M, Infante C, Asensio E, Planas J, Cañavate J (2008) Thyroid hormones down-regulate thyrotropin β subunit and thyroglobulin during metamorphosis in the flatfish Senegalesesole (*Solea senegalensis* Kaup). Gen Comp Endocrinol 155: 447–455.
7. Rousseau K, Martin P, Boeuf G, Dufour S (2012). Salmonid secondary metamorphosis: smoltification. *In*: Dufour S, Rousseau K and Kapoor BG, editors. 'Fish Metamorphosis': *Science Publishers, Enfield (NH), USA* pp. 167-215.
8. Sudo R, Okamura A, Kuroki M, Tsukamoto K (2014) Changes in the role of the thyroid axis during metamorphosis of the Japanese eel, *Anguilla japonica*. J Exp Zool A Ecol Genet Physiol 321: 357–364.
9. Klein JR (2003) Physiological relevance of thyroid stimulating hormone and thyroid stimulating hormone receptor in tissues other than the thyroid. Autoimmunity 36: 417–421.
10. Krassas GE, Poppe K, Glinoer D (2010) Thyroid function and human reproductive health. Endocr Rev 31: 702–755.
11. Williams GR (2011) Extrathyroidal expression of TSH receptor. Annales d'Endocrinologie 72: 68–73.
12. Duarte-Guterman P, Navarro-Martin L, Trudeau VL (2014) Mechanisms of crosstalk between endocrine systems: Regulation of sex steroid hormone synthesis and action by thyroid hormones. Gen Comp Endocrinol 203: 69–85.
13. Pierce JG, Parsons TF (1981) Glycoprotein hormones: structure and function. Ann Rev Biochem 50: 465–495.
14. Dos Santos S, Mazan S, Vankatesh B, Cohen-Tannoudji J, Quérat B (2011) Emergence and evolution of the glycoprotein hormone and neurotrophin gene families in vertebrates. BMC Evol Biol 11: 332.
15. Van de Peer Y, Maere S, Meyer A (2009) The evolutionary significance of ancient genome duplications. Nature Rev Genet 10: 725–732.
16. MacKenzie DS, Jones RA, Miller TC (2009) Thyrotropin in teleost fish. Gen Comp Endocrinol 161: 83–89.
17. Hoegg S, Brinkmann H, Taylor JS, Meyer A (2004) Phylogenetic timing of the fish-specific genome duplication correlates with the diversification of teleost fish. J Mol Evol 59: 190–203.

18. Kitano J, Lema SC, Luckenbach JA, Mori S, Kawagishi Y, et al. (2010) Adaptive divergence in the thyroid hormone signaling pathway in the stickleback radiation. Current Biology 20: 2124–2130.

19. Szkudlinski MW, Fremont V, Ronin C, Weintraub BD (2002) Thyroid-stimulating hormone and thyroid-stimulating hormone receptor structure-function relationships. Physiol Rev 82: 473–502.

20. Ponce M, Infante C, Manchado M (2010) Molecular characterization and gene expression of thyrotropin receptor (TSHR) and a truncated TSHR-like in Senegalese sole. Gen Comp Endocrinol 168: 431–439.

21. Chauvigné F, Tingaud-Sequeira A, Agulleiro MJ, Calusinska M, Gómez A, et al. (2010) Functional and evolutionary analysis of flatfish gonadotropin receptors reveals cladal- and lineage-level divergence of the teleost glycoprotein receptor family. Biol Reprod 82: 1088–1102.

22. Venkatesh B, Lee AP, Ravi V, Maurya AK, Lian MM, et al. (2014) Elephant shark genome provides unique insights into gnathostome evolution. Nature 505: 174–179.

23. Amores A, Catchen J, Ferrara A, Fontenot Q, Postlethwait JH (2011) Genome evolution and meiotic maps by massively parallel DNA sequencing: spotted gar, an outgroup for the teleost genome duplication. Genetics 188: 799–808.

24. Amemiya CT, Alföldi J, Lee AP, Fan S, Philippe H, et al. (2013) The African coelacanth genome provides insights into tetrapod evolution. Nature 496: 311–316.

25. Liang D, Shen XX, Zhang P (2013) One thousand two hundred ninety nuclear genes from a genome-wide survey support lungfishes as the sister group of tetrapods. Mol Biol Evol 30: 1803–1807.

26. Henkel CV, Burgerhout E, de Wijze DL, Dirks RP, Minegishi Y, et al. (2012)a Primitive duplicate hox clusters in the European eel's genome. PLoS One 7: e32231.

27. Henkel CV, Dirks RP, de Wijze DL, Minegishi Y, Aoyama J et al. (2012) First draft genome sequence of the Japanese eel, Anguilla japonica. Gene 511(2): 195–201.

28. Faircloth BC, Sorenson L, Santini F, Alfaro ME (2013) A phylogenomic perspective on the radiation of ray-finned fishes based upon targeted sequencing of ultraconserved elements (UCEs). PLoS One 8: e65923.

29. Chen JN, López JA, Lavoué S, Miya M, Chen WJ (2014) Phylogeny of the Elopomorpha (Teleostei): evidence from six nuclear and mitochondrial markers. Mol Phylogenet Evol 70: 152–161.

30. Altschul SF, Gish W, Miller W, Myers EW, Lipman DJ (1990) Basic local alignment search tool. J Mol Biol 215: 403–410.

31. Dereeper A, Guignon V, Blanc G, Audic S, Buffet S, et al. (2008) Phylogeny. fr: robust phylogenetic analysis for the non-specialist. Nucleic Acids Research 36. 465–469.

32. Aroua S, Maugars G, Jeng SR, Weltzien FA, Rousseau K et al. (2012) Pituitary gonadotropins FSH and LH are oppositely regulated by the activin/follistatin system in a basal teleost, the eel. Gen Comp Endocrinol 175: 82–91.

33. Untergrasser A, Cutcutache I, Koressaar T, Ye J, Faircloth BC, et al. (2012) Primer3 - new capabilities and interfaces.Nucleic Acids Research 40: 115.

34. Koressaar T, Remm M (2007) Enhancements and modifications of primer design program Primer3. Bioinformatics 23: 1289–1291

35. Pasquier J, Lafont A-G, Jeng S-R, Morini M, Dirks R et al. (2012) Multiple kisspeptin receptors in early osteichthyans provide new insights into the evolution of this receptor family. PLoS One 7: e48931.

36. Dethleffsen K, Heinrich G, Lauth M, Knapik EW, Meyer M (2003) Insert-containing neurotrophins in teleost fish and their relationship to nerve growth factor. Mol Cell Neuroscience 24: 380–394.

37. Quérat B, Arai Y, Henry A, Akama Y, Longhurst TJ, et al. (2004). Pituitary glycoprotein hormone β-subunits in the Australian lungfish and estimation of the relative evolution rate of these subunits within vertebrates. Biol Reprod 70: 356–363.

38. Levavi-Sivan B, Bogerd J, Mañanos EL, Gomez A, Lareyre JJ (2010) Perspectives on fish gonadotropins. Gen Comp Endocrinol 165: 412–437.

39. Quérat B, Sellouk A, Salmon C (2000) Phylogenetic analysis of the vertebrate glycoprotein hormone family including new sequences of sturgeon Acipenser baeri, β-subunits of the two gonadotropins and the thyroid-stimulating hormone. Biol Reprod 63: 222–228.

40. Dos Santos S, Bardet C, Bertrand S, Escriva H, Habert D, et al. (2009) Distinct expression patterns of glycoprotein hormone-α2 and - β5 in a basal chordate suggest independent developmental functions. Endocrinology 150: 3815–3822.

41. Kano S (2010) Genomics and developmental approaches to an acidian adenohypophysis primordium. Integr Comp Biol 50: 1–35–52.

42. Blair JE, Hedges SB (2005) Molecular phylogeny and divergence times of deuterostome animals. Mol Biol Evol 22: 2275–2284.

43. Williams R, Ma X, Schott RK, Mohammad N, Ho CY, Li CF, et al (2014) Encoding asymmetry of the N-glycosylation motif facilitates glycoprotein evolution. PLoS One 9: e86088.

44. Choi JK, Kim SC (2007) Environmental effects on gene expression phenotype have regional biases in the human genome. Genetics 175: 1607–1613.

45. Harewood L, Schütz F, Boyle S, Perry P, Delorenzi M et al (2010) The effect of translocation-induced nuclear reorganization on gene expression. Genome Res. 20: 554–564.

46. Oba Y, Hirai T, Yoshiura Y, Kobayashi T, Nagahama Y (2000) Cloning, functional characterization, and expression of thyrotropin receptors in the thyroid of amago salmon (Oncorhynchus rhodurus). Biochem Biophys Res Commun 276: 258–263.

47. Angers B, Gharbi K, Estoup A (2002) Evidence of gene conversion events between paralogous sequences produced by tetraploidization in Salmoninae fish. J Mol Evol 54: 501–510.

48. Costagliola S, Panneels V, Bonomi M, Koch J, Many MC, et al. (2002) Tyrosine sulfation is required for agonist recognition by glycoprotein hormone receptors. EMBO J 21: 504–513.

49. Krause G, Kreuchwig A, Kleinau G (2012) Extended and structurally supported insights into extracellular hormone binding, signal transduction and organization of the thyrotropin receptor. PLoS One 7: e52920.

50. Hurles M (2004) Gene duplication: the genomic trade in spare parts. PLoS Biol 2: e206.

51. Lema SC, Dickey JT, Schultz IR, Swanson P (2009) Thyroid hormone regulation of mRNAs encoding thyrotropin β-subunit, glycoprotein α-subunit, and thyroid hormone receptors a and b in brain, pituitary gland, liver, and gonads of an adult teleost, Pimephales promelas. J Endocrinol 202: 43–54.

52. Wang Y, Zho L, Yao B, Li CJ, Gui JF (2004) Differential expression of thyroid-stimulating hormone β subunit in gonads during sex reversal of orange-spotted and red-spotted groupers. Mol. Cell. Endocrinol. 220: 77–88.

53. Nakane Y, Ikegami K, Iigo M, Ono H, Takeda K, et al. (2013) The saccus vasculosus of fish is a sensor of seasonal changes in day length. Nat Commun 4, 2108.

54. Vischer H, Bogerd J (2003) Cloning and functional characterization of a testicular TSH receptor cDNA from the African catfish (Clarias gariepinus). J Mol Endocrinol 30: 227–238.

55. Goto-Kazeto R, Kazeto Y, Trant JM (2003) Cloning and seasonal changes in ovarian expression of a TSH receptor in the channel catfish, Ictalurus punctatus. Fish Physiology and Biochemistry 28: 339–340.

56. Kumar RS, Ijiri S, Kight K, Swanson P, Dittman A (2000) Cloning and functional characterization of a thyrotropin receptor from the gonads of a vertebrate (bony fish): potential thyroid-independent role for thyrotropin in reproduction. Mol. Cell Endocrinol 167: 1–9.

57. Rocha A, Gomez A, Galay-Burgos M, Zanuy S, Sweeney G.E., et al. (2007) Molecular characterization and seasonal changes in gonadal expression of a thyrotropin receptor in the European sea bass. Gen Comp Endocrinol 152: 89–101.

58. Davies TF, Ando T, Lin RY, Tomer Y, Latif R (2005) Thyrotropin receptor-associated diseases: from adenomata to Graves disease. J Clin Invest 115:1972–1983.

59. Bodó E, Kany B, Gáspár E, Knüver J, Kromminga A, et al. (2010) Thyroid-stimulating hormone, a novel, locally produced modulator of human epidermal functions, is regulated by thyrotropin-releasing hormone and thyroid hormones. Endocrinology 151: 1633–1642.

60. Lu S, Guan Q, Liu Y, Wang H, Xu W, et al (2012) Role of extrathyroidal TSHR expression in adipocyte differentiation and its association with obesity. Lipids in Health and Disease 11: 17.

61. Stavreus-Evers A (2012) Paracrine interactions of thyroid hormones and thyroid stimulation hormone in the female reproductive tract have an impact on female fertility. Front Endocrinol 3: 50.

4

Meta-Analysis of Gene Expression Signatures Reveals Hidden Links among Diverse Biological Processes in Arabidopsis

Liming Lai, Steven X. Ge*

Department of Mathematics and Statistics, South Dakota State University, Brookings, South Dakota, United States of America

Abstract

The model plant Arabidopsis has been well-studied using high-throughput genomics technologies, which usually generate lists of differentially expressed genes under various conditions. Our group recently collected 1065 gene lists from 397 gene expression studies as a knowledgebase for pathway analysis. Here we systematically analyzed these gene lists by computing overlaps in all-vs.-all comparisons. We identified 16,261 statistically significant overlaps, represented by an undirected network in which nodes correspond to gene lists and edges indicate significant overlaps. The network highlights the correlation across the gene expression signatures of the diverse biological processes. We also partitioned the main network into 20 sub-networks, representing groups of highly similar expression signatures. These are common sets of genes that were co-regulated under different treatments or conditions and are often related to specific biological themes. Overall, our result suggests that diverse gene expression signatures are highly interconnected in a modular fashion.

Editor: Francisco J. Esteban, University of Jaén, Spain

Funding: This work was supported by the National Institute of General Medical Studies at the National Institutes of Health (GM083226 to SXG, in part) and this material is based upon work supported partially by the National Science Foundation/EPSCoR Award No. IIA-1355423 and by the state of South Dakota. The funders had no role in study design, data collection and analysis, decision to publish, or preparation of the manuscript.

Competing Interests: The authors have declared that no competing interests exist.

* Email: xijin.ge@sdstate.edu

Introduction

Because of its small genome size, *Arabidopsis* thaliana has been a valuable model system for genetic mapping, sequencing and gene expression analysis [1]. Until March 2013, 1787 studies on gene expression of *Arabidopsis* were indexed in Gene Expression Omnibus (GEO) website in National Center for Biotechnology Information (NCBI) [2]. These studies investigated various biological processes by monitoring the gene expression level using the high-throughput genomics technologies such as DNA microarrays and RNA sequencing. The results were usually a set of genes associated with particular biological processes based on different experimental designs. Even though DNA microarrays suffer from noise and reproducibility issues [3], we believe that many of the noise could be filtered out by statistical analysis and that there are significant associations among these numerous results, or common modules in the transcriptional program.

Some studies have showed the relationships among gene lists in different species. Most researchers analyzed these gene lists using methodology of meta-analysis [4–7], which combines the results of studies that address a set of related research hypotheses, focusing on a special individual topic such as cancer or special treatment [8]. Several databases of gene lists have been created, such as L2L [9], LOLA [10], and MSigDB [11]. An network-based method was developed by Ge [12] to define associations among a large number of gene sets in human. Associations are defined as statistically significant overlaps between two gene lists. The method was applied successfully to a large number of human

gene lists [12], and identified molecular links among diverse biological processes.

In this study, we used the methodology in [12] to analyze a set of *Arabidopsis* gene lists identified by genome wide expression studies. These lists were collected for AraPath [13], an *Arabidopsis* gene lists database we created recently. The objective was to systematically evaluate relationships among the gene lists and interpret the relationships. This process provides not only a new tool to uncover hidden links among vast amounts of gene lists, but a quantitative measure to describe the global gene expression of the *Arabidopsis* system under diverse conditions.

Materials and Methods

Data in this study was extracted from the AraPath [13], which is a gene lists database in *Arabidopsis* we created (Availability: http://bioinformatics.sdstate.edu/arapath/). As part of the database, the data contains a total of 1,065 co-expression gene lists, which were manually retrieved from published papers linked to GEO [2] before February, 2011.

Methodology of the analysis includes four steps. Step 1 is to evaluate overlapping genes among the 1,065 gene lists. A Perl programs was written to evaluate overlapping genes between all 566,580 pairs of lists. An overlap refers to a pair of gene lists, which has at least two common genes. And overlaps from the same paper were considered trivial and were removed. Because there are too much overlaps and microarray experiments tends to produce noisy data, we selected significant overlaps using stringent threshold. Step 2 computes p-values and q-values to identify significant overlaps. Based on the Hypergeometric distribution, we first calculate the likelihood (p-value) of observing the number of overlapping genes if these two gene lists are randomly drawn without replacement from a collection of 28,024 unique genes in terms of R program [14] we compiled. Then, p-values were translated into q-values based on the false discovery rate (FDR) [15] to correct that for multiple testing. Overlaps with very small q-value were significant overlaps. In this case, significant overlaps were identified with a q-value $= 5.0E\text{-}9$ as a cutoff. In step 3, network of significant overlaps was constructed based on outputs of the step 2 using Cytoscape[16]. Because this network includes too many nodes and edges, we need to further break the big clusters into smaller subclusters. In step 4, There are many algorithms that could decompose large networks into small, densely connected subnetworks such as those in [17,18]. We chose a simply algorithm that is available as a plug-in to Cytoscape. MCODE [19] is used to identify interconnected sub-networks and their clusters within the network of the step 3. To generally find locally dense regions (or clusters) of a graph is based on the clustering coefficient [19], C_i, which measures "clique" of the neighborhood of a vertex: $C_i = 2n/k_i\ (k_i - 1)$, where k_i is the vertex size of the neighborhood of vertex i, n is the number of edges in the neighborhood. According to the MCODE algorithm [19], however, clustering the main network into sub-networks is by means of vertex weighting, which is to weight all vertices based on their local network density using the highest k-core of the vertex neighborhood rather than the clustering coefficient C_i. A k-core is a graph of minimal degree k. The highest k-core of a graph is the central most densely connected sub-graph. Given a highly connected vertex, in a dense region of a graph, v may be connected to many vertices of degree one. These low degree vertices do not interconnect within the neighborhood of v and thus would reduce the clustering coefficient, but not the core-clustering coefficient (for detailed information about the MCODE algorithms, see the paper [19]). Here we created the sub-networks and found the modules and clusters using MCODE algorithms based on the following parameters: Node Score Cutoff $= 0.15$; k-core $= 2$; Degree Cutoff $= 2$; Max. Depth $= 100$. The DAVID web site [20,21] was applied to analyze the most significant functions of most frequently shared genes in each of sub-networks.

Results

A total of 1,065 gene lists were analyzed in this study. They include 277,349 gene entries corresponding to 28,024 unique genes. The average size of these gene lists is 87 genes, ranging from 1 to 2,952 genes. Its distribution is close to normality on a log10 scale (Figure 1). The results of analysis of the data are as follows.

Significant overlaps

By comparing all pairs of 1,065 gene lists using the Perl program, 16,261 significant overlaps were identified from a total of 192,642 overlaps. Based on the Hyper-geometric distribution, the probabilities (p-values) of observing the number of overlapping genes or more were first calculated if these two gene lists were randomly drawn without the replacement from a collection of 28,024 unique genes. The p-values were translated into q-values according to the false discovery rate (FDR) [15] to correct for multiple testing. Overlaps from the same paper were considered trivial and were removed. With a q-value $= 5 \times 10^-$ as a conservative cutoff, 16,261 significant overlaps were identified.

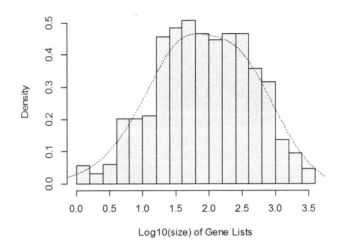

Figure 1. Histogram of log10 scale of size of gene lists.

Main network

The 16,261 significant overlaps are represented as an undirected network (Figure 2). In the network, nodes correspond to gene lists and edges indicate number of overlapping genes between two nodes within significant overlaps. This network highlights the correlation across gene expression signatures of diverse biological processes. It, thus, constitutes a "molecular signature map" in which the individual perturbations are placed in the context defined by others. This is a highly connected network with an average of 20.10 connections per gene list. The 809 nodes (75.96% of the 1,065 gene lists) and 16,261 edges are connected to a dominant main network. Most nodes are connected to a small number of gene lists. The network shows some different colors "cliques", which are some of the most connected graphs in terms of a vertex-weighting scheme based on the highest k-core of the vertex neighborhood. They are intuitively denser links within some neighborhoods.

Modules

To further explore these neighborhoods, we used the MCODE algorithm [19] to decompose the network into a total of 20 sub-networks. Of them, nine modules were further analyzed and their clustered information was shown in Table 1. The others were ignored because they are much lower score of density (less than 1.6) and have few nodes and edges (less than 6). The nine sub-networks are highly interconnected, suggesting that those genes are involved in common metabolic pathways or interact with each other under similar biological perturbations. The first three sub-networks are described in the following section. The remaining six sub-networks description and all the sub-networks figures and their composite outcomes tables are shown in Figures S1–S9 and Tables S1–S9 in File S1.

Sub-network 1

The sub-network 1 includes 46 nodes and 969 edges (Figure 3). The score of cluster density is 21.065, which is the highest score among nine sub-networks. This indicates it is the most densely connected. In Figure 3, the dark red nodes represent higher network density based on MCODE [19]. Dark green edges represent very small p-values. There are 31 nodes that represent up-regulated, eight down-regulated, and seven differently regulated. Most gene lists (67.39%) involving up-regulated nodes are related to seven biological themes and 25 treatments or conditions.

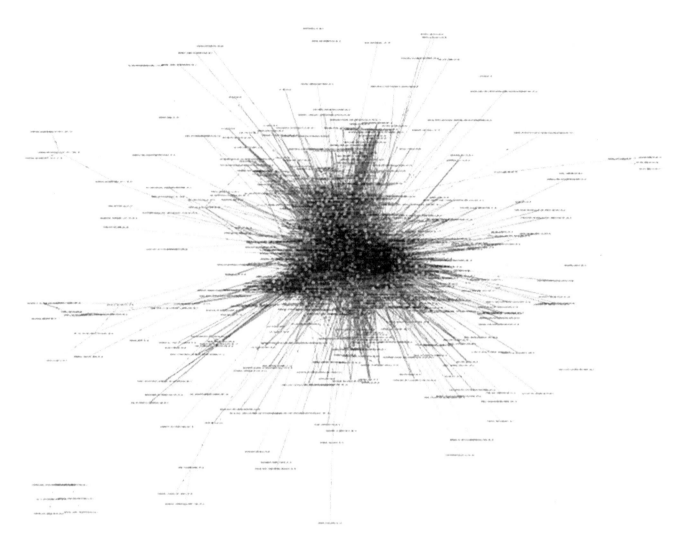

Figure 2. The main network created by Cytoscape. Node = name of gene list. Node Color = MCODE_Scores from small to large and corresponds to color from light green to dark red. Edge Color = p-values from large to small and corresponds to color from grey to dark green.

Table S1 in File S1 shows its composite outcomes. There are 46 gene lists and 256 frequently shared genes identified in this sub-network. They are regulated by 32 treatments or conditions from 32 publications related to 11 biological themes involving development, metabolism, disease, yield, function, genome analysis, immune, pathogen, mechanism, energy, virus, and photosynthesis in *Arabidopsis*. The top 10 most frequently shared genes with their gene descriptions were specifically listed corresponding to different gene lists, different biological themes, and treatments or conditions. For example, gene AT4G14365 ("putative E3 ubiquitin-protein ligase XBAT34") has the highest frequency of 35, which indicates it is the most active gene because it is regulated simultaneously under 35 gene lists in sub-network 1, namely, the gene connects directly 35 gene lists.

The most significant function of sub-network 1 is biological process in response to chitin (i.e. the most enriched term corresponding to the most frequently shared genes in sub-network 1 is "response to chitin") based on results of analysis of DAVID (Table 1). This indicates sub-network 1 is specifically associated with the chitin signaling pathway rather than by random chance. The other significant functions of sub-network 1 are responding to carbohydrate stimulus, organic substance, defense response, and bacterium based on the analysis of DAVID with a cutoff of

1.60×10^{-16} p-value. This suggests that sub-network 1 involves multiple signaling pathways.

Sub-network 2

Sub-network 2 is shown in Figure 4 and Table S2 in File S1. It includes 54 nodes (gene lists) and 168 frequently shared genes, which are regulated under 38 different treatments or conditions from 38 publications related to 10 biological themes. The score of cluster density is 9.907. There are 17 nodes to be up-regulated, 34 to be down-regulated, and three to be differently regulated. Most gene lists (62.96%) involving down-regulated nodes are related to nine biological themes and 23 treatments or conditions. Compared to sub-network 1, sub-network 2 has a lower cluster density score with even more treatments or conditions. Nine themes in sub-network 2 are common with sub-network 1: development, disease, function, genome analysis, mechanism, metabolism, photosynthesis, virus, and yield. This indicates the two sub-networks have relationships linked by same themes. No gene is common between the 256 frequently shared genes in sub-network 1 and the 168 frequently shared genes in sub-network 2. The two sub-networks have relatively independent functions. The most significant function of sub-network 2 is biological process of plastid thylakoid membrane based on results of DAVID (Table 1), suggesting that

Table 1. Summary of nine modules consisting of highly interconnected gene lists.

ID	Score Density†	#Nodes	#Edges	Unique genes	Shared genes*	Highest frequency	Most significantly enriched GO Term*	P-value*
1	21.065	46	969	10581	256	35	response to chitin	1.70E-38
2	9.907	54	535	12163	168	20	plastid thylakoid membrane	1.80E-59
3	9.545	33	315	9501	124	17	response to chitin	8.80E-13
4	9.062	48	435	13930	155	18	response to auxin stimulus	9.00E-10
5	2.559	34	87	9751	109	10	cell wall	5.30E-11
6	2.111	9	19	2565	34	6	External encapsulating structure organization	5.40E-07
7	2	15	30	6725	53	8	glycoside biosynthetic process	2.00E-05
8	2	6	12	5212	66	6	membrane-enclosed lumen	6.00E-14
9	1.846	13	24	3567	23	6	response to abiotic stimulus	6.80E-08
T	-	258	2426	-	988	-	-	-

Note: †Score Density = #Edges/#Nodes. *Most significantly enriched GO Term and p-value are the results of analysis of the DAVID in terms of the most frequently shared genes (i.e. Shared genes in Table 1) in each sub-network.

sub-network 2 is specifically associated with plastid thylakoid membrane, i.e. the lipid bilayer membrane of any thylakoid within a plastid. The other significant functions of sub-network 2 are response to chloroplast thylakoid membrane, thylakoid membrane, plastid thylakoid, and chloroplast thylakoid based on DAVID with cut-off p-value of 6.8×10^{-58}. The top 10 most frequently shared genes with their gene descriptions corresponding to gene lists, biological themes, and treatments or conditions were specifically listed in Table S2 in File S1. Gene AT4G27030 (fatty acid desaturase A), for example, has the highest frequency of 20, indicating it is the most active gene in sub-network 2.

Sub-network 3

The sub-network 3 includes 33 nodes (gene lists) and 124 most frequently shared genes (Figure 5 and Table S3 in File S1). There are 28 nodes to be up-regulated, four to be down-regulated, and one to be differently regulated. Most gene lists (84.85%) involving up-regulated nodes are related to nine biological themes and 20 treatments or conditions. By contrast to sub-networks 1 and 2, sub-network 3 is smaller in size, has a lower cluster density score, and less treatments or conditions for gene lists. Sub-network 3 are regulated by 25 treatments or conditions from 25 publications associated with 11 biological themes. Nine themes in sub-network 3 are common with sub-network 1: development, disease, energy, function, immune, mechanism, metabolism, photosynthesis, and virus. There are seven common themes (development, disease, function, mechanism, metabolism, photosynthesis, and virus) between sub-networks 3 and 2. These indicate sub-networks 3 and 1 or 2 have relationships linked by the same themes.

The top 10 most frequently shared genes with their gene descriptions corresponding to each gene list in sub-network 3 are specifically listed in Table S3 in File S1. Gene AT2G18690 has the highest frequency at 17, indicating it is the most active genes in sub-network 3. Other shared genes in sub-network 3 have lower frequency, which means they are less active than those in sub-networks 1 and 2. There is no common gene between the 168 most frequently shared genes in sub-network 2 and the 124 most frequently shared genes in sub-network 3. However, there are 72 genes of intersection between sub-networks 1 and 3. This indicates sub-networks 2 and 3 have relatively independent functions and sub-networks 1 and 3 have dependent relationship linked by the common shared genes. The most significant function of sub-network 3 is biological process in response to chitin based on results of analysis of DAVID (Table 1). It is specifically associated with the chitin signaling pathway, which is the same as sub-network 1 but different from sub-networks 2.

Discussion

The gene lists in our data are highly connected. Out of the 1,065 gene lists, 75.96% are connected in the main network in which many seemingly unrelated stimuli/perturbation may activate or deactivate the same molecular pathways. All the gene lists within each sub-network are highly connected by the most frequently shared genes. For example, in sub-network 8 (Figure S8 and Table S8 in File S1), AT1G56110 ("homolog of nucleolar protein NOP56"), AT3G05060 ("putative SAR DNA-binding protein"), and AT3G44750 (HDA3 histone deacetylase HDT1) are regulated by six different treatments or conditions from five publications corresponding to five special biological themes, which involves reproduction, photosynthesis, metabolism, development, and yield in *Arabidopsis* (Table S8 in File S1). And the most enriched term in sub-network 8 is membrane-enclosed lumen based on functional analysis of DAVID (Table 1). Therefore, the

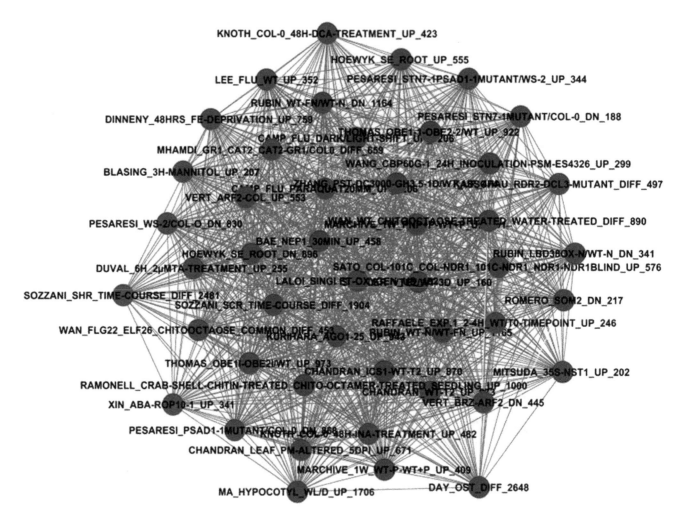

Figure 3. Sub-network 1 corresponding to the module 1/cluster 1 (see note in Figure 2 for meanings of node and edge and their color).

three genes not only connect the six gene lists, but have multiple functions by which we could propose a hypotheses that the three genes' interaction controls the reproduction, photosynthesis, metabolism etc. Furthermore, the three genes associated with the rapidly proliferating nature of the endosperm at 4 DA, with similar expression patterns to the early endosperm markers SUC5, PHE1, FWA, and FIS2 [22], were regulated by interploidy crosses, fis1X2x crosses at 5 DAP (two biological replicates of each), and unfertilized msi1 siliques at 7 DAF [23], kin10, starvation conditions, and sugar availability increase [24], sucrose [25], and 4h-carbon fixcation [26]. These all became the organized links among the six gene lists because they associated with the three genes.

However, there are significant differences among the nine sub-networks. Based on Table 1, sub-networks 1–5 have more nodes than sub-networks 6–9. This does not mean the genes in sub-network 6–9 are less important than those in sub-networks 1–5. Generally, the most significantly enriched GO terms in sub-networks 1–9 are different except for sub-networks 1 and 3, which have the same theme "response to chitin". The second, third, and fourth most significantly enriched GO Terms in sub-network 1 are response to carbohydrate stimulus, organic substance, and defense response, respectively, which are different from those in sub-network 3. This indicates there are significantly different functions

in sub-networks 1–9. Furthermore, "cliques" of all sub-networks are different in the whole network with 16,261 significant overlaps. These "cliques" are some of the most connected graphs in the NETWORK in terms of a vertex-weighting scheme based on the highest k-core of the vertex neighborhood. Therefore, they specify different meanings and information. Finally, all the most frequently shared genes of the sub-networks are different. For instance, sub-network 7 has the second smallest score of 2, with 15 nodes, and 30 edges, but possesses 53 most frequently shared genes, which are completely different from that of sub-network 1.

The most frequently shared genes are the strongest links within each of nine sub-networks and provide genomics research with important insights. They are the most important results we found in this study. For example, the gene AT5G39670 ("putative calcium-binding protein CML45", function as calcium ion binding) has the second highest frequency of 34 in the sub-network 1 (Table S1 in File S1). Its function as calcium ion binding indicates calcium-binding proteins participate in calcium cell signaling pathways by binding to Ca^{2+}. These proteins are expressed in many cell types during various growth stages in plants, and contribute to all aspects of the cell's functioning [24]. In the present study, we found that this gene responded to 24 treatments or conditions such as necrosis-ethylene, diurnal cycle, salicylic acid, iron deprivation, etc. according to various reports.

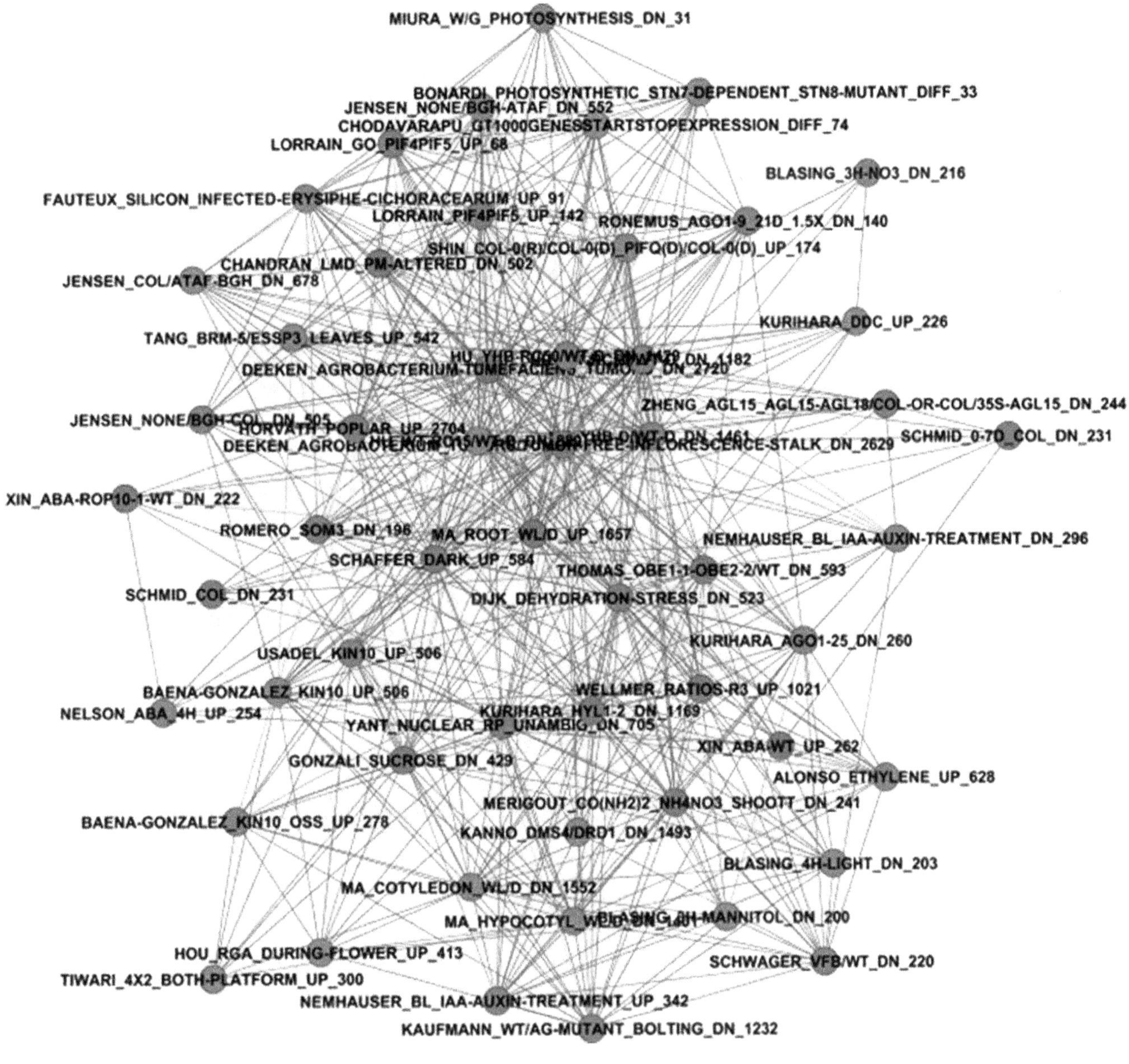

Figure 4. Sub-network 2 corresponding to the module 2/cluster 2 (see note in Figure 2 for meanings of node and edge and their color).

Furthermore, this gene mediates 10 crucial biological themes: immune, yield, disease, development, metabolism, function, photosynthesis, pathogen, energy, and virus. Also, the gene belongs to 24 up-regulated gene lists, seven down-regulated gene lists, and three different-regulated gene lists. In most cases, this gene is up-regulated, indicating that when the experimental treatments listed above were applied, there was an increased expression of the gene AT5G39670. However, some treatments or stimuli may cause a decreased expression of the above gene in order to protect its cells. Therefore, AT5G39670 is the second most active gene and second strongest link in sub-network 1. Similarly, gene AT4G14365 ("XBAT34", molecular functions: protein binding and zinc ion binding) is the strongest link as it is related to 35 gene lists in sub-network 1. Gene AT3G50930 ("BCS1", molecular functions: ATP binding and ATPase activity) is the third strongest link because it is associated with 33 gene lists

in sub-network 1. Also, the most frequently shared genes are significantly different in these nine sub-networks. For instance, there are 124 most frequently shared genes in sub-network 3 and 155 most frequently shared genes in sub-network 4. However, there are only two common genes between these two sub-networks. These important results and their biological mechanisms need to be further addressed.

The results from this study, summarized as a molecular signature map, provide key insights into the underlying connections of diverse perturbations. More importantly, compared to previous reports that focused on specific themes, this study explored and established the hidden links among the gene lists on a global scale in *Arabidopsis*. These sub-networks will provide new putative gene targets for future research. For example, sub-network 4 shows that the top three genes AT1G74670, AT1G04240, and AT1G69530 are down-regulated by bioactive

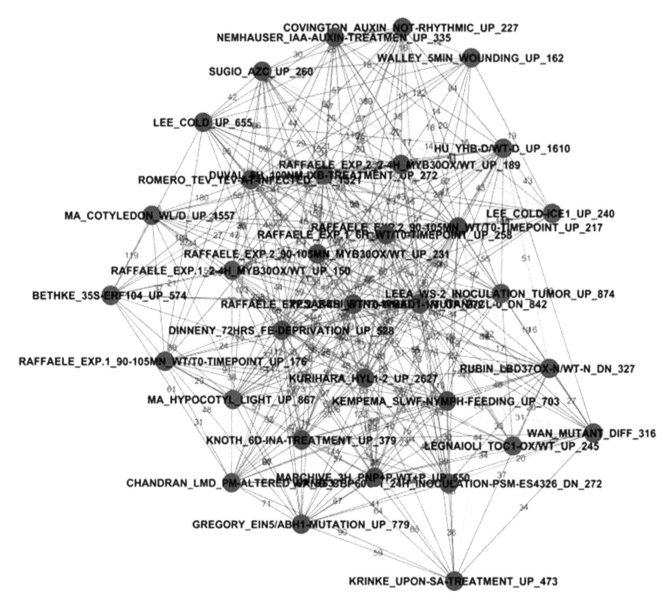

Figure 5. Sub-network 3 corresponding to the module 3/cluster 3 (see note in Figure 2 for meanings of node and edge and their color. edge label = number of overlapping genes between two nodes).

gibberellins corresponding to the gene list ZENTELLA_DEX_-VECTOR_DN_244 (Table S4 in File S1). This information provides some possible clues for future research regarding the mechanism of the regulation of plant growth by plant hormone gibberellins. Another example is gene AT4G27030, which has the highest frequency of 20 in sub-network 2. This gene is regulated by 14 treatments or conditions such as agrobacterium tumefaciens, kin10 and kin 11, dark, far-red light, etc. (Table S2 in File S1). This gene could be used to genetically modify crops for new and useful functions.

Conclusions

There are hidden links among the gene lists from the published papers concerning *Arabidopsis*. After performing systematic overlap analysis, we created 10 networks, including network and sub-networks 1–9 where there are a number of links among gene lists. Many seemingly unrelated stimuli/perturbation may activate or deactivate the same molecular pathways. These links are actually a set of overlapping genes. Of them, a total of 988 most frequently shared genes were identified from each sub-network. These genes are regulated by multiple treatments or conditions from different gene lists and related to different biological themes based on their sub-networks. They construct more active (stronger) links among the gene lists in our data.

Compared to previous reports focusing on specific themes, this study explored and established hidden links among the gene lists on a global scale in *Arabidopsis*. These results provide significant information about target genes or models for future research. In the future, it will be necessary for us to extend gene lists and develop more effective analysis methods to further explain the booming gene lists of microarray data.

Supporting Information Legends

File S1   Fig. S1. Sub-network 1 corresponding to cluster 1. Node = name of gene list. Node Color = MCODE_Scores from small to large and corresponds to color from light green to dark red. Edge Color = p-values from large to small and corresponds to color from grey to dark green. Fig. S2. Sub-network 2 corresponding to cluster 2. Fig. S3. Sub-network 3 corresponding to cluster 3. Fig. S4. The sub-network 4 correspoding to cluster 4. Fig. S5. The sub-network 5 corresponding to Cluster 5. Fig. S6. The sub-network 6 corresponding to Cluster 6. Fig. S7. The sub-network 7 corresponding to Cluster 7. Fig. S8. The sub-network 8 corresponding to Cluster 8. Fig. S9. The sub-network 9 corresponding to Cluster 9. Table S1. Results of sub-network 1 corresponding to cluster 1. Table S2. Results of sub-network 2 corresponding to cluster 2. Table S3. Results of sub-network 3 corresponding to cluster 3. Table S4. Results of sub-network 4 corresponding to cluster 4. Table S5. Results of sub-network 5 corresponding to cluster 5. Table S6. Results of sub-network 6 corresponding to cluster 6. Table S7. Results of sub-network 7 corresponding to cluster 7. Table S8. Results of sub-network 8 corresponding to cluster 8. Table S9. Results of sub-network 9 corresponding to cluster 9.

Author Contributions

Conceived and designed the experiments: SXG. Performed the experiments: LL. Analyzed the data: LL. Wrote the paper: LL SXG.

References

1. (2008) Arabidopsis thaliana. Wikipedia http://enwikipediaorg/wiki/Arabidopsis_thaliana: Wikipedia.
2. (2012). NCBI http://wwwncbinlmnihgov/geo/.
3. Ioannidis JP, Allison DB, Ball CA, Coulibaly I, Cui X, et al. (2009) Repeatability of published microarray gene expression analyses. Nat Genet 41: 149–155.
4. Miller BG, Stamatoyannopoulos JA (2010) Integrative meta-analysis of differential gene expression in acute myeloid leukemia. PLoS One 5: e9466.
5. Rogic S, Pavlidis P (2009) Meta-analysis of kindling-induced gene expression changes in the rat hippocampus. Front Neurosci 3: 53.
6. Yang XN, Sun X (2007) Meta-analysis of several gene lists for distinct types of cancer: A simple way to reveal common prognostic markers. BMC Bioinformatics 8.
7. Edwards YJK, Bryson K, Jones DT (2008) A Meta-Analysis of Microarray Gene Expression in Mouse Stem Cells: Redefining Stemness. PLoS One 3.
8. Glass GV Meta-analysis. Wikipedia http://enwikipediaorg/wiki/Meta-analysis. http://en.wikipedia.org/wiki/Meta-analysis: Wikipedia.
9. Newman JC, Weiner AM (2005) L2L: a simple tool for discovering the hidden significance in microarray expression data. Genome Biol 6: R81.
10. Cahan P, Ahmad AM, Burke H, Fu S, Lai YL, et al. (2005) List of lists-annotated (LOLA): A database for annotation and comparison of published microarray gene lists. Gene 360: 78–82.
11. Liberzon A, Subramanian A, Pinchback R, Thorvaldsdottir H, Tamayo P, et al. (2011) Molecular signatures database (MSigDB) 3.0. Bioinformatics 27: 1739–1740.
12. Ge SX (2011) Large-scale analysis of expression signatures reveals hidden links among diverse cellular processes. Bmc Systems Biology 5.
13. Lai LM, Liberzon A, Hennessey J, Jiang GX, Qi JL, et al. (2012) AraPath: a knowledgebase for pathway analysis in Arabidopsis. Bioinformatics 28: 2291–2292.
14. Team RC R: A language and environment for statistical computing. (2012) R Foundation for Statistical Computing, Vienna, Austria ISBN 3-900051-07-0, URL http://wwwR-projectorg/.
15. Benjamini Y, Hochberg Y (1995) Controlling the False Discovery Rate - a Practical and Powerful Approach to Multiple Testing. Journal of the Royal Statistical Society Series B-Methodological 57: 289–300.
16. Shannon P, Markiel A, Ozier O, Baliga NS, Wang JT, et al. (2003) Cytoscape: A software environment for integrated models of biomolecular interaction networks. Genome Research 13: 2498–2504.
17. Guimera R, Nunes Amaral LA (2005) Functional cartography of complex metabolic networks. Nature 433: 895–900.
18. Hsieh MH, Magee CL (2008) An algorithm and metric for network decomposition from similarity matrices: Application to positional analysis. Social Networks 30: 146–158.
19. Bader GD, Hogue CW (2003) An automated method for finding molecular complexes in large protein interaction networks. BMC Bioinformatics 4: 2.
20. Huang DW, Sherman BT, Lempicki RA (2009) Systematic and integrative analysis of large gene lists using DAVID bioinformatics resources. Nature Protocols 4: 44–57.
21. Huang DW, Sherman BT, Lempicki RA (2009) Bioinformatics enrichment tools: paths toward the comprehensive functional analysis of large gene lists. Nucleic Acids Research 37: 1–13.
22. Day RC, Herridge RP, Ambrose BA, Macknight RC (2008) Transcriptome analysis of proliferating Arabidopsis endosperm reveals biological implications for the control of syncytial division, cytokinin signaling, and gene expression regulation. Plant Physiology 148: 1964–1984.
23. Tiwari S, Spielman M, Schulz R, Oakey RJ, Kelsey G, et al. (2010) Transcriptional profiles underlying parent-of-origin effects in seeds of Arabidopsis thaliana. BMC Plant Biol 10: 72.
24. Baena-Gonzalez E, Rolland F, Thevelein JM, Sheen J (2007) A central integrator of transcription networks in plant stress and energy signalling. Nature 448: 938–942.
25. Gonzali S, Loreti E, Solfanelli C, Novi G, Alpi A, et al. (2006) Identification of sugar-modulated genes and evidence for in vivo sugar sensing in Arabidopsis. J Plant Res 119: 115–123.
26. Blasing OE, Gibon Y, Gunther M, Hohne M, Morcuende R, et al. (2005) Sugars and circadian regulation make major contributions to the global regulation of diurnal gene expression in Arabidopsis. Plant Cell 17: 3257–3281.

5

Insights to Genetic Characterization Tools for Epidemiological Tracking of *Francisella tularensis* in Sweden

Tara Wahab[1]*, **Dawn N. Birdsell**[2], **Marika Hjertqvist**[1], **Cedar L. Mitchell**[2], **David M. Wagner**[2], **Paul S. Keim**[2], **Ingela Hedenström**[1], **Sven Löfdahl**[1]

1 Public Health Agency of Sweden, Department of Microbiology, Stockholm, Sweden, 2 Northern Arizona University, Center for Microbial Genetics and Genomics, Flagstaff, AZ, United States of America

Abstract

Tularaemia, caused by the bacterium *Francisella tularensis*, is endemic in Sweden and is poorly understood. The aim of this study was to evaluate the effectiveness of three different genetic typing systems to link a genetic type to the source and place of tularemia infection in Sweden. Canonical single nucleotide polymorphisms (canSNPs), MLVA including five variable number of tandem repeat loci and *PmeI*-PFGE were tested on 127 *F. tularensis* positive specimens collected from Swedish case-patients. All three typing methods identified two major genetic groups with near-perfect agreement. Higher genetic resolution was obtained with canSNP and MLVA compared to PFGE; *F. tularensis* samples were first assigned into ten phylogroups based on canSNPs followed by 33 unique MLVA types. Phylogroups were geographically analysed to reveal complex phylogeographic patterns in Sweden. The extensive phylogenetic diversity found within individual counties posed a challenge to linking specific genetic types with specific geographic locations. Despite this, a single phylogroup (B.22), defined by a SNP marker specific to a lone Swedish sequenced strain, did link genetic type with a likely geographic place. This result suggests that SNP markers, highly specific to a particular reference genome, may be found most frequently among samples recovered from the same location where the reference genome originated. This insight compels us to consider whole-genome sequencing (WGS) as the appropriate tool for effectively linking specific genetic type to geography. Comparing the WGS of an unknown sample to WGS databases of archived Swedish strains maximizes the likelihood of revealing those rare geographically informative SNPs.

Editor: Yousef Abu Kwaik, University of Louisville, United States of America

Funding: This work was supported by grants from the Swedish Emergency Management Agency and by the US Department of Homeland Security Science and Technology Directorate via award HSHQDC-10-C-00139. The funders had no role in study design, data collection and analysis, decision to publish, or preparation of the manuscript.

Competing Interests: The authors have declared that no competing interests exist.

* Email: tara.wahab@folkhalsomyndigheten.se

Introduction

Francisella tularensis is a highly virulent, facultative intracellular pathogen, which causes tularaemia in humans and animals [1]. Transmission occurs via arthropod bites (mosquitoes and ticks), inhalation of contaminated dust, or ingestion of contaminated food or water. Tularaemia is endemic in Sweden and has been reported since 1931 causing between 100–700 infections annually [2]. The most common clinical form is ulceroglandular tularaemia and all reported human cases of tularaemia in Sweden have been caused by *F. tularensis* subspecies *holarctica* (type B). The disease occurs with a seasonal pattern – being especially prevalent in summer and autumn. It is most common in Northern and Middle Sweden but during the last decade the infection has spread further south (SmiNet2, Swedish National Surveillance System).

Recently, several molecular typing methods have been utilized in studies of genetic population structure of *F. tularensis* including: PFGE, whole genome microarrays, multi-locus variable-number of tandem repeat (VNTR) analysis (MLVA), insertion-deletion markers (INDELs), and single nucleotide polymorphism (SNP) [3–12]. SNPs are point mutations that are evolutionarily stable in clonally reproducing organisms such as *F. tularensis* [12]. This stability makes them useful for classifying bacterial populations into specific genetic groups where phylogenetic relationships among groups can be accurately inferred [13]. Several studies have constructed a global phylogenetic tree using canSNPs, subdividing the subspecies *holarctica* samples into 30 subpopulations found worldwide [6,8,11,12,14]. MLVA has been very useful for several bacterial species, which, like *F. tularensis*, have little genomic variation [15,16]. MLVA analysis using 25 VNTR markers on 139 *F. tularensis* subspecies *holarctica* samples from North America, Europe and Asia, revealed five subpopulations, which with one exception were found in several well separated geographic areas [7].

The aim of present study was to evaluate canSNPs, MLVA, and *PmeI*-PFGE for practical uses in epidemiological investigation of

F. tularensis infections in Sweden and in combination with geomapping to possibly predict sources of infection and reservoirs.

Results

Molecular typing

To evaluate the effectiveness of SNP, MLVA and PFGE typing as methods for tracing source and place of infection within an endemic country, we analysed 127 clinical specimens (Table S1). We discovered that all three typing methods identified two major genetic groups with near-perfect agreement. Six samples were removed from canSNP analysis due to DNA quality issues. Analysis with canSNPs revealed that all *F. tularensis* samples were assigned to two major groups: B.7/8 (n = 24) and B.12 (n = 97) (Figure 1A). The proportion of B.12 phylogroup to B.7/8 was in agreement with previous publication [8]. MLVA analysis resulted in two major clusters, Tul-I and Tul-II that corresponded with the B.12 and B.7/8 lineages, respectively (Table S1; Figure 1A). Two samples falling within the B.12 lineage formed a distinct MLVA cluster, Tul-III (Table S1). The two major MLVA clusters (Tul-I and Tul-II) were based on differences in the two less discriminating markers, Ft-M22 and Ft-M24, with only two allelic variants each. Tul-III MLVA cluster differed from all other MLVA types in the allele combination of VNTR markers Ft-M24 and Ft-M22 with 1 and 4 copies, respectively. Two other canSNP groups (B.4 and B.10) that were not found in this study have been previously reported in Sweden [8,11,12]. However, samples of these phylogroups are rather rare in Sweden so their lack of presence in this study may be due to our smaller sample size.

PFGE analysis of the 124 clinical samples revealed three different but rather similar PFGE profiles, types 1–3 (Figure 2). Comparison of PFGE data to MLVA and canSNP data (Table S1) revealed that PFGE types 1 and 3 corresponded to the two major canSNP groups B.12 (Tul-I) and B.7/8 (Tul-II), respectively (Table S1). MLVA cluster Tul-III corresponded with PFGE type 2. Taken together, canSNP, MLVA, and PFGE were in general agreement when classifying samples into major groups.

Higher genetic resolution was obtained with SNP and MLVA analyses compared to PFGE. Samples within the B.12 SNP lineage were further classified into one of nine minor phylogroups (B.12/13, n = 11; B.14, n = 5; B.20/21/33, n = 13; B.21/22, n = 13; B.22, n = 22; B.23/14/25, n = 24, B.33/34, n = 6; B.34/35, n = 1; and B.35/36, n = 2) (Figure 1A; Table S1) using SNP-signatures previously described [6,11,12]. Combining all five VNTR markers resulted in 33 unique MLVA subtypes wherein 17 unique subtypes were the result of variation at the Ft-M3 locus, which was the most rapidly mutating marker. Tul-I samples were assigned into one of five smaller subgroups (A–E), with each alpha code genotype further divided into Ft-M3 subtypes. Tul-II samples were less diverse than Tul-I, resulting in 3 unique MLVA-types referred to as #8, #10, and #33. The number of alleles of the five markers varied exhibiting moderate to high diversity (D) ranging from 0.15–0.90 as previous described [7] (Table 1).

At this higher resolution level, MLVA and canSNP assignment of samples were not in consistent agreement. Samples within identical MLVA genotype did not fall into a single canSNP group, but rather fell into multiple SNP phylogroups (Figure 1A; Table S1). Several canSNP groups contained multiple MLVA genotypes (Figure 1A; Table S1). This lack of grouping agreement is due to the type of genetic markers (SNPs or VNTRs) targeted by each typing system. SNP mutations are highly stable and therefore are informative of the genetic relationships among groups of isolates [13]. MLVA typing is based on VNTR loci that can be prone to mutational instability and, therefore, often result in homoplasy,

making inferences about relationships among groups of isolates unreliable. When SNP analysis and MLVA are used in a hierarchical scheme, accurate genetic relatedness among SNP-defined groups of *F. tularensis* samples can be confidently known (Figure 1A) [12,13] and the MLVA data provided finer levels of discrimination among samples within the same phylogroup.

Geographic distribution of SNP groups

A highly complex geographic pattern among the phylogroups exists at a national and regional scale in Sweden (Figure 1). Our data present a pattern of wide distribution of multiple phylogroups that are found in multiple relatively distant counties in Sweden. Samples from both major groups (B.7/8 and B.12) are represented in middle and northern Sweden, with the highest density found in middle Sweden. Southern Sweden is sparse and is represented by samples classified in closely related terminal phylogroups within B.12 lineage (B.33/34 and B.34/35). Nearly all phylogroups identified in this study are present in middle Sweden, making this region the center of diversity, as previously described [8].

As a consequence of wide distribution of multiple phylogroups, extensive phylogenetic diversity was found within individual counties in middle Sweden. The richest diversity is found in Stockholm area (Figure 1B, county AB), representing seven diverse phylogroups, each with multiple MLVA subtypes. Örebro, a city in middle Sweden, was co-localized with 3 distinct phylogroups and MLVA subtypes (Table S1 and Figure 1, county T). Most samples appeared to cluster along major waterways, such as rivers and coastal areas of the Swedish east coast, the Baltic Sea. There was no obvious geographical correlation to age and gender of the patients (data not shown), but adults were significantly more commonly infected than children. Water bodies, like the Dalälven river, appears to be linked to multiple phylogroups that are diverse (Figure 1B, county W).

In contrast, Ljusnan river (county X in Figure 1B) is linked to seventeen case-patient samples that are highly genetically similar despite the 12 year span (1995–2006). All samples, except one, belonged to subgroup B.22 MLVA D4. The remaining sample fell in the B.21/22 subgroup, which is the closest relative to B.22 samples. Despite this pattern, 3 B.22 samples were found in 3 other nearby counties in middle Sweden, including Stockholm (Figure 1B), which may reflect recent dispersal from the founding source. Taken together, small regional sections or water bodies are co-localized with multiple phylogroups with great genetic diversity.

Discussion

The complex phylogeographic pattern of tularemia distribution in Sweden poses a great challenge to accurately identify a source and place of infection for any given *F. tularensis* specimen within Sweden (Figure 1). Our attempts to correlate geographic origin of the samples to specific genetic types did not generate a clear cut result (Figure 1B) despite employing a canSNP typing scheme that provided higher genetic resolution [6] than in the study performed by Karlsson et al 2013 and colleagues. This SNP typing scheme allowed us to place 121 clinical specimens, collected throughout Sweden over a span of 16 years, on the existing global phylogenetic tree for *F. tularensis* subsp. *holarctica* (Figure 1A) [6]. All phylogroups identified in Sweden have also been found in distant nations abroad, except B.22, which is restricted to Sweden. Given this broader dispersal range, it is no surprise that samples within these specific phylogroups are broadly dispersed in Sweden across multiple counties and not restricted to a small geographic region. The broad distribution of closely related phylogroups is central to the argument that *F. tularensis* is a rapidly dispersed

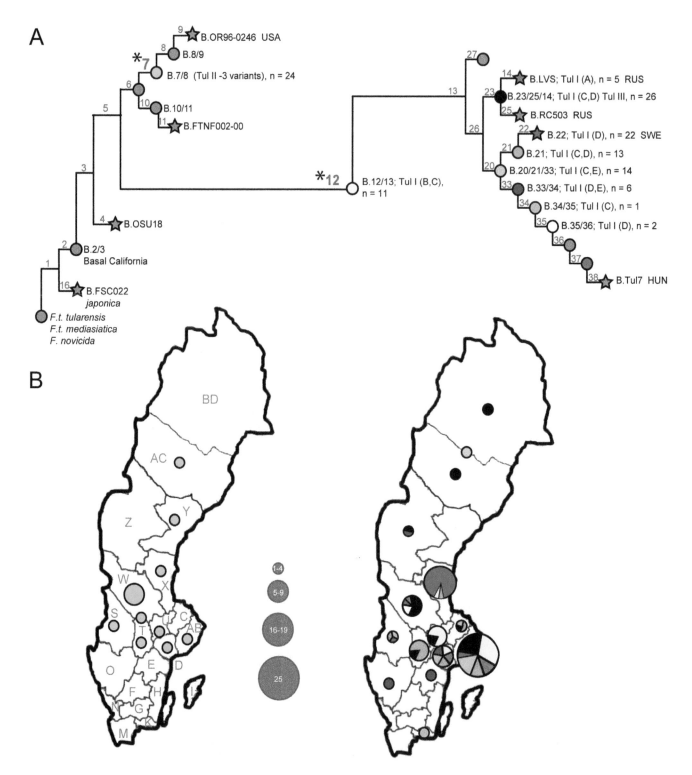

Figure 1. Detailed phylogeographic patterns of 103 human patient samples from Sweden. A) Existing global canSNP phylogeny of *F. tularensis* subsp. *holarctica* (Gyuranecz et al) wherein subgroups are indicated as circles and reference strains as stars. Gray coloration indicates subgroups not identified in this study. Noted for each mapped subgroup are the MLVA genotypes and n values (i.e. number of strains). The country code for each sequence genome is indicated: HUN, RUS, SWE, USA. B) Geographic distribution of groups on separate maps of Sweden based on membership to one of the two major subgroups (*B.7/8 and *B.12). County code is indicated on the map (left). Total number of samples per county is represented by the circle size. Multiple subgroups within a single county are represented proportionally on a pie chart comprised of the colors corresponding to subgroups.

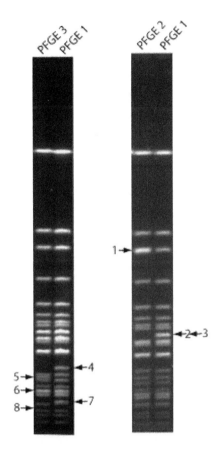

Figure 2. *PmeI* **pulsed-field gel electrophoresis (PFGE) patterns for** *F. tularensis* **subsp.** *holarctica.* Polymorphic band position 1 consists of two fragments in PFGE type 2. Polymorphic band position 2 and 3 consist of two fragments at the same position, both missing in PFGE type 2. Polymorphic band position 6 consists of two fragments in PFGE type 3.

organism. The basis for this rapid dispersal remains unclear, but recent reports suggest dispersal could be facilitated by the migration of birds [19,20].

Despite the phylogeographic complexity, patterns emerge that suggest the possibility of identifying SNP markers that could be meaningfully linked to geographic regions or at least narrow the geographic range of possible places. An example of this is the SNP for B.22 phylogroup, which is comprised of samples found only in

Sweden [6,11,12]. It is interesting to note that unlike all other phylogroups in this study, B.22 SNP was identified from a Swedish genome (FSC200) linked to the Ljusnan river in county X (Figure 1). This B.22 SNP was highly specific to FSC200 genome. All other phylogroups are defined by SNPs discovered from genomes found in other nations (USA, Russia, and Hungary) [6,11,12]. Most case-patients (16/17) linked to the Ljusnan river, collected over a 12 year time frame (1995–2006) (Figure 1B), typed as B.22 MLVA D4 (Table S1). The striking genetic similarity suggests that they all recently emerged from a common ancestor. The temporal pattern rules out a single outbreak season and provides insight into the stability of this genotype. Taken together, these data suggest that the B.22 D4 genotype originated from a common ecological niche that spanned the approximately 70 kilometres distance of the river. Intense localized sampling of beaver populations may verify this hypothesis. Beavers, which are common on this river, could be a viable source given that these semi-aquatic rodent species have shown evidence of seroconversion to *F. tularensis* [21]. Three B.22 samples were found in other neighboring counties, one B.22 D4 type was found in Stockholm and two B.22 samples with D25 & D32 subtypes were found in counties W and S (Figure 1B). The B.22 samples located in multiple counties may reflect very recent dispersal events, which is supported by the MLVA subtype data, or errors in epidemiological records.

The B.22 SNP provides a striking line of evidence that supports the pattern that closely genetically related samples tend to have closer geographic proximity despite the complex phylogeographic landscape found in Sweden. Extrapolating from this model, SNPs that are highly specific to the sequenced genome may be found most frequently among samples recovered from the same location where the reference genome originated. Such SNPs would be both relationally and geographically informative and, therefore, useful in identifying a likely place of infection. That said, due to the rapid dispersal of *F. tularensis*, the geographical attribution of the B.22 SNP may be time limited.

The results of the present study indicate that SNP typing schemes, designed from geographically informative SNPs, combined with a MLVA typing scheme have the potential to be used as a standalone typing method in outbreak investigations. However, since our attempts to correlate geographic origin of the samples to specific genetic types did not generate a clear cut result despite employing a canSNP typing scheme that provided high genetic resolution we conclude that whole-genome sequencing (WGS) would be the most appropriate tool for effectively linking specific genetic type to geography. Comparing the WGS of an unknown sample to WGS databases of archived Swedish strains

Table 1. VNTR markers.

VNTR marker	Repeat size (nt)	No. of repeats*		No. of alleles*	Diversity*†	Inside orf††
		Min	Max			
Ft-M3	9	8	25	17	0.90	Yes
Ft-M6	21	4	6	3	0.61	Yes
Ft-M20	12	2	4	3	0.15	Yes
Ft-M22	6	3	4	2	0.34	Yes
Ft-M24	21	1	2	2	0.36	No

*Data obtained in this study.
†The individual marker diversity (D) was calculated as $D = [1 - \sum(\text{allele frequency})^2]$.
††Location within an open reading frame.

maximizes the likelihood of revealing those rare geographically informative SNPs among genetic near matches. This insight may prove useful for future epidemiological investigation practices.

Materials and Methods

Clinical samples

The Public Health Agency of Sweden receives continuously clinical specimens for primary diagnostics of *F. tularensis* from physicians. All samples were received during 1994 to 2010 from patients of both genders, varying ages (1–89 years), and from diverse regions in Sweden (Table S1). Since tularaemia is a noticeable disease in Sweden, cases had been reported to the Swedish National Surveillance System by the treating physician. If no likely place of exposure had been included, the patients were contacted. We extracted *F. tularensis* subspecies *holarctica* DNA from patients suffering from ulceroglandular tularaemia: 3 complex clinical samples taken directly from the wound site and 124 cultured samples. Genomic DNA was prepared using two commercially available DNA extraction kits, the QIAamp tissue protocol (Qiagen, Stockholm, Sweden) for samples from 1994 to 2005 and the NucliSens magnetic extraction protocol (Biomérieux, Gothenburg, Sweden) for *F. tularensis* samples and wound specimens from 2006–2010.

canSNP

CanSNP analysis using 26 previously published assays was performed on the 127 clinical samples as described (Figure 1A) [6,11,12].

MLVA

The markers Ft-M3, Ft-M6, Ft-M20, Ft-M22 and Ft-M24 were amplified as described [7]. The forward primers (Invitrogen Life Technologies, Paisley, United Kingdom), Ft-M3 and Ft-M20 were fluorescent labelled with NED, Ft-M6 and Ft-M24 with 6-FAM, and HEX for Ft-M22 respectively. PCR was performed in 12,5 µl reaction mixture containing 10 mM Tris-HCl, pH 8.3, 50 mM KCl, 2,5 mM MgCl$_2$, 0.5 U AmpliTaq DNA polymerase (Applied Biosystems, Stockholm, Sweden), 0,1 mM deoxynucleoside tri-phosphates, 0,6 µM of each primer with the addition of 0,5–1,0 ng template. The reaction mixture was incubated at 94°C for 5 minutes and then cycled at 94°C for 30 s, 58°C for 30 s, and 72°C for 30 s, and finally at 72°C for 5 minutes. Amplicons were diluted 30 times and pooled into two combinations a) Ft-M3, Ft-

M6, and Ft-M22 and b) Ft-M20, and Ft-M24, respectively. 1 µl of each pool was analysed with capillary electrophoresis (3130 Genetic Analyzer, POP7-polymer, and. GeneScanTM-500 ROX TM size standards, Applied Biosystems, Stockholm, Sweden). The GeneMapper (Applied Biosystems) software was used to determine the size of the amplicons and to calculate the number of repeats at each VNTR marker. The diversity (D) for each VNTR marker was calculated as $D = 1 - \sum (\text{allele frequency})^2$ [17].

PFGE

PFGE analysis was performed on *F. tularensis* samples [18]. Agarose plugs were sliced and incubated in 10 U of restriction enzyme *PmeI* (Biolabs, New England) for 3 hours at 37°C. Electrophoresis was performed in 1% agarose with a switch time of 1.79 to 10.71 s at 6 V/cm for 24 hours at 14°C. *Salmonella enterica* serotype Braenderup strain H9812 restricted with *XbaI* was used for gel normalization. Gels were stained with gel red and gel images captured by using a Gel Doc 1000 imager (Bio-Rad).

PFGE images were analysed using Bionumerics v 6.01 (Applied Maths, Sint-Martens-Latem, Belgium). Unique PFGE patterns were analysed and compared manually for band polymorphism.

Geomapping

To obtain phylogeographic patterns we mapped the phylogenetic groups on a geographic map of Sweden at the county level resolution (Figure 1B). Of the 127 patients, 24 were excluded from this analysis due to unknown or uncertain location of exposure or lack of genotype information. The study protocol was approved by the Regional Ethical Review Board in Stockholm (# 2008/1020-31/2).

Author Contributions

Conceived and designed the experiments: TW DB SL PK. Performed the experiments: TW IH CM DW DB. Analyzed the data: TW DB MH SL. Contributed reagents/materials/analysis tools: DB TW SL PK. Wrote the paper: TW DB DW PK SL.

References

1. Ellis J, Oyston PC, Green M, Titball RW (2002) Tularemia. Clin Microbiol Rev 15: 631–646.
2. Payne L, Arneborn M, Tegnell A, Giesecke J (2005) Endemic tularemia, Sweden. Emerg Infect Dis 11: 1440–1442.
3. Broekhuijsen M, Larsson P, Johansson A, Byström M, Eriksson U, et al. (2003) Genome-wide DNA microarray analysis of Francisella tularensis strains demonstrates extensive genetic conservation within the species but identifies regions that are unique to the highly virulent F. tularensis subsp. tularensis. J Clin Microbiol 41: 2924–2931.
4. Farlow J, Smith KL, Wong J, Abrams M, Lytle M, et al. (2001) Francisella tularensis strain typing using multiple-locus, variable-number tandem repeat analysis. J Clin Microbiol 39: 3186–3192.
5. Garcia Del Blanco N, Dobson ME, Vela AI, De La Puente VA, Gutierreza CB, et al. (2002) Genotyping of Francisella tularensis strains by pulsed-field gel electrophoresis, amplified fragment length polymorphism fingerprinting, and 16S rRNA gene sequencing. J Clin Microbiol 40: 2964–2972.
6. Gyuranecz M, Birdsell DN, Splettstoesser W, Seibold E, Beckström-Sternberg SM, et al. (2012) Phylogeography of Francisella tularensis subsp. holarctica, Europe. Emerg Infect Dis 18: 290–293.
7. Johansson A, Farlow J, Larsson P, Dukerich M, Chambers E, et al. (2004) Worldwide genetic relationships among Francisella tularensis isolates determined by multiple-locus variable-number tandem repeat analysis. J Bacteriol 186: 5808–5818.

8. Karlsson E, Svensson K, Lindgren P, Bystrom M, Sjodin A, et al. (2013) The phylogeographic pattern of Francisella tularensis in Sweden indicates a Scandinavian origin of Eurosiberian tularaemia. Environ Microbiol 15: 634–645.
9. Larsson P, Svensson K, Karlsson L, Guala D, Granberg M, et al. (2007) Canonical insertion-deletion markers for rapid DNA typing of Francisella tularensis. Emerg Infect Dis 13: 1725–1732.
10. Staples JE, Kubota KA, Chalcraft LG, Mead PS, Petersen JM (2006) Epidemiologic and molecular analysis of human tularemia, United States, 1964–2004. Emerg Infect Dis 12: 1113–8.
11. Svensson K, Back E, Eliasson H, Berglund L, Granberg M, et al. (2009) Landscape epidemiology of tularemia outbreaks in Sweden. Emerg Infect Dis 15: 1937–1947.
12. Vogler AJ, Birdsell D, Price LB, Zhgenti E, Babuadze G, et al. (2009) Phylogeography of Francisella tularensis: Global expansion of a highly fit clone. J Bacteriol 191: 2474–2484.
13. Keim P, Van Ert MN, Pearson T, Vogler AJ, Huynh LY, et al. (2004) Anthrax molecular epidemiology and forensics: using the appropriate marker for different evolutionary scales. Infect Genet Evol 4: 205–213.
14. Chanturia G, Birdsell DN, Kekelidze M, Zhgenti E, Babuadze G, et al. (2011) Phylogeography of Francisella tularensis subspecies holarctica from the country of Georgia. BMC Microbiol 11: 139.

15. Keim P, Price LB, Klevytska AM, Smith KL, Schupp JM, et al. (2000) Multiple-locus variable-number tandem repeat analysis reveals genetic relationships within Bacillus anthracis. J Bacteriol 182: 2928–3296.

16. Klevytska AM, Price LB, Schupp JM, Worsham PL, Wong J, et al. (2001) Identification and characterization of variable-number tandem repeats in the Yersinia pestis genome. J Clin Microbiol 39: 3179–3185.

17. Weir BS (1990) Genetic data analysis: methods for discrete population genetic data analysis. Sinauer Associates, Inc., Sunderland, Mass.

18. Swaminathan B, Barrett TJ, Hunter SB, Tauxe RV, CDC PulseNet Task Force (2001) PulseNet: the molecular subtyping network for foodborne bacterial disease surveillance, United States. Emerg Infect Dis 7: 382–389.

19. Carvalho DD, Klein S, Akkus Z, ten Kate G, Schinkel A et al. (2012) Estimating 3D lumen centerlines of carotid arteries in free-hand acquisition ultrasound. Int J Comput Assist Radiol Surg 7: 207–215.

20. Padeshki PI, Ivanov IN, Popov B, Kantardjiev TV (2010) The role of birds in dissemination of Francisella tularensis: first direct molecular evidence for bird-to-human transmission. Epidemiol Infect 138: 376–379.

21. Morner T, Sandstedt K (1983) A serological survey of antibodies against Francisella tularensis in some Swedish mammals. Nord Vet Med 35: 82–85.

6

Bioinformatic Analysis Reveals Genome Size Reduction and the Emergence of Tyrosine Phosphorylation Site in the Movement Protein of New World Bipartite Begomoviruses

Eric S. Ho[1]*, Joan Kuchie[2], Siobain Duffy[3]

1 Department of Biology, Lafayette College, Easton, Pennsylvania, United States of America, **2** New Jersey City University, Jersey City, New Jersey, United States of America, **3** Department of Ecology, Evolution and Natural Resources, Rutgers University, New Brunswick, New Jersey, United States of America

Abstract

Begomovirus (genus Begomovirus, family *Geminiviridae*) infection is devastating to a wide variety of agricultural crops including tomato, squash, and cassava. Thus, understanding the replication and adaptation of begomoviruses has important translational value in alleviating substantial economic loss, particularly in developing countries. The bipartite genome of begomoviruses prevalent in the New World and their counterparts in the Old World share a high degree of genome homology except for a partially overlapping reading frame encoding the pre-coat protein (PCP, or AV2). PCP contributes to the essential functions of intercellular movement and suppression of host RNA silencing, but it is only present in the Old World viruses. In this study, we analyzed a set of non-redundant bipartite begomovirus genomes originating from the Old World (N = 28) and the New World (N = 65). Our bioinformatic analysis suggests ~120 nucleotides were deleted from PCP's proximal promoter region that may have contributed to its loss in the New World viruses. Consequently, genomes of the New World viruses are smaller than the Old World counterparts, possibly compensating for the loss of the intercellular movement functions of PCP. Additionally, we detected substantial purifying selection on a portion of the New World DNA-B movement protein (MP, or BC1). Further analysis of the New World MP gene revealed the emergence of a putative tyrosine phosphorylation site, which likely explains the increased purifying selection in that region. These findings provide important information about the strategies adopted by bipartite begomoviruses in adapting to new environment and suggest future *in planta* experiments.

Editor: Darren P. Martin, Institute of Infectious Disease and Molecular Medicine, South Africa

Funding: ESH is supported by NIH K12 GM093854-01. JK is supported by New Jersey City University and the RiSE program at Rutgers. SD is supported by NSF DEB 1026095 and BMGF/DFID OPP1052391. The funders had no role in study design, data collection and analysis, decision to publish, or preparation of the manuscript.

Competing Interests: The authors have declared that no competing interests exist.

* Email: hoe@lafayette.edu

Introduction

Begomoviruses (genus Begomovirus, family *Geminiviridae*) are single-stranded DNA viruses of dicots with small genomes - one or two circular segments of ~2.5–2.9 K nucleotides (nts). Begomoviruses are transmitted by the whitefly *Bemisia tabaci* [1,2] and their damaging infections pose a severe threat to commercial and subsistence production of key crops worldwide, including tomato, squash, cassava and bean [3]. Understanding the molecular biology and adaptation of begomoviruses to novel hosts has an important socioeconomic impact as they are emerging problems in developing countries [3]. The vast majority of begomovirus sequences also exhibit a classic biogeographic pattern: they fall into clades of New World (the Americas, and Caribbean) and Old World (rest of the world) viruses, with New World viruses thought to be derived from those in the Old World [4–6]. Bipartite begomoviruses, which have two similarly-sized, ambisense genomic segments termed DNA-A and DNA-B, are found worldwide,

with monopartite begomoviruses largely restricted to the Old World [7]. The DNA-A segment contains five or six genes, including the capsid protein (CP, also known as AV1), the replication-associated protein (REP, also known as AC1), a transcriptional activator (TrAP, also known as AC2), a replication enhancer (REn, also known as AC3) that overlaps with both the REP and TrAP genes and a virulence factor (AC4) that overlaps the reading frame within REP. The DNA-B segment contains two non-overlapping genes: the nuclear shuttle protein (NSP, also known as BV1), and the movement protein (MP, also known as BC1).

Old and New World bipartite begomoviruses share a high degree of homology, with the largest exception being the gene for the pre-coat protein (PCP, also known as AV2), which partially overlaps the CP gene and is only present in Old World viruses [8]. PCP and the monopartite V2 has been shown to localize at the cell periphery and is thought to act as a "movement protein" by increasing the size exclusion limit of the plasmodesmata [9,10].

They also suppresses RNA silencing by binding to the host's SGS3 protein [11]. V2 is thought to be the key movement protein in monopartite Old World viruses, but two genes on the DNA-B segment (NSP and MP) also contribute to systemic infection of plants by bipartite begomoviruses [12]. Virulent New World begomoviruses must rely on their other seven proteins to cope with the loss of PCP, and this is frequently invoked as the reason the DNA-B segment is required for infectivity of the overwhelming majority of New World begomoviruses [13]. Despite this assumption, the selective pressures imposed by the loss of PCP on the remaining New World viral genes have not been examined.

In this report we have compared the genome size, degree of variability and purifying selection of the viral genes between the Old and New World. Results indicate a loss of 100 nts in PCP's promoter region, stronger purifying selection on the two DNA-B genes in the New World, and the emergence of a putative tyrosine phosphorylation site in the New World MP. Studies with RNA plant viruses have shown that phosphorylation of MP regulates their localization and may account for cell-to-cell movement [14]. We speculate that the reduction in viral cell-to-cell movement caused by the loss of the PCP in the New World begomoviruses may be compensated by systematic genome size reduction and/or the gain of additional phosphorylation activity in the MP.

Materials and Methods

Compilation of bipartite begomovirus genomes

Genomes of begomovirus were downloaded from the June-2012 release of the viral genome database hosted in NCBI (ftp://ftp. ncbi.nih.gov/refseq/release/viral/). Only genomes containing the distinct, invariant nonamer "TAATATT|AC" were included in this study (the vertical bar represents the cleavage site). The pairing of DNA-A and DNA-B genomes, and the classification of genomes into Old and New Worlds were done semi-automatically according to the information stated in NCBI's RefSeq records [15] and ICTV report [16]. To ease sequence comparison, the beginning of the cleavage site "AC" was adopted as reference position 1 and the original genomic coordinates stated in NCBI's RefSeq records of the begomoviruses were adjusted accordingly. 33 and 83 Old and New World bipartite begomoviruses were collected, respectively, before further redundancy checking.

Identification of common regions

The DNA-A and DNA-B genomes of a bipartite begomovirus share a 200- to 250-nt long highly identical segment (>85%), namely the common region (CR), in which the invariant nonamer "TAATATT|AC" resides near to the middle of it. To determine the 5′ and 3′ termini of the CR, a pair of segments consisting of 250 nts upstream and downstream flanking regions of the invariant nonamer from DNA-A and DNA-B was aligned. Based on the alignment, the longest stretch of highly identical (at least 20 nts long and 80% identity) segment flanking the invariant nonamer was taken as the CR.

Identification of non-redundant genomes and ORFs

We clustered DNA-As together if their CRs shared >80% similarity. If more than one species was found in a cluster, only one species was retained arbitrarily for further analysis. A Peruvian begomovirus, Tomato leaf deformation virus (ToLDeV), was confirmed to be the first New World monopartite begomovirus in 2013 [7], but this was after our dataset had been finalized. ToLDeV does not appear to have a PCP gene. As a result, 26 out of 33 (85%) and 65 out of 83 (78%) non-redundant Old World and New World bipartite begomovirus genomes were included in this

analysis (Table 1). The full list of bipartite begomovirus genomes used and their sizes can be found in the Table S1 in File S1. Additionally, ORFs specified in RefSeq records were verified. We required the stated coding sequences or ORFs be translated exactly to the protein sequences specified in the RefSeq records. Genes failed to meet this requirement were excluded from this study (Table 1). Genomes and viral protein sequences used in this study can be downloaded as Data S1 or through this web link: http://sites.lafayette.edu/hoe/files/2014/01/bipartite_seqs_eh_jk_ sd.tar_.gz.

dN/dS calculation

dN/dS represents the log ratio of the rate of non-synonymous substitutions to the rate of synonymous (silent) substitutions. A negative, zero, or positive dN/dS value indicates purifying (negative), neutral, or positive selection, respectively. Protein sequences were aligned by T_COFFEE [17] using default parameters. Protein alignments were converted to codon alignments using pal2nal v14 [18]. The codon alignments were submitted to the tool SLAC [19] hosted in the Datamonkey web server http://www.datamonkey.org/ [20] for site dN/dS calculation. Substitution models were selected by iterating the likelihood ratio tests between nested and non-nested models. This procedure is implemented in Datamonkey web server and detailed discussion of the procedure can be found in [21]. The results calculated by SLAC were downloaded in CSV format for analysis.

Pairwise protein sequence alignment

As dynamic programming approach to local pairwise sequence alignment produces the optimal alignment for a given scoring scheme. We used the percentage of identity calculated by an implementation of such approach i.e. Smith-Waterman water program [22], to determine the diversity of each viral protein for either Old or New World regions. BLOSUM62 score matrix was used and gap opening penalty and gap extension penalty were 10 and 0.5, respectively.

D-statistic of the Kolmogorov-Smirnov test

In order to ascertain the statistical significance of the difference between two non-Gaussian, cumulative distributions of protein sequence similarities and dN/dS values, we quantified the difference using the D-statistic of the two-sample Kolmogorov-Smirnov (KS) test. In both worlds, the viral protein AC4 exhibited the highest diversity. Thus, AC4 was chosen as the reference for two-sample D-statistic calculation. D-statistics were computed using the R function ks. test () [23]. All the values of D-statistic calculated showed significant differences between the two worlds with p-value in the range of 10^{-16}.

Scanning of functional sites in the movement protein

We developed a Python script (available upon request) to scan for functional sites in protein sequences using the BioPython scanProsite package [24], where the option for skipping of high probability of occurrence was turned off. In addition, our script used the bootstrap approach to compute the p-value of hits through these steps: 1. Obtain the list of functional sites detected in the input sequences through scanProsite, 2. Scramble input sequences, 3. Scan for functional sites in scrambled sequences, 4. Register the list of functional sites found in scrambled sequences, 5. Repeat steps 2 to 4 100 times (a user-defined parameter), 6. Estimate the p-value of a functional site by dividing the occurrence of the functional site in scrambled sequences by the occurrence of the same site in the original input sequences.

Table 1. Number of bipartite begomovirus genomes and proteins included in this study.

	Old World (28)	New World (65)
Coat protein (CP/AV1)	28	65
Pre-coat protein (PCP/AV2)	23	0
Replication-associated protein (REP/AC1)	28	65
Transcription activator protein (TrAP/AC2)	27	63
Replication enhancer (REn/AC3)	27	64
AC4	26	42
Nuclear shuttle protein (NSP/BC1)	28	65
Movement protein (MP/BV1)	28	64

The bracketed numbers in the column head is the number of genomes included in this report. Note that not all genes from included genomes were automatically accepted in this study because we found some of the ORFs documented in NCBI RefSeq database showed discrepancies with the associated protein sequences.

Results and Discussion

New World begomoviruses have smaller segments

We discovered that the genome size of DNA-A in the New World is on average 121 nts shorter than their counterparts in the Old World (Figure 1C). Intriguingly, though no apparent gene loss event was reported previously in the New World DNA-B, their genomes (mean size is 2,589 nts, standard deviation or s.d. 43) are also on average 113 nts smaller than the Old World DNA-B (mean is 2,702 nts and s.d. 55) as shown in Figure 1C. This commensurate genome size reduction does not seem to be coincidental as bipartite genome segments (DNA-A and DNA-B) in the New World begomoviruses show a higher correlation in size (R = 0.91, p-value $<2.2 \times 10^{-16}$) than those in the Old World (R = 0.74, p-value $<8.1 \times 10^{-6}$). Besides, the genome size differences between DNA-A and DNA-B concurred this point as we found smaller and less variable differences between DNA-A and DNA-B in the New World (mean 37 nts, s.d. 18) than the Old World (mean 45 nts, s.d. 37). Regardless of the geographical factor, this result may suggest size codependency of the bipartite genomes, which is still largely unknown. Our findings are unlikely confounded by biased samples as viral genes AC4 (pink) and REP (blue) exhibit similar spectra of sequence diversity between the two worlds (Figure 2). We further investigated whether or not deletions are localized at a particular region and how it may explain the loss of PCP in the New World begomoviruses.

Deletions are localized at PCP's promoter region

We compared dinucleotide profiles in the 400-nt upstream, homologous region of all viral genes using a 60-nt sliding window between the two worlds (see Materials and Methods, and Figure S1A–G in File S1). We found that dinucleotides were better than single nucleotides in insulating the profiles from random nucleotide fluctuation. If short (<5 nts) insertions or deletions are scattered, dinucleotide profiles between the two worlds should exhibit similar patterns; otherwise we should see a direct shift between the two profiles. Among dinucleotide profiles of all genes, only C+G profiles, i.e. CC, CG, GC, and CG, of the CP gene were found to differ between the two worlds in which the region with high concentration of C+G in the New World was shifted ~100 nts closer to the start of the ORF (Figure 1A). The elevated C+G content is chiefly due to the stem of the highly conserved hairpin structure found in all begomoviruses in which the loop region contains the invariant "TAATATT|AC" nonamer ("|" represents the cleavage site during complementary strand synthesis). Corroborating results were found when we examined the

distance between the cleavage site "AC" and the start of the CP genes in both worlds (Figure 1B) where the New World's CP gene is on average 100 nts closer to the cleavage site "AC" than those in the Old World. This accounts for much of the 121 nts shorter average genome size of DNA-A of the New World viruses compared to those of the Old World (Figure 1C). In New World begomoviruses the distance from the cleavage site to CP is highly correlated with DNA-A size (R = 0.93), but to a lesser extent in the Old World (R = 0.72). Additionally, the C+G content in the non-overlapping region of PCP (from −164 to 0 in Figure 1A) remains at similar level between the two worlds. Therefore our analysis indicates one or more deletions totaling more than 100 nts were mainly localized in the proximal promoter region of PCP, not in other genomic regions, and that these deletions may have led to PCP inactivation in the New World begomoviruses.

Currently, little is known about the effect of genome size on cell-to-cell transport through plasmodesma but studies have shown that the plasmodesmata impose a size limit [25,26]. Effective shuttling of viral genomes between cells without passing through the cell wall is critical for maintaining infectivity of plant viruses as small viruses do not encode enzymes to breakdown the cell wall, which other phytopathogens such as fungi employ [27]. This finding suggests genome size reduction may be one of the evolutionary paths selected for in the New World begomoviruses in order to maintain virulence despite the loss of cell-to-cell movement conferred by PCP.

New World NSP and MP are under enhanced purifying selection

The compact begomovirus genome encodes only a small number of highly overlapping genes in ambisense, most known to have multiple functions during infection. The lost functions of the PCP gene are likely compensated by remaining genes in New World begomoviruses. Therefore, we took a comparative approach to identify the presence of purifying selection in the New World viral proteins. We measured the within-world diversity of each gene by pairwise protein sequence alignment. A high sequence similarity indicates strong conservation pressures on the genes. Figure 2 shows the cumulative distributions of pairwise identity (%id) of seven or eight viral proteins from the two worlds. In the Old World (Figure 2A), AC4 exhibits the highest variability followed by the two DNA-B proteins NSP and MP, then REn, TrAP, REP and finally CP. The CP is known to be the most conserved of all begomovirus proteins, and under the greatest amount of purifying selection [12,28]. All distributions were tested

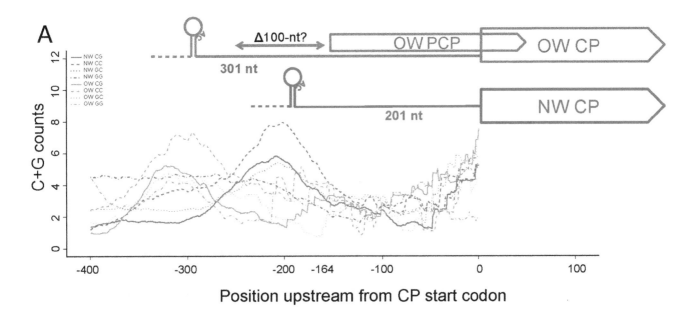

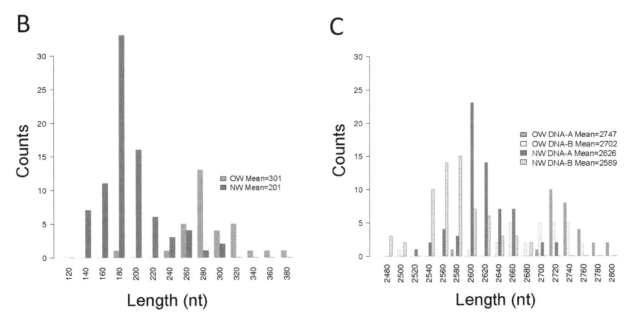

Figure 1. The loss of 100 nts from the promoter region of the New World PCP. A) C+G profiles of the homologous regions upstream from the CP from Old and New World bipartite begomoviruses. All positions labeled in the gene structure diagram are average values. Each plot represents the average number of CC, CG, GC, or GG in a 60-nt window. B) Distributions of the distance between the cleavage site "AC" of the invariant nonamer and the beginning of CP gene. C) Distribution of genome size.

for statistical significance (p-value $\sim 10^{-26}$) according to the two-sample Kolmogorov-Smirnov test with AC4 as the reference protein. Results from the New World viral proteins show much lower levels of diversity except for AC4 and REP. Such results are consistent with the presumed more recent origin of New World begomoviruses [4], but show a different pattern in protein variability (Figure 2B). The seven proteins are still bounded by AC4 as the most variable protein, and CP being the most conserved. The most striking difference is in the reduced variability of the New World MP (black plot in Figure 2B), which has become the most conserved protein after CP. Additionally, the New World NSP (gray plot in Figure 2B) is also found to show significant reduction in variability, comparable to the essential

replication protein REP (blue plot in Figure 2B). It appears that both DNA-B genes are under stronger selective pressure in the absence of PCP. These results suggest that the less genomically compressed DNA-B genomic segment was more able to accommodate new or enhanced functions than the more constrained DNA-A segment, which already has several overlapping open reading frames.

To further confirm this point, we sought evidence for adaptive evolution at the nucleotide level to corroborate these protein sequence analyses. Adaptive evolution is measured by the log ratio of the rate of non-synonymous substitutions versus synonymous substitutions (dN/dS). If the rate of non-synonymous substitution is lower than synonymous substitution, dN/dS will yield a negative

A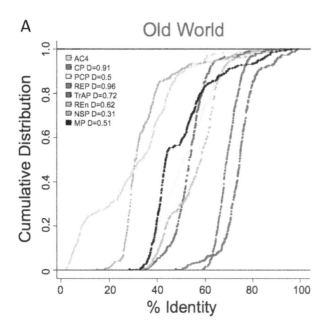

B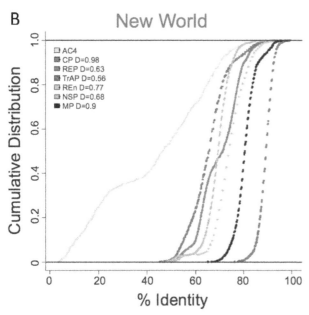

Figure 2. Protein sequences variability by gene. A) Cumulative distributions of percentage of identity (%id) of viral proteins from the Old World bipartite begomoviruses. The D values printed beside the protein name in the legend represent the magnitude of deviation of the plot from the AC4's curve and it was determined by two-sample Kolmogorov test. Larger the D value, the great is the deviation from AC4. B) Proteins from the New World.

value, indicating amino acid substitution is unfavorable. Conversely, a positive dN/dS value indicates amino acid substitution is permissible, suggesting the protein is under positive or adaptive selection. Aligned protein sequences were converted to corresponding codon alignments before dN/dS calculation using the Single Likelihood Ancestor Counting (SLAC) method from the Datamonkey website [20,29]. Figure 3A–B show the cumulative dN/dS ratios for MP and NSP. The New World MP shows the biggest deviation (D = 0.54, p-value = 0) from the Old World counterpart and nearly all dN/dS values fall in the negative

region, reconfirming elevated purifying selection in the New World MP. But we did not see this in other viral genes (Figure S2 in File S1). We further explored whether or not purified residues in the New World MP constitute to any functional motif(s).

The emergence of tyrosine phosphorylation site in the New World MP

In order to uncover the specific nucleotides subjected to elevated purifying selection in the New World MP, we compared the functional sites of MP in both worlds. Among all functional sites discovered, a putative tyrosine phosphorylation site [RK]-x(2,3)-[DE]-x(2,3)-Y (PROSITE ID: PS00007; the notation means the site starts with either R or K, followed by any 2 to 3 residues, and then a D or E residue, followed by any 2 to 3 residues, and ends with Y) shows the greatest difference between the two worlds: 62/65 New World MP sequences were found to carry the tyrosine phosphorylation site compared to only 1/28 from the Old World.

We also evaluated the likelihood for the emergence of this site by comparing the putative tyrosine phosphorylation site in the New World MP with the homologous region in the Old World MP. We aligned the eight-residue site and the corresponding codons. The amino acid consensus of the Old World (Figure 3C) shows only two residue substitutions are needed to transform the functionally indeterminate eight-residue site in the Old World MP to the tyrosine phosphorylation site found in the New World MP. From the codon perspective, four nucleotide substitutions from the first and fifth codons are sufficient to transform the site (Figure 3D).

Conclusions

Our analysis strongly suggests one or more deletions of 100 nts in the promoter region of the New World PCP, which may be linked to the inactivation of PCP. The resultant shrunken genome may have had an advantage in cell-to-cell movement through plasmodesmata. Furthermore, our genome size analysis unraveled putative size codependency of the bipartite genomes. As the New World begomoviruses are presumably originated from the Old World counterparts recently [4], the conspicuous correlation between the New World DNA-A and DNA-B could be alluded to bottleneck effect. However, the more diverse Old World begomoviruses still maintain a high level of correlation (R = 0.74, p-value $<8.1\times10^{-6}$) between segment size of their bipartite genomes. DNA-B's functional sequences – the common region (~200 nts), ORFs of NSP (~800 nts) and MP (~900 nts) and their promoter regions (~200 nts) – occupy ~2,100 nts of the 2,700-nt genome on average, leaving ~600 nts (22% of the genome) available for size reduction. According to our data (Table S1 in File S1), the mean, median and maximum difference between the bipartite genomes of the Old World viruses are only 45, 40, and 170 nts, respectively, which are far smaller than the 600 nts permissible range without interrupting the genomic structure of the viruses. This result is surprising as begomoviruses are fast mutating [30] and recombining [31,32] ssDNA viruses, indicating the presence of unknown constraints that limit the variance in size between segments in bipartite genomes.

Our prediction aligns with findings in closely related monopartite begomoviruses. PCP has been reported previously to perform some MP functions, such as intracellular movement and cell periphery localization [9,25,26]. Additionally, in-vitro phosphorylation activity was reported in MP of Abutilon mosaic virus [33]. Our thorough bioinformatic comparison of geographically separated begomovirus species has produced a candidate region for detailed wet lab analysis. If the tyrosine phosphorylation site is

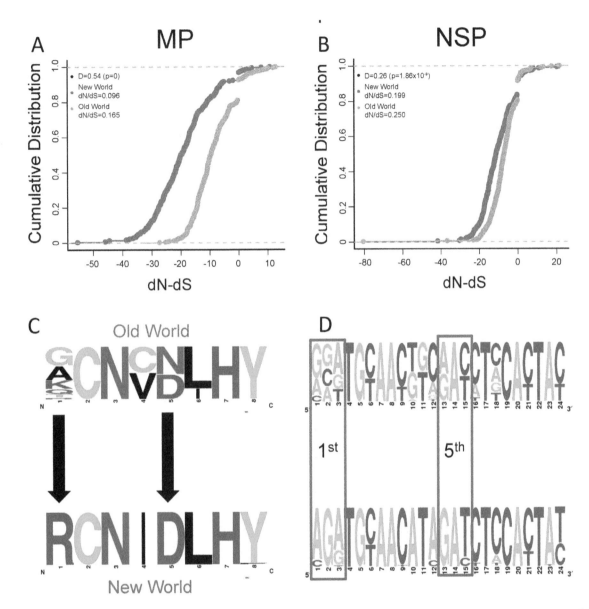

Figure 3. Cumulative distributions of site dN/dS values of the viral proteins. D-value, with p-value, represents the deviation of the New World curve from the Old World curve. D-value was calculated by the two-sample Kolmogorov test. Averaged site dN/dS is displayed on the top left, which reflects the overall selection pressure on the protein. A) MP. B) NSP. C) The emergence of putative tyrosine phosphorylation site in the New World MP. Consensus sequence pictures were created using Weblogo [34]. Searching is based on PROSITE database [35]. PROSITE ID of the tyrosine phosphorylation site is PS00007 where its consensus is [RK]-x(2,3)-[DE]-x(2,3)-Y. D) Codon alignment of the homologous region of the site.

critical to infectivity of New World begomoviruses, it will be a novel target for sequence-specific, anti-viral strategies.

Supporting Information

File S1 Contains the following files: **Table S1:** Selected bipartite begomoviruses and their genome size. **Figure S1:** Dinucleotide profiles in 400-nt upstream regions. Window size is 60 nts. Y-axis denotes the average occurrences of the specified dinucleotide in the 60-nt window. Plots of dinucleotides AA, AC, ..., TG, TT are arranged from top left to bottom right. **Figure S2:** Cumulative dN/dS values by gene.

Data S1 Genomes and protein sequences used in this study.

Author Contributions

Conceived and designed the experiments: ESH JK SD. Performed the experiments: ESH JK. Analyzed the data: ESH SD. Contributed reagents/materials/analysis tools: ESH JK. Contributed to the writing of the manuscript: ESH SD.

References

1. Nault LR (1997) Arthropod transmission of plant viruses: A new synthesis. Annals of the Entomological Society of America 90: 521–541.
2. Zhang WM, Fu HB, Wang WH, Piao CS, Tao YL, et al. (2014) Rapid Spread of a Recently Introduced Virus (Tomato Yellow Leaf Curl Virus) and Its Vector Bemisia tabaci (Hemiptera: Aleyrodidae) in Liaoning Province, China. Journal of Economic Entomology 107: 98–104.
3. Seal SE, Jeger MJ, Van den Bosch F (2006) Begomovirus evolution and disease management. Plant Virus Epidemiology. 297–316.
4. Rybicki EP (1994) A phylogenetic and evolutionary justification for 3 genera of geminiviridae. Archives of Virology 139: 49–77.
5. Xu XZ, Liu QP, Fan LJ, Cui XF, Zhou XP (2008) Analysis of synonymous codon usage and evolution of begomoviruses. Journal of Zhejiang University Science B 9: 667–674.
6. Rojas MR, Hagen C, Lucas WJ, Gilbertson RL (2005) Exploiting chinks in the plant's armor: evolution and emergence of geminiviruses. Annu Rev Phytopathol 43: 361–394.
7. Melgarejo TA, Kon T, Rojas MR, Paz-Carrasco L, Zerbini FM, et al. (2013) Characterization of a new world monopartite begomovirus causing leaf curl disease of tomato in Ecuador and Peru reveals a new direction in geminivirus evolution. J Virol 87: 5397–5413.
8. Ha C, Coombs S, Revill P, Harding R, Vu M, et al. (2008) Molecular characterization of begomoviruses and DNA satellites from Vietnam: additional evidence that the New World geminiviruses were present in the Old World prior to continental separation. The Journal of general virology 89: 312–326.
9. Rothenstein D, Krenz B, Selchow O, Jeske H (2007) Tissue and cell tropism of Indian cassava mosaic virus (ICMV) and its AV2 (precoat) gene product. Virology 359: 137–145.
10. Poornima Priyadarshini CG, Ambika MV, Tippeswamy R, Savithri HS (2011) Functional characterization of coat protein and V2 involved in cell to cell movement of Cotton leaf curl Kokhran virus-Dabawali. PLoS ONE 6: e26929.
11. Glick E, Zrachya A, Levy Y, Mett A, Gidoni D, et al. (2008) Interaction with host SGS3 is required for suppression of RNA silencing by tomato yellow leaf curl virus V2 protein. Proc Natl Acad Sci U S A 105: 157–161.
12. Padidam M, Beachy RN, Fauquet CM (1995) Classification and identification of geminiviruses using sequence comparisons. Journal of General Virology 76: 249–263.
13. Briddon RW, Patil BL, Bagewadi B, Nawaz-ul-Rehman MS, Fauquet CM (2010) Distinct evolutionary histories of the DNA-A and DNA-B components of bipartite begomoviruses. BMC Evol Biol 10: 97.
14. Modena NA, Zelada AM, Conte F, Mentaberry A (2008) Phosphorylation of the TGBp1 movement protein of Potato virus X by a Nicotiana tabacum CK2-like activity. Virus Res 137: 16–23.
15. Pruitt KD, Brown GR, Hiatt SM, Thibaud-Nissen F, Astashyn A, et al. (2014) RefSeq: an update on mammalian reference sequences. Nucleic Acids Res 42: D756–763.
16. King AMQ, Adams MJ, Carstens EB, Lefkowitz EJ, editors (2012) Virus taxonomy: classification and nomenclature of viruses: Ninth Report of the International Committee on Taxonomy of Viruses. San Diego: Elsevier.
17. Notredame C, Higgins DG, Heringa J (2000) T-Coffee: A novel method for fast and accurate multiple sequence alignment. J Mol Biol 302: 205–217.
18. Suyama M, Torrents D, Bork P (2006) PAL2NAL: robust conversion of protein sequence alignments into the corresponding codon alignments. Nucleic Acids Res 34: W609–612.
19. Kosakovsky Pond SL, Frost SDW (2005) Datamonkey: rapid detection of selective pressure on individual sites of codon alignments. Bioinformatics 21: 2531–2533.
20. Delport W, Poon AF, Frost SD, Kosakovsky Pond SL (2010) Datamonkey 2010: a suite of phylogenetic analysis tools for evolutionary biology. Bioinformatics 26: 2455–2457.
21. Posada D, Buckley TR (2004) Model selection and model averaging in phylogenetics: advantages of akaike information criterion and bayesian approaches over likelihood ratio tests. Syst Biol 53: 793–808.
22. Rice P, Longden I, Bleasby A (2000) EMBOSS: the European Molecular Biology Open Software Suite. Trends Genet 16: 276–277.
23. Team RDC (2012) R: a language and environment for statistical computing. Vienna: R Foundation for Statistical Computing.
24. Cock PJ, Antao T, Chang JT, Chapman BA, Cox CJ, et al. (2009) Biopython: freely available Python tools for computational molecular biology and bioinformatics. Bioinformatics 25: 1422–1423.
25. Gilbertson RL, Sudarshana M, Jiang H, Rojas MR, Lucas WJ (2003) Limitations on geminivirus genome size imposed by plasmodesmata and virus-encoded movement protein: insights into DNA trafficking. Plant Cell 15: 2578–2591.
26. Rojas MR, Jiang H, Salati R, Xoconostle-Cazares B, Sudarshana MR, et al. (2001) Functional analysis of proteins involved in movement of the monopartite begomovirus, Tomato yellow leaf curl virus. Virology 291: 110–125.
27. Tonukari NJ, Scott-Craig JS, Walton JD (2000) The Cochliobolus carbonum SNF1 gene is required for cell wall-degrading enzyme expression and virulence on maize. Plant Cell 12: 237–248.
28. Duffy S, Holmes EC (2009) Validation of high rates of nucleotide substitution in geminiviruses: phylogenetic evidence from East African cassava mosaic viruses. J Gen Virol 90: 1539–1547.
29. Kosakovsky Pond SL, Frost SDW (2005) Not so different after all: a comparison of methods for detecting amino acid sites under selection. Mol Biol Evol 22: 1208–1222.
30. Duffy S, Shackelton LA, Holmes EC (2008) Rates of evolutionary change in viruses: patterns and determinants. Nat Rev Genet 9: 267–276.
31. Monjane AL, Pande D, Lakay F, Shepherd DN, van der Walt E, et al. (2012) Adaptive evolution by recombination is not associated with increased mutation rates in Maize streak virus. BMC Evol Biol 12: 252.
32. Rocha CS, Castillo-Urquiza GP, Lima AT, Silva FN, Xavier CA, et al. (2013) Brazilian begomovirus populations are highly recombinant, rapidly evolving, and segregated based on geographical location. J Virol 87: 5784–5799.
33. Kleinow T, Holeiter G, Nischang M, Stein M, Karayavuz M, et al. (2008) Post-translational modifications of Abutilon mosaic virus movement protein (BC1) in fission yeast. Virus Res 131: 86–94.
34. Crooks GE, Hon G, Chandonia JM, Brenner SE (2004) WebLogo: a sequence logo generator. Genome research 14: 1188–1190.
35. Sigrist CJ, de Castro E, Cerutti L, Cuche BA, Hulo N, et al. (2013) New and continuing developments at PROSITE. Nucleic Acids Res 41: D344–347.

7

CollaborationViz: Interactive Visual Exploration of Biomedical Research Collaboration Networks

Jiang Bian[1]*, Mengjun Xie[2], Teresa J. Hudson[5,3], Hari Eswaran[4,1], Mathias Brochhausen[1], Josh Hanna[6], William R. Hogan[7,8]

1 Division of Biomedical Informatics, University of Arkansas for Medical Sciences, Little Rock, AR 72205, United States of America, 2 Department of Computer Science, University of Arkansas at Little Rock, Little Rock, AR 72204, United States of America, 3 Department of Psychiatry and Behavioral Sciences, University of Arkansas for Medical Sciences, Little Rock, AR 72205, United States of America, 4 Department of Obstetrics & Gynecology Research, University of Arkansas for Medical Sciences, Little Rock, AR 72205, United States of America, 5 Department of Veterans Affairs HSR&D Center for Mental Healthcare and Outcomes Research, Central Arkansas Veterans Healthcare System, Little Rock, AR 722205, United States of America, 6 Clinical and Translational Science Informatics and Technology, University of Florida, Gainesville, FL 32610, United States of America, 7 Department of Health Outcomes & Policy, University of Florida, Gainesville, FL 32610, United States of America, 8 Clinical and Translational Science Institute, University of Florida, Gainesville, FL 32610, United States of America

Abstract

Social network analysis (SNA) helps us understand patterns of interaction between social entities. A number of SNA studies have shed light on the characteristics of research collaboration networks (RCNs). Especially, in the Clinical Translational Science Award (CTSA) community, SNA provides us a set of effective tools to quantitatively assess research collaborations and the impact of CTSA. However, descriptive network statistics are difficult for non-experts to understand. In this article, we present our experiences of building meaningful network visualizations to facilitate a series of visual analysis tasks. The basis of our design is multidimensional, visual aggregation of network dynamics. The resulting visualizations can help uncover hidden structures in the networks, elicit new observations of the network dynamics, compare different investigators and investigator groups, determine critical factors to the network evolution, and help direct further analyses. We applied our visualization techniques to explore the biomedical RCNs at the University of Arkansas for Medical Sciences – a CTSA institution. And, we created CollaborationViz, an open-source visual analytical tool to help network researchers and administration apprehend the network dynamics of research collaborations through interactive visualization.

Editor: Zhong-Ke Gao, Tianjin University, China

Funding: The work described in this manuscript is supported by award UL1TR000039 through National Center for Advancing Translational Sciences (i.e., formerly UL1RR029884 through the NIH National Center for Research Resources). The content is solely the responsibility of the authors and does not necessarily represent the official views of the NIH. The funders had no role in study design, data collection and analysis, decision to publish, or preparation of the manuscript.

Competing Interests: The authors have declared that no competing interests exist.

* Email: jbian@uams.edu

Introduction

Clinical translational science embraces inter-disciplinary collaborations. One of the key objectives of the Clinical Translational Science Award (CTSA) is to promote cross-disciplinary collaborations that can accelerate the translation and application of biomedical research discoveries into clinical settings. To better understand, facilitate, and direct clinical and translational research efforts, it is essential to analytically assess the quality and efficiency of existing research collaborations in a CTSA institution and promptly identify those potential collaborations that are more likely to be productive and make significant impact. Social network analysis (SNA) has been deemed as an effective tool to assess inter- and intra-institution research collaborations in the CTSA community [1]. Studying different collaborative relationships (e.g., co-authorships in scientific publication and collaborations on grants), a number of studies on research collaboration networks (RCNs) [2–8] have provided insights into the networks' topological characteristics and the network dynamics of research collaborations. For example, using various network centrality measures [8], we can identify key entities/components of the collaboration network, which enables us to allocate resources

strategically and therefore boost the overall network efficiency, e.g., attract new investigators to join the network and spawn new collaborations.

Although quantitative metrics of RCNs are valuable, the interpretations of descriptive network statistics are difficult for non-experts. Visualization of a RCN, e.g., through a graph where nodes in the graph represent social entities and links among them indicate their interactions, is beneficial to a layperson to understand its topology and dynamics. Visualization has been shown effective to present large amount of information and to stimulate visual thinking. And, visualizing social networks (and network visualization in general) has a rich history [9–12]. However, the majority of literature on social network visualization is based on static graph drawing. And most of the visualization tools used by social network analysts focus predominantly on automatic graph layout algorithms. Many SNA studies leverage one of the general-purpose network analysis toolkits such as iGraph [13], NetworkX [14] and Pajek [15] that provides some basic visualization capabilities. However, due to the limitation of those tools, often only static visualization of the networks are presented in those SNA studies. Our goal in this study is to create an interactive visualization platform that can support a variety of social network analysis tasks pertaining to studying collaborative research relationships. Interactive network visualization techniques can reinforce human recognition and have a profound impact on how best we can represent, analyze, and communicate network data.

In this paper, we present our experiences in exploring various network visualization techniques to create CollaborationViz, an open-source web-based informative and interactive visual analytical tool for studying biomedical RCNs. Specifically, we demonstrate CollaborationViz through analyzing network dynamics and characteristics of the biomedical RCN at the University of Arkansas for Medical Sciences (UAMS) – a CTSA institution. All the resources including the source code of CollaborationViz, the scripts of our network analyses and the anonymized network data can be found at https://github.com/bianjiang/rcna. While in this paper we use a particular dataset to present our work, CollabrationViz supports a set of visual analysis tasks applicable to networks in general and may be adopted by other exploratory visual analysis systems.

Methods and Technologies

Dataset and social network analysis of biomedical research collaboration

The biomedical research collaboration networks we study are unique in that those RCNs are formed based on collaborative research grants rather than publication co-authorships [8]. The Office for Research and Sponsored Programs (ORSP) at UAMS uses an in-house developed software system to track detailed information of research grants such as the requested budget amount, the budget start and end dates, the funding agencies, as well as investigators and their roles on each grant. Table 1 shows the statistics of the research grant data we have obtained from the ORSP. Our dataset included all grants that were awarded from 2006 to 2012 (fiscal years). We use these meta-data of grants to construct seven RCNs for each fiscal year from 2006 to 2012, and two aggregated RCNs (one spanning four fiscal years from 2006 to 2009 and the other spanning three years from 2010 to 2012). Besides the ORSP, we also used data collected by the Translational Research Institute (TRI, UAMS) to identify investigators that are supported by the CTSA program at UAMS. The TRI supports all CTSA activities at UAMS since July 2009.

We formalize a biomedical RCN as an ***undirected weighted graph*** to reflect the degree of collaboration, i.e., $G = (V, E)$, where each investigator is represented by a vertex or node ($v_i \in V$), and the collaborative relationship between two investigators (v_i and v_j) is evident by an edge or link between the two nodes ($e_{ij} \in E$). The weight (w_{ij}) of an edge (e_{ij}) is the number of research grants the two investigators have collaborated on during the time period of interest. Many previous studies on scientific collaborations [2–6] model a RCN as a binary network, where an edge is either present or not. In real world, however, the strength of the collaborative ties among different pairs of investigators may vary. One tends to feel more comfortable to work with existing collaborators rather than finding new peers. Therefore, our graph model incorporates non-binary edge weights in network generation and adopts the number of collaborated grants to indicate the extent of collaboration. Clearly, this is a rough approximation as some investigators spend more time than other investigators on the same grant. However, in the absence of other data, using the number of collaborated grants to indicate the strength of the social tie between two investigators is a reasonable approximation [22].

We studied a variety of network characteristic measures pertaining to RCNs, including clustering coefficient, characteristic path length, and number of disjointed components, once a biomedical RCN is generated. In our previous social network analysis of the biomedical RCNs at UAMS [8], we have investigated the effectiveness of the CTSA program and its impact on promoting collaborative research within an institution by observing the temporal evolution of those measures prior to and after the CTSA program at UAMS. Further, we can identify "influential" (or "important") investigators in the RCNs (in terms of network topology) based on four different network centrality measures–degree, betweenness, closeness, and eigenvector centralities–of the nodes. We have obtained quantitative evidence that the biomedical RCN at UAMS is moving towards favoring cross-disciplinary research after the CTSA award with the help of the diversity measure. Last but not least, we have created a collaboration recommendation model leveraging the random walk with restart (RWR) algorithm for suggesting potential new collaborations. The benchmarks of our recommendation method on the RCNs of UAMS show promising results.

Table 1. Statistics of the research grants dataset at the University of Arkansas for Medical Sciences.

Fiscal Year	Number of Awarded Grants	Number of Investigators	Number of CTSA Investigators[1]	Number of CTSA Supported Investigators
2006	477	326	N/A	N/A
2007	479	409	N/A	N/A
2008	601	469	N/A	N/A
2009	516	414	N/A	N/A
2006–2009	**2073**	**759**	**N/A**	**N/A**
2010	603	431	34	114
2011	538	443	26	115
2012	549	434	23	322
2010–2012	**1690**	**650**	**34**	**551**

[1]The CTSA at UAMS started on July 14th, 2009. The "Number of CTSA Investigators" and "Number of CTSA Supported Investigators" are not applicable to fiscal years from 2006 to 2009.

Modern Web technologies for interactive network visualization

Although static graphs are useful in presenting network structures, they limit the amount of information that can be conveyed and always present the network from a fixed perspective. To deepen our understanding of RCNs and assist nontechnical users in comprehending important network metrics and their implications, we created CollaborationViz, a web-based interactive network visual analytics tool. CollaborationViz is built using a number of cutting-edge web-based visualization technologies, especially the Scalable Vector Graphics (SVG)–a language for building rich graphical content [16], d3.js–a JavaScript library for manipulating SVG objects [17], and Bootstrap–a front-end Web development framework [18]. Network data are stored in Java-Script Object Notation (JSON), a lightweight web-friendly data-store and data-interchange format [19].

Results

An important goal of our study on RCNs is to provide a set of analytical tools for nontechnical biomedical researchers and administration to understand the nature and evolution of collaboration. As interactive visualization is direct, informative, and user friendly for a person to apprehend data and derive accurate observations and useful insights, CollaborationViz has been created to not only better disseminate the results of our network analyses on biomedical RCNs, but also to support visual analytics. Figure 1 illustrates the main interface of Collaboration-Viz. Based on our previous study on UAMS's RCN [8], our design of CollaborationViz starts by considering an analysis process to support exploration and assessment of a research collaboration network with respect to the following objectives: (1) representing collaboration networks in a meaningful format (e.g., a force-directed graph layout); (2) visualizing the strength of the collaborative relationships; (3) visualizing and tracking global and individual changes over time; (4) emphasizing relative importance and possible correlation between nodes (investigators); and (5) demonstrating the predictive power of our collaboration recommendation model. A live demo of CollaborationViz can be found at http://bianjiang.github.io/rcna/.

Informative representations and interactive network visualization

CollaborationViz provides an informative and intuitive user interface with theoretically-motivated abstractions for nontechnical users to interact with and study a collaboration network. As shown in Figure 1, each circle (node) represents an investigator in the collaboration network, and a curved line connecting two nodes indicates the collaborative relationship between the two investigators. Nodes are colored to distinguish CTSA (green) supported investigators from non-CTSA (gray) supported investigators. The strength of collaboration between two investigators is represented by the thickness of line.

To realize vivid, accurate, interactive representation, networks in CollaborationViz are rendered using a physically-based force-directed graph layout [17]. We can consider the network as a particle system, and the force-directed graph layout in d3.js implements the position Verlet integration to determine moving trajectories of nodes (particles) in the network. Typically, in implementations of particle systems, each particle has two main variables–its position x and its velocity v. Vertlet integration is a velocity-less schema, where we only store the current position x and its previous position x' of each particle. The velocity can be implicitly computed and consequently it is easier to keep velocity

and position in sync, which makes the simulation more stable [23]. Further, the physically-based model not only considers repulsive charge forces that spread nodes evenly on the canvas, but also takes into account the gravity forces that keep nodes centered in the visible area and avoid expulsion of isolated components [25]. One immediate benefit of using a force-directed graph layout for rendering networks is the clustering effect that manifests. A cluster of nodes that are highly connected will naturally be grouped together because of the gravity forces. For more details, Kobourov has an excellent review article on force-directed graph drawing algorithms that provides more technical background of the implementations [24].

One of the goals in CollaborationViz is to integrate various contextual information along with the node-edge graph. Network characteristics such as the numbers of nodes, edges and isolated components of a network are readily available along with the network diagram. A user can hover her mouse cursor over each node to see the node's local network characteristics including its local clustering coefficient and four centrality measures (degree, betweenness, closeness and eigenvector centralities). These network topological features help understand the structure of the overall network as well as the importance and position of each investigator in the RCN. A user can also drag a node to a different position and the nodes that are incident to this node will also be repositioned according to the physically-based graph rendering model. The parameters (i.e., charge, gravity, and link distance) of the force-directed layout algorithm are adjusted and the changes will be reflected immediately on the canvas.

Temporal evolution of research collaboration networks

The ability to visually exam the research collaboration networks at an institution is crucial to the understanding of the evolution of the network dynamics, therefore the development direction of the research environment under study. CollaborationViz not only provides a timeline that shows snapshots of the overall network of interest at different time periods, but also gives the ability to track individual investigator's development in the network across different time spans.

Figure 2 shows a use case of using CollaborationViz to explore the advancement of an investigator's collaborative relationships within UAMS's RCNs from 2007 to 2010. The chosen investigator is one of many who have received the TRI pilot awards, which was developed as part of the CTSA program at UAMS to "stimulate and solidify new, innovative research collaborations and promote high-quality translational research". In Figure 2, the investigator of interest is highlighted in red. The top part of Figure 2 shows four snapshots of the RCN at UAMS from 2007 to 2010– one of each year, and gives us a sense of the relative positions of the particular investigator in the network; while the bottom figures present a focused view of the investigator's immediate-connections and their changes over the four year, respectively. Through analyzing these figures, we can make the following observations. In 2007, the investigator only collaborated with researchers in an isolated small group (four investigators). In 2008, the size of the group and the number of internal connections increased; however, the group was still disconnected from other parts of the network and the particular investigator still had very few collaborations. In 2009, in preparation of the CTSA program, this group eventually made connections to the largest component (i.e., connected subgraph) of the network. We can easily see in the 2009 graph in Figure 2 that this investigator became a bridge connecting different small clusters. In 2010, the first year after the CTSA, the investigator was drawn towards the center of the network, and her "influence"

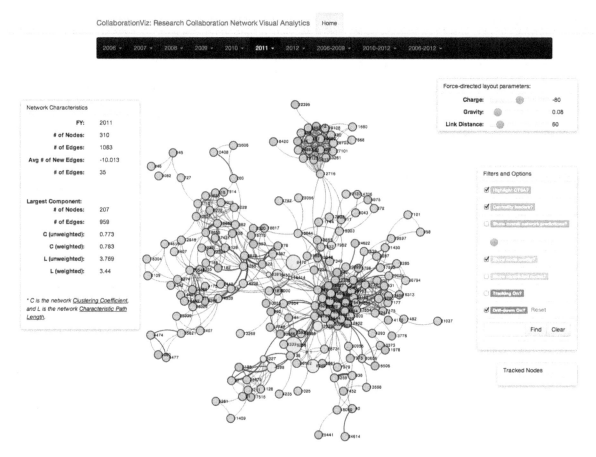

Figure 1. The main interface of CollaborationViz, an interactive visual analytical tool for exploration of biomedical research collaboration networks.

in the network increased drastically. Moreover, these visual patterns echo our quantitative social network analysis of the investigator's collaboration network. Positive changes of the investigator's network characteristics also suggest her increased productivity in research collaborations from 2007 to 2010. For example, the degree of her node in the network increased from 1 in 2007 to 98 in 2010. Furthermore, all of the four centrality measures of this investigator had increased. In particular, the closeness centrality had risen from 1.007 in 2007 to 3.664 in 2010, which coincides with our visual analysis that her position in the RCN became more "central" from 2007 to 2010. Many of other TRI pilot awardees exhibit similar temporal evolutions in network dynamics with increased degree of collaboration and became more "influential" in the network after the awards. Further, we also examined non-CTSA supported investigators' network developments within the UAMS RCN, and found that their collaboration circles (collaborative relationships) were less developed during the same time period comparing to the CTSA-supported group. These findings are consistent with our previous quantitative analyses [8] which suggest that the CTSA program has a positive effect in promoting research collaboration and such effect is more evident within the group of investigators who are supported by the CTSA.

Modeling influence in a social network through centrality measures

In network analysis, a variety of centrality measures are used to determine the relative importance of a node in the network.

However, each centrality measure defines the meaning of importance from a different perspective [26]. Within the context of research collaboration network, centrality measures of an investigator can be interpreted as how influential or important the person is with respect to the structure of the network. To identify influential nodes in a comprehensive manner, we investigated four widely used network centrality measures–degree centrality, betweenness, closeness, and eigenvector centrality [27]–to rank investigators' relative influence (or importance, contribution) and combine multiple rankings of nodes using rank aggregation techniques [28]. An influential investigator with a high consensus ranking is called a centrality leader who affects others in ways such as propagating an idea or an advertisement across the network. CollaborationViz visualizes a node's relative influence through adjusting the size of each node according to its ranking of relative influence in the RCN. Combined with other visual analytical tools in CollaborationViz, we can easily identify, analyze and reason with investigators' relative importance in the collaboration network. Figure 3 (a) demonstrates a visualization of ranking investigators' relative importance in CollaborationViz based on UAMS's 2012 RCN. Further, as shown in Figure 3 (b), CollaborationViz gives us the ability to drill down to a specific centrality leader (id: 32923) and it is obvious that this investigator is not only highly connected (a high degree node) but also acts as a hub connecting three communities in the network. Such observations are hard to make and comprehend through a quantitative network analysis, but self-evident in CollaborationViz through novel visualizations.

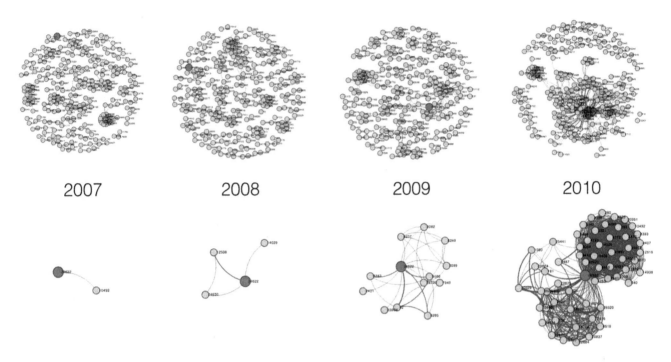

Figure 2. Temporal evolution of an investigator in the research collaboration network at UAMS.

Exploration and interaction through highlighting, filtering and visual overlays

It is important for a user to have the ability to narrow down the scope and reduce the complexity of the data by filtering based on her domain knowledge or interests. Such functionality facilitates users in discovering patterns and data points of interest; and it helps to focus the visual analysis process. However, it is not always easy to translate an analysis task into proper interfaces since the user may not have a well-defined hypothesis and simply wants to explore and learn the data. CollaborationViz implements a

number of viewing control mechanisms—highlighting, filtering, and visual overlays—to offer services for visual navigation and visual analytics. For example, as shown in Figure 1, the centrality leaders and CTSA supported investigators are highlighted in different color and size. Highlighting helps to attract users' attention to a small portion of highly relevant information and nodes that is directly beneficial for their analyses [29]. Further, transparency is an efficient transient highlighting techniques to dissolve the context around the object of interests. In CollaborationViz, we adjust objects' alpha levels to render the focused

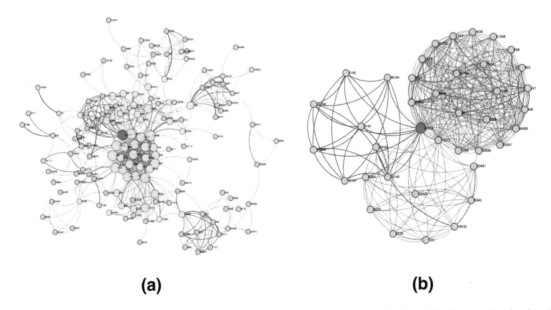

(a)   **(b)**

Figure 3. Visualizing "centrality leaders": Figure 3 (a) demonstrates a visualization of the identified "centrality leaders" and their relative "importance" to the network based on UAMS's 2012 research collaboration network; and Figure 3 (b) zooms in to one of the centrality leaders and shows her immediate collaborative relationships.

objects more obvious in the display (Figure 4). Moreover, filtering and visual overlays are two other important information visualization techniques. Through filtering, we can greatly reduce the data complexity by narrowing down the scope of interests. As demonstrated in Figure 3, through filtering out non-incident nodes and edges, we can zoom in to examine the collaborative relationships of a particular node (Figure 3b), by which it eliminates the noises to the analysis problem in hand and reveals hidden patterns (e.g., the bridging and clustering effects) that were not self-evident (as in Figure 3a).

Collaboration recommendation through link prediction

Social networks such as research collaboration networks are highly dynamic, whereas new interactions among social entities are commonly manifested through additions and deletions of edges in the network. One of the main questions in studying research collaborations is how we can find promising new collaborations (new edges in the network). Such question can be tackled through applying link prediction techniques with network data. In this study, using the random walks with restarts (RWRs) method, we can accurately discover missing links (overlooked collaborations) and the links that could appear in the future (potential new collaborations). Despite the conceptual differences, the same prediction model applies to both tasks [8]. In CollaborationViz, we can depict the predicted links as dotted lines between nodes (Figure 5), which gives the user a quick overview of the predicted new collaborations and how it would affect the network dynamics.

Discussion and Conclusion

In this study, we presented our efforts in building meaningful interactive network visualizations with theoretically based information visualization approaches to support a visual analysis process of studying research collaborations. Our result, CollaborationViz, is a novel interactive visual analytical tool for understanding social interactions among research collaborators through

network analysis. The design of CollaborationViz is driven by the needs of understanding the generative mechanisms of research collaborations and helping nontechnical users in comprehending social network analysis results of RCNs in an intuitive manner. CollaborationViz provides a convenient mechanism for interactive data interrogation and exploration that enables analysts to "synthesize information and derive insight from massive, dynamic, ambiguous, and often conflicting data" and "detect the expected and discover the unexpected" [20]. The interactive visual representations in CollaborationViz make it easy for users to perceive salient aspects of the dynamics and characteristics of RCNs quickly.

CollaborationViz is designed to facilitate analytical reasoning by helping a user understand historical and current situations and enhancing user's ability to recognize both expected and unexpected patterns in many ways. For example, as shown in Figure 2, the centripetal trend manifests in the evolution of the investigator's collaborative relationship. The collaboration of the investigator has grown significantly, which pushes the node to move towards the center of the collaboration network at UAMS. Such a phenomenon is difficult to perceive without a visual analytical tool.

Last but not least, the ultimate goal of studying biomedical RCNs in the CTSA community is to assist administration and leaderships of research institutions to strategically allocate resources and shape policies to attain an effective, transdisciplinary collaboration environment. CollaborationViz facilitates the dissemination of a quantitative SNA of RCNs and helps a layperson to explore, perceive, understand, and reason about complex network dynamics of the collaborative research environment. For example, a visual representation of the collaboration recommendation model [8] in CollaborationViz, as shown in Figure 5, helps to quickly identify potential new collaborations that are likely to succeed. Furthermore, the open-source nature makes CollaborationViz highly customizable and easy to be adopted by other CTSA institutions.

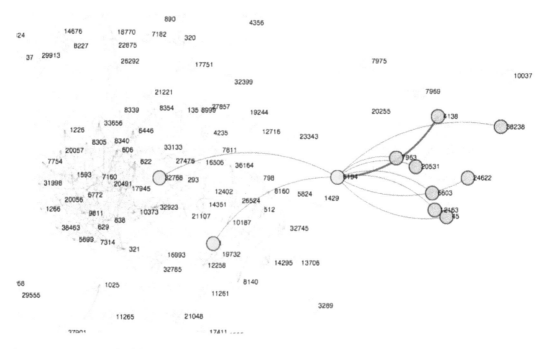

Figure 4. Using transparency to highlight areas of interests while preserving the context (e.g., a particular investigator's direct collaborators).

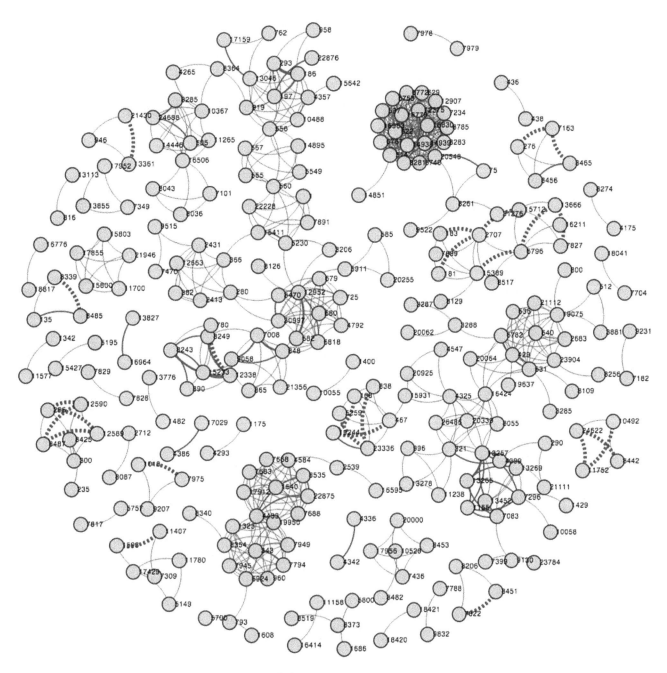

Figure 5. A visualization of collaboration recommendations.

Efforts to develop software libraries and frameworks for network visualization have been underway in several different areas. A number of general purposed network analysis tools such as iGraph [13], NetworkX [14] and Pajek [15] have graph drawing components that provide some basic visualization functionalities. However, most of these including tools that are specialized in network (or graph) visualization (e.g., Hive plots [32] and GraphViz [30]) merely focus on graph layout algorithms to provide a static aesthetically pleasing view of the network and few of them can provide interactive user experiences (e.g., iGraph and Pajek). A few of the network visualization tools (e.g., Pajek and Gephi [31]) provide infrastructures to support time-varying and dynamic networks. And, tools such as LaNet-vi [35], Tulip [36], and Cytoscape [37] focus on visualizing large-scale networks.

Further, numerous efforts have also been spurred on building domain specific network visualization to assist visual thinking and solve domain analytical problems. For example, Cytoscape [37], BioLayout [34] and Arean3D [33] are all well-known in the biomedical domain for visualizing biological networks. And, vizster [38] has been successful in allowing end-user exploration of large-scale online social networks. CollaborationViz falls into the category of a domain specific network visualization study. Nevertheless, CollaborationViz is unique in the sense that it integrates contextual information to facilitate a complete visual analysis process (e.g., analysis tasks such as observing temporal evolution of a network, studying relative importance of investigators, and predicting potential successful new collaborations) pertaining to studying and understanding of research collaboration environment. Furthermore, CollaborationViz is important for large-scale national efforts (e.g., CTSA) that promote interdisciplinary collaborations as it gives program evaluators and team science researchers a meaningful instrument to assess the impact of such programs on building a collaborative research environment and incubating new multidisciplinary collaborations.

Complex networks are commonly seen in biomedical research. Although CollaborationViz is built to specialize in exploring research collaboration networks, the underlying network visualization methods and principles can potentially be translated to other network studies such as brain connectivity networks and gene networks. Future work involves further iterations of new interactive visualization features to support more visual analysis tasks. For example, we are exploring the possibility of labeling the clusters (i.e., community structures [6]) in the network with research topics through mining grant abstracts with topic modeling methods (e.g., Latent dirichlet allocation [21]). To allow identifying relations between these topics and identify higher-level domains and disciplines, we can use a machine-understandable hierarchy that allows automated inference. Additionally, we will use more sophisticated topic relations to identify RCNs where, for example, the researchers focus on the use of a specific drug or even drugs with a specific mechanism of action (e.g., beta blockers or other antihypertensive medications). To accomplish these goals, we will use a realism-based knowledge representation system coded in Web Ontology Language (OWL) to define the topics and their relations to each other. These additions will benefit the analysis of RCNs in multiple ways, among others: a) automatically identifying existing research priorities in a network, b) identifying larger research domains that are relevant in the network, and c) automatically identifying unused research potential for research collaborations within an network.

Acknowledgments

The work describe in this manuscript is supported by award UL1TR000039 through National Center for Advancing Translational Sciences (i.e., formerly UL1RR029884 through the NIH National Center for Research Resources). The content is solely the responsibility of the authors and does not necessarily represent the official views of the NIH.

Author Contributions

Conceived and designed the experiments: JB TH HE MB JH WH. Performed the experiments: JB. Analyzed the data: JB. Contributed reagents/materials/analysis tools: JB. Wrote the paper: JB MJX.

References

1. CTSA Consortium: Evaluation Key Function Committee (2011) Evaluation - social network analysis. Available: https://www.ctsacentral.org/committee/evaluation-social-network-analysis. Accessed 2014 April 18.

2. Newman ME (2001) The structure of scientific collaboration networks. Proc Natl Acad Sci USA 98: 404–409.

3. Newman ME (2004) Coauthorship networks and patterns of scientific collaboration. Proc Natl Acad Sci USA 101 Suppl 1: 5200–5205.

4. Uddin S, Hossain L, Rasmussen K (2013) Network effects on scientific collaborations. PLoS ONE 8: e57546.

5. Nagarajan R, Lowery CL, Hogan WR (2011) Temporal evolution of biomedical research grant collaborations across multiple scales–a CTSA baseline study. AMIA Annu Symp Proc 2011: 987–993.

6. Nagarajan R, Kalinka AT, Hogan WR (2013) Evidence of community structure in Biomedical Research Grant Collaborations. J Biomed Inform 46: 40–46.

7. Bian J, Xie M, Topaloglu U, Hudson T, Hogan W (2013) Understanding biomedical research collaborations through social network analysis: A case study. In: Bioinformatics and Biomedicine (BIBM), 2013 IEEE International Conference on. 9–16. doi:10.1109/BIBM.2013.6732728.

8. Bian J, Xie M, Topaloglu U, Hudson T, Eswaran H, et al. (2014) Social network analysis of biomedical research collaboration networks in a CTSA institution. J Biomed Inform. doi:10.1016/j.jbi.2014.01.015.

9. Freeman LC (2000) Visualizing social networks. Journal of Social Structure 1.

10. Heer J, Boyd D (2005) Vizster: visualizing online social networks. In: Information Visualization, 2005. INFOVIS 2005. IEEE Symposium on. 32–39. doi:10.1109/INFVIS.2005.1532126.

11. Shen Z, Ogawa M, Teoh ST, Ma KL (2006) Biblioviz: A system for visualizing bibliography infor- mation. In: Proceedings of the 2006 Asia-Pacific Symposium on Information Visualisation - Volume 60. Darlinghurst, Australia, Australia: Australian Computer Society, Inc., APVis '06, 93–102.

12. Alsukhni M, Zhu Y (2012) Interactive visualization of the social network of research collaborations. In: Information Reuse and Integration (IRI), 2012 IEEE 13th International Conference on. 247–254. doi:10.1109/IRI.2012.6303017.

13. Csardi G, Nepusz T (2006) The igraph software package for complex network research. Inter Journal Complex Systems: 1695.

14. Hagberg AA, Schult DA, Swart PJ (2008) Exploring network structure, dynamics, and function using NetworkX. In: Proceedings of the 7th Python in Science Conference (SciPy2008). Pasadena, CA USA, 11–15.

15. Batagelj V, Mrvar A (2003) Pajek - analysis and visualization of large networks. In: Graph Drawing Software. Springer, 77–103.

16. W3C SVG Working Group (2011) Scalable Vector Graphics (SVG) 1.1 (Second Edition). Available: http://www.w3.org/TR/2011/REC-SVG11-20110816/. Accessed 2014 April 18.

17. Bostock M, Ogievetsky V, Heer J (2011) D3: Data-driven documents. IEEE Trans Visualization & Comp Graphics (Proc InfoVis).

18. Twitter Inc. (2012) Bootstrap. Available: http://getbootstrap.com/. Accessed 2014 April 18.

19. EMCA International (2013) The JSON Data Interchange Format, 1st Edition. Available: http://www.ecma-international.org/publications/files/ECMA-ST/ECMA-404.pdf. Accessed 18 April 2014].

20. Thomas JJ, Cook KA (2006) A visual analytics agenda. Computer Graphics and Applications, IEEE, 26(1), 10–13.

21. Blei DM, Ng AY, Jordan MI (2003) Latent dirichlet allocation. Journal of machine Learning research, 3, 993–1022.

22. Newman ME (2001) *Scientific collaboration networks. II. Shortest paths, weighted networks*, and centrality. Physical review E. 64(1): p. 016132.

23. Verlet L (1967) Computer "experiments" on classical fluids. I. Thermodynamical properties of Lennard-Jones molecules. Physical review,159(1), 98.

24. Kobourov SG (2012) Spring embedders and force directed graph drawing algorithms. arXiv preprint arXiv: 1201.3011.

25. Dwyer T (2009) Scalable, versatile and simple constrained graph layout. In Computer Graphics Forum (Vol. 28, No. 3, 991–998). Blackwell Publishing Ltd.

26. Newman ME (2010) Networks: an introduction. Oxford University Press.

27. Opsahl T, Agneessens F, Skvoretz J (2010) Node centrality in weighted networks: Generalizing degree and shortest paths. Social Networks, 32(3), 245–251.

28. Dwork C, Kumar R, Naor M, Sivakumar D (2001) Rank aggregation methods for the web. In Proceedings of the 10th international conference on World Wide Web (613–622). ACM.

29. Liang J, Huang ML (2010) Highlighting in information visualization: A survey. In Information Visualisation (IV), 2010 14th International Conference (79–85). IEEE.

30. Gansner ER, North SC (2000) An open graph visualization system and its applications to software engineering. Software Practice and Experience, 30(11), 1203–1233.

31. Bastian M, Heymann S, Jacomy M (2009) Gephi: an open source software for exploring and manipulating networks. ICWSM, 8, 361–362.

32. Krzywinski M, Birol I, Jones SJ, Marra MA (2012) Hive plots–rational approach to visualizing networks. Briefings in bioinformatics, 13(5), 627–644.

33. Pavlopoulos GA, O'Donoghue SI, Satagopam VP, Soldatos TG, Pafilis E, et al. (2008) Arena3D: visualization of biological networks in 3D. BMC Systems Biology, 2, 104.

34. Enright AJ, Ouzounis CA (2001) BioLayout–an automatic graph layout algorithm for similarity visualization. Bioinformatics, 17(9), 853–854.

35. Alvarez-Hamelin JI, Dall'Asta L, Barrat A, Vespignani A (2005) k-core decomposition: A tool for the visualization of large scale networks. arXiv preprint cs/0504107.

36. Auber D, Archambault D, Bourqui R, Lambert A, Mathiaut M, et al. (2012) The tulip 3 framework: A scalable software library for information visualization applications based on relational data.

37. Shannon P, Markiel A, Ozier O, Baliga NS, Wang JT, et al. (2003) Cytoscape: a software environment for integrated models of biomolecular interaction networks. Genome research, 13(11), 2498–2504.

38. Heer J, Boyd D (2005) Vizster: Visualizing online social networks. In Information Visualization, 2005. INFOVIS 2005. IEEE Symposium on (32–39). IEEE.

8

Transcriptome of the Invasive Brown Marmorated Stink Bug, *Halyomorpha halys* (Stål) (Heteroptera: Pentatomidae)

Michael E. Sparks[1], Kent S. Shelby[2], Daniel Kuhar[1], Dawn E. Gundersen-Rindal[1]*

1 USDA-ARS Invasive Insect Biocontrol and Behavior Laboratory, Beltsville, Maryland, United States of America, **2** USDA-ARS Biological Control of Insects Research Laboratory, Columbia, Missouri, United States of America

Abstract

Halyomorpha halys (Stål) (Heteroptera: Pentatomidae), the brown marmorated stink bug, is an invasive agricultural and nuisance pest rapidly expanding its incidence in North America. This voracious pest poses a significant threat to rural and urban agriculture, especially to specialty crops such as apples, grapes and ornamentals, as well as staple crops including soybean and corn. The object of this study was to generate transcript sequence resources for *H. halys*. RNA-seq libraries derived from distinct developmental stages and sexes were sequenced and assembled into 248,569 putatively unique transcripts (PUTs). PUTs were segmented into three disjoint tiers of varying reliability, with 4,794 classified as gold tier (highest quality), 16,878 as silver, and 14,357 as bronze. The gold-tier PUTs associated with 2,580 distinct non-redundant protein sequences from the NCBI NR database—1,785 of these (69%) mapped to annotated UniProtKB database proteins, from which 1,273 unique Pfam families and 459 unique Molecular Function GO terms were encountered. Of the silver tier's 6,527 PUTs associated with unique proteins, 4,193 mapped to UniProtKB (64%), from which 1,941 and 640 unique Pfam and Molecular Function GO terms were extracted. *H. halys* PUTs related to important life processes like immunity, endocrinology, reproduction, development, behavior, neurotransmission, neurotoxicity, olfaction, and small RNA pathways were validated through quantitative Real-Time PCR (qRT-PCR) for differential expression during distinct life stages (eggs, 2nd instar nymphs, 4th instar nymphs, female adults, male adults). PUTs similar to hypothetical proteins identified in symbiont microbes, including *Pantoea* and *Nosema* species, were more abundantly expressed in adults *versus* nymphs. These comprehensive *H. halys* transcriptomic resources can be utilized to aid development of novel control methodologies to disrupt life processes; to conduct reverse genetic screens to determine host gene function; and to design environmentally unobtrusive means to control host populations or target specific *H. halys* life stages, such as molecular biopesticides.

Editor: Omprakash Mittapalli, The Ohio State University/OARDC, United States of America

Funding: The authors have no support or funding to report.

Competing Interests: The authors have declared that no competing interests exist.

* Email: dawn.gundersen-rindal@ars.usda.gov

Background

Halyomorpha halys (Stål) (Heteroptera: Pentatomidae), the brown marmorated stink bug (BMSB), is an invasive insect native to Asia (China, Taiwan, Korea, and Japan) that has emerged in the last decade as an important major insect pest in the United States, Canada and Europe and has become the top invasive insect research priority for the USDA Agricultural Research Service. *H. halys* is a polyphagous piercing/sucking feeder having over 300 known plant hosts. It poses a considerable ecological and economic threat—tens of billions of dollars annually—to specialty crops such as apples, stone and pome fruits, grapes, ornamental plants, vegetables, seed crops, as well as such staple crops as soybean and corn. *H. halys* has rapidly expanded its range from the original single point of accidental introduction and establishment in the Allentown, Pennsylvania area in the late 1990s [1]. Damage has been particularly extensive in the U.S. Mid-Atlantic Region (DE, MD, PA, NJ, VA, and WV) and this voracious pest continues to spread. Currently, *H. halys* has been detected in 40 states and Canada [2], as well as Europe [3]. In addition to its status as a major invasive agricultural pest, *H. halys* is also considered a structural nuisance pest as it invades homes and indoor spaces in high numbers in fall to overwinter as adults before re-emerging in spring [2].

The threat to agriculture from spread of *H. halys* populations has continued to increase, spurring development of management tools; these include traditional classical biological control strategies using natural enemies or predators [2], as well as development of novel management tools including pheromone lures for monitoring and trapping [4,5], and newer biologically- and genetically-based control methods employing entomopathogenic [6] or molecular [7] biopesticides. The characterization of *H. halys* genomic and transcriptomic sequence data has been needed to aid development of novel, specifically-targeted, effective and environmentally sound means to mitigate the extensive damage produced by this insect, and to slow its aggressive geographic expansion. Because *H. halys* represents one of a broad group of agriculturally significant, highly invasive stink bug pests of the insect family Pentatomidae—which include southern green stink bug (*Nezara viridula*), green stink bug (*Chinavia hilaris*) [8], brown stink bug (*Euschistus servus*), and red-banded stink bug (*Piezodorus guildinii*), to name a few— the *H. halys* transcriptome is needed as a reference transcriptome for genetic marker development and comparative analyses of the functional array of transcripts deployed by this class of insects. The current study obtained a comprehensive RNA-Seq transcriptome dataset from four distinct *H. halys* developmental life stages (2nd instar nymphs, 4th instar nymphs, adult females, adult males); a set of high quality *H. halys* gene structures was delineated and functionally annotated, and the transcriptome-level activity at each developmental stage was assessed and compared. Differentially expressed transcripts were further validated across developmental stages by quantitative real time PCR (qRT-PCR) analyses to gain insight into stage-specific genes that could serve as targets for improved biopesticides. In addition, these *H. halys* transcript resources will be critical for annotation of the *H. halys* genome (currently in process), as well as enabling identification of inherent defense mechanisms against proposed control measures, the ability to defend against entomopathogens, and mechanisms that may enable resistance development.

Results and Discussion

Qualitative analysis of *H. halys* RNA-Seq data

Figure 1 shows the RNA-Seq assembly and analysis pipeline used in this study, which is further detailed in Materials and Methods. The 439,615,225 RNA-Seq reads surviving quality control procedures were assembled into a total of 248,569 putatively unique transcripts (PUTs). Of these, 4,794 were classified into the gold tier, 16,878 into the silver, and 14,357 into the bronze. The gold-tier PUTs associated with 2,580 distinct non-redundant protein sequences obtained from the NCBI NR database—1,785 of these NR proteins (69%) could be mapped to annotated proteins in the Swiss-Prot subset of the UniProtKB database, from which 1,273 unique Pfam families and 459 unique GO terms from the Molecular Function aspect were encountered. (Gold-tier PUT sequences and their associated annotations are available in Table S1.) The process was similarly repeated for the silver-tiered data: Of the silver tier's 6,527 unique GI numbers, 4,193 mapped to UniProtKB entries (64%), from which 1,941 and 640 unique Pfam and Molecular Function-specific GO terms were extracted. Figures 2 and 3 illustrate the relative abundances of the ten most frequently encountered Pfam family definitions and GO Molecular Function terms encountered in this data set, respectively.

A total of 31 genes were apparently highly differentially expressed, exhibiting a 20-fold or greater difference in expression levels in the 2nd-instar *versus* 4th-instar comparison. In the nymphs *versus* adult comparison, 41 genes were highly (20+ fold) differentially expressed; in the nymphs *versus* adults comparison, 150 genes were highly differentially expressed. Table 1 shows the five genes having the greatest level of perturbation for each of the three comparisons made, and Table S1 shows RNA-Seq-inferred fold differences in gene expression as observed for all genes.

qRT-PCR-based validation of *H. halys* expressed transcripts

Numerous *H. halys* differentially expressed transcripts were associated with functions in critical life processes, including immune response, endocrinology, reproduction, growth, development, behavior, neurotransmission, neurotoxicity, olfaction, de-

toxification, insecticide resistance, and other categories. Individual *H. halys* transcripts examined using gene-specific primers (detailed in Table S2) displayed a variety of interesting differential expression patterns observed in males *versus* females and across discrete developmental stages, and these correlated well to initial RNA-seq profiles. For example, various tubulin-related and heat shock protein genes were found to be more highly expressed in males *versus* females; females had higher expression levels of orthodenticle; the egg-related gene, vitellogenin-2; and a decaprenyl diphosphate synthase subunit 1-like gene associated with coenzyme Q production [9]. A LIM homeobox transcription factor beta gene was found preferentially expressed in early nymphal stages (Figure 4). Most patterns were expected; for example, vitellogenin encodes the vitellin protein present in oocytes, and is expressed as an egg yolk precursor in female insects and in the hemolymph of drones and sterile worker bees, as well as in other insects [10,11]. LIM homeobox transcription factor beta, highly expressed in early instar nymphs, is an evolutionarily conserved gene important in gene regulation during embryonic and early stages of development [12], particularly limb development. The phosphopantothenoylcysteine decarboxylase/phosphopantothenate-cysteine ligase, which functions in coenzyme A biosynthesis, was preferentially highly expressed in *H. halys* eggs and appears to have originated from gammaproteobacteria. The high levels of expression in eggs with substantial expression in adult females suggest this could be associated with symbionts vertically transmitted to eggs by adult females [13,14].

Detection of abundant symbiont-associated *H. halys* transcripts: *Pantoea*, *Nosema*, and other spp. and a novel iflavirus

A large percentage of abundantly expressed *H. halys* transcripts originated from apparent microbial organisms, including *Pantoea* and *Nosema* species as well as other microbes (*Nosema* transcripts detailed in Tables 1 and 2, additional microbial transcripts detailed in Table S3). This was not surprising based on recent evidence highlighting the importance of gut symbionts in the overall survival and success of *H. halys* in the field [13]: Surface sterilization of eggs to remove vertically transmitted gut colonizing bacteria (primarily *Pantoea agglomerans*) resulted in smaller clutches in the first generation and dramatically reduced survivorship in the second generation. Bansal et al [14] recently examined the gammaproteobacterial endosymbiont harbored in midgut gastric caeca and identified *Candidatus* "Pantoea carbekii", a close relative of *P. agglomerans*, as the primary bacterial symbiont of *H. halys* based on 16S rRNA sequences. In the present *H. halys* transcriptome data, more than 50 PUTs similar to hypothetical proteins from various *Pantoea* species were identified and were more abundantly expressed in adults *versus* nymphs (nymphs: 2nd and 4th instars combined). Over 20 PUTs similar to hypothetical proteins of *Nosema ceranae*, a honeybee parasite, were also more abundantly expressed in *H. halys* adults *versus* nymphs, as well as PUTs homologous to ribosomal and histone proteins identified in the silkworm parasite, *Nosema bombycis* (Table 2 and Table S1). PCR amplification of 18S rRNA confirmed presence of a novel *Nosema* species in *H. halys* adults— these genes were preferentially expressed in males relative to females (Figure 5). Interestingly, several *H. halys* individuals field collected in Maryland did not display detectable *Nosema* species infections (data not shown), which may indicate the Beltsville lab colony is distinct in this regard. No *Wolbachia*-associated transcripts were identified in the *H. halys* transcriptome, nor were any detected by DNA PCR using *Wolbachia*-specific primers (data not shown), though *Wolbachia* have been observed in association

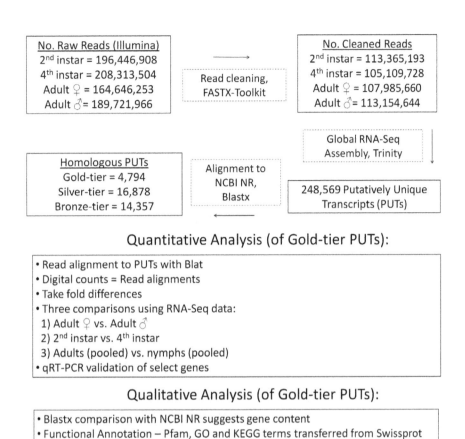

Figure 1. RNA-Seq Assembly and Analysis Protocol. Following data cleaning and assembly into putatively unique transcripts (PUTs), the *H. halys* gene space captured by these data was functionally annotated using information collected from the highly reliable Swiss-Prot subset of UniProtKB. RNA-Seq data was also used quantitatively, in order to identify potential differentially expressed genes for further validation using qRT-PCR assays.

with *H. halys* [13]. Finally, by similar comparative PUT analyses and methodologies, a novel RNA iflavirus was recognized and discovered as being associated with *H. halys*; this iflavirus was the subject of a prior publication [15].

Immunity-related transcripts identified in *H. halys* non-induced and immune-induced transcriptome

Insects have complex immune systems that enable them to defend against infections by microbial pathogens. These immune responses are critical to insect survival and must be overcome to effect biological control; thus immune-related PUTs were examined in detail for *H. halys*. All key components of the innate insect immune response were identified in *H. halys*, including core immune signaling, cellular response/immobilization, and RNA interference pathways (discussed separately below). The immune response is triggered in response to systemic infection by pathogen-associated molecular patterns (PAMPs) such as bacterial cell wall or flagellar components in the presence of host damage-associated molecular patterns and chemokines [16]. Pattern recognition receptors located on hemocytes and other tissues bind PAMPs, activating signal transduction pathways that induce antimicrobial peptide biosynthesis. Insects possess an innate immune defense separated into humoral and cell-mediated responses, which may be constitutive or induced following microbial incursion. Though no attempt was made in this study to induce the *H. halys* immune response with microbial elicitors, it was expected that some

constitutively expressed components would be present. Surprisingly, several inducible response components were noted in non-immune-stimulated *H. halys* (Figure 4). It is possible that expression of inducible immune pathway gene components is elevated in response to the possible presence of microbial pathogens, including species from the genus *Pantoea* (summarized in Tables 1 and 2, as well as Table S3). Among the PAMPS, pattern recognition receptors, and immune-associated PUTs expressed in the non-immune-induced *H. halys* transcriptome were peptidoglycan recognition protein S2, peptidoglycan-recognition protein precursor, and pattern recognition serine proteinase precursor. Increased expression of selected putative immune-related PUTs was subsequently confirmed by qRT-PCR of immune-induced male and female adults 24 hours following immune induction by non-sterile septic puncture (Figure 6). Proteins responsible for immune recognition of foreign glycoproteins were identified, including C-type lectins, hemocytin, scavenger receptor, and leucine-rich repeat proteins. C-type lectin was up-regulated 4.2-fold and a scavenger receptor PUT up-regulated 2.6-fold in immune-induced adult males (Figure 6).

Pathogen invasion activates core innate immune signaling pathways, including Toll, Imd, and JAK/STAT [17]. These pathways effect the production of a suite of antimicrobial peptides, enzymes, and inhibitors that limit growth of pathogens [17]. *H. halys* PUTs homologous to Toll pathway components included nuclear factor kappa-B kinase, spaetzle, spaetzle 4, spatzle 5, dorsal and snake. PUTs homologous to antibacterial peptides of

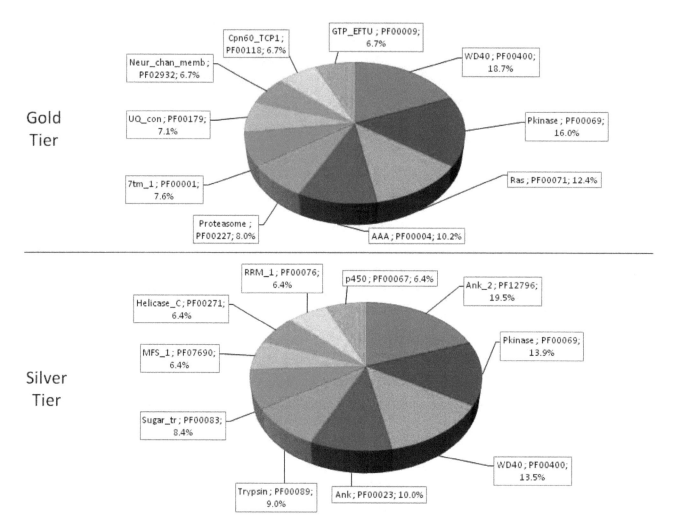

Figure 2. Relative Frequencies of the Ten Most Abundant Pfam Families. For each of the gold and silver PUT tiers, the ten Pfam families most frequently encountered among associated Swiss-Prot exemplars, and their relative abundances, are indicated.

other insects identified included an antibacterial peptide homolog of *Tribolium castaneum* hyphantrin and a lysozyme transcript— these are normally expressed at extremely low levels in uninfected insects, but were relatively abundant in *H. halys*. Immune stimulation slightly up-regulated a Toll-like PUT by 1.2-fold in adult males and 1.5-fold in females (Figure 6). Within Heteroptera, the model insect *Rhodnius prolixus*, closely related to *H. halys*, has been shown to possess components of the insect signal transduction eicosanoid pathway interacting with trypanosomal and bacterial infection [18,19]. Homologs of eicosanoid pathway components were noted in the *H. halys* non-induced transcriptome assembly, including a calcium-independent phospholipase A2 enzyme, phospholipase A2-activating protein, 15-hydroxy-prostaglandin dehydrogenase, prostaglandin E synthase, prostaglandin GH synthase, and prostaglandin reductase.

Many constitutively expressed proteins related to the cellular mobilization response (phagocytosis, autophagy, melanization, and coagulation) were sampled in *H. halys*, such as homologs of cadherin, annexin, cell adhesion molecule 3, hemicentins and beta-integrins. PUTs encoding an engulfment and cell motility protein and lingerer were identified. A PUT corresponding to an insect gap junction protein, innexin, was identified, suggesting monomers involved in gap junction formation following cellular

activation were present; this innexin was up-regulated 3.9-fold in immune-stimulated males, but was not up-regulated in immune-stimulated females (Figure 6). Components of the melanization reaction, which is catalysed by phenoloxidase and initiates synthesis of melanin, leading to crosslinked proteins and cytotoxic free radicals [17,20,21], were numerous. Transcripts corresponding to prophenoloxidase, putative serpins, and serine proteases of the prophenoloxidase regulatory cascade were recognized: these included a full length homolog of prophenol oxidase subunit 2, as well as prophenoloxidase activating factor, serpins, clip-domain serine protease, and hemolymph proteinase-5. Clip-domain serine protease expression was increased 3.2-fold as a result of activation of the immune response (Figure 6). Additional melanization pathway enzymes such as DOPA decarboxylase, dopamine N-acetyltransferase, and dopachrome conversion enzyme, and laccases were up-regulated; DOPA decarboxylase was increased 1.8-fold in females and 4.3-fold in immune-stimulated males (Figure 6). Additionally laccase, multicopper oxidases, Ebony, and proteins associated with cuticular melanization and coloration were identified, with laccase transcription elevated 3.1-fold in immune-stimulated males (Figure 6). Phenoloxidase-activated hemolymph coagulation defence pathways are utilized against multicellular invaders [22]. Components of these pathways were

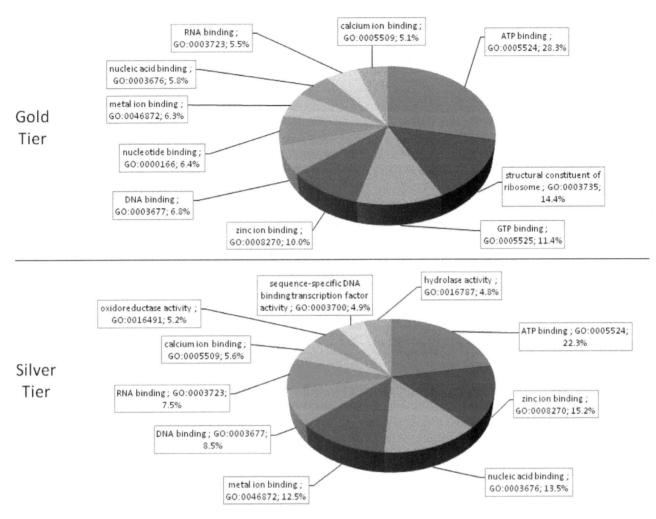

Figure 3. Relative Frequencies of the Ten Most Abundant (Molecular Function) GO Terms. Terms obtained from the Molecular Function aspect of the Gene Ontology were analyzed for their frequency of occurrence in this PUT dataset. The ten terms most frequently encountered among associated Swiss-Prot exemplars, and their relative abundances, are presented.

identified in *H. halys*, including transcripts encoding anticoagulant serine protease, clotting factor B-like, coagulation factor XI, proclotting enzyme-like, limulus clotting factor c and a multiple coagulation factor deficiency protein.

Cytotoxic reactive oxygen and nitrogen species generated by hemocytes and other tissues elicit a non-specific defense against all invaders [23]. *H. halys* PUTs similar to the plasma membrane reactive oxygen generator NADPH oxidase, which drives the respiratory burst phenomenon [24], and nitric oxide synthase, an antimicrobial free nitrogen radical generator [25], were identified. Enzymes responsible for inactivation of reactive oxygen species—for example, superoxide dismutase (up-regulated 1.7-fold in immune-stimulated females; 6.2-fold in males) and catalase (up-regulated 1.4-fold in immune-stimulated males and females)—were identified. Dual oxidase transcripts were elevated 2.1-fold in females, and 4.8-fold in immune-stimulated males (Figure 6). A transcript encoding the iron storage and transporting protein ferritin was up-regulated 3.9-fold in immune-stimulated males (Figure 6).

Up-regulation of arginine kinase transcription suggested that immune stimulation altered energy metabolism. Arginine kinase levels were elevated 2.3-fold and 2.7-fold, respectively, in immune-stimulated males and females (Figure 6).

Transcripts Related to Endocrinology, Reproduction, Growth and Development

Both male and female adults were sampled separately, resulting in identification of assemblies homologous to reproduction-related transcripts of other insects. Proteins required for vitellogenesis, follicle and egg maturation–including vitellogenin and vitellogenin carboxypeptidases, vitelline membrane proteins, and chorion peroxidases–were identified. qRT-PCR results demonstrated differential expression of vitellogenin in adult females (Figure 4). This protein is synthesized and secreted by the fat body and shuttled to developing follicles in the ovaries. Vitellogenin transcripts were up-regulated by septic puncture of adult females (Figure 6), which was expected since its increased transcription is a known insect antibacterial response [26]. Transcripts encoding components of the male reproductive system also were noted, among them testis- and spermatogenesis-related proteins; sperm membrane proteins; sperm flagellar components; and ejaculatory and accessory gland proteins comprising proteases and aconitase.

H. halys undergoes incomplete metamorphosis, molting through five nymphal stadia to become an adult. Insect molting is rigorously choreographed, regulated by precise timing of release of several peptide hormones, and coordinated fluctuations in the titers of both juvenile hormone and ecdysone. Disruption of the

Table 1. *Halyomorpha halys* genes having the most pronounced expression level perturbations as suggested by fold changes in RNA-Seq read abundances.

4th Instar expression relative to 2nd Instar

FoldDiff	Direction	2nd Instar	4th Instar	NRgene
110.55	up	1.76E-08	1.95E-06	ref|XP_001656025.1| tubulin beta chain
74.06	up	2.65E-08	1.96E-06	dbj|BAB88643.1| platyfish HSP70-1
63.36	up	3.53E-08	2.24E-06	ref|ZP_06714235.1| GTP-binding protein YchF
61.48	up	8.82E-09	5.42E-07	gb|AFP62029.1| Phosphoenolpyruvate carboxykinase
58.24	up	9.70E-08	5.65E-06	gb|AAM33784.1| ribosomal protein S12

Female expression relative to Male

FoldDiff	Direction	Male	Female	NRgene
24,885.78	down	2.30E-04	9.26E-09	dbj|BAB88643.1| platyfish HSP70-1
23,383.69	down	2.17E-04	9.26E-09	ref|XP_001656025.1| tubulin beta chain
22,865.49	down	2.12E-04	9.26E-09	ref|XP_002731505.1| GL12416-like
10,414.30	down	4.82E-04	4.63E-08	ref|XP_003708589.1| tubulin alpha chain-like
8,891.39	down	1.65E-04	1.85E-08	gb|AFP62029.1| Phosphoenolpyruvate carboxykinase

Nymph expression relative to Adult

FoldDiff	Direction	Adult	Nymph	NRgene
1,821.93	down	2.67E-04	1.46E-07	pdb|2JNF| Fly Troponin C, Isoform F1
1,668.64	down	7.64E-06	4.58E-09	gb|EFR25008.1| AND_10038, hypothetical
1,110.95	down	1.02E-05	9.15E-09	ref|XP_002424596.1| protein kinase subunit
1,083.78	down	4.96E-06	4.58E-09	ref|XP_002971910.1| SELMODRAFT_172529
657.97	down	3.01E-06	4.58E-09	ref|NP_001155541.1| density-regulated protein

Results for each of the three comparisons performed are presented.

molting process through chemical means, including growth and development hormone mimics, has been a promising method of insect control [27]. Plant-expressed RNAi targeting the insect-specific metamorphosis regulation gene HaHR3 was shown to be lethal in *Helicoverpa armigera* [27]. Thus, acquisition of tools to study this vital life process in *H. halys* was an objective of this study. Inclusion of an RNA pool containing earlier nymphal instars and molting individuals allowed sampling of *H. halys* nymphal and adult cuticular proteins, resulting in the identification of PUTs putatively involved in cuticle assembly, pigmentation and integrity (*e.g.*, chitin synthase, chitin deacetylase, chitotriosidase, laccases, cuticulins). Peritrophin and chitin-binding peritrophin precursor PUTs were also identified. Peptide hormones and corresponding receptors utilized during development and molting were recognized in *H. halys*, including prothoracicotropic hormone, allatostatin and its receptor, bursicon, eclosion hormone, and ecdysis triggering hormone precursor. Contigs orthologous to enzymes in the insect steroid synthesis/degradation pathways also were identified (17-β-hydroxysteroid dehydrogenases, 7-dehydrocholesterol reductase, sterol desaturases, and sterol o-acyltransferases) as well as PUTs similar to the isoprenoid juvenile hormone (JH) synthesis and degradation enzymes of other insects, including JH acid methyltransferases, JH epoxide hydrolases, JH esterases, epoxide hydrolases, and farnesoic acid O-methyltransferase. Also present were homologs of known haemocoelic hormone transporters such as lipophorins, JH binding proteins, oxysterol binding proteins and sterol carrier proteins.

Additional peptide hormones and receptors involved in regulation of metabolism were identified, including leptin receptor-like protein, calcitonin and its receptor, cardioacceleratory peptide receptor, gonadotropin-releasing hormone receptor-like, PDGF- and VEGF-related factors, octopamine receptor, retinoid X receptor, and tachykinin receptor. Also present were PUTs for the corticotropin releasing factor/diuretic hormone and CAPA receptor, 5-hydroxytryptamine receptor system regulating diuresis in *R. prolixus* [28]. *H. halys* PUTs for insulin and mTOR pathways involved in energy metabolism included glycogen synthase, glycogen debranching enzyme, glycogen phosphorylase, trehalase, trehalose 6-phosphate synthase, insulin-like peptide, insulin-like peptide receptor, insulin receptor substrate, and insulin-degrading enzyme.

Eggs were included as a developmental stage in qRT-PCR analyses, though sampling all stages of embryonic development was not undertaken. A number of *H. halys* PUTs homologous to developmental proteins identified in other insects were identified, including instances of armadillo, caudal, bicaudal, bicoid, decapentaplegic, mothers against decapentaplegic, and ultrabithorax. Availability of these sequences should facilitate evolutionary developmental (evo-devo) studies using hemipteran bugs as an experimental system.

Transcripts Related to Behavior, Neurotransmission, Neurotoxicity, and Olfaction

Insect nervous systems have a critical role in coordinating all behaviors, from vision and locomotion, to mating and host plant location. Many PUTs similar to neurotransmitter receptors, G-protein coupled receptors, and enzymes involved in neurotransmitter synthesis/degradation were identified. Resistance to (or

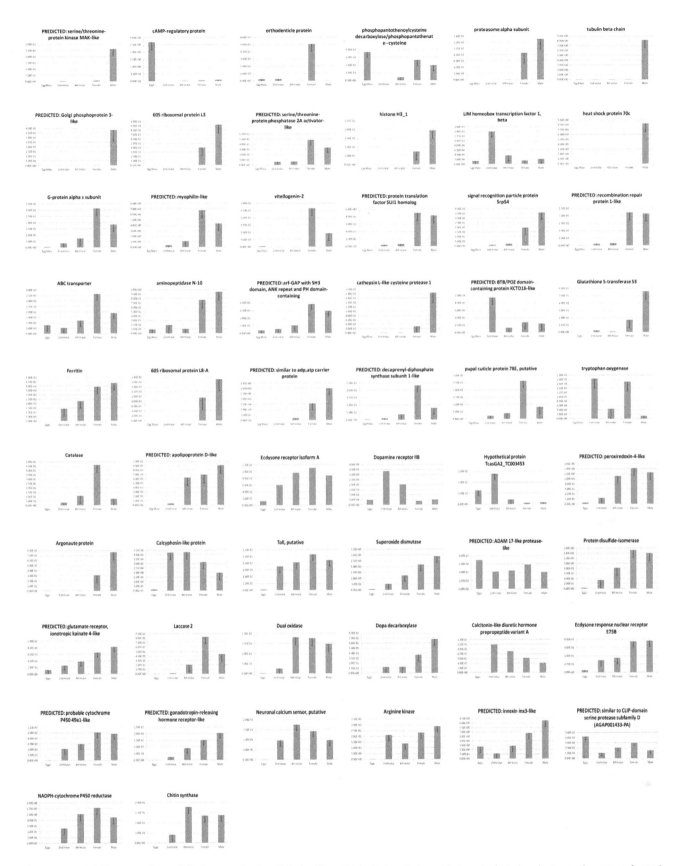

Figure 4. qRT-PCR transcript validation results for *H. halys.* Three biological replicates with three technical replicates each were performed. Bar height denotes the mean average of sample-specific $2^{-\Delta Ct}$ values, and error bars represent the standard error of the mean. Thirty-two selected transcripts are shown including certain genes predominantly expressed in adult males (e.g., Golgi phosphoprotein 3-like and tubulin beta chain); predominantly expressed in adult females (e.g., orthodenticle proteins, vitellogenin-2, decaprenyl diphosphate synthase subunit 1-like);

predominantly expressed in nymphs (e.g., LIM-homeobox transcription factor beta, BTB/POZ domain containing protein KCTD16-like); and those differentially expressed across various life stages (e.g., apolipoprotein D-like, neuronal calcium sensor). The transcript identified as TcasGA2_TC003453 associates with the NCBI NR protein having GI no. 270004135.

detoxification of) insecticides and plant-based toxic secondary metabolites are major contributors to the survival of herbivorous insects. Insect detoxification enzymes include cytochrome P450s and esterases, and many distinct homologs of these were present in *H. halys*. Glutathione S-transferase transcript levels were elevated 9.8-fold in females subjected to septic puncture, and 6.1-fold in males (Figure 6). Numerous multidrug transporters and ABC transporters responsible for xenobiotics efflux were noted. Transcripts encoding genes involved in olfaction and gustation were also present, including odorant binding and receptor PUTs, olfactory receptors, pheromone binding and degrading enzymes, and signal transduction pathway intermediates.

Transcripts Related to Small RNA Pathways

Components either directly composing or associated with the double-stranded (ds) RNA processing systems required for effective gene silencing in insects were present in *H. halys*. Transcripts encoding proteins involved in dsRNA cleavage and endonuclease activity, including cytoplasmic subunit argonaute-2, piwi, dicer-2, helicases, and RISC-loading complex subunits, were discernable. Interestingly, no *sid* or *sid*-like [29] PUTs were detected; these have been reported in all insect systems (except dipterans) to be involved in initial dsRNA uptake and transport pathways [30]. PUTs for scavenger receptors and lipophorins, thought to have roles in cellular uptake of RNA [31,32], were found in *H. halys* assemblies.

Insect transcriptomes have become critical for evaluation of differential transcript expression profiles for biotechnological use

[33], and a principal motivation in this study was to identify suitable gene silencing targets for ongoing *H. halys* control research efforts. Numerous differentially-expressed or stage-specific PUTs identified constitute excellent targets for further experimentation. For example, dsRNA synthesized from *Anthonomus grandis* chitin synthase 1 gene has been shown in injected cotton boll weevil female adults to silence chitin synthase 1, and has similarly been reported for silencing the laccase gene [33]. Both transcripts are highly and differentially expressed in *H. halys*. Several bacterial symbiont-associated transcripts also represent gene silencing targets, including those associated with symbiont microbial species.

Collectively, the *H. halys* transcriptome identifies a wide variety of differentially expressed transcripts, providing a reliable source of candidate genes involved in key physiological processes. This resource will enable multiple control projects for this insect pest, especially those targeting specific life stages, including identification and characterization of pathological agents with possible utility for the biological control of *H. halys* populations [15] and the identification of novel RNAi targets, including both bacterial symbionts and key *H. halys* transcripts associated with specific life stages or sexes. These sequence resources will also facilitate annotation of the *H. halys* genome, and provide a needed reference for comparative transcriptomics with other species of stink bug pests. Likewise, genes induced in certain *H. halys* life stages (e.g., vitellogenin-2 and tubulin) or associated with specific biological systems (e.g., ecdysone-related peptide binding proteins, laccase, chitin synthase and cytochrome p450) represent key genes

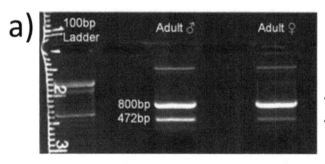

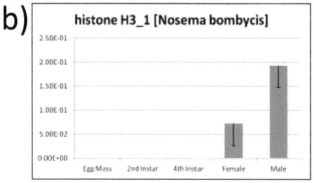

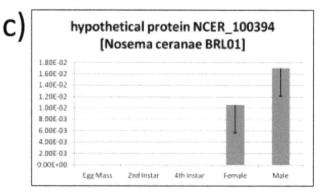

Figure 5. Identification and Quantification of *Nosema* sp. Gene Expression in *H. halys*. A) PCR confirmation of a *Nosema* sp. 18S rRNA gene from cDNA. Amplicon sequencing confirmed a *Nosema* origin of the 472bp band (data not shown). B) qRT-PCR amplification of a histone protein gene similar to a homologous instance from *Nosema bombycis*. C) qRT-PCR amplification of a protein similar to a hypothetical protein identified in *Nosema ceranae*.

Table 2. Fold changes in RNA-Seq read abundances for six representative homologs of various *Nosema* genes identified in the *Halyomorpha halys* transcriptome data.

4th Instar expression relative to 2nd Instar

FoldDiff	Direction	2nd Instar	4th Instar	NRgene
0.00	up	0.00E+00	9.51E-09	gb|ACJ24176.1| histone H2A [Nosema bombycis]
0.00	up	0.00E+00	9.51E-09	gb|ACU00734.1| 60S ribosomal protein L3 [Nosema bombycis]
0.00	up	0.00E+00	9.51E-09	gb|ADZ95692.1| 60S ribosomal protein L4 [Nosema bombycis]
1.08	up	8.82E-09	9.51E-09	Ref|XP_002995330.1| NCER_101816 [Nosema ceranae]
0.00	up	0.00E+00	9.51E-09	Ref|XP_002995933.1| NCER_101048 [Nosema ceranae]
0.00	up	0.00E+00	4.76E-08	Ref|XP_002995188.1| NCER_102023 [Nosema ceranae]

Female expression relative to Male

FoldDiff	Direction	Male	Female	NRgene
4.19	down	3.49E-06	8.33E-07	gb|ACJ24176.1| histone H2A [Nosema bombycis]
2.01	down	2.51E-06	1.25E-06	gb|ACU00734.1| 60S ribosomal protein L3 [Nosema bombycis]
3.18	down	2.65E-06	8.33E-07	gb|ADZ95692.1| 60S ribosomal protein L4 [Nosema bombycis]
2.12	down	8.74E-06	4.12E-06	Ref|XP_002995330.1| NCER_101816 [Nosema ceranae]
3.51	down	2.83E-06	8.06E-07	Ref|XP_002995933.1| NCER_101048 [Nosema ceranae]
2.11	down	8.97E-06	4.25E-06	Ref|XP_002995188.1| NCER_102023 [Nosema ceranae]

Nymph expression relative to Adult

FoldDiff	Direction	Adult	Nymph	NRgene
479.15	down	2.19E-06	4.58E-09	gb|ACJ24176.1| histone H2A [Nosema bombycis]
413.95	down	1.89E-06	4.58E-09	gb|ACU00734.1| 60S ribosomal protein L3 [Nosema bombycis]
385.30	down	1.76E-06	4.58E-09	gb|ADZ95692.1| 60S ribosomal protein L4 [Nosema bombycis]
708.36	down	6.48E-06	9.15E-09	Ref|XP_002995330.1| NCER_101816 [Nosema ceranae]
402.09	down	1.84E-06	4.58E-09	Ref|XP_002995933.1| NCER_101048 [Nosema ceranae]
291.25	down	6.67E-06	2.29E-08	Ref|XP_002995188.1| NCER_102023 [Nosema ceranae]

for further assessment, and RNAi-based gene knockdown experiments are currently in progress. If they prove to be sufficiently species-specific, these genes could suggest possible targets for RNAi-mediated gene disruption that may be useful towards diminishing this destructive insect pest.

Materials and Methods

Insect Rearing and Dissection

H. halys (BMSB) insects were reared as previously described [4] in a colony maintained at USDA-ARS in the Beltsville Agricultural Research Center, Beltsville, MD; this colony was established in 2007 from adults collected in Allentown, PA, and supplemented annually with several Beltsville, MD-collected individuals. Briefly, insects were reared in ventilated plastic cylinders (21×21 cm OD) on a diet of organic green beans, shelled sunflower and buckwheat seeds (2:1, w/w), and distilled water supplied in cotton-stopped shell vials. Eggs were collected weekly, hatched in plastic Petri dishes with a water vial and, after molting to second-instars, nymphs were transferred to larger rearing cages for the remaining four instars. Adults, males and females were separated 1 to 2 days post emergence, and subsequently maintained in different containers. Insects were maintained in Thermo Forma chambers (Thermo Fisher Scientific) at 25°C and 72% relative humidity, under a 16L:8D photoperiod. Insects of all developmental life stages were collected for RNA extraction, including eggs that originated from a single non-washed egg mass collected <20h

after laying. Four discrete developmental life stages were selected for transcriptome analyses: 2nd-instar nymphs, 4th-instar nymphs, adult males and adult females. Adult males and females were seven days old and had reached maturity. A separate set of adult male and female individuals were also immune-stimulated by septic puncture to the ventral side using a non-sterile minutien pin, followed by RNA extraction 24 hours after puncture, to facilitate analyses of immunity-related and other transcripts.

RNA Extraction

In each of the four developmental life stages characterized, five individuals were pooled and placed in a tube on ice to calm the insects. Tubes were then placed in liquid nitrogen for approximately 30 sec. Denaturing solution provided from the Totally RNA kit (Life Technologies, Grand Island, NY) was added to the tubes totaling 5 ml. Using an ultra-turrax T25, samples were homogenized until all individuals were fully dispersed (1–2 min., depending on insect size) and samples were placed on ice. RNA was extracted immediately thereafter following the Totally RNA protocol. RNAs were aliquoted as 10 µg in 100 µl of DEPC-treated water and stored at −80°C until sent to University of Georgia Genomics Facility for RNA-seq processing.

RNA-Seq Library Construction and Sequencing

TruSeq RNA libraries were prepared from total RNA. rRNA depletion was performed, and SE100 reads were sequenced from

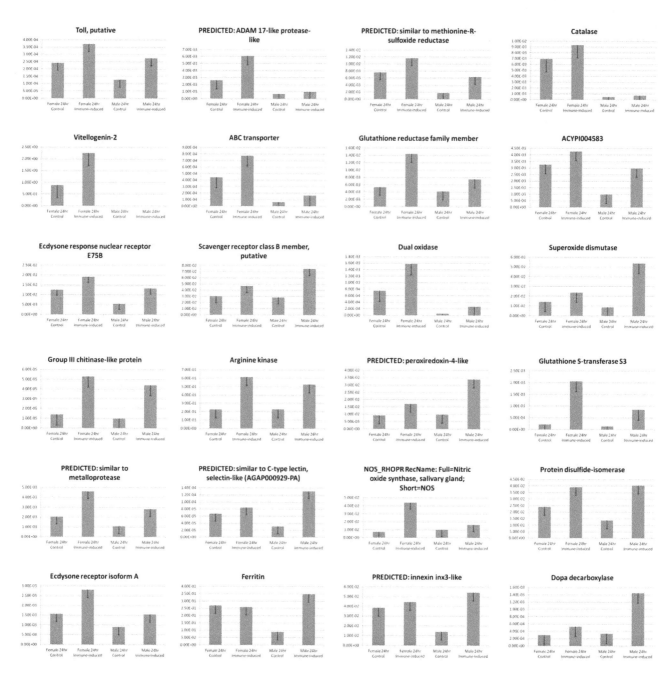

Figure 6. qRT-PCR Transcript Validation Results for Select Transcripts of Immune-Induced Adult Male and Adult Female _H. halys_ 24 Hours After Septic Puncture. Three biological replicates with three technical replicates were performed. Bar height denotes the mean average of sample-specific $2^{-\Delta Ct}$ values, and error bars represent the standard error of the mean. Twenty-eight selected transcripts are shown including those associated with immune response (e.g., toll, vitellogenin, ecdysone response nuclear receptor, group III chitinase-like, metalloprotease, ecdysone receptor isoform A, DOPA decarboxylase, Adam 17-like, ABC transporter, scavenger receptor class B, ACYP1004583, arginine kinase, C-type lectin, ferritin, innexin); energy metabolism (e.g., methionine-r-sulfoxide reductase, glutathione reductase family, dual oxidase, peroxiredoxin-4-4like, arginine kinase, glutathione-s-transferase, protein disulfide isomerase); and the oxidative stress response (e.g., Met-r-sulfoxide reductase, catalase, dual oxidase, peroxiredoxin-4-4like, nitric oxide synthase, superoxide dismutase, ferritin). The transcript identified as ACYPI004583 associates with the NCBI NR protein having GI no. 239791403.

resulting libraries using an Illumina HiSeq 1000 instrument. These data have been made available at the NCBI Sequence Read Archive [SRA BioProject Acc. No. SRP040652].

RNA-Seq Data

The FASTX-toolkit (http://hannonlab.cshl.edu/fastx_toolkit) was used to clean sequenced reads. The process eliminated artifact reads, and terminal spans of bases having Phred scores less than 21 were clipped, thereby forcing read ends to have error rates of less than 1%. Trimmed reads of less than 36 bases were purged, as were reads for which 10% or more of bases had a Phred score of 20 or less. Among surviving reads, bases having Phred quality scores less than 21 were masked with the symbol 'N'. In total, 58% of reads originally sequenced were retained for analysis, as well as 58% of bases originally sequenced (see Table 3).

Sequence Analysis and *de novo* assembly of transcripts

Figure 1 presents a graphical overview of the RNA-Seq data analysis approach used. Cleaned RNA-Seq reads were globally pooled and assembled into putatively unique transcripts (PUTs) using the Trinity assembler [34]. These were aligned to the non-redundant protein database, NCBI NR, using Blastx [35]. Homology information was used to identify PUTs that were likely non-spurious, and these were partitioned into three mutually exclusive sets on the basis of alignment quality. The gold-tier gene set represented the most highly reliable set of transcripts, and inclusion required that the associated Blastx hit consisted of a single high-scoring segment pair (HSP), that the PUT query was at least 300 bases in length, that the alignment's subject sequence (i.e., an NR protein) was at least 100 amino acid residues in length, that 75% or more of aligned residues were positively similar, and that the ratio of hit length to subject sequence length was at least 90%. Only the top-scoring hit per PUT was considered. End sequences from PUTs that were not incorporated into Blastx-derived alignments were clipped, and the remaining coding sequences were translated into high-quality *H. halys* protein sequences using the EMBOSS package's Transeq utility [36]. For inclusion in the silver-tier gene class, a PUT had to be at least 100 nucleotides in length and exhibit a hit length covering at least 75% of the NR subject sequence's length. Finally, PUTs of the bronze-tier class were required to be at least 100 nucleotides long and have a hit covering at least 30% of the NR protein's length.

Functional Annotation

To identify functional capacity in the gold-tiered data, GI numbers for these PUTs' best NCBI NR exemplars were mapped to UniProtKB entries using the "ID Mapping" tab from the UniProt website [37]. These mappings enabled the transfer of associated GO, Pfam and KEGG annotation terms from UniProtKB entries onto *H. halys* gold-tier PUTs. Immune-, developmental- and olfaction-related transcripts contained in the silver and bronze data tiers were identified using GO and InterPro descriptors generated with Blast2GO [38]. Significant hits were confirmed by multiple sequence alignment to homologous arthropod transcripts.

Sample-specific Gene Expression Quantification

Following quantitative protocols established in a previous insect transcriptome investigation [39], RNA-Seq data were used to suggest potentially up- or down-regulated genes among the gold-tier gene set. Three comparisons were performed: 4th instar against 2nd instar, adult female against adult male, and nymph against adult. No pooling of sequencing lanes was necessary for the first two of these comparisons, though for the last, the 4th and 2nd instar nymph data were pooled to create the nymphal representation, and the adult female and male samples were pooled to create the adult test set. To generate sample-specific gene expression levels, unassembled, cleaned reads were aligned to trimmed gold-tier PUT sequences using Blat [40]. An aligned read incremented a PUT's digital expression level if not less than 95% of its length aligned with 100% sequence identity. If a read mapped to multiple PUTs under these criteria, only its highest-scoring alignment was considered. (If multiple alignments shared this highest score, at most one representative PUT was chosen on an arbitrary basis.) In cases where multiple gold-tier PUTs corresponded to the same NR protein—resulting from such phenomena as gene duplication or alternative splicing—then the counts of all such PUTs were summed and attributed to the responsible protein coding gene. Normalization of the resulting digital expression counts was performed by dividing each protein coding gene's absolute digital count by the total number of unassembled, cleaned reads in the sample. Fold differences in relative gene expression levels were ranked to suggest differentially expressed *H. halys* genes. These candidate transcripts were then flagged for further inspection using qRT-PCR.

Validation of select transcripts using quantitative real-time PCR (qRT-PCR)

A panel of *H. halys* genes having RNA-Seq fold-level changes suggesting significant differential gene expression was statistically validated using qRT-PCR analysis, performed using three biological and three technical replicates. Quantitative real-time expression experiments were conducted using primers designed from PUT templates with PrimerPlex 2.62 (PREMIER Biosoft, Palo Alto, CA); primer sequences are provided in Table S2. In addition to 2nd and 4th instar, adult male and adult female cDNAs, qRT-PCR was performed for an egg mass sample. Reactions were conducted using an ABI 7500 Real Time PCR System (Applied Biosystems, Carlsbad CA). For each replicate, first strand cDNA was synthesized from 1–5 ug RNA using Superscript Reverse Transcriptase II (Life Technologies, Carlsbad, CA). Each qRT-PCR reaction consisted of 6.25 µl of Power SYBR Green PCR Master Mix (Life Technologies, Carlsbad, CA), 50 ng of diluted cDNA and 1 µM of each primer in a total volume of 12.5 µl. Reactions were performed in triplicate to ensure consistent technical replication and run in 96-well plates under the following conditions: 50°C for 2 min, 95°C for 10 min, and 40 cycles of 95°C for 15 sec and 60°C for 1 min. Melting curves (60°C to 95°C) were derived for each reaction to ensure a single product. Relative gene expression was evaluated with DataAssist Software version 3.0 (Applied Biosystems/Life Technologies), using *H. halys* 18S rRNA and the ER-associated endoreticulocalbin housekeeping gene [41] as endogenous controls for RNA load and gene expression, respectively. 18S rRNA is commonly used for control purposes in quantitative eukaryotic transcriptome studies [42], and endoreticulocalbin was bioinformatically identified as a quality expression control gene for *H. halys* normalization—its transcription level was shown to be the most minimally perturbed across all three comparisons and suitable primers could be designed for it

Table 3. Sample-specific and global RNA-Seq data sizes for *H. halys* pre- and post-quality control.

		2nd instar	4th instar	Adult male	Adult female	Total
Raw	Reads	196,439,408	208,313,504	189,721,966	164,646,253	759,121,131
	Bases	19,643,940,800	20,831,350,400	18,972,196,600	16,464,625,300	75,912,113,100
Cleaned	Reads	113,365,193	105,109,728	113,154,644	107,985,660	439,615,225
	Bases	11,304,674,285	10,477,330,878	11,288,454,095	10,774,361,340	43,844,820,598

using the PrimerPlex software. A basic geometric argument demonstrated its expression consistency: Because fold changes in gene expression levels were calculated by placing the greater abundance level in the ratio's numerator, these ratios are strictly ≥ 1 for instances in which counts were detected in both samples being compared (i.e., both numerator and denominator were positive-valued). Thus, in three-dimensional space, an idealized reference point denoting an unperturbed transcript is $(x,y,z) = (1,1,1)$, where x, y and z denote 4th instar *versus* 2nd instar, adult female *versus* adult male, and nymph *versus* adult comparisons, respectively. Reticulocalbin minimized the Euclidean distance from this reference point (data not shown), which was calculated using the equation:

$$\sqrt{(x-1)^2+(y-1)^2+(z-1)^2}$$

in which variables x, y and z correspond to the absolute fold change values for the three comparisons listed above.

Supporting Information

Table S1 *Halyomorpha halys* **gold-tier PUTs BLAST2GO annotations using the NCBI NR database.**

Table S2 **Primers designed in this study for** *Halyomorpha halys* **qRT-PCR transcript validation, including GenBank gene identifying information for each transcript.**

Table S3 **Select microbial-origin transcripts identified in the** *Halyomorpha halys* **transcriptome that exhibit possible differential gene expression according to fold changes in RNA-Seq read abundances.** Data are presented for three comparisons: 2nd instar *versus* 4th instar, male adults *versus* female adults, and adults (males and females combined) *versus* nymphs (2nd and 4th instar combined).

Acknowledgments

The authors thank Robert Bennett and Megan Herlihy for rearing insects used in this study.

Author Contributions

Conceived and designed the experiments: DEGR. Performed the experiments: MES KSS DK. Analyzed the data: MES KSS DK DEGR. Wrote the paper: MES KSS DK DEGR.

References

1. Xu J, Fonseca DM, Hamilton GC, Hoelmer KA, Nielson AL (2014) Tracing the origin of US brown marmorated stink bugs, *Halyomorpha halys*. Biological Invasions 16: 153–166.
2. Leskey TC, Hamilton G, Nielsen A, Polk D, Rodrigues-Saona C, et al. (2012) Pest status of the brown marmorated stink bug, *Halyomorpha halys* (Stål) in the USA. Outlooks on Pest Management 23: 218–226.
3. Zhu G, Bu W, Gao Y, Liu G (2012) Potential geographic distribution of brown marmorated stink bug invasion (*Halymorpha halys*). PLOS One 7: e31246.
4. Khrimian A, Zhang A, Weber DC, Ho H-Y, Aldrich JR, et al. (2014) Discovery of the aggregation pheromone of the brown marmorated stink bug (*Halymorpha halys*) through the creation of stereoisomeric libraries of 1-bisabolen-3-ols. Journal of Natural Products (in press). doi: 10.1021/np5003753
5. Weber DC, Leskey TC, Cabrera Walsh G, Khrimian A (2014) Synergy of aggregation pheromone with methyl (E,E,Z)-2,4,6-decatrienoate in attraction of *Halyomorpha halys* (Hemiptera: Pentatomidae). Journal of Economic Entomology 107: 1061–1068.
6. Gouli V, Gouli S, Skinner M, Hamilton G, Kim JS, et al. (2012) Virulence of select entomopathogenic fungi to the brown marmorated stink bug, *Halymorpha halys* (Stal) (Heteroptera: Pentatomidae). Pest Manag Sci 68: 155–157.
7. Hunter WB, VanEngelsdorp D, Hayes J, Westervelt, et al. (2010) Large-scale field application of RNAi technology reducing Israeli Acute Paralysis Virus disease in Honey Bees (*Apis mellifera*, Hymenoptera: Apidae). PLOS Pathogens 6: e1001160.
8. van Kretschmar JBD, Donahue KV, Cabrera AR, Magalhaes LC, Sorenson CE, et al. (2012) Illumina sequencing of green stink bug nymph and adult cDNA to identify potential RNAi gene targets. Beltwide Cotton Conf: 1090–1096.
9. Zhang H, Li ZX (2013) *In vitro* and *in vivo* characterization of a novel insect decaprenyl diphosphate synthase: a two major step catalytic mechanism is proposed. Biochem Biophys Res Commun. 442: 105–111. doi: 10.1016/j.bbrc.2013.11.025.
10. Engels W, Kaatz H, Zillikens A, Simoes ZLP, Trube A, et al. (1990) Honey bee reproduction: vitellogenin and caste-specific regulation of fertility. Advances in Invertebrate Reproduction 5: 495–502.
11. Hrassnigg N, Crailsheim K (2005) Differences in drone and worker physiology in honeybees (*Apis mellifera*). Apidologie 36: 255–277.
12. Hobert O, Westphal H (2000) Functions of LIM-homeobox genes. Trends Genet. 16(2): 75–83.
13. Taylor CM, Coffey PL, DeLay BD, Dively GP (2014) The Importance of Gut Symbionts in the Development of the Brown Marmorated Stink Bug, *Halyomorpha halys* (Stål). PLoS ONE 9(3): e90312. doi:10.1371/journal.pone.0090312.
14. Bansal R, Michel AP, Sabree ZL (2014) The Crypt-Dwelling Primary Bacterial Symbiont of the Polyphagous Pentatomid Pest *Halyomorpha halys* (Hemiptera: Pentatomidae). Environmental Entomology, 43(3): 617–625.
15. Sparks ME, Gundersen-Rindal DE, Harrison RL (2013) Complete genome sequence of a novel Iflavirus from the transcriptome of *Halyomorpha halys*, the brown marmorated stink bug. Genome Announcements 1: e00910–00913.
16. Blander JM, Sander LE (2012) Beyond pattern recognition: five immune checkpoints for scaling the microbial threat. Nature Revs Immunol 12: 215–225.
17. Jiang H, Vilcinskas A, Kanost MR (2011) Immunity in Lepidopteran insects. Invertebrate Immunity. pp.163–180.
18. Defferari MS, Lee DH, Fernandes CL, Orchard I, Carlini CR (2013) A phospholipase A$_2$ gene is linked to jack bean urease toxicity in the Chagas' disease vector *Rhodnius prolixus*. Biochimica Biophysica Acta 1840: 396–405.
19. Garcia ES, Castro DP, Figueiredo MB, Genta FA, Azambuja P (2009) *Trypanosoma rangeli*: a new perspective for styding the modulation of immune reactions of *Rhodnius prolixus*. Parasites and Vectors 2: 33.
20. Nappi AJ, Christensen BM (2005) Melanogenesis and associated cytotoxic reactions: Applications to insect innate immunity. Insect Biochemistry and Molecular Biology 35: 443–449.
21. Kanost MR, Gorman MJ (2008) Phenoloxidases in insect immunity. In: Beckage N, editor.Insect Immunology. 1 ed.New York: Academic Press. pp.69–96.
22. Schmidt O, Soderhall K, Theopold U, Faye I (2010) Role of adhesion in arthropod immune recognition. Annual Review of Entomology 54: 485–504.
23. Broderick NA, Welchman DP, Lemaitre B (2009) Recognition and response to microbial infection in *Drosophila*. In: Rolff J, Reynolds SE, editors.Insect Infection and Immunity: Evolution, Ecology, and Mechanisms.New York: Oxford University Press. pp.13–33.
24. Renwick J, Reeves EP, Wientjes FB, Kavanagh K (2007) Translocation of proteins homologous to human neutrophil p47phox and p67phox to the cell membrane in activated hemocytes of *Galleria mellonella*. Dev Comp Immunol 31: 347–359.
25. Eleftherianos I, Felfoldi G, ffrench-Constant RH, Reynolds SE (2009) Induced nitric oxide synthesis in the gut of *Manduca sexta* protects against oral infection by the bacterial pathogen *Photorhabdus luminescens*. Insect Molecular Biology 18: 507–516.
26. Singh NK, Pakkianathan BC, Kumar M, Prasad T, Kannan M, et al. (2013) Vitellogenin from the Silkworm, *Bombyx mori*: An Effective Anti-Bacterial Agent. PLoS ONE 8: e73005. doi:10.1371/journal.pone.0073005.
27. Xiong Y, Zeng H, Zhang Y, Xu D, Qiu D (2013) Silencing the HaHR3 Gene by Transgenic Plant-mediated RNAi to Disrupt *Helicoverpa armigera* Development. Int J Biol Sci 9: 370–381. doi:10.7150/ijbs.5929.
28. Paluzzi J-PV, Young P, Defferrari MS, Orchard I, Carlini CR, et al. (2012) Investigation of the potential involvement of eicosanoid metabolites in anti-diuretic hormone signaling in *Rhodnius prolixus*. Peptides 34: 127–134.
29. Winston WM, Molodowitch C, Hunter CP (2002) Systemic RNAi in *C. elegans* requires the putative transmembrane protein SID-1. Science 295(5564): 2456–2459. doi:10.1126/science.1068836.
30. Zha W, Peng X, Chen R, Du B, Zhu L, et al. (2011) Knockdown of Midgut Genes by dsRNA Transgenic Plant-Mediated RNA Interference in the Hemipteran Insect *Nilaparvata lugens*. PLoS ONE 6(5): e20504. doi:10.1371/journal.pone.0020504.
31. Wynant N, Duressa TF, Santos D, Van Duppen J, Proost P, et al. (2014) Lipophorins can adhere to dsRNA, bacteria and fungi present in the hemolymph of the desert locust: A role as general scavenger for pathogens in

the open body cavity. Journal of Insect Physiology 64: 7–13. doi: 10.1016/j.jinsphys.2014.02.010.

32. Wynant N, Santos D, Van Wielendaele P, Vanden Broeck J (2014) Scavenger receptor-mediated endocytosis facilitates RNA interference in the desert locust, *Schistocerca gregaria*. Insect Molecular Biology 23: 320–329. doi: 10.1111/imb.12083.

33. Firmino AAP, Fonseca FCA, Pepino de Macedo L, Coelho RR, de Souza Jr JDA, et al. (2013) Transcriptome Analysis in Cotton Boll Weevil (*Anthonomus grandis*) and RNA Interference in Insect Pests. PLoS One 8(12): e85079. doi: 10.1371/journal/pone.0085079.

34. Grabherr MG, Haas BJ, Yassour M, Levin JZ, Thompson DA, et al. (2011) Full-length transcriptome assembly from RNA-Seq data without a reference genome. Nature Biotechnology 8: 469–477.

35. Altschul SF, Madden TL, Schaffer AA, Zhang J, Zhang Z, et al. (1997) Gapped BLAST and PSI-BLAST: a new generation of protein database search programs. Nucleic Acids Res 25: 3389–3402.

36. Rice P, Longden I, Bleasby A (2000) EMBOSS: the European Molecular Biology Open Software Suite. Trends Genet 16: 276–277.

37. The Uniprot Consortium (2012) Update on activities at the Universal Protein Resource (UniProt) in 2013. Nucleic Acids Res 41: D43–D47.

38. Gotz S, Garcia-Gomez JM, Terol J, Williams TD, Naagaraj SH, et al. (2008) High-throughput functional annotation and data mining with the Blast2GO suite. Nucleic Acids Res 36: 3420–3435.

39. Sparks ME, Blackburn MB, Kuhar D, Gundersen-Rindal DE (2013) Transcriptome of the *Lymantria dispar* (Gypsy Moth) Larval Midgut in Response to Infection by *Bacillus thuringiensis*. PLOS One 8(5): e61190. doi: 10.1371/journal/pone.0061190.

40. Kent WJ (2002) BLAT—the BLAST-like alignment tool. Genome Res 12: 656–664.

41. Ozawa M, Muramatsu T (1993) Reticulocalbin, a novel endoplasmic resident Ca(2+)-binding protein with multiple EF-hand motifs and carboxyl-terminal HDEL sequence. Journal of Biological Chemistry 268: 699–705.

42. Matoušková P, Bártíková H, Boušová I, Hanušová V, Szotáková B, et al. (2014) Reference Genes for Real-Time PCR Quantification of Messenger RNAs and MicroRNAs in Mouse Model of Obesity. PLOS One 9(1): e86033. doi: 10.1371/journal.pone.0086033.

9

Exploring the Genetic Basis of Adaptation to High Elevations in Reptiles: A Comparative Transcriptome Analysis of Two Toad-Headed Agamas (Genus *Phrynocephalus*)

Weizhao Yang[1,2], Yin Qi[1], Jinzhong Fu[1,3]*

1 Chengdu Institute of Biology, Chinese Academy of Sciences, Chengdu, China, **2** University of Chinese Academy of Sciences, Beijing, China, **3** Department of Integrative Biology, University of Guelph, Guelph, Ontario, Canada

Abstract

High elevation adaptation offers an excellent study system to understand the genetic basis of adaptive evolution. We acquired transcriptome sequences of two closely related lizards, *Phrynocephalus przewalskii* from low elevations and *P. vlangalii* from high elevations. Within a phylogenetic framework, we compared their genomic data along with green anole, chicken and Chinese softshell turtle, and identified candidate genes and functional categories that are potentially linked to adaptation to high elevation environments. More than 100 million sequence reads were generated for each species via Illumina sequencing. A *de novo* assembly produced 70,919 and 62,118 transcripts for *P. przewalskii* and *P. vlangalii*, respectively. Based on a well-established reptile phylogeny, we detected 143 positively selected genes (PSGs) along the *P. vlangalii* lineage from the 7,012 putative orthologs using a branch-site model. Furthermore, ten GO categories and one KEGG pathway that are over-represented by PSGs were recognized. In addition, 58 GO categories were revealed to have elevated evolutionary rates along the *P. vlangalii* lineage relative to *P. przewalskii*. These functional analyses further filter out PSGs that are most likely involved in the adaptation process to high elevations. Among them, ADAM17, MD, and HSP90B1 likely contributed to response to hypoxia, and POLK likely contributed to DNA repair. Many other candidate genes involved in gene expression and metabolism were also identified. Genome-wide scan for candidate genes may serve as the first step to explore the genetic basis of high elevation adaptation. Detailed comparative study and functional verification are needed to solidify any conclusions. High elevation adaptation requires coordinated changes in multiple genes that involve various physiological and biochemical pathways; we hope that our genetic studies will provide useful directions for future physiological or molecular studies in reptiles as well as other poikilothermic species.

Editor: Ulrich Joger, State Natural History Museum, Germany

Funding: This work is supported by the Key Laboratory of Mountain Ecological Restoration and Bioresource Utilization (CAS), the Ecological Restoration & Biodiversity Conservation Key Laboratory of Sichuan Province, the 100 Talents Programme of Sichuan Province (Y1D3011), the Chinese Academy of Sciences Knowledge Innovation Program (grant Y1C2021203), and the NSERC Discovery Program (Canada). The funders had no role in study design, data collection and analysis, decision to publish, or preparation of the manuscript.

Competing Interests: The authors have declared that no competing interests exist.

* Email: jfu@uoguelph.ca

Introduction

Understanding the genetic basis of adaptive changes is one of the central goals in evolutionary biology [1], and organisms living in extreme environments often provide the best study systems [2]. High elevation environments impose considerable physiological challenges to their residents, particularly these associated with low temperature, low oxygen density, and strong ultraviolet (UV) radiation [3,4]. In order to survive these extreme stressors, high elevation adaptation may require coordinated structural and transcriptional changes in multiple genes that interact at different levels and involve various physiological and biochemical pathways [3]. Therefore, elucidating how animals cope with high elevation environments provides unique insights in the process of adaptive evolution, especially its intertwined genetic and regulatory basis. A

A number of studies have revealed aspects of the genetic mechanisms for high elevation adaptation, particularly for endo-

thermic species [4]. Genes associated with response to hypoxia appeae to play a key role in the adaptation process. For example, several studies of Tibetan human populations reported that genes EGLN1, PPARA, and EPAS1, all part of the hypoxia-inducible factor (HIF) pathway, were involved in high elevation adaptation [5,6,7]. For other high elevation mammals, Qiu *et al.* [8] screened the genome of yak (*Bos grunniens*), and detected signatures of positive selecton for three HIF pathway related genes, ADAM17, ARG2, and MMP3. Ge *et al.* [9] also identified a set of candidate gene in the Tibetan antelope (*Pantholops hodgsonii*) that were under positive selection and likely associated with the HIF pathway, including CCL2 and PKLR. Studies of poikilothermic species are few. Yang *et al.* [10] compared the transcriptomes of the plateau frog (*Ranakukunoris*) and its low elevation relative *R. chensinensis*, and found that genes related to oxygen binding may have been involved in high elevation adaptation, but there was no evidence of involvement among the HIF pathway genes.

Poikilotherms represent the majority of animal biodiversity, and they differ from endotherms both physiologically and behaviourally [11]. To generate widely applicable hypotheses, more studies on poikilotherms are needed.

Reptiles are excellent model systems for studying high elevation adaptation of poikilothermic organisms. Similar to mammals, reptiles are terrestrial amniotes and spend most of their time on land. Frequently observed basking behaviour in reptiles also increases their UV exposure [11]. Several toad-headed agamas (genus *Phrynocephalus*) are true high elevation dwellers of the Tibetan Plateau, and live at elevations as high as 5,300 m above sea level (a.s.l.) [12]. Recent phylogenetic studies found that all high elevation species formed a monophyletic group, which nested within the low elevation species [13]. This relationship suggests that the high elevation species may have evolved from low elevation ancestors. Therefore, a comparison between the high elevation species and low elevation species may provide information regarding the high elevation adaptation process. *Phrynocephalus vlangalii* is a high elevation species and primarily distributed in the Tibetan Plateau with altitudes of 2,000–4,600 m a.s.l. It possesses a series of physiological traits that likely represent adaptation to high elevation environments, including remarkably high hemoglobin concentration, hematocrit, mean corpuscular hemoglobin concentration, heart weight to body mass ratio, myocardium capillary density, and succinate dehydrogenase activity [14]. On the other hand, *P. przewalskii* is widely distributed in northern China and Mongolia and mainly occurs at low altitudes of 500–1,500 m a.s.l. [12]. A comparison between them may reveal the genetic basis of high elevation adaptation in reptiles.

The objective of this study is to identify candidate genes and gene functions that may have facilitated adaptation to high elevation environments in *Phrynocephalus* lizards. We sequenced transcriptomes of *P. przewalskii* and *P. vlangalii*, and acquired genomic data of three other reptile species from online databases. Using a branch-site model within a phylogenetic framework, genes that might have experienced positive selection along the *P. vlangalii* lineage were identified. Furthermore, gene functional categories that revealed an accelerated evolutionary rate or were over-represented by positively selected genes were also identified.

Materials and Methods

Ethics statement

All animal specimens were collected legally. Animal collection and utility protocols were approved by the Chengdu Institute of Biology Animal Use Ethics Committee.

Sample collection

Six different tissue types (brain, liver, heart, muscle, and testicle/ootheca) from six individuals (three males and three females) of each species were sampled in order to obtain as many expressed genes as possible. Samples of *P. przewalskii* were collected from the vicinity of Yinchuan City, China (106.87°E, 38.32°N) with an altitude of 1,153 m a.s.l. Samples of *P. vlangalii* were collected from the Zoige County, Sichuan Province, China (102.48°E, 33.72°N) with an altitude of 3,464 m a.s.l. Lizards were captured by hand and euthanized on-site by intracoelomic injection of overdose pentobarbital solution, typically within one hour of capture. Tissue samples were removed and stored in Sample Protector (*Takara*) immediately following euthanasia and dissection.

Illumina sequencing and *de novo* assembly

RNA was extracted separately from each tissue according to the TRIzol protocol (*Invitrogen*) and then mixed using approximately the same quantity. A single cDNA library was constructed for each species. mRNAs were purified from total RNA by poly (T) oligo-attached magnetic beads (*Life Technologies*). Random oligonucleotides and M-MuLV Reverse Transcriptase (RNase H-) were used to synthesize the first cDNA strand, and the second cDNA strand was synthesized using DNA Polymerase I and RNase H. The cDNA library with an insert size of ~200 base pairs (bps) was targeted and purified with AMPure XP beads system (*Beckman Coulter*), and subsequently sequenced on an Illumina HiSeq 2000 platform. Paired-end reads were generated with a read length of 100 bps. Both cDNA library construction and Illumina sequencing were carried out by *Novogene* (Beijing, China).

The raw sequence reads were first cleaned by filtering the exact duplicates from both sequencing directions. Subsequently, the sequence reads were trimmed using Trimmomatic [15] by removing adapter sequences, sequences with unknown base call (N) more than 5%, and low quality sequences (<Q20). Reads likely derived from human and *Escherichia coli* contaminants were also filtered using Bowtie [16,17].

De novo assembly of clean reads was performed using a combination of multiple K-mer lengths and coverage cut-off values [18,19]. We selected five K-mer lengths (21, 31, 41, 51, and 61) and six coverage cut-off values (2, 3, 6, 10, 15, and 20), and generated 30 raw assemblies for each species using ABYSS [20,21]. A final assembly was produced by eliminating redundancies and integrating sequence overlaps for each transcriptome using CD-HIT-EST [22] and CAP3 [23]. All clean reads were mapped back to the final assembly using Bowtie, and single nucleotide variable (SNP) sites were identified using SAMtools pipeline [24]. For all SNP sites, the base call with the most mapped reads was chosen as the consensus using an in-house Python script.

Orthology determination and dataset construction

We selected another three closely related vertebrate species to construct our orthologous gene dataset for comparison, including the green anole (*Anolis carolinensis*), the Chinese softshell turtle (*Pelodiscus sinensis*), and chicken (*Gallus gallus*). These three species have well-annotated genomic data, which formed the foundation for orthology determination and gene function analysis.

We used an analytical pipeline that identifies only single-copy orthologous genes in a relatively conservative fashion. The coding sequences of a 1:1:1 orthologous gene dataset shared by *A. carolinensis*, *G. gallus*, and *P. sinensis* was first downloaded from bioMart (Ensembl Genes 74). A best reciprocal hit (BRH) method [25] was then applied to identify 1:1 orthologs from the final transcriptome assemblies of *P. przewalskii* and *P. vlangalii*. We performed the first tBlastx search using the orthologous coding DNA sequences (CDS) of *A. carolinensis* against each assembly (e-value threshold of 1e-10), and a second tBlastx search with each assembly against the full CDSs of *A. carolinensis*. Only sequences with a significant BRH on the same CDS were considered orthologs [26].

The identified orthologous sequences of *P. przewalskii* and *P. vlangalii* were added to the above 1:1:1 orthologous gene dataset and aligned using the "codon alignment" option in Prank [27,28]. The alignments were further trimmed using Gblocks [29] to remove unreliable regions with "codons" option ("-t = c") and the default parameters. Sequences with unexpected stop codons and alignment length less than 200 bps were discarded to reduce the chance of false-positive prediction. A saturation test was also performed for all orthologs to remove sequences with saturation at synonymous sites [30]. All third codon position sequences of each orthologous gene were extracted and used to estimate branch lengths of the species tree with the general time reversible model and the program BASEML (in PAML package [31]). If any branch length ≥ 1, the gene was considered saturated, and was discarded from further analysis.

Candidate gene and gene function identification

A composite phylogeny of the five vertebrate species was constructed based on well-established phylogenetic hypotheses (Figure 1) [13,32]. Based on this phylogeny, we assumed that evolution along the *P. vlangalii* lineage likely represented an adaptation process to a high elevation environment. Genes that have experienced positive selection (or positively selected genes; PSGs) along this lineage were likely involved in high elevation adaptation, and therefore were considered candidate genes. In addition, gene functional categories that have elevated evolutionary rates along this lineage likely have experienced either positive selection or relaxed purifying selection [8,33]. Gene Ontology (GO) [34] and the Kyoto Encyclopedia of Genes and Genomes (KEGG) [35] pathways were used to define gene functions.

Positively selected genes. We used a branch-site model implemented in the program CODEML (in PAML package [31]) to identify PSGs. The *P. vlangalii* lineage was set as the foreground branch, and the optimized branch-site model was used. A likelihood ratio test was conducted to compare the model with positive selection on the foreground branch to a null model with no positive selection on the foreground branch for each orthologous gene [36,37]. PSGs were inferred only if their P values were less than 0.05.

We also identified GO categories and KEGG pathways that were over-represented by PSGs. Functional annotation of PSGs was performed using the DAVID pipeline [38]. Both the enrichment P-value and enrichment score (ES) for each category, which is equivalent to the geometric mean of all the enrichment P-values of each annotation term that genes in the category are involved in, were calculated. All P-values were estimated with a modified Fisher's exact test. Categories with ES greater than 1.3 and P-value less than 0.05 were considered over-represented by PSGs [38,39]. Corrections for multiple tests were also applied in the DAVID pipeline. Similarly, the KEGG pathways that were over-represented by PSGs were also identified using the DAVID pipeline.

Elevated evolutionary rate. We used the Ka/Ks ratio to measure the evolutionary rate along a lineage. The values of Ka, Ks, and Ka/Ks ratio were estimated using the *free-ratio* model in

CODEML for the *P. przewalskii* branch and *P. vlangalii* branch [35]. The lineage-specific mean values were estimated by concatenated alignments from all orthologs. A comparison of evolutionary rates based on non-synonymous substitution between *P. przewalskii* and *P. vlangalii* was conducted using a binomial test (see [33] for detailed method). Functional categories that had experienced a relatively accelerated evolution were identified. Only GO categories with more than 20 orthologs were included in the analyses, and a Holm test [40] was applied to correct for multiple comparisons.

Sanger sequencing confirmation

To confirm the accuracy of the Illumina sequencing and assemblies, we randomly selected 20 fragments and re-sequenced them using Sanger sequencing. The lengths of target sequences were limited to below 500 bps to reduce the possibility of sequences spanning across exon boundaries. Primers for PCR amplification and sequencing were designed using Primer3 [41]. Standard PCR with optimized annealing temperature was conducted and the PCR products were directly sequenced. Sequencing was carried out with BigDye chemistry on an ABI 3730 DNA Analyzer. The primer information and PCR conditions are provided in Table S1.

Results

Illumina sequencing and *de novo* assembly

A total of 111,576,922 sequence reads of *P. przewalskii* and 108,689,778 sequence reads of *P. vlangalii* were generated. Defective reads, 3,319,392 and 3,750,648 respectively, were first removed, and the *de novo* assembly of clean reads produced final assemblies with 115.9 mega base pairs (Mb) and 111.6 Mb, respectively. For *P. przewalskii*, 70,989 transcripts were obtained with an N50 length of 2,284 bps and a mean length of 1,632 bps. For *P. vlangalii*, 62,118 transcripts were obtained with an N50 length of 2,728 bps and a mean length of 1,796 bps. Detailed information of the sequence data is summarized in Table 1, and the length distribution of assembled transcripts is shown in Figure 2. All original data are deposited in the NCBI Sequence Read Archive repository (Accession Number: SRR1298770 for *P. przewalskii* and SRR1298771 for *P. vlangalii*).

Our Sanger sequencing confirmed the accuracy of the Illumina sequences and our final assemblies. For *P. przewalskii*, nine fragments were successfully sequenced with a total length of 2,799 bps, and we found 12 nucleotide sites that were different. Similarly, 15 fragments were successfully sequenced for *P. vlangalii* with a total length of 4,485 bps, and we found three sites that were different (Table S1). Overall, the consistency was high, 99.57% for *P. przewalskii* and 99.93% for *P. vlangalii*. Some of the discrepancies were likely derived from individual variations rather than errors. Five of the sites with different calls were putative SNP sites; when individuals were pooled for Illumina sequencing, only the genome with a dominant amount of RNA would be selected in the final assemblies. Ten of the 12 sites with different calls in *P. przewalskii* were from a single fragment, suggesting our PCR likely amplified more than one target, possibly paralogous genes. Other sources of differences might include RNA editing, sequencing errors, or assembly errors. The high consistency between Sanger sequencing and our assembly confirmed the effectiveness of our methods and the accuracy of the final assemblies.

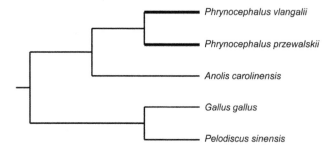

Figure 1. A composite phylogeny of the five vertebrate species examined. The bold lines represent the two *Phrynocephalus* species. The unrooted tree used in CODEML is (((*P. vlangalii, P. przewalskii*), *A. carolinensis*), *G. gallus, P. sinensis*).

Table 1. Summary of transcriptome data for *Phrynocephalus przewalskii* and *P. vlangalii*.

	P. przewalskii	P. vlangalii
Total number of raw reads	111,576,922	108,689,778
Total number of clean reads	108,257,530	104,939,130
Total sequences of assembly	70,989	62,118
Total length of assembly (Mb)	115.9	111.6
N50 length of assembly (bp)	2,284	2,728
Mean length of assembly (bp)	1,632	1,796
Median length of assembly (bp)	1,124	1,136

bp = base pair; Mb = mega base pair.

Putative orthologous genes

A total of 7,275 putative orthologs were first identified for both species. After removing the low quality and short sequences, 7,012 orthologs were preceded to downstream analyses. Therefore, our final dataset included five species, *P. przewalskii*, *P. vlangalii*, *A. carolinensis*, *G. gallus*, and *P. sinensis*, and 7,012 genes.

Functional categories with elevated evolutionary rates

The mean values of Ka, Ks, and Ka/Ks ratio along the *P. vlangalii* lineage were 0.0039, 0.0295, and 0.1306, respectively, and the values along the *P. przewalskii* lineage were 0.0033, 0.0272, and 0.1223, respectively. The *P. vlangalii* lineage

demonstrated slightly higher evolutionary rates than *P. przewalskii* (Figure 3).

A total of 58 GO categories revealed relatively accelerated evolutionary rates ($P<0.05$) in the *P. vlangalii* lineage, compared to *P. przewalskii* (Figure 4 and Table S2). Among them, the majority were involved in ion transport, gene expression, and organ development, such as ion transport (GO: 0006811), ion channel activity (GO: 0005216), negative regulation of gene expression (GO: 0010629), DNA-dependent transcription (GO: 0006351), heart development (GO: 0007507), and kidney development (GO: 0001822). Notably, the category of response to hypoxia (GO: 0001666) revealed an accelerated evolutionary rate in the *P. vlangalii* lineage. Similarly, 24 GO categories revealed relatively accelerated evolutionary rates in the *P. przewalskii*

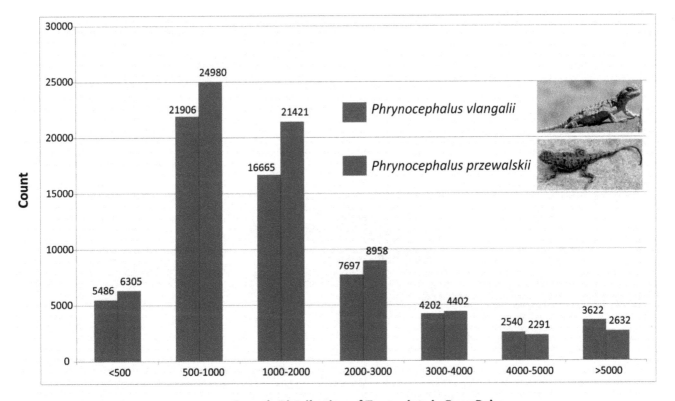

Length Distribution of Transcripts in Base Pairs

Figure 2. Length distribution of assembled transcripts in base pairs. The numbers of transcripts are shown on top of each bar.

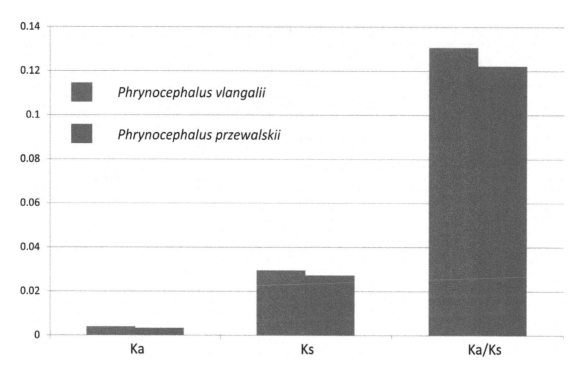

Figure 3. Comparison of evolutionary rates between the *P. vlangalii* and *P. przewalskii* lineages. The mean Ka, Ks, and Ka/Ks ratio of both lineages are presented.

lineage, compared to *P. vlangalii* (Figure 4 and Table S2). Categories involving molecular binding were dominant, such as identical protein binding (GO: 0042802), heme binding (GO: 0020037), and ATP binding (GO: 0005524).

Positively selected genes

The branch-site model and likelihood ratio test identified 143 PSGs ($P<0.05$) along the *P. vlangalii* lineage (Table S3). Interestingly, three genes from the 'response to hypoxia' GO category, MB, ADAM17, and HSP90B1, were among them. MB

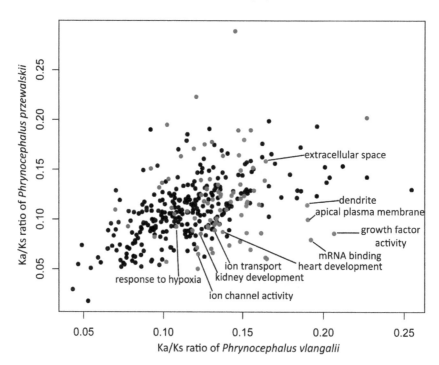

Figure 4. Comparison of Ka/Ks ratios between *P. vlangalii* and *P. przewalskii* by GO functional categories. Blue dots represent categories with an elevated evolutionary rate along the *P. przewalskii* lineage. Red dots represent categories with an elevated evolutionary rate along the *P. vlangalii* lineage. A full list of the categories is presented in Table S2.

encodes myoglobin, which is an oxygen-binding hemoprotein, and plays a key role in dealing with chronic hypoxia (e.g. [42,43]). ADAM17 encodes a crucial regulator of hypoxia-inducible factor-1α (HIF-1α), which is associated with the cellular response to hypoxia [44,45]. HSP90B1 is one of the heat shock protein members and plays important roles in folding proteins in the secretory pathways [46]. In addition, POLK from the GO category of DNA repair also experienced positive selection. POLK is a well-studied gene, and plays an important role in response to DNA damage [47]. Furthermore, three other PSGs, INPPL1, PPP2CB, and HDAC2, are associated with transcription and gene expression [48,49,50].

Based on gene annotation, 10 GO categories were over-represented by 42 PSGs with ESs greater than 1.3 and P values less than 0.05, including RNA metabolic process (GO: 0016070, ES = 2.8), gene expression (GO: 0010467, ES = 2.0), ion binding (GO: 0043167, ES = 1.6), and several others (Table 2). These categories were generally in three functional groups: metabolism, ion binding, and gene expression. Similarly, one KEGG pathway (endocytosis, ko04144) was over-represented by PSGs with an ES of 3.3.

Discussion

Transcriptomes of *Phrynocephalus*

We reported transcriptome data for two lizard species. A total of 70,989 transcripts were generated for *P. przewalskii*, and 62,118 transcripts were generated for *P. vlangalii*. Squamates represent one of the most diverse vertebrate groups; however, genomic data of squamates are limited. At present time, only one species (the green anole, *A. carolinensis*) has a completed whole genome sequence [51]. Although the draft genomes of the Burmese python (*Python molurus bivittatus*) and king cobra (*Ophiophagus hannah*) have been recently published, the annotation and orthologous identification is far from being complete [52,53]. Transcriptome data represent a feasible and inexpensive alternative to whole genome sequencing for many genome level studies. In our case, the two transcriptomes allow us to examine 7,012 orthologous coding genes and their potential involvement in the adaptation process to high elevation environments.

We pooled RNA samples from multiple tissue sources in order to obtain sequences of a large number of expressed genes. With this method, we were able to recover more than 60,000 transcripts with N50 lengths greater than 2,000 bps for each species. Nevertheless, there are certain drawbacks associated with this

approach. For example, we were unable to recover any gene expression data, which limited this study to sequence level only. In addition, pooling tissues together may reduce the number of detected transcripts and cause problems in the assembly process, such as in the case of alternative splicing producing different transcripts in different tissues.

Candidate genes and their functions

The two *Phrynocephalus* species demonstrated relatively low evolutionary rates. Their Ka/Ks ratios are 0.1306 and 0.1223, much lower than those of human (0.208), chimpanzee (0.194), and dolphin (0.237), but similar to mouse (0.142) and rat (0.137) [30,33]. The low rates suggest that most genes in both lineages were under purified selection. Their large population size may also contribute to their low Ka/Ks ratio [33]. Between the two species, *P. vlangalii* has a slightly higher evolutionary rate than *P. przewalskii*. There are many more GO categories with accelerated evolutionary rates in the *P. vlangalii* lineage (58) than in the *P. przewalskii* lineage (24). This is consistent with our assumption that *P. vlangalii* may have evolved from a low elevation ancestor, and the evolutionary change along the lineage may represent adaptation process to high elevations.

We identified 143 genes that may have experienced positive selection along the evolution of the high elevation *P. vlangalii* lineage. Among them, 42 are in the ten GO categories that are over-represented by PSGs, and 61 are associated with 40 GO categories with accelerated evolutionary rates (Table S3). The over-represented categories are mostly in three functional groups: metabolism, ion binding, and gene expression. The categories with elevated evolutionary rates primarily involve ion transport, gene expression, and organ development. Some gene functions are clearly associated with high elevation adaptation while others are less obvious.

The GO category of response to hypoxia (GO: 0001666) is particularly interesting. Hypobaric hypoxia is one of the main environmental stressors at high elevations, and is generally difficult to mitigate by behavioural avoidance [54]. We found that genes in this category have an elevated average evolutionary rate, suggesting their potential involvement in high elevation adaptation in *Phrynocephalus* lizards. Similar findings were also reported in endothermic species living in high altitude environments, including yak [8] and ground tit [55]. Moreover, three genes in the category, ADAM17, MB, and HSP90B1, have experienced positive selection. ADAM17 encodes a regulator at upstream of the HIF-1α pathway, which affects the stability of HIF-1α by

Table 2. List of GO functional categories that are over-represented by positively selected genes.

ID	GO categories	Count	*P*-value	Enrichment score (ES)
GO: 0016070	RNA metabolic process	7	3.20E-02	2.8
GO: 0010467	gene expression	12	2.20E-02	2.0
GO: 0044267	cellular protein metabolic process	17	2.10E-02	1.7
GO: 0044260	cellular macromolecule metabolic process	26	2.70E-03	1.6
GO: 0046872	metal ion binding	22	1.70E-02	1.6
GO: 0043169	cation binding	22	2.10E-02	1.6
GO: 0043167	ion binding	22	2.20E-02	1.6
GO: 0043170	macromolecule metabolic process	26	1.60E-02	1.5
GO: 0044238	primary metabolic process	30	2.00E-02	1.4
GO: 0044237	cellular metabolic process	28	2.80E-02	1.4

regulating the production of tumor necrosis factor α [44,45]. HIF-1α is a key regulator of cellular reaction to hypoxia, and it regulates transcription of a wide range of genes associated with energy metabolism, vasodilatation, and angiogenesis [56]. Notably, ADAM17 was also found under positive selection in yak [8], a high-altitude mammal. These results reinforce the inference that this gene plays a role in the adaptation to high elevation environments. MB encodes a hemoglobin-related protein, myoglobin, which is an oxygen-binding hemoprotein and has several key functions in hypoxic conditions, including oxygen transport, oxygen storage, oxygen utilization, and oxygen reduction [42]. Hypoxia-inducible myoglobin is expressed not only in muscle tissues but also in non-muscle tissues, particularly in blood [43]. The MB gene is very likely involved in high altitude adaptation of *P. vlangalii*. Our understanding of hypoxia adaptation of these lizards at phenotypic level is limited, though a recent physiological study of *P. vlangalii* suggested that it has special anatomical, physiological, and biochemical adaptive features to live in a hypoxic environment [14]. No direct link has been established between these features and any of our PSGs.

Strong UV radiation is another major physiological stressor on animals at high altitudes, which may damage DNA molecules by generating highly reactive chemical intermediates such as oxygen radicals [57,58]. It is particularly acute for reptiles because they often use basking for thermoregulation [11]. One candidate gene, POLK, is in the functional category of DNA repair. It encodes a low-fidelity DNA polymerase, which enables DNA to be synthesized across damaged bases [47]. POLK also involves several other functional categories that are over-represented by PSGs (Table S3). The potential involvement of POLK in high elevation adaptation provides clues of how *P. vlangalii* may resist increased DNA damage.

The adaptation to high altitudes may occur at the transcription and expression level in addition to nucleotide substitutions at the DNA sequence level. Several GO categories involving gene expression in *P. vlangalii* lineage have accelerated evolutionary rates (Table S2). The GO category of gene expression (GO: 0010467) is over-represented by PSGs (Table 2). In addition, three key regulators of transcription and expression, INPPL1, PPP2CB, and HDAC2, are among the PSGs in the *P. vlangalii* lineage. INPPL1 encodes protein that regulates insulin, epidermal growth, and actin [48]. PPP2CB is implicated in a series of biological processes of controlling cell growth and division [49]. HDAC2 encodes an enzyme that is responsible for the deacetylation on the N-terminal of lysine residues of the core histones [50]. These results demonstrate the complexity of the adaptive process to high elevation environments. We did not directly examine gene expression levels due to the limits of our sampling strategy.

Future directions

Genome-wide scan for PSGs may serve as the first step to explore the genetic basis of high elevation adaptation. It has several advantages over the candidate gene approach. Multiple genes at multiple levels (genes, pathways, functional groups) are examined simultaneously. This allows the interactions of genes to be inferred, which is essential for high elevation adaptation [4]. In addition, without pre-defined targets, it is likely to yield previously unknown pathways or functions. Nevertheless, PSGs do not necessarily represent high elevation adaption. There are many reasons that a gene may experience positive selection. For example, genes associated with the host-pathogen interaction or immune system are frequently under positive selection [59], and they may not specifically contribute to high elevation adaptation. Furthermore, without corroboration from phenotypic data and functional verification, these PSGs are no more than "candidate" genes in any adaptive processes.

For future studies, other reptile groups that live at high-altitude environments should be examined and potential convergent evolution can be investigated. As well, population level comparisons of candidate genes would detect positive selection at a more recent temporal scale. Finally, research at gene expression level and, perhaps more importantly, at physiological (phenotypic) level are essential to understand the adaptation process to high elevation environments.

Conclusions

Using transcriptome data and a branch-site model, we evaluated positive selection and evolutionary rates of 7,012 genes along the high elevation *P. vlangalii* lineage. A total of 143 candidate genes were identified and several gene functional categories that are likely associated with high elevation adaption were also detected. These functional analyses further sift out candidate genes that are of particular interests. Among them, ADAM17, MD, and HSP90B1 likely contribute to response to hypoxia, and POLK likely contributes to DNA repair. These genes and their function should be the priority for future studies of high elevation adaptation in poikilothermic animals.

High elevation adaptation is a very exciting area of research. Direct examinations of phenotypic traits and a better understanding of their molecular and cellular processes are essential. We hope that our genetic studies will provide useful directions for future physiological or molecular studies in reptiles as well as other poikilothermic species.

Acknowledgments

We would like to thank B. Lu, L. Qiao, and J. Hu for assisting with lab work. Drs. J. P. Bogart and K. Bi and Ms M. Fu kindly provided valuable comments on an early version of this manuscript.

Author Contributions

Conceived and designed the experiments: JF WY. Performed the experiments: WY YQ. Analyzed the data: WY. Contributed reagents/materials/analysis tools: JF. Wrote the paper: WY JF.

References

1. Rose MR (2001) Adaptation. In Encyclopedia of Biodiversity, Edited by Levin RA. San Diego: Academic Press: 17–23.

2. Rothschild LJ, Mancinelli RL (2001) Life in extreme environments. Nature 409: 1092–1101.

3. Scheinfeldt LB, Tishkoff SA (2010) Living the high life: high-altitude adaptation. Genome Biology 11: 133.

4. Cheviron ZA, Brumfield RT (2011) Genomic insights into adaptation to high-altitude environments. Heredity 108: 354–361.

5. Beall CM, Cavalleri GL, Deng L, Elston RC, Gao Y, et al. (2010) Natural selection on EPAS1 (HIF2) associated with low hemoglobin concentration in Tibetan highlanders. Proceedings of the National Academy of Sciences USA 107: 11459–11464.

6. Simonson TS, Yang Y, Huff CD, Yun H, Qin G, et al. (2010) Genetic evidence for high-altitude adaptation in Tibet. Science 329: 72–75.

7. Yi X, Liang Y, Huerta-Sanchez E, Jin X, Cuo ZXP, et al. (2010) Sequencing of 50 human exomes reveals adaptation to high altitude. Science 329: 75–78.

8. Qiu Q, Zhang G, Ma T, Qian W, Wang J, et al. (2012) The yak genome and adaptation to life at high altitude. Nature Genetics 44: 946–949.

9. Ge R-L, Cai Q, Shen Y-Y, San A, Ma L, et al. (2013) Draft genome sequence of the Tibetan antelope. Nature Communications 4: 1858.

10. Yang W, Qi Y, Bi K, Fu J (2012) Toward understanding the genetic basis of adaptation to high-elevation life in poikilothermic species: a comparative transcriptomic analysis of two ranid frogs, *Rana chensinensis* and *R. kukunoris*. BMC genomics 13: 588.

11. Huey RB (1982) Temperature, physiology, and the ecology of reptiles. Biology of the Reptilia 12: 25–91.

12. Zhao E-M, Zhao K-T, Zhou K-Y (1999) Fauna Sinica, Reptilia Vol. 2: Squamata, Lacertilia. Beijing: Science Press.

13. Guo X, Wang Y (2007) Partitioned Bayesian analyses, dispersal–vicariance analysis, and the biogeography of Chinese toad-headed lizards (Agamidae: *Phrynocephalus*): a re-evaluation. Molecular Phylogenetics and Evolution 45: 643–662.

14. He J, Xiu M, Tang X, Yue F, Wang N, et al. (2013) The different mechanisms of hypoxic acclimatization and adaptation in lizard *Phrynocephalus vlangalii* living on Qinghai-Tibet Plateau. Journal of Experimental Zoology Part A: Ecological Genetics and Physiology 319: 117–123.

15. Lohse M, Bolger AM, Nagel A, Fernie AR, Lunn JE, et al. (2012) RobiNA: a user-friendly, integrated software solution for RNA-Seq-based transcriptomics. Nucleic Acids Research 40: W622–W627.

16. Langmead B, Trapnell C, Pop M, Salzberg SL (2009) Ultrafast and memory-efficient alignment of short DNA sequences to the human genome. Genome Biology 10: R25.

17. Bi K, Vanderpool D, Singhal S, Linderoth T, Moritz C, et al. (2012) Transcriptome-based exon capture enables highly cost-effective comparative genomic data collection at moderate evolutionary scales. BMC Genomics 13: 403.

18. Surget-Groba Y, Montoya-Burgos JI (2010) Optimization of *de novo* transcriptome assembly from next-generation sequencing data. Genome Research 20: 1432–1440.

19. Gruenheit N, Deusch O, Esser C, Becker M, Voelckel C, et al. (2012) Cutoffs and k-mers: implications from a transcriptome study in allopolyploid plants. BMC Genomics 13: 92.

20. Birol I, Jackman SD, Nielsen CB, Qian JQ, Varhol R, et al. (2009) *De novo* transcriptome assembly with ABySS. Bioinformatics 25: 2872–2877.

21. Simpson JT, Wong K, Jackman SD, Schein JE, Jones SJM, et al. (2009) ABySS: a parallel assembler for short read sequence data. Genome Research 19: 1117–1123.

22. Li W, Godzik A (2006) Cd-hit: a fast program for clustering and comparing large sets of protein or nucleotide sequences. Bioinformatics 22: 1658–1659.

23. Huang X, Madan A (1999) CAP3: a DNA sequence assembly program. Genome Research 9: 868–877.

24. Li H, Handsaker B, Wysoker A, Fennell T, Ruan J, et al. (2009) The sequence alignment/map format and SAMtools. Bioinformatics 25: 2078–2079.

25. Altenhoff AM DC (2009) Phylogenetic and functional assessment of orthologs inference projects and methods. PLoS Computational Biology 5: e1000262.

26. Chiari Y, Cahais V, Galtier N, Delsuc F (2012) Phylogenomic analyses support the position of turtles as the sister group of birds and crocodiles (Archosauria). BMC Biology 10: 65.

27. Loytynoja A (2005) From the cover: an algorithm for progressive multiple alignment of sequences with insertions. Proceedings of the National Academy of Sciences USA 102: 10557–10562.

28. Loytynoja A, Goldman N (2008) Phylogeny-aware gap placement prevents errors in sequence alignment and evolutionary analysis. Science 320: 1632–1635.

29. Castresana J (2000) Selection of conserved blocks from multiple alignments for their use in phylogenetic analysis. Molecular Biology and Evolution 17: 540–552.

30. Sun YB, Zhou WP, Liu HQ, Irwin DM, Shen YY, et al. (2012) Genome-wide scans for candidate genes involved in the aquatic adaptation of dolphins. Genome Biology and Evolution 5: 130–139.

31. Yang Z (2007) PAML 4: phylogenetic analysis by maximum likelihood. Molecular Biology and Evolution 24: 1586–1591.

32. Wang Z, Pascual-Anaya J, Zadissa A, Li W, Niimura Y, et al. (2013) The draft genomes of soft-shell turtle and green sea turtle yield insights into the development and evolution of the turtle-specific body plan. Nature Genetics 45: 701–706.

33. The Chimpanzee Sequencing and Analysis Consortium (2005) Initial sequence of the chimpanzee genome and comparison with the human genome. Nature 437: 69–87.

34. Ashburner M, Ball CA, Blake JA, Botstein D, Butler H, et al. (2000) Gene ontology: tool for the unification of biology. Nature Genetics 25: 25–29.

35. Kanehisa M, Goto S (2000) KEGG: kyoto encyclopedia of genes and genomes. Nucleic Acids Research 28: 27–30.

36. Yang Z, Nielsen R (2002) Codon-substitution models for detecting molecular adaptation at individual sites along specific lineages. Molecular Biology and Evolution 19: 908–917.

37. Zhang J, Nielsen R, Yang Z (2005) Evaluation of an improved branch-site likelihood method for detecting positive selection at the molecular level. Molecular Biology and Evolution 22: 2472–2479.

38. Huang DW, Sherman BT, Lempicki RA (2009) Systematic and integrative analysis of large gene lists using DAVID bioinformatics resources. Nature Protocols 4: 44–57.

39. McGowen MR, Grossman LI, Wildman DE (2012) Dolphin genome provides evidence for adaptive evolution of nervous system genes and a molecular rate slowdown. Proceedings of the Royal Society B: Biological Sciences 279: 3643–3651.

40. Holm S (1979) A simple sequentially rejective multiple test procedure. Scandinavian Journal of Statistics: 65–70.

41. Koressaar T, Remm M (2007) Enhancements and modifications of primer design program Primer3. Bioinformatics 23: 1289–1291.

42. Merx MW, Flögel U, Stumpe T, Gödecke A, Decking UK, et al. (2001) Myoglobin facilitates oxygen diffusion. The FASEB Journal 15: 1077–1079.

43. Fraser J, de Mello LV, Ward D, Rees HH, Williams DR, et al. (2006) Hypoxia-inducible myoglobin expression in nonmuscle tissues. Proceedings of the National Academy of Sciences USA 103: 2977–2981.

44. Srour N, Lebel A, McMahon S, Fournier I, Fugère M, et al. (2003) TACE/ADAM-17 maturation and activation of sheddase activity require proprotein convertase activity. FEBS Letters 554: 275–283.

45. Zhou J, Schmid T, Brüne B (2003) Tumor necrosis factor-α causes accumulation of a ubiquitinated form of hypoxia inducible factor-1α through a nuclear factor-κB-dependent pathway. Molecular Biology of the Cell 14: 2216–2225.

46. Randow F, Seed B (2001) Endoplasmic reticulum chaperone gp96 is required for innate immunity but not cell viability. Nature Cell Biology 3: 891–896.

47. Bavoux C, Hoffmann J, Cazaux C (2005) Adaptation to DNA damage and stimulation of genetic instability: the double-edged sword mammalian DNA polymerase κ. Biochimie 87: 637–646.

48. Habib T, Hejna JA, Moses RE, Decker SJ (1998) Growth factors and insulin stimulate tyrosine phosphorylation of the 51C/SHIP2 protein. Journal of Biological Chemistry 273: 18605–18609.

49. Glatter T, Wepf A, Aebersold R, Gstaiger M (2009) An integrated workflow for charting the human interaction proteome: insights into the PP2A system. Molecular Systems Biology 5: 237.

50. Hua F, Xia Y, Wu D, Chen R, Wang Y, et al. (2012) Effect of down-regulation of histone deacetylase 2 protein expression on cell proliferation and cell cycle in cervical carcinoma. Chinese Journal of Pathology 41: 466.

51. Alföldi J, Di Palma F, Grabherr M, Williams C, Kong L, et al. (2011) The genome of the green anole lizard and a comparative analysis with birds and mammals. Nature 477: 587–591.

52. Castoe TA, de Koning APJ, Hall KT, Card DC, Schield DR, et al. (2013) The Burmese python genome reveals the molecular basis for extreme adaptation in snakes. Proceedings of the National Academy of Sciences USA 110: 20645–20650.

53. Vonk FJ, Casewell NR, Henkel CV, Heimberg AM, Jansen HJ, et al. (2013) The king cobra genome reveals dynamic gene evolution and adaptation in the snake venom system. Proceedings of the National Academy of Sciences USA 110: 20651–20656.

54. Storz JF, Scott GR, Cheviron ZA (2010) Phenotypic plasticity and genetic adaptation to high-altitude hypoxia in vertebrates. Journal of Experimental Biology 213: 4125–4136.

55. Qu Y, Zhao H, Han N, Zhou G, Song G, et al. (2013) Ground tit genome reveals avian adaptation to living at high altitudes in the Tibetan Plateau. Nature Communications 4: 2071.

56. Koh MY, Spivak-Kroizman TR, Powis G (2008) HIF-1 regulation: not so easy come, easy go. Trends in Biochemical Sciences 33: 526–534.

57. Blumthaler M, Ambach W, Ellinger R (1997) Increase in solar UV radiation with altitude. Journal of Photochemistry and Photobiology B: Biology 39: 130–134.

58. Svobodová AR, Galandáková A, Šianská J, Doležal D, Lichnovská R, et al. (2012) DNA damage after acute exposure of mice skin to physiological doses of UVB and UVA light. Archives of Dermatological Research 304: 407–412.

59. Li W, Saunders MA (2005) The chimpanzee and us. Nature 437: 50–51.

10

Comparative Genomic Analysis Shows That Avian Pathogenic *Escherichia coli* Isolate IMT5155 (O2:K1:H5; ST Complex 95, ST140) Shares Close Relationship with ST95 APEC O1:K1 and Human ExPEC O18:K1 Strains

Xiangkai Zhu Ge[1ⓢ], Jingwei Jiang[2,3ⓢ], Zihao Pan[1], Lin Hu[1], Shaohui Wang[4], Haojin Wang[1], Frederick C. Leung[2,3], Jianjun Dai[1]*, Hongjie Fan[1]

1 College of Veterinary Medicine, Nanjing Agricultural University, Nanjing, China, **2** Bioinformatics Center, Nanjing Agricultural University, Nanjing, China, **3** School of Biological Sciences, University of Hong Kong, Hong Kong SAR, China, **4** Shanghai Veterinary Research Institute, Chinese Academy of Agricultural Sciences, Shanghai, China

Abstract

Avian pathogenic *E. coli* and human extraintestinal pathogenic *E. coli* serotypes O1, O2 and O18 strains isolated from different hosts are generally located in phylogroup B2 and ST complex 95, and they share similar genetic characteristics and pathogenicity, with no or minimal host specificity. They are popular objects for the study of ExPEC genetic characteristics and pathogenesis in recent years. Here, we investigated the evolution and genetic blueprint of APEC pathotype by performing phylogenetic and comparative genome analysis of avian pathogenic *E. coli* strain IMT5155 (O2:K1:H5; ST complex 95, ST140) with other *E. coli* pathotypes. Phylogeny analyses indicated that IMT5155 has closest evolutionary relationship with APEC O1, IHE3034, and UTI89. Comparative genomic analysis showed that IMT5155 and APEC O1 shared significant genetic overlap/similarities with human ExPEC dominant O18:K1 strains (IHE3034 and UTI89). Furthermore, the unique PAI I$_{5155}$ (GI-12) was identified and found to be conserved in APEC O2 serotype isolates. GI-7 and GI-16 encoding two typical T6SSs in IMT5155 might be useful markers for the identification of ExPEC dominant serotypes (O1, O2, and O18) strains. IMT5155 contained a ColV plasmid p1ColV$_{5155}$, which defined the APEC pathotype. The distribution analysis of 10 sequenced ExPEC pan-genome virulence factors among 47 sequenced *E. coli* strains provided meaningful information for B2 APEC/ExPEC-specific virulence factors, including several adhesins, invasins, toxins, iron acquisition systems, and so on. The pathogenicity tests of IMT5155 and other APEC O1:K1 and O2:K1 serotypes strains (isolated in China) through four animal models showed that they were highly virulent for avian colisepticemia and able to cause septicemia and meningitis in neonatal rats, suggesting zoonotic potential of these APEC O1:K1 and O2:K1 isolates.

Editor: Mikael Skurnik, University of Helsinki, Finland

Funding: This work was supported by the Fundamental Research Funds for the Central Universities (KYZ201326), the Fund of Priority Academic Program Development of Jiangsu Higher Education Institutions (PAPD) and the Fundamental Research Funds for the Central Universities (KYZ201214). The funders had no role in study design, data collection and analysis, decision to publish, or preparation of the manuscript.

* Email: daijianjun@njau.edu.cn

ⓢ These authors contributed equally to this work.

Introduction

Escherichia coli generally colonizes the mammalian intestinal tract commensally, but highly adapted *E. coli* clones can become true pathogens called "pathotypes", some of which cause various lethal diseases after acquisition of specific virulent factors [1,2]. These *E. coli* pathotypes can be broadly classified as intestinal pathogenic *E. coli* or extraintestinal pathogenic *E. coli* (ExPEC) based on the pathogenic types [3]. Intestinal pathogenic *E. coli* strains (IPEC) cause infection in the gastrointestinal system, while ExPEC strains cause urinary tract infections, newborn meningitis, abdominal sepsis, and septicemia in the extraintestinal system [2,4]. ExPEC pathotypes are classically divided into four groups,

based on the disease pathology, namely avian pathogenic *E. coli* (APEC), uropathogenic *E. coli* (UPEC), neonatal meningitis *E. coli* (NMEC), and septicemic *E. coli* [5–7].

In order to discriminate ExPEC from commensal and intestinal pathogenic *E. coli*, several molecular epidemiology approaches are used for ExPEC typing. The classical typing method is the identification of *E. coli* (O: K: H) serotypes, and highly virulent ExPEC isolates can be classified as several specific and predominant O1, O2 and O18 serotypes strains, which can express K1 capsule and are popularly isolated from human and avian colibacillosis [6,8–10]. Related to above mentioned three O serotypes, O6 serotype strains are also highly virulent and popular among UPEC isolates [6,11], and APEC O78 serotype strains are also frequently isolated from avian colibacillosis [6,12]. The phylogroup typing method based on multilocus enzyme electrophoresis (MLEE) and several relevant DNA markers are generally used for identification of *E. coli* genetic and evolutionary characteristics. *E. coli* can be classified as four major phylogroups (A, B1, D and B2) in accordance with the studies of Clermont et al. [13–16], and an additional fifth group (E) [17–19]. Most ExPEC isolates belong to the mainly phylogroup B2 and a lesser group D, especially highly virulent ExPEC strains, while intestinal pathogens and commensals *E. coli* mainly belong to group A and B1 [20]. In addition, the phylogroup E contains almost all serotype O157:H7 strains [18,19,21]. Multilocus sequence typing (MLST) is currently most powerful typing system for the discrimination of bacterial population genetics [22]. The molecular epidemiology shows that phylogenetic diversity of *E. coli* isolates are unambiguously differentiated based on *E. coli* MLST data (clonal complexes and sequence types data) [17,23]. ExPEC and IPEC isolates are generally distributed in distinct clonal complexes i.e. sequence type complexes, containing numerous sequence types (ST) for *E. coli* MLST database. The majority of ExPEC isolates are located in several specific ST complexes (95, 73, 131, 127, 141, et al.), which are called ExPEC dominated clonal complexes[24–27]. Phylogroup B2 ExPEC strians of serotypes O1, O2 and O18 are generally located in ST complex 95, and ExPEC isolates of ST complex 95 are popular objects for ExPEC genetic characteristics and pathogenesis in recent years [5,6,19,27–29].

After its entry via inhalation of fecal dust, APEC colonizes at the avian respiratory tract, and causes local infections and then spreads to various internal organs, resulting in systemic infection in poultry. These APEC-associated systemic infections have been proven economically devastating to global poultry industries [6,29–31]. The phylogroup B2 APEC strains isolated from avian colibacillosis mainly belong to O1:K1, O2:K1, and another O78 serotypes [6,9]. The complete genomic sequence of APEC O1 (an O1:K1:H7 strain; ST95) is first determined, which shares high similarities with the genomes of human UPEC isolates [5]. APEC and NMEC ST95 serotype O18 isolates can both cause meningitis in the rat model and disease in poultry, suggesting that they might have no or minimal host specificity [32]. APEC O78 strain χ7122 (ST23) is the second genome that has been sequenced in APEC isolates, which keeps close relationship with human ST23 ETEC than that of APEC O1 and human ExPEC strains. APEC wild-type strain IMT5155 (O2:K1:H5; ST complex 95, ST140; B2 phylogroup) is often used as a classic infection strain of APEC pathogenicity to identify APEC virulence factors [33–35]. Due to close relationship of ExPEC O2:K1 serotype strains with extraintestinal infection between humans and animals, we reported the complete genome sequence of IMT5155 in order to unravel the evolutionary and genomic features of APEC O2 isolates. We further compared IMT5155 genome with other *E. coli* strains to identify APEC/ExPEC genetic characteristics. In addition, virulence and zoonotic potentials of APEC O1:K1 and O2:K1 serotypes isolates were assessed through animal models for pathogenicity testing.

Materials and Methods

APEC strain and the total DNA extraction

The avian pathogenic *E. coli* strain IMT5155 was isolated from a chicken with the typical clinical symptoms of avian colibacillosis at a German chicken farm in the year 2000 and were provided by Lothar H Wieler and Christa Ewers [33]. The IMT5155 cells were cultured in LB media to its exponential growth phase and harvested by centrifuge. The bacteria genomic DNA extraction

was extracted using the Bacterial DNA Kit (Omega Bio-Tek, America).

454 pyrosequencing of the IMT5155 genome and assembly

A whole genome shotgun library was produced with 5 μg of the genomic DNA of IMT5155. The shotgun sequencing procedure followed the instruction of 454 GS Junior General Library Preparation Kit (Roche). In addition, an 8 kb insert paired end library was produced with 15 μg of the genomic DNA of IMT5155. The paired end sequencing procedure followed the instruction of 454 GS Junior Paired-end Library Preparation Kit (Roche). Paired-end reads were used to orientate the contigs into scaffolds. The DNA libraries were amplified by emPCR and sequenced by FLX Titanium sequencing chemistry (Roche). Two shotgun runs and one paired-end runs were performed based on their individual library. After sequencing, the raw data were assembled by Newbler 2.7 (Roche) with default parameters. Primer pairs were designed along the sequences flanking the gap regions for PCR gap filling. The complete sequences of IMT5155 chromosome and two plasmids have been deposited in GenBank (Accession numbers: CP005930, CP005931, and CP005932, respectively).

Genome annotation of IMT5155

Glimmer 3.02 was used for gene prediction of IMT5155 complete genome [36]. The Glimmer results were corrected manually, and pseudogenes were investigated through genome submission check process for GenBank (http://www.ncbi.nlm.nih.gov/genomes/frameshifts/frameshifts.cgi), and small CDSs in intergenic regions were identified by IASPLS (Iteratively adaptive sparse partial least squares) [37]. Then, all the predicted ORF sequences were translated into protein sequences. BLASTp was applied to align all the above protein sequences against the NCBI non-redundant database (January, 2013) [38]. Protein sequences with alignment length over 90% of its own length and over 50% identity were chosen and the name of the best hit will be assigned to the corresponding predicted gene. rRNA operons were annotated by RNAmmer (http://www.cbs.dtu.dk/services/RNAmmer/), tRNA genes tRNAscan-SE Search Server (http://lowelab.ucsc.edu/tRNAscan-SE/), and tmRNA were annotated by tmRNA Database (http://rth.dk/resources/rnp/tmRDB/) with default parameters.

Phylogenomic analysis of IMT5155 with other *E. coli* pathotypes

46 complete genomes and 1 draft genome of *E. coli* strains were downloaded from NCBI GenBank (File A in File S3). The othologous genes were identified by using the predicted genes of IMT5155 to align to all annotated genes of 47 *E. coli* by BLAT (the BLAST-like alignment tool) [39]. Those single copy IMT5155 genes over 90% of alignment length against all other *E. coli* strains were considered as the common genes, which composed the common genome of 47 *E. coli* strains. Then, all the common genes were aligned by MUSCLE and concatenated together [40]. Finally, the concatenated aligned genes were submitted to MrBayes with the GTR+G+I substitution model [41]. The chain length was set to 10,000,000 (1 sample/1000 generations). The first 2,000 samples were discarded as burn in after scrutinizing the trace files of two independent runs with Tracer v1.4 (http://tree.bio.ed.ac.uk/software/tracer/).

Virulence genes and Genomic islands of IMT5155

The annotated genes were submitted to IslandViewer (http://www.pathogenomics.sfu.ca/islandviewer/genome_submit.php) and PAIDB (https://www.gem.re.kr/paidb/about_paidb.php) with default parameters for the identification of genomic islands s, i.e., pathogenecity island-like region [42,43]. Then the annotated genes were submitted to VFDB database (http://www.mgc.ac.cn/VFs/) for the identification of virulence genes [38,44]. Protein sequences with alignment length over 90% of its own length and over 50% identity were chosen from VFDB database, and the name of the best hit will be assigned to the corresponding predicted gene. Through online prediction and manual inspection, we obtained the detailed and precise information for IMT5155 GIs and virulence genes.

Comparative genomic analysis

For comparative studies, common genes in chromosomes of other *E. coli* strains (APEC O1, CFT073, χ7122, MG1655, SE15, O157Sakai, IHE3034, CE10, 83972, NA114, UMN026, UTI89, E2348/69, RM12579, NRG857c, and UM146) shared with *E. coli* IMT5155 were identified and plotted along with all predicted genes in *E. coli* IMT5155 (with >90% alignment length and >50% identity). The similarities and differences of the predicted genes located in IMT5155 genomic islands were highlighted among the other *E. coli* strains.

p1ColV5155 and 5 plasmids (pAPEC-O2-ColV, pAPEC-O1-ColBM, pUTI89, pMAR2, and pO83-CoRR) were used for plasmid comparative analysis and synteny analysis. The common genes in 5 plasmids shared with p1ColV$_{5155}$ were identified and plotted along with all predicted genes in p1ColV$_{5155}$ as well as some functional genes. All genes of 5 plasmids were aligned with all genes predicted in p1ColV$_{5155}$ respectively. Then, the aligned genes (with >90% alignment length and >50% identity) were shown for synteny analysis. The scripts for comparative ORF analysis and GIs distribution between IMT5155 and other *E. coli* strains were shown in File B in File S3.

The distribution analysis of 10 sequenced B2 ExPEC pan-genome virulence genes among all sequenced *E. coli* strains

The homologous and non-orthologous genes in genomes of 10 sequenced B2 ExPEC strains (NA114, UTI89, IHE3034, IMT5155, APEC O1, S88, CFT073, Clone Di14, ABU83972, 536) were identified by this standard: homology genes, gene sequence identity ≥80% and coverage ≥80%, otherwise it was a non-orthologous gene. The total genes of the homologous and non-orthologous genes of those genomes represent the pan-genome of 10 sequenced B2 ExPEC genomes. The genes of pan-genome for 10 sequenced B2 ExPEC were translated into protein, and then protein of 10 sequenced B2 ExPEC pan-genome were submitted to VFDB database (with >90% alignment length and >50% identity) [38,44]. Then all predicted virulence genes were one by one manually verified through a large number of references about ExPEC virulence factors, and the confirmed virulence-associated genes were classified as six categories: adhesins, invasins, toxins, iron acquisition/transport systems, polysialic acid synthesis, and other virulence genes. For distribution analysis of virulence genes, common genes in 46 *E. coli* genomes (selected consistent with phylogenomic analysis) (File A in File S3) shared with virulence genes of 10 sequenced B2 ExPEC pan-genome were identified with >90% alignment length and >50% identity, and highlighted among all 46 sequenced *E. coli* strains expect draft PCN033 genome sequence. The scripts for virulence genes statistics and heat-map for virulence gene distribution were shown in File B in File S3.

Pathogenicity testing

All animal experimental protocols were approved by the Laboratory Animal Monitoring Committee of Jiangsu Province, China.

(i) Chicken embryo lethality assay (ELA). The ELA model was performed to evaluate lethality in chicken embryos for IMT5155 and other APEC strains, as previously described [5,32]. Briefly, approximately 500 CFU of each cultured bacterial were inoculated into the allantoic cavity of a 12-day-old, embryonated, specific-pathogen-free egg (Jinan SAIS Poultry Co. Ltd.), and 20 eggs were successively inoculated for every experimental group. PBS-inoculated and uninoculated were used as negative controls. The inoculated eggs were checked daily, and embryo deaths were recorded for 4 days.

(ii) Chick colisepticemia model. IMT5155 and other APEC strains to cause avian colibacillosis were assessed for chick lethality, as previously described [5,32]. Briefly, group of 10 1-day-old SPF chicks (QYH Biotech) were inoculated intratracheally with 0.1 ml bacteria suspensions (approximately 10^7 CFU) for APEC and other strains. The groups for chicks inoculated with PBS and MG1655 acted as negative controls. Measuring time for mortality were 7 days after postinfection. Deaths were recorded, and the survivors after 7 days were euthanatized, and all tested chicks in each group were dissected and examined for lesion scores (ranked from 0 to 3 in accordance with the presence of airsacculitis, pericarditis, and perihepatitis). The air sacs, blood in heart, and brain of all tested chicks were picked using inoculation loops, and then plates of MacConkey agar were crossed by inoculation loops and cultured at 37°C overnight.

(iii) Mouse sepsis model. The mouse sepsis model for virulence evaluation of ExPEC isolates was performed on the basis of previously described methods [28,45,46]. Approximately 10^7 CFU (0.2 ml) of bacteria suspensions for APEC and other strains were injected intraperitoneally into 8-week-old imprinting control region (ICR) mice, and every group contained 10 mice. Mice for health status were observed twice daily during 3 days postinfection, which was score on a 5-step scale (1 = healthy, 2 = minimally ill, 3 = moderately ill, 4 = severely ill, 5 = dead) with the worst score as the score for that day, as described by Johnson et al. [28]. The mean of the 3 daily health status scores represented each mouse's infection process during 3 days postinfection. The blood in heart and brain of all tested mouse were picked using inoculation loops, and then plates of MacConkey agar were crossed by inoculation loops and cultured at 37°C overnight.

(iv) Rat neonatal meningitis model. The abilities to induce septicemia and enter the central nerves system (CNS) for APEC strains were assessed by 5 days old, specific-pathogen-free Sprague-Dawley rats, as previously described [28,32]. And *E. coli* MG1655 and NMEC strain RS218 acted as negative and positive controls, respectively. Groups of 12 rat pups were intraperitoneally inoculated with approximately 200 CFU of bacteria suspensions (20 μl) [32]. At 24 h postinoculation, rats were subsequently euthanized, and 25 μl of blood and 10 μl of cerebrospinal fluid (CSF) from each survivor for infected rat pup were obtained for quantitative cultures. The blood and CSF were plated on MacConkey agar to measure the bacteria concentration in the blood and indicate meningitis, respectively.

Results and Discussion

Sequencing and overview of the complete genome of APEC strain IMT5155

The complete genome of APEC strain IMT5155 was determined by initial *de novo* assembly of two shotgun sequencing runs and one paired-end sequencing run (8-kb insert paired-end library) followed by PCR gap-filling. The raw shotgun reads and paired-end reads were assembled into 121 contigs which were further assembled into eight scaffolds. The N50 contig size was 177,509 bp. The largest scaffold size was 4,907,543 bp (containing 56 large contigs). The second largest scaffold size was 191,765 bp (containing 14 large contigs) indicating that our raw assembly was highly continuous and that might be sequence of *E. coli* large plasmids. Primer pairs were designed to amplify the gaps between contigs. The PCR products were directly sequenced using a Sanger sequencer ABI 3730. For the shotgun runs, one run generated 132,755 reads (~53 Mb) and the other generated 108,804 reads (~47 Mb). The average read length of both shotgun runs was approximately 400 bp. The paired-end run generated 90,792 reads (~26 Mb) with an average read length of approximately 300 bp. Over 99% of the total reads were assembled, resulting in approximately 23-fold coverage of the genome of APEC strain IMT5155.

The complete genome of APEC strain IMT5155 comprises 5,126,057 bp, existing as a circular chromosome of 4,929,051 bp and two plasmids of 194,170 bp and 2,836 bp. Glimmer 3.02 annotated 4,804 CDSs covering 87.87% of IMT5155 chromosome. In addition, 27 pseudogenes and 30 small CDSs in intergenic regions were identified (File C in File S3). p1ColV$_{5155}$ contained 270 Glimmer-predicted CDSs (File D in File S3), and 6 CDSs were identified in p2$_{5155}$. Moreover, 88 tRNA genes, 19 rRNA genes, and 1 tmRNA gene were identified in the IMT5155 chromosome (File C in File S3). The GC content of the IMT5155 chromosome is approximately 50.65%, which is similar to other reported *E. coli* genomes. By contrast, the two plasmids have GC% contents of 49.84% (p1ColV$_{5155}$) and 42.21% (p2$_{5155}$). The large plasmid, p1ColV$_{5155}$, was identified as a ColV plasmid, which was widespread in ExPEC pathotypes, particularly in APEC pathotype[47,48]. Table A in File S2 summarizes the general genomic features of IMT5155 genome. Among 5,144 Glimmer-annotated CDSs found in IMT5155 genome, 5,053 (~98.2%) could be matched to genes in the NCBI nr database (December, 2013).

Whole-genome phylogenetic analysis of IMT5155 compared with other *E. coli* pathotypes

Whole-genome-derived phylogeny of common genomes can accurately illustrate evolutionary relationships among different commensal and pathogenic *E. coli* variants [49]. The genomes of IMT5155 and another 46 *E. coli* strains were selected for mapping the whole-genome evolutionary phylogeny, ranging from a commensal K12 strain, through intestinal pathogenic strains, to the highlighted extraintestinal pathogenic strains (Figure 1). MrBayes was used to construct a BMCMC phylogenetic tree to define the evolutionary phylogeny of 47 whole genome sequenced *E. coli* strains, based on *E. coli* common genes. The common genes identified from IMT5155 and the others 46 *E. coli* genomes comprised 1,782 genes and covered approximately 1.61 Mb. The result of phylogeny showed that 47 *E. coli* strains could be clearly divided into six monophyletic groups, which was similar to the whole-genome-based phylogeny by both Rasko and McNally et al. [26,50] (Figure 1). In the phylogenetic tree, APEC strains IMT5155 and APEC O1 were located in B2 ExPEC cluster

(Figure 1), and an APEC O78 strain χ7122 was located in B1 clade (Figure 1). The phylogenomic tree showed that ST complex 95 APEC dominant O1:K1 and O2:K1 serotypes strains (APEC O1 and IMT5155) have the closest evolutionary relationships with human ExPEC dominant O18:K1 (ST95 complex) strains (UTI89 and IHE3034).

Identification of virulence determinants and genomic islands in the IMT5155 genome

Many virulence-associated factors were identified in IMT5155 genome (Table B in File S2). Adhesins, invasins, and iron uptake systems were critical for APEC/ExPEC pathogenesis, which typically promote motility, achieve the capability of adhesion to and invasion of host tissues, and conduct iron uptake for survival [51–53]. The predicted adhesins of IMT5155 genome were listed in Table B in File S2. Six different chaperone-usher adhesion determinants were identified at IMT5155 genome, including *fim*, *yqi*, *yad*, *auf*, *yfc*, and *fml* operons. APEC strains shared common invasion genes with NMEC strains isolated from patients with neonatal meningitis [28,51]. Several microbial invasion determinants, including *Ibe* proteins, *yijP*, *aslA*, K1 capsule, and *Hcp* family proteins (Table B in File S2) which contribute to invasion of brain microvascular endothelial cells (BMECs), were identified at both APEC and NMEC pathotypes [46,54,55]. IMT5155 possessed ferrous iron transporters *FeoABC* and *SitABCD* (Table B in File S2). Unlike widespread siderophore enterobactin, IMT5155 contained three ExPEC specific pathogen-related siderophores for salmochelin, aerobactin, and yersiniabactin, which took important roles in APEC virulence [52,56] (Table B in File S2).

The distinct genomic islands (GIs) of pathogens that encode various virulence factors are called pathogenicity islands (PAIs), which have a significant difference in GC content compared with the core genome, and some PAIs are usually integrated into tRNA genes [57]. In this study, 20 GIs, ranging from 4 to 96-kb, were annotated on the IMT5155 chromosome via PAIDB and IslandViewer (Table C in File S2). 14 GIs contained several potential virulence factors, as predicted by PAIDB forecast and NCBI BLAST analysis, and these islands could be considered as confirmed or presumed PAIs. Moreover, 5 prophage islands (GI-5, -6, -13, -18, and -19) were identified at IMT5155 chromosome. Among the five prophages, it seemed that GI-13 was a P4 family phage and GI-18 was a P2 family member. The coexistence of these two phages (a satellite and helper phage pair) was quite reasonable [58]. It was also likely that the GI-18 phage could produce two types of tail fibers by DNA inversion like phage Mu and several other phages [59,60]. The detailed and precise information for each GI had been elucidated and listed at Table C in File S2. We then focused on a novel APEC O2 PAI (GI-12) and two GIs (GI-8 and GI-22) coding Type VI secretion systems.

A novel APEC O2 PAI (GI-12), termed PAI I$_{5155}$, was identified from the IMT5155 chromosome, which inserted between the *cadC* and *yidC* genes of *E. coli* core genome, was adjacent to tRNA-Phe (Figure 2 and Table C in File S2). The total GC content of this island was 48.76%, below to the average GC content(50.65%)of IMT5155 chromosome. The size of PAI I$_{5155}$ was approximately 94 kb, composed 105 ORFs. Proteins encoded by ORFs of PAI I$_{5155}$ were shown in Figure 2 and Table C in File S2. PAI I$_{5155}$ was absent in APEC O1 and other ExPEC genomes in this study, and only partial CDSs including several virulence/fitness factors (*aatA*, ireA, *fecIRABCDE*, and *pgtABCP*) were identified in pathogenicity islands of other *E. coli* pathotypes. For virulence factors encoded in PAI I$_{5155}$, AatA of APEC auto-transporter adhesin, IreA of iron-regulated virulence factor have

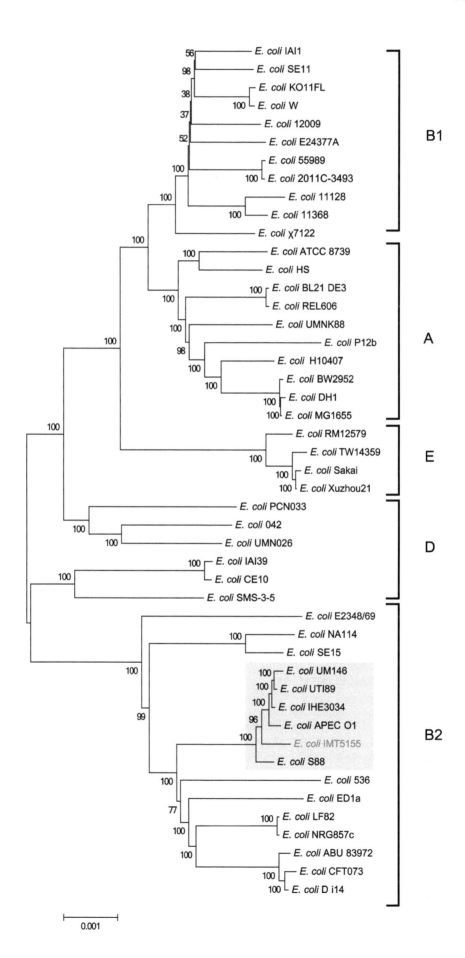

Figure 1. Phylogenomic tree (1,782 concatenated core genes, 1.61 Mb) of 47 *E. coli* strains. All MrBayes with the GTR+G+I substitution model (BMCMC) was used for the reconstruction of the phylogenomic tree. The chain length was set to 10,000,000 (1 sample/1000 generations). 47 *E. coli* strains clearly divided into monophyletically phylogroups (A, B1, B2, D, and E), and ST complex 95 strains were highlighted in phylogenomic tree. 47 *E. coli* genomes data was listed in File A in File S3.

been confirmed that they were involved in the pathogenicity of APEC/ExPEC [33,61,62], and other putative virulence genes need to be further identified (Figure 2 and Table C in File S2). Unlike other ExPEC, IMT5155 contained the ferric dicitrate transport system, which was previously reported to maintain *E. coli* growth under iron-limited circumstances and widespread among *E. coli* K-12, intestinal pathogenic *E. coli*, and *Shigella* strains [63]. For the putative metabolism/biosynthesis-related systems, those annotated genes of PAI I$_{5155}$ were mainly distributed in ExPEC strains by BLASTN analysis. A putative transketolase-like protein, which was adjacent to a putative ascorbate-specific IIABC component of a PTS system, was also annotated in PAI I$_{5155}$. In addition, like typical PAIs, PAI I$_{5155}$ contained many mobility elements, including four integrases and multiple transposons, suggesting that horizontal gene transfer and genomic recombination were possibly involved in the evolution of PAI I$_{5155}$ (Figure 2 and Table C in File S2). We identified a PAI I$_{5155}$ analogue located in the chromosome of APEC strain DE205B (O2:K1), which was isolated in China (unpublished data) [45]. Therefore, PAI I$_{5155}$ could be considered as a novel arrangement of these virulence factors and metabolism/biosynthesis-related systems. This island currently was only identified in APEC serotype O2 strains. Furthermore, roles of the putative virulence factors and metabolism/biosynthesis-related systems in pathogenicity and fitness of bacterial demands pending further research.

Type VI secretion systems (T6SSs) are distributed widely in many Gram-negative pathogenic bacteria [64]. IMT5155 carried two putative type VI secretion systems, which were located in GI-7 (32.2 kb) and GI-16 (28.2 kb) (Table C in File S2). GI-7, which was inserted between the *mltA* and *serA*-1 genes of B2 ExPEC core genome, was a region (GC content: 52.81%) adjacent to the tRNA-Met. GI-16 (GC content: 51.95%) located directly downstream of a tRNA-Asp, was inserted between the *yafT* and *ramA*-1 genes of *E. coli* core genome. GI-7 and GI-16 were respectively corresponding to T6SS1 and T6SS2, both of which have been recently described by Ma et al. [65]. The genes encoding secretion assembly components, including conserved core components of T6SS and additional unknown proteins [65], were located in GI-7 and GI-16 (Figure A in File S1). The typical T6SS1 (GI-7) was widely prevalent among the B2 and D ExPEC strains, and was elaborated to take roles in pathogenesis of APEC [28,66]. However, it was reported that the T6SS2 was mainly encoded in virulent isolated of B2 ExPEC and might be a potential marker for B2 ExPEC, but not associated with ExPEC virulence [28,65]. In order to identify whether T6SS2 can act as a potential marker for ExPEC dominant serotypes (O1, O2, and O18) strains, we detected almost all of the reported ExPEC O1:K1, O2:K1 and O18:K1 strains (genome sequences available online) and APEC isolates in our laboratory as previously described by Ma et al. [65] (Table D in File S2). We speculated that T6SS2 might be associated with ST95 ExPEC (serotypes O1, O2 and O18) strains, and those B2 phylogroup ExPEC (O1, O2, and O18) strains almost simultaneously contained two T6SSs (T6SS1 and T6SS2) (Table D in File S2).

Comparative genomic analysis of IMT5155 with other *E. coli* pathotypes

Comparative genomic analysis was performed using one by one alignment between IMT5155 genome and other 16 representative

E. coli strains based on their evolutionary relationships and phenotypes. The general comparison of IMT5155 genome content with 16 *E. coli* strains was shown in Table A in File S2. The 16 representative strains encompassed typical commensal *E. coli*, highly pathogenic diarrhoeagenic *E. coli*, and extraintestinal *E. coli* strains. Four of these 16 *E. coli* strains were used as control references for comparative genomic analysis, including the commensal strains (MG1655 and SE15), EHEC strain O157 Sakai, and EPEC strain RM12579. IMT5155 shared different numbers of common chromosomal genes with these strains (Table E in File S2). The comparative chromosomal atlas of IMT5155 with those *E. coli* genomes is shown in Figure 3. The results showed that significant differences in genome content mainly focus on IMT5155 GIs regions (Figure 3). The distribution of IMT5155 GIs among these strains was shown in Table C in File S2. The commensal *E. coli* genomes were usually smaller than *E. coli* pathotypes, and harbored fewer genes, especially accessory genes i.e., genomic islands by genomic recombination than *E. coli* pathotypes [19,49]. As described above, MG1655 harbored merely IMT5155 GIs homology loci (Figure 3 and Table C in File S2). Comparison between B2 phylogroup SE15 and IMT5155 reflected a similar result that only 4 IMT5155 GIs were present in SE15. The EHEC O157:H7 pathotype is a typical highly pathogenic diarrhoeagenic *E. coli* and highlighted the genomic plasticity for lateral gene transfer. EPEC strain RM12579 (O55:H7) is a precursor to O157:H7 pathotype [67,68]. Both E phylogroup Sakai and RM12579 harbored merely IMT5155 GIs homology loci (Figure 3 and Table C in File S2), and Sakai shared the least numbers of chromosomal common genes with IMT5155 (Table E in File S2). The typical EPEC strain E2348/69 (serotype O127:H6) shares close evolutionary relationship with B2 ExPEC pathotypes, but has no common GIs with IMT5155. Two AIEC strains (UM146 and NRG857c) shared relatively largest numbers of common genes with IMT5155. UM146 and NRG857c had12 and 9 common GIs with IMT5155, respectively.

For 9 ExPEC strains in the comparative genomic analysis, APEC O1, IHE3034, and UTI89 exhibited closest phylogenetic relationship with IMT5155 (Figure 1). CFT073, ABU83972 and NA114 were in different subclades of phylogenetic tree relative to IMT5155, respectively (Figure 1). Our phylogenetic tree and previous studies revealed APEC ST23 serotype O78 strain χ7122 arose from distinct lineages with APEC O1 and IMT5155 [12]. In addition, CE10 and UMN026 belong to phylogroup D. The comparative genomic analysis showed that IMT5155 GIs, excepting for PAI I$_{5155}$ and several prophage GIs, were highly conserved in APEC O1, IHE3034, and UTI89 (Figure 3 and Table C in File S2). Furthermore, IMT5155 shared the highest number of common chromosomal genes with IHE3034 (3,948; 83.0% of the total annotated CDSs in IHE3034 genome) (Table E in File S2). In contract, IMT5155 GIs were not widespread among CFT073, ABU83972, NA114, CE10, UMN026, and χ7122 (Table C in File S2). Moreover, 16 of the 20 genomic islands of IMT5155 were absent or poorly conserved in χ7122, and this result further reinforced the fact that ST23 APEC O78 strains lacked of conservation of virulence-associated genomic islands with ST95 APEC serotypes O1 and O2 strains (Figure 3 and Table C in File S2). Interestingly, the results showed that prophage GIs in IMT5155 exhibited partial or no homology among these

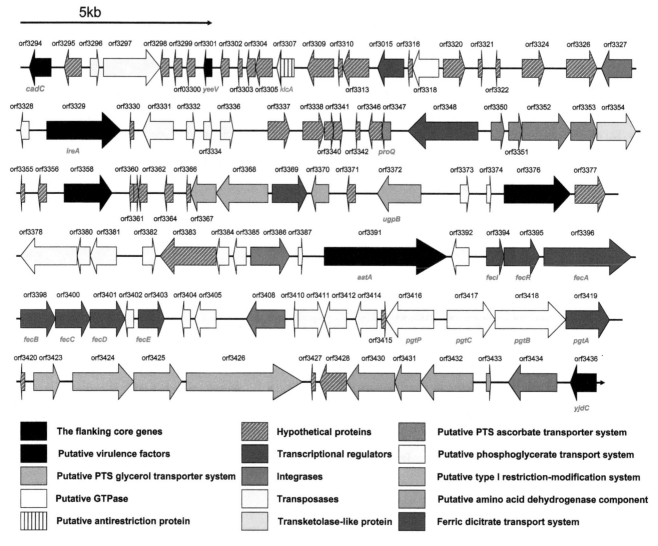

Figure 2. Chimeric feature and genetic context of PAI I$_{5155}$ (GI-12). PAI I$_{5155}$ was inserted between the *cadC* and *yidC* genes of *E. coli* core genome. Proteins encoded by the ORFs of PAI I$_{5155}$ represented by arrows, and the direction of the arrows indicated the direction of transcription. The color keys for functions of these proteins were shown at the bottom.

ExPEC strains. These results showed that genomes of APEC O1 and IMT5155 shared significant genetic overlap/similarities with human ExPEC O18 strains UTI89 and IHE3034. Moreover, those GIs of IMT5155 that were widespread among APEC O1, IHE3034, and UTI89 might be involved in or contribute to the pathogenicity and niche adaptation of ExPEC O1/O2/O18 strains (phylogroup B2; ST complex 95).

Sequence analysis and characterization of IMT5155 ColV plasmid p1ColV5155

(i) Analysis and characterization of the structure of p1ColV$_{5155}$. The IMT5155 strain harbored a 194-kb ColV plasmid, termed p1ColV$_{5155}$, which have been described elsewhere [69]. p1ColV$_{5155}$, which was depicted in a circular map (Figure 4), comprised 214 CDSs, encoding virulence-related proteins, plasmid conjugal transfer proteins, mobile genetic elements, and hypothetical proteins. The number and percentage of common genes of p1ColV$_{5155}$ and the other *E. coli* pathotypes' plasmids were listed in Table F in File S2. p1ColV$_{5155}$ shared more common genes with pAPEC-O2-ColV and pAPEC-O1-

ColBM than the other large plasmids in other *E. coli* pathotypes (Table F in File S2). In an effort to better define p1ColV$_{5155}$ backbone, classical circular genetic map was applied for comparative CDSs analysis of the p1ColV$_{5155}$ with five other large plasmids (pAPEC-O2-ColV, pAPEC-O1-ColBM, pUTI89, pMAR2, and pO83-CoRR), three (pUTI89, pMAR2, and pO83-CoRR) of which acted as references for homology analysis (Figure 4). Plasmids pUTI89, pMAR2, and pO83-CoRR were respectively present in UTI89, E2348/69 and NRG 857C, which shared close evolutionary relationships with IMT5155 in the preceding section. In addition, synteny analysis between CDSs in p1ColV$_{5155}$ and the above five plasmids were also performed (Figure B in File S1). For the Tra genes region, we identified the detailed locations of p1ColV$_{5155}$ homologous genes among those five plasmids. The common genes of p1ColV$_{5155}$ with pAPEC-O2-ColV and pAPEC-O1-ColBM were mainly concentrated in virulence and plasmid conjugal transfer regions. The conjugative transfer system regions of pUTI89 and pMAR2 also shared high identity with that regions of p1ColV$_{5155}$. However, the common

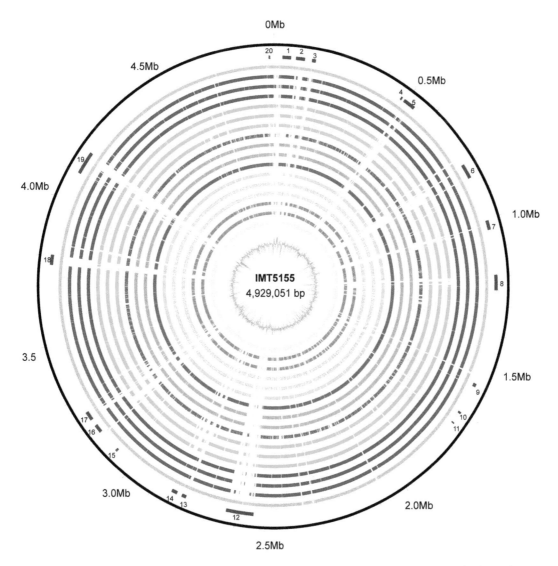

Figure 3. Comparative ORF analysis between IMT5155 and other *E. coli* strains. From outside to inside, the circles represent that: a) coordinate of IMT5155 genome; b) IMT5155 genomic island regions (red); c) IMT5155 (pink); d) APEC O1, IHE304, and UTI189 (blue); e) CFT073, ABU 83972 and NA114 (green); f) χ7122 (olive); g) UM146 and NRG857c (orange); h) SE15 (magenta); i) E2348/69 (cyan); j) CE10 and UMN026 (skyblue); k) O157 Sakai and O55:H7 RM12579 (purple); l) MG1655 (yellow); GC% of IMT5155 (calculated by 500 bp sliding window).

genes between pO83-CoRR and p1ColV$_{5155}$ were mainly located in the virulence region (Figure 4).

(ii) Virulence-associated genes of p1ColV$_{5155}$. ColV plasmids are generally present in ExPEC strains and contain a series of virulence genes [70]. Several genes of ColV plasmids, identified as being involved in APEC virulence and defined the APEC pathotype [47,48,71,72], were found at two virulence regikbons of p1ColV$_{5155}$. The first virulence region with the size of 62.1 kb was from *iroBCDEN* of the salmochelin cluster to *iucABCD* and *iutA* of the aerobactin cluster (Figure 4). The second region was a 24.3-kb virulence gene region from *cvaA* and *cvaB* of the ColV operon to *eitABCD* of a putative iron transport system (Figure 4). In particular, the first virulence region of p1ColV$_{5155}$ was nearly identical to the conserved portion of pAPEC-O2-CoLV and pAPEC-O1-CoLBM [47,48]. The second virulence region of p1ColV$_{5155}$ was homologous to the variable portion of pAPEC-O2-CoLV and pAPEC-O1-CoLBM, including *cvaAB*, *tsh*, and *eitABCD* [47,48] (Figure 4). However, the virulence genes' locus in p1ColV$_{5155}$ variable portion was completely inverted to that of

pAPEC-O2-CoLV (Figure 4 and Figure B in File S1). Further analysis of variable portion revealed that p1ColV$_{5155}$ contained intact *cvaA* and *cvaB* genes for ColV export, but lacked the *cvaC* gene for ColV synthesis and the *cvi* gene for ColV immunity (Figure 4). Obviously, p1ColV$_{5155}$ neither contained ColB and ColM operons, which were the namesake traits of ColBM plasmids [48] (Figure 4). Therefore, this plasmid named as ColBM plasmid can be excluded, due to the namesake traits of ColBM plasmids. Even though without encoding *cvaC* and *cvi*, p1ColV$_{5155}$ was preferred to be classified as a ColV plasmid, which might lose the intact ColV operon during p1ColV$_{5155}$ evolution. One speculation is that p1ColV$_{5155}$ may be a novel type of ColV plasmid with rearrangements during its evolution. The pathogenic role of the two virulence regions of p1ColV$_{5155}$ might be correspondent to pVM01 of APEC strain E3, which was highly similar to pAPEC-O2-CoLV and pAPEC-O1–CoLBM [47,48,72]. The conserved section of the pVM01 virulence region was clearly shown to be associated with the virulence of APEC strains. However, the variable sections of this plasmid were not directly

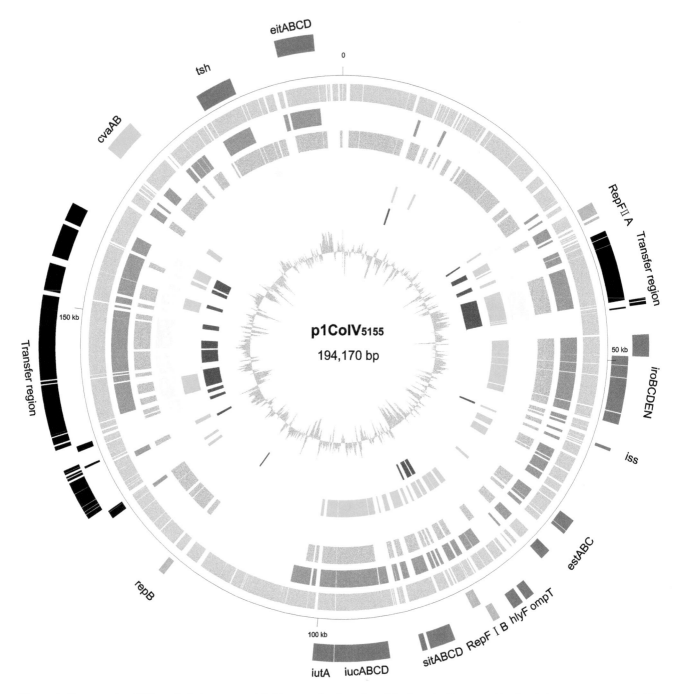

Figure 4. Comparative ORF analysis between p1ColV₅₁₅₅ and other plasmids. From inside to outside, the circles represent that: a) GC% (calculated by 500 bp sliding window); b) common ORFs in pUTI89 (brown); c) common ORFs in pO83_CORR (green); d) common ORFs in pMAR2 (yellow); e) common ORFs in pAPEC-O2-ColV (grey); f) common ORFs in pAPEC-O1-ColBM (purple); g) p1ColV₅₁₅₅ (pink); i) highlighted functional ORFs in the negative strand of p1ColV₅₁₅₅; j) highlighted functional ORFs in the positive strand of p1ColV₅₁₅₅ (orange: RepF IIA, RepF IB, repB; blue: Transfer regions; red: virulence related genes; green: cvaAB locus).

associated with APEC virulence [72]. We speculated that the conserved section of p1ColV₅₁₅₅ virulence region might be involved in virulence of IMT5155.

(iii)Replication and transfer regions of p1ColV₅₁₅₅. Two replication regions were found in the chromosome of p1ColV₅₁₅₅: RepFIIA and RepFIB replicons (Figure 4). The first is a 33.4 kp region encompassing mostly predicted conjugal transfer genes of p1ColV₅₁₅₅, and the second is a 7.8 kp region contained another three conjugal transfer genes adjoining RepFIIA (Figure 4). The

plasmid transfer region of p1ColV₅₁₅₅ was slightly different from that of pAPEC-O2-ColV, which contained a complete plasmid conjugal transfer region [47].

The distribution of 10 sequenced B2 ExPEC pan-genome virulence genes among 46 sequenced *E. coli* strains

E. coli is highly evolved and adapted to the different specific environment. Recent findings show that the frequency of core genome recombination appears a striking decrease from intestinal commensal, through intestinal pathogenic strains, to phylogroup B2 ExPEC strains. Phylogroup B2 ExPEC strains are pathogenic variants, which show highly environmental adaptability with recombination being restricted [26,73]. Comparative genomic analysis of IMT5155 with other *E. coli* pathotypes showed that APEC dominant O1 and O2 serotypes strains (phylogroup B2; ST complex 95) shared significant genetic overlap/similarities with human ExPEC dominant O18 strains (IHE3034, and UTI89), and could be distinguished from APEC O78 strain χ7122, commensal *E. coli*, and IPEC. Accordingly, B2 ExPEC strains should harbor typical ExPEC-specific virulence factors, which could endue ExPEC a selective advantage to adapt/colonize to extraintestinal specific niches during infection relative to intestinal pathogenic strains.

In order to understand the relationship between virulence factors and genetic landscape of B2 ExPEC pathotypes, the distribution of 10 sequenced B2 ExPEC pan-genome virulence genes among 46 sequenced *E. coli* strains was conducted to examine whether B2 ExPEC strains harbored typical ExPEC-specific virulence factors (i.e., determining whether there were significant differences for the distribution of B2 ExPEC virulence genes among different *E. coli* pathotypes) [51]. The pan-genome of sequenced 10 B2 ExPEC strains contained 10,399 orthologous gene families. The VFDB database predicted 287 virulence genes among these orthologous genes. 73 virulence-associated genes were manually confirmed among these 287 virulence genes and classified as six categories: adhesins, invasins, toxins, iron acquisition/transport systems, polysialic acid synthesis, and other virulence genes. The details of 73 virulence genes of 10 sequenced B2 ExPEC pan-genome and their distributions among 46 sequenced strains were shown in Figure 5 and Table B in File S2. The distribution diagram showed that 10 sequenced B2 ExPEC pan-genome virulence genes were significant occurring in extraintestinal pathogenic strains compared with commensal and diarrhoeagenic *E. coli*, and several virulence genes were only present among ExPEC strains, such as fimbrial adhesins (*yqi*, *auf*, and *papG*), invasins (*ibeA* and *Hcp*), almost of toxins, and others (Figure 5 and Table B in File S2). The distribution of 10 sequenced B2 ExPEC pan-genome virulence factors provided a meaningful information for ExPEC-specific virulence factors, including several adhesins, invasions, toxins, iron acquisition systems, and others (Figure 5 and Table B in File S2), which were conserved in ExPEC pathotypes and contributed to ExPEC to adapte/colonize extraintestinal specific niches during infection. Moreover, these specific virulence factors might also provide valuable targets for the vaccines design.

Certainly, there may be strain-to-strain variation of the distribution of virulence genes in any specific strains (Figure 5). For example, compared with other B2 ExPEC strains, IMT5155 does not have F1C, P, and S fimbariaes, which are involved in UPEC pathogenesis [53]. We wondered whether there were specific genes or virulence factors to define the APEC pathotype. For 10,399 orthologous genes of 10 sequenced ExPEC pan-genome, 239 genes were identified in IMT5155 genome relative to the other 9 B2 ExPEC strains (Table G in File S2), and 202 genes were present only in APEC O1, and 24 genes were only common present in APEC strains (IMT5155 and APEC O1) compared with the other 8 B2 ExPEC strains (data not shown). The hypothetical genes and prophage genes were predominant among those specific genes for each APEC strains, and only five virulence genes (*aatA*, *eitA*, *eitB*, *eitC*, and *eitD*) were identified among 24 common genes. Moreover, 600 orthologous genes were identify as NMEC-specific genes. Similarly, the majority of NMEC-specific genes were prophage genes and hypothetical genes, and no virulence

factors were only present in NMEC (data not shown). Even though 3462 UPEC-specific genes among 10,399 orthologous genes of 10 sequenced ExPEC pan-genome were identified in six UPEC strains, almost all virulence genes identified in UPEC strains were present among some APEC and UPEC strains. Therefore, there may be slight different distributions of virulence genes for an individual ExPEC strain, but no specific type of virulence genes to define B2 ExPEC subpathotype. The distribution analysis of 10 sequenced B2 ExPEC pan-genome virulence factors were further considered that phylogroup B2 APEC might not be differentiated from group B2 human ExPEC pathotypes (NMEC/UPEC), because two APEC O1 and O2 strains shared ExPEC-specific virulence factors with human ExPEC pathotypes. Furthermore, these results also support the previous findings that phylogroup B2 APEC isolates share remarkable similarities with human ExPEC pathotypes, and might pose a potential zoonosis threat [5,9,10,27,74].

Virulence assessment of APEC O1:K1, O2:K1 and O78 serotypes isolates

The pathogenicity and zoonotic potential of APEC O1:K1 and O2:K1 serotypes isolates, including IMT5155 and several strains isolated in China, were assessed with four animal models [5,28,32,45,46]. In addition, one ST23 APEC O78 strain CVCC1553 and an APEC non-dominant serotype strain Jnd2 (B2; ST95; O39:K1) were also included in the virulence assessment. The strains APEC O1, NMEC RS218, and UPEC CFT073 were used as the positive control, while *E. coli* K-12 MG1655 and CVCC1531 were used as negative control [5,28,32,45,46]. The detail information of these 13 selected strains was shown in Table H in File S2.

The virulence of the selected APEC O1:K1, O2:K1, and O78 strains for natural reservoir were assessed by chicken embryo lethality assay (ELA) and chick colisepticemia model for avian colisepticemia. In ELA assay, the mortalities for un-inoculated, PBS-inoculated, Jnd2, and CVCC1531 inoculated embryos were not obviously different from the negative control MG1655, while seven APEC O1:K1, O2:K1, and O78 strains were significantly different from the negative control MG1655 ($P<0.05$) (Table 1). No significant differences existed among the seven APEC O1:K1, O2:K1, and O78 strains compared to the ELA-positive control strain APEC O1 (high pathogenicity) (Table 1). For chick colisepticemia assay, the mortalities, rates of reisolation from the chick organs, and lesion scores were evaluated. Similarly to ELA results, seven APEC O1:K1, O2:K1, and O78 strains were significantly different from the negative control MG1655 ($P<0.05$) (Table 2) (the original data shown in File E in File S3), while no significant differences were observed among the seven APEC O1:K1, O2:K1, and O78 strains compared to the high-pathogenicity control strain APEC O1 (Table 2). Therefore, based on the results of two models for avian colisepticemia, seven selected APEC O1:K1, O2:K1, and O78 strains was categorized as being highly virulent for natural reservoir. Recent reports show ExPEC isolates of same clonal group could be different for virulence genotypes, because acquisition of accessory virulence traits might be distinct evolutionary paths for strain-to-strain variation [8,9,32]. The virulence genotypes among APEC O1:K1 and O2:K1 strains showed slight differences (Table H in File S2), although the virulence for avian colisepticemia were similar ($P\geq 0.05$). Four APEC O2:K1 strains showed almost similar virulence genotypes, and *iucD* and *iroN* were absent in Fy26 and DE205B (Table H in File S2). For the virulence genotypes among three APEC O1:K1 strains, the two O1:K1 isolates (Jnd25 and CVCC249) in China did not harbor *ibeA* (GimA island) and

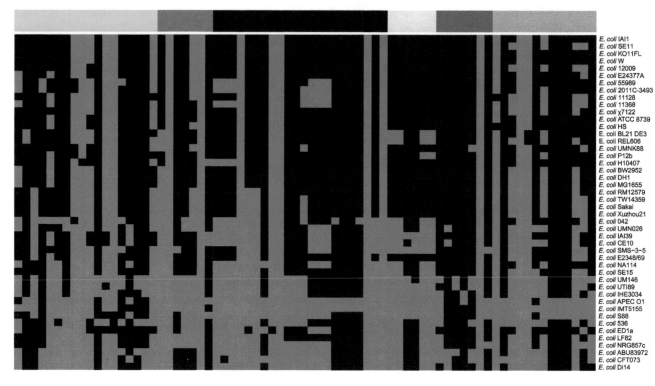

Figure 5. The distribution diagram of 10 sequenced B2 ExPEC pan-genome virulence genes among 46 *E. coli* strains. The uppermost row showed six classified clusters: 1, adhesins, green; 2, invasins, magenta; 3, iron acquisition/transport systems, blue; 4, polysialic acid synthesis, aquamarine; 5, toxins, purple; 6, others, darksalmon. Right side of the vertical line showed *E. coli* strains that were consistent with phylogenetic tree (Figure 1). The red and black body showed distribution of virulence genes among these strains. A red line meant that the virulence gene of interest was present at a particular strain, while a black line implied the gene was absent.

aatA genes (APEC autotransporter adhesion) compared to APEC O1. The results of ELA assay and chick colisepticemia model showed that Jnd2 was a low-pathogenicity isolate compared to APEC O1 (*P*<0.05), even though previous studies claimed that ST95 B2 strains exhibited enhanced ExPEC virulence [8,75]. There were significant differences between Jnd2 and APEC O1:K1/O2:K1 isolates that Jnd2 genomic did not harbor the typical T6SS1 (GI-7 for IMT5155), *vat*, and *ireA*, which are specifically required for survival and virulence during APEC infection [28,62,66,76] (Table H in File S2). In short, combined pathogenicity tests with comparative genomic analysis, we confirmed that APEC O1:K1 and O2:K1 strains, including IMT5155 and several strains isolated in China, are extraintestinal pathogenic variants for high pathogenicity during infecting avian hosts, which is consistent with previous studies [5,24,26–29,32].

Previous reports put forward the hypothesis that APEC strains have zoonotic potential [6,8,9], and it is confirmed that a subset of APEC ST95 serotype O18 isolates could cause systemic disease in chickens and murine models of human ExPEC-caused septicemia and meningitis [32]. Our comparative genomic analysis further showed that IMT5155 shared significant genetic overlap/similarities with APEC O1 and human ExPEC O18 strains (IHE3034, and UTI89), and O1:K1/O2:K1 strains are common among APEC isolates but which also found among human NMEC and septicemic isolates [6,9]. Certainly, APEC O1 is unable to cause bacteremia or meningitis in the neonatal rat model and keep host specificity by unknown mechanisms [28]. Here, we assessed the zoonotic potential of IMT5155 and the other O1:K1/O2:K1 isolates through two murine models of human ExPEC-caused septicemia and meningitis. For mouse sepsis assay, no mortalities

were observed among mouse intraperitoneally inoculated (approximately 10^7 CFU) with Jnd2, CVCC1531, APEC O1, CFT073, and MG1655 (Table 3) (the original data shown in File F in File S3). The data also showed that six APEC O1:K1/O2:K1 isolates (Jnd25, CVCC249, IMT5155, Fy26, DE164, and DE205B) and O78 strain CVCC1553 were not significantly different from the positive ExPEC reference strain RS218 (rate of mortality:100%)(*P*≥0.05) (Table 3), suggesting that those strains could have its ability to cause sepsis in the mouse through intraperitoneal inoculation. For rat neonatal meningitis assay, CVCC1531 and APEC strain jnd2 were unable to induce bacteremia in blood and CSF in neonatal rats (Table 4) (the original data shown in File G in File S3). The number of bacteria reisolated from the blood and CSF of rats infected with seven strains (Jnd25, CVCC249, IMT5155, Fy26, DE164, DE205B, and CVCC1553) were significantly higher than that of negative control (*P*<0.05) (Table 4). Moreover, IMT515 and five O1:K1/O2:K1 isolates in China showed comparable septicemia and meningitis in neonatal rats, since no significant differences in the blood and CSF counts were observed (*P*≥0.05). Our data demonstrated that IMT515 and five O1:K1/O2:K1 isolates were close to the high-level bacteremia in blood and CSF of RS218-inoculated neonatal rats, suggesting that these APEC O1:K1/O2:K1 isolates were able to cause septicemia and meningitis in neonatal rats. Like the subset of APEC ST95 serotype O18 isolates, our data confirmed that APEC O1:K1 and O2:K1 strains had zoonotic potential.

A subset of APEC ST23 serotype O78 isolates could be acknowledged as APEC-specific pathogens, because APEC O78 strains were clearly differentiated from serotypes O1, O2, and O18 by MLST, phylogroup, and virulence genotypes [9]. The

Table 1. Mortality rates among chick embryos infected with APEC strains.

Strain	Mortality rate[d]	P value vs[a]:	
		MG1655	APEC O1
Uninoculated	0/10	1.0	<0.001
PBS	1/10	0.416	<0.001
MG1655[b]	3/20		<0.001
IMT5155	17/20	<0.001	0.306
Fy26	19/20	<0.001	0.179
DE164	17/20	<0.001	0.306
DE205B	18/20	<0.001	0.271
Jnd25	17/20	<0.001	0.306
CVCC249	16/20	<0.001	0.276
Jnd2	6/20	0.162	<0.001
CVCC1553	16/20	<0.001	0.276
CVCC1531	4/20	0.296	<0.001
APEC O1[c]	25/30	<0.001	

[a]P value measured by Fisher's exact test.
[b]Negative control for the ELA.
[c]Positive control for the ELA.
[d]Data mean the number of dead embryos/total number of embryos tested.

APEC O78 strain χ7122 was used as a classic infection strain of APEC pathogenicity to identify O78-specific virulence genotype [12]. Comparative genomic analysis of IMT5155 with χ7122 was consistent with the description by Dziva et al. that χ7122 were distinct from APEC O1 and IMT5155, and close to human ST23 serotype O78 human ETEC strain [12]. We compared the virulence and zoonotic potential of APEC O78 strain CVCC1553 with ST23 intestinal pathogenic strain CVCC1531. Like APEC O1:K1 and O2:K1 isolates, CVCC1553 was categorized as being highly virulent for natural reservoir, and CVCC1531 was avirulent

in ELA and chick colisepticemia model (Table 1 and Table 2). Meanwhile, both CVCC1553 and χ7122 caused low pathogenicity in the neonatal meningitis mode compared to RS218 and APEC O1:K1/O2:K1 isolates (Table 4) [32]. As discussed by Dziva et al., χ7122 acquired a different virulence gene repertoire via variation in the accessory genome enabling success in avian species, including virulence-associated large plasmids [12]. The virulence genotype of CVCC1553 showed that it also contained the conserved regions of large virulence plasmids (Table H in File S2). Our investigation further confirmed that APEC O78 strains

Table 2. Lethality in 1-day-old chicks for intratracheal inoculation with APEC isolates.

strain	Mortality rate[cf]	Reisolation rate (air sacs)[df]	Reisolation rate (blood)[df]	Reisolation rate (brain)[df]	Mean lesion score[e]
PBS	0/10[f]	1/10[f]	0/10[f]	0/10[f]	0.1[f]
MG1655[a]	0/10	2/10	0/10	0/10	0.2
IMT5155	6/10	10/10	8/10	8/10	2.3
Fy26	6/10	10/10	9/10	7/10	2.5
DE164	5/10	9/10	9/10	7/10	2.3
DE205B	7/10	10/10	9/10	9/10	2.5
Jnd25	7/10	10/10	10/10	8/10	2.5
CVCC249	6/10	9/10	9/10	7/10	2.3
Jnd2	1/10[f]	5/10	3/10	0/10	0.9
CVCC1553	8/10	10/10	10/10	4/10	2.5
CVCC1531	0/10[f]	3/10[f]	0/10[f]	0/10[f]	0.3
APEC O1[b]	6/10	9/10	8/10	6/10	2.3

[a]Negative control for chick colisepticemia model.
[b]Positive control for chick colisepticemia model.
[c]Data mean the number of dead chicks/total number of chicks tested.
[d]Data mean the number of chicks from which the APEC strain was reisolated/total number of chicks tested.
[e]Mean of lesion scores (ranked from 0 to 3 due to occurrence of airsacculitis, pericarditis, and perihepatitis) for 10 chicks tested.
[f]Values are not significantly different ($P \geq 0.05$ by Fisher's exact test) with the negative control.

Table 3. Lethality of ICR mouse for intraperitoneal inoculation with APEC isolates and human ExPEC strains.

strain	Mortality rate[cf]	Reisolation rate (blood)[df]	Reisolation rate (brain)[df]	Mean lesion score[e]
PBS	0/10[f]	0/10[f]	0/10[f]	1.0[f]
MG1655[a]	0/10	0/10	0/10	1.0
IMT5155	10/10	10/10	10/10	5.0
Fy26	10/10	10/10	10/10	4.9
DE164	10/10	10/10	10/10	4.9
DE205B	10/10	10/10	10/10	5.0
Jnd25	9/10	9/10	9/10	4.7
CVCC249	10/10	10/10	10/10	4.9
Jnd2	0/10[f]	4/10	0/10[f]	1.1[f]
CVCC1553	10/10	10/10	7/10	5
CVCC1531	0/10[f]	0/10[f]	0/10[f]	1.0[f]
APEC O1	0/10[f]	7/10	0/10[f]	1.5[f]
RS218[b]	10/10	10/10	10/10	4.9
CFT073	0/10[f]	8/10	0/10[f]	1.5[f]

[a]Negative control for mouse sepsis model.
[b]Positive control for mouse sepsis model.
[c]Data mean the number of dead mouse/total number of mouse tested.
[d]Data mean the number of mouse from which the APEC/ExPEC strain was reisolated/total number of mouse tested.
[e]Mean of lesion scores (1 = healthy, 2 = minimally ill, 3 = moderately ill, 4 = severely ill, 5 = dead) for 10 mouse tested.
[f]Values are not significantly different ($P \geq 0.05$ by Fisher's exact test) with the negative control.

could act as avian host-specific extraintestinal pathogenic variant of ST23 lineage to adapt/colonize to extraintestinal specific niches and establish a specific infection by an intratracheal route in avian host.

Conclusions

The study presented here enriches our knowledge of IMT5155 and complements the *E. coli* genome data of O2 serotype and ST140 (ST complex 95). Our phylogeny analyses confirmed that IMT5155 was closest evolutionary relationship with APEC O1

Table 4. Pathogenicities of APEC isolates in the neonatal rat meningitis model.

Strain	Inoculum (log₁₀ CFU per animal)	Mortality rate[c]	Reisolation rate from blood of survivors[d]	Mean log₁₀ CFU ml⁻¹ (blood)[e]	Reisolation rate from CSF of survivors[d]	Mean log₁₀ CFU ml⁻¹ (CSF)[e]
PBS	0	0/12[f]	0/12[f]	0	0/12	0
MG1655[a]	2.36	0/12	0/12	0	0/12	0
IMT5155	2.33	1/12[f]	10/11	3.54	10/11	4.02
Fy26	2.34	0/12[f]	12/12	3.57	10/12	4.10
DE164	2.31	0/12[f]	12/12	3.41	11/12	3.95
DE205B	2.25	1/12[f]	10/11	3.51	10/11	4.18
Jnd25	2.35	1/12[f]	10/11	3.64	10/11	4.3
CVCC249	2.32	0/12[f]	12/12	3.50	12/12	4.16
Jnd2	2.32	0/12[f]	2/12[f]	3.17	0/12[f]	0
CVCC1553[f]	2.34	0/12[f]	7/12	2.85	7/12	3.51
CVCC1531	2.31	0/12[f]	0/12[f]	0	0/12[f]	0
APEC O1[a]	2.34	0/12[f]	0/12[f]	0	0/12[f]	0
RS218[b]	2.34	3/12	9/9	3.82	9/9	>4.57

[a]Negative control for the neonatal rat meningitis model.
[b]Positive control for the neonatal rat meningitis model.
[c]Data mean the number of dead rats/total number of rats tested.
[d]Data mean the number of rats from which the APEC/ExPEC strain was reisolated/total number of rat survivors.
[e]Mean number of *E. coli* isolates recovered from the blood and CSF of the rat survivors.
[f]Values are not significantly different ($P \geq 0.05$ by Fisher's exact test) with the negative control.

serotype and human ExPEC O18 serotype strains (APEC O1, IHE3034, and UTI89; ST complex 95), which all belonged to phylogroup B2 and ST complex 95. Comparison of IMT5155 genome with other *E. coli* strains facilitated the identification of APEC/ExPEC genetic characteristics. Our results of comparative genomics showed that APEC dominant O1 and O2 serotypes strains (APEC O1 and IMT5155) shared significant genetic overlap/similarities with human ExPEC dominant O18 strains (IHE3034, and UTI89). The unique PAI I_{5155} (GI-12) was identified and conserved in APEC O2 isolates, and GI-7 and GI-16 encoding two typical T6SSs might be useful markers for the identification of ExPEC dominant serotypes (O1, O2, and O18) strains. IMT5155 contained a ColV plasmid p1ColV$_{5155}$, and virulence genes in p1ColV$_{5155}$ also defined the APEC pathotype. The distribution of 10 sequenced B2 ExPEC pan-genome virulence factors among 47 sequenced *E. coli* provided a meaningful evidence for phylogroup B2 APEC/ExPEC-specific virulence factors, including several adhesins, invasins, toxins, iron acquisition systems, and others, which contributed to ExPEC to adapte/colonize extraintestinal specific niches during infection. The pathogenicity tests of IMT515 and other APEC O1:K1 and O2:K1 serotypes isolates in China through four animal models showed that they were high virulent for avian colisepticemia and able to cause septicemia and meningitis in neonatal rats, suggesting these APEC O1:K1 and O2:K1 isolates had zoonotic potential. Our comparative genomics studies and the pathogenicity tests will promote the investigation of APEC/ExPEC pathogenesis and zoonotic potential of APEC, and pave the way to development of strategies in their prevention and treatment.

Supporting Information

File S1 Figure A. Gene clusters of T6SS1 (GI-7) and T6SS2 (GI-16) in IMT5155 chromosome. Genes encoding conserved domain proteins were represented by the bule colors. And white arrows indicate other unknown proteins, which were not identified as part of the conserved core described by Ma et al. [65]. The flanking core genes were indicated by the black arrows. A) IMT5155 T6SS1 (GI-7); B) IMT5155 T6SS2 (GI-16). Figure B. Synteny analysis based on common ORFs between p1ColV$_{5155}$ and 5 plasmids (pAPEC-O1-ColBM, pAPEC-O2-ColV, pMAR2, pO8 3_CORR, and pUTI89). Grey ribbons are common ORFs in p1ColV5155 and pAPEC-O2-ColV; Pink ribbons are common

ORFs in p1ColV$_{5155}$ and pAPEC-O1-ColBM; Yellow ribbons are common ORFs in p1ColV5155 and pMAR2; Purple ribbons are common ORFs in p1ColV5155 and PO83-CORR; Green ribbons are common ORFs in p1ColV5155 and PUTI89. Red blocks are repA genes; Purple blocks are *repB* genes; Blue blocks are *Tra* genes.

File S2 Table A. General feature of IMT5155 genome and other *E. coli* strains. Table B. The virulence factors in B2 ExPEC pan-genome among 10 *E. coli* strains. Table C. The genomic islands of IMT5155. Table D. The information of 15 ExPEC isolates for simultaneous presence of T6SS1 and T6SS2. Table E. Common genes shared with IMT5155 for 15 *E. coli* strains. Table F. The number and percentage of common genes of other *E. coli* pathotype's plasmids shared with p1ColV$_{5155}$. Table G. The specific genes of IMT5155 relative to other 9 B2 ExPEC strains. Table H. The detail information of the 13 selected strains for pathogenicity testing.

File S3 File A. Detailed description for 47 *E. coli* genomes data. File B. The scripts for comparative genomic analysis. File C. Detailed description for annotated ORFs in the chromosome sequence of IMT5155. File D. Detailed description for annotated ORFs in p1ColV$_{5155}$. File E. The original data for chick colisepticemia assay. File F. The original data for mouse sepsis assay. File G. The original data for rat neonatal meningitis assay.

Acknowledgments

We gratefully acknowledge Lothar H. Wieler (Institute of Microbiology and Epizootics, Freie Universitaet BerlinBerlin, Germany) for the gift of IMT5155 strain. We acknowledge Qiang Li and his colleagues for genome sequencing and analysis at Shanghai Majorbio Bio-pharm Technology Co., Ltd.

Author Contributions

Conceived and designed the experiments: JJD XKZG ZHP. Performed the experiments: XKZG LH SHW HJW. Analyzed the data: XKZG JWJ FCL. Contributed reagents/materials/analysis tools: FCL HJF. Wrote the paper: XKZG. Designed the pathogenicity experiments: JJD XKZG.

References

1. Diard M, Garry L, Selva M, Mosser T, Denamur E (2010) Pathogenicity-associated islands in extraintestinal pathogenic *Escherichia coli* are fitness elements involved in intestinal colonization. J Bacteriol 192: 4885–4893.
2. Kaper JB, Nataro JP, Mobley HL (2004) Pathogenic *Escherichia coli*. Nat Rev Microbiol 2: 123–140.
3. Croxen MA, Finlay BB (2010) Molecular mechanisms of Escherichia coli pathogenicity. Nat Rev Microbiol 8: 26–38.
4. Russo TA, Johnson JR (2000) Proposal for a new inclusive designation for extraintestinal pathogenic isolates of *Escherichia coli*: ExPEC. J Infect Dis 181: 1753–1754.
5. Johnson TJ, Kariyawasam S, Wannemuehler Y, Mangiamele P, Johnson SJ (2007) The genome sequence of avian pathogenic *Escherichia coli* strain O1:K1:H7 shares strong similarities with human extraintestinal pathogenic *E. coli* genomes. J Bacteriol 189: 3228–3236.
6. Ewers C, Li G, Wilking H, Kiessling S, Alt K (2007) Avian pathogenic, uropathogenic, and newborn meningitis-causing *Escherichia coli*: how closely related are they? Int J Med Microbiol 297: 163–176.
7. Ron EZ (2006) Host specificity of septicemic *Escherichia coli*: human and avian pathogens. Curr Opin Microbiol 9: 28–32.
8. Johnson TJ, Wannemuehler Y, Johnson SJ, Stell AL, Doetkott C (2008) Comparison of extraintestinal pathogenic *Escherichia coli* strains from human and avian sources reveals a mixed subset representing potential zoonotic pathogens. Appl Environ Microbiol 74: 7043–7050.
9. Moulin-Schouleur M, Reperant M, Laurent S, Bree A, Mignon-Grasteau S (2007) Extraintestinal pathogenic *Escherichia coli* strains of avian and human

origin: link between phylogenetic relationships and common virulence patterns. J Clin Microbiol 45: 3366–3376.
10. Moulin-Schouleur M, Schouler C, Tailliez P, Kao MR, Bree A (2006) Common virulence factors and genetic relationships between O18:K1:H7 Escherichia coli isolates of human and avian origin. J Clin Microbiol 44: 3484–3492.
11. Brzuszkiewicz E, Bruggemann H, Liesegang H, Emmerth M, Olschlager T (2006) How to become a uropathogen: comparative genomic analysis of extraintestinal pathogenic *Escherichia coli* strains. Proc Natl Acad Sci U S A 103: 12879–12884.
12. Dziva F, Hauser H, Connor TR, van Diemen PM, Prescott G (2013) Sequencing and functional annotation of avian pathogenic *Escherichia coli* serogroup O78 strains reveal the evolution of E. coli lineages pathogenic for poultry via distinct mechanisms. Infect Immun 81: 838–849.
13. Gordon DM, Clermont O, Tolley H, Denamur E (2008) Assigning *Escherichia coli* strains to phylogenetic groups: multi-locus sequence typing versus the PCR triplex method. Environ Microbiol 10: 2484–2496.
14. Wirth T, Falush D, Lan R, Colles F, Mensa P (2006) Sex and virulence in *Escherichia coli*: an evolutionary perspective. Mol Microbiol 60: 1136–1151.
15. Clermont O, Bonacorsi S, Bingen E (2000) Rapid and simple determination of the *Escherichia coli* phylogenetic group. Appl Environ Microbiol 66: 4555–4558.
16. Boyd EF, Hartl DL (1998) Chromosomal regions specific to pathogenic isolates of *Escherichia coli* have a phylogenetically clustered distribution. J Bacteriol 180: 1159–1165.
17. Tenaillon O, Skurnik D, Picard B, Denamur E (2010) The population genetics of commensal *Escherichia coli*. Nat Rev Microbiol 8: 207–217.

18. Escobar-Paramo P, Clermont O, Blanc-Potard AB, Bui H, Le Bouguenec C (2004) A specific genetic background is required for acquisition and expression of virulence factors in *Escherichia coli*. Mol Biol Evol 21: 1085–1094.

19. Touchon M, Hoede C, Tenaillon O, Barbe V, Baeriswyl S (2009) Organised genome dynamics in the *Escherichia coli* species results in highly diverse adaptive paths. PLoS Genet 5: e1000344.

20. Picard B, Garcia JS, Gouriou S, Duriez P, Brahimi N (1999) The link between phylogeny and virulence in *Escherichia coli* extraintestinal infection. Infect Immun 67: 546–553.

21. Kaas RS, Friis C, Ussery DW, Aarestrup FM (2012) Estimating variation within the genes and inferring the phylogeny of 186 sequenced diverse *Escherichia coli* genomes. BMC Genomics 13: 577.

22. Maiden MC, Bygraves JA, Feil E, Morelli G, Russell JE (1998) Multilocus sequence typing: a portable approach to the identification of clones within populations of pathogenic microorganisms. Proc Natl Acad Sci U S A 95: 3140–3145.

23. Jaureguy F, Landraud L, Passet V, Diancourt L, Frapy E (2008) Phylogenetic and genomic diversity of human bacteremic *Escherichia coli* strains. BMC Genomics 9: 560.

24. Kohler CD, Dobrindt U (2011) What defines extraintestinal pathogenic *Escherichia coli*? Int J Med Microbiol 301: 642–647.

25. Tartof SY, Solberg OD, Manges AR, Riley LW (2005) Analysis of a uropathogenic *Escherichia coli* clonal group by multilocus sequence typing. J Clin Microbiol 43: 5860–5864.

26. McNally A, Cheng L, Harris SR, Corander J (2013) The evolutionary path to extraintestinal pathogenic, drug-resistant *Escherichia coli* is marked by drastic reduction in detectable recombination within the core genome. Genome Biol Evol 5: 699–710.

27. Mora A, Lopez C, Dabhi G, Blanco M, Blanco JE (2009) Extraintestinal pathogenic *Escherichia coli* O1:K1:H7/NM from human and avian origin: detection of clonal groups B2 ST95 and D ST59 with different host distribution. BMC Microbiol 9: 132.

28. Johnson TJ, Wannemuehler Y, Kariyawasam S, Johnson JR, Logue CM (2012) Prevalence of avian-pathogenic *Escherichia coli* strain O1 genomic islands among extraintestinal and commensal *E. coli* isolates. J Bacteriol 194: 2846–2853.

29. Rodriguez-Siek KE, Giddings CW, Doetkott C, Johnson TJ, Nolan LK (2005) Characterizing the APEC pathotype. Vet Res 36: 241–256.

30. Antao EM, Glodde S, Li G, Sharifi R, Homeier T (2008) The chicken as a natural model for extraintestinal infections caused by avian pathogenic *Escherichia coli* (APEC). Microb Pathog 45: 361–369.

31. Dho-Moulin M, Fairbrother JM (1999) Avian pathogenic *Escherichia coli* (APEC). Vet Res 30: 299–316.

32. Tivendale KA, Logue CM, Kariyawasam S, Jordan D, Hussein A (2010) Avian-pathogenic *Escherichia coli* strains are similar to neonatal meningitis *E. coli* strains and are able to cause meningitis in the rat model of human disease. Infect Immun 78: 3412–3419.

33. Dai J, Wang S, Guerlebeck D, Laturnus C, Guenther S (2010) Suppression subtractive hybridization identifies an autotransporter adhesin gene of *E. coli* IMT5155 specifically associated with avian pathogenic *Escherichia coli* (APEC). BMC Microbiol 10: 236.

34. Antao EM, Ewers C, Gurlebeck D, Preisinger R, Homeier T (2009) Signature-tagged mutagenesis in a chicken infection model leads to the identification of a novel avian pathogenic *Escherichia coli* fimbrial adhesin. PLoS One 4: e7796.

35. Li G, Laturnus C, Ewers C, Wieler LH (2005) Identification of genes required for avian *Escherichia coli* septicemia by signature-tagged mutagenesis. Infect Immun 73: 2818–2827.

36. Delcher AL, Bratke KA, Powers EC, Salzberg SL (2007) Identifying bacterial genes and endosymbiont DNA with Glimmer. Bioinformatics 23: 673–679.

37. Chen S, Zhang CY, Song K (2013) Recognizing short coding sequences of prokaryotic genome using a novel iteratively adaptive sparse partial least squares algorithm. Biol Direct 8: 23.

38. Altschul SF, Madden TL, Schaffer AA, Zhang J, Zhang Z (1997) Gapped BLAST and PSI-BLAST: a new generation of protein database search programs. Nucleic Acids Res 25: 3389–3402.

39. Kent WJ (2002) BLAT–the BLAST-like alignment tool. Genome Res 12: 656–664.

40. Edgar RC (2004) MUSCLE: multiple sequence alignment with high accuracy and high throughput. Nucleic Acids Res 32: 1792–1797.

41. Ronquist F, Huelsenbeck JP (2003) MrBayes 3: Bayesian phylogenetic inference under mixed models. Bioinformatics 19: 1572–1574.

42. Yoon SH, Park YK, Lee S, Choi D, Oh TK (2007) Towards pathogenomics: a web-based resource for pathogenicity islands. Nucleic Acids Res 35: D395–400.

43. Yoon SH, Hur CG, Kang HY, Kim YH, Oh TK (2005) A computational approach for identifying pathogenicity islands in prokaryotic genomes. BMC Bioinformatics 6: 184.

44. Chen L, Yang J, Yu J, Yao Z, Sun L (2005) VFDB: a reference database for bacterial virulence factors. Nucleic Acids Res 33: D325–328.

45. Zhuge X, Wang S, Fan H, Pan Z, Ren J (2013) Characterization and Functional Analysis of AatB, a Novel Autotransporter Adhesin and Virulence Factor of Avian Pathogenic *Escherichia coli*. Infect Immun.

46. Wang S, Niu C, Shi Z, Xia Y, Yaqoob M (2011) Effects of ibeA deletion on virulence and biofilm formation of avian pathogenic *Escherichia coli*. Infect Immun 79: 279–287.

47. Johnson TJ, Siek KE, Johnson SJ, Nolan LK (2006) DNA sequence of a ColV plasmid and prevalence of selected plasmid-encoded virulence genes among avian *Escherichia coli* strains. J Bacteriol 188: 745–758.

48. Johnson TJ, Johnson SJ, Nolan LK (2006) Complete DNA sequence of a ColBM plasmid from avian pathogenic *Escherichia coli* suggests that it evolved from closely related ColV virulence plasmids. J Bacteriol 188: 5975–5983.

49. Sims GE, Kim SH (2011) Whole-genome phylogeny of *Escherichia coli*/Shigella group by feature frequency profiles (FFPs). Proc Natl Acad Sci U S A 108: 8329–8334.

50. Sahl JW, Steinsland H, Redman JC, Angiuoli SV, Nataro JP (2011) A comparative genomic analysis of diverse clonal types of enterotoxigenic *Escherichia coli* reveals pathovar-specific conservation. Infect Immun 79: 950–960.

51. Logue CM, Doetkott C, Mangiamele P, Wannemuehler YM, Johnson TJ (2012) Genotypic and phenotypic traits that distinguish neonatal meningitis-associated *Escherichia coli* from fecal *E. coli* isolates of healthy human hosts. Appl Environ Microbiol 78: 5824–5830.

52. Gao Q, Wang X, Xu H, Xu Y, Ling J (2012) Roles of iron acquisition systems in virulence of extraintestinal pathogenic *Escherichia coli*: salmochelin and aerobactin contribute more to virulence than heme in a chicken infection model. BMC Microbiol 12: 143.

53. Wright KJ, Hultgren SJ (2006) Sticky fibers and uropathogenesis: bacterial adhesins in the urinary tract. Future Microbiol 1: 75–87.

54. Zhou Y, Tao J, Yu H, Ni J, Zeng L (2012) Hcp family proteins secreted via the type VI secretion system coordinately regulate *Escherichia coli* K1 interaction with human brain microvascular endothelial cells. Infect Immun 80: 1243–1251.

55. Wang S, Shi Z, Xia Y, Li H, Kou Y (2012) IbeB is involved in the invasion and pathogenicity of avian pathogenic *Escherichia coli*. Vet Microbiol 159: 411–419.

56. Schubert S, Picard B, Gouriou S, Heesemann J, Denamur E (2002) Yersinia high-pathogenicity island contributes to virulence in *Escherichia coli* causing extraintestinal infections. Infect Immun 70: 5335–5337.

57. Juhas M, van der Meer JR, Gaillard M, Harding RM, Hood DW (2009) Genomic islands: tools of bacterial horizontal gene transfer and evolution. FEMS Microbiol Rev 33: 376–393.

58. Bobay LM, Rocha EP, Touchon M (2013) The adaptation of temperate bacteriophages to their host genomes. Mol Biol Evol 30: 737–751.

59. Saha RP, Lou Z, Meng L, Harshey RM (2013) Transposable prophage Mu is organized as a stable chromosomal domain of *E. coli*. PLoS Genet 9: e1003902.

60. Harshey RM (2012) The Mu story: how a maverick phage moved the field forward. Mob DNA 3: 21.

61. Li G, Feng Y, Kariyawasam S, Tivendale KA, Wannemuehler Y (2010) AatA is a novel autotransporter and virulence factor of avian pathogenic *Escherichia coli*. Infect Immun 78: 898–906.

62. Russo TA, Carlino UB, Johnson JR (2001) Identification of a new iron-regulated virulence gene, ireA, in an extraintestinal pathogenic isolate of *Escherichia coli*. Infect Immun 69: 6209–6216.

63. Grim CJ, Kothary MH, Gopinath G, Jarvis KG, Beaubrun JJ (2012) Identification and characterization of Cronobacter iron acquisition systems. Appl Environ Microbiol 78: 6035–6050.

64. Shrivastava S, Mande SS (2008) Identification and functional characterization of gene components of Type VI Secretion system in bacterial genomes. PLoS One 3: e2955.

65. Ma J, Sun M, Bao Y, Pan Z, Zhang W (2013) Genetic diversity and features analysis of type VI secretion systems loci in avian pathogenic *Escherichia coli* by wide genomic scanning. Infect Genet Evol 20: 454–464.

66. de Pace F, Nakazato G, Pacheco A, de Paiva JB, Sperandio V (2010) The type VI secretion system plays a role in type 1 fimbria expression and pathogenesis of an avian pathogenic *Escherichia coli* strain. Infect Immun 78: 4990–4998.

67. Kyle JL, Cummings CA, Parker CT, Quinones B, Vatta P (2012) *Escherichia coli* serotype O55:H7 diversity supports parallel acquisition of bacteriophage at Shiga toxin phage insertion sites during evolution of the O157:H7 lineage. J Bacteriol 194: 1885–1896.

68. Eppinger M, Mammel MK, Leclerc JE, Ravel J, Cebula TA (2011) Genomic anatomy of *Escherichia coli* O157:H7 outbreaks. Proc Natl Acad Sci U S A 108: 20142–20147.

69. Böhnke U (2010) Charakterisierung und Bedeutung der Plasmide p1ColV 5155 und p2 5155 für den aviären pathogenen *E. coli*-Stamm IMT5155. Dissertation, Humboldt-Universität zu Berlin, Faculty of Mathematics and Natural Sciences.

70. Johnson TJ, Jordan D, Kariyawasam S, Stell AL, Bell NP (2010) Sequence analysis and characterization of a transferable hybrid plasmid encoding multidrug resistance and enabling zoonotic potential for extraintestinal *Escherichia coli*. Infect Immun 78: 1931–1942.

71. Mellata M, Ameiss K, Mo H, Curtiss R 3rd (2010) Characterization of the contribution to virulence of three large plasmids of avian pathogenic *Escherichia coli* chi7122 (O78:K80:H9). Infect Immun 78: 1528–1541.

72. Tivendale KA, Noormohammadi AH, Allen JL, Browning GF (2009) The conserved portion of the putative virulence region contributes to virulence of avian pathogenic *Escherichia coli*. Microbiology 155: 450–460.

73. Willems RJ, Top J, van Schaik W, Leavis H, Bonten M (2012) Restricted gene flow among hospital subpopulations of Enterococcus faecium. MBio 3: e00151–00112.

74. Rodriguez-Siek KE, Giddings CW, Doetkott C, Johnson TJ, Fakhr MK (2005) Comparison of *Escherichia coli* isolates implicated in human urinary tract infection and avian colibacillosis. Microbiology 151: 2097–2110.

75. Johnson JR, Clermont O, Menard M, Kuskowski MA, Picard B (2006) Experimental mouse lethality of *Escherichia coli* isolates, in relation to accessory traits, phylogenetic group, and ecological source. J Infect Dis 194: 1141–1150.

76. Salvadori MR, Yano T, Carvalho HE, Parreira VR, Gyles CL (2001) Vacuolating cytotoxin produced by avian pathogenic Escherichia coli. Avian Dis 45: 43–51.

11

Distinct Strains of *Toxoplasma gondii* Feature Divergent Transcriptomes Regardless of Developmental Stage

Matthew McKnight Croken[1], **Yanfen Ma**[2], **Lye Meng Markillie**[3], **Ronald C. Taylor**[4], **Galya Orr**[3], **Louis M. Weiss**[2,5]*, **Kami Kim**[1,2,5]*

1 Department of Microbiology and Immunology, Albert Einstein College of Medicine, Bronx, New York, United States of America, **2** Department of Pathology, Albert Einstein College of Medicine, Bronx, New York, United States of America, **3** Environmental Molecular Sciences Laboratory, Pacific Northwest National Laboratory, Richland, Washington, United States of America, **4** Computational Biology and Bioinformatics Group, Biological Sciences Division, Pacific Northwest National Laboratory, Richland, Washington, United States of America, **5** Department of Medicine, Albert Einstein College of Medicine, Bronx, New York, United States of America

Abstract

Using high through-put RNA sequencing, we assayed the transcriptomes of three different strains of *Toxoplasma gondii* representing three common genotypes under both *in vitro* tachyzoite and *in vitro* bradyzoite-inducing alkaline stress culture conditions. Strikingly, the differences in transcriptional profiles between the strains, RH, PLK, and CTG, is much greater than differences between tachyzoites and alkaline stressed *in vitro* bradyzoites. With an FDR of 10%, we identified 241 genes differentially expressed between CTG tachyzoites and *in vitro* bradyzoites, including 5 putative AP2 transcription factors. We also observed a close association between cell cycle regulated genes and differentiation. By Gene Set Enrichment Analysis (GSEA), there are a number of KEGG pathways associated with the *in vitro* bradyzoite transcriptomes of PLK and CTG, including pyrimidine metabolism and DNA replication. These functions are likely associated with cell-cycle arrest. When comparing mRNA levels between strains, we identified 1,526 genes that were differentially expressed regardless of culture-condition as well as 846 differentially expressed only in bradyzoites and 542 differentially expressed only in tachyzoites between at least two strains. Using GSEA, we identified that ribosomal proteins were expressed at significantly higher levels in the CTG strain than in either the RH or PLK strains. This association holds true regardless of life cycle stage.

Editor: Laura J. Knoll, University of Wisconsin Medical School, United States of America

Funding: Research was supported by National Institutes of Health (NIH) grants AI095094 (LMW), AI087625 (KK), and by grant 40070 (LMW) from Environmental Molecular Sciences Laboratory (EMSL) Pacific Northwest National Laboratory. MMC was supported by the Training Program in Cellular and Molecular Biology and Genetics, funded by NIH T32 GM007491 awarded to the Albert Einstein College of Medicine. A portion of the research was performed using EMSL, a national scientific user facility sponsored by the Department of Energy's Office of Biological and Environmental Research and located at Pacific Northwest National Lab. This work was also supported in part by the Center for AIDS Research at the Albert Einstein College of Medicine and Montefiore Medical Center funded by the National Institutes of Health (NIH AI-051519). The funders had no role in study design, data collection and analysis, decision to publish, or preparation of the manuscript.

Competing Interests: The authors have declared that no competing interests exist.

* Email: louis.weiss@einstein.yu.edu (LMW); kami.kim@einstein.yu.edu (KK)

Introduction

Toxoplasma gondii is an obligate intracellular parasite belonging to the phylum Apicomplexa. It has a complicated life cycle marked by sexual reproduction in the gastrointestinal tract of a feline host and asexual replication in any warm-blooded animal [1]. The asexual cycle itself is divided into a fast-growing tachyzoite stage and slow-growing bradyzoite stage. The bradyzoite form is thought to persist indefinitely within infected hosts within cysts and can reactivate if a host's immune function wanes. The ability to shift between acute and chronic phases of its life cycle is critical for disease pathogenesis and thus the subject of intense investigation [1].

One mark of the success of *Toxoplasma gondii* is its global distribution. It is estimated to infect around 30% of the human population. The parasite is transmitted through water contaminated with cat feces as well as being clonally propagated from animal to animal via carnivorism. The transmission strategies of *T.*

gondii has led to a complex structure of populations within the species. Fourteen different haplogroups have been identified around the world with each lineage containing multiple distinct strains [2]. Research has focused on parasites belonging to groups 1, 2, and 3 (also designated types I, II, and III) isolated in North America and Europe. Although these parasites diverged relatively recently (~10 kya) [33], they are marked by distinct differences in phenotype, most prominently virulence. Type I tachyzoites are less able to convert to bradyzoites, thereby causing acute disease in their hosts [34]. Type III strains readily differentiate causing their hosts to become chronically infected, but these strains are infrequently associated with clinical disease in humans [34]. Type II strains tend to be intermediate to types I and III in terms of differentiation competence and virulence [34]. Despite significant differences in phenotypes, there appears to be very little difference in genome sequence [3]. Forward genetics studies have attributed most of the difference in virulence to the ROP18 and ROP5 loci [4] [5] [6].

Few studies currently exist describing the differences among the transcriptomes of *T. gondii* lineages and how these transcriptomes change following differentiation from tachyzoite to bradyzoite [25]. What studies do exist are often stymied by lack of gene annotation. Roughly half of *T. gondii* genes are described only as "hypothetical proteins". Gene Set Enrichment Analysis (GSEA) is a software tool designed to test whether functionally related sets of genes are collectively up or down regulated between experimental conditions [7].

It has been shown that *T. gondii*, like other Apicomplexa, exerts tight control over gene expression [8], but little is known about the effectors that make this control possible. In 2005, a family of genes containing the AP2 DNA-binding domain were identified in the phylum Apicomplexa [9]. Follow up work found 68 AP2 genes in *T. gondii* [10]. Members of this family regulate important life cycle developments in *Plasmodium* [11] [12] [13] [14] and *Toxoplasma* [15]. As many more of these genes are expected to be key transcription factors, observed differences in AP2 expression levels between strains and across life cycle development are of keen importance.

Results and Discussion

Inter-strain differences in gene expression much larger than those between tachyzoites and bradyzoites

We analyzed steady state mRNA levels from three different strains of *T. gondii*, RH (Type I, the most common laboratory strain), PLK (Type II, a clone of ME49 the genome reference strain), and CTG (Type III). We grew each strain under both "normal" tachyzoite tissue culture (pH 7, 5% CO_2) conditions as well as bradyzoite-cyst inducing stress conditions (pH 8, low CO_2), resulting in six total groups. Each condition was sampled in three biological replicates at a single time point. We had expected that this simple experimental design would yield groups of genes linked to the stress response, but the most striking observation is that the genes' steady state RNA levels vary much more between strains than between different stages of their life cycles. Figure 1B illustrates multi-dimensional scaling (MDS) of samples by condition, based on the top five hundred most divergent genes between each condition. The conditions cluster first by strain and then by life cycle stage. While tachyzoites and bradyzoites from different strains have many functional similarities, these results reinforce the divergence of gene expression of these parasites despite relatively modest differences in genome sequence.

The MDS plot only examines those genes with the most divergent expression levels. We also examined differences between conditions for all genes. First, we computed the differences in gene expression between tachyzoites and bradyzoites for each strain (three comparisons). We then examined differences between strains for both tachyzoites and bradyzoites (six more comparisons). The results are illustrated in Figure 1C. For all nine comparisons, the median and the interquartile ranges change very little and remain relatively close to zero. The mRNA levels of the majority of genes are not widely different between the strains and life cycle stage. To measure the total amount of change between compared groups, we calculate the root mean square difference (RMSD) for each of the nine comparisons. The RMSD values, plotted as blue crosses on Figure 1C, are much greater for the inter-strain comparisons than for the alkaline stressed/CO_2 starved parasites of the same strain. This supports the observations shown in Figure 1B and further suggests that variation between the groups is driven by relatively small subsets of genes.

Comparisons between transcriptomes of tachyzoites and in vitro bradyzoites of the same strain are consistent with what is known about the propensity of each of these strains to differentiate. Type III (CTG) parasites readily switch from tachyzoite to bradyzoite and showed the greatest change in mRNA steady state levels, whereas Type I (RH) parasites fail to differentiate under these stress conditions and likewise showed almost no difference in mRNA between tachyzoite and bradyzoite conditions. Type II (PLK) parasites are intermediate to types I and III both in terms of differentiation competence as well as overall changes in its transcriptome. This is an important proof of principle that this type of global transcriptomic analysis does correlate with actual biological states of the parasite.

Strain specific expression differences

Globally, we see a much greater difference between the transcriptomes of different strains than we do between stressed and unstressed parasites of the same strain (Figures 1B and 1C). To identify which genes are expressed differently between strains, we used edgeR. We compared each strain against the other two under both tachyzoite (unstressed) and bradyzoite (stressed) conditions (FDR 10%). This created six lists of differentially expressed genes that are differentially expressed between strains in either tachyzoites or bradyzoites as well those genes that were differentially expressed in both stages (Figure 2A). The number in the center of the diagram represents the number of genes differentially expressed between all three strains. A full gene list is in Table S2. Genes in the outer intersections differed in only one strain and those not falling into any intersection are cases where the expression level is different between two strains, but the strain's expression level was not significantly different. It is important to note that the number differentially expressed genes between any two strains is always equal to or larger than number of genes affected by differentiation.

If differential gene expression has indeed played an important in the evolution of *T. gondii* lineages, then regulators of transcription are likely candidates as drivers of evolution. Therefore, we examined whether AP2 genes are differentially expressed between strains. mRNA of seven AP2 differed in tachyzoites and mRNA levels of twenty- four AP2 differed among the bradyzoite transcriptomes. Five AP2 genes are differentially expressed between strains regardless of developmental stage. The AP2 genes that are differentially expressed in at least two comparisons are shown in Figure 2A and a full list is available in the Supplementary tables.

Steady state mRNA levels of AP2III-1 are significantly higher in PLK parasites than in either RH or CTG. It is a defining feature of the PLK strain regardless of developmental stage. Compared to PLK and CTG, expression of AP2VIIa-7 is lower in CTG tachyzoites, while expression of AP2IV-2 is higher. In CTG bradyzoites, expression of AP2X-10 and AP2XI-1 is lower than the other strains. RH tachyzoites express AP2IX-9 mRNA at significantly higher levels than either of the other strains examined. This is consistent with this transcription factors' reported role as a repressor of bradyzoite commitment [15], but differs from the pattern of expression initially reported. This difference may reflect that in our study parasites were predominantly the more stressed extracellular forms, in contrast to the intracellular parasites characterized previously. One can hypothesize that high levels of AP2IX-9 contributes to the parasite's ability to withstand stress and its inability to differentiate. Ten AP2 genes are differentially expressed in RH under stress conditions. This may reflect that RH does not differentiate into bradyzoites.

Expression of a number of AP2 genes in our study differs from previous reports that have compared AP2 expression in different strains. Some of these differences may be due to technical reasons

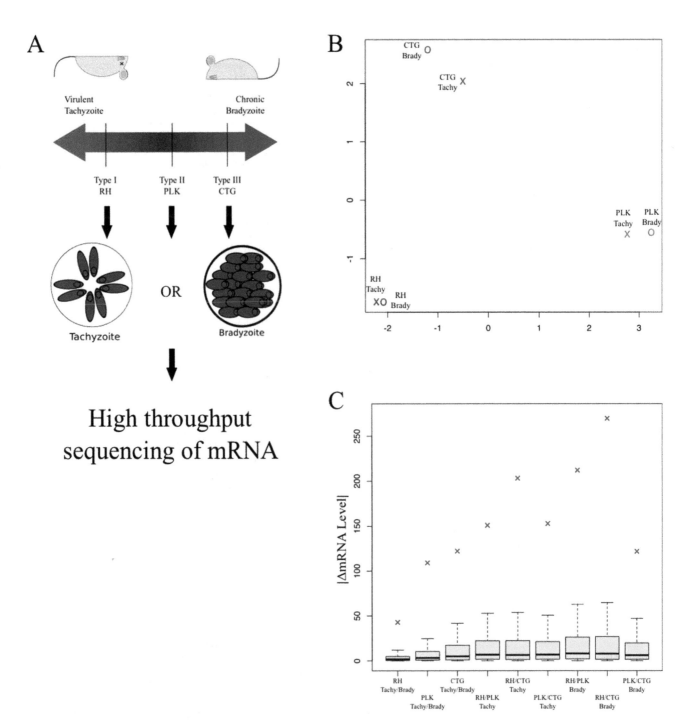

Figure 1. Patterns of gene expression vary more by strain than by developmental stage. A) A representative strain from *T. gondii* lineages Types I (RH), II (PLK), and III (CTG) was selected and grown in tissue culture in either pH neutral conditions, conducive to tachyzoite growth or alkaline conditions, inducing bradyzoite differentiation. B) Multi-dimensional scaling (MDS) plot based on pairwise comparisons for each of the six experimental conditions. This is calculated as the root mean square deviation for the 500 most differentially expressed genes between any two conditions. The distance between any two points represents the average difference in expression levels (RPKM) of the most dissimilar genes, relative to differences observed between other conditions. In effect, the MDS plot provides an overview of the total amount of variation between samples. The axes show arbitrary distances. Experimental conditions include parasite strain (red = RH, green = PLK, blue = CTG) and by life cycle stage (X = tachyzoite, O = bradyzoite). Distances calculated using the 'plotMDS' function in the 'limma' Bioconductor package [30]. C) Boxplot represents absolute value of expression level difference between conditions. Interquartile regions are in gold, median differences are plotted as a solid black line. The root mean square deviation for each comparison is represented as a blue cross. From left to right, the first three groups are the intrastrain comparisons, tachyzoite vs. bradyzoite. The next three groups are interstrain comparisons between tachyzoite (unstressed) groups. The final three are are interstrain comparisons between bradyzoite (alkaline-stressed) groups.

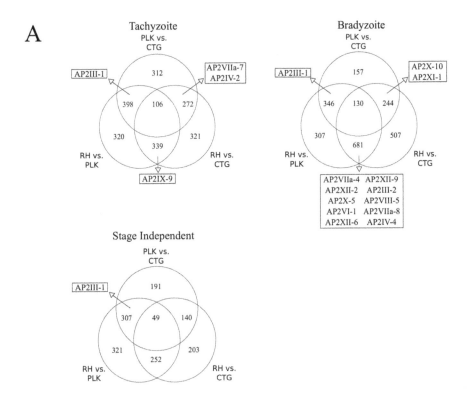

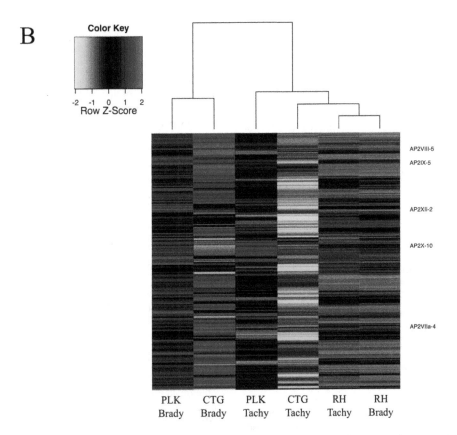

Figure 2. Hundreds of genes differentially expressed between strains including potential AP2 regulators. A) Using edgeR, we identify genes that are differentially expressed between strains (FDR <10%), generating three gene lists for tachyzoite condition and three for the bradyzoite condition. We generated Venn diagrams showing the overlap between the lists in the tachyzoite condition and bradyzoite condition. We also compared tachyzoite and bradyzoite gene lists to each other. Venn diagrams shows comparison of genes that appear in both the tachyzoite and the bradyzoite lists and therefore are "stage independent". AP2 containing genes appearing on more than one list (any intersection) are indicated. The

complete set of genes that are differentially expressed are listed in Table S2 and RPKM values for all replicates are listed in Table S1. B) Heat map of genes differentially expressed following CTG bradyzoite differentiation in all six conditions. Red indicates up regulation compared to that gene's expression level under other conditions, whereas green indicates down regulation. Conditions (columns) are clustered based on similarity of expression levels. The five AP2 genes that are differentially expressed are indicated on the right. Heat map was generated using the 'heatmap.2' function in the 'gplots' package for R. Hierarchical clustering of both the rows (genes) and columns (conditions) computed by the 'hclust' function in the R 'stats' package. Based on mean of replicate RPKM values.

such as inaccurate gene models that resulted in incorrect hybridization probes. Other differences are likely due to differences in experimental conditions. As proposed in earlier studies [16] and confirmed by GSEA analysis [22], extracellular tachyzoites represent an intermediate cell cycle arrested state with upregulation of stress-response genes that may be amongst the first that are induced during bradyzoite formation.

If experimental evidence supports the hypothesized role of AP2 genes as bona fide transcription factors, then the genes which they regulate are likely critical in determining phenotypic differences between strains. Differences in expression of AP2 in extracellular vs intracellular parasites may reflect expression differences seen in different biological states.

Genes and genes pathways associated with *in vitro* stage differentiation

Using the edgeR package from the Bioconductor project, we identified 241 genes that were differentially expressed between CTG tachyzoites and bradyzoites with a false discovery rate (FDR) of 10%. Figure 2B is a heatmap of these genes across all six groups. Both PLK and CTG showed differential expression of these genes, whereas RH parasites are largely insensitive to alkaline stress treatment. Notably, only 33 of the 241 genes (13.7%) are down-regulated in the CTG bradyzoites.

Of the 241 genes related to CTG differentiation identified, there are five genes that are predicted to have an AP2 DNA binding domain [10]. AP2VIIa-4, AP2VIII-5, AP2IX-5, and AP2XII-2 are all up-regulated after 72 hours of *in vitro* bradyzoite conditions, while AP2X-10 is down-regulated. Members of this family have been shown to regulate transcription in malarial parasites, including differentiation to gametocytes [11] [12] [13]. One possibility is that these AP2 transcription factors are important for long-term maintenance of tissue cysts, either promoting the expression of bradyzoite-specific factors or repressing tachyzoite differentiation. Alternatively, these may be only transiently expressed during differentiation, and their temporal expression may reflect a cascade of events that occurs during developmental transitions. Some of the AP2 previously reported to be induced in bradyzoites [22] [23] were down-regulated in stressed CTG, supporting this hypothesis (Table S3). The expression of AP2VIIa-4 and AP2XII-2 are both linked to the cell cycle [8]. Given the associated between cell cycle and differentiation [24], it is not surprising that putative cell cycle transcription factors are differentially expressed following differentiation.

Examining individual genes can be a useful method of analyzing expression data. Understanding how many genes are affected and how much their expression changes provides an important global overview of the transcriptome under different conditions. This type of analysis also provides an unbiased way testing whether particular genes of interest are differentially expressed. In this case, we identified five potential transcription factors belonging to the family AP2. This association is intriguing and suggests a series of genetics experiments that could test if these factors contribute to *in vitro* cyst formation and maintenance.

There are, however, limits to a gene-by-gene analysis. For instance, we were unable to detect differentially expressed genes in either of the RH or PLK strains. RH is a type I parasite and therefore known to be resistant to stress-induced differentiation, but the PLK strain belongs to the type II lineage and is competent to differentiate. Although many of the genes differentially expressed in CTG had a similar pattern of expression PLK, the difference in expression was too low or the variance between replicates too high to achieve statistical significance. The number of required replicates to conclusively discriminate consistent differences is often prohibitively high. In addition, since analyses of this kind involve testing several thousand hypotheses, managing false positive inferences very often makes it impossible to distinguish signal from noise.

Using GSEA, we compared the expression data to a set of genes shown to be differentially expressed after Compound 1 induced differentiation [22]. As Figure 3 shows, we are able to characterize both CTG and PLK, but not RH, as strongly enriched for bradyzoite genes. CTG has quantifiably more enrichment with a normalized enrichment score (NES) of 2.5 (p = 0.000) than PLK with an NES of 1.7 (p = 0.001). This is consistent with a continuum of differentiation competence with the type I lineage very resistant to bradyzoite development, type III differentiating readily, and type II parasites falling somewhere in the middle. Interestingly, the enrichment plot for RH (fig. 3B) is actually shaped like those of PLK, CTG (figs. 3C & 3D), even though the enrichment in RH is not statistically significant. This is consistent with data from other groups that indicates that RH is able to induce many of the stress-associated genes linked with bradyzoite differentiation, but is not able to complete the developmental transition.

Strain specific metabolic differences

Presently, sequence homology is the primary method of predicting gene function. This poses a difficult problem for divergent eukaryotes like *T. gondii*, where approximately half of protein coding genes remain unannotated. The Kyoto Encyclopedia of Genes and Geneomes (KEGG) curates a collection of molecular pathways [17]. To begin parsing out the biological meaning of many differences in transcriptomes between the strains we used Gene Set Enrichment Analysis (GSEA) software [7] a tool that examines expression data holistically using "functionally related gene sets", rather than testing genes individually. 33 KEGG pathways have been identified in *Toxoplasma* and are an appropriate size for use with GSEA. Tables 1 and 2 summarize the significant results for the interstrain comparisons in tachyzoites and bradyzoites, respectively.

We find very few KEGG pathways enriched in any of the examined conditions. The most prominent result from this analysis is the much higher expression level of ribosomal proteins in CTG. In the absence of other stress, depletion of ribosomal protein RPS13 has been shown to arrest the cell cycle and induce BAG1 expression, but the parasites do not form a mature cyst wall, suggesting a state of partial differentiation [18]. It is not immediately clear why CTG expresses more ribosome components, but translational regulation has been linked to both the stress response and bradyzoite differentiation in *T. gondii* [19].

A

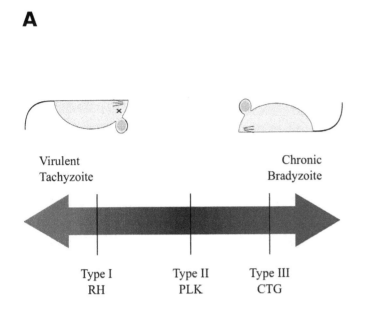

Virulent
Tachyzoite

Chronic
Bradyzoite

Type I
RH

Type II
PLK

Type III
CTG

B

RH

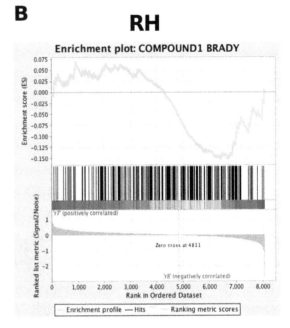

Normalized Enrichment Score: 0.55
P value: 0.996

C

PLK

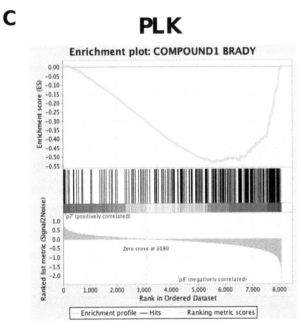

Normalized Enrichment Score: 1.70
P value: 0.001

D

CTG

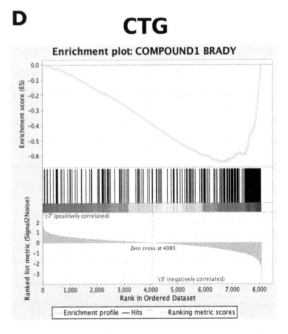

Normalized Enrichment Score: 2.52
P value: 0.000

Figure 3. GSEA detects bradyzoite-induced genes in PLK and CTG, but not RH parasites. (A) A schematic of strain virulence of the strains used as a function of ability to differentiate into bradyzoites. (B) GSEA enrichment plot for RH parasites under differentiation conditions compared to compound1 induced genes. Position of black bars indicate ranking of compound 1 genes relative to all other genes. Green line represents strength of enrichment under bradyzoite conditions (right) or tachyzoite conditions (left). (C) Enrichment plot for PLK parasites under differentiation conditions compared to compound 1 induced genes. (D) Enrichment plot for CTG parasites under differentiation conditions compared to compound 1 induced genes.

Table 1. Differential expression of KEGG pathways between strains in the tachyzoite stage.

RH vs. PLK		RH vs. CTG		PLK vs. CTG	
RH	PLK	RH	CTG	PLK	CTG
			TGO03010: Ribosome		TGO03010: Ribosome
			TGO03008: Ribosome Biogenesis in Eukaryote		TGO03013: RNA Transport
			TGO03040: Spliceosome		TGO03008: Ribosome Biogenesis in Eukaryote
			TGO03013: RNA Transport		TGO03020: RNA Polymerase

Thorough annotation of the *Toxoplasma* gene pathways will likely yield more insights into the biological processes underlying the divergence of the strains. The Liverpool Library of Apicomplexan Metabolic Pathways (LAMP) is one such thorough annotation and a promising starting point to address strain-specific differences [20]. However, by GSEA, we were unable to detect enrichment of any LAMP pathway (data not shown). The pathways we tested may not be expressed differently between strains, or the small size of the pathways may contribute to false negative results.

It is possible that despite the large differences in expression we observed between strains, there are not significant changes in the overall biological processes of the parasite between tachyzoites and bradyzoites. Recently Behnke showed that by principal components analysis, the transcriptomes of tachyzoites and bradyzoites group closely when compared to the transcriptomes of merozoite sexual stages harvested from cat intestines or the transcriptome of oocysts [21]. These findings speak to the importance of pathway analysis and global analysis over more traditional gene-by-gene testing.

Differentiation influences the cell cycle

By examining DNA content, it has been shown that cell cycle arrest accompanies bradyzoite differentiation [24]. More recent work has identified two large sets of cell cycle regulated genes, with one set corresponding to the G_1 phase and the other related to genes involved in S-phase and mitosis (S/M) [8]. To test how these cell cycle genes are affected by differentiation stress, we plotted the difference of each gene's expression level between tachyzoite conditions and bradyzoite-inducing stress conditions for each of the three parasite strains.

In keeping with the existing model, Figure 4A shows that S/M genes are more highly expressed in bradyzoite populations while G_1 genes are more closely associated with tachyzoites. In bradyzoite differentiated parasites, there is an up regulation of

S/M associated genes, while tachyzoites have higher steady state expression levels of G_1-linked genes. The mean difference of each group (red cross) also illustrates these relationships. Further, there is again a clear difference in how each strain is affected by stress (significant difference of means by ANOVA). The cell cycle genes of RH are relatively unaffected by differentiation stress, while PLK experiences significant changes in expression of these genes and CTG more so. These data underscore the fundamental link between cell cycle regulation and life cycle advancement.

In the present model, the "switch" between tachyzoite and bradyzoite occurs in the late S phase [25]. This fits with the observed changes in gene expression, since not every cell cycle regulated gene is influenced the same way following differentiation stress. In Figure 4A, we show that the mean expression values change proportionate to each strain's ability to differentiate, but so does the variance. Not only are many of these gene unaffected by stress, but many of their expression values change in the "wrong" direction, with S/M annotated genes being up regulated in tachyzoites and G_1 genes up regulated in bradyzoites.

To understand more precisely how bradyzoite development affects expression of cell cycle genes, we again employed GSEA. This time, we assigned cell-cycle genes into gene sets based on their peak time of expression [26]. In figure 4B, PLK and CTG bradyzoites show clear enrichment of multiple S phase gene sets, while tachyzoites are enriched for G_1 gene sets with peak expression between hours four and six. Interestingly, many later G_1 gene sets are actually associated with bradyzoites. In this analysis, we also find that the RH cell cycle is affected by the stress conditions, but to a much lesser extent than PLK or CTG.

The cell cycle transcriptome is temporally linked with differentiation stress. Using GSEA, we are able to identify specific cell cycle genes, grouped by time of peak expression, that are linked with bradyzoites or tachyzoites. Once again, the continuum of virulence (Figure 3) is observable. Both the number of the gene sets enriched and the magnitude of the enrichment is great in

Table 2. Differential expression of KEGG pathways between strains in treated with alkaline stress bradyzoite induction conditions.

RH vs. PLK		RH vs. CTG		PLK vs. CTG	
RH	PLK	RH	CTG	PLK	CTG
	TGO03030: DNA Replication		TGO03010: Ribosome		TGO03010: Ribosome
			TGO03008: Ribosome Biogenesis in Eukaryotes		TGO03008: Ribosome Biogenesis in Eukaryotes
			TGO03030: DNA Replication		TGO03013: RNA Transport
			TGO00240: Pyrimidine Metabolism		TGO00240: Pyrimidine Metabolism
					TGO03020: RNA Polymerase
					TGO03050: Proteasome

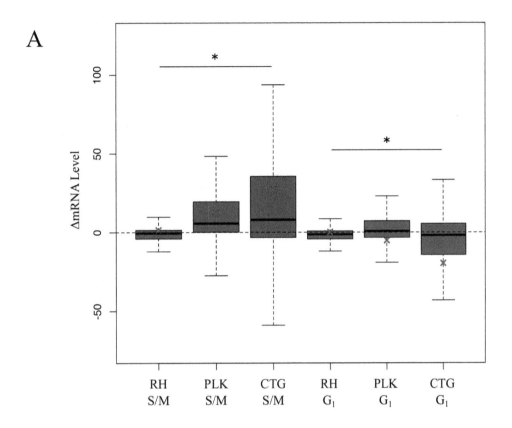

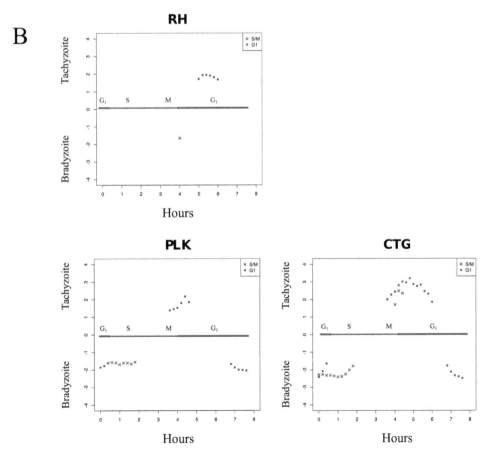

Figure 4. Expression of cell-cycle genes altered during differentiation. A) Boxplot represents differences in expression levels of cell cycle-dependent genes following differentiation conditions. Green boxes represent changes in S/M gene expression, blue boxes represent changes in G_1 gene expression. A positive difference indicates up regulation of the gene in tachyzoite conditions, while a negative difference in expression values indicates greater expression in the alkaline stress induced bradyzoites. The black bar indicates median value; the red cross indicates mean value. Significance tested by one-way ANOVA. A star (*) indicates: $p < 0.001$. B) Cell cycle genes are annotated as either G_1 or S/M [8]. We then sorted genes into groups based on time of peak expression. Each of these gene sets was tested by GSEA [26]. Gene sets with significant (FWER-p value <0.05) normalized enrichment scores (NES) are plotted. Positive scores indicate association with the unstressed (tachyzoite) condition, negative scores indicate association with the stress (bradyzoite) condition. Blue and green bar across middle of plots represent an eight hour RH tachyzoite cell cycle. Counter-clockwise from the top, the plots show cell cycle gene sets influenced following RH differentiation, cell cycle gene sets influenced following PLK differentiation, cell cycle gene sets influenced following CTG differentiation. Note that time of expression is based on the RH cell cycle as defined, which is shorter than that of either PLK or CTG.

CTG than PLK. What is most interesting is that the cell cycle of RH parasites does appear to affected by differentiation stress, albeit to a much lesser extent than either of the other two strains. This was the only indication that RH parasites reacted to the alkaline stress conditions and probably speaks to the fact that disruption of the cell cycle precedes the bradyzoite developmental switch.

Conclusions

In summary our integrative analysis of RNA-seq points to strain specific differences in gene expression that are more prominent than changes in gene expression associated with exposure to alkaline stress. The comparison of strains with different virulence phenotypes and capacity to differentiation using various tools has enabled us to identify pathways and genes that may be conserved between strains as well as those that regulate strain-specific traits.

Materials and Methods

This work did not involve human subject or animal research. All procedures were approved by the appropriate biosafety committees at the Albert Einstein College of Medicine.

Parasite culture

Human foreskin fibroblasts (HFF) cells grown in eight 150 mm tissue culture plates were infected with RH (type I), PLK (type II), and CTG (type III) strain in regular medium (pH 7 DMEM with 10% fetal bovine serum, incubated in 5% CO_2). The uninvaded RH free parasites were removed 2 hours after inoculation while the CTG and PLK strain free parasites were removed 4 hours later by washing with PBS. Inoculation medium was and then replaced with regular medium (pH 7, 5% CO_2) or differentiation medium (pH 8.1 DMEM with 5% fetal bovine serum, 10 mM HEPES, incubated in 0.5% CO_2). Thethe RH infection duration was two days while CTG and PLK strain were three days. Tachyzoite preparations were a mix of freshly lysed extracellular parasites and mature vacuoles on the verge of lysis as were alkaline-shocked RH strain. Afterwards, cells were harvested, passed through 27G needle twice to lyse HFF cells and filtered through 3 μm pore polycarbonate membrane to remove HFF cells. Purified parasites were pelleted at 1000 xg for 20 minutes 4°C. Pellets were stored in TRIzol Reagent (Invitrogen) in −80°C.

Library preparation and sequencing

RNA was extracted using Invitrogen TRIzol Reagent (cat#15596018), followed by genomic DNA removal and cleaning using Qiagen RNase-Free DNase Set kit (cat#79254) and Qiagen Mini RNeasy kit (cat#74104). Agilent 2100 Bioanalyzer was used to assess the integrity of the RNA samples. Only RNA samples having RNA Integrity Number between 9–10 were used. Ambion MicroPoly(A)Purist Kit (cat#AM1919) was used for enrichment of transcripts. The SOLiD Total RNA-Seq Kit (cat#4445374) was used to construct template cDNA for RNA-Seq following the protocol recommended by Applied Biosystems. Briefly, mRNA

was fragmented using chemical hydrolysis followed by ligation with strand specific adapters and reverse transcript to generate cDNA. The cDNA fragments, 150 to 250 bp in size, were subsequently isolated by electrophoresis in 6% Urea-TBE acrylamide gel. The isolated cDNA was amplified through 15 amplification cycles to produce the required number of templates for the SOLiD EZ Bead system, which was used to generate template bead library for the ligation base sequencing by the SOLiD4 instrument.

We aligned sequenced RNA fragments against release 6.1, ME49 strain of *Toxoplasma gondii* [27] using TopHat-1.2 [28]. We set minimum intron size at 30 bp and maximum at 1500 bp, encompassing $>98\%$ of predicted introns [27]. All other parameters were left at their default values. We assigned aligned reads to predicted gene models using BEDTools [29] and generated a table describing how many reads are aligned to each gene.

Using this "counts" table, we generated the unsupervised clustering or multi-dimensional scaling plot in figure 1A with the "plotMDS" function from the Limma package [30] and "predFC" from edgeR package [31]. Both packages are available through the Bioconductor project. Presented data is the mean of three RPKM normalized [32] replicates for each condition. All data generated in this study are accessible at the GEO database under accession number GSE60305. A summary of RPKM for each version 6.1 gene is listed in Table S1. Data have also been provided to the community database www.toxodb.org.

Detection of differential gene expression

We used the edgeR software package to infer differential expression [31]. Briefly, each gene across all eighteen samples was fitted with a log-linear model, then the regression coefficients for each group (both strain and growth conditions) are compared. Inequality of regression coefficients strongly suggests differential expression. Differentially expressed genes are listed in Table S2.

Gene Set Enrichment Analysis

GSEA is a pathway analysis tool supported by available through the Broad Institute (http://www.broadinstitute.org/gsea/index.jsp). Subramanian and colleagues describe the algorithm in detail [7]. We permuted by gene sets, not phenotypes and used the "Signal2Noise" ranking metric. Gene sets were based on KEGG pathway annotation [17], while gene sets related to cell cycle and differentiation were developed for implementation of GSEA for *T. gondii* [26].

Supporting Information

Table S1 RPKM normalized expression values for all genes, across all samples (TgME49_6.1). RNA-seq transcriptome data expressed as RPKM for each of 3 biological replicates grown and harvested at pH 7 or pH 8. r = RH; p = PLK; c = CTG.

Table S2 Membership table for genes differentially expressed in different pairwise comparisons. The genes are as listed in Table S1, using the version 6.1 gene ID's obtained from www.toxodb.org used to initially map the reads. All genes that were found to be differentially expressed in the comparisons discussed in the text are marked with an 'x'. Cell cycle regulated genes (G1 and S/M) and AP2 genes as defined by Behnke [8] are also indicated. Definition of abbreviations: RH → RH – Tachy vs Brady; PLK → PLK – Tachy vs Brady; CTG → CTG – Tachy vs Brady; rpt → RH vs PLK (Tachyzoite); rct → RH vs CTG (Tachyzoite); pct → PLK vs CTG (Tachyzoite); rpb → RH vs PLK (Bradyzoite); rcb → RH vs CTG (Bradyzoite); pcb → PLK vs CTG (Bradyzoite); g1 → Annotated as G1 cell cycle gene; sm → Annotated as S/M cell cycle gene; ap2 → Predicted or confirmed AP2 DNA-binding domain.

Table S3 RPKM expression values for annotated AP2 genes. Product names are those conferred by a community annotation group as available on www.toxodb.org. Gene ID's are version 6.1. Developmental assignments are per Behnke [8] and Walker Mol Micro [23]. Mean RPKM for each strain and condition are shown: r7 (RH strain pH 7); r8 (RH strain pH 8); p7 (PLK strain pH 7); p8 (PLK strain pH 8); c7 (CTG strain pH 7); c7 (CTG strain pH 8);

Acknowledgments

Some of this work was published in a thesis submitted in partial fulfillment of the requirements for a Doctor of Philosophy conferred by the Graduate Program in Biomedical Sciences of the Albert Einstein College of Medicine (MMC). We thank Michael White and Bill Sullivan for ongoing discussions throughout the course of this work.

Author Contributions

Conceived and designed the experiments: MMC GO LMW KK. Performed the experiments: MMC YM LMM. Analyzed the data: MMC LMM RCT GO LMW KK. Contributed reagents/materials/analysis tools: RCT. Wrote the paper: MMC LMW KK.

References

1. Kim K, Weiss LM (2008) Toxoplasma: the next 100years. Microbes Infect Inst Pasteur 10: 978–984. doi:10.1016/j.micinf.2008.07.015.
2. Khan A, Miller N, Roos DS, Dubey JP, Ajzenberg D, et al. (2011) A monomorphic haplotype of chromosome Ia is associated with widespread success in clonal and nonclonal populations of Toxoplasma gondii. mBio 2: e00228–00211. doi:10.1128/mBio.00228-11.
3. Khan A, Taylor S, Su C, Mackey AJ, Boyle J, et al. (2005) Composite genome map and recombination parameters derived from three archetypal lineages of Toxoplasma gondii. Nucleic Acids Res 33: 2980–2992. doi:10.1093/nar/gki604.
4. Sibley LD, Khan A, Ajioka JW, Rosenthal BM (2009) Genetic diversity of Toxoplasma gondii in animals and humans. Philos Trans R Soc Lond B Biol Sci 364: 2749–2761. doi:10.1098/rstb.2009.0087.
5. Behnke MS, Khan A, Wootton JC, Dubey JP, Tang K, et al. (2011) Virulence differences in Toxoplasma mediated by amplification of a family of polymorphic pseudokinases. Proc Natl Acad Sci USA 108: 9631–9636.
6. Reese ML, Zeiner GM, Saeij JPJ, Boothroyd JC, Boyle JP (2011) Polymorphic family of injected pseudokinases is paramount in Toxoplasma virulence. Proc Natl Acad Sci U S A 108: 9625–9630. doi:10.1073/pnas.1015980108.
7. Subramanian A, Tamayo P, Mootha VK, Mukherjee S, Ebert BL, et al. (2005) Gene set enrichment analysis: a knowledge-based approach for interpreting genome-wide expression profiles. Proc Natl Acad Sci USA 102: 15545–15550.
8. Behnke MS, Wootton JC, Lehmann MM, Radke JB, Lucas O, et al. (2010) Coordinated progression through two subtranscriptomes underlies the tachyzoite cycle of Toxoplasma gondii. PLoS ONE 5: e12354.
9. Balaji S, Babu MM, Iyer LM, Aravind L (2005) Discovery of the principal specific transcription factors of Apicomplexa and their implication for the evolution of the AP2-integrase DNA binding domains. Nucleic Acids Res 33: 3994–4006.
10. Altschul SF, Wootton JC, Zaslavsky E, Yu YK (2010) The construction and use of log-odds substitution scores for multiple sequence alignment. PLoS Comput Biol 6: e1000852.
11. Iwanaga S, Kaneko I, Kato T, Yuda M (2012) Identification of an AP2-family protein that is critical for malaria liver stage development. PLoS ONE 7: e47557.
12. Yuda M, Iwanaga S, Shigenobu S, Kato T, Kaneko I (2010) Transcription factor AP2-Sp and its target genes in malarial sporozoites. Mol Microbiol 75: 854–863.
13. Yuda M, Iwanaga S, Shigenobu S, Mair GR, Janse CJ, et al. (2009) Identification of a transcription factor in the mosquito-invasive stage of malaria parasites. Mol Microbiol 71: 1402–1414.
14. Sinha A, Hughes KR, Modrzynska KK, Otto TD, Pfander C, et al. (2014) A cascade of DNA-binding proteins for sexual commitment and development in Plasmodium. Nature 507: 253–257. doi:10.1038/nature12970.
15. Radke JB, Lucas O, De Silva EK, Ma Y, Sullivan WJ, et al. (2013) ApiAP2 transcription factor restricts development of the Toxoplasma tissue cyst. Proc Natl Acad Sci USA 110: 6871–6876.
16. Lescault PJ, Thompson AB, Patil V, Lirussi D, Burton A, et al. (2010) Genomic data reveal Toxoplasma gondii differentiation mutants are also impaired with respect to switching into a novel extracellular tachyzoite state. PLoS One 5: e14463. doi:10.1371/journal.pone.0014463.
17. Kanehisa M, Goto S, Sato Y, Furumichi M, Tanabe M (2012) KEGG for integration and interpretation of large-scale molecular data sets. Nucleic Acids Res 40: D109–114.

18. Hutson SL, Mui E, Kinsley K, Witola WH, Behnke MS, et al. (2010) T. gondii RP promoters & knockdown reveal molecular pathways associated with proliferation and cell-cycle arrest. PLoS One 5: e14057. doi:10.1371/journal.pone.0014057.
19. Konrad C, Wek RC, Sullivan WJ Jr (2014) GCN2-like eIF2α kinase manages the amino acid starvation response in Toxoplasma gondii. Int J Parasitol 44: 139–146. doi:10.1016/j.ijpara.2013.08.005.
20. Shanmugasundram A, Gonzalez-Galarza FF, Wastling JM, Vasieva O, Jones AR (2013) Library of Apicomplexan Metabolic Pathways: a manually curated database for metabolic pathways of apicomplexan parasites. Nucleic Acids Res 41: D706–713. doi:10.1093/nar/gks1139.
21. Behnke MS, Zhang TP, Dubey JP, Sibley LD (2014) Toxoplasma gondii merozoite gene expression analysis with comparison to the life cycle discloses a unique expression state during enteric development. BMC Genomics 15: 350. doi:10.1186/1471-2164-15-350.
22. Behnke MS, Radke JB, Smith AT, Sullivan WJ Jr, White MW (2008) The transcription of bradyzoite genes in Toxoplasma gondii is controlled by autonomous promoter elements. Mol Microbiol 68: 1502–1518. doi:10.1111/j.1365-2958.2008.06249.x.
23. Walker R, Gissot M, Croken MM, Huot L, Hot D, et al. (2013) The Toxoplasma nuclear factor TgAP2XI-4 controls bradyzoite gene expression and cyst formation. Mol Microbiol 87: 641–655. doi:10.1111/mmi.12121.
24. Radke JR, Guerini MN, Jerome M, White MW (2003) A change in the premitotic period of the cell cycle is associated with bradyzoite differentiation in Toxoplasma gondii. Mol Biochem Parasitol 131: 119–127.
25. White MW, Radke JR, Radke JB (2014) Toxoplasma development - turn the switch on or off? Cell Microbiol 16: 466–472. doi:10.1111/cmi.12267.
26. Croken MM, Qiu W, White MW, Kim K (2014) Gene Set Enrichment Analysis (GSEA) of Toxoplasma gondii expression datasets links cell cycle progression and the bradyzoite developmental program. BMC Genomics 15: 515. doi:10.1186/1471-2164-15-515.
27. Gajria B, Bahl A, Brestelli J, Dommer J, Fischer S, et al. (2008) ToxoDB: an integrated Toxoplasma gondii database resource. Nucleic Acids Res 36: D553–556.
28. Trapnell C, Pachter L, Salzberg SL (2009) TopHat: discovering splice junctions with RNA-Seq. Bioinformatics 25: 1105–1111.
29. Quinlan AR, Hall IM (2010) BEDTools: a flexible suite of utilities for comparing genomic features. Bioinformatics 26: 841–842.
30. Smyth GK (2005) Limma: linear models for microarray data. In: Gentleman R, Carey V, Dudoit S, Irizarry R, Huber W, editors. Bioinformatics and Computational Biology Solutions Using R and Bioconductor. New York: Springer. pp. 397–420.
31. Robinson MD, McCarthy DJ, Smyth GK (2010) edgeR: a Bioconductor package for differential expression analysis of digital gene expression data. Bioinformatics 26: 139–140.
32. Mortazavi A, Williams BA, McCue K, Schaeffer L, Wold B (2008) Mapping and quantifying mammalian transcriptomes by RNA-Seq. Nat Methods 5: 621–628.
33. Su C, Evans D, Cole RH, Kissinger JC, Ajioka JW, et al. (2003) Recent expansion of Toxoplasma through enhanced oral transmission. Science 299: 414–416.
34. Knoll LJ, Tomita T, Weiss LM (2014) Bradyzoite Development. In: Weiss LM, Kim K, editors. *Toxoplasma gondii The Model Apicomplexan: Perspectives and Methods.* 2nd edition. New York: Academic Press. pp. 521–551.

12

Results of a "GWAS Plus:" General Cognitive Ability Is Substantially Heritable and Massively Polygenic

Robert M. Kirkpatrick[1]*, Matt McGue[1], William G. Iacono[1], Michael B. Miller[1], Saonli Basu[2]

1 University of Minnesota, Department of Psychology, Minneapolis, Minnesota, United States of America, **2** University of Minnesota, School of Public Health, Division of Biostatistics, Minneapolis, Minnesota, United States of America

Abstract

We carried out a genome-wide association study (GWAS) for general cognitive ability (GCA) plus three other analyses of GWAS data that aggregate the effects of multiple single-nucleotide polymorphisms (SNPs) in various ways. Our multigenerational sample comprised 7,100 Caucasian participants, drawn from two longitudinal family studies, who had been assessed with an age-appropriate IQ test and had provided DNA samples passing quality screens. We conducted the GWAS across ~2.5 million SNPs (both typed and imputed), using a generalized least-squares method appropriate for the different family structures present in our sample, and subsequently conducted gene-based association tests. We also conducted polygenic prediction analyses under five-fold cross-validation, using two different schemes of weighting SNPs. Using parametric bootstrapping, we assessed the performance of this prediction procedure under the null. Finally, we estimated the proportion of variance attributable to all genotyped SNPs as random effects with software *GCTA*. The study is limited chiefly by its power to detect realistic single-SNP or single-gene effects, none of which reached genome-wide significance, though some genomic inflation was evident from the GWAS. Unit SNP weights performed about as well as least-squares regression weights under cross-validation, but the performance of both increased as more SNPs were included in calculating the polygenic score. Estimates from *GCTA* were 35% of phenotypic variance at the recommended biological-relatedness ceiling. Taken together, our results concur with other recent studies: they support a substantial heritability of GCA, arising from a very large number of causal SNPs, each of very small effect. We place our study in the context of the literature–both contemporary and historical–and provide accessible explication of our statistical methods.

Editor: Dmitri Zaykin, NIH - National Institute of Environmental Health Sciences, United States of America

Funding: The reported research was made possible by NIH grants AA09367, AA11886, DA05147, DA13240, DA024417, and MH066140. While conducting the reported analyses and drafting the manuscript, the first author was supported by a Doctoral Dissertation Fellowship from the University of Minnesota Graduate School, and while finalizing the manuscript for publication, was supported by NIH grant R25DA026119. The funders had no role in study design, data collection and analysis, decision to publish, or preparation of the manuscript.

Competing Interests: The authors have declared that no competing interests exist.

* Email: rkirkpatrick2@vcu.edu

Introduction

Candidate-Gene Association

General cognitive ability (GCA) is that mental capacity which is involved to some extent in every cognitively demanding task. It is an important individual-differences variable, and correlates non-trivially with other variables in a considerable variety of domains [1,2,3,4]. Decades of research from twin, family, and adoption studies have established that general cognitive ability (GCA) is a substantially heritable trait. Estimates of its heritability (h^2), the proportion of its variance that is attributable to genetic factors, typically range from 0.50 to 0.70 [5,6,7], and are sometimes as high as ~0.80 [8]. In light of the empirical fact that genes influence cognitive ability, a natural subsequent question to ask is *which* genetic polymorphisms contribute to individual variation in the trait

Association analysis is merely a test for whether the allelic state of a genetic polymorphism systematically covaries with the disease or quantitative trait of interest (typically via regression analysis). It can implicate a specific polymorphism provided that the "causal" polymorphism actually be typed, or alternately, lie in close chromosomal proximity–linkage disequilibrium (LD)–to a marker that is typed. (Linkage disequilibrium is the logical consequence of recombination, over many generations, in entire populations. The result is that loci very close to one another on a chromosome are least likely to be sundered by a recombination event, and therefore, polymorphisms within small "blocks" of DNA on a given chromosome tend to be transmitted together in the population. This essentially induces correlation between markers in tight proximity to one another on the same chromosome.) For a number of years, the dense genotyping needed for association analysis was costly, so association analysis saw use primarily in candidate-gene studies.

The rationale behind the candidate-gene study is simple: typing markers within genes that are *a priori* plausibly related to the phenotype is a focused use of limited genotyping resources, which is (presumably) more likely to identify genetic variants that are truly associated with the phenotype. Unfortunately, the candidate-gene association literature has been plagued by apparent false positives that fail to replicate. This has occurred in human genetics at large [9,10], and has occurred in candidate-gene association research for GCA since its inception [11]. In fact, one recent article concluded that "most reported genetic associations with general intelligence are probably false positives"[12].

Rather presciently, Risch & Merikangas [13] foreshadowed the advent of the genome-wide association (GWAS) study in their remark that an "approach (association studies) that utilizes candidate genes has far greater power, *even if one has to test every gene in the genome*" (p. 1516, emphasis supplied). The genome-wide association scan (GWAS) grew naturally out of researchers' (1) demand for denser and denser coverage of variation in more and more genes, and (2) growing dissatisfaction with replication failures in association studies of *a priori* biologically-hypothesized candidate genes. GWAS in the modern sense involves typing individuals on at least 300,000 SNPs throughout the genome [14]; due to LD, SNPs that are typed can "speak on behalf" of non-genotyped SNPs and other polymorphisms that are nearby on the same chromosome. It is only within the past five years or so that biotechnology reached such sophistication that researchers can feasibly genotype a sample of participants on hundreds of thousands of SNPs, and engage in the atheoretical brute-force empiricism that is GWAS. Needless to say, there is an inherent multiple-testing problem in GWAS; the currently accepted standard for "genome-wide significance" is $p < 5 \times 10^{-8}$.

GWAS

In a sense, the IQ QTL Project [15] carried out the first "genome-wide association study" of GCA (via DNA pooling [16]), with only 1,847 markers; it failed to uncover replicable association. A "low-density GWAS" for IQ has been reported by Pan, Wang, & Aragam [17], with no genome-wide significant hits. The first two "true" GWAS for GCA both used samples of children from the Twins Early Development Study (TEDS). Butcher, Davis, Craig, and Plomin [18] reported the first; subsequently, Davis et al. [19] ran a similar study. Butcher et al. reported that, at the uncorrected $\alpha = 0.05$, their full-sample association analysis would have 100%, 98%, and 71% power to detect an additive SNP accounting for 1%, 0.5%, and 0.2%, respectively, of the phenotypic variance. With a Bonferroni correction for 28 hypothesis tests yielding a per-comparison $\alpha = 0.001786$, Davis et al.'s full-sample association analysis would have 99.5% and 82% power to detect a SNP accounting for 1% and 0.5%, respectively, of the phenotypic variance.

Butcher et al. [18] observed nominally significant association from 6 of 37 SNPs entered into the full-sample association analysis. After implementing Benjamini and Hochberg's [20] step-up procedure to control false discovery rate, only one of these SNPs, rs1378810, was resolved as a discovery ($r^2 = 0.004$, corrected $p < 0.03$). Of Davis et al.'s [19] 28 SNPs entered into the full-sample association analysis, 9 were nominally significant, but none survived Bonferroni correction or Benjamini and Hochberg's procedure.

The largest effect-size estimate that Davis et al. [19] reported is $r^2 = 0.0024$. The largest effect-size estimate that Butcher et al. [18] reported is $r^2 = 0.004$; the sum of effect sizes of their six nominally significant SNPs was only 1.2% of the variance. Butcher et al. commented accordingly, and succinctly summarized the main lesson of GWAS for quantitative traits (p. 442, emphasis in original):

One possible reason for not observing larger, common, single-locus SNP effects for *g* is that they do not exist…[I]t may be that for…quantitative traits…the main finding is the *exclusion* of SNPs of large effect size to the extent that coverage for common variants is virtually complete…[W]innowing the wheat from the chaff will be difficult, requiring

extremely large samples, multiple-stage designs, and replication in independent samples.

As others have pointed out, the same lesson is apparent from GWAS for human height [21,22]. Height is highly heritable, uncontroversial in definition, and easily measured, almost without error. And yet, the SNPs identified by initial GWAS for height (reviewed in Ref [22]) each accounted for around 0.3% or less of the phenotypic variance, and in total, 3%. It would appear that variation in quantitative traits is attributable to a very large number of polymorphisms of very small effect. (Non-additivity of genetic effects is another possible explanation. However, this appears to be unlikely for GCA, since there is little evidence of non-additive genetic variance from twin, family, and adoption studies of this trait [23]).

Clearly, it is necessary to move beyond analyses of one SNP at a time. We refer to GWAS, combined with analyses that aggregate across multiple SNPs in some fashion, as "GWAS plus." We describe three such multi-SNP analyses: *VEGAS*, polygenic scoring, and *GCTA*.

GWAS Plus: Polygenic Scoring

Both TEDS GWAS [18,19] illustrated a simple approach to combining the effect of multiple SNPs: for each participant, aggregate those alleles suggestively implicated in the GWAS into a "genetic score" for him/her. From the six nominally significant SNPs from the GWAS, Butcher et al. simply counted how many of the putative increaser alleles each participant carried. This score ranged from 1 to 11 in the subsample of 2,676 children in which it was calculated, and correlated $r \approx 0.10$ with general ability–a very significant result ($p < 3 \times 10^{-8}$). Similarly, Davis et al. created a score from the nine nominally significant SNPs from the GWAS, which ranged from 6 to 16, and accounted for 1.2% of phenotypic variance. Davis et al. acknowledge that they conducted the genetic scoring analysis with the same participants in which they conducted the GWAS, so the analysis is almost certainly capitalizing on chance.

S. Purcell (with the International Schizophrenia Consortium [24]) appears to be the first to have performed genetic scoring by weighting each selected SNP by its GWAS regression coefficient, and cross-validating in a separate sample. Not surprisingly, the genetic score's predictive performance upon cross-validation depended upon the GWAS p-value threshold set for a SNP to be included toward the score (Ref [24], supplemental online material); at best, the genetic score could predict around 3% of disease risk in the cross-validation sample.

Lango Allen et al. [25] (the GIANT Consortium) utilized genetic scoring subsequent to a GWAS for human height on a titanic scale: a combined sample of 133,653 participants, with called or imputed genotypes on over 2.8 million SNPs, and a replication sample of 50,074 participants. The GIANT Consortium ultimately identified 180 SNPs robustly associated with height. The genetic score from these loci predicted around 10% of the phenotypic variance in each cross-validation sample. When additional SNPs at varying significance thresholds were counted toward the score, it predicted as much as 16.8% of the variance in a cross-validation sample.

GWAS plus: VEGAS

VEGAS (Versatile Gene-based Association Study [26]) is a program that tests each *gene* (specifically, all genotyped SNPs in each gene) for association with the phenotype, via parametric bootstrapping. A rather clever program, it takes GWAS results as its input, requiring only the rs numbers and GWAS p-values of each SNP. If an Internet connection is available, the program "knows" (from bioinformatic databases) which of 17,787 autosomal gene(s), if any, contain each SNP. Within each gene, the program first converts each SNP p-value to the corresponding quantile from a central chi-square distribution on $1df$, and sums them to produce an observed test statistic T_{obs} for that gene. The null hypothesis is that there is no association of any SNP in the gene with the phenotype. Under the null, and if there were zero LD among the gene's m SNPs, then $T \sim \text{chi}^2(m)$. Under the null, but at the other extreme of perfect LD among the m SNPs, then $T/m \sim \text{chi}^2(1)$.

But, *VEGAS* also "knows" the LD structure from reference datasets for three populations: HapMap CEU (Caucasians of European ancestry), CHB and JPT (Han Chinese and Japanese), and YRI (West Africans). *VEGAS* assumes that, under the null hypothesis, the LD pattern among SNPs in a gene dictates the correlation pattern among the single-SNP test statistics–an assumption made, for example, in methods for controlling Type I Error rate in association studies of SNPs in LD with one another [27,28]. The matrix of pairwise LD correlations for the user-specified population, Σ, is employed in the random generation of test statistics under the null hypothesis. Specifically, in each iteration, an order-m vector is drawn from a multivariate normal distribution with zero mean and covariance matrix equal to Σ. The elements of this vector are squared and summed, yielding the value of the test statistic for that iteration. The proportion of test statistics exceeding T_{obs} provides the p-value for the gene-based test of association. Liu et al. [26] recommend a Bonferroni-corrected significance level of $p < 0.05/17,787$, or 2.8×10^{-6}, which is slightly conservative since genes' boundaries overlap to some extent.

GWAS Plus: *GCTA*

GCTA (Genome-wide Complex Trait Analysis) [29] is a software package that implements what some [30] have referred to as GREML, for "genomic-relatedness restricted maximum-likelihood." Instead of regressing a quantitative trait onto one marker at a time, *GCTA* instead assesses how much of the phenotypic variance is attributable to *all* the typed markers at once, which is accomplished by treating all the markers as random effects, and entering them into a mixed linear model fit by restricted maximum likelihood. *GCTA* thereby provides an unbiased estimate of the variance attributable to the typed SNPs, and a matrix of (roughly) genome-wide SNP correlations among participants–a genetic relationship matrix, obtainable from a genotyped sample of classically unrelated participants. Put simply, *GCTA* attempts to predict phenotypic similarity among individuals from their genetic similarity, and to predict phenotypic variance that would otherwise be treated as error. *GCTA* may be expected to outperform polygenic scoring, because it does not rely upon estimates of individual SNP effects, which are prone to sampling error [31].

For n participants typed on m SNPs, the *GCTA* model [29] is expressed as

$$\mathbf{y} = \mathbf{X}\boldsymbol{\beta} + \mathbf{W}\mathbf{u} + \boldsymbol{\varepsilon} \qquad (1)$$

where $\mathbf{y}$ is a random $n \times 1$ vector of scores on a quantitative trait, $\mathbf{X}$ is a model matrix of scores on covariates, $\boldsymbol{\beta}$ is a vector of the covariates' regression coefficients (fixed effects), and residual vector $\boldsymbol{\varepsilon} \sim N_n(0, \mathbf{I}\sigma_\varepsilon^2)$. Further, $\mathbf{u}$ is an $m \times 1$ vector of random SNP effects, such that $\mathbf{u} \sim N_n(0, \mathbf{I}\sigma_\varepsilon^2)$; $\mathbf{W}$ is an $n \times m$ matrix of

participants' reference-allele counts, expressed as z-scores (i.e., columns are standardized).

We hereby condition upon the observed value of $\mathbf{X}$. Since the random effects have zero expectation, $E(\mathbf{y}|\mathbf{X}) = \mathbf{X}\boldsymbol{\beta}$. Now define the phenotypic variance matrix, $\mathbf{V}$:

$$\mathbf{V} = \text{var}(\mathbf{y}|\mathbf{X}) = \mathbf{W}\mathbf{W}^T \sigma_u^2 + \mathbf{I}\sigma_\varepsilon^2 \qquad (2)$$

Matrix $\mathbf{V}$ is the model-predicted covariance matrix of participants' phenotype scores. Intuitively, each off-diagonal (covariance) element of $\mathbf{V}$ is the degree of phenotypic similarity between the two participants, as predicted from their genotypic similarity. Now, further define genetic relationship matrix, $\mathbf{A}$:

$$\mathbf{A} = \frac{1}{m} \mathbf{W}\mathbf{W}^T \qquad (3)$$

Matrix $\mathbf{A}$ is $n \times n$, and roughly, may be regarded as a matrix of correlations between different participants' genotypes. However, this is not strictly correct, since $\mathbf{W}$ is standardized by column (SNP) rather than by row (participant), and therefore the elements of $\mathbf{A}$ may exceed unity in absolute value.

Let $\sigma_g^2 = m\sigma_u^2$, the variance attributable to all SNPs. The model may now be written:

$$\mathbf{y} = \mathbf{X}\boldsymbol{\beta} + \mathbf{g} + \boldsymbol{\varepsilon} \qquad (4)$$

where $\mathbf{g}$ is an $n \times 1$ vector of random genetic effects, distributed as $N_n(0, \mathbf{A}\sigma_\varepsilon^2)$. Now,

$$\mathbf{V} = \text{var}(\mathbf{y}|\mathbf{X}) = \mathbf{A}\sigma_g^2 + \mathbf{I}\sigma_\varepsilon^2 \qquad (5)$$

Where σ_g^2 is the component of variance attributable to all typed SNPs and all untyped "causal" mutations in close LD with them. The model-predicted phenotypic variance $\sigma_p^2 = \sigma_g^2 + \sigma_\varepsilon^2$. Herein, we refer to the ratio of σ_g^2 to σ_p^2 as h_{SNP}^2, for it is a lower bound on the additive heritability of the phenotype. Estimation is carried out via restricted maximum-likelihood; details of the algorithm may be found in Ref [29].

Recent Developments

Davies et al. [32] reported a "GWAS Plus" for cognitive abilities. The discovery sample contained 3,511 unrelated participants, combined from 5 cohorts of older adults in the United Kingdom. The replication cohort comprised 670 Norwegian participants of a wide range of ages (18–79). Davies et al. extracted composite scores for both crystallized and fluid ability from the ability measures in each cohort, and conducted separate analyses for fluid and crystallized ability.

Davies et al. [32] combined association results from the 5 UK cohorts via meta-analytic techniques. No single SNP achieved genome-wide significance ($p < 5 \times 10^{-8}$). Gene-based tests in *VEGAS* implicated only one gene, *FNBP1L*, which was not confirmed in the replication cohort. Davies et al. performed polygenic scoring using the most lenient SNP inclusion threshold possible: *all* genotyped SNPs, irrespective of GWAS p-value. In the UK samples, this score predicted between 0.45% and 2.19% of the variance. Under cross-validation in the replication cohort, this score predicted less than 1% of the variance (statistically significant for both fluid and crystallized ability). Davies et al. emphasized that, when treating SNPs as single fixed effects, their individual effect sizes will be quite small, and estimated with considerable sampling error.

Instead, GCTA, though it is silent with regard to the individual contribution of each marker, treats all SNPs as random effects and estimates a single omnibus variance component. (In this report, we are chiefly interested in the simplest application of GCTA, when only variance components and fixed-effects regression coefficients are computed. If the original genotypic data used to calculate **A** is available, then it is also possible to obtain empirical best linear unbiased predictions (eBLUPs) of the individual SNP effects in vector **u** from Equation (1).) This seems to be one of its major advantages. In any event, the most notable results from Davies et al. [32] were from GCTA, which produced variance-component estimates equivalent to 40% of the variance in crystallized ability, and 51% of the variance in fluid ability. Davies et al. (p. 1) conclude that "human intelligence is highly heritable and polygenic.".

A recent study of GCA in children and adolescents reported by the Childhood Intelligence Consortium (CHIC)[33] has borne out that same conclusion. The CHIC study represented a collaboration of six discovery cohorts (total $N = 12,441$) and three replication cohorts ($N = 5,548$). One of the replication cohorts was a sample of Caucasian adolescent participants from studies conducted at the Minnesota Center for Twin & Family Research (MCTFR, $N = 3,367$), which is a subset of the present study's sample. The phenotype in all cohorts was either Full-Scale IQ score or a composite score derived from a battery of both verbal and non-verbal tests. GWAS SNP results were combined across discovery cohorts by meta-analysis. No SNP reached genome-wide significance. Among the top 100 SNPs from the discovery GWAS, none was significant after Bonferroni correction in any of the replication cohorts, though discovery sample's estimated regression coefficients for these 100 SNPs were moderately positively correlated with those from two of the three replication cohorts, but not the MCTFR cohort.

Gene-based analysis with VEGAS in Benyamin et al.'s [33] discovery sample suggested association with FNBP1L (formin binding protein 1-like, on chromosome 1; $p = 4 \times 10^{-5}$), which "is involved in a pathway that links cell surface signals to the actin cytoskeleton" (p. 3). This was also the most significantly associated gene in Davies et al.'s [32] discovery cohort. However, one cohort was common to both studies–Davies et al. used adult IQ scores from the Lothian Birth Cohorts, whereas Benyamin et al. used their childhood IQ scores. When Benyamin et al. combined VEGAS results across all of their cohorts except the Lothian Birth Cohorts, the association with FNBP1L remained nominally significant ($p = 0.0137$), as did the top SNP in the gene ($p = 4.5 \times 10^{-5}$). Benyamin et al. regarded this as robust evidence of association between GCA and polymorphisms in FNBP1L.

Benyamin et al. [33] also reported results of polygenic scoring analyses conducted in the replication cohorts. These analyses calculated polygenic scores from the SNP regression weights obtained in the meta-analytic GWAS results from the discovery sample. Eight such analyses were conducted in each replication cohort, with a different p-value cutoff for each. That is, polygenic score for each such analysis was computed from a set of SNPs the p-values of which exceeded some threshold in the discovery sample. The proportion of variance attributable to the polygenic score varied by p-value cutoff and by replication cohort, but was statistically significant for at least one analysis in each replication cohort. The best achieved in the MCTFR cohort was 0.5% of variance ($p = 5.52 \times 10^{-5}$). Finally, Benyamin et al. reported GCTA results for the three largest cohorts in the study, one of which was

the MCTFR cohort. Estimates of h^2_{SNP} varied from 0.22 to 0.46, with the MCTFR estimate in between at 0.40; all three estimates were significantly different from zero. Based on all results, Benyamin et al. conclude that "[c]hildhood intelligence is heritable, highly polygenic and associated with FNBP1L" (p. 1).

In the present study, we report the detailed results of our "GWAS Plus" from our *full* sample of 7,100 Caucasian MCTFR participants, both adolescents and adults. We conducted our GWAS using over 2.6 million SNPs and a method appropriate for the complicated family structures in our dataset. We then conducted gene-based association tests in VEGAS with the SNP p-values calculated in our GWAS. We also carried out polygenic scoring analyses with five-fold cross-validation, at different p-value cutoffs (a la Benyamin et al. [33]) and under two different schemes of weighting SNPs to compute the score. Finally, we ran GCTA to estimate how much of the phenotypic variance is attributable to all genotyped SNPs.

Methods

Ethics Statement

Both longitudinal family studies, the Minnesota Twin Family Study (MTFS) and the Sibling Interaction & Behavior Study (SIBS), and the collection, genotyping, and analysis of DNA samples, were approved by the University of Minnesota Institutional Review Board's Human Subjects Committee. Written informed assent or consent was obtained from all participants; parents provided written consent for their minor children.

Sample

Participants. Our participants came from two longitudinal family studies conducted by the MCTFR. MTFS [34,35,36] is a longitudinal study of same-sex twins, born in the State of Minnesota between 1972 and 1994, and their parents. There are two age cohorts in this community-based sample, an 11-year-old cohort (10–13 years old at intake, mean age = 11.78) and a 17-year-old cohort (16–18 years old at intake, mean age = 17.48). Zygosity has been genomically confirmed for all DZ twins included in the present study [37]. SIBS [38] is a longitudinal adoption study of sibling pairs and their parents. This community-based sample includes families where both siblings are adopted, where both are biologically related to the parents, or where one is adopted and one is biologically related. As required by SIBS inclusion criteria, any sibling in the sample who was adopted into the family will not be biologically related to his or her co-sibling, which has been genomically verified for all SIBS participants in the present study [37]. The age range at intake was 10–19 for the younger sibling, and 12–20 for the older. For the purposes of our analyses, the sample comprises six distinct family types:

1. Monozygotic- (MZ) twin families ($N = 3,939$ in 1143 families),
2. Digyzotic- (DZ) twin families ($N = 2,114$, in 638 families),
3. SIBS families with two adopted offspring ($N = 291$, in 224 families),
4. SIBS families with two biological offspring ($N = 472$, in 184 families),
5. "Mixed" SIBS families with 1 biological and 1 adopted offspring ($N = 204$, in 107 families),
6. Step-parents ($N = 80$).

As explained below, our method of analysis accounted for the clustering of individual participants within families. However, family-type #6, step-parents, do not fit neatly into a four-member family unit; we treated them as independent observations (in a sense, as one-person families) in our analysis. A total of $N = 7,100$ participants were included in our analyses. Descriptive characteristics of the sample are provided in Table 1. Details concerning families' patterns of data availability are provided in Table S1. Genotype and phenotype data have been submitted to dbGaP (accession number phs000620.v1.p1).

Genotyping. Participants who provided DNA samples were typed on a genome-wide set of markers with the Illumina Human660W-Quad array. Both DNA samples and markers were subject to thorough quality-control screens. 527,829 SNPs on the array were successfully called and passed all QC filters, which filters include call rate <99%, minor allele frequency <1%, and Hardy-Weinberg equilibrium p-value $< 10^{-7}$. After excluding DNA samples that failed quality-control screening, a genotyped GWAS sample of 8,405 participants was identified.

Population stratification occurs when one's sample of participants represents heterogeneous populations across which allele frequencies differ appreciably, and can produce spurious genetic association (or suppress genuine association). We therefore restricted our analyses only to participants who are Caucasian, of European ancestry ("White"), based upon both self-reported ancestry as well as principal components from EIGENSTRAT [41]. These principal components were extracted from an $n \times n$ covariance matrix of individuals' genotypes across SNPs (similar to matrix **A** described above). A White GWAS sample of 7,702 participants was identified. The sample for the present study is the 7,100 out of 7,702 White participants with available phenotype data. Details concerning genotyping, quality-control, and ancestry determination can be found in Ref [37].

Imputation. Many known SNPs exist that are not on our Illumina array. But, by combining observed SNP genotypes with what is known–*a priori*, from reference data–about haplotype frequencies in the population, the allelic state of common untyped SNPs can often be imputed with a high degree of accuracy. For SNP imputation, using HapMap2 [42] as the reference panel, we first phased our observed genotypes into expected haplotypes with *BEAGLE* [43], which takes information from genotyped relatives into account to improve phasing. We then input phased data into *Minimac*, a version of *MaCH* [44], to impute SNP states for a total of 2,094,911 SNPs not on the Illumina array. In our GWAS, we used the allelic dosages of these SNPs, which are individuals' posterior expected reference-allele counts on each SNP so imputed. The quality of the imputation for an untyped SNP may be assessed by its imputation R^2 [44], which is the ratio of the variance of its imputed dosages to its population variance (from reference data). Our GWAS only included dosages of imputed SNPs with imputation $R^2 > 0.5$, of which there were 2,018,818.

Between these imputed SNPs and the 527,829 from the array, we analyzed a total of 2,546,647 SNPs in our GWAS.

Phenotypic measurement. Measurement of GCA was included in the design of the intake assessment for most participants, by way of an abbreviated form of the Wechsler Intelligence Scale for Children-Revised (WISC-R) or Wechsler Adult Intelligence Scale-Revised (WAIS-R), as age-appropriate (that is, 16 or younger, and older than 16, respectively). The short forms consisted of two Performance subtests (Block Design and Picture Arrangement) and two Verbal subtests (Information and Vocabulary), the scaled scores on which were prorated to determine Full-Scale IQ (FSIQ). FSIQ estimates from this short form have been shown to correlate 0.94 with FSIQ from the complete test [45]. Parents in the SIBS sample were an exception, in that they were not tested with this short form of WAIS-R until the first SIBS follow-up assessment. By design, only one parent per SIBS family returned for this follow-up, which was usually the mother. As a result, IQ data for SIBS fathers is very limited in its availability.

IQ-testing was also included in the design of the second follow-up for both age cohorts of MTFS twins, and for the fourth follow-up for the 11-year-old cohort. At these assessments, twins received a further abbreviated form of WAIS-R, consisting only of the Vocabulary and Block Design subtests, the scaled scores on which were again prorated to determine FSIQ. Of the 3,226 twins entered into our analysis, 903 were tested twice, and 337 were tested three times. Multiple testing occasions were spaced approximately seven years apart. To achieve a more reliable assessment of the phenotype, we simply averaged all available measures of FSIQ for each participant, and used these single within-person averages in analysis. FSIQ among participants entered into analysis ranged from 59 to 151 (also see Table 1). Twelve participants with FSIQ of 70 or below were included in analyses. Despite their low scores, these participants were not noticeably impaired and were capable of completing the multifaceted MTFS/SIBS assessment during their visit. They are therefore unlikely to meet diagnostic criteria for mental retardation [46], and instead, likely represent the low end of the normal-range distribution of GCA. (Participants who are discovered to have a physical or mental disability severe enough to prevent them from completing the intake assessment are retroactively ruled ineligible to participate. This has occurred for five MTFS twin pairs and one SIBS adoptee, whose data were eliminated from the studies' databases.).

Analyses

Statistical power. Because our participants are clustered within 2,376 families, our effective sample size is less than 7,100 participants. We conducted two sets of power calculations in

Table 1. Descriptive characteristics of Study #1 sample.

	Parents	Twins (17yo)	Twins (11yo)	Non-twin Biological Offspring	Adoptees	Step-parents
N	3,264	1,146	2,080	414	116	80
Female(%)	60.2%	55.3%	50.1%	52.2%	46.6%	8.8%
Mean Age at Intake (SD)	43.3 (5.46)	17.5 (0.45)	11.8 (0.43)	14.9 (1.89)	15.1 (2.17)	40.6 (7.45)
Mean FSIQ (SD)	105.8 (14.2)	100.4 (14.1)	103.6 (13.5)	108.5 (13.1)	105.7 (14.3)	103.4 (15.7)

Table notes: Total $N = 7100$, in 2376 families. FSIQ = Full-Scale IQ; 17yo = 17-year-old cohort; 11yo = 11-year-old cohort. For a minority of twins (38%), FSIQ represents a within-person average of FSIQ scores from more than one assessment (see text). FSIQ range: 151−59 = 92. Parental intake age range: 65−28 = 37. Offspring intake age range: 20−10 = 10.

Quanto [47], one that assumed 7,000 independent participants (an aggressive estimate of our effective sample size) and one that assumed 2,000 independent participants (a conservative estimate of our sample size). Both assume a Type I error rate of $\alpha = 5 \times 10^{-8}$, i.e. genome-wide significance. With 7,000 independent participants, our GWAS would have at least 80% power to detect a SNP accounting for 0.6% of phenotypic variance. With 2,000 independent participants, our GWAS would have at least 80% power to detect a SNP accounting for 2% of phenotypic variance

GWAS. Our GWAS consisted of a large number of least-squares regressions of FSIQ onto the genotype (or imputed dosage) of each SNP, along with covariates, which were sex, birth year, and the first 10 principal components from EIGENSTRAT [41], to control for any crypto-stratification (i.e., lurking population stratification in a sample of apparently homogeneous ancestry) within this White sample. (There are three reasons why we covaried out birth year, rather than age-at-testing. First, IQ tests are age-normed in the first place. Second, a minority of our twins would in a sense have more than one age-at-testing, since their FSIQ scores entered into analysis are actually within-person averages from more than one testing occasion. Third, the nuisance confound of chief concern is the Flynn Effect (first reported in Refs [39] and [40])–the secular trend of increasing IQ scores with each generation–which is directly related to birth year, and not to age *per se*. Surprisingly, at a glance, our data are not consistent with the Flynn Effect. In the covariates-only FGLS regression, the estimated coefficient for birth year was -0.09 (Table S2), indicating that later birth year corresponded on average to lower IQ.) One notable example of this kind of stratification came from a study [48] in which a SNP in the gene for lactase (*LCT*) was significantly, but spuriously, associated with height among European-Americans. Allele frequency for the SNP in question is known to vary among regions of Europe, and no association was observed when participants were matched on grandparental country-of-origin. Instead, the SNP appeared to mark participants' ancestral origins along a northwest-southeast axis running through the continent of Europe.

Because our participants are clustered within families, they were not sampled independently. To further complicate matters, the within-family covariance structure will depend upon the kind of family in question. We therefore employed a feasible generalized least-squares (FGLS) method in our GWAS, via *RFGLS*, a package for the R statistical computing environment designed for FGLS regression in datasets with complicated family structures [49]. (As is widely known (see Ref [49]), in multiple regression, when the residuals are uncorrelated and have mean zero and constant variance, the best linear unbiased estimate of the regression parameters is obtained as $\hat{\boldsymbol{\beta}}_{OLS} = \left(\mathbf{X}^T\mathbf{X}\right)^{-1}\mathbf{X}^T\mathbf{y}$; if the residuals are further normally distributed and stochastically independent, $\hat{\boldsymbol{\beta}}_{OLS}$ is also the maximum-likelihood estimator. If the residuals are not uncorrelated, $\hat{\boldsymbol{\beta}}_{OLS}$ will not be maximally efficient, and the degrees-of-freedom for its test statistics will be mis-specified. In practice, the (non-diagonal) residual covariance matrix must be estimated from data. If $\mathbf{V}$ is a consistent such estimator, then the feasible generalized least-squares estimator of the regression coefficients is obtained as $\hat{\boldsymbol{\beta}}_{FGLS} = \left(\mathbf{X}^T\mathbf{V}^{-1}\mathbf{X}\right)^{-1}\mathbf{X}^T\mathbf{V}^{-1}\mathbf{y}$).

RFGLS has a "rapid-FGLS" approximation, which we used to run the GWAS and which works as follows. First, an FGLS regression of the phenotype onto covariates only is run, in which the regression coefficients and the residual covariance matrix are both estimated. Then, that residual covariance matrix is saved to disk, so it can then be "plugged in" for use in all subsequent single-SNP regressions, with covariates. The approximation saves a considerable amount of computation time, since the residual covariance matrix is calculated only once. It produces negligible bias in the resulting *p*-values, so long as no SNP accounts for more than 1% of phenotypic variance [49] (which is a very reasonable assumption).

GWAS Plus: *VEGAS*. We conducted gene-based association tests in *VEGAS*, inputting 2,485,149 autosomal SNPs, both observed and imputed, and specifying HapMap CEU as the reference data for pairwise LD correlations. We also ran *VEGAS* inputting only the 515,385 autosomal SNPs on the Illumina array.

GWAS Plus: polygenic scoring. We conducted polygenic scoring with five-fold cross-validation. Since the family is the independent unit of observation in our dataset, we first randomly divided the sample into five subsamples of approximately equal numbers of families, and with each family type approximately equally represented in each. Then, we ran a GWAS with the observed SNPs only, five times over, each time including four of the five subsamples–the calibration sample for that iteration. Then, the left-out subsample served as that iteration's validation sample.

Each iteration, we used *PLINK* [50] to produce polygenic scores for the participants in the validation sample based on the GWAS statistics from the calibration sample, at the same eight *p*-value cutoffs used by Benyamin et al. [33]: $p \leq 0.001$, $p \leq 0.005$, $p \leq 0.01$, $p \leq 0.05$, $p \leq 0.1$, $p \leq 0.25$, $p \leq 0.5$, and $p \leq 1$ (i.e., all SNPs). We used two different weighting methods to calculate polygenic scores. The first simply used the GWAS regression coefficients from the calibration sample. The second weighted each SNP as either -1 or 1, depending on the sign of its coefficient. Thus, with eight *p*-value cutoffs and two weighting schemes, we produced 16 polygenic-score vectors in each validation sample.

To evaluate the performance of the polygenic scores under cross-validation in each iteration, we first ran a FGLS regression of the phenotype onto covariates only in the validation sample, and retained the residualized FSIQs. We then did another FGLS regression of the residualized FSIQ onto polygenic score, from which we calculated Buse's R^2 [51]. Buse's R^2 is the coefficient of determination from OLS regression, except that each sum is instead replaced by a quadratic or bilinear form in the vector of terms, with a weight-matrix coefficient (for our purposes, this weight matrix is the inverse of the residual covariance matrix obtained from regressing the residualized phenotype onto the score). (We also calculated Nagelkerke's [52] generalized R^2, and the squared Pearson correlation between polygenic score and residualized phenotype. Nagelkerke's R^2 was typically very close to Buse's. The squared Pearson correlation was generally close to the other two, but tended to be higher, sometimes as much as twice as high as Buse's).

With parametric bootstrapping, we assessed the performance of polygenic scoring under the null hypothesis of residualized FSIQ being independent of the SNPs, as follows. First, new phenotype scores were simulated by generating a new residual vector for each family and adding it to the family's vector of predicted scores from the GWAS covariates-only regression. Each new residual vector was drawn from a multivariate-normal distribution with zero mean and covariance matrix as estimated for that family in the covariates-only regression. Thus, in each newly simulated dataset, the within-family covariance structure and the associations among covariates and phenotype in the real data are expected to be preserved, but the phenotype is generated independently of SNP genotypes (conditional on covariates). However, the procedure does assume that multivariate normality is a reasonable distribution for the residuals.

The simulated sample was then randomly divided so that 80% of families were assigned to the calibration subsample, and the remaining 20% to the validation subsample. A GWAS was then run in the calibration sample, the results of which were used to conduct polygenic scoring in the validation sample, in the same way as done in the real data. We repeated this process a total of only 50 times, as it was somewhat computationally demanding.

GWAS Plus: *GCTA*. We first computed the genetic relationship matrix **A** from all 7,702 White participants with genome-wide SNP data (which includes those for whom FSIQ scores were not available), using the 515,385 autosomal SNPs passing QC. We then ran *GCTA* to estimate h^2_{SNP}, with FSIQ as the phenotype, and with the same covariates as used in the GWAS, as fixed effects. An exploratory analysis involving *GCTA* (described in Material S1) showed that including close relatives in the analysis can upwardly bias $\hat{h}^2_{SNP}$ by confounding variance attributable to genotyped SNPs with variance attributable to shared environment. We therefore restricted the analysis only to participants whose degrees of genetic relatedness (from **A**) were 0.025 or smaller. To assess how well the distributional assumptions of the GREML method were met, we computed empirical best linear unbiased predictions (eBLUPs) of participants' total genetic effects–**g** in Equation (4)–and residuals, both of which are assumed to be normally distributed.

Results

GWAS

Estimates of the fixed and random effects from the covariates-only FGLS regression are presented in Table S2. *P*-values from the GWAS are depicted in Figures 1, 2, S1, and S2. Figure 1 is a "Manhattan plot" of the GWAS *p*-values from the 2,546,647 observed and imputed SNPs. The *y*-axis of a Manhattan plot is $-\log_{10}(p)$. The *x*-axis is divided into chromosomes, and within each chromosome, SNPs are ordered by base-pair position. Chromosomes above #22 refer to different parts of the sex chromosomes and to mitochondrial DNA (see figure captions). No SNPs reached genome-wide significance, which in this metric would be $-\log_{10}(p)$ >7.30. The association signal exceeding 6 on chromosome 1 is due to 11 SNPs (9 imputed) spanning about 14 kb, not within a known gene. The signal exceeding 6 on chromosome 16 is due to a single imputed SNP in the *FA2H* gene, rs16947526, of borderline imputation quality ($R^2 = 0.52$). On chromosome 21, the signal exceeding 6 is due to a single imputed SNP in the *ERG* gene, rs9982370. When only the observed SNPs are plotted (Figure S1), the only elevation above 6 occurs on chromosome 1.

Under the null hypothesis, *p*-values are uniformly distributed on interval (0, 1). Figures 2 and S2 are uniform quantile-quantile (QQ) plots of the GWAS *p*-values from, respectively, the 2,546,647 observed and imputed SNPs, and the 527,829 observed SNPs only. Under the null hypothesis, *p*-values from independent statistical tests are expected to follow the diagonal red line. Both QQ plots show some divergence from the null distribution, where the observed *p*-values tend to be more extreme than expected. To quantify this deviation, we can convert the *p*-values to quantiles from a chi-square distribution on 1 *df*, and compare their median and mean to the null values of 0.455 and 1, respectively. The ratio of the observed to the expected median is known as the genomic inflation factor, λ [53]. When this is done with observed and imputed SNPs together, median = 0.475 (λ = 1.044) and mean = 1.037; when done with observed SNPs only, the median = 0.471 (λ = 1.035) and mean = 1.031. This departure from the

null may indicate massively polygenic inheritance of FSIQ, wherein few if any SNPs yield genome-wide significant association signals, but the overall distribution of test statistics reflects the presence of a large number of nonzero effects [54].

There are clearly some *p*-values that lie outside the confidence limits in Figures 2 and S2. However, because of LD among SNPs, the assumption of independent statistical tests is violated to begin with, and so one extreme result usually carries others with it. It stands to reason that this effect of LD would be more pronounced when imputed SNPs are included, since imputation methods rely on the LD (correlation) structure among SNPs to achieve denser coverage of the genome.

Our statistical inference from FGLS regression assumes that families' vectors of residuals follow a multivariate-normal distribution in the population. If this assumption is met, then family members' residuals will be marginally distributed as univariate normal, and the squared Mahalanobis distance from the origin of families' residual vectors will be distributed as chi-square. Figures S3 and S4 present QQ plots that respectively check the observed distributions of individual residuals and family Mahalanobis distances against their theoretical distributions. The plots do not show severe departures from the theoretical distributions (though logically, these checks can only disconfirm, and not confirm, multivariate normality). The departure from normality evident in Figure S3 likely reflects that the far lower tail of the population IQ distribution is poorly represented in our sample.

VEGAS

The resulting gene-based *p*-values from *VEGAS* (inputting 2,485,149 autosomal SNPs, both observed and imputed) are depicted in Figure 3, a Manhattan plot, and Figure 4, a QQ plot. Figure 4 suggests that *VEGAS* has a somewhat conservative bias in these data. No gene in Figure 3 reaches the genome-wide significance level recommended for *VEGAS*, which in this metric would be $-\log_{10}(p)$ >5.55. As shown in Figures S5 and S6 (results when inputting only 515,385 genotyped autosomal SNPs), our conclusions would be substantially unchanged if we had restricted our analyses to observed SNPs only. Our data do not support association of *FNBP1L* with GCA ($p = 0.727$).

Polygenic scoring

Figure 5 depicts cross-validation performance (Buse's R^2) of polygenic score, averaged across subsample, and plotted in black by *p*-value cutoff and weighting scheme (in Figure S7, the R^2s from each subsample are plotted as separate trendlines). The red lines in Figure 5 depict the 98th percentiles of Buse's R^2, among the 50 iterations of parametric bootstrapping under the null, for each combination of *p*-value cutoff and weighting scheme. One notable result here is that the polygenic score, when calculated from signed unit-weighted SNPs, performed about as well as when it was calculated from the actual single-SNP GWAS regression weights. Another result evident in Figure 5 is the trend in cross-validation performance across *p*-value cutoffs: the predictive accuracy is maximized when using all genotyped SNPs (with best R^2 around 0.55%). This conclusion is further supported by comparing the black and red lines, which indicates that the "signal" in the real data was only reliably distinguishable from simulated "noise" at lenient *p*-value cutoffs.

GCTA

At Yang et al.'s [29] suggested genetic-relatedness ceiling of 0.025 in our dataset, *N* = 3,322 of our participants were included in analysis, yielding $\hat{h}^2_{SNP} = 0.35$ (*SE* = 0.11). Figure S8 presents

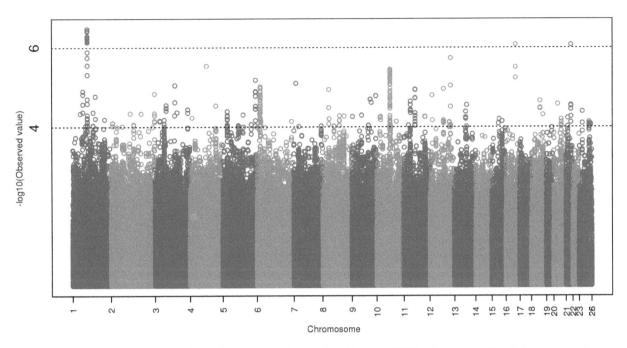

Figure 1. Manhattan plot of GWAS *p*-values, all 2,546,647 observed and imputed SNPs. Chromosome 23 = X chromosome, chromosome 25 = pseudoautosomal region of sex chromosome. Chromosome 26 indicates mitochondrial DNA. SNPs are plotted by serial position on each chromosome. Genome-wide significance is $-\log_{10}(p) > 7.30$, which no SNP reaches. The peak on chromosome 1 is due to 11 SNPs (rs10922924, rs3856228, plus 9 others imputed nearby) that span about 14 kb not within a known gene. The peaks on chromosomes 16 and 21 are each due to a single imputed SNP, respectively rs16947526 and rs9982370.

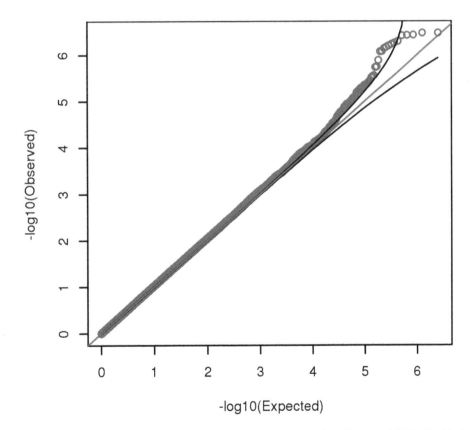

Figure 2. Uniform quantile-quantile plot of GWAS *p*-values, all 2,546,647 observed and imputed SNPs. The black curves delineate 95% confidence limits.

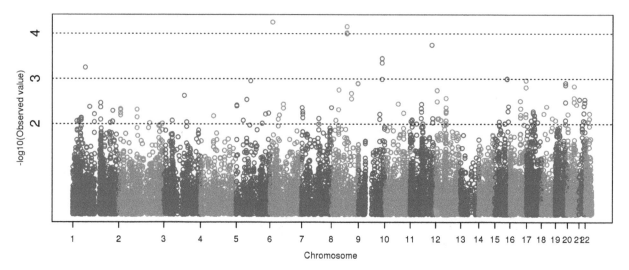

Figure 3. Manhattan plot for gene-based *p*-values from *VEGAS*. Analysis input was GWAS *p*-values from 2,485,149 autosomal SNPs, both observed and imputed. Abscissa position of each point is the gene's beginning base-pair position, NCBI genome build 36. Genome-wide significance is −log₁₀(*p*) >5.55, which no gene reaches.

normal QQ plots of individuals' total genetic-effect eBLUPs and residuals. These plots resemble those of the FGLS residuals (Figure S3). However, the QQ plot of the eBLUPs may not be very informative about the true distribution of the random effects, since the eBLUPs were computed from a model that assumes normality in the first place, and the observed distribution of BLUPs can

greatly depend upon the random effects' assumed theoretical distribution (e.g., Ref [55]).

Discussion

The present study is a "GWAS Plus" for general cognitive ability, conducted in a sample of over 7,000 Caucasian partici-

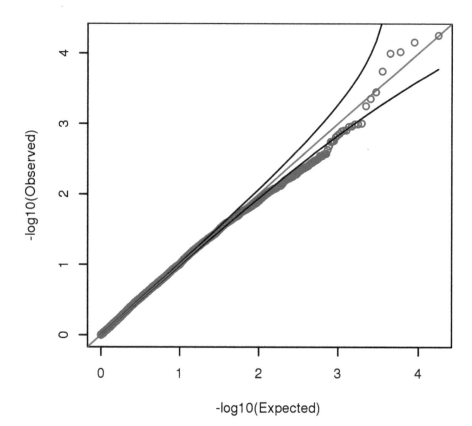

Figure 4. Uniform quantile-quantile plot for gene-based *p*-values from *VEGAS*. Analysis input was GWAS *p*-values from 2,485,149 autosomal SNPs, both observed and imputed. Black curves delineate 95% confidence limits.

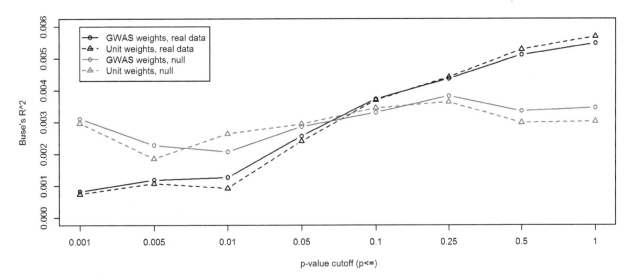

Figure 5. Five-fold cross-validation R^2 of polygenic score (averaged across subsamples, in black) for predicting FSIQ residualized for covariates, compared to results from simulated null data (98th percentiles, in red). Black lines represent cross-validation Buse's R^2 [51] for predicting residualized FSIQ, averaged across the 5 subsamples. In each subsample, residualized FSIQ was predicted from polygenic score calculated from regression weights obtained in the other 4 subsamples. "P-value cutoff" dictated how small a SNP's p-value had to be in the calibration GWAS to be included in calculating polygenic score for the validation sample. Red lines represent the results of 50 iterations of parametric bootstrapping, which conducted polygenic scoring under cross-validation using data simulated under the null of independence between phenotype and SNP genotypes (conditional on covariates). Each point plotted for the red lines is the 98th percentile, among the 50 iterations of parametric bootstrapping, of R^2 at that p-value cutoff. Polygenic score was either calculated directly from the GWAS weights (solid lines) or from signed unit weights (dashed lines; see text).

pants from two longitudinal family studies. We conducted the GWAS *per se* using 2,546,647 SNPs: 527,829 from the Illumina 660W–Quad array, plus 2,018,818 imputed with reasonable reliability (imputation $R^2 > 0.5$). The "Plus" in "GWAS Plus" refers to our additional analyses that involve predicting the phenotype from more than one SNP at a time. These analyses were (1) gene-based association tests in *VEGAS*, (2) polygenic scoring with five-fold cross-validation, and (3) a genomic-relatedness restricted maximum-likelihood analysis in *GCTA*.

Our least interesting results were from *VEGAS* (Figures 3 and 4). What *VEGAS* essentially does is test whether all SNP p-values in a gene significantly differ in distribution from the null. No gene achieved genome-wide significance ($p < 2.8 \times 10^{-6}$ or $-\log_{10}(p) > 5.55$), and the method appears to be slightly conservatively biased in our dataset, possibly because of differences between our actual LD structure and that of *VEGAS*' reference dataset, HapMap CEU. Running *VEGAS* with LD estimated from data is possible, but it seems doubtful that the LD misspecification could be so severe as to suppress a robustly significant association signal. Certainly the most *a priori* plausible gene, *FNBP1L*, is not supported in our sample ($p = 0.727$).

Polygenic scoring is another way of combining the predictive power of multiple SNPs. At best, the polygenic score could predict 0.7% of variance in our analyses (Figure S7), which occurred when calculating the score from all genotyped SNPs. Presumably, better results could be obtained at stricter p-value cutoffs when the calibration sample is larger. Interestingly, our cross-validation analysis showed that signed unit SNP weights performed about as well as GWAS regression weights. This suggests that, at least when the calibration sample is relatively small, there is negligible loss in predictive accuracy when fixing all SNP effects to the same absolute magnitude, and using GWAS merely to determine the direction of each SNP's effect. We attempted the unit-weighting to strike a different balance between bias and variance. The GWAS regression weights, while unbiased, are estimated with consider-

able sampling error. On the other hand, unit weights are presumably biased, but possibly less variable over repeated sampling. In fact, unit weights can rival optimal least-squares weights in terms of predictive accuracy, especially when the overall amount of predictive error is large [56].

We are somewhat surprised at the relative performance of the polygenic score at inclusive vis-à-vis exclusive p-value cutoffs. We expected that the peak would occur at a relatively stringent cutoff, and that most SNPs with p greater than 0.25 or so would be irrelevant noise. Peak R^2 occurred at stricter cutoffs for the three replication cohorts of Benyamin et al. [33], including the one from MCTFR (at $p \leq 0.01$), which is a subsample of the present study sample. Likewise, in Lango Allen et al.'s [25] report on height, the average R^2 across five validation samples was highest at $p \leq 0.001$. However, both Benyamin et al. and Lango Allen et al. had the advantage of larger calibration samples than we did here. With larger calibration samples, estimates of SNP weights have less sampling error, and a given non-null effect size corresponds to a smaller expected p-value in the calibration sample. Evidently, our most significant SNPs had limited predictive power, but a heap of non-significant SNPs can better contribute to prediction in the aggregate. Polygenic scores calculated from all 527,829 genotyped SNPs at best account for about 0.7% of phenotypic variance, a value that contrasts sharply with parameter estimates from *GCTA*, even though both represent the proportion of variance attributable to every SNP on the array.

No single SNP has yet been replicably associated with human intelligence at genome-wide significance levels, and our GWAS results do not change that fact. This is not surprising, though, in light of our GWAS' limited power. Given a conservative estimate of our effective sample size, we would have slightly above 80% power to detect a SNP accounting for 2% of phenotypic variance, which constitutes rather poor power. Even given an aggressive estimate of effective sample size, we would have slightly above 80% power to detect a SNP accounting for 0.6% of variance. But if realistic effect sizes are even smaller, like on the order of 0.2% to 0.4%[18,19], this would still be inadequate. Needless to say, the major limitation of the present study was its limited sample size and commensurately limited power.

Even though we lacked sufficient power to detect a realistic SNP effect at genome-wide significance levels, the overall distribution of our test statistics and p-values differs slightly but appreciably from the null. This kind of genomic inflation can reflect population stratification(e.g., Ref [57]), but as shown analytically, through simulation, and through analysis of data from the GIANT Consortium [54], such genomic inflation is expected when there is no lurking population structure and the number of causal SNPs is large. Population stratification is doubtful in our case, because we carefully ensured that all our participants are White, and included 10 principal components from EIGENSTRAT as covariates. Even so, we cannot rule it out completely, so we cautiously interpret our observed genomic inflation as evidence of the massive polygenicity of GCA.

We regard our *GCTA* results as the most impressive and informative. The performance of our polygenic score at inclusive p-value cutoffs, plus the genomic inflation evident in our GWAS, suggest that there is a very large number of trait-relevant polymorphisms, each with a very small individual effect on FSIQ. Our results from *GCTA*–which were similar to those of earlier studies [32,33]–provide even stronger evidence that this is so. We surmise that few behavior geneticists, once they understood the GREML method, were surprised that a substantial proportion of variance in cognitive ability and in height [58] could be attributed to genotyped SNPs on a chip. But, that is precisely why *GCTA* is so monumental: it has furnished molecular genetics with the result that quantitative genetics has predicted for decades, in support of the classical theory of polygenic inheritance. We see now how truly R. A. Fisher wrote when he penned these words in 1918 [59]: "the statistical properties of any feature determined by a *large number* of Mendelian factors have been successfully elucidated...In general, the hypothesis of cumulative Mendelian factors seems to fit the facts very accurately" (p. 432–433, emphasis supplied).

Readers may wonder at the discrepancy between the proportions of variance explainable by polygenic scoring from all genotyped SNPs and by *GCTA*, even though both methods attempt to use SNPs to account for phenotypic variance. The discrepancy is explainable by important differences between the two methods [31]. The essential reason is that the performance of polygenic scoring depends upon accurate calibration of many SNP weights, whereas the performance of GREML methods does not. The multiple SNP weights used to compute the polygenic score are estimated with sampling error, which error is expected to decrease its validation R^2. In contrast, GREML does not predict the phenotype from a linear composite of weighted genotypes. Instead, it estimates the extent to which genetic similarity among participants corresponds to their phenotypic similarity, based on the same principle as biometric analysis in, say, a twin study. It differs from biometric modeling in that it uses genome-wide marker data to calculate genetic similarity between participants who are not closely related, instead of relying on the expected genetic similarity between biological relatives according to quantitative-genetic theory. Visscher et al. [31] discuss the contrast between polygenic scoring and the GREML method, commenting that "the accuracy of prediction from estimated SNP effects can be very different from the proportion of variance explained in the population by those effects" (p. 524).

GCTA provided us with an h^2_{SNP} estimate of 35%, within the range of GREML effect sizes previously observed for cognitive ability [32,33]. But, biometrical heritability estimates for GCA are typically in the range of 50% to 70%. This outcome, that through GREML methods common SNPs on a genome-wide array can account for most but not all of the heritability of a trait, also appears typical for cognitive ability, and for that archetypal polygenic quantitative trait, height [58]. This is known as the problem of "hidden heritability"[60]. Of course, biometrical analysis and GREML each estimate different quantities: $\hat{h}^2_{SNP}$ is only a lower-bound estimate of a phenotype's additive heritability. What, then, might be the molecular basis for the heritability that is not captured by GREML estimates? Since h^2_{SNP} represents the proportion of phenotypic variance attributable to common SNPs on the array (and variants in tight LD with them), it stands to reason that the hidden heritability might be due to polymorphisms that are not common, or are not SNPs (such as copy-number variants), or are not tagged in the population by common SNPs. In any event, if specific polymorphisms underlying variation in GCA are to be discovered, gargantuan sample sizes, such as in the GIANT Consortium [25], will be necessary. But in the meantime, we can conclude that there are a great many unspecified polymorphisms associated with GCA, each with a very small effect–general cognitive ability is indeed "heritable [and] highly polygenic" (Ref [35], p. 1). The trait-relevant SNPs are each Lilliputian in effect size, but together, are legion in number.

Supporting Information

Figure S1 Manhattan plot of GWAS p-values from 527,829 observed SNPs only. Chromosome 23 = X chromosome, chromosome 25 = pseudoautosomal region of sex chromosome. Chromosome 26 indicates mitochondrial DNA. SNPs are plotted by serial position on each chromosome. Genome-wide significance is $-\log_{10}(p) > 7.30$, which no SNP reaches.

Figure S2 Uniform quantile-quantile plot for GWAS p-values from 527,829 observed SNPs only. The black curves delineate 95% confidence limits.

Figure S3 Normal quantile-quantile plots of FGLS residuals, graphed separately by family member. Plotted residuals were obtained from the covariates-only regression. The number of points in each plot is provided in the y-axis label. If families' residual vectors are multivariate-normal in the population, then family members' residuals are expected to be marginally univariate-normal. It can be seen that univariate normality provides a reasonably good approximation, except for some divergence in the lower tail.

Figure S4 Chi-square quantile-quantile plots of squared Mahalanobis distances (from the origin) of families' FGLS residual vectors, graphed separately by family size.

Figure S5 Manhattan plot for gene-based p-values from *VEGAS*, inputting observed SNPs only. Analysis input was GWAS p-values from 515,385 autosomal SNPs on the Illumina array. Abscissa position of each point is the gene's beginning base-pair position, NCBI genome build 36. Genome-wide significance is $-\log_{10}(p) > 5.55$, which no gene reaches.

Figure S6 Uniform quantile-quantile plot for gene-based p-values from *VEGAS*, inputting observed SNPs only. Analysis input was GWAS p-values from 515,385 autosomal SNPs on the Illumina array. Black curves delineate 95% confidence limits.

Figure S7 Five-fold cross-validation of polygenic score, predicting FSIQ residuallized for covariates. Figure depicts cross-validation Buse's R^2 for predicting residuallized FSIQ in the indicated subsample from polygenic score calculated from regression weights obtained in the other 4 subsamples. "P-value cutoff" dictated how small a SNP's p-value had to be in the calibration GWAS to be included in calculating polygenic score for the validation sample. Polygenic score was either calculated directly from the GWAS weights (solid lines) or from signed unit weights (dashed lines; see text).

Figure S8 Normal quantile-quantile plots of predicted *GCTA* random effects. The left-hand panel depicts empirical best linear unbiased predictions (eBLUPs) of 3,322 participants' total genetic effects, i.e. **g** in main-text Equation (4), conditional on the fixed effects. The right-hand panel depicts those participants' residuals, given the fixed effects and the eBLUPs of **g**. As explained in the text, quantile-quantile plots of eBLUPs should be interpreted cautiously.

Table S1 Family patterns of GWAS data availability.

Table S2 *RFGLS* parameter estimates for regression of FSIQ onto covariates only.

Material S1 Supplementary Appendix: $\hat{h}^2_{SNP}$ as function of genetic-relatedness cutoff. Includes Figures A1, A2, and A3

Acknowledgments

The authors give their special thanks to Niels G. Waller for his helpful comments on a draft of this paper.

Author Contributions

Analyzed the data: RMK. Contributed reagents/materials/analysis tools: SB MBM. Wrote the paper: RMK. Oversaw data collection: MM WGI. Planned the data analysis: RMK MBM MM.

References

1. Gottfredson LS (2003) *g*, Jobs, and Life. In: Nyborg H, editor. The Scientific Study of General Intelligence: Tribute to Arthur R. Jensen. New York: Pergamon. 293–342.
2. Herrnstein RJ, Murray C (1994) The Bell Curve: Intelligence and Class Structure in American Life. New York: Simon & Schuster, Inc.
3. Jensen AR (1998) The g Factor: The Science of Mental Ability. London: Praeger.
4. Deary IJ (2012) Intelligence. Annual Review of Psychology 63: 453–482. doi:10.1146/annurev-psych-120710-100353.
5. Bouchard TJ, McGue M (1981) Familial studies of intelligence: A review. Science 212: 1055–1059.
6. Bouchard TJ, McGue M (2003) Genetic and environmental influences on human psychological differences. Journal of Neurobiology 54: 4–45.
7. Deary IJ, Spinath FM, Bates TC (2006) Genetics of intelligence. European Journal of Human Genetics 14: 690–700. doi:10.1038/sj.ejhg.5201588.
8. Rijsdijk FV, Vernon PA, Boomsma DI (2002) Application of hierarchical genetic models to Raven and WAIS subtests: A Dutch twin study. Behavior Genetics 32: 199–210.
9. Ioannidis JPA, Ntzani EE, Trikalinos TA, Contopoulos-Ioannidis DG (2001) Repication validity of genetic association studies. Nature Genetics 29: 306–309.
10. Hirschorn JN, Lohmueller K, Byrne E, Hirschorn K (2002) A comprehensive review of genetic association studies. Genetics in Medicine 4: 45–61.
11. Payton A (2006) Investigating cognitive genetics and its implications for the treatment of cognitive deficit. Genes, Brain and Behavior 5: 44–53. doi:10.1111/j.1601-183X.2006.00194.x.
12. Chabris CF, Hebert BM, Benjamin DJ, Beauchamp J, Cesarini D, et al. (2012) Most reported genetic associations with general intelligence are probably false positives. Psychological Science 23: 1314–1323. doi:10.1177/0956797611435528.
13. Risch N, Merikangas M (1996) The future of genetic studies of complex human diseases. Science 273: 1516–1517.
14. Balding DJ (2006) A tutorial on statistical methods for population association studies. Nature Reviews Genetics 7: 781–791.
15. Plomin R (2003) Molecular genetics and *g*. In: Nyborg H, editor. The Scientific Study of General Intelligence: Tribute to Arthur R. Jensen. New York: Pergamon. 275–292.
16. Daniels J, Holmans P, Williams N, Turic D, McGuffin P, et al. (1998) A simple method for analyzing microsatellite allele image patters generated from DNA pools and its application to allelic association studies. American Journal of Human Genetics 62: 1189–1197.
17. Pan Y, Wang K-S, Aragam N (2011) NTM and NR3C2 polymorphisms influencing intelligence: Family-based association studies. Progress in Neuro-Psychopharmacology & Biological Psychiatry 35: 154–160. doi:10.1016/j.pnpbp.2010.10.016.
18. Butcher LM, Davis OSP, Craig IW, Plomin R (2008) Genome-wide quantitative trait locus association scan of general cognitive ability using pooled DNA and 500 K single nucleotide polymorphism microarrays. Genes, Brain and Behavior 7: 435–446. doi:10.1111/j.1601-183X.2007.00368.x.
19. Davis OSP, Butcher LM, Docherty SJ, Meaburn EL, Curtis CJC, et al. (2010) A three-stage genome-wide association study of general cognitive ability: Hunting the small effects. Behavior Genetics 40: 759–767. doi:10.1007/s10519-010-9350-4.
20. Benjamini Y, Hochberg Y (1995) Controlling the false discovery rate: A practical and powerful approach to multiple testing. Journal of the Royal Statistical Society, Series B (Methodological) 57: 289–300.
21. Visscher PM (2008) Sizing up human height variation. Nature Genetics 40: 488–489.
22. Turkheimer E (2011) Still missing. Research in Human Development 8: 227–241.
23. Bouchard TJ (2004) Genetic influence on human psychological traits. Current Directions in Psychological Science 13: 148–151.
24. The International Schizophrenia Consortium (2009) Common polygenic variation contributes to risk of schizophrenia and bipolar disorder. Nature 460: 748–752. doi:10.1038/nature08185.
25. Lango Allen H, Estrada K, Lettre G, Berndt SI, Weedon MN, et al. (2010) Hundreds of variants clustered in genomic loci and biological pathways affect human height. Nature 467: 832–838. doi:10.1038/nature09410.
26. Liu JZ, Mcrae AF, Nyholt DR, Medland SE, Wray NR, et al. (2010) A versatile gene-based test for genome-wide association studies. The American Journal of Human Genetics 87: 139–145. doi:10.1016/j.ajhg.2010.06.009.
27. Nyholt DR (2004) A simple correction for multiple testing for single-nucleotide polymorphisms in linkage disequilibrium with each other. The American Journal of Human Genetics 74: 765–769.
28. Li J, Ji L (2005) Adjusting multiple testing in multilocus analyses using the eigenvalues of a correlation matrix. Heredity 95: 221–227.
29. Yang J, Lee SH, Goddard ME, Visscher PM (2011) GCTA: A tool for genome-wide complex trait analysis. The American Journal of Human Genetics 88: 76–82.
30. Benjamin DJ, Cesarini D, van der Loos MJHM, Dawes CT, Koellinger PD, et al. (2012) The genetic architecture of economic and political preferences. Proceedings of the National Academy of Sciences 109: 8026–8031.
31. Visscher PM, Yang J, Goddard ME (2010) A commentary on 'Common SNPs Explain a Large Proportion of the Heritability for Human Height' by Yang, et al. (2010). Twin Research and Human Genetics 13: 517–524.
32. Davies G, Tenesa A, Payton A, Yang J, Harris SE, et al. (2011) Genome-wide association studies establish that human intelligence is highly heritable and polygenic. Molecular Psychiatry 16: 996–1005.
33. Benyamin B, St Pourcaine B, Davis OS, Davies G, Hansell NK, et al. (2013) Childhood intelligence is heritable, highly polygenic and associated with FNBP1L. Molecular Psychiatry. doi:10.1038/mp.2012.184.
34. Iacono WG, Carlson SR, Taylor J, Elkins IJ, McGue M (1999) Behavioral disinhibition and the development of substance-use disorders: Findings from the Minnesota Twin Family Study. Development and Psychopathology 11: 869–900.
35. Iacono WG, McGue M (2002) Minnesota Twin Family Study. Twin Research 5: 482–487.
36. Keyes MA, Malone SM, Elkins IJ, Legrand LN, McGue M, et al. (2009) The Enrichment Study of the Minnesota Twin Family Study: Increasing the yield of twin families at high risk for externalizing psychopathology. Twin Research and Human Genetics 12: 489–501.
37. Miller MB, Basu S, Cunningham J, Eskin E, Malone SM, et al. (2012) The Minnesota Center for Twin and Family Research Genome-Wide Association Study. Twin Research & Human Genetics 15: 767–774.
38. McGue M, Keyes M, Sharma A, Elkins I, Legrand L, et al. (2007) The environments of adopted and non-adopted youth: Evidence on range restriction

from the Sibling Interaction and Behavior Study (SIBS). Behavior Genetics 37: 449–462.

39. Flynn JR (1984) The mean IQ of Americans: Massive gains 1932 to 1978. Psychological Bulletin 95: 29–51.

40. Flynn JR (1987) Massive IQ gains in 14 nations: What IQ tests really measure. Psychological Bulletin 101: 171–191.

41. Price AL, Patterson NJ, Plenge RM, Weinblatt ME, Shadick NA, et al. (2006) Principal components analysis corrects for stratification in genome-wide association studies. Nature Genetics 38: 904–909. Software and documentation available as *EIGENSOFT*, at http://genetics.med.harvard.edu/reich/Reich_Lab/Software.html.

42. The International HapMap Consortium (2007) A second generation human haplotype map of over 3.1 million SNPs. Nature 449: 851–862. doi:10.1038/nature06258.

43. Browning BL, Browning SR (2009) A unified approach to genotype imputation and haplotype-phase inference for large data sets of trios and unrelated individuals. The American Journal of Human Genetics 84: 210–223. doi:10.1016/j.ajhg.2009.01.005.

44. Li Y, Willer CJ, Ding J, Scheet P, Abecasis GR (2010) *MaCH*: Using sequence and genotype data to estimate haplotypes and unobserved genotypes. Genetic Epidemiology 34: 816–834. doi:10.1002/gepi.20533. (*Minimac* software and documentation available at http://genome.sph.umich.edu/wiki/Minimac).

45. Sattler JM (1974) *Assessment of Children (Revised)*. Philadelphia: W. B. Saunders Company.

46. American Psychiatric Association (1994) *Diagnostic and Statistical Manual of Mental Disorders* (4th ed.). Washington DC: Author.

47. Gauderman WJ, Morrison JM (2006) QUANTO 1.1: A computer program for power and sample size calculations for genetic-epidemiology studies [software and manual]. Available at http://hydra.usc.edu/gxe/.

48. Campbell CD, Ogburn EL, Lunetta KL, Lyon HN, Freedman ML, et al. (2005) Demonstrating stratification in a European American population. Nature Genetics 8: 868–872. doi:10.1038/ng1607.

49. Li X, Basu S, Miller MB, Iacono WG, McGue M (2011) A rapid generalized least squares model for genome-wide quantitative trait association analysis.

Human Heredity 71: 67–82. Package and manual available at http://www.cran.r-project.org/web/packages/RFGLS/.

50. Purcell S, Neale B, Todd-Brown K, Thomas L, Ferreira MAR, et al. (2007) *PLINK*: A tool set for whole-genome association and population-based linkage analyses. American Journal of Human Genetics 81: 559–575. doi:10.1086/519795. Software and documentation available at http://pngu.mgh.harvard.edu/~purcell/plink/.

51. Buse A (1973) Goodness of fit in generalized least squares estimation. The American Statistician 27: 106–108.

52. Nagelkerke NJD (1991) A note on a general definition of the coefficient of determination. Biometrika 78: 691–692.

53. Devlin B, Roeder K (1999) Genomic control for association studies. Biometrics 55: 997–1004.

54. Yang J, Weedon MH, Purcell S, Lettre G, Estrada K, et al. (2011) Genomic inflation factors under polygenic inheritance. European Journal of Human Genetics 19: 807–812. doi:10.1038/ejhg.2011.39.

55. McCulloch CE, Neuhaus JM (2011) Prediction of random effects in linear and generalized linear models under model misspecification. Biometrics 67: 270–279. doi:10.1111/j.1541-0420.2010.01435.x.

56. Dana J, Dawes RM (2004) The superiority of simple alternatives to regression for social science predictions. Journal of Educational and Behavioral Statistics 29: 317–331.

57. Marchini J, Cardon LR, Phillips MS, Donnelly P (2004) The effects of human population structure on large genetic association studies. Nature Genetics 36: 512–517. doi:10.1038/ng1337.

58. Yang J, Benyamin B, McEvoy BP, Gordon S, Henders AK, et al. (2010) Common SNPs explain a large proportion of the heritability for human height. Nature Genetics 42: 565–569.

59. Fisher RA (1918) The correlation between relatives on the supposition of Mendelian inheritance. Transactions of the Royal Society of Edinburgh 52: 399–433.

60. Gibson G (2010) Hints of hidden heritability in GWAS. Nature Genetics 42: 558–560.

13

Accelerating the Switchgrass (*Panicum virgatum* L.) Breeding Cycle Using Genomic Selection Approaches

Alexander E. Lipka[1¤a*], Fei Lu[1], Jerome H. Cherney[2], Edward S. Buckler[1,3,4], Michael D. Casler[5,6], Denise E. Costich[1,3¤b]

1 Institute for Genomic Diversity, Cornell University, Ithaca, New York, United States of America, **2** Department of Crop and Soil Sciences, Cornell University, Ithaca, New York, United States of America, **3** Agricultural Research Service, United States Department of Agriculture, Ithaca, New York, United States of America, **4** Department of Plant Breeding and Genetics, Cornell University, Ithaca, New York, United States of America, **5** Agricultural Research Service, United States Department of Agriculture, Madison, Wisconsin, United States of America, **6** Department of Agronomy, University of Wisconsin–Madison, Madison, Wisconsin, United States of America

Abstract

Switchgrass (*Panicum virgatum* L.) is a perennial grass undergoing development as a biofuel feedstock. One of the most important factors hindering breeding efforts in this species is the need for accurate measurement of biomass yield on a per-hectare basis. Genomic selection on simple-to-measure traits that approximate biomass yield has the potential to significantly speed up the breeding cycle. Recent advances in switchgrass genomic and phenotypic resources are now making it possible to evaluate the potential of genomic selection of such traits. We leveraged these resources to study the ability of three widely-used genomic selection models to predict phenotypic values of morphological and biomass quality traits in an association panel consisting of predominantly northern adapted upland germplasm. High prediction accuracies were obtained for most of the traits, with standability having the highest ten-fold cross validation prediction accuracy (0.52). Moreover, the morphological traits generally had higher prediction accuracies than the biomass quality traits. Nevertheless, our results suggest that the quality of current genomic and phenotypic resources available for switchgrass is sufficiently high for genomic selection to significantly impact breeding efforts for biomass yield.

Editor: David D. Fang, USDA-ARS-SRRC, United States of America

Funding: This work was supported by Department of Energy-United States Department of Agriculture Plant Feedstock Genomics for Bioenergy Program Project Number DE-A102-07ER64454 (http://genomicscience.energy.gov/research/DOEUSDA/) and United States Department of Agriculture—Agricultural Research Services (http://www.ars.usda.gov/main/main.htm). The funders had no role in study design, data collection and analysis, decision to publish, or preparation of the manuscript.

Competing Interests: The authors have declared that no competing interests exist.

* Email: alipka@illinois.edu

¤a Current address: Department of Crop Sciences, University of Illinois, Urbana, Illinois, United States of America
¤b Current address: International Maize and Wheat Improvement Center (CIMMYT), Texcoco, Mexico

Introduction

Switchgrass (*Panicum virgatum* L.) is undergoing development as a biofuel feedstock due to its high biomass yield, broad adaptation, perennial growth habit, and long-standing presence in the seed industry [1]. Once inhabiting prairie and savanna ecosystems from Canada to Mexico and east of the Rocky Mountains, native switchgrass is now confined to thousands of prairie and savanna remnants that range in size from a few plants to a few hundred hectares [2]. Driven largely by photoperiod and temperature, latitude is the principal source of adaptive phenotypic variability across a broad landscape [3,4].

Switchgrass contains three principal taxa: a tetraploid $(2n = 4x = 28)$ lowland ecotype, a tetraploid upland ecotype, and an octoploid $(2n = 8x = 56)$ upland ecotype [5]. Upland ecotypes originated from upland prairie and savanna habitats that were frequently exposed to drought, especially toward the western portion of the range [6]. Lowland ecotypes originated in low-lying riverine or lacustrine habitats that were exposed to seasonal wet periods [6]. Upland ecotypes tend to be more northern adapted,

while lowland ecotypes tend to be more southern adapted, with a transition zone where both can be found, sometimes within a single prairie or savanna remnant [5]. Upland and lowland ecotypes are highly cross-fertile and significant gene flow has occurred between the ecotypes during glacial maxima of the past million years [7]. Ploidy is the secondary taxonomic division within the species, primarily within the upland ecotype; lowland plants at the octoploid level are rare [8]. Gene flow has occurred between tetraploid and octoploid levels, largely by 2n gametes (4x to 8x) or haploidy (8x to 4x), but at relatively low frequencies due to the role of ploidy as a hybridization barrier [9].

Since the establishment of switchgrass as the herbaceous model species for cellulosic biofuel feedstock development in 1992 [1], a total of 12 breeding programs have been developed in North America [5]. Due to phenotypic differences among the three principal taxa and to the magnitude of adaptive phenotypic variation for flowering time and temperature (cold and heat) tolerance, there is very little overlap or duplication among these breeding programs. Collectively, their target population of environments covers eastern North America, but their individual target regions are realistically broken down into a minimum of eight regional gene pools or cultivar deployment zones [5]. Because adaptive phenotypic variation is a strong driver of both adaptation and production traits, genotype × environment interactions are a dominant force and individual cultivars are rarely adapted to more than three hardiness zones, as defined by [10].

Due to the length of the breeding cycle and the need for frequent (perhaps constant) phenotypic assessment of adaptive traits, few cultivars have been developed with documented improvement in biomass production traits. 'Liberty' is the most notable example, demonstrating both an increase in biomass yield and broader adaptation into USDA hardiness zone 3 [11]. Recent advances in the development of genomic tools for measuring and quantifying DNA marker diversity and sophisticated statistical tools to associate marker variation with phenotypic variation have the potential to revolutionize switchgrass breeding methodology [12]. Switchgrass breeding is complicated by the perennial nature of the species and the need for accurate measurement of biomass yield on a per-hectare basis, the single trait that is most limiting for sustainable and economically viable biomass production [13]. Simple-to-measure surrogate traits are needed to speed up the breeding cycle. Genomic selection [14,15] offers such an opportunity by developing predictive equations that allow breeders to measure DNA markers on seedlings and to predict which seedlings will have the highest biomass yield potential as adult plants [12].

The potential of genomic selection for improving the effectiveness of breeding programs has been successfully demonstrated in livestock [16–18], annual crops [19–23], and forest trees [24–26]. In these species, genomic selection has been shown to increase selection accuracy, reduce evaluation cost per genotype, and reduce breeding cycle time compared to phenotypic selection. More specifically, a recent evaluation of genomic selection methods concluded that genomic selection for perennial biofuel crops, such as switchgrass, is most advantageous when biomass yield on a per-hectare basis is difficult or expensive to measure, when it is difficult or impossible to apply meaningful selection pressure on plants within families, and when cycle times are >5 years, which is typically the case with switchgrass [12].

The purpose of this study was to explore the potential for genomic selection to increase the breeding cycle in switchgrass, particularly for seven morphological traits and 13 biomass quality traits. For most of these traits, reasonably high prediction accuracies were obtained. Our analysis was conducted within an association panel of 515 genotypes defined as a random sample of switchgrass from the northern USA gene pools. The population was evaluated using a set of 16,669 single nucleotide polymorphisms (SNPs) obtained using genotyping by sequencing (GBS) techniques [27,28] that were subsequently mapped to the recently available *Panicum virgatum* genome sequence v1.1 reference genome [29].

Materials and Methods

Germplasm

We analyzed the switchgrass association panel described in [27]. Briefly, this panel included 66 diverse switchgrass populations derived from predominantly northern adapted upland germplasm. Both tetraploid and octoploid germplasm were included. This panel was grown from seed planted at the greenhouse in the USDA-ARS Dairy Forage Research Center in Madison, Wisconsin in 2007. Ten clones or genotypes from each population were vegetatively propagated, then planted in Ithaca, New York in 2008

in a randomized complete block design with two replicates. Subsequently, a total of 540 plants from the Ithaca location were used for genotypic and phenotypic evaluation.

Morphological traits

The association panel was evaluated for seven morphological traits in 482 of the plants grown in Ithaca, NY during the 2009, 2010, and 2011 field seasons. These traits included anthesis date, heading date, standability, leaf length, leaf width, plant height, and total plant height. Descriptions of how each of these traits was measured are presented in Table 1, and the tools used to obtain the measurements are described at http://www.maizegenetics.net/phenotyping-tools [30]. Prior to subsequent analysis, the heading and anthesis dates were converted to growing degree days (GDD) as follows:

1) The first day in which GDD was recorded occurs the day after the first five consecutive days where the average temperature is >32° F.

2) After this day, GDD for a single day is calculated as:

$$[(Adj.Min + Adj.Max)/2] - 32$$

where *Adj. Min* is the maximum of the minimum daily temperature and 32°F, and *Adj.Max* is the minimum of the of the maximum daily temperature and 86°F. Intuitively, *Adj. Min* and *Adj.Max* limits the recorded minimum and maximum daily temperatures to 32°F and 86°F, respectively.

3) For each day after the first day in which GDD is recorded, the cumulative GDD is also recorded. The cumulative GDD is used to record heading date and anthesis date.

Biomass Quality traits

Near-infrared reflectance spectroscopy (NIRS, described in [31]) was used to estimate 42 biomass quality traits for a total 515 genotypes grown during two field seasons at the Ithaca, NY location. Samples were ground in Ithaca, NY, shipped to Madison, WI, and scanned on an NIRS unit at the U.S. Dairy Forage Research Center, as described in [31]. A total of 42 biomass quality traits were predicted using equations developed by [31], but only 13 of those traits were analyzed in this study due to their direct relevance and practical value in a breeding program focused on improving conversion efficiency, and to minimize redundancy from collinear traits. Specifically, these traits include acid detergent lignin, minerals (total ash), carbon, high heating value, cell wall concentration, ethanol/g dry forage, etherified ferulates, in vitro dry matter digestibility, pentose sugars release/g dry forage, total soluble carbohydrates, starch, sucrose, and total sugar. No sample had an H-statistic >3.0, indicating that none of the samples could be classified as outliers.

Description of SNPs

The Universal Network-Enabled Analysis Kit (UNEAK) discovery pipeline [27] was used to generate 29,221 SNPs with a minimum call rate of 0.5 and minimum minor allele frequency (MAF) of 0.05 among the 540 plants grown at the Ithaca location. These SNPs were then aligned to the *Panicum virgatum* genome sequence v1.1 [29]. The resulting 16,669 uniquely aligned SNPs were used for subsequent analysis.

Table 1. Phenotyping protocol for seven morphology traits measured in three summer environments, in Ithaca, NY across three years.

Trait Name (units)	Trait Description	Measured in Following Years
Anthesis Date	50% of panicles have 50% open florets	2009–2011
Heading Date	at least 50% of stems are 50% emerged (panicle branches still upright, just starting to spread)	2009–2011
Standability	0 = prostrate	2010–2011
	10 = upright	
Leaf length (mm)	Leaf below flag; base to tip	2009–2011
Leaf width (mm)	Leaf below flag; widest part	2009–2011
Plant Height (cm)	Base of longest flowering stem to the node at the base of the panicle	2009–2011
Total Plant Height (cm)	Base of the longest flowering stem to the tip of the panicle	2009–2011

Phenotypic evaluation

A subset of the 540 plants that yielded sufficient biomass for at least one field season was evaluated for morphological and quality traits. Specifically, 482 plants were evaluated for seven morphological traits and 515 plants were evaluated for 13 quality traits. All 20 traits were examined for outliers using Studentized deleted residuals [32] from a mixed linear model including year, field, block, and population as random effects in SAS version 9.3 [33]. For each trait, best linear unbiased predictors (BLUPs) were obtained for each line across years and replicates, using a mixed linear model fitted in ASReml version 3.0 [34]. Details of the model fitting procedure have been described in [35]. The relationship between each of these BLUPs was then evaluated using the Pearson correlation coefficient (r). Variance component estimates from the model used to obtain BLUPs were also used to estimate repeatability on a clone mean basis ($\hat{h}_i^2$) [36,37]. These repeatability estimates are upper bounds of the heritabilities for each trait. The delta method was used to approximate the standard error of the repeatability estimates [36]. Finally, the Box-Cox procedure [38] was implemented to find the optimal transformation of the BLUPs, as described in [39].

Genomic Selection

Prior to evaluating the genomic selection models, missing allelic values among the 16,669 SNPs anchored to the *Panicum virgatum*

genome sequence v1.1 reference genome were imputed using fastPhase version 1.4.0 [40]. The allele frequencies of these SNPs were calculated among the 482 plants evaluated for the morphology traits and again among the 515 plants evaluated for the quality traits. Within each of these two subsets, SNPs with MAF <0.05 were removed. Consequently, 11,857 SNPs were used in the genomic selection models for the morphology traits, and 12,180 SNPs were used in the models for the quality traits.

To assess the capability of our imputed markers to predict morphological and quality trait values, three genomic selection approaches were tested, namely ridge regression-best linear unbiased prediction (RR-BLUP) [14], least absolute shrinkage and selection operator (LASSO) [41], and elastic net [42]. Although these three approaches have been shown to produce similar results in practice (e.g., [21]), the performance of each approach could depend on the genetic architecture of the evaluated traits. Specifically, RR-BLUP should theoretically outperform LASSO for complex traits, while LASSO should be superior for simpler traits. The elastic net, whose penalty is a weighted average of the penalties of RR-BLUP and LASSO, is considered to be a compromise between the two approaches. In this study, the mixing parameter for the elastic net was set to $\alpha = 0.5$, meaning that the RR-BLUP and LASSO penalties were given equal weights. The RR-BLUP approach was conducted using the rrBLUP package [43] in the R programming language

Table 2. Means and ranges for best linear unbiased predictors (BLUPs) of seven morphological traits evaluated on a switchgrass association panel, and estimated repeatability on a clone-mean basis in three summer environments, in Ithaca, NY across three years.

Trait	No. Lines	BLUP Mean	BLUP SD[b]	BLUP Range	Repeatability	Repeatability SE[c]
Anthesis Date (GDD[a])	481	3840.53	450.21	2630.25–5272.48	0.93	0.01
Heading Date (GDD)	482	2870.47	343.81	2111.75–4547.04	0.91	0.01
Standability (0–10 scale)	481	5.36	1.60	1.47–8.59	0.88	0.01
Leaf Length (mm)	482	528.88	73.30	294.62–708.48	0.85	0.02
Leaf Width (mm)	482	13.32	1.91	6.56–20.75	0.82	0.02
Plant Height (cm)	482	88.78	16.45	44.75–146.16	0.75	0.03
Total Plant Height (cm)	482	162.22	20.24	105.43–222.81	0.85	0.02

[a]GDD, Growing degree dates
[b]SD, Standard deviation
[c]SE, Standard error

Table 3. Means and ranges for best linear unbiased predictors (BLUPs) of 13 quality traits evaluated on a switchgrass association panel, and estimated repeatability on a clone-mean basis in two summer environments, in Ithaca, NY, across two years.

Trait (µg/g)	No. Lines	BLUP Mean	BLUP SD[a]	BLUP Range	Repeatability	Repeatability SE[b]
Acid detergent lignin	514	75.62	5.45	61.47–90.02	0.81	0.02
Minerals (total ash)	514	69.20	4.60	54.47–83.62	0.67	0.03
Carbon	514	443.86	2.19	438.78–452.85	0.67	0.03
High Heating Value	514	4182.59	17.6	4136.14–4237.54	0.76	0.02
Cell wall concentration	514	673.11	47.31	564.12–832.92	0.87	0.01
Ethanol/g dry forage	514	82.73	7.46	60.83–106.78	0.78	0.02
Etherified ferulates	514	0.88	0.10	0.64–1.28	0.83	0.48
In vitro dry matter digestibility	514	410.54	35.16	311.86–494	0.82	0.01
Pentose sugars release/g dry forage	515	191.29	8.30	167.13–218.05	0.77	0.02
Total soluble carbohydrates	514	51.27	8.58	29.22–74.16	0.71	0.03
Starch	514	6.35	2.72	0.67–17.27	0.59	0.04
Sucrose	514	28.29	5.71	13.71–45.13	0.72	0.02
Total sugar	514	625.44	19.01	572.91–691.56	0.79	0.02

[a]SD, Standard deviation
[b]SE, Standard error

[44], while LASSO and elastic net were conducted using the glmnet R package [45].

For any genomic selection model, it is important to ensure that SNP effects arising from overall differences in population structure are factored out [17]. Given the genetic differences attributable to the observed ecotypes and ploidies in our association panel, it is crucial to account for such SNP effects prior to conducting our genomic selection study. Based on the results presented in [27], we hypothesized that the first two principal components (PCs) of a principal component analysis (PCA) of the 16,669 SNPs imputed with fastPhase would sufficiently account for these genetic differences. Accordingly, we fitted a model to each trait where the trait was the response variable and the first two PCs from the PCA of these SNPs were the explanatory variables. The residuals from each model were used for genomic selection.

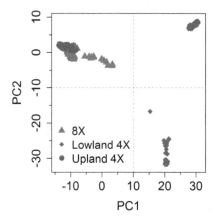

Figure 1. First two principal components of 16,669 single nucleotide polymorphisms separate plants by ploidy and ecotype. The first and second principal components (x- and y-axis, respectively) from a principal component analysis of 540 switchgrass closes separate octoploid (8X) and upland tetraploid (4X) accessions from lowland 4X accessions. The lowland accessions are also separated into two distinct clusters.

The performance of each model was assessed through ten-fold cross validation, as described in [46]. Briefly, the association panel was partitioned into ten equally-sized subgroups. Nine of the ten subgroups (i.e., the training set) were used to fit each prediction model while the remaining subgroup (the prediction set) was used to assess the correlation between the observed and predicted trait values. This process was repeated ten times, with each subgroup being the prediction set exactly once. For each trait, prediction accuracies were calculated by dividing the average Pearson's correlation coefficient across the ten folds by the square root of the repeatability [25]. To prevent inflated prediction accuracies arising from clones nested within populations, the data were partitioned for ten-fold cross validation so that none of the populations were in both the training and prediction sets. All phenotypic and genotypic data used to conduct this analysis are included in File S1.

Results

Extensive Phenotypic Variability among Clones

Substantial variation was observed for each of the seven morphological traits, with differences between minimum and maximum values of each trait ranging from 2-fold for anthesis date to 5.84-fold for standability (Table 2). In general, the majority of the morphological traits were highly correlated, with the strongest Pearson's correlation being between heading date and anthesis date ($r = 0.92$; Table S1). High correlations between leaf width, plant height, and total plant height were also observed (Pearson correlations ranging from $r = 0.53$ to $r = 0.88$). The average repeatability among the seven morphological traits was 0.86, with a range from 0.75 for plant height to 0.93 for anthesis date (Table 2). These high repeatabilities suggest that the majority of the phenotypic variation is attributable to genetic effects, and that genomic selection could be a useful breeding approach for morphological traits in switchgrass.

In comparison to the morphological traits, a greater range of fold differences between the minimum and maximum values of each trait was observed for the quality traits (Table 3). Although many of the correlations between the quality traits were generally

Table 4. Prediction accuracies of seven morphological traits in a switchgrass association panel.

Trait	Mean prediction accuracy	Prediction accuracy: RR-BLUP[a]	Prediction accuracy: Elastic net	Prediction accuracy: LASSO[b]
Anthesis Date	0.44	0.55 (0.21)	0.38 (0.23)	0.38 (0.23)
Heading Date	0.36	0.39 (0.14)	0.34 (0.20)	0.34 (0.19)
Standability	0.52	0.51 (0.27)	0.53 (0.19)	0.52 (0.19)
Leaf Length	0.40	0.55 (0.21)	0.34 (0.30)	0.32 (0.29)
Leaf Width	0.19	0.32 (0.29)	0.13 (0.24)	0.13 (0.24)
Plant Height	0.25	0.34 (0.18)	0.21 (0.26)	0.20 (0.26)
Total Plant Height	0.15	0.30 (0.28)	0.09 (0.19)	0.06 (0.19)

Standard errors of prediction accuracies are provided in parentheses.
Mean prediction accuracies were obtained by averaging results across ridge regression best linear unbiased prediction (RR-BLUP), least absolute shrinkage and selection operator (LASSO), and elastic net analysis.
[a]RR-BLUP, Ridge regression-best linear unbiased prediction
[b]LASSO, Least absolute shrinkage and selection operator

lower than those between the morphology traits, some individual quality traits were strongly correlated. For example, a Pearson correlation coefficient of $r = 0.95$ was observed between sucrose and total soluble carbohydrates (Table S2). Although lower than observed among the morphology traits, the estimated repeatabilities of the quality traits were sufficiently high enough to merit investigation into the utility of genomic selection.

First Two Principal Components of SNPs Sufficiently Account for Ploidy and Ecotype Differences

The first two PCs of the imputed GBS markers subdivided the plants used in this study into three genetically distinct subgroups (Figure 1). Specifically, the octoploid and upland tetraploid plants were clustered into one group, while the lowland tetraploid plants were subdivided into two distinct clusters. Collectively, these results suggest that the first two PCs of the SNPs capture a substantial amount of the major genetic differences between the ploidies and ecotypes of the plants included in our association panel. Moreover, these results justify our use of the first two PCs to factor out the SNP effects arising from overall population structure differences prior to conducting our genomic selection study.

Genomic Selection has Considerable Potential in Switchgrass

As expected, the observed prediction accuracies were similar across the three GS approaches (Tables 4–5). The predictive ability of the morphological traits were generally higher than those of the quality traits, with the highest prediction accuracies

Table 5. Prediction accuracies of 13 quality traits in a switchgrass association panel.

Trait	Mean prediction accuracy	Prediction accuracy: RR-BLUP[a]	Prediction accuracy: Elastic net	Prediction accuracy: LASSO[b]
Acid detergent lignin	0.34	0.41 (0.25)	0.31 (0.21)	0.30 (0.21)
Minerals (total ash)	−0.08	−0.09 (0.18)	−0.06 (0.13)	−0.10 (0.15)
Carbon	0.12	0.21 (0.25)	0.09 (0.27)	0.07 (0.27)
High Heating Value	0.22	0.26 (0.14)	0.21 (0.16)	0.20 (0.17)
Cell wall concentration	0.23	0.30 (0.23)	0.21 (0.19)	0.19 (0.18)
Ethanol/g dry forage	0.43	0.46 (0.20)	0.42 (0.20)	0.41 (0.21)
Etherified ferulates	0.22	0.27 (0.23)	0.20 (0.16)	0.19 (0.15)
In vitro dry matter digestibility	0.35	0.43 (0.27)	0.32 (0.25)	0.30 (0.25)
Pentose sugars release/g dry forage	0.06	0.15 (0.20)	0.03 (0.26)	0.01 (0.25)
Total soluable carbohydrates	0.30	0.39 (0.21)	0.26 (0.23)	0.25 (0.23)
Starch	0.08	0.19 (0.26)	0.03 (0.16)	0.03 (0.15)
Sucrose	0.32	0.44 (0.20)	0.26 (0.24)	0.25 (0.24)
Total sugar	0.04	0.16 (0.17)	0.00 (0.14)	−0.03 (0.17)

Standard errors of prediction accuracies are provided in parentheses.
Mean prediction accuracies were obtained by averaging results across ridge regression best linear unbiased prediction (RR-BLUP), least absolute shrinkage and selection operator (LASSO), and elastic net analysis.
[a]RR-BLUP, Ridge regression-best linear unbiased prediction
[b]LASSO, Least absolute shrinkage and selection operator

(averaged across all three tested GS models) obtained for standability (0.52), anthesis date (0.44), ethanol/g dry forage (0.43), leaf length (0.40), and heading date (0.36). We also obtained relatively strong positive Spearman's rank correlation coefficients between repeatabilities and unstandardized prediction accuracies for both the morphology ($r_{SP} = 0.61$) and the quality ($r_{SP} = 0.44$) traits. Consistent with the findings of previous studies (e.g., [25]), this result suggests that all three GS approaches successfully use the larger genetic contribution to phenotypic variability of the more heritable traits to obtain higher prediction accuracies.

Discussion

We evaluated the ability of three popular genomic selection approaches to predict the phenotypic values of seven morphological traits and 13 quality traits in a switchgrass association panel. Such a study is important because the successful application of genomic selection to switchgrass could significantly reduce the breeding cycle of this important biofuel feedstock. In general, our prediction accuracies are comparable to those reported in previous studies (e.g., [17] and [23]) that identified quantifiable advantages of genomic selection compared to traditional breeding programs. For perennial grasses such as switchgrass, one important quantity to consider is the expected genetic gain per unit of time. Because genomic selection does not require on-site phenotyping to identify accessions with superior trait values, multiple cycles of breeding could be completed with a genomic selection breeding program during the same amount of time required to achieve one cycle of breeding using traditional breeding programs [17,23]. For instance, it is demonstrated in [23] that it is possible for genomic selection breeding programs in maize and winter wheat to respectively achieve three cycles and two cycles of breeding during the same amount of time to complete one cycle of marker-assisted selection breeding. Moreover, the same study concluded that the expected genetic gain per year from a genomic selection breeding program will exceed that of a marker-assisted selection breeding program for traits with prediction accuracies as low as 0.20 in maize and 0.30 in winter wheat. Because many of our tested traits had prediction accuracies that exceed these thresholds, we believe that it is possible for similar advantages in expected genetic gain per unit of time to be achieved in switchgrass genomic selection breeding programs.

To our knowledge, the genetic architectures of the traits we evaluated are unknown in switchgrass. In particular, little is known about the number of genes underlying each trait. Therefore, we used three genomic selection models that have been hypothesized to perform differently under various genetic architectures. In general, we obtained similar prediction accuracies for all three genomic selection models. This result is especially apparent if we consider the standard errors of the prediction accuracies. Suppose we use the prediction accuracies and their standard errors from each genomic selection model (presented in Tables 4 and 5) to construct 95% confidence intervals. For each trait, the confidence intervals from the three genomic selection approaches overlap. This suggests that there are no discernible differences in prediction accuracies among the three genomic selection models. Indeed, this finding has been reported in other studies (e.g. [46]) and is theoretically justified in [47]. Nevertheless, we recommend repeating our study because we anticipate that the sampling, genotyping, and phenotypic resources available to the switchgrass community will continue to expand and improve, and it is imperative to confirm that these conclusions still hold given the new information we expect to obtain from these resources.

We observed a wide range of prediction accuracies across the traits. We suspect that this result was obtained because our markers provided incomplete coverage of the switchgrass genome, and it is likely that they tagged only a subset of the loci underlying the genetic sources of variation for each trait. It is therefore plausible that traits with higher prediction accuracies have causal loci that were in higher linkage disequilibrium with our markers compared to traits with lower prediction accuracies. Nonetheless, the prediction accuracies for many of the studied traits were suitably high enough to justify further investigation into the application of genomic selection to switchgrass breeding programs. Indeed one major factor contributing to our observed prediction accuracies was the availability of the *Panicum virgatum* genome sequence v1.1 reference genome. Because of this reference genome, we were able to use genotypic information from neighboring markers to impute missing genotypic data, and ultimately obtain substantial increases in the predictive abilities of our genomic selection models. Thus, we strongly recommend that switchgrass genomic selection breeding programs only use markers that are anchored to a reference genome. This will enable accurate imputation of missing data, and should ultimately result in genomic selection models with higher predictive abilities.

In general, lower prediction accuracies were obtained for the biomass quality traits relative to the morphology traits. We suspect that this result could have arisen from two different sources. In contrast to the morphological traits, the process of obtaining the quality traits was a lengthy procedure that was conducted in the laboratory. As such, it is possible that a greater amount of variability was introduced into the quality traits, which ultimately resulted in lower prediction accuracies. Factors such as spatial variability in the field, diurnal variation in biomass quality traits manifested by variation in sampling time, variation in grinding time and blade sharpness, and moisture content of the samples may all introduce variability to the measurement of biomass quality traits.

Our study suggests that the implementation of genomic selection approaches to switchgrass breeding programs will be highly beneficial. We believe that such an approach will revolutionize switchgrass breeding programs just as it has in at least four dairy cattle breeding programs [17]. Indeed, the large body of theoretical and empirical studies conducted in plant and animal species [15,22,25,46,48,49] suggests that genomic selection is a cost-effective approach that will substantially speed up breeding cycles, and we expect that these advantages will significantly benefit the development of switchgrass as a biofuel feedstock. As high as the prediction accuracies were in our study, we expect them to increase as more attention is focused on the characterization and exploitation of switchgrass phenotypic and genotypic resources. Specifically, we believe that increased prediction accuracies will arise from improvements to the switchgrass reference genome, improvements in phenotyping techniques, and the development of markers with higher levels of genomic coverage and density.

Supporting Information

Table S1   Correlation matrix for untransformed BLUPs of the seven morphological traits. Pearson correlation coefficients are presented in the upper triangle, and the P-values for the significance of associations are in the lower triangle.

Table S2   Correlation matrix for untransformed BLUPs of the 13 quality traits. Pearson correlation coefficients are presented in the upper triangle, and the P-values for the significance of associations are in the lower triangle.

File S1 Data files used to conduct analysis. All files used to conduct the genomic selection analysis are included in this file.

Acknowledgments

We would like to thank the propagators on our team, Ken Paddock (Cornell) and Nick Baker (USDA-ARS, Madison, Wisconsin), as well as the legions of undergraduate students who assisted in growing and phenotyping switchgrass, and preparing samples for both phenotypic and genotypic analyses. Nick Lepak (USDA-ARS, Ithaca, New York) provided valuable support at the Ithaca field site and contributed to the GDD calculations

and selection of the appropriate formula. We also thank the Cornell University Genomics Core Facility and the staff at the Institute for Genomic Diversity (Cornell) for their support: they made the development of our GBS markers possible. AEL acknowledges the USDA-ARS for providing a Postdoctoral Fellowship to pursue this research. Pre-publication data for the *Panicum virgatum* genome sequence v1.1 reference genome were provided by the Department of Energy Joint Genome Institute.

Author Contributions

Conceived and designed the experiments: ESB DEC JHC MDC. Performed the experiments: FL DEC JHC MDC. Analyzed the data: AEL FL. Contributed reagents/materials/analysis tools: FL DEC MDC JHC. Wrote the paper: AEL MDC DEC.

References

1. Sanderson MA, Adler PR, Boateng AA, Casler MD, Sarath G (2006) Switchgrass as a biofuels feedstock in the USA. Can J Plant Sci 86: 1315–1325.
2. Stubbendieck JL, Hatch SL, Butterfield CH (1992) North American range plants: U of Nebraska Press.
3. Casler M, Vogel K, Taliaferro C, Ehlke N, Berdahl J, et al. (2007) Latitudinal and longitudinal adaptation of switchgrass populations. Crop Sci 47: 2249–2260.
4. Casler M, Vogel K, Taliaferro C, Wynia R (2004) Latitudinal adaptation of switchgrass populations. Crop Sci 44: 293–303.
5. Casler MD (2012) Switchgrass breeding, genetics, and genomics. Switchgrass: Springer. pp. 29–53.
6. Porter CL Jr (1966) An analysis of variation between upland and lowland switchgrass, Panicum virgatum L., in central Oklahoma. Ecology: 980–992.
7. Zhang Y, Zalapa J, Jakubowski AR, Price DL, Acharya A, et al. (2011) Natural hybrids and gene flow between upland and lowland switchgrass. Crop Sci 51: 2626–2641.
8. Zhang Y, Zalapa JE, Jakubowski AR, Price DL, Acharya A, et al. (2011) Post-glacial evolution of Panicum virgatum: centers of diversity and gene pools revealed by SSR markers and cpDNA sequences. Genetica 139: 933–948.
9. Martinez-Reyna J, Vogel K (2002) Incompatibility systems in switchgrass. Crop Sci 42: 1800–1805.
10. Cathey HM (1990) USDA plant hardiness zone map.
11. Vogel KP, Mitchell R, Casler M, Sarath G (2014) Registration of 'Liberty' switchgrass. J Plant Regist.
12. Simeão Resende RM, Casler MD, Vilela de Resende MD (2014) Genomic selection in forage breeding: accuracy and methods. Crop Sci 54: 143–156.
13. Perrin R, Vogel K, Schmer M, Mitchell R (2008) Farm-scale production cost of switchgrass for biomass. Bioenerg Res 1: 91–97.
14. Meuwissen T, Hayes B, Goddard M (2001) Prediction of total genetic value using genome-wide dense marker maps. Genetics 157: 1819–1829.
15. de los Campos G, Hickey JM, Pong-Wong R, Daetwyler HD, Calus MP (2013) Whole-genome regression and prediction methods applied to plant and animal breeding. Genetics 193: 327–345.
16. Schaeffer L (2006) Strategy for applying genome-wide selection in dairy cattle. J Anim Breed Genet 123: 218–223.
17. Hayes B, Bowman P, Chamberlain A, Goddard M (2009) Invited review: Genomic selection in dairy cattle: Progress and challenges. J Dairy Sci 92: 433–443.
18. VanRaden P, Van Tassell C, Wiggans G, Sonstegard T, Schnabel R, et al. (2009) Invited Review: Reliability of genomic predictions for North American Holstein bulls. J Dairy Sci 92: 16–24.
19. Asoro FG, Newell MA, Beavis WD, Scott MP, Jannink JL (2011) Accuracy and training population design for genomic selection on quantitative traits in elite North American oats. Plant Gen 4: 132–144.
20. Zhao Y, Gowda M, Liu W, Würschum T, Maurer HP, et al. (2012) Accuracy of genomic selection in European maize elite breeding populations. Theor Appl Genet 124: 769–776.
21. Riedelsheimer C, Czedik-Eysenberg A, Grieder C, Lisec J, Technow F, et al. (2012) Genomic and metabolic prediction of complex heterotic traits in hybrid maize. Nat Genet 44: 217–220.
22. Heffner EL, Sorrells ME, Jannink JL (2009) Genomic selection for crop improvement. Crop Sci 49: 1–12.
23. Heffner EL, Lorenz AJ, Jannink JL, Sorrells ME (2010) Plant breeding with genomic selection: gain per unit time and cost. Crop Sci 50: 1681–1690.
24. Resende MD, Resende MF, Sansaloni CP, Petroli CD, Missiaggia AA, et al. (2012) Genomic selection for growth and wood quality in Eucalyptus: capturing the missing heritability and accelerating breeding for complex traits in forest trees. New Phytol 194: 116–128.
25. Resende MF, Muñoz P, Resende MD, Garrick DJ, Fernando RL, et al. (2012) Accuracy of genomic selection methods in a standard data set of loblolly pine (Pinus taeda L.). Genetics 190: 1503–1510.
26. Resende M, Munoz P, Acosta J, Peter G, Davis J, et al. (2012) Accelerating the domestication of trees using genomic selection: accuracy of prediction models across ages and environments. New Phytologist 193: 617–624.
27. Lu F, Lipka AE, Glaubitz J, Elshire R, Cherney JH, et al. (2013) Switchgrass genomic diversity, ploidy, and evolution: novel insights from a network-based SNP discovery protocol. PLoS Genet 9: e1003215.
28. Elshire RJ, Glaubitz JC, Sun Q, Poland JA, Kawamoto K, et al. (2011) A robust, simple genotyping-by-sequencing (GBS) approach for high diversity species. PLoS One 6: e19379.
29. Joint Genome Institute (2014) Phytozome 10. Panicum virgatum v1.1 DOE-JGI. Available: http://phytozome.jgi.doe.gov.
30. Buckler Lab for Maize Genetics and Diversity (nd) Buckler lab phenotyping tools. Available: http://www.maizegenetics.net/phenotyping-tools.
31. Vogel KP, Dien BS, Jung HG, Casler MD, Masterson SD, et al. (2011) Quantifying actual and theoretical ethanol yields for switchgrass strains using NIRS analyses. Bioenerg Res 4: 96–110.
32. Kutner MH, Nachtsheim CJ, Neter J, Li W (2004) Applied Linear Statistical Models. Boston, MA: McGraw-Hill.
33. SAS Institute (2012) The SAS system for Windows. Release 9.3. SAS Institute. Institute SAS: Sas Inst.
34. Gilmour AR, Gogel B, Cullis B, Thompson R, Butler D, et al. (2009) ASReml user guide release 3.0. VSN International Ltd, Hemel Hempstead, UK.
35. Chandler K, Lipka AE, Owens BF, Li H, Buckler ES, et al. (2013) Genetic Analysis of Visually Scored Orange Kernel Color in Maize. Crop Sci 53: 189–200.
36. Holland JB, Nyquist WE, Cervantes-Martínez CT (2003) Estimating and interpreting heritability for plant breeding: An update. Plant Breed Rev 22: 9–112.
37. Hung HY, Browne C, Guill K, Coles N, Eller M, et al. (2012) The relationship between parental genetic or phenotypic divergence and progeny variation in the maize nested association mapping population. Heredity (Edinb) 108: 490–499.
38. Box GEP, Cox DR (1964) An Analysis of Transformations. J Roy Stat Soc B Met 26: 211–252.
39. Lipka AE, Gore MA, Magallanes-Lundback M, Mesberg A, Lin H, et al. (2013) Genome-wide association study and pathway-level analysis of tocochromanol levels in maize grain. G3: Genes, Genomes, Genet 3: 1287–1299.
40. Scheet P, Stephens M (2006) A fast and flexible statistical model for large-scale population genotype data: applications to inferring missing genotypes and haplotypic phase. Am J Hum Genet 78: 629–644.
41. Tibshirani R (1996) Regression shrinkage and selection via the lasso. J Roy Stat Soc B Met: 267–288.
42. Zou H, Hastie T (2005) Regularization and variable selection via the elastic net. J Roy Stat Soc B Met 67: 301–320.
43. Endelman JB (2011) Ridge regression and other kernels for genomic selection with R package rrBLUP. Plant Gen 4: 250–255.
44. Team RC (2012) R: A language and environment for statistical computing.
45. Friedman J, Hastie T, Tibshirani R (2010) Regularization paths for generalized linear models via coordinate descent. J Stat Softw 33: 1.
46. Heslot N, Yang HP, Sorrells ME, Jannink JL (2012) Genomic selection in plant breeding: a comparison of models. Crop Sci 52: 146–160.
47. Gianola D (2013) Priors in whole-genome regression: the Bayesian alphabet returns. Genetics 194: 573–596.
48. Jannink J, Lorenz AJ, Iwata H (2010) Genomic selection in plant breeding: from theory to practice. Brief Funct Genomics 9.2 166–177.
49. Wolc A, Stricker C, Arango J, Settar P, Fulton JE, et al. (2011) Breeding value prediction for production traits in layer chickens using pedigree or genomic relationships in a reduced animal model. Genet Sel Evol 43.

14

Toxin-Antitoxin Systems in the Mobile Genome of *Acidithiobacillus ferrooxidans*

Paula Bustamante[1], Mario Tello[2], Omar Orellana[1]*

1 Programa de Biología Celular y Molecular, ICBM, Facultad de Medicina, Universidad de Chile, Santiago, Chile, **2** Centro de Biotecnología Acuícola, Departamento de Biología, Facultad de Química y Biología, Universidad de Santiago de Chile, Santiago, Chile

Abstract

Toxin-antitoxin (TA) systems are genetic modules composed of a pair of genes encoding a stable toxin and an unstable antitoxin that inhibits toxin activity. They are widespread among plasmids and chromosomes of bacteria and archaea. TA systems are known to be involved in the stabilization of plasmids but there is no consensus about the function of chromosomal TA systems. To shed light on the role of chromosomally encoded TA systems we analyzed the distribution and functionality of type II TA systems in the chromosome of two strains from *Acidithiobacillus ferrooxidans* (ATCC 23270 and 53993), a Gram-negative, acidophilic, environmental bacterium that participates in the bioleaching of minerals. As in other environmental microorganisms, *A. ferrooxidans* has a high content of TA systems (28-29) and in twenty of them the toxin is a putative ribonuclease. According to the genetic context, some of these systems are encoded near or within mobile genetic elements. Although most TA systems are shared by both strains, four of them, which are encoded in the active mobile element ICE*Afe*1, are exclusive to the type strain ATCC 23270. We demostrated that two TA systems from ICE*Afe*1 are functional in *E. coli* cells, since the toxins inhibit growth and the antitoxins counteract the effect of their cognate toxins. All the toxins from ICE*Afe*1, including a novel toxin, are RNases with different ion requirements. The data indicate that some of the chromosomally encoded TA systems are actually part of the *A. ferrooxidans* mobile genome and we propose that could be involved in the maintenance of these integrated mobile genetic elements.

Editor: Finbarr Hayes, University of Manchester, United Kingdom

Funding: This work was supported by grants from Fondecyt Chile 1110203 to OO (http://www.conicyt.cl/fondecyt/) and Proyecto Bicentenario PDA20 (www.conicyt.cl) and Proyecto FIA PYT20120056 to MT (www.fia.cl). PB was the recipient of a graduate studies fellowship and supporting fellowship AT-24100112 from Conicyt (www.conicyt.cl), Chile. The funders had no role in study design, data collection and analysis, decision to publish, or preparation of the manuscript.

Competing Interests: The authors have declared that no competing interests exist.

* Email: oorellan@med.uchile.cl

Introduction

Toxin-antitoxin (TA) systems are small genetic modules widely distributed in bacteria and archaea [1] that are comprised of a pair of genes encoding a stable toxin and an unstable antitoxin capable of inhibiting toxin activity [1,2]. In contrast to bacteriocins [3] and toxins from contact-dependent inhibition systems [4], TA toxins are not secreted and inhibit cell growth by targeting key molecules in essential cellular processes such as DNA replication, mRNA stability or protein, cell-wall or ATP biosynthesis [1].

TA systems were first discovered as systems that contribute to plasmid maintenance by a phenomenon denoted as "post-segregational killing" or "addiction" [5,6]. When a plasmid encoding a TA system is lost from a cell, the toxin is released from the existing TA complex as the unstable antitoxin decays, resulting in cell growth inhibition and eventually death [7]. In addition to plasmids, TA systems are also found in bacterial chromosomes, particularly in free-living prokaryotic cells [8,9], but their function is not well understood [10]. Although chromosomal TA systems are not essential for normal cell growth [11], it is believed that they play key roles in stress response [12], persister phenotype [13] and stabilization of horizontally acquired genetic elements [14].

Five types of TA systems have been proposed to date. All of them comprise a toxic protein (toxin) and an antitoxin that can be either a small non-coding RNA (type I and type III [15,16]) or a low molecular weight protein (types II, IV and V [17–19]). Recent studies have identified an ever-increasing number of experimentally defined, or putative, type I, type II and type III TA systems [8,9,15,16]. On the other hand, type IV and type V TA systems were recently discovered and to date have only a few representatives [17,18,20,21].

Type II TA systems, the most well known and the interest of this work, are encoded in operons consisting of genes that overlap (or are a few bases apart); the toxin and its cognate antitoxin form a stable protein TA complex that prevents the toxic effect [1]. Type II TA systems are diverse and are classified in 12 toxin and 20 antitoxin super-families based on sequence similarity [19]. Targets of type II toxins are also diverse, most frequently acting to cleave mRNA at specific sequences to inhibit translation in a ribosome-dependent or independent manner [22,23].

Type II systems are thought to move from one genome to another by horizontal gene transfer (HGT) [9]. In fact, some TA systems (besides plasmidial TA) are localized within mobile genetic elements (MGEs) such as transposons and superintegrons [24,25].

Chromosomally encoded TA systems have also been shown to have a role in the stabilization of large genomic fragments and integrative-conjugative elements (ICEs) [14,26]. Thus, it is possible that TA systems considered to be chromosomally encoded could actually be associated with active or inactive integrated genetic elements.

The number of type II TA systems in an organism varies greatly, not only from one bacterial species to another, but also between isolates from the same species [9,19]. Most of the organisms that have many TA systems grow in nutrient-limited environments and/or are chemolithoautotrophs (although a high TA content is observed in some obligate intracellular bacterial genomes [19]), leading to the proposal that these systems might be beneficial for this type of slow-growing microorganisms [9].

Acidithiobacillus ferrooxidans is an environmental acidophilic, chemolithoautotrophic Gram-negative γ-proteobacterium (although some discrepancies exist concerning its classification in this bacterial class [27]) that obtains its energy from the oxidation of ferrous ions or reduced sulfur compounds [28]. It belongs to the consortium of microorganisms that participate in the bioleaching of minerals, being a model organism for the study of bioleaching, metabolic and genomic studies of acidophilic bacteria [28,29]. Although no genetic system has been developed for this microorganism, the genome sequences of two strains are available in public databases (ATCC 23270 and ATCC 53993 strains). A number of MGE-related DNA sequences have been described in its genome as insertion sequence elements, transposons and plasmids [28,30,31], including a large genomic island [32] and an actively excising integrative-conjugative element (ICE*Afe*1) [33]. As these MGEs are stably integrated into the chromosome of *A. ferrooxidans* and a number of TA-related proteins have been annotated in the genome of the two sequenced strains [28], it is possible that this environmental bacterium relies on TAs to avoid the loss of these mobile elements.

To shed light into the role of chromosomally encoded TA systems from *A. ferrooxidans* and their relation with MGEs, we studied the distribution of type II TA systems in the two available sequenced genomes in public databases. We also studied the functionality of the systems encoded in the actively excising ICE*Afe*1. Based on our data we propose that type II TA systems from *A. ferrooxidans* could be part of its mobile genome and might be involved in the maintenance of its MGEs.

Materials and Methods

Bioinformatic analysis

In silico screening for type II TA systems in *A. ferrooxidans* ATCC 23270 (NCBI RefSeq NC_011761) and ATCC 53993 (NCBI RefSeq NC_011206) was conducted using the web-based search tool TADB (http://bioinfo-mml.sjtu.edu.cn/TADB/) [34], an online resource of type II TA loci-relevant data from 'wet' experimental data as well as information garnered by bioinformatics analyses. We also used the data from RASTA-Bacteria (http://genoweb1.irisa.fr/duals/RASTA-Bacteria/) [35], an automated method allowing identification of TA loci in sequenced prokaryotic genomes, whether they are annotated open reading frames or not.

The classification of putative toxin and antitoxins in superfamilies was according to Leplae et al. [19]. Using BLASTP, each putative toxin and antitoxin from *A. ferrooxidans* was compared against the sequences of toxins and antitoxins from the different super-families described by Leplae et al. [19], either 'original', 'similar' or validated sequences. An E-value score threshold of 0.001 and 50% query residues aligned were used to select

candidates. Each toxin or antitoxin was assigned to the super-family with the best hit and a name was given according to the best protein hit. Protein structure predictions were assayed by Phyre 2.0 server [36].

The Integrated Microbial Genomes platform (IMG, http://img.jgi.doe.gov/cgi-bin/w/main.cgi) [37] was used for the visualization of genome contexts and characteristics of each gene and protein.

Phylogenetic analysis

Multi-alignment between nucleotide sequences encoding TA toxins was performed using ClustalW [38]. The parameters were set up to align codons using Gonnet as substitution matrix [39]. The evolutionary history was inferred using the Neighbor-Joining method [40]. The optimal tree with the sum of branch length = 380.7 is shown. The confidence probability (multiplied by 100) that the interior branch length is greater than 0, as estimated using the bootstrap test (1000 replicates), is shown next to the branches [41]. The evolutionary distances were computed using the Maximum Composite Likelihood method [42]. The rate of variation among sites was modeled with a gamma distribution (shape parameter = 1). The analysis involved 72 nucleotide sequences. All ambiguous positions were removed for each sequence pair. There were a total of 618 positions in the final dataset. Multialignment and evolutionary analyses were conducted in MEGA5 [43].

Bacterial strains and growth conditions

Escherichia coli JM109 strain was used for cloning and plasmid maintenance. *E. coli* BL21(DE3)pLysS strain was used for recombinant protein expression and BL21(DE3) strain for plasmid maintenance tests. The strains were grown in Luria-Bertani (LB) or on LB agar at 37°C with 1% glucose. When appropriate, media were supplemented with ampicillin (100 μg/ml) or chloramphenicol (34 μg/ml). When both antibiotics were used together, they were added to half of the concentration.

Cloning of TA systems

Toxin and antitoxin genes were amplified by PCR using PfuUltra II Fusion HS DNA Polymerase (Agilent Technologies), *A. ferrooxidans* ATCC 23270 chromosomal DNA as a template and the oligonucleotides indicated in Table 1. The pETDuet-1 expression vector (Novagen) was used for cloning. The amplified genes and vector DNA were double digested with *Bam*HI/*Hind*III or *Nde*I/*Xho*I according to the protocols indicated by the manufacturer (ThermoScientific), ligated with T4 DNA Ligase (New England Biolabs), and used to transform *E. coli* JM109 by a chemical method [44]. Three types of recombinant vectors were constructed: pETDuet-T, with toxin genes cloned into multiple cloning site-1 (MCS1) so that the toxins are expressed as N-terminal (His)₆-tagged proteins; pETDuet-A, with the antitoxin genes cloned into MCS1; and pETDuet-TA, corresponding to pETDuet-T vectors with the cognate antitoxin genes cloned into MCS2. Transformants were selected with ampicillin and checked by colony PCR with the oligonucleotides indicated in Table 1. Cloned genes were analyzed by DNA sequencing (Macrogen, USA). Recombinant plasmids were used for transformation of *E. coli* BL21(DE3)pLysS cells by a chemical method [44].

For the plasmid maintenance test (see below) we constructed pACYCDuet-A plasmids, corresponding to the pACYCDuet-1 vector (Novagen) with antitoxin genes cloned into its MCS2. DNA fragments containing the antitoxin genes were obtained from the corresponding pETDuet-TA plasmids double digested with *Nde*I/ *Xho*I. The fragments were ligated to pACYCDuet-1 double

Table 1. Oligonucleotides used.

Name	Sequence 5'-3'	Use
HtoxinDuet-F	AGA TCT TCT GAT GGG CGC TGC	Forward oligonucleotide for cloning the toxin gene from MazEF-1 system on pGEM-T Easy and further sub-cloning into the MCS1 from pETDuet-1.
HtoxinDuet-R	AAG CTT CTC CCA ATA GCT ATG CC	Reverse oligonucleotide for cloning the toxin gene from MazEF-1 system on pGEM-T Easy and further sub-cloning into the MCS1 from pETDuet-1.
AntitoxinDuet-F	ACC ATA TGC GGG TGA TTG TG	Forward oligonucleotide for cloning the toxin gene from MazEF-1 system on pGEM-T Easy and further sub-cloning into the MCS2 from pETDuet-1.
AntitoxinDuet-R	ATC TCG AGC GCC CAT CAG AG	Reverse oligonucleotide for cloning the toxin gene from MazEF-1 system on pGEM-T Easy and further sub-cloning into the MCS1 from pETDuet-1.
AFE1361_NdeI	GCC AGA GGC ATA TGA TTA CAA TG	Forward oligonucleotide for cloning of the antitoxin gene from StbC/VapC-3 system into the MCS2 from pETDuet-1
AFE1361_XhoI	GGT CTC GAG CAA AAT CAT GC	Reverse oligonucleotide for cloning of the antitoxin gene from StbC/VapC-3 system into the MCS2 from pETDuet-1
AFE1362_BamHI	ATA GGA TCC CAT GAT TTT GCT GG	Forward oligonucleotide for cloning of the toxin gene from StbC/VapC-3 system into the MCS1 from pETDuet-1
AFE1362_HindIII	CAT TAA GCT TGT CTC ATG TCT C	Reverse oligonucleotide for cloning of the toxin gene from StbC/VapC-3 system into the MCS1 from pETDuet-1
AFE1367_NdeI	TGT GCA TAT GCT TGA TAA GC	Oligonucleotide forward for cloning of the antitoxin gene from TA system number 9 into the MCS2 from pETDuet-1
AFE1367_XhoI	TCT CTC GAG TTG CGC ATC AAC	Reverse oligonucleotide for cloning of the antitoxin gene from TA system number 9 into the MCS2 from pETDuet-1
AFE1368_BamHI	GGG GAT CCG AAA TTT TTA GTT G	Forward oligonucleotide for cloning of the toxin gene from TA system number 9 into the MCS1 from pETDuet-1
AFE_1368_HindIII	CGA TAA GCT TCT TCA CTG ATG G	Reverse oligonucleotide for cloning of the toxin gene from TA system number 9 into the MCS1 from pETDuet-1
AFE1383_NdeI	CAT CCA TAT GAG CGG TGG CAA TG	Forward oligonucleotide for cloning of the antitoxin gene from EcoA1/EcoT1-1 system into the MCS2 from pETDuet-1
AFE1383_XhoI	CGA TCT CGA GTC ATA GCG CAC	Reverse oligonucleotide for cloning of the antitoxin gene from EcoA1/EcoT1-1 system into the MCS2 from pETDuet-1
AFE1384_BamHI	GCA GGA TCC TTT GCT CTG GGT G	Forward oligonucleotide for cloning of the toxin gene from EcoA1/EcoT1-1 system into the MCS1 from pETDuet-1
AFE1384_HindIII	GAC ATA AGC TTC GCT CAT CTC G	Reverse oligonucleotide for cloning of the toxin gene from EcoA1/EcoT1-1 system into the MCS1 from pETDuet-1
pET Upstream Primer	ATG CGT CCG GCG TAG A	Oligonucleotide for sequencing genes inserted into MCS1 from pETDuet-1
DuetDOWN-1 Primer	GAT TAT GCG GCC GTG TAC AA	Oligonucleotide for sequencing genes inserted into MCS1 from pETDuet-1
DuetUP2 Primer	TTG TAC ACG GCC GCA TAA TC	Oligonucleotide for sequencing genes inserted into MCS2 from pETDuet-1 and pACYCDuet-1
T7 Terminator Primer	GCT AGT TAT TGC TCA GCG G	Oligonucleotide for sequencing genes inserted into MCS2 from pETDuet-1 and pACYCDuet-1

digested with the same enzymes and the constructs were used to transform *E. coli* JM109 by a chemical method [44]. Transformants were selected with chloramphenicol and checked by colony PCR with the oligonucleotides indicated in Table 1. Recombinant plasmids were used for transformation of *E. coli* BL21(DE3) cells by a chemical method [44].

Evaluation of toxicity in *E. coli*

The toxicity of toxin proteins in *E. coli* BL21(DE3)pLysS was determined by the growth pattern of cultures on liquid and solid media in the presence or absence of the inducer IPTG. Overnight cultures of *E. coli* BL21(DE3)pLysS cells with plasmids containing toxin, antitoxin or both genes of each TA system were diluted 100-fold and grown in LB broth until an OD_{600} of 0.2-0.3. At this point, 1 mM IPTG was added and growth was monitored by measuring OD_{600} of the cultures in a microplate spectrophotometer (Epoch). Three hours after the induction, aliquots of each culture were 10-fold serial diluted, and 5 μl of each dilution were

spotted on LB agar without IPTG and growth at 37°C for 16 hours. In addition, following the induction with IPTG, a viability assay was performed. At different time intervals culture samples were serially diluted (10-fold) and aliquots were seeded on LB plates to determine the number of colony-forming units (CFU/ml).

Plasmid maintenance test

E. coli BL21(DE3) was double-transformed with the corresponding pETDuet-T and pACYCDuet-A or pETDuet-1 and pACYCDuet-A vectors. With these cultures a plasmid maintenance test was performance as in [45].

Protein expression and purification of (His)$_6$-toxins

Toxins were expressed in *E. coli* BL21(DE3)pLysS carrying the corresponding plasmids after induction with 1 mM IPTG for three hours and purified by Ni^{+2}-affinity chromatography.

(His)$_6$-MazF-1 was purified under native conditions from *E. coli* carrying pETMazF-1. The cells were harvested by centrifugation

Table 2. Putative type II TA systems encoded on *A. ferrooxidans*§.

TA	Antitoxin locus	Accession gi	Hits in CDD	Antitoxin super-family[a] (name)	Toxin locus	Accession gi	Hits in CDD	Toxin super-family[a] (name)	Chromosomal or in a MGE[b]
1	AFE_0085	218668122	Phd super family [cl18766]; COG4118	Phd (Phd-1)	AFE_0086	218666107	PIN_MT3492 [cd09874]	NI (tox1)	Chr
	Lferr_0087	198282235	Phd super family [cl18766]; COG4118	Phd (Phd-1)	Lferr_0088	198282236	PIN_MT3492 [cd09874]	NI (tox1)	Chr
2	AFE_0089	218666717	HTH_XRE [cd00093]	HigA (HigA-1)	AFE_0088	218665352	Plasmid_killer super family [cl01422]	RelE/ParE (HigB-1)	Chr
	Lferr_0091	198282239	HTH_XRE [cd00093]	HigA (HigA-1)	Lferr_0090	198282238	Plasmid_killer super family [cl01422]	RelE/ParE (HigB-1)	Chr
3	AFE_0414	218665317	Phd super family [cl18766]; COG4118	Phd (Phd-2)	AFE_0413	218666088	PIN_SlI0205 [cd09872]	VapC (VapC-1)	Chr
	Lferr_0577	198282717	Phd super family [cl18766]; COG4118	Phd (Phd-2)	Lferr_0576	198282716	PIN_SlI0205 [cd09872]	VapC (VapC-1)	Chr
4	AFE_0477	218665855	VagC super family [cl18787]	VapB (VapB-1)	AFE_0478	218667984	PIN_VapC-FitB [cd09881]	VapC (VapC-2)	Chr
	Lferr_0637	198282777	VagC super family [cl18787]	VapB (VapB-1)	Lferr_0638	198282778	PIN_VapC-FitB [cd09881]	VapC (VapC-2)	Chr
5	AFE_0869	218667933	PhdYeFM_antitox [pfam02604]	NI (antitox5)	AFE_0870	218667345	Plasmid_Txe super family [cl17389]	RelE/ParE (YoeB-1)	Chr
	Lferr_0994	198283126	PhdYeFM_antitox [pfam02604]	NI (antitox5)	Lferr_0995	198283127	Plasmid_Txe super family [cl17389]	RelE/ParE (YoeB-1)	Chr
6	AFE_0889	218667173	PhdYeFM_antitox super family [cl09153]	Phd (StbD-1)	AFE_0890	218665915	RelE [COG2026]	RelE/ParE (StbE-1)	Chr
	Lferr_1011	198283139	PhdYeFM_antitox super family [cl09153]	Phd (StbD-1)	Lferr_1012	198283140	RelE [COG2026]	RelE/ParE (StbE-1)	Chr
7	AFE_1413	218667280	PRK09974; AbrB [COG2002]	NI (antitox7)	AFE_1412	218665529	Toxin_YhaV [pfam11663]	NI (tox7)	Chr
	Lferr_1133	198283260	PRK09974; AbrB [COG2002]	NI (antitox7)	Lferr_1132	198283259	Toxin_YhaV [pfam11663]	NI (tox7)	Chr
8	AFE_1418	218665082	COG4453	NI (antitox8)	AFE_1417	218665278	Acetyltransf_1 [pfam00583]	NI (tox8)	Chr
	Lferr_1137	198283264	COG4453	NI (antitox8)	Lferr_1136	198283263	Acetyltransf_1 [pfam00583]	NI (tox8)	Chr
9	AFE_1560	218667662	DUF4415 [pfam14384]	NI (antitox9)	AFE_1559	218665905	NI	NI (tox9)	ICEAfe2-23270
	Lferr_0133	198282280	DUF4415 [pfam14384]	NI (antitox9)	Lferr_0132	198282279	NI	NI (tox9)	GI
10	AFE_1579	218667623	DUF2191 [pfam09957]	RelB (RelB-1)	AFE_1578	218666342	VapC [COG1487]	NI (tox10)	ICEAfe2-23270
	Lferr_0230	198283374	DUF2191 [pfam09957]	RelB (RelB-1)	Lferr_0229	198282373	VapC [COG1487]	NI (tox10)	ICEAfe2-53993
	Lferr_1290	198283414	DUF2191 [pfam09957]	RelB (RelB-1)	Lferr_1289	198283413	VapC [COG1487]	NI (tox10)	GI
11	AFE_1614	218666352	Excise [TIGR01764]	NI (antitox11)	AFE_1613	218668111	PIN_3 [pfam13470]	NI (tox11)	ICEAfe2-23270
	Lferr_0234	198282378	Excise [TIGR01764]	NI (antitox11)	Lferr_0233	198282377	PIN_3 [pfam13470]	NI (tox11)	GI
12	AFE_1631	218665941	HTH_XRE [cd00093]	NI (antitox12)	AFE_1630'		upstrm_HI1419 [TIGR02683]	NI (tox12)	ICEAfe2-23270
	Lferr_1332	198283452	HTH_XRE [cd00093]	NI (antitox12)	Lferr_1331	198283451	upstrm_HI1419 [TIGR02683]	NI (tox12)	ICEAfe2-53993
13	AFE_1700	218667519	NI	RelB (Paa1-1)	Pseudo		ParE [COG3668]	NI (tox13)	ICEAfe2-23270
	Lferr_0263	198282407	NI	RelB (Paa1-1)	Lferr_0264	198282408	ParE [COG3668]	NI (tox13)	ICEAfe2-53993
	Lferr_1399	198283518	NI	RelB (Paa1-1)	Lferr_1400	198283519	ParE [COG3668]	NI (tox13)	GI

Table 2. Cont.

TA	Antitoxin locus	Accession gi	Hits in CDD	Antitoxin super-family[a] (name)	Toxin locus	Accession gi	Hits in CDD	Toxin super-family[a] (name)	Chromosomal or in a MGE[b]
14	AFE_1732	218667149	YcfA super family [cl00752]	NI (antitox14)	AFE_1733	218666062	UPF0150 [pfam03681]	NI (tox14)	ICEAfe2-23270
	Lferr_1422	198283540	YcfA super family [cl00752]	NI (antitox14)	Lferr_1423	198283541	UPF0150 [pfam03681]	NI (tox14)	ICEAfe2-53993
15	AFE_1779	218665129	StbC super family [cl01921]	NI (antitox15)	AFE_1780	218665399	PIN_VapC-FitB [cd09881]	VapC (VapC-4)	Chr
	Lferr_1455	198283572	StbC super family [cl01921]	NI (antitox15)	Lferr_1456	198283573	PIN_VapC-FitB [cd09881]	VapC (VapC-4)	Chr
16	AFE_2130	218665450	VagC [COG4456]	VapB (MvpA-1)	AFE_2129	218668039	PIN_VapC-FitB [cd09881]	VapC (VapC-5)	Chr
	Lferr_1789	198283896	VagC [COG4456]	VapB (MvpA-1)	Lferr_1788	198283895	PIN_VapC-FitB [cd09881]	VapC (VapC-5)	Chr
17	AFE_2415	218666500	DUF4415 [pfam14384]	NI (antitox17)	AFE_2414	218666978	DUF497 super family [cl01108]	NI (tox17)	Chr
	Lferr_1314	198283435	DUF4415 [pfam14384]	NI (antitox17)	Lferr_1315	198283436	DUF497 super family [cl01108]	NI (tox17)	ICEAfe2-53993
	Lferr_2046	198284147	DUF4415 [pfam14384]	NI (antitox17)	Lferr_2045	198284146	DUF497 super family [cl01108]	NI (tox17)	Chr
18	AFE_2658	218666707	DUF4415 [pfam14384]	NI (antitox18)	AFE_2657'		NI	NI (tox18)	Chr
	Lferr_2284	198284371	DUF4415 [pfam14384]	NI (antitox18)	Lferr_2283	198284370	NI	NI (tox18)	Chr
19	AFE_2771	218665366	VagC super family [cl18787]	VapB (VapB-2)	Pseudo		PIN_VapC-FitB [cd09881]	NI (tox19)	Chr
	Lferr_2392	198284478	VagC super family [cl18787]	VapB (VapB-2)	Lferr_2391	198284477	PIN_VapC-FitB [cd09881]	NI (tox19)	Chr
20	AFE_2886	218668170	Antitoxin-MazE super family [cl00877]	VapB (MazE-2)	AFE_2885	218665972	PemK [pfam02452]	CcdB/MazF (PemK-1)	Chr
21	Lferr_2506	198284586	Antitoxin-MazE super family [cl00877]	VapB (MazE-2)	Lferr_2505	198284585	PemK [pfam02452]	CcdB/MazF (PemK-1)	Chr
	AFE_2889	218666996	Antitoxin-MazE super family [cl00877]	VapB (VapB-3)	AFE_2888	218666880	PIN_VapC-Smg6-like [cd09855]	VapC (NspT2-1)	Chr
	Lferr_2509	198284589	Antitoxin-MazE super family [cl00877]	VapB (VapB-3)	Lferr_2508	198284588	PIN_VapC-Smg6-like [cd09855]	VapC (NspT2-1)	Chr
22	AFE_2981	218665144	NI	NI (antitox22)	AFE_2982	218667184	NI	RelE/ParE (CcrT1-1)	Chr
	Lferr_2595'		NI	NI (antitox22)	Lferr_2595''		NI	RelE/ParE (CcrT1-1)	Chr
23	AFE_2983	218666488	Phd [COG4118]	NI (antitox23)	AFE_2984	218665493	PIN_MT3492 [cd09874]	NI (tox23)	Chr
	Lferr_2596	198284676	Phd [COG4118]	NI (antitox23)	Lferr_2597	198284677	PIN_MT3492 [cd09874]	NI (tox23)	Chr
24	AFE_3174	218665847	Phd super family [cl18766]	NI (antitox24)	AFE_3173	218665111	PIN_2 [pfam10130]	NI (tox24)	Chr
	Lferr_2770	198284847	Phd super family [cl18766]	NI (antitox24)	Lferr_2769	198284846	PIN_2 [pfam10130]	NI (tox24)	Chr
25	AFE_3268	218667137	PhdYeFM_antitox [pfam02604]	Phd (YefM-1)	AFE_3269	218665388	PIN_3 super family [cl17397]	NI (tox25)	Chr
	Lferr_2866	198284937	PhdYeFM_antitox [pfam02604]	Phd (YefM-1)	Lferr_2867	198284938	PIN_3 super family [cl17397]	NI (tox25)	Chr
26	AFE_1098	218667753	MazE [COG2336]	VapB (MazE-1)	AFE_1099	218666923	PemK super family [cl00995]	CcdB/MazF (MazF-1)	ICEAfe1
27	AFE_1361	218667301	StbC super family [cl01921]	NI (antitox27)	AFE_1362	218667390	PIN_VapC-FitB [cd09881]	VapC (VapC-3)	ICEAfe1
28	AFE_1367	218667849	DUF433 [pfam04255]	NI (antitox28)	AFE_1368	218665288	COG4634 super family [cl18792]	NI (tox28)	ICEAfe1
29	AFE_1383	218666557	HTH_XRE [cd00093]; HipB [COG1396]	HigA (EcoA1-1)	AFE_1384	218667318	Gp49 super family [cl01470]	RelE/ParE (EcoT1-1)	ICEAfe1

§Locus, accession gi and hits in CDD are according to the NCBI.
[a]according to the classification by Leplae et al., [19]; NI: not identified.
[b]Chr: chromosomal TA II; when a TA II is encoded in a MGE, the name of the element is indicated; in the case of ICEAfe2, the name is followed by the number of A. ferrooxidans ATCC strain where the TA is present.

at 3800 g at 4°C for 10 minutes, resuspended in native lysis buffer (50 mM NaH$_2$PO$_4$, 300 mM NaCl, 20 mM imidazole, pH 8.0) with 1 mM PMSF and subjected to lysis by sonication. The protein extract was cleared by centrifugation at 15350 g at 4°C for 30 minutes and the supernatant was applied to a column containing 500 μl of Ni^{+2}-Sepharose resin (GE Healthcare). The resin was washed with 30 column volumes of washing buffer (50 mM NaH$_2$PO$_4$, 300 mM NaCl, 150 mM imidazole, pH 8.0) and the retained proteins were eluted with the same buffer containing 250 mM imidazole. The purified proteins were dialyzed against storage buffer (25 mM Tris-HCl pH 8.0, 100 mM NaCl, 20% glycerol, 0.5 mM dithiothreitol) at 4°C for 16 hours followed by a second dialysis for 4 hours against fresh storage buffer and stored at −20°C.

(His)$_6$-VapC-3, (His)$_6$-tox28 and (His)$_6$-EcoT1-1 were purified from *E. coli* carrying the corresponding pETDuet-TA plasmids. Cells were harvested by centrifugation at 3800 g at 4°C for 10 minutes, resuspended in denaturing lysis buffer (100 mM NaH$_2$PO$_4$, 10 mM Tris-HCl, 6 M GuHCl, pH 8.0) and incubated at ambient temperature for 1 h with agitation to achieve the TA complexes dissociation. Protein extracts were cleared by centrifugation at 15350 g at ambient temperature for 30 minutes and the supernatant applied to a column containing 500 μl of Ni^{+2}-Sepharose resin (GE Healthcare). The resin was washed with 30 column volumes of denaturing wash buffer (100 mM NaH$_2$PO$_4$, 10 mM Tris-HCl, 8 M urea, 20 mM imidazole, pH 8.0). The elution of bound proteins was achieved by increasing the imidazole concentration in the buffer to 50 mM (for (His)$_6$-VapC-3 and (His)$_6$-tox28) or 100 mM (for (His)$_6$-EcoT1-1). The purified proteins were refolded by dialysis against storage buffer as before and stored at -20°C.

All proteins were quantified by the method of Bradford (Bio-Rad Protein Assay) in a microplate spectrophotometer (Epoch), analyzed by Tricine-SDS-PAGE [46] and visualized by staining with Coomassie brilliant blue.

RNase activity

The digestion reaction mixture (20 μl) consisted of 1.6 μg of MS2 RNA substrate (Roche) in 10 mM Tris-HCl (pH 7.8) with or without 10 mM MgCl$_2$ or MnCl$_2$, 40 U RNase inhibitor Ribolock (ThermoScientific) and 100 pmol of each purified toxin. Parallel reactions with 12 mM EDTA were used as controls. The reactions were incubated for 15 or 30 minutes at 37°C and stopped by adding 4 μl of 6X electrophoresis loading buffer. The reaction products were run on a 1% agarose gel (in 1X TAE) and visualized by staining with GelRed (Biotium).

Results

Content of type II TA systems in *A. ferrooxidans*

To further understand the role of chromosomally encoded TA systems in environmental microorganisms, we searched for type II TA systems (hereafter named as TA) in the publicly available genome sequences from two strains (ATCC 23270 and ATCC 53993) of the bioleaching bacterium *A. ferrooxidans*.

To identify shared TA between both strains, BLASTP searches were conducted, using toxin and antitoxin protein sequences from one strain as query (based on the information available in TADB) to search the proteins encoded by the other strain. From this analysis, 29 TA are encoded in *A. ferrooxidans* ATCC 23270 (including TA 13 and 19 in which the toxin gene corresponds to a pseudogene; Table 2 and Figure 1) and 28 in ATCC 53993 (including TA 10, 13 and 17 which have two identical copies; Table 2 and Figure 1). A total of 13 new putative TA were

identified that were either not assigned or erroneously assigned by TADB (Supporting information S1). In support of this, we note that *A. ferrooxidans* has a high TA content and it is expected that this characteristic is shared with other bioleaching bacteria. When we analyzed the TA content of other sequenced acidophilic bioleaching bacteria with the RASTA-Bacteria platform (because they are not available in TADB), we found that *A. caldus* SM-1, *Leptospirillum ferriphilum* ML-04, *L. ferrooxidans* C2-3 and *A. ferrivorans* SS3 encode at least, 30, 16, 29 and more than 50 putative TA, respectively (data not shown).

As is described in some TA (mainly in *higBA* family) [47–49], an organization opposite to the classical gene arrangement (toxin gene encoded after the antitoxin gene) was found in six systems from *A. ferrooxidans* (TA 2, 9, 12, 17, 18 and 29).

All TA from *A. ferrooxidans* ATCC 53993 have counterparts in the other strain (sharing 94-100% amino acid identity; Figure 1, TA 1-25). Strikingly, type strain ATCC 23270 contains four exclusive TA (TA 26-29), encoded in a MGE as discussed below (Figure 1, highlighted in red). As TA 1 to 25 are the same in both strains, we will refer only to TA from ATCC 23270 strain hereafter (if not otherwise indicated).

Nowadays, TA systems are classified as independent toxin and antitoxin super-families instead of TA families as before [19]. Based on this classification, we assigned 14 antitoxins and 13 toxins to a given super-family according to amino acid sequence similarity (Table 2). The prevalent antitoxin super-families in *A. ferrooxidans* are Phd and VapB (4 and 5 representative of each respectively), whereas the toxins that we could assign to a super-family belong to VapC, RelE/ParE and CcdB/MazF super-families, with 6, 5 and 2 representatives each, respectively. Specifically, toxins containing PIN domains are the most abundant in *A. ferrooxidans* (thirteen TA, 48% of the toxins). It is known that TA toxins show limited sequence similarity, despite having common folds [50] and this might explain why sixteen toxins from *A. ferrooxidans* could not be assigned in the current classification. Indeed, there are seven PIN domain toxins in *A. ferrooxidans* (TA 1, 10-11, 19 and 23-25, Table 2) that do not show a suitable sequence similarity with VapC super-family proteins (those containing PIN domains). Nonetheless, these toxins show high structural homology with characterized VapC toxins (Supporting information S2) and are clustered within the VapC super-family in a phylogenetic analysis (Figure 2, green squared). Using the same phylogenetic approach, the rest of the unclassified toxins grouped within different super-families, with some of them forming a different clade (e. g. TA 1, 9, 10, 23 and 28; Figure 2, shown in open symbols).

Based on the conserved domain database (CDD [51]) hits and the super-families of each toxin identified in *A. ferrooxidans*, we predicted that twenty toxins might be ribonucleases that possibly function as translation inhibitors. Functional analysis of some of these ribonucleases associated with MGEs is described below.

TA encoded in MGEs

TA may be associated with MGEs allowing their movement between microorganisms by HGT [25,52]. To elucidate whether chromosomal TA systems from *A. ferrooxidans* form part of MGEs and to predict whether they have been acquired or they have the potential to be mobilized by HGT, we analyzed their genetic context.

Recently, we identified and characterized ICE*Afe*1, an active 291-kbp ICE from *A. ferrooxidans* type strain ATCC 23270; this element is excised from the chromosome of the bacterium and has the potential to be transferred by conjugation [33]. *A. ferrooxidans* ATCC 53993 also encodes a 164-kbp genomic island (GI) that

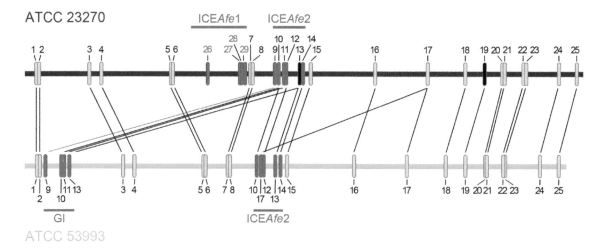

Figure 1. Comparison of the relative genomic locations of *A. ferrooxidans* TA systems. Using BLASTP, TA from each *A. ferrooxidans* genome were paired according to protein similarity. TA encoded in MGEs are shown in red (ICE*Afe*1), pink (ICE*Afe*2) and blue (Genomic island, GI). In black are shown TA in which the gene that must encode the toxin are pseudo genes. Black lines link TA that have 94-100% amino acid identity between the two strains. The blue line links a TA that has 49% (antitoxin) and 52% (toxin) amino acid identity with its counterpart in the other strain. Numbers of the TA are according to Table 2.

provides additional copper resistance to the bacterium [32]. Further other putative ICE, ICE*Afe*2, is shared by both strains, although these elements are not identical (176-kbp and 159-kbp in ATCC 23270 and ATCC 53993, respectively). A detailed analysis of TA encoded in these MGEs revealed that ICE*Afe*1, ICE*Afe*2 and the GI contain four, five (six in ATCC 23270 including a pseudo gene) and four of them, respectively (Figure 1 highlighted in red, pink and blue). Remarkably, TA from ICE*Afe*1 (TA 26-29, Figure 1 highlighted in red) are exclusive to ATCC 23270, consistent with the unique presence of this ICE in this strain. On the other hand, ICE*Afe*2 is present in both strains and thus TA encoded within this MGE are shared (TA 9-14 and 17, Figure 1 highlighted in pink). Some of these TA are also encoded in the GI from ATCC 53993 (TA 9-11 and 13, Figure 1, highlighted in blue) suggesting a duplication of these TA systems in this strain. Interestingly, TA encoded in the GI are close to transposon-related sequences and integrases genes and have a different genomic context to their counterparts in the ICE*Afe*2 (not shown). These findings reinforce the notion that certain chromosomal TA in *A. ferrooxidans* have the potential to be mobilized by HGT and to form part of its mobile genome. Other TA in *A. ferrooxidans* are also encoded near to transposases or transposon related-genes (e.g. TA systems from ICE*Afe*1, Figure S1).

TA from ICE*Afe*1 are functional and their toxins are ribonucleases

Because TA systems have been proposed to participate in the maintenance of MGEs, we hypothesize that TAs encoded in ICE*Afe*1, ICE*Afe*2 and the GI might contribute to prevent the loss of these elements from the *A. ferrooxidans* chromosome. Indeed, although we do not know yet the function of ICE*Afe*1 or the advantage for strain ATCC 23270 to carry it, it is stably maintained in laboratory conditions despite being unique to this strain among the other 12 strains that we have analyzed [33]. We therefore carried out a functional analysis of TA from ICE*Afe*1.

Three out of four TA from ICE*Afe*1 (TA 26, 27 and 29) share sequence similarity to well-known super-families (Table 2) and are grouped within their corresponding super-families on phylogenetic trees (Figure 2).

TA 26 (MazEF-1) is similar to the MazEF system from *E. coli* [53–56]. The putative toxin (MazF-1) is 51.8% identical (65.8% similar) with its counterpart from *E. coli* (Figure S2A). On the other hand, the putative antitoxin (MazE-1) is 42.7% identical (65.9% similar) to the orthologue from *E. coli* (Figure S2B). A number of conjugation genes and genes from a transposon are encoded both upstream and downstream to this TA system, respectively (Figure S1A).

TA 27 has conserved domains similar to StbC antitoxins and VapC toxins (Table 2). The toxin, VapC-3, has low sequence identity with VapC proteins but it conserves the three acidic residues from PIN-domains that are important for toxin activity (Figure S3). It is encoded near a cluster of genes that are involved in the biosynthesis and export of exopolysaccharides (Figure S1B).

TA 29 is encoded by AFE_1383/AFE_1384 genes. This system is encoded near to two other TA and close to transposition-related sequences (Figure S1B). The antitoxin is encoded by AFE_1383 and has a HTH_XRE conserved domain present on HigA and VapB antitoxins [2,35]. Similar to the classical TA loci *higBA* [43], this TA is unusual because the toxin-encoding gene is located upstream of the antitoxin-encoding gene. The toxin encoded by AFE_1384 has a Gp49 super family conserved domain and amino acid similarity with RelE/ParE super-family. The highest amino acid identity found is with a new toxin EcoT1$_{EDL933}$ identified and validated by Leplae et al [19], thus we named it EcoT1-1.

Phylogenetic data revealed that TA toxins 26, 27 and 29 clustered within their corresponding toxin super-families, but in a different clade from their chromosomal counterparts (Figure 2). These data reinforces the fact that these systems are part of the mobile genome from *A. ferrooxidans*.

TA 28, encoded by AFE_1367/AFE_1368 genes, has no orthologue described to date and it was ascribed as a TA system based on the characteristic of the operon by RASTA-Bacteria (Supporting information S1). On the phylogenetic analysis this toxin is closer to a putative RelE/ParE toxin from TA 22 but within a heterogeneous clade involving CcdB and not classified toxins (Figure 2). According to the information from the Integrated Microbial Genomes platform, tox28 contains a Mut7-C domain (pfam01927), which corresponds to a C-terminal RNase domain with a PIN fold [57]. Indeed, structural homology

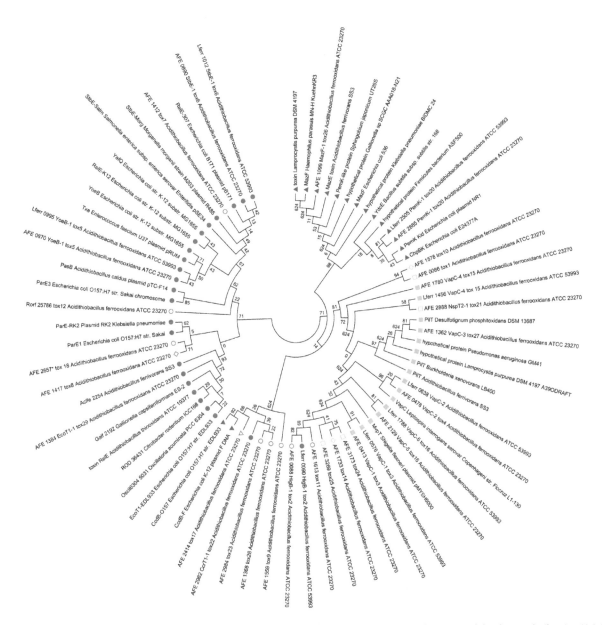

Figure 2. Phylogenetic relationship between TA toxins of *A. ferrooxidans* ATCC 23270. Circular unrooted dendogram built using Neighbor-Joining method. Scale shows the evolutionary distance in number of base substitutions per site. Toxins described by Leplae et al [19] belonging to RelE/ParE (red full-filled circle), CcdB/MazF (blue full-filled triangles) and VapC (green full-filled squared) super-families were introduced in the analysis as reference. Toxin classifications performed according the homologs with lower evolutionary distance (Table S1) are show in open symbols. The sequences whose homologs with lower evolutionary distance correspond to a non previously classified toxin are show in open rhomboid. The accession numbers of the sequences used in the analysis are in Supporting information S3.

searches predicted in tox28 the presence of a putative fold like a 3-phosphoglycerate dehydrogenase (PDB ID: 2EKL; 77% coverage) and low structural homology with PIN domain proteins (PDB ID: 1O4W, 39% coverage; PDB ID: 3H87, 26% coverage). According to BLASTP results, this toxin is conserved in different species, especially in cyanobacteria and Gram-positive bacteria. Therefore, this TA system might be a novel system with an RNase toxin related to PIN domain proteins. In *A. ferrooxidans* TA 28 is encoded very close to TA 27 and transposon-related sequences (Figure S1B).

The functionality of TA from ICE*Afe*1 was tested by transformation of *E. coli* BL21(DE3)pLysS with a multicopy plasmid (pETDuet-1 derivatives) carrying genes encoding either the toxin, the antitoxin or both (see Table 3 and Methods for a

description of each plasmid). Induction of VapC-3 and tox28 expression caused cell growth arrest of *E. coli* (Figure 3, blue lines). As expected, the co-induction of cognate antitoxins restored cell growth (Figure 3, green lines). Growth of cells expressing only the antitoxins was not affected (Figure 3, red lines). Overexpression of MazF-1 did not caused cell growth arrest of *E. coli* (Figure 3A). Conversely, overexpression of VapC-3 and tox28 seems to be bactericidal. In these cases the growth is not restored when the cells are transferred to a non-inducer medium (Figure 3B and C, lower panels). These results are consistent with a decrease in the CFU count (Figure S4). On the other hand, EcoT1-1 could not be cloned in the absence of its cognate antitoxin gene, which sheds light on its high toxicity in *E. coli* cells. These results indicated that, as all these toxins are RNases (bellow), they could target

Table 3. Plasmids used.

Plasmid	Characteristics	Reference
pGEM-T Easy	*E. coli* cloning vector. Ampicillin resistance.	Promega
pETDuet-1	*E. coli* expression vector. Ampicillin resistance. This vector is designed for the co-expression of two target genes. The vector contains two multiple cloning site (MCS1 and MCS2), each of which is preceded by a T7 promoter/lac operator and a ribosome binding site. ColE1 replicon.	Novagen
pACYCDuet-1	*E. coli* expression vector. Chloramphenicol resistance. This vector is designed for the co-expression of two target genes. The vector contains two multiple cloning site (MCS1 and MCS2), each of which is preceded by a T7 promoter/lac operator and a ribosome binding site. P15A replicon.	Novagen
pETMazE-1	pETDuet-1 derivative. Expressing the antitoxin gene from TA 26 system.	This work
pETMazF-1	pETDuet-1 derivative. Expressing the toxin gene from TA 26 system with a His$_6$ tag at the N-terminal.	This work
pETMazEF-1	pETDuet-1 derivative. Expressing TA 26 system. In this construction the toxin gene has a His$_6$ tag at the N-terminal.	This work
pETantitox27	pETDuet-1 derivative. Expressing the antitoxin gene from the TA 27 system.	This work
pETVapC-3	pETDuet-1 derivative. Expressing the toxin gene from TA 27 system with a His$_6$ tag at the N-terminal.	This work
pETStbC-VapC-3	pETDuet-1 derivative. Expressing the TA 27 system. In this construction the toxin gene has a His$_6$ tag at the N-terminal.	This work
pETantitox28	pETDuet-1 derivative. Expressing the antitoxin gene from TA 28 system.	This work
pETtox28	pETDuet-1 derivative. Expressing the toxin gene from TA 28 system with a His$_6$ tag at the N-terminal.	This work
pETTA28	pETDuet-1 derivative. Expressing the TA 28 system. In this construction the toxin gene has a His$_6$ tag at the N-terminal.	This work
pEcoA1/EcoT1-1	pETDuet-1 derivative. Expressing the TA 29 system. In this construction the toxin gene has a His$_6$ tag at the N-terminal.	This work
pACYCantitox27	pACYCDuet-1 derivative with the antitoxin27 gene cloned at its MCS2.	This work
pACYCantitox28	pACYCDuet-1 derivative with the antitoxin28 gene cloned at its MCS2.	This work

different cellular RNAs and/or have different sequence specificities. VapC-3, tox28 and EcoT1-1 probably target important RNAs in *E. coli* cells, while no target (or underrepresented targets) is present for MazF-1 in this host.

According to bioinformatic data all these toxins were predicted to be ribonucleases. To test the ability of these proteins to

hydrolyze RNA, we performed *in vitro* cleavage of viral MS2 RNA assays with purified toxins (Figure S5). MazF-1 digested the RNA only in the absence of Mg^{+2} ions (Figure 4, lane 2). Surprisingly, RNA cleavage by MazF-1 apparently is blocked by Mg^{+2} and it appears to be insensitive to Mn^{+2} ions (Figure 4B, lane 2-4), a phenomenon not yet described for a MazF toxin to our

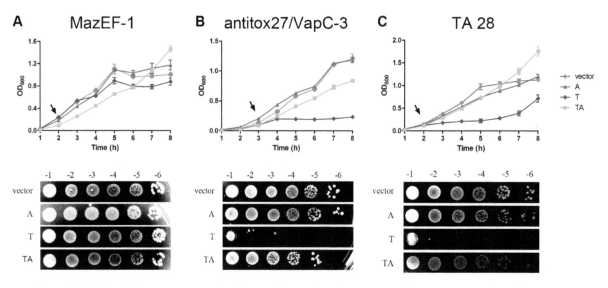

Figure 3. Effect of ICE*Afe*1 TA systems expression in *E. coli* growth. Cellular growth of *E. coli* BL21(DE3)pLysS cells harboring plasmids containing toxin (T, blue curves), antitoxin (A, red curves) or both (TA, green curves) genes of TA 26 (A), TA 27 (B) and TA 28 (C) was monitored by measuring the OD$_{600}$. Cells containing the empty vector (gray curves) were used as a control. The arrows indicate the moment when 1 mM IPTG was added to each culture. 3 hours after the induction 10-fold serial dilutions of each culture were spotted on LB plates without IPTG (panels below each graph). The means and standard deviation of three different experiments are plotted.

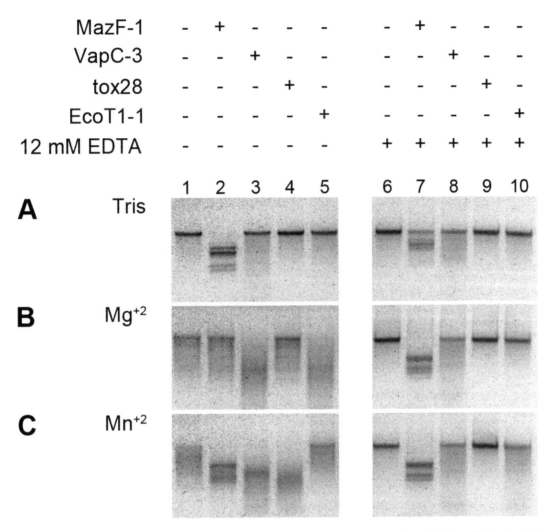

Figure 4. *In vitro* RNase assay of ICE*Afe*1 toxins. 1.6 µg of MS2 RNA was incubated with (+) or without (−) the purified toxins in 10 mM Tris-HCl (pH 7.8) in the absence of divalent ions (A) or with 10 mM $MgCl_2$ (B) or $MnCl_2$ (C). The reactions were incubated at 37°C for 15 (A and C) or 30 minutes (B). 12 mM EDTA was added to some reactions as a control (lanes 6-10).

knowledge. Consistent with this, EDTA addition restored the RNase activity (Figure 4B, lane 7). Conversely, VapC-3 exhibited RNase activity only when Mg^{+2} or Mn^{+2} ions were present (Figure 4B and C, lane 3). Strikingly, under our tested conditions tox28 was active only in the presence of Mn^{+2} ions (Figure 4C, lane 4). According to our knowledge there are no TA toxins that required Mn^{+2} ions for their RNase activity. Some VapC toxins

bind Mg^{+2} and/or Mn^{+2} [58] or have been crystallized with bound Mn^{+2}, as in the case of VapC toxin PAE0151 from *Pyrobaculum aerophilum* [59], but its activity has been assayed only with Mg^{+2}. In contrast to tox28, in the analyzed conditions EcoT1-1 was an active RNase only in the presence of Mg^{+2} ions (Figure 4B, lane 5). All Mg^{+2}/Mn^{+2}-dependent RNase activities

Table 4. Plasmid maintenance test. *E. coli* BL21(DE3) was double transformed with the plasmids indicated.

Culture	Plasmid maintenance (%)[a]			
	15 days	**20 days**	**26 days**	**30 days**
pETVapC-3+pACYCantitox27	70.87±37.93	88.10±16.83	89.03±13.51	76.67±33.00
pETDuet-1+pACYCantitox27	52.77±33.56	44.67±27.15	44.97±22.13	35.03±31.94
pETtox28+pACYCantitox28	62.23±34.59	55.42±37.93	55.83±41.05	51.43±40.88
pETDuet-1+pACYCantitox28	64.70±44.87	60.83±43.03	40.73±29.02	28.20±21.25

[a]percentage of chloramphenicol-resistant bacteria (resistance gene encoded on pACYCDuet-1) when cultured on ampicillin-containing media (resistance gene encoded on pETDuet-1) for the days indicated. The data are expressed as the means of three independent cultures ± standard deviation.

were inhibited in the presence of EDTA (Figure 4, lane 6-10), confirming that the divalent ions are necessary for the activity.

Thus, three out of four TA encoded in ICE*Afe*1 (with the exception of MazF-1) are active in a heterologous system, i.e. the expression of toxins in *E. coli* arrest growth and the cognate antitoxins suppress this toxicity. Furthermore, these results show that all ICE*Afe*1 TA toxins are RNases with different ions requirements that could inhibit translation via RNA cleavage. Cellular targets and cleavage sites of these toxins are our future interest to study.

TA systems from ICE*Afe*1 might allow plasmid maintenance

Given that TA from ICE*Afe*1 are functional and in general TA systems have been proposed to participate avoiding the loss of MGEs from their hosts, we hypothesize that these TA might be responsible of the stable maintenance of ICE*Afe*1 in *A. ferrooxidans* chromosome. To determine whether TA systems from ICE*Afe*1 mediate plasmid stability, we assay the capacity of TA 27 and TA 28 to avoid the loss of pACYCDuet-1, a vector carrying chloramphenicol resistance. We could not assay TA 26 and TA 29 given that MazF-1 (TA 26) did not affect the growth of *E. coli* (Figure 3A) and, on the other hand, the gene encoding EcoT1-1 (TA 29) could not be cloned in *E. coli*.

The assay consisted on monitoring the stability of pACYCDuet-A vectors during cultivation in the presence of selective antibiotic pressure towards pETDuet-T vectors [45]. After 30 days of culture in the absence of chloramphenicol, although they were not fully maintained (and that we obtained high standard deviations in the experiment), pACYCantitox27 and pACYCantitox28 were lost to a lower level in the absence of their cognate pETDuet-T vectors in comparison to cultures with the pETDuet-1 empty vector (Table 4). As *E. coli* BL21(DE3) contains its native chromosomal TA systems, the failure to pACYCantitox27 and pACYCantitox28 to be fully maintained, may be due to cross-interaction between ICE*Afe*1 toxins with cognate antitoxins from *E. coli*. This may have made the presence of ICE*Afe*1 antitoxins dispensable and thus the pACYCDuet-A vectors lost. Functional interaction between chromosomal and plasmidial TA systems has been demonstrated before [60]. Nevertheless, these data demonstrate that TA 27 and TA 28 encoded on a MGE from *A. ferrooxidans* could have a plasmid-stabilizing role.

Discussion

In this study, the content of type II TA systems and their relationship with MGEs in the environmental bacterium *A. ferrooxidans* were investigated. According to the data presented here, *A. ferrooxidans* encodes at least 29 and 28 TA in ATCC 23270 and ATCC 53993 strains, respectively (representing 1.8 and 2% of total number of CDSs, respectively). Given this content of TA and considering the number of putative TA proteins that we could not classify within a super-family, it is expected that this microorganism could be a source of novel systems, expanding the repertoire currently known. It seems to be the case for TA 28 characterized in this work; a TA present in a MGE encoding a novel toxin that causes a bactericidal state in *E. coli* and has a Mn^{+2}-dependent RNase activity. The described number of TA in *A. ferrooxidans* could be underestimated because of the several hypothetical proteins encoded in a TA-like gene organization as well as putative orphan toxins. Additionally, we must consider that type I, III, IV and V TA systems, that were not the subject of this study, might contribute to the total number of TA systems in *A. ferrooxidans*.

Putative roles of ICE*Afe*1 TA systems

In the ICE SXT from *V. cholera*, the MosAT system promotes the maintenance of the element. The mRNA levels of MosAT system are enhanced when the element is excised, preventing its loss [14]. Since the levels of TA mRNAs from ICE*Afe*1 do not increase upon their excision (based on qRT-PCR, data not shown), it seems that these systems do not behave in the same way as the MosAT system. We cannot rule out that there might be changes at a protein level in different growth conditions.

Plasmid-encoded TA systems prevent the proliferation of plasmid-free progeny and thereby contribute to the maintenance of their replicons. By a similar mechanism, chromosomal genes closely linked to a TA locus could have a selective advantage; as a consequence the maintenance of specific genes (like TA genes) might have an effect on the stability and spread of MGEs. Here we have shown that two TA from *A. ferrooxidans* ICE*Afe*1 (TA 27 and TA 28) seem to have a role in the maintenance of MGEs (Figure 4). Thus, the presence of TA on MGEs in *A. ferrooxidans* could explain why they are stably maintained in this bacterium.

Based on the genomic contexts, we hypothesize that TA from ICE*Afe*1 might be involved in the conjugal transfer and/or biofilm formation, putative roles ascribed to this MGE [33]. The MazEF-1 system (TA 26) is encoded very close to the conjugation cluster probably responsible for the horizontal transfer of this element (Figure S1A). On the other hand, TA 27, TA 28 and TA 29 are encoded near to a cluster of genes predicted to be involved in the biosynthesis and export of exopolysaccharides which could be linked to biofilm formation in this bacterium (Figure S1B). To determine whether TA systems from ICE*Afe*1 contribute to biofilm formation is to be further analyzed. However, we can not rule out that each system might have a different function under different physiological conditions.

Elucidation of the sequence specificity and thus the cellular targets of each toxin from ICE*Afe*1 might be crucial to determine their role in the physiology of *A. ferrooxidans*.

Type II TA systems, chromosomal or mobile TA systems?

Hitherto TA systems are classified as chromosomal (stable) or plasmid encoded (mobile). All TA in ICE*Afe*1 are encoded near to transposon-related sequences (Figure S1). Similar distribution occurs with TA from the genomic island of *A. ferrooxidans* ATCC 53993. As it is known that ICEs are modular elements [61], it is possible that TA are part of modules that have been acquired by HGT and contributed to the creation of ICE*Afe*1. Thus we propose that most *A. ferrooxidans* TA systems may belong to either active or inactive MGEs that are inserted in the bacterial chromosome. A similar case has been reported in *Acidithiobacillus caldus*, another acidophilic bacterium [62].

Supporting Information

Figure S1   Genetic overview of ICE*Afe*1 TA and the flanking DNA regions. The genetic contexts of TA 26 (A), TA 27, TA 28 and TA 29 (B) are indicated. Each gene is colored by COG according to the information on the Integrated Microbial Genomes platform (IMG, http://img.jgi.doe.gov/cgi-bin/w/main.cgi [37]). Color codes of function category for COGs are indicated in the insert below the images.

Figure S2   Alignment of MazEF-1 system from ICE*Afe*1 with its ortholog from *E. coli*. Protein sequences from toxin (A) and antitoxin (B) were aligned using ClustalW. GenBank accession numbers: MazF_Ec, BAA03918.1; MazF ICEAfe1, YP_002425571.1; MazE_Ec, BAA41177.1; MazE ICEAfe1,

YP_002425570.1. Identical and similar amino acids are shown in black and grey, respectively. Functionally important conserved regions [51] are indicated below the MazF and MazE sequences by black lines.

Figure S3 Alignment of VapC toxins from *A. ferrooxidans* ATCC 23270. Protein sequences were aligned using ClustalW. Identical and similar amino acids are shown in black and grey, respectively. The three conserved acidic residues of the PIN-domain are highlighter in green. GenBank accession numbers: VapC-1, YP_002424909; VapC-2, YP_002424974; VapC-3, YP_002425797; VapC-4, YP_002426198; and VapC-5, YP_002426529.

Figure S4 Effect of ICE*Afe*1 toxins expression on *E. coli* CFU. Cellular growth of *E. coli* BL21(DE3)pLysS cells harboring plasmids containing toxin (T, blue curves) of TA 26 (A), TA 27 (B) and TA 28 (C) post IPTG addition was monitored by measuring the CFU/ml. Cells containing the empty vector (gray curves) were used as a control. The means and standard deviation of two different experiments are plotted.

Figure S5 ICE*Afe*1 toxins purification. Tricine-SDS-PAGE of (His)$_6$-tagged toxin proteins purified as it is described at Materials and Methods. The proteins were visualized by staining with Coomassie brilliant blue. The molecular weights of some reference bands (M, PageRuler Unstained Broad Range Protein Ladder, Thermo Scientific) are indicated at the left of the figure.

Figure S6 *In vitro* RNase assay of MazEF-1 system. 1.6 μg of MS2 RNA was incubated with (+) or without (−) 50 picomoles of the purified MazF-1 toxin and/or MazE-1 antitoxin in 10 mM Tris-HCl (pH 7.8). The reactions were incubated at 37°C for 15 minutes. Lanes 5-7: the reactions contain 100, 150 and 200 picomoles of MazF-1, respectively. Lane 8-10: the reactions contain 100, 150 and 200 picomoles of MazF-1, respectively.

Table S1 Evolutionary distances among toxins from *A. ferrooxidans*.

Supporting Information S1 Identification of new TA II not describe in TADB.

Supporting Information S2 Structural homologous of PIN domain toxins from *A. ferrooxidans*.

Supporting Information S3 Gene ID or locus tag of nucleotide sequences used in the phylogenetic analysis.

Acknowledgments

We thank to Dr. Jonathan Iredell from the University of Sydney to review and to correct the manuscript and to María Catalina Aranda for her generous assistance in some experiments.

Author Contributions

Conceived and designed the experiments: PB MT OO. Performed the experiments: PB MT. Analyzed the data: PB MT OO. Wrote the paper: PB OO.

References

1. Yamaguchi Y, Park J-H, Inouye M (2011) Toxin-antitoxin systems in bacteria and archaea. Annu Rev Genet 45: 61–79.
2. Gerdes K, Christensen SK, Løbner-Olesen A (2005) Prokaryotic toxin-antitoxin stress response loci. Nat Rev Microbiol 3: 371–382.
3. Riley MA, Wertz JE (2002) Bacteriocins: evolution, ecology, and application. Annu Rev Microbiol 56: 117–137.
4. Hayes CS, Aoki SK, Low DA (2010) Bacterial contact-dependent delivery systems. Annu Rev Genet 44: 71–90.
5. Gerdes K, Bech FW, Jørgensen ST, Løbner-Olesen A, Rasmussen PB, et al. (1986) Mechanism of postsegregational killing by the hok gene product of the parB system of plasmid R1 and its homology with the relF gene product of the E. coli relB operon. EMBO J 5: 2023–2029.
6. Gerdes K, Rasmussen PB, Molin S (1986) Unique type of plasmid maintenance function: postsegregational killing of plasmid-free cells. Proc Natl Acad Sci U S A 83: 3116–3120.
7. Yamaguchi Y, Inouye M (2011) Regulation of growth and death in Escherichia coli by toxin-antitoxin systems. Nat Rev Microbiol 9: 779–790.
8. Makarova KS, Wolf YI, Koonin EV (2009) Comprehensive comparative-genomic analysis of type 2 toxin-antitoxin systems and related mobile stress response systems in prokaryotes. Biol Direct 4: 19.
9. Pandey DP, Gerdes K (2005) Toxin-antitoxin loci are highly abundant in free-living but lost from host-associated prokaryotes. Nucleic Acids Res 33: 966–976.
10. Magnuson RD (2007) Hypothetical functions of toxin-antitoxin systems. J Bacteriol 189: 6089–6092.
11. Tsilibaris V, Maenhaut-Michel G, Mine N, Van Melderen L (2007) What is the benefit to Escherichia coli of having multiple toxin-antitoxin systems in its genome? J Bacteriol 189: 6101–6108.
12. Norton JP, Mulvey MA (2012) Toxin-antitoxin systems are important for niche-specific colonization and stress resistance of uropathogenic Escherichia coli. PLoS Pathog 8: e1002954.
13. Fasani RA, Savageau MA (2013) Molecular mechanisms of multiple toxin-antitoxin systems are coordinated to govern the persister phenotype. Proc Natl Acad Sci U S A 110: E2528–2537.
14. Wozniak RAF, Waldor MK (2009) A toxin-antitoxin system promotes the maintenance of an integrative conjugative element. PLoS Genet 5: e1000439.
15. Fozo EM, Makarova KS, Shabalina SA, Yutin N, Koonin EV, et al. (2010) Abundance of type I toxin-antitoxin systems in bacteria: searches for new candidates and discovery of novel families. Nucleic Acids Res 38: 3743–3759.
16. Blower TR, Short FL, Rao F, Mizuguchi K, Pei XY, et al. (2012) Identification and classification of bacterial Type III toxin-antitoxin systems encoded in chromosomal and plasmid genomes. Nucleic Acids Res 40: 6158–6173.
17. Masuda H, Tan Q, Awano N, Wu K-P, Inouye M (2012) YeeU enhances the bundling of cytoskeletal polymers of MreB and FtsZ, antagonizing the CbtA (YeeV) toxicity in Escherichia coli. Mol Microbiol 84: 979–989.
18. Dy RL, Przybilski R, Semeijn K, Salmond GPC, Fineran PC (2014) A widespread bacteriophage abortive infection system functions through a Type IV toxin-antitoxin mechanism. Nucleic Acids Res 42: 4590–4605.
19. Leplae R, Geeraerts D, Hallez R, Guglielmini J, Drèze P, et al. (2011) Diversity of bacterial type II toxin-antitoxin systems: a comprehensive search and functional analysis of novel families. Nucleic Acids Res 39: 5513–5525.
20. Sala A, Bordes P, Genevaux P (2014) Multiple toxin-antitoxin systems in Mycobacterium tuberculosis. Toxins 6: 1002–1020.
21. Wang X, Lord DM, Cheng H-Y, Osbourne DO, Hong SH, et al. (2012) A new type V toxin-antitoxin system where mRNA for toxin GhoT is cleaved by antitoxin GhoS. Nat Chem Biol 8: 855–861.
22. Cook GM, Robson JR, Frampton RA, McKenzie J, Przybilski R, et al. (2013) Ribonucleases in bacterial toxin-antitoxin systems. Biochim Biophys Acta 1829: 523–531.
23. Yamaguchi Y, Inouye M (2009) mRNA interferases, sequence-specific endoribonucleases from the toxin-antitoxin systems. Prog Mol Biol Transl Sci 85: 467–500.
24. Cambray G, Guerout A-M, Mazel D (2010) Integrons. Annu Rev Genet 44: 141–166.
25. Guérout A-M, Iqbal N, Mine N, Ducos-Galand M, Van Melderen L, et al. (2013) Characterization of the phd-doc and ccd toxin-antitoxin cassettes from Vibrio superintegrons. J Bacteriol 195: 2270–2283.
26. Szekeres S, Dauti M, Wilde C, Mazel D, Rowe-Magnus DA (2007) Chromosomal toxin-antitoxin loci can diminish large-scale genome reductions in the absence of selection. Mol Microbiol 63: 1588–1605.
27. Williams KP, Gillespie JJ, Sobral BWS, Nordberg EK, Snyder EE, et al. (2010) Phylogeny of gammaproteobacteria. J Bacteriol 192: 2305–2314.

28. Valdés J, Pedroso I, Quatrini R, Dodson RJ, Tettelin H, et al. (2008) Acidithiobacillus ferrooxidans metabolism: from genome sequence to industrial applications. BMC Genomics 9: 597.

29. Bonnefoy V, Holmes DS (2012) Genomic insights into microbial iron oxidation and iron uptake strategies in extremely acidic environments. Environ Microbiol 14: 1597–1611.

30. Holmes DS, Zhao HL, Levican G, Ratouchniak J, Bonnefoy V, et al. (2001) ISAfe1, an ISL3 family insertion sequence from Acidithiobacillus ferrooxidans ATCC 19859. J Bacteriol 183: 4323–4329.

31. Oppon JC, Sarnovsky RJ, Craig NL, Rawlings DE (1998) A Tn7-like transposon is present in the glmUS region of the obligately chemoautolithotrophic bacterium Thiobacillus ferrooxidans. J Bacteriol 180: 3007–3012.

32. Orellana LH, Jerez CA (2011) A genomic island provides Acidithiobacillus ferrooxidans ATCC 53993 additional copper resistance: a possible competitive advantage. Appl Microbiol Biotechnol 92: 761–767.

33. Bustamante P, Covarrubias PC, Levicán G, Katz A, Tapia P, et al. (2012) ICE Afe 1, an actively excising genetic element from the biomining bacterium Acidithiobacillus ferrooxidans. J Mol Microbiol Biotechnol 22: 399–407.

34. Shao Y, Harrison EM, Bi D, Tai C, He X, et al. (2011) TADB: a web-based resource for Type 2 toxin-antitoxin loci in bacteria and archaea. Nucleic Acids Res 39: D606–611.

35. Sevin EW, Barloy-Hubler F (2007) RASTA-Bacteria: a web-based tool for identifying toxin-antitoxin loci in prokaryotes. Genome Biol 8: R155.

36. Kelley LA, Sternberg MJE (2009) Protein structure prediction on the Web: a case study using the Phyre server. Nat Protoc 4: 363–371.

37. Markowitz VM, Chen I-MA, Palaniappan K, Chu K, Szeto E, et al. (2012) IMG: the Integrated Microbial Genomes database and comparative analysis system. Nucleic Acids Res 40: D115–122.

38. Thompson JD, Higgins DG, Gibson TJ (1994) CLUSTAL W: improving the sensitivity of progressive multiple sequence alignment through sequence weighting, position-specific gap penalties and weight matrix choice. Nucleic Acids Res 22: 4673–4680.

39. Gonnet GH, Cohen MA, Benner SA (1992) Exhaustive matching of the entire protein sequence database. Science 256: 1443–1445.

40. Saitou N, Nei M (1987) The neighbor-joining method: a new method for reconstructing phylogenetic trees. Mol Biol Evol 4: 406–425.

41. Dopazo J (1994) Estimating errors and confidence intervals for branch lengths in phylogenetic trees by a bootstrap approach. J Mol Evol 38: 300–304.

42. Tamura K, Nei M, Kumar S (2004) Prospects for inferring very large phylogenies by using the neighbor-joining method. Proc Natl Acad Sci U S A 101: 11030–11035.

43. Tamura K, Peterson D, Peterson N, Stecher G, Nei M, et al. (2011) MEGA5: molecular evolutionary genetics analysis using maximum likelihood, evolutionary distance, and maximum parsimony methods. Mol Biol Evol 28: 2731–2739.

44. Chung CT, Niemela SL, Miller RH (1989) One-step preparation of competent Escherichia coli: transformation and storage of bacterial cells in the same solution. Proc Natl Acad Sci U S A 86: 2172–2175.

45. Bukowski M, Lyzen R, Helbin WM, Bonar E, Szalewska-Palasz A, et al. (2013) A regulatory role for Staphylococcus aureus toxin-antitoxin system PemIKSa. Nat Commun 4: 2012.

46. Schägger H (2006) Tricine-SDS-PAGE. Nat Protoc 1: 16–22.

47. Budde PP, Davis BM, Yuan J, Waldor MK (2007) Characterization of a higBA toxin-antitoxin locus in Vibrio cholerae. J Bacteriol 189: 491–500.

48. Christensen-Dalsgaard M, Gerdes K (2006) Two higBA loci in the Vibrio cholerae superintegron encode mRNA cleaving enzymes and can stabilize plasmids. Mol Microbiol 62: 397–411.

49. Tian QB, Ohnishi M, Tabuchi A, Terawaki Y (1996) A new plasmid-encoded proteic killer gene system: cloning, sequencing, and analyzing hig locus of plasmid Rts1. Biochem Biophys Res Commun 220: 280–284.

50. Blower TR, Salmond GPC, Luisi BF (2011) Balancing at survival's edge: the structure and adaptive benefits of prokaryotic toxin-antitoxin partners. Curr Opin Struct Biol 21: 109–118.

51. Marchler-Bauer A, Zheng C, Chitsaz F, Derbyshire MK, Geer LY, et al. (2013) CDD: conserved domains and protein three-dimensional structure. Nucleic Acids Res 41: D348–352.

52. Wozniak RAF, Fouts DE, Spagnoletti M, Colombo MM, Ceccarelli D, et al. (2009) Comparative ICE genomics: insights into the evolution of the SXT/R391 family of ICEs. PLoS Genet 5: e1000786.

53. Amitai S, Kolodkin-Gal I, Hananya-Meltabashi M, Sacher A, Engelberg-Kulka H (2009) Escherichia coli MazF leads to the simultaneous selective synthesis of both "death proteins" and "survival proteins." PLoS Genet 5: e1000390.

54. Kamada K, Hanaoka F, Burley SK (2003) Crystal structure of the MazE/MazF complex: molecular bases of antidote-toxin recognition. Mol Cell 11: 875–884.

55. Mittenhuber G (1999) Occurrence of mazEF-like antitoxin/toxin systems in bacteria. J Mol Microbiol Biotechnol 1: 295–302.

56. Zhang Y, Zhang J, Hoeflich KP, Ikura M, Qing G, et al. (2003) MazF cleaves cellular mRNAs specifically at ACA to block protein synthesis in Escherichia coli. Mol Cell 12: 913–923.

57. Anantharaman V, Koonin EV, Aravind L (2002) Comparative genomics and evolution of proteins involved in RNA metabolism. Nucleic Acids Res 30: 1427–1464.

58. Arcus VL, McKenzie JL, Robson J, Cook GM (2011) The PIN-domain ribonucleases and the prokaryotic VapBC toxin-antitoxin array. Protein Eng Des Sel PEDS 24: 33–40.

59. Bunker RD, McKenzie JL, Baker EN, Arcus VL (2008) Crystal structure of PAE0151 from Pyrobaculum aerophilum, a PIN-domain (VapC) protein from a toxin-antitoxin operon. Proteins 72: 510–518.

60. Wilbaux M, Mine N, Guérout A-M, Mazel D, Melderen LV (2007) Functional Interactions between Coexisting Toxin-Antitoxin Systems of the ccd Family in Escherichia coli O157:H7. J Bacteriol 189: 2712–2719.

61. Wozniak RAF, Waldor MK (2010) Integrative and conjugative elements: mosaic mobile genetic elements enabling dynamic lateral gene flow. Nat Rev Microbiol 8: 552–563.

62. Acuña LG, Cárdenas JP, Covarrubias PC, Haristoy JJ, Flores R, et al. (2013) Architecture and gene repertoire of the flexible genome of the extreme acidophile Acidithiobacillus caldus. PloS One 8: e78237.

15

Genomic Assortative Mating in Marriages in the United States

Guang Guo[1,2,3]*, **Lin Wang**[4], **Hexuan Liu**[1,2], **Thomas Randall**[5]

1 Department of Sociology, the University of North Carolina at Chapel Hill, Chapel Hill, North Carolina, the United States of America, 2 Carolina Population Center, the University of North Carolina at Chapel Hill, Chapel Hill, North Carolina, the United States of America, 3 Carolina Center for Genome Sciences, the University of North Carolina at Chapel Hill, Chapel Hill, North Carolina, the United States of America, 4 Center for Child and Family Policy, Duke University, Durham, North Carolina, the United States of America, 5 National Institute of Environmental Health Sciences, Research Triangle Park, North Carolina, the United States of America

Abstract

Assortative mating in phenotype in human marriages has been widely observed. Using genome-wide genotype data from the Framingham Heart study (FHS; number of married couples = 989) and Health Retirement Survey (HRS; number of married couples = 3,474), this study investigates genomic assortative mating in human marriages. Two types of genomic marital correlations are calculated. The first is a correlation specific to a single married couple "averaged" over all available autosomal single-nucleotide polymorphism (SNPs). In FHS, the average married-couple correlation is 0.0018 with $p = 3 \times 10^{-5}$; in HRS, it is 0.0017 with $p = 7.13 \times 10^{-13}$. The marital correlation among the positively assorting SNPs is 0.001 ($p = .0043$) in FHS and 0.015 ($p = 1.66 \times 10^{-24}$) in HRS. The sizes of these estimates in FHS and HRS are consistent with what are suggested by the distribution of the allelic combination. The study also estimated SNP-specific correlation "averaged" over all married couples. Suggestive evidence is reported. Future studies need to consider a more general form of genomic assortment, in which different allelic forms in homologous genes and non-homologous genes result in the same phenotype.

Editor: Margaret M. DeAngelis, University of Utah, United States of America

Funding: Funding provided by Challenge Grant RC1 DA029425-01, National Institutes of Health, http://www.nih.gov/. The funders had no role in study design, data collection and analysis, decision to publish, or preparation of the manuscript.

Competing Interests: The authors have declared that no competing interests exist.

* Email: guang_guo@unc.edu

Introduction

Assortative mating refers to a systematic departure from random mating. Positive assortative mating or homogamy occurs when mating individuals have similar traits, and negative assortative mating or heterogamy occurs when mating individuals have dissimilar traits. Human assortative mating in phenotype has been investigated for more than a century. In 1903, Pearson and colleagues report that the correlations in height, the span of arms, and the length of left forearm between husband and wife are 0.28, 0.20, and 0.20, respectively, drawing on extensive family records of 1,000 husband-wife pairs. Since Pearson's work, marriage partners have been shown to assort on a wide range of traits including race and ethnicity, age, propinquity in geography, religious belief, socio-economic status (such as educational attainment, occupation, and income), cognitive ability, anthropometric measures (such as weight, height, skin pigmentation, and other related measures), personality characteristics, mental and psychiatric conditions, and political attitudes (e.g., [1,2–13]).

If marriages are assorted to a degree by individual traits and if these traits are to a degree associated with genetic variation, it would be reasonable to hypothesize a degree of genetic assortment in human marriages. As an illustrative example, the heritability of human height is about 0.80 in developed countries [14]. Recent genome-wide association studies (GWAS) have found at least 180 independent regions of the genome that are associated with height

[15–19]. Figure 1 shows the correlation of height for different types of pairs using data from the Framingham Heart Study (FHS), with height standardized within each sex. The data show a correlation of about one half for same-sex as well as opposite-sex full-sibling pairs and parent-child pairs. The correlation for randomly paired individuals is essentially zero. The correlation for married couples in FHS after adjusting for population structure is about 0.27. This marital assortment in height likely has a major genetic component.

Genetic assortative mating may have reproductive consequences. Thiessen and Gregg [6] hypothesize that positive assortative mating outside nuclear families increases the genetic relatedness within a family, which in turn increases inclusive fitness without an extra reproductive effort. Lewontin [3] suggests that human assortative mating may play a major role in redistributing genes in contemporary times, particularly because selection through death has largely been replaced by selection through birth due to sharply-reduced mortality. If mating partners do share similar genetic variants related to, for example, obesity or psychiatric conditions, the impact of these genetic variants on the couples' offspring may be compounded. The role of genetic assortative mating may evolve with social trends. For example, college-educated Americans are increasingly more likely to marry each other rather than those with less education in comparison to a half-century ago [20]. This educational assortative mating reinforces a

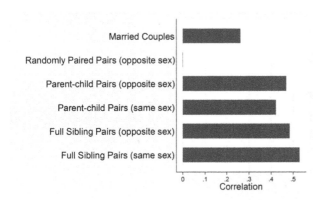

Figure 1. FHS data – the correlation of height (standardized within each sex) for married couples (N of couples = 989), opposite-sex random pairs from permuted individuals in FHS (N = 200,000), opposite-sex parent-child pairs (N = 3,447), same-sex parent-child pairs (N = 3,511), opposite-sex full sibling pairs (N = 2,815), and same-sex full sibling pairs (N = 2,898).

growing social divide between those with very low levels of education and those with more education, magnifying social class differences. This growing social divide could be partially genetic because of assortative mating.

Pearson [21] conjectures that, on average, a husband and wife are more alike than first cousins, whose coefficient of genetic relatedness is 0.125 and probably as much alike as uncle and niece, whose coefficient of genetic relatedness is 0.25, apparently basing the conjectures on the correlation findings over anthropometric measures. Pearson compares human homogamy to self-fertilization in plants; nevertheless, he realizes that human homogamy may have any degree of intensity and may be restricted to certain traits because genetic assortment can only be accomplished through phenotype.

In this project, we assess the extent to which marriage partners assort genetically using genome-wide genotype (GWAS) data from two independent studies in the United States for replication: 989 married couples in the Framingham Heart Study [22] (FHS) and 3,474 married couples in the Health and Retirement Survey (HRS). We carry out three sets of analyses: the first analysis uses 989 married couples and 287,294 SNPs in FHS; the second uses 3,474 couples and 66,526 SNPs (these 66,526 SNPs are common to both genotyping platforms used in the FHS and HRS studies); and the third analysis repeats the FHS analysis using the same 66,526 SNPs that are commonly available in FHS and HRS.

This analysis focuses on genomic assortative mating beyond race and ethnicity. It is well-known that marriages in the United States assort on race and ethnicity (e.g., [9,23]). To estimate genetic correlation within married couples net of race and ethnicity, population stratification must be controlled. In our analysis, population stratification is controlled directly in the regression models that estimate genomic assortment.

To estimate genetic assortative mating at the genomic level, we calculate two types of genome-wide marital correlations. The first is a correlation specific to a single married couple (couple correlation) "averaged" over all available autosomal SNPs. For FHS, this calculation yields 989 correlation estimates, one for each married couple averaged over 287,294 SNPs. Married-couple correlations provide a global or genomic estimate of the correlation averaged over the human genome. Such a measure is possible and attempted in this project because assortative mating

may occur over a number of human traits. Negative genomic assortment is a potential complication that may cancel negative and positive genomic assortment within a single married couple. Although assortative mating is generally considered positive, negative assortment or that opposites attract is likely to be present [1,6]. To address this issue, we estimate two additional correlations for each married couple. One is based on about half of the 287,294 SNPs that assort more positively and the other is based on the other half that assort more negatively.

The second marital correlation is a SNP correlation "averaged" over all married couples. For FHS, the SNP correlation analysis yields 287,294 correlations, one for each SNP averaged over 989 married couples. The analysis of couple correlations is quite distinct from GWAS studies. It is concerned with genetic similar within a couple averaged over the genome; it is also far more computationally demanding than a GWAS analysis. The analysis of SNP correlations appears to resemble a GWAS analysis: a GWAS study examines each SNP's association with a single phenotype in a collection of individuals and a SNP-correlation analysis estimates the average correlation over a collection of married couples with respect to a SNP. However, an important difference between the two is that married couples may assort on different phenotypes and thus assort at different genetic loci, which makes it more difficult for the analysis of SNP correlations to produce reliable estimates than a GWAS analysis.

Recent work by Domingue et al. [24] provides an estimate of genome-wide genetic similarity and an estimate of educational similarity within spousal pairs, concluding that the spousal genetic similarity over the genome is about one third or one fourth of the spousal educational similarity. Although using the same two data sources of FHS and HRS, our analysis was independently performed and reveals a number of additional insights. We use a different measure of spousal genomic similarity, calculate additional two measures of couple correlation for each married couple, and estimate SNP-correlations.

Results

Figure 2 shows the FHS distribution of couple correlation for married couples (N = 989), opposite-sex random pairs from permuted individuals in FHS (N = 200,000), opposite-sex random pairs from permuted individuals among married couples (N = 246,870), full-sibling pairs (N = 5,713), and parent-child pairs (N = 6,958). After controlling for population admixture, the married-couple correlations average 0.0018 relative to the average of randomly paired individuals (Panel 1 of Table 1). The correlation is highly significant according to both permutation tests. In contrast, the pair-specific correlations for full-sibling pairs and parent-child pairs are both centered on 0.50 with a mean of 0.503 (SD = 0.053) and 0.499 (SD = 0.007), respectively. As expected, the standard deviation of the parent-child pairs is much smaller than that of the full siblings.

Figure 3 shows the effect of controlling for population admixture via adding seven main principal components in FHS. The figure presents two estimated distributions of married-couple correlation (Panels 1 and 2) and the distribution of pair correlations estimated from random pairs (Panel 3). The results in Panels 1 and 2 are without and with control for population admixture, respectively. Once population admixture is controlled, the couple correlations that are larger than 0.02 have vanished (Panel 2).

Figure 4 shows the HRS distribution of pair correlation, for married couples (N = 3,474), opposite-sex random pairs from permuted individuals in HRS (N = 200,000), and opposite-sex

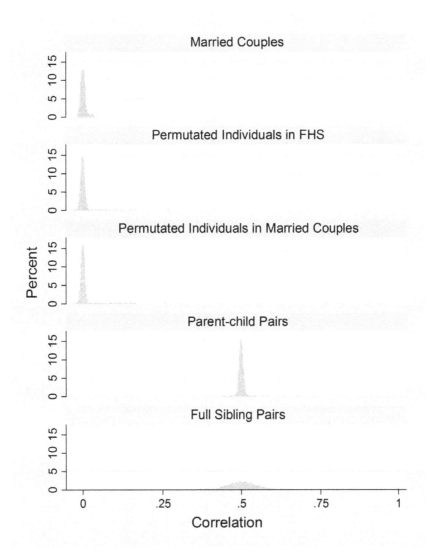

Figure 2. FHS data – the empirical density distribution of couple correlation for married-couples (N = 989), opposite-sex random pairs from permuted individuals in FHS (N = 200,000), opposite-sex random pairs from permuted individuals among married couples (N = 246,870), parent-child pairs (N = 6,958), and full sibling pairs (N = 5,713), with each mixed-model regression estimating a within-a-single-pair correlation "averaged" over 287,294 SNPs.

random pairs from permuted individuals among married couples (N = 200,000), with each mixed-model regression estimating a within-a-single-pair correlation "averaged" over the 66,526 SNPs. The results from the two permutation tests in Panel 2 of Table 1 suggest that averaged over the genome, married couples in HRS has a correlation of 0.0016–0.0017 relative to permuted random pairs. The results from both tests are highly significant. This HRS finding is similar to that from FHS.

Panel 1 of Table 2 presents FHS distribution of within-pair allelic combination for married couples, random pairs permuted among married couples, random pairs permuted among all FHS subjects, parent-child pairs, and full-sibling pairs. Large differences exist between genetically-related pairs (GRPs) and genetically non-related pairs (GNPs). Consistent with our hypothesis, GRPs tend to have a much higher percentage in allelic combinations of 22, 12 or 21, and 00 that contribute to positive assortment than GNPs. GNPs tend to have a much higher percentage than GRPs in allelic combinations of 02 or 20, 01 or 10, and 11 that contribute to negative assortment. Consistent with Figure 2, married couples

exhibit an allelic distribution that is almost identical to those from the two sets of random pairs. However, a careful comparison reveals that married couples have slightly higher proportions of positive-assorting SNP combinations (22, 12 or 21, and 00) than those among the two types of random pairs, suggesting that the positive genomic correlation for married couples be slightly higher than that of random pairs. For the negatively assorting combinations (02 or 20, 10 or 01, and 11), the differences between married couples and random pairs are small and the directions are mixed. Compared with random pairs, married couples have a lower proportion in 02 or 20, and 10 or 01, but a higher proportion in 11, suggesting that the negative genomic correlation for married couples be zero or extremely small.

Panel 2 of Table 2 provides the observed HRS distribution of within-pair allelic combination for different types of pairs for the 66,526 SNPs. Comparing married couples against random pairs in HRS yields a similar pattern to that in FHS: the proportions of positively assorting allelic combinations in married couples are consistently higher than those in random pairs. These allelic data

Table 1. FHS and HRS data – Two permutation tests for married-couple correlations within "negative" and "positive" SNPs: (1) permuted individuals in 989 (FHS) and 3,474 (HRS) married couples, respectively, and (2) permuted all individuals in FHS.

FHS data

		Permuted individuals in 989 married couples	Permuted all individuals in the FHS
All SNPs	Mean difference in correlation: (Married couples minus random pairs)	0.0018	0.0018
	Average p-values	0.00003	0.0001
	Proportion of p-values <0.05	99.98%	99.94%
Negative "half" of SNP combinations: 20/02, 01/10, and 11	Mean difference in correlation: (Married couples minus random pairs)	−0.000076	0.00036
	Average p-values	0.417	0.178
	Proportion of p-values <0.05	8.94%	36.14%
Positive "half" of SNP combinations: 00,12/21, and 22	Mean difference in correlation: (Married couples minus random pairs)	0.00095	0.0012
	Average p-values	0.0043	0.0088
	Proportion of p-values <0.05	98.14%	96.32%

HRS data

		Permuted individuals in 3,474 married couples	Permuted all individuals in the HRS
All SNPs	Mean difference in correlation: (Married couples minus random pairs)	0.0017	0.0016
	Average p-values	7.13×10^{-13}	8.39×10^{-12}
	Proportion of p-values <0.05	100%	100%
Negative "half" of SNP combinations: 20/02, 01/10, and 11	Mean difference in correlation: (Married couples minus random pairs)	−0.0012	−0.0012
	Average p-values	0.0023	0.0016
	Proportion of p-values <0.05	99.2%	99.3%
Positive "half" of SNP combinations: 00, 12/21, and 22	Mean difference in correlation: (Married couples minus random pairs)	0.015	0.020
	Average p-values	1.66×10^{-24}	7.75×10^{-41}
	Proportion of p-values <0.05	100%	100%

in HRS suggest that the "positive" half of the SNPs for married couples have a positive correlation while the negative correlation may be zero or extremely small. Comparing FHS and HRS, the proportion of positive assorting allelic combinations in married couples relative to random pairs appears considerably higher in HRS than in FHS, suggesting that the "positive" half of the SNPs for married couples in HRS have a larger positive correlation than those in FHS. These expectations are confirmed by regression findings.

Figure 5 provides the FHS empirical distribution of the "positive" and "negative" pair correlation, for married couples (N = 989), opposite-sex random pairs from permuted individuals in FHS (N = 200,000), and opposite-sex random pairs from permuted individuals among married couples (N = 246,870), with each mixed-model regression estimating the within a single-pair correlation "averaged" over about one half of the 287,294 SNPs.

The second half of Panel 1 of Table 1 shows the FHS results of two permutation tests for the married-couple correlations within the "negative" and "positive" SNPs. The two tests yield essentially identical findings. For the "negative" SNPs, the difference between the married-couple correlation and the random-pair correlation is small and statistically non-significant. In contrast, for

the "positive" SNPs, the average of the married-couple correlation minus the random-pair correlation is about 0.001 and statistically significant according to the average p-values (0.0043 and 0.0088).

Figure 6 presents the HRS distribution of the "positive" and "negative" pair-specific correlation, for married couples (N = 3,474), opposite-sex random pairs from permuted individuals in the HRS (N = 200,000), and opposite-sex random pairs from permuted individuals among married couples (N = 200,000), with each mixed-model regression estimating the within a single-pair correlation "averaged" over about one half of the 66,526 SNPs.

The second half of Panel 2 of Table 1 presents two permutation tests for HRS data – Two permutation tests for couple-specific correlations within "negative" and "positive" SNPs. Like in the FHS data, the two tests yield very similar findings. For the "negative" SNPs, on average, married couples have a small and statistically significant negative correlation (−0.0012, p = 0.0023; −0.0012, p = 0.0016). For the "positive" SNPs, on average married couples show a correlation of about 0.015 and 0.020, respectively, with extremely small p-values of 1.66×10^{-24} and 7.75×10^{-41}.

Panel 1 of Figure 7 plots the genome-wide SNP-specific correlation for each of the 287,294 SNPs in 989 married couples

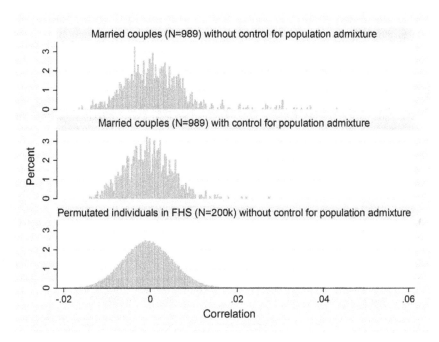

Figure 3. FHS data – the empirical density distribution of married-couple correlation over the 287,295 SNPs; (1) married couples (N = 989) without control for population admixture, (2) married couples (N = 989) with control for population admixture, and (3) opposite-sex random pairs from permuted individuals in FHS (N = 200,000). Panels (2) and (3) are the same as Panels (1) and (2) in Figure 2 and enlarged.

in FHS. The correlation was estimated using the mixed model that allows positive and negative correlations. A large majority of the SNP correlations are scattered around 0 with a range of −0.10–0.10. Panel 2 of Figure 7 parallels Panel 1 of Figure 7 except it is based on HRS with a much larger sample of 3,474 married couples. The large sample explains the much narrower ranges of estimates of SNP correlations for HRS, ranging mostly between − 0.05 and 0.05.

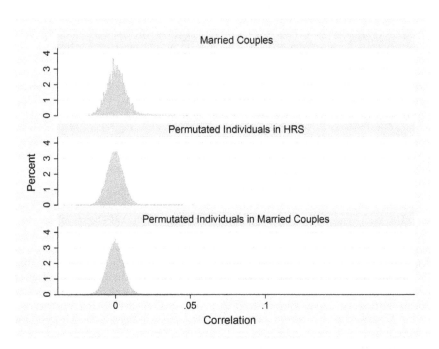

Figure 4. HRS data – the empirical density distribution of couple correlation for married-couples (N = 3,474), opposite-sex random pairs from permuted individuals (N = 200,000), and opposite-sex random pairs from permuted individuals among married couples (N = 200,000), with each mixed-model regression estimating a within-a-single-pair correlation "averaged" over 66,526 SNPs. These 66,526 SNPs are also available in FHS.

Table 2. FHS and HRS data – the observed distribution of within-pair allelic combination for different types of pairs [%(standard deviation)] for a total of 287,294 SNPs (FHS), 66,526 SNPs (HRS), and 66,526 SNPs (FHS common to those in HRS).

Panel 1: FHS

Within-pair combination	Married Couples N = 989	Random pairs permuted among married Couples N = 246,870	Random pairs permuted among all FHS subjects N = 200,000	Parent-child Pairs N = 6,958	Full sibling Pairs N = 5,713
02/20	6.457(0.21)	6.474(0.21)	6.457(0.22)	0.024(0.02)	1.606(0.30)
01/10	32.508(0.26)	32.560(0.25)	32.578(0.26)	22.661(0.23)	19.344(1.87)
11	12.725(0.22)	12.714(0.21)	12.737(0.21)	16.260(0.23)	19.560(1.23)
00	40.061(0.32)	40.021(0.32)	40.009(0.38)	48.190(0.32)	49.050(1.10)
12/21	7.069(0.14)	7.058(0.12)	7.050(0.12)	9.922(0.16)	6.690(0.60)
22	1.180(0.06)	1.173(0.05)	1.169(0.05)	2.943(0.12)	3.757(0.41)
Total	100%	100%	100%	100%	100%

Panel 2: HRS

Within-pair combination	Married Couples N = 3,474	Random pairs permuted among married Couples N = 200,000	Random pairs permuted among all FHS subjects N = 200,000
02/20	6.728(0.44)	7.360(1.24)	7.580(1.40)
01/10	31.971(0.72)	32.688(1.26)	32.905(1.41)
11	13.192(0.35)	12.956(0.60)	12.865(0.66)
00	37.146(0.67)	36.470(1.22)	36.251(1.37)
12/21	8.819(0.22)	8.583(0.43)	8.512(0.48)
22	2.143(0.22)	1.943(0.33)	1.888(0.37)
Total	100%	100%	100%

Panel 3: HRS for a total of 66,526 SNPs in FHS that are also available in HRS

Within-pair combination	Married Couples N = 989	Random pairs permuted among married Couples N = 246,870	Random pairs permuted among all FHS subjects N = 200,000	Parent-child Pairs N = 6,958	Full sibling Pairs N = 5,713
02/20	6.708(0.22)	6.729(0.23)	6.714(0.23)	0.027(0.03)	1.669(0.30)
01/10	33.459(0.29)	33.513(0.27)	33.524(0.28)	23.390(0.25)	19.948(1.88)
11	13.233(0.23)	13.224(0.23)	13.241(0.22)	16.815(0.25)	20.246(1.26)
00	38.037(0.36)	37.993(0.35)	37.988(0.40)	46.407(0.35)	47.300(1.12)
12/21	7.338(0.15)	7.327(0.14)	7.321(0.14)	10.308(0.18)	6.947(0.62)
22	1.224(0.07)	1.215(0.06)	1.212(0.06)	3.054(0.13)	3.901(0.42)
Total	100%	100%	100%	100%	100%

To evaluate our measure of correlation, Figure 8 plots the genome-wide SNP correlation for each of the 287,294 SNPs in 5,713 full sibling pairs from FHS. Both same-sex and opposite-sex full sibling pairs are included. The large majority of the SNP correlations are scattered around 0.50 with a range of 0.40–0.60. Figure 9 presents the genome-wide SNP correlation for each of the 287,294 SNPs in 6,958 parent-child pairs. Again, both same-sex and opposite-sex parent-child pairs are included. The large majority of the SNP-specific correlations are scattered around 0.50 with a range of 0.45–0.55. As expected, the spread of the correlations for parent-child pairs is considerably narrower than that of full sibling pairs. The results in Figures 8 and 9 demonstrate that our method can produce the known patterns of genetic similarity in full sibling pairs and parent-child pairs.

Potentially problematic SNPs are those with a correlation estimate that is much less than 0.50 in the full-sibling analysis and the parent-child analysis. These SNPs do not affect our results of SNP correlations because each SNP correlation is independently calculated. In the calculation of the couple correlations where all SNPs were used in each regression, we excluded 231 out of the 287,525 SNPs. These excluded SNPs have either a full-sibling correlation less than 0.2 or greater than 0.8, or a parent-child correlation less than 0.3. The findings of couple correlations are not affected by whether these SNPs are included or excluded.

Figure 10 shows the FHS permutation tests for the SNP-specific correlations in married couples against random pairs. As will be shown in Table 3, a small number of SNPs achieve a genome-wide significance with a p-value of 5×10^{-8} or smaller. The Q–Q plot of p-values from the SNP-specific correlations is presented in Figure 11, showing that some signals remain after removing the SNPs that have genome-wide significance (Panel 2 of Figure 11).

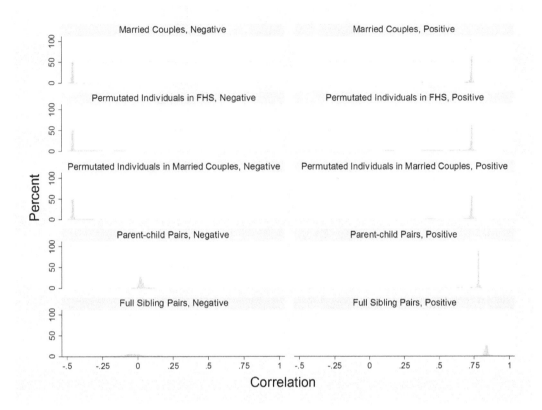

Figure 5. FHS data – the empirical density distribution of the "positive" and "negative" couple correlation, for married couples (N = 989), opposite-sex random pairs from permuted individuals in FHS (N = 200,000), opposite-sex random pairs from permuted individuals among married couples (N = 246,870), parent-child pairs (N = 6,958), and full sibling pairs (N = 5,713), with each mixed-model regression estimating the within a single-pair correlation "averaged" over about one half of the 287,294 SNPs.

Table 3 lists 10 SNPs with the smallest p-values for the SNP-specific correlations in 989 married couples out of the 287,294 SNPs from FHS. The table lists SNP name, chromosome position, gene name when available, gene location, reference allele frequency, SNP correlation for married couples and p value from the permutation test, correlation for full sibling pairs and p value, and correlation for parent-child pairs and p value. Eight SNPs have a p-value 5×10^{-8} or smaller. The largest ten correlations are all positive. The SNP correlations from full-sibling pairs and parent-child pairs are in the expected ranges.

Our replication of the top ten SNPs from FHS (Table 3) using HRS yielded two SNPs (rs16871467 and rs9483869) that are statistically significant at 0.057 and 0.050, respectively. The correlations of these two SNPs are also positive, but smaller (0.026 and 0.027, respectively) than those in FHS. Overall, three of the SNPs in the HRS analysis with 66,526 SNPs achieve a genome-wide significance with a p-value of 5×10^{-8} or smaller.

Our final analysis is an FHS-66,526-SNP analysis for couple correlation. Panel 3 of Table 2 provides the observed distribution of within-pair allelic combination for different types of pairs for these SNPs in FHS. The table indicates that the distribution is much closer to the FHS distribution based on the full set of 287,294 SNPs with the same set of individuals than that in HRS based on the exactly the same set of SNPs but a different set of individuals. The regression analysis of couple correlation of these 66,526 SNPs in FHS confirm the findings from Panel 3 of Table 2 (not shown), providing evidence that married couple correlations are predominantly determined by individuals rather than SNPs

and that the HRS 66,526-SNP analysis is likely generalizable to the full-SNP analysis.

Discussion

In FHS, the two estimates of genome-wide couple correlation are 0.0018 (p = 3×10^{-5}) and 0.0018 (p = 10^{-4}). These couple correlation estimates in HRS are 0.0016 (p = 8.29×10^{-12}) and 0.0017 (p = 7.13×10^{-13}). The much smaller p values from HRS in these estimates as well as other estimates are likely due to the much larger samples of HRS (3,474 couples) than FHS (989 couples). These estimates of couple correlations are not threatened by multiple testing.

Consistent with the estimates of Domingue et al [24], we show positive overall similarity in genomic assortment in married couples; however, our estimates seem much smaller than theirs (0.0016–0.0018 vs. 0.02–0.045). This is the case after taking into account that the two sets of estimates are not exactly comparable. As demonstrated in this analysis (Figures 2, 8, and 9), our estimates are essentially coefficients of genetic relatedness (r) and their estimates are quartile-transformed coefficients of kinship (F) with $r = 2F$, where F is untransformed coefficient of kinship. Our estimates in spousal correlation of educational attainment or years of education with standardization within each sex are 0.59 and 0.52 for HRS and FHS, respectively. One fifth to one third of these quantities are much larger than our estimated genome-wide couple correlation of 0.0016–0.0018. The variation in couple correlation across racial/ethnic groups is examined only in HRS. Less than 1% of the couples in FHS are ethnic minorities. In HRS,

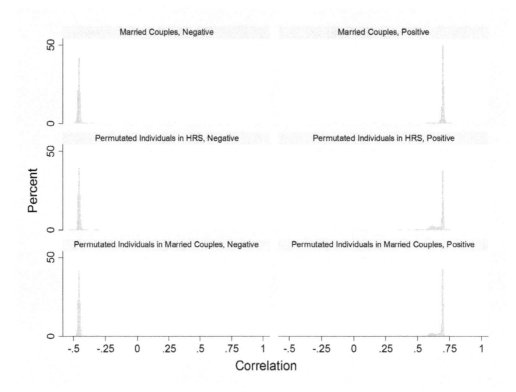

Figure 6. HRS data – the empirical density distribution of the "positive" and "negative" couple correlation for married couples (N = 3,474), opposite-sex random pairs from permuted individuals in the HRS (N = 200,000), and opposite-sex random pairs from permuted individuals among married couples (N = 200,000), with each mixed-model regression estimating the within a single-pair correlation "averaged" over about one half of the 66,526 SNPs.

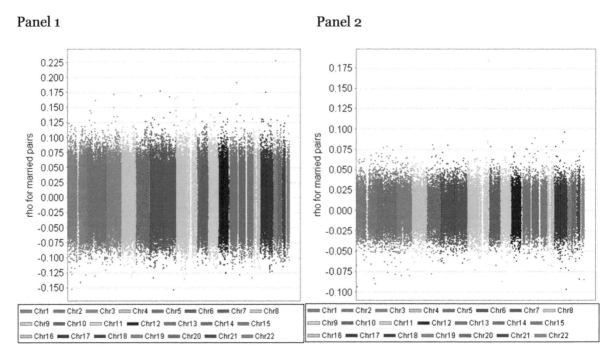

Figure 7. Panel 1: FHS data – genome-wide SNP-specific correlation for each of the 287,294 SNPs in 989 married couples. Panel 2: HRS data – genome-wide SNP-specific correlation for each of the 66,526 SNPs in 3,474 married couples (these 66,525 SNPs also available in FHS). The correlation was estimated using the mixed models with AR(1) covariance structure, controlling for population admixture.

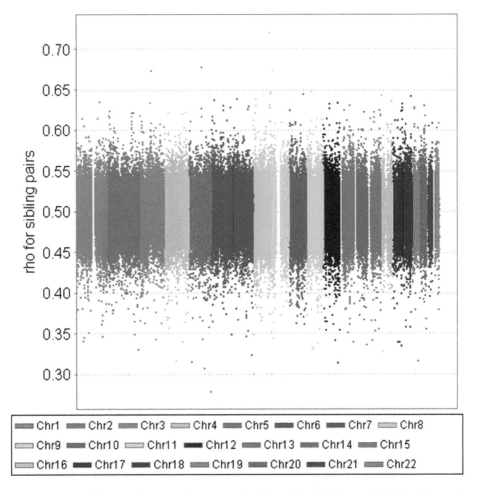

Figure 8. FHS data – genome-wide SNP-specific correlation for each of the 287,294 SNPs in 5,747 full sibling pairs. Both same-sex and opposite-sex full sibling pairs are included. The correlation was estimated using the mixed models with AR(1) covariance structure, controlling for population admixture.

constraining the sample to non-Hispanic whites yields a somewhat smaller and statistically significant couple correlation of 0.0012.

The negative couple correlations in FHS are small and statistically non-significant ($-.00008$, p = .41;.00036, p = .18). The negative marital correlations in HRS are small and statistically significant (-0.0012, p = .0023; -0.0012, p = .0016). The positive couple correlations are much larger than negative correlations in absolute values in both FHS (0.001, p = .0043; 0.0012, p = .0088) and HRS (0.015, p = 1.66×10^{-24}; 0.020, p = 7.75×10^{-41}). The sizes of these estimates in FHS and HRS are consistent with what are suggested by the distribution of the allelic combination in Panels 1 and 2 of Table 2. The data in Table 2 can be considered findings that are more closely based on raw data than those from regression analysis. In both FHS and HRS, the positive correlation is much larger and more statistically significant than the negative correlation suggesting that genetic assortative mating is primarily positive.

For the analysis of SNP-specific correlation based on FHS, of the 287,294 SNP correlations, eight have a p-value 5×10^{-8} or smaller. These SNPs are all positively correlated between married couples, with a range of 0.16–0.27. We repeated the analysis of SNP correlations for these eight SNPs using HRS data. In HRS, two of these eight SNPs (rs9483869 and rs16871467) are statistically significant at about 0.05 and also correlated positively. However, these replications are suggestive rather than definitive

because the two correlations in HRS are considerably smaller than those in FHS.

Neither rs9483869 nor rs16871467 has itself been identified as a statistically significant association in any previous GWAS analysis [25]. Rs9483869 is within an ncRNA called LINC00271, which is expressed in the brain [26]. Another SNP within LINC00271 (rs9494266) has been found to be a statistically significant hit in a GWAS on type 2 diabetes [27]. LINC00271 is in a region of high LD with the immediately adjacent gene AHI1, a gene involved in neurodevelopment and implicated in schizophrenia [27,28]. Rs16871467 is approximately 246 kb downstream of ARHGF28, a member of the Rho guanine nucleotide exchange factor family. This protein interacts with low molecular weight neurofilament mRNA and may be involved in the formation of amyotrophic lateral sclerosis neurofilament aggregates [29]. Opposite, towards the chr5 telomere, the closest defined element is the retrogene C17orf76 antisense RNA 1, approximately 36 kb away. This SNP does reside in a DNAse I hypersensitive site defined by the ENCODE project [30,31].

Genomic assortment in human marriages may vary over a number of factors. Different couples may assort on entirely different phenotypes and thus different genetic variants, which is expected to decrease the power of detecting SNP-specific correlations among couples. Genomic assortment may also be influenced by social and cultural contexts that vary across

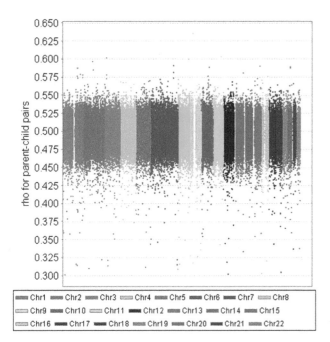

Figure 9. FHS data – genome-wide SNP-specific correlation for each of the 287,294 SNPs in 6,958 parent-child pairs. Both same-sex and opposite-sex parent-child pairs are included. The correlation was estimated using the mixed models with AR(1) covariance structure, controlling for population admixture.

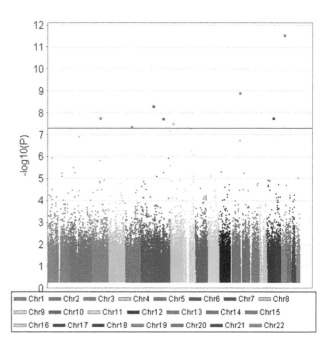

Figure 10. FHS data – the significance tests of SNP-specific correlations: the within-pair correlation of married couples against randomly-paired pairs. The tests for the 287,294 SNPs are shown in a Manhattan plot. The larger dots representing individual SNPs above the blue line indicate statistical significance at $p < 5 \times 10^{-8}$.

historical periods and geographic locations. American marriage is considerably different from marriage in other Western countries [32], not to mention marriage in non-Western countries. Pawlowski et al. [33] report an effect of World War II on mate preference in height. The advantage of taller males in the marriage market is evident among individuals born in the 1940 s, 1950 s and 1960 s, but not in the 1930 s. The authors suggest that this may be due to the relative scarcity of young men immediately after WWII. The genomic assortment may vary across geographic regions within the United States.

Overall, our data suggest a degree of genomic assortative mating at the allelic level in married couples who were born in the first half of the 20th century in the United States. Apparently, this degree of genetic assortment averaged over the human genome is much smaller than the 0.20 Pearson had conjectured based on the observed correlations in height and arm span between husband and wife. As alluded earlier, certain genetic variants such as those underlying height are likely to be heavily assorted; however, the level of overall assortment in the genome seems much less.

However, a genomic correlation of 0.015–0.02 with married couples, estimated for the "positive" assorting SNPs in HRS, can represent an important genomic assortment for at least two reasons. A married-couple correlation may be compared with genetic relatedness among biological relatives. A genomic correlation of 0.015–0.02 is close to the average genomic correlation (0.0312) among second cousins (or the genomic correlation [0.0312] of an individual with his grandfather's grandfather). While an individual passively and unselectively inherits half of his or her genes from each of the two parents, married individuals consciously or unconsciously assort on genes that play a strategic role in their reproductive marriages.

Our analysis of HRS reports a small but statistically significant negative genomic assortment, suggesting that negative genomic may, indeed, exist. This negative assortment contrasts conspicu-

ously with the only-positive assortment among genetic relatives (see Figures 2 and 4).

Our interest is in assortative mating rather than genomic similarity related to population stratification and marriages between distant relatives. The principal components included in the analysis are effective (Figure 3); nevertheless, it might be difficult to differentiate low-level genomic similarity due to assortative mating from low-level genetic similarity due to distant genetic relatives marrying each other.

There is one important methodological limitation in the current analysis. As Wright [34] pointed out decades ago, assortative mating can only be done through external phenotypes and the same phenotype may result from different DNA sequences or non-homologous genes. For example, a married couple may assort by body weight, but the body weight of the husband and the wife may depend on different sets of genes (e.g., *FTO* vs *MC4R*). Such cases of genetic assortment are missed by direct allelic comparison between homologous genes, an approach used in this analysis.

The methodological limitation underestimates a more general form of genomic assortment, in which different allelic forms cause the same phenotype within the same gene or different genes. Assortative mating may actually occur at a higher level than we estimated in this project. Only when the general form of genomic assortment is taken into account could the impact of assortative mating suggested by Lewontin [3] and Thiessen and Gregg [6] be adequately evaluated.

Methods

The Framingham Heart Study (FHS) is a community-based, prospective, longitudinal study following three generations of participants: (i) the Original Cohort enrolled in 1948 (N = 5,209); (ii) the Offspring Cohort consist of the children of the Original Cohort and their spouses, who were enrolled in 1971 (N = 5,124);

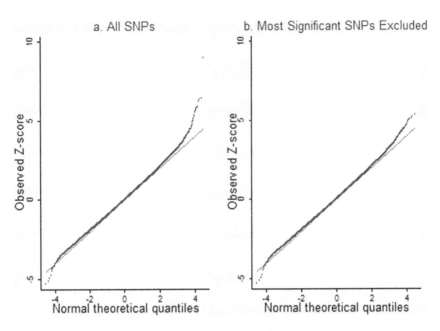

Figure 11. The QQ plot of observed Z-scores vs. expected Z-scores. The plot on the left side includes all 287,294 SNPs while the one on the right side excludes 8 SNPs with p-values smaller than 5×10^{-8}.

and (iii) the Generation Three Cohort consists of the grandchildren of the Original Cohort, who were enrolled in 2002 (N = 4,095). More information on FHS can be found online [22]. Our analysis uses the 1,978 individuals or 989 married couples whose genotype data are available. These individuals are predominantly of European origin. Less than 1% of FHS respondents were racial/ethnic minorities.

Of the 14,428 study subjects in FHS, a total of 9,237 consenting individuals have been genotyped including 4,986 women and 4,251 men. Genotyping for FHS participants was performed by Affymetrix (Santa Clara, CA, USA) using the Affymetrix 500K GeneChip array. The Y chromosome was not genotyped. The standard quality control filter is applied. Individuals with 5% or more missing genotype data are excluded from analysis. X chromosome SNPs, SNPs with a call rate $\leq 99\%$ or a minor allele frequency ≤ 0.01 are also eliminated from analysis. The application of the quality control filter leaves 8,738 individuals with 287,525 SNPs from the 500K genotype data.

The Health and Retirement Survey (HRS), launched in 1992, is a longitudinal study, surveying more than 22,000 Americans over the age of 50 every two years and collecting information on labor force participation and health transitions. The HRS began collecting salivary DNA in 2006 and has approximately > 13,000 such DNA samples stored in repository. The genotyping for HRS was completed using the Illumina HumanOmni2.5-4v1 array, which includes more than one million SNPs. A total of 12,857 samples were genotyped and passed CIDR's quality control (QC) process. The HRS analysis used samples of 6,948 individuals or 3,474 married couples that have passed the QC. A total of 66,526 SNPs out of 287,525 SNPs used in FHS were also genotyped in HRS.

In all our analyses, the outcome variable is the dosage of minor alleles for a SNP, which is standardized with mean = 0 and SD = 1; a correlation coefficient is used to measure genetic similarity. A correlation coefficient has a range of -1 to 1 allowing measurement of positive as well as negative assortment, and was used widely in measuring phenotypic similarity in studies of assortative mating. Correlation coefficients based on dosages of

minor alleles are essentially coefficients of genetic relatedness (r). Because a coefficient of genetic relatedness is the most widely-used measurement of genetic relatedness among genetic relatives, our findings of genetic assortment among married couples can be readily understood and compared with the well-known genetic relatedness among full siblings ($r = 0.5$) and identical twins ($r = 1$).

Both married-couple-specific correlation and SNP-specific correlation are estimated by the following mixed linear model [35]:

$$Y = X\beta + \varepsilon \qquad (1)$$

where Y stands for standardized SNP dosage, X is a matrix of observed variables such as those used for controlling for population admixture, β is a coefficient vector of X including a standard intercept, and $\mathrm{Var}(Y|X) = \mathrm{Var}(\varepsilon) = \begin{pmatrix} W & \cdots & 0 \\ \vdots & \ddots & \vdots \\ 0 & \cdots & W \end{pmatrix}$

with $W = \sigma^2 \begin{pmatrix} 1 & \rho \\ \rho & 1 \end{pmatrix}$ in which ρ is either a couple correlation or a SNP correlation, depending on input data in Y. Model (1) is a special case of the auto-regressive AR(1) model. This AR(1) model allows for both positive and negative correlations, which correspond to positive and negative marital assortment.

For the couple correlation, Y_{ij} in Y is the SNP dosage for individual i and SNP j where $i = 1,2$ indexing husband and wife in a married couple and $j = 1,...,287,294$ indexing the SNPs for FHS. Note that in the calculation for the couple correlation, the input data for a single mixed model FHS are a vector of SNP dosage with an extremely large dimension of $287,294 \times 2 = 574,588$. This dimension exceeds 2,000,000 if the entire set of HRS genome-wide genotype data are used for couple correlation analysis. For the SNP correlation, Y_{ij} in Y is the SNP dosage for individual i and married couple j where $i = 1,2$ indexing husband and wife in a married couple and $j = 1,...,989$ indexing married couples for FHS. The mixed models for both couple correlations and SNP correlations were implemented in SAS [36].

Table 3. FHS data – ten SNPs with the smallest p-values for the SNP-specific correlation in 989 married couples out of the 287,294 SNPs, with the correlation estimated from the mixed model after controlling for population admixture.

SNP	Chromosome (position)		Gene	Location	Reference Allele (Freq.)		Married Pairs		Sibling Pairs		Parent-child Pairs	
							corr	p	corr	p	corr	p
rs16974794	19	(41499094)	CYP2B6	Intronic	A	(0.922)	0.27	0	0.47	0	0.35	0
rs1021652	17	(71403890)	SDK2	WNCG	A	(0.089)	0.20	9.30E-11	0.34	0	0.49	0
rs951954	2	(110459505)		Intergenic	T	(0.189)	0.20	1.11E-10	0.56	0	0.61	0
rs3007246	13	(105822046)		Intergenic	C	(0.928)	0.19	2.56E-10	0.56	0	0.55	0
rs16871467	5	(73484420)		Intergenic	G	(0.968)	0.18	2.43E-09	0.50	0	0.54	0
rs352416	8	(28452799)		Intergenic	C	(0.865)	0.17	9.45E-09	0.50	0	0.55	0
rs9483869	6	(136022914)	LINC00271	Noncoding RNA	T	(0.904)	0.17	1.59E-08	0.45	0	0.51	0
rs4449354	3	(105998897)		Intergenic	T	(0.090)	0.17	1.82E-08	0.49	0	0.52	0
rs16852244	3	(105993897)		Intergenic	T	(0.961)	0.16	5.15E-08	0.48	0	0.52	0
rs17155256	7	(81238711)	AY927633	WNCG	A	(0.843)	0.16	9.14E-08	0.46	0	0.53	0

Information is provided on SNP name, chromosome position, gene name when available, gene location, reference allele frequency, SNP correlation for married couples and p value from the permutation tests, correlation for full sibling pairs and p value, and correlation for parent-child pairs and p value.
WNCG: within noncoding gene&intronic.
NMDT: NMD transcript&intronic.

More intuitively, our mixed model is analogous to a multilevel model in which IQ measures of students are clustered into schools [37]. IQ measures would be equivalent to SNP dosages and schools would be equivalent to couples. In FHS, each SNP-correlation regression model estimates the correlation of a SNP averaged over 989 couples, which is equivalent to a multilevel model that estimates the intra-class or within-school correlation of an IQ measure averaged over the schools in the analysis sample. The analogy may also be applied to our couple-correlation regression where the multilevel model analyzes only one school on a large number of different cognitive measures. The multilevel model would estimate a within-school correlation averaged over the large number of cognitive measures. The model can be identified because of multiple measures of cognitive outcomes. The model makes sense because we estimate an average genomic correlation within a couple, which is similar to genomic correlation within a pair of biological siblings. In FHS, our mixed couple-correlation model estimates a correlation within a couple averaged over 287,294 SNPs. In FHS, 989 couples yielded 989 such couple estimates.

To verify that our estimated correlation coefficients are essentially coefficients of genetic relatedness, the couple correlation and SNP correlation were also performed on 5,713 pairs of full siblings and 6,958 parent-child pairs. For full-sibling pairs, each couple correlation is based on all SNPs for a single full-sibling pair and each SNP correlation is based on all sibling pairs. The parent-child estimates parallel those of full-sibling pairs. The known genetic relatedness in full siblings and parent-children can be used as a benchmark against which the genetic similarity estimates from married couples can be evaluated. The SNP correlation based on full sibling pairs and parent-child pairs can also be used to check the quality of individual SNPs. If the sibling and parent-child correlation for a specific SNP deviate severely from what is expected, the quality of that particular SNP may be questioned.

To remove the effects of race and ethnicity on genomic assortment, principal components (PCs) were estimated in FHS and in HRS by Eigensoft [38,39] and then included in regression analysis of couple and SNP correlations. Since principle components are influenced by correlation data, we excluded some of the correlated SNPs and correlated individuals when constructing PCs. To remove correlated SNPs, we used Plink to run LD-based SNP pruning and only kept the SNPs with pair-wise $r^2 < 0.2$. To remove the correlated individuals, we used Plink to get the pairwise identity-by-descent (IBD) estimates, and kept those with estimated genome-wide pair-wise IBD <0.1. The PCs for the subjects that were excluded for the construction of PCs were subsequently calculated using the parameter coefficients obtained from those included in the PC estimation. For both FHS and HRS, seven largest PCs were used. Previous work shows that adjusting a small number of PCs is usually sufficient to account for population admixture [38]. For FHS, 92,648 SNPs were used to construct the PCs; for HRS, the PCs were constructed on the basis of the 67,385 SNPs.

Our mixed-model approach allows controlling population stratification in the regression analysis. For the SNP correlation, the seven largest PCs were included in Equation (1) as individual predictors. For the couple correlation, the seven largest PCs were used in a regression to predict the minor allele dosage of each SNP; the resulting residuals were then used as the outcome variable in Equation (1).

The statistical significance tests for couple correlations and SNP correlations are performed following the same principles in FHS and HRS. The couple correlations are evaluated via two permutation tests. Two permutation tests based on two quite different populations provide a robustness check for the results of significance tests. For FHS, the first permutation test is based on the individuals in the 989 married couples. We obtained 246,870 random pairs from these individuals who are genetically unrelated, unmarried, of the opposite sex, and with the male no more than 5 years older and no more than 2 years younger than the female. In the second permutation test based on all FHS individuals, we first randomly select a subset of 200,000 pairs from about 20 million possible unrelated opposite-sex pairs in FHS. A subset is selected to reduce computation. In both permutation tests, we (1) compute couple correlations for all these married couples and random pairs, (2) randomly draw 5,000 samples (N = 989) from the large pool of 200,000 (or 246,870) pairs without replacement, (3) randomly draw 5,000 samples (N = 989) from married couples with replacement, and (4) compare each of the 5,000 bootstrapped samples of married couples with the 5,000 random-pair samples using a t test.

A potential limitation of a couple correlation is that the positive and negative assortment within each married couple may cancel each other. To address this issue, we calculate two correlations for each couple, one using about half of the SNPs that contribute to the more "positive" assortment and the other using the half of SNPs that contribute to the more "negative" assortment.

The division of the entire set of the SNPs into "positive" and "negative" groups is based on the combination of minor allele dosage at each SNP for each couple. We use "02" to indicate that the minor allele dosage for a particular SNP for one spouse is "0" and for the other is "2". The combination can only take one of the six forms: 02 or 20, 01 or 10, 11, 00, 12 or 21, and 22, where 0, 1 and 2 represent a minor allele dosage. A simulation based on the observed distribution of these combinations in the married couples of FHS yields an order of 02 or 20, 01 or 10, 11, 00, 12 or 21, and 22 according to how positive a contribution each of the six combinations makes to the overall couple correlation. These simulated results were used to order the SNPs in each couple dataset.

To provide more information on the simulation, we simulated paired data with six possible combinations of 02 or 20, 01 or 10, 11, 00, 12 or 21, and 22, assuming the distribution of each combination is the same as that in the observed genome-wide genotype data. We then compared each pair of the combinations with respect to their contributions to the overall correlation. For example, when comparing the contributions of 11 and 22, we assessed the change in the overall correlation as a response to increasing the proportion of 22 and reducing the proportion of 11, while keeping the same the proportions of other combinations. Comparing all possible pairs found that increasing the proportions of 00, 12 or 21, and 22 results in an increase of the overall correlation, whereas an increase in the proportions of 20 or 02, 10 or 01, and 11 results in a decrease of the overall correlation.

For each couple, the SNPs with the combinations of 20 or 02, 10 or 01, and 11 are included in the negative group and the SNPs with the combinations of 00, 12 or 21, and 22 are included in the positive group. The statistical tests for these positive and negative correlations are performed in a similar fashion as those for the overall couple correlation.

A Z-test and its associated p-value were obtained for each SNP correlation in both FHS and HRS. For FHS, each test is a comparison of the SNP correlation based on 989 married couples against the distribution of the same-SNP correlation calculated from the 5,000 samples of randomly paired opposite-sex pairs based on the entire FHS sample. Each of the 5,000 samples has a sample size of 989 pairs.

To summarize, this study consists of three parts. The first part is an FHS analysis; it uses all available SNPs (287,294) in FHS for both couple-correlation and SNP-correlation analysis. Part-2 is an HRS analysis. Part-2 SNP-correlation analysis only uses the 10 SNPs in HRS that have the smallest P-values in FHS; and part-2 couple-correlation analysis uses 66,526 SNPs in HRS that are also available in FHS. These SNPs are the only SNPs available in both FHS and HRS. Using exactly the same set of SNPs from two independent studies offers an opportunity to replicate the findings. A non-trivial reason for not using all SNPs available in HRS in couple-correlation analysis is computational. The analysis would have to estimate an extremely large number of mixed models for permutation tests, each model using a dataset with $2 \times 2,000,000 = 4,000,000$ rows of data. Part-3 analysis is a couple-correlation analysis using the 66,526 SNPs in FHS that are available in HRS. Thus, this part-3 FHS analysis uses exactly the same set of the 66,526 SNPs that the HRS analysis of couple correlation used, but a different set of individuals in FHS to calculate couple correlations. Comparing the findings from the FHS 287,294-SNP analysis and the FHS 66,526-SNP analysis provides evidence whether the findings from the 66,526-SNP analysis in HRS can be generalized to those of the 2,000,000-SNP analysis in HRS.

Acknowledgments

Many thanks to Yunfei Wang and Qianchuan He for their invaluable support in this project.

Author Contributions

Conceived and designed the experiments: GG. Analyzed the data: LW HL. Contributed reagents/materials/analysis tools: TR. Contributed to the writing of the manuscript: GG.

References

1. Vandenberg SG (1972) Assortative mating, or who marries whom? Behavior Genetics 2: 127–157.
2. Risch N, Choudhry S, Via M, Basu A, Sebro R, et al. (2009) Ancestry-related assortative mating in Latino populations. Genome Biology 10.
3. Lewontin R, Kir D, Crow J (1968) Selective mating, assortative mating, and inbreeding: Definitions and implications. Biodemography and Social Biology 15: 141–143.
4. Ramsoy NR (1966) Assortative Mating and the Structure of Cities. American Sociological Review 31: 773–786.
5. Speakman JR, Djafarian K, Stewart J, Jackson DM (2007) Assortative mating for obesity. American Journal of Clinical Nutrition 86: 316–323.
6. Thiessen D, Gregg B (1980) Human assortative mating and genetic equilibrium: An evolutionary perspective. Ethology and Sociobiology 1: 111–140.
7. Merikangas KR (1982) Assortative Mating for Psychiatric Disorders and Psychological Traits. Arch Gen Psychiatry 39: 1173–1180.
8. Nielsen J (1964) Mental disorders in married couples (assortative mating). British Journal of Psychiatry 110: 683–697.
9. Qian Z (1998) Changes in Assortative Mating: The Impact of Age and Education, 1970–1990. Demography 35: 279–292.
10. Mare RD (1991) 5 Decades of Educational Assortative Mating. American Sociological Review 56: 15–32.
11. Torche F (2010) Educational Assortative Mating and Economic Inequality: A Comparative Analysis of Three Latin American Countries. Demography 47: 481–502.
12. Smits J, Park H (2009) Five Decades of Educational Assortative Mating in 10 East Asian Societies. Social Forces 88: 227–255.
13. Heath AC, Berg K, Eaves LJ, Solaas MH, Sundet J, et al. (1985) No Decline in Assortative Mating for Educational-Level. Behavior Genetics 15: 349–369.
14. Silventoinen K, Kaprio J, Lahelma E, Koskenvuo M (2000) Relative effect of genetic and environmental factors on body height: Differences across birth cohorts among Finnish men and women. American Journal of Public Health 90: 627–630.
15. Weedon MN, Lettre G, Freathy RM, Lindgren CM, Voight BF, et al. (2007) A common variant of HMGA2 is associated with adult and childhood height in the general population. Nature Genetics 39: 1245–1250.
16. Weedon MN, Lango H, Lindgren CM, Wallace C, Evans DM, et al. (2008) Genome-wide association analysis identifies 20 loci that influence adult height. Nature Genetics 40: 575–583.
17. Allen HL, Estrada K, Lettre G, Berndt SI, Weedon MN, et al. (2010) Hundreds of variants clustered in genomic loci and biological pathways affect human height. Nature 467: 832–838.
18. Lettre G, Jackson AU, Gieger C, Schumacher FR, Berndt SI, et al. (2008) Identification of ten loci associated with height highlights new biological pathways in human growth. Nature Genetics 40: 584–591.
19. Sanna S, Jackson AU, Nagaraja R, Willer CJ, Chen WM, et al. (2008) Common variants in the GDF5-UQCC region are associated with variation in human height. Nature Genetics 40: 198–203.
20. Schwartz CR, Mare RD (2005) Trends in Educational Assortative Marriage from 1940 to 2003. Demography 42: 621–646.
21. Pearson K (1903) Assortative mating in man. Biometrika 2: 481–489.
22. FHS (2012) Framingham Heart Study: www.framinghamheartstudy.org. Accessed 2014 Oct 17.
23. Qian ZC, Lichter DT (2007) Social boundaries and marital assimilation: Interpreting trends in racial and ethnic intermarriage. American Sociological Review 72: 68–94.
24. Domingue BW, Fletcher J, Conley D, Boardman JD (2014) Genetic and educational assortative mating among US adults. Proceedings of the National Academy of Sciences of the United States of America 111: 7996–8000.
25. Hindorff L, MacArthur J, Morales J, Junkins H, Hall P, et al. (2013) A Catalog of Published Genome-Wide Association Studies. pp. www.genome.gov/gwastudies. Accessed 2014 Oct 17.
26. Amann-Zalcenstein D, Avidan N, Kanyas K, Ebstein RP, Kohn Y, et al. (2006) AHI1, a pivotal neurodevelopmental gene, and C6orf217 are associated with susceptibility to schizophrenia. European Journal of Human Genetics 14: 1111–1119.
27. Salonen JT, Uimari P, Aalto JM, Pirskanen M, Kaikkonen J, et al. (2007) Type 2 diabetes whole-genome association study in four populations: The DiaGen consortium. American Journal of Human Genetics 81: 338–345.
28. Slonimsky A, Levy I, Kohn Y, Rigbi A, Ben-Asher E, et al. (2010) Lymphoblast and brain expression of AHI1 and the novel primate-specific gene, C6orf217, in schizophrenia and bipolar disorder. Schizophrenia Research 120: 159–166.
29. Volkening K, Leystra-Lantz C, Strong MJ (2010) Human low molecular weight neurofilament (NFL) mRNA interacts with a predicted p190RhoGEF homologue (RGNEF) in humans. Amyotrophic Lateral Sclerosis 11: 97–103.
30. Dunham I, Kundaje A, Aldred SF, Collins PJ, Davis C, et al. (2012) An integrated encyclopedia of DNA elements in the human genome. Nature 489: 57–74.
31. Thurman RE, Rynes E, Humbert R, Vierstra J, Maurano MT, et al. (2012) The accessible chromatin landscape of the human genome. Nature 489: 75–82.
32. Cherlin CJ (2009) The Marriage-Go-Round: The State of Marriage and the Family in America Today. New York: Alfred A. Knop.
33. Pawlowski B, Dunbar RIM, Lipowicz A (2000) Evolutionary fitness - Tall men have more reproductive success. Nature 403: 156–156.
34. Wright S (1921) Systems of mating. III. Assortative mating based on somatic resemblance. Genetics 6: 144–161.
35. Searle SR (1971) Linear Models. New York: Wiley and Sons.
36. SAS Institute Inc. (1961–2005) www.sas.com. Accessed 2014 Oct 17.
37. Goldstein H (2011) Multilevel Statistical Models. 4th ed. London: Wiley.
38. Price AL, Patterson NJ, Plenge RM, Weinblatt ME, Shadick NA, et al. (2006) Principal components analysis corrects for stratification in genome-wide association studies. Nature Genetics 38: 904–909.
39. Ma J, Amos CI (2012) Principal Components Analysis of Population Admixture. Plos One 7.

16

Computational Surprisal Analysis Speeds-Up Genomic Characterization of Cancer Processes

Nataly Kravchenko-Balasha[1], Simcha Simon[2], R. D. Levine[3,4], F. Remacle[3,5], Iaakov Exman[2]*

1 NanoSystems Biology Cancer Center, Division of Chemistry, Caltech, Pasadena, California, United States of America, **2** Software Engineering Department, The Jerusalem College of Engineering, Azrieli, Jerusalem, Israel, **3** The Institute of Chemistry, The Hebrew University, Jerusalem, Israel, **4** Department of Molecular and Medical Pharmacology, David Geffen School of Medicine, University of California Los Angeles, Los Angeles, California, United States of America, **5** Département de Chimie, Université de Liège, Liège, Belgium

Abstract

Surprisal analysis is increasingly being applied for the examination of transcription levels in cellular processes, towards revealing inner network structures and predicting response. But to achieve its full potential, surprisal analysis should be integrated into a wider range computational tool. The purposes of this paper are to combine surprisal analysis with other important computation procedures, such as easy manipulation of the analysis results – e.g. to choose desirable result sub-sets for further inspection –, retrieval and comparison with relevant datasets from public databases, and flexible graphical displays for heuristic thinking. The whole set of computation procedures integrated into a single practical tool is what we call *Computational Surprisal Analysis*. This combined kind of analysis should facilitate significantly quantitative understanding of different cellular processes for researchers, including applications in proteomics and metabolomics. Beyond that, our vision is that *Computational Surprisal Analysis* has the potential to reach the status of a routine method of analysis for practitioners. The resolving power of *Computational Surprisal Analysis* is here demonstrated by its application to a variety of cellular cancer process transcription datasets, ours and from the literature. The results provide a compact biological picture of the thermodynamic significance of the leading gene expression phenotypes in every stage of the disease. For each transcript we characterize both its inherent steady state weight, its correlation with the other transcripts and its variation due to the disease. We present a dedicated website to facilitate the analysis for researchers and practitioners.

Editor: Jose M. Sanchez-Ruiz, Universidad de Granada, Spain

Funding: This work was supported by an EMBO postdoctoral fellowship to N.K.B. and European Commission FP7 Future and Emerging Technologies–Open Project BAMBI 618024 (to FR and RDL). The funders had no role in study design, data collection and analysis, decision to publish, or preparation of the manuscript.

Competing Interests: The authors have declared that no competing interests exist.

* Email: iaakov@jce.ac.il

Introduction

Surprisal Analysis, in its most general sense, is a procedure to characterize the probability of different states of a system, states that may have a rich internal structure. Furthermore the system may not be in a steady state. The procedure begins by assuming that a set of a relatively small number of constraints is known. These constraints are considered to be sufficient to characterize the deviations of the distribution from the steady state due to the imposed conditions on the system. If the assumed constraints are insufficient to actually reproduce the probability distribution, one is *surprised* and therefore must search for modified and/or additional constraints.

Surprisal Analysis has its basis in the physical sciences and has been successfully applied to a plethora of physical, chemical and engineering problems and convincingly demonstrated to be relevant, useful and producing verifiable results [1–4].

The present work belongs to a series of papers [5–9] whose purpose is to show that Surprisal Analysis is also relevant and applicable to biological phenomena, in particular cellular cancer processes. A recent commentary on the approach in Biology is [10]. Using surprisal analysis we identify the most stable balanced mRNA distributions at every stage of the disease from the

experimental data and also the less stable mRNA networks that maintain the cells away from the balanced state. These networks underlie the process of cancer development. We compare between the cell system/patient networks participating in cancer transformation and relate them to the networks contributing mostly to the balanced state.

This paper has two additional specific purposes.

First, to combine Surprisal Analysis with other important computation procedures, such as easy manipulation of the analysis results – e.g. to choose desirable result sub-sets for further inspection –, retrieval and comparison with relevant data sets from public databases, and flexible graphical displays for heuristic thinking. The whole set of computation procedures integrated into a single practical tool is what we call *Computational Surprisal Analysis*. This combined kind of analysis should be much faster for practitioners and researchers, than having independent but mismatched tools to be integrated into logical and practical consistency.

Second, over a longer time-scale, our vision is to reach the status that *Computational Surprisal Analysis* will be a routine analysis for cancer diagnostics. Thus besides, imaging techniques, minimally invasive surgery, chemotherapy, controlled radiation treatments, it is expected that *Computational Surprisal Analysis* will find its place in clinical practice, speeding-up diagnostics.

Therefore, this paper aims to show:

- the relevance of Surprisal Analysis to the *understanding* of biological phenomena, by discussing novel results in the area of Cellular Cancer Processes in the laboratory environment;
- that *Computational Surprisal Analysis* indeed accelerates Surprisal Analysis, by first describing the integrative aspects of the tool, and then explaining the speed-up gains in computation and in heuristic thinking;
- the applicability of *Computational Surprisal Analysis* to diagnostic of Cellular Cancer Processes, by comparing results obtained for diseased as opposed to healthy subjects.

Cellular Cancer Processes

Cancer is a highly heterogeneous disease displaying a considerable phenotypic variation among patients with a same type of cancer. Therefore understanding of the underlying oncogenic processes, involved in the process of transformation, requires system-level approaches allowing identification and characterization of the system constituents.

Recent technical advances including cDNA microarrays and mass spec analysis of the cell proteomes, enable to establish global and quantitative functional profiles of cancer cells and tissues. Therefore there is a growing demand for theoretical-computational tools assisting with for the deeper understanding of the data.

Using a theoretical-computational approach we analyzed several gene expression datasets, including renal cancer patients, HPV16 induced transformed keratinocytes and WI-38 transformed fibroblasts [7,8]. Furthermore the method of analysis can be applied not only to messenger RNAs, mRNAs as we do here but also to microRNAs [9] and beyond to the all –omics datasets, including proteomics and metabolomics.

In this paper we center attention on an analysis of the mRNA levels utilizing the same quantitative principles as in non-equilibrium multicomponent systems in physics and chemistry. Utilizing biological systems evolving in time in response to perturbations we aim to define the mRNA signatures at the most stable, steady state of the system and the groups of mRNAs that deviate from the steady state due to perturbation. For this purpose we utilize surprisal analysis as a technique that enables us to apply thermodynamic principles in biology [4,6,8,14].

The output of surprisal analysis includes several groups of mRNAs, those that contribute mostly to the steady state and other group of mRNAs contributing significantly to the deviations from the steady state at every stage of transformation. The last group comprises highly heterogeneous unstable transcription phenotypes [6] underlying the process of transformation. In addition to identification cancer specific gene/protein signatures, surprisal analysis allows comparing of the disease mRNA phenotypes to the most stable and resistant to perturbations steady state transcription patterns at every stage of the disease, adding a new layer to the characterization of varying parts in the cancer transcriptome.

Surprisal Analysis

Surprisal Analysis is based upon the principle of maximal entropy. Entropy is a physical quantity that originated in the discipline of Thermodynamics, then appeared in Statistical Mechanics and later on in Information Theory. Qualitatively speaking entropy is a measure of disorder or lack of information. Entropy increases when the chance of a system to be in a given state among its many possible states is more uniform. If the probability of the system to be in a certain state is much larger than the probabilities to be in any other state, we do not lack the information about the system and entropy is minimal.

The approach based upon the principle of maximal entropy, says that our information about a distribution of the system states is obtained by maximizing the entropy under the known information constraints. In absence of any information, the disorder is maximal and the information is minimal.

We impose the constraints using a method introduced by Lagrange (for further details see File S1). It requires maximizing the expression for the Lagrangian as a function of the Lagrange multipliers:

$$\pounds = Entropy - \sum_\alpha \lambda_\alpha \, Constraint_\alpha \qquad (1)$$

Each $Constraint_\alpha$ is multiplied by a coefficient λ_α a Lagrange multiplier whose numerical value tells about the relative importance of the respective constraint in the particular circumstance. All the weighted constraints are summed and constrain the Entropy to be reduced from its absolute maximal value.

In our application of this technique to cellular cancer processes, constraints are viewed as so-called transcription/translation patterns/cancer signatures e.g. related to specific cellular processes. These biological patterns prevent cancer cells to reach the maximal entropy that is expected to exist at the balanced state of the biological system. Surprisal analysis identifies both states at every stage of the disease: the balanced state and the constrained state, where specific cancer patterns are most active [6–8]. At any given point in time certain patterns contribute more than others. Thereby one can infer about the relative importance of specific cellular processes in different stages of the cancer onset. In this analysis every transcript can participate in more than one transcription pattern, underlying the process of cancer development.

Computational Surprisal Analysis

In order to demonstrate the concept and obtained speed-up of *Computational Surprisal Analysis*, an integrated tool was designed and implemented, having the overall software architecture shown in Figure 1. Its software modules (from now on called softmodules) will be described in detail in the Methods section of the paper (for further details see also the File S1).

In order to get the integrative flavor of the *Computational Surprisal Analysis* tool, we now mention the four softmodules' inputs and the final output of the analysis:

1. *Surprisal Analysis* – input is a large rectangular matrix of data of gene expression levels obtained from measurements in a chip array. One of the dimensions of the data matrix is much larger than the other one (for example, 4 time stamps by approximately 22,000 genes). A goal of the surprisal analysis is to reduce the data matrix to manageable dimensions, viz. to obtain a square matrix whose dimension is smaller or at most equal to the small dimension of the data matrix;

2. *Gene Profiling* – input is a small matrix of data whose size is set by the number of patterns relevant to the information measured, say a 4 by 4 matrix, relevant to 4 time stamps in the cellular processes;

3. *DB Retrieval* – input consists of sub-sets of genes obtained by the gene profiling. Each sub-set contains the more influential genes in the respective pattern;

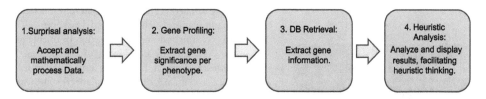

Figure 1. *Computational Surprisal Analysis.* Software Architecture of the integrated tool.

4. *Heuristic Analysis* – input is data obtained in the previous softmodules. Computation is performed to analyze, and interactively display to further analyze heuristically.

A sample output is seen in two heat maps, describing protein connectivity, in Figure 2.

Results

In this section we present results of our work as viewed from three different perspectives: a- genomic characterization of cancer processes: b- the nature of *Computational Surprisal Analysis*; c- the vision of *Computational Surprisal Analysis* as a practical cancer diagnosis tool.

A- Genomic Characterization of Cancer Processes

For genomic characterization of cancer processes the relevant experimental input are the transcription levels of the different mRNAs. The constraints α in the surprisal analysis label the phenotypes and a suitable terminology is given by an application and specialization of equation (1) above, as follows:

$$\ln X_i = -\sum_\alpha G_{\alpha i} \lambda_\alpha \qquad (2)$$

where the indices refer to gene i and to the phenotype. $\alpha = 0,1,2,...$ X_i is the experimental expression level of gene i, $G_{\alpha i}$ is the (time-independent) extent of participation of a given transcript i in the transcription pattern α and λ_α, the Lagrange multiplier of equation (1) is here the weight of the respective transcription pattern α. This terminology will be further clarified in the Methods section with particular reference to the special role of the $\alpha = 0$ term.

The final output of the *Computational Surprisal Analysis* is the heatmaps showing the extent of participation of the transcripts in particular transcription patterns indexed by α. These theoretical heatmaps are compared to the experimental heatmaps describing the functional connectivity of the examined transcripts, using the connectivity scores from the STRING database (See Methods section). In this way we relate $G_{\alpha i}$ values to the functional networks, having the highest STRING connectivity scores, which were verified experimentally.

The G_{0i} coefficients, where the index 0 refers to the zeroth phenotype, have negative values, meaning that the transcripts most contributing to the *steady state* have the lowest G_{0i} values. G_{1i} values – for the first phenotype – represent the extent of participation of a particular transcript in the most important transcription pattern underlying the *process of cellular transformation*. G_{1i} values can be both negative and positive, pointing to the correlation or inverse correlation of the transcripts within the transcription pattern. The transcripts are labeled according to Gene Ontology categories.

HF1 cells – HPV16 Immortalized keratinocytes. Using HPV-16 induced immortalized keratinocytes, we analyzed gene expressions between different stages of HPV-16 induced transfor-mation of keratinocytes [11]. Gene expression levels were measured at *four discrete time points,* called respectively:

- K (normal cells untransformed by the papilloma virus),
- E (HPV16 transformed cells from an *early* stage of transfor-mation),
- L (transformed cells from a *late* stage of transformation)
- BP (the cells from the late stage that were treated by *benzo[a]pyrene*) [11].

Using surprisal analysis we identified the major transcription pattern $\alpha = 1$ contributing at all time-points (For more details see [8]). This transcription pattern included the transcripts responsible for the shrinkage in the pathways controlling apoptosis and enhancement in the cell cycle networks in the late stages of transformation. All these signatures were validated by biochemical means [11].

Surprisal analysis also identifies secondary transcription patterns that are not significant at all the stages of the HF1 transformation [8]. In this work we examine the most stable transcripts contributing to the balanced, invariant state of the HF1 system and compare them to the major transcription pattern involved in the process of transformation. We use *Computational Surprisal Analysis* to build symmetric matrices – in order to generate heatmaps –, e.g. whose ij element is $G_{0i}G_{0j}$.

In Figure 3 one can see results for HF1 cells (HPV16 Immortalized keratinocytes) of *Computational Surprisal Analysis* in five different forms. These are respectively:

a) Upper left – Heatmap representing $G_{0i}G_{0j}$ values;

b) Upper middle – Heatmap of the same transcripts list in (a) using STRING DB scores;

c) Upper right – Heatmap of the same transcripts list in (a) with $G_{1i}G_{1j}$ values;

d) Lower left – Connectivity Map of the most stable transcripts in (a) using STRING DB;

e) Lower right – Connectivity Map of the highest G_{1i}.

From Figure 3 one can observe that, the most stable transcripts (with the lowest values of G_{0i} belong mostly to the protein synthesis category. There is a good correspondence between (Fig.3A) and (Fig.3B) heatmaps, meaning that the most stable transcripts, as defined by surprisal analysis, are more functionally connected as shown in the STRING DB heatmap. The heatmap (Fig. 3B) is the quantitative representation of the connectivity maps (Fig. 3D and 3E).

The (Fig. 3C) heatmap of the same gene list with $G_{1i}G_{1j}$ values is uncorrelated with the (Fig. 3A) and (Fig. 3B), meaning that the transcripts with the largest contribution to the stable invariant state hardly participate in the process of transformation. Those transcripts contributing mostly to the process of transformation generate less connected map (Fig.3B, 3E) in comparison with the

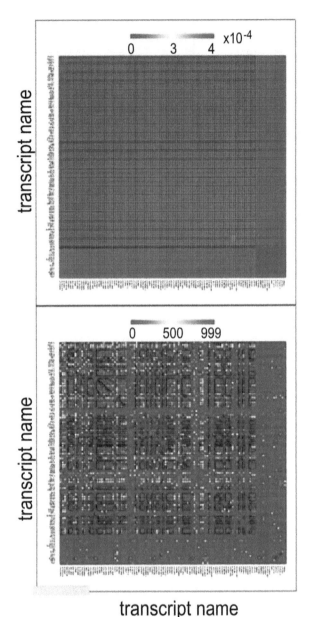

Figure 2. Heat Maps. The upper heat map is obtained by means of Surprisal Analysis. The lower heat map is based upon totally independent data obtained by DB Retrieval. The axes in both heatmaps are identical, viz. they contain the same transcription names in the same order. As usual for heatmaps, colors stand for relative intensities (numerical scales seen above each heatmap): red is high intensity and blue is low intensity. The regions with the same color in both heatmaps clearly overlap, i.e. their results fit very well, implying that *Computational Surprisal Analysis* – in the upper heatmap - can yield predictive information about transcriptional and protein network structures – in the lower heatmap. White dots in the lower heatmap denote lack of information for the specific transcripts.

most stable transcripts (Fig. 3B and 3D) that have very small relative changes (the lowest values of G_{0i}).

WI-38 cells – WI-38 transformed fibroblasts. In Figure 4 one can see results for WI-38 cells (WI-38 transformed fibroblasts) of *Computational Surprisal Analysis* in the same five forms and conventions as in Figure 3. This cellular system includes 12 stages of cancer transformation in which different genetic alterations

were applied [12]. This cell system underwent about 12 molecular manipulations such as hTERT insertion, cell doublings, repression of p53 function and the insertion of oncogenic H-Ras as reported in [12], thereby developing of the normal WI-38 immortalized non-transformed fibroblasts into fully transformed cells. In this cancer cellular system the balanced state was stable during all 12 time points of transformation, whereas the significance of the transcription patterns involved in the process of transformation varied at different time points [7].

From Figure 4 one makes the same observations as above: there is a good fitness between (Fig. 4A) and (Fig. 4B) heatmaps; the (C) $G_{1i}G_{1j}$ values heatmap is uncorrelated with (Fig. 4A) and (Fig. 4B). The heatmap (Fig. 4B) is the quantitative representation of the connectivity maps (Fig. 4D and Fig. 4E). Transcripts with the highest G_{0i} values and the biggest absolute G_{1i} generate less connected maps (Fig. 4E) with several biological modules (not to be confused with softmodules). The main network module in the Figure 4E includes transcripts participating in the NFκB (Nuclear factor kappa B) signaling. Interestingly this module belongs to the additional (minor) transcription pattern $\alpha = 3$ that has large weights in the last stages of cancer development [7]. This module was validated and defined previously as "tumor-forming genetic signature" in the WI-38 cancer model system [12].

One summarizes the Genomic Characterization sub-section by the following points:

1. *Stable networks* (transcripts with the lowest G_{0i} values) generate strong functional connections according to STRING DB. Each protein there is a hub protein, with numerous connections and bridges that can be quantitatively visualized in the surprisal and STRING DB heatmaps. The probability that a lethal mutation, such as deletion, in that hub protein would lead to a cell death is expected to be higher in comparison with the less connected proteins.

2. *Transformation networks and connectivity*– transcripts with the highest G_{1i} values, contributing mostly to the process of transformation, generate less connected group in all datasets. Thus deletion of one of them or replacement by another protein may not affect significantly the G_{1i} network. The same result was obtained for the transcripts with the lowest G_{1i} values [6]. As shown above, the G_{1i} map usually contains several separated networks modules (see for example Fig. 4E). These modules can be further examined as potential targets for the drug therapy.

B- The Nature of Computational Surprisal Analysis

Here we describe the nature of *Computational Surprisal Analysis*. It essentially consists of the three following aspects: a- synergistic integration of various kinds of computation; b- quantitative speed-up; c- novel kind of inferences exclusively based on surprisal analysis.

Synergistic Integration of Diverse Kinds of Computation. Following the softmodules depicted in Figure 1, there are two modes of operation of the *Computational Surprisal Analysis* system:

1- *Sequential* – to concatenate the softmodules exactly as shown in Figure 1, using each softmodule output as the input to the next softmodule.

2- *Cyclical* – certain softmodules are chosen to be cyclically repeated, with possibly varying inputs until one exits the loop, with satisfactory results.

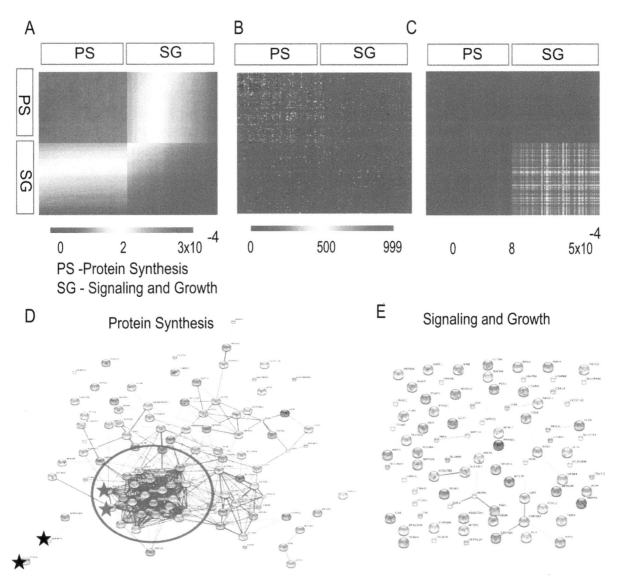

Figure 3. HPV16 Immortalized keratinocytes. (A) A heatmap of the 100 most stable (seen in (a) in red color) and the 100 most contributing to the main transcription pattern $\alpha = 1$ (highest G_{1i}) and up-regulated transcripts (seen in (a) in blue color) as obtained by surprisal analysis. In this figure: PS – protein synthesis, SG – Signaling and Growth. (B) A heatmap of the same transcript list in (A) using STRING DB scores. (C) The same transcripts list was utilized to generate $G_{1i}G_{1j}$. (D) Connectivity Map of the 100 most stable transcripts as using STRING DB; the red color ellipse encloses the most stable and connected transcripts involved in the protein synthesis. The thickness of the lines reflect the approximate probability of the protein-protein functional link for the related transcripts as provided by the String score (see Methods sections for more details). For instance, thick lines (as for the proteins highlighted by red stars inside the ellipse, String score = 0.999) represent high probability for the functional connectivity based on biochemical verification, whereas thin lines (as for the proteins highlighted by black stars, in the left bottom outside the ellipse, String score = 0.507) represent smaller probability for the functional connection. (E) Connectivity map of the 100 transcripts most contributing to the main transcription pattern $\alpha = 1$ (blue color).

In both ways an efficient computation is essentially limited only by the interactions with the human user. These interactions may be as simple as choosing/reading input/output. They may be more sophisticated, as for example dedicating time to heuristic thinking and making inferences of several types.

In order to enable cyclical repetitions, one must be able to arbitrarily start with a softmodule, independently of other softmodules. This is indeed possible as softmodules are built such that they can either directly receive the output of a previous softmodule in a chain fashion or to get another external input. There is no need to waste time on explicit data manipulation, such

as converting formats in between softmodules. This is automatically done, being an intrinsic feature of the synergistic integration.

Concerning the 1st softmodule – Surprisal Analysis – we have already seen that its output includes several groups of e.g. mRNAs: those that participate in the steady state and others that contribute significantly to the deviations from the steady state. The softmodules synergism is necessary to understand the biological meaning of these groups, viz. we utilize e.g. STRING DB access [15] to draw functional networks for every group.

The 2nd softmodule – Gene Profiling – is an efficient integrating bridge between the 1st and 3rd softmodules. It allows selection of

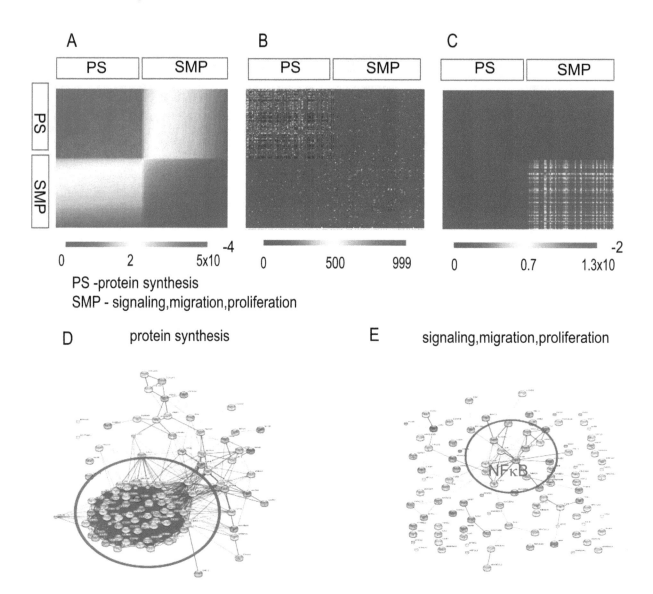

Figure 4. WI-38 transformed fibroblasts. (A) A heatmap of the 100 most stable (seen in (A) in red color) and the 100 most contributing to the main transcription pattern $\alpha = 1$ (highest G_{1i}) and upregulated transcripts (seen in (A) in blue color) as obtained by surprisal analysis. (PS – protein synthesis, SMP – Signaling, migration, proliferation). (B) A heatmap of the same transcript list in (A) using STRING DB scores. (C) The same transcripts list was utilized to generate $G_{1i}G_{1j}$. (D) Connectivity Map of the 100 most stable transcripts as using STRING DB; the red color ellipse encloses the most stable and connected transcripts involved in the protein synthesis. (E) Connectivity map of the 100 transcripts most contributing to the transcription pattern $\alpha = 1$ (blue color).

the significant genes from surprisal analysis results to retrieve the relevant information from publicly available databases.

Regarding the 3rd softmodule, the access to a database such as STRING DB is done through a suitable interface – transparent to the human user – allowing straightforward selection and retrieval of the desired data into the softmodule, for forward computations. The system modularity enables simple future interfaces to additional databases of interest.

Finally, the 4th softmodule enables relating quantitatively the output of surprisal analysis to the functional connectivity between mRNAs. Two kinds of heatmaps are provided:

1- theoretical heatmap of connectivity using degrees of participations of e.g. mRNAs at the steady state/deviations from the steady state as computed by Surprisal analysis (from the 1st softmodule) and selected by means of Gene Profiling (the 2nd softmodule);

2- functional heatmap calculated from the STRING DB combined scores.

These integrated procedures allow very *efficient and quantitative* understanding of the functional connectivity between mRNAs contributing to the different stages of transformation.

Quantitative Speed-Up Evaluation. As seen above, *Computational Surprisal Analysis* involves diverse kinds of computation procedures. These have duration times with very different order of magnitudes, which can be classified as follows:

- *Automatic purely computational procedure* – for instance the Surprisal Analysis performed by the 1st softmodule. The duration of such a computation can be and has actually been measured very precisely. This duration can be certainly shortened by efficient sequential computation in the usual sense or say by parallelization. On the other hand, this is so much faster than the next procedures, that for all evaluation purposes a rough time upper bound of the order of a few seconds is sufficiently satisfactory.

- *Human interactive procedure* – for instance the Gene Profiling of the 2nd softmodule or the slightly longer heatmaps comparison. These are the rate determining steps of the *Computational Surprisal Analysis*. Their duration could be in principle shortened by means of human-computer interaction analysis techniques. On the other hand, it is reasonably safe to assume that its lower bound is limited by human capabilities, roughly estimated to take a time of the order of minutes.

In order to evaluate the quantitative speed-up obtained by the modules of *Computational Surprisal Analysis*, the above duration times should be compared with non-synergistic performance:

- *Manual data conversion and manipulation* – for instance, manually moving the data obtained from databases, while converting them to a suitable format to a heatmap depiction procedure. It could take a roughly estimated duration at least of the order of tens of minutes even for expert software engineers.

From the above estimates, one evaluates the overall quantitative speed-up obtained by *Computational Surprisal Analysis*, to be of the order of ten. This is the ratio between the longest possible duration, viz. the *manual data manipulation* to the shorter rate determining step, viz. the *human interactive procedure* mediated by synergistic automatic data conversion and manipulation.

This faster turnaround enables researchers and practitioners to use the gained time for profitable analysis. In this sense, it speeds-up the potential heuristic thinking. Heuristic thinking has an associative character, as was hinted to by putting side-by-side (for instance in Figures 3 and 4 of the present paper) diverse result displays as Surprisal Analysis generated heatmaps and connectivity maps.

An Important Inference: Stability of the steady state. Besides the integration of diverse types of computation with surprisal analysis, the analysis enables new kinds of inferences. Here we discuss the inference of the stability of the basic, housekeeping cellular processes, such as protein synthesis.

The quantitative argument uses eq.(2) that implies that the experimental expression levels of the transcripts with significant (negative) G_{0i} values and small G_{1i} values will be well reproduced using the steady state term only, $G_{0i}\lambda_0$. This means that experimental expression levels of these transcripts are not very much influenced by the ongoing deviation processes, as represented by $-G_{\alpha i}\lambda_\alpha$ for $\alpha = 1,2...$, and therefore these transcripts are more stable. By more stable we mean that their expression level may change but only by a fraction, since $-G_{0i}\lambda_0 >> -G_{1i}\lambda_1$.

Figure 5 shows HF1 cells and WI-38 cells results from the previous sub-section together, in which $G_{0i}\lambda_0$ values are plotted against $G_{1i}\lambda_1$ values (representing extent of participation in the carcinogenic process). One can see that the transcripts with the biggest $G_{0i}\lambda_0$ values (those that have lowest values of G_{0i}) usually have poor participation in the ongoing oncogenic processes (their $G_{1i}\lambda_1$ values are close to 0). These transcripts are usually highly expressed in comparison with the less stable and deviating transcripts [6].

Less stable transcripts with significant $G_{1i}\lambda_1$ absolute values (transcripts contributing significantly to the deviations from the steady state) correspond to smaller absolute $G_{0i}\lambda_0$ values. In summary, stable transcripts (with the biggest absolute $G_{0i}\lambda_0$ values) have much smaller fold changes and are influenced less by the

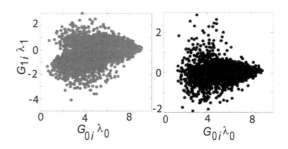

Figure 5. Homeostasis: The stability of the steady state. $G_{0i}\lambda_0$ values for all analyzed transcripts in HF1 cells (left-hand-side red graph) and WI-38 cells (right-hand-side black graph) were plotted against corresponding $G_{1i}\lambda_1$ values. Stable transcripts that have small relative alterations contribute less to the process of transformation. The biggest $G_{0i}\lambda_0$ values correspond to low $G_{1i}\lambda_1$ absolute values.

process of transformation in comparison with the unstable ones (with $G_{0i}\lambda_0$ values close to 0 but significant absolute $G_{1i}\lambda_1$ values).

This example of stability of the steady state is interesting as it uses exclusively $G_{\alpha i}$ and λ_α values obtained from surprisal analysis; this kind of inference was motivated by the application of surprisal analysis to cancer characterization.

C- Computational Surprisal Analysis as a Cancer Diagnostic Tool

What are the advantages of *Computational Surprisal Analysis* as a cancer diagnostic tool? We offer a combination of different reasons. The first refers to types of available information; the second refers to cancer itself as a disease and the third to cancer patients.

Regarding available types of information, recent technical advances enabling quantitative functional profiles of cancer cells and tissues require generation of bio-informatics software tools providing a deeper understanding of the data at the systems level.

Concerning understanding cancer – a very complex disease – working with networks, and not with the individual proteins, is appropriate since many mutations may emerge at the same time due to molecular changes, such as gene mutations and chromo-somal instability [16]. Cells that have spontaneous mutations with a survival advantage would proliferate. There is no "golden list" of specific proteins or pathways that provide these advantages. For example, alterations in the "death" network during the transformation is a hallmark of cancer, but different proteins or pathways may lead to that alteration that eventually would result in the same phenotype – cell survival [17,18]. Surprisal analysis identifies major and minor networks, as represented by transcription patterns, participating in the process of transformation and classifies them according to the importance of every one at each stage of the disease [7,8].

With respect to patients, cancer is highly heterogeneous, showing a dramatic phenotypic variation between different cancer types and among patients with the same type of cancer [6]. Thus *Computational Surprisal Analysis* has the advantage of enabling fast identification of the patient specific protein/gene signatures along with the characterization of the invariant stable genomic/proteomic reference related to all patients.

As a final example, we present results of the *Computational Surprisal Analysis* of renal cancer patients. We deal with development of renal cancer in three patients [13] and surprisal analysis is carried separately for each patient. We analyze three stages of the disease, namely normal tissues, primary tumor and metastases, and identify the stable balance state in each stage and the deviations thereof. The major transcription pattern accounting for the deviation from the stable state ($\alpha = 1$) contributed at all stages of the disease in all patients and differentiating between normal and tumor/metastatic tissues.

A list of the most stable (in the balance state) and least stable transcripts (participating in the pattern $\alpha = 1$) was generated for the patients with renal metastatic cancer. The most stable transcripts (with the lowest values of G_{0i}) belong mostly to the protein synthesis category and have similar G_{0i} values in all patients.

A bigger heterogeneity was observed among less stable transcripts. As was previously mentioned the stable transcripts remained unchanged among the patients, whereas the transcripts participated in the process of transformation varied significantly [6]. Similar results were obtained for two patients with colon carcinoma and for four patients with prostate cancer [6]. Figure 6 shows the relative stability of the protein synthesis network for two of the renal cancer patients.

Although data and respective heatmaps differ in their details, comparison of the patients' heatmaps with that obtained from STRING DB data reveals good correlation. The important point here is that in addition to fast generation of the specific cancer phenotypes for each patient *Computational Surprisal Analysis* identifies a common invariant stable network that remains unchanged between different patients with renal cancer and other types of cancer.

The less stable pattern that strongly contributes to the development of renal cancer differs significantly between examined patients ([6] and Fig. 6D and 6E). This pattern includes proteins participating in the EGFR (Epidermal growth factor receptor) network, such as EGFR and IL6 (interleukin 6), in one patient (Fig. 6F) but not in the other two. EGFR and IL6 are markers of highly invasive tumors, including renal carcinoma [19,20]. These results point to the potential usefulness of Computational Surprisal Analysis as a candidate patient-oriented cancer diagnostic tool.

Discussion

We discuss here the results obtained, on-going and future work, and open issues from the three perspectives: a- genomic characterization of cancer processes; b- usage and speed-up due to *Computational Surprisal Analysis*; c- the vision of *Computational Surprisal Analysis* as a potential practical cancer diagnosis tool.

Genomic Characterization of Cancer Processes

Surprisal analysis identifies a small number of independent transcription patterns that fully describe the process of transformation. At every stage of cancer transformation the importance of every transcription pattern can decrease or increase, thereby giving a very descriptive picture of cancer development process [6,8]. The most stable transcription pattern remains similar between different cell lines or patients as was shown in this study and earlier [6,9].

Transcripts that belong to the steady state pattern generate very connected network maps, whereas the transcripts underlying the process of transformation generate much less connected maps with separated small modules. We suggest that a high connectivity of the stable pattern does not allow a big variation between stable patterns of model cell systems or cancer patients in comparison with the unstable and most contributing transcription patterns participating in the process of cancer development.

Using *Computational Surprisal Analysis* the invariant stable transcription pattern along with the unstable patterns are identified. Several small connected modules inside unstable transcription patterns can be usually observed and further examined as drug potential targets, such as the NFκB module in the WI-38 cancer module system or EGFR module in the renal cancer patient.

Usage and Speed-Up due to Computational Surprisal Analysis

Surprisal Analysis is a formal procedure to test a priori hypotheses about complex phenomena. If the hypotheses are reasonable, the same procedure obtains compact descriptions of the relevant probability distributions of the system states, by a few parameters. If the hypotheses are not satisfactory, Surprisal Analysis – as implied by its name – *surprises* us, indicating that the hypotheses must be modified or more parameters added.

In this work we refer to genomic characterization of cancer processes. In these systems the hypotheses being tested can be classified by the following characteristics:

- *Nature and number of intensive variables* – The intensive variables in our systems are the lambda coefficients (the Lagrange multipliers) of the surprisal analysis. As illustrated in the Computational Methods section, the rank of the small matrix used to characterize the cancer process – i.e. the number of phenotypes – is at most the number of the respective intensive variables. Intensive variables determine the kind of comparisons that we wish and can perform.

A typical kind of comparison refers to *time points*. For this case, researchers should decide, based upon a priori biological knowledge, in which time points to perform measurements that are embedded into a chip-array. In such a system, the lambda coefficients, the "potentials", are time dependent and constitute the relevant intensive variables. For instance, in the HF1 cells – HPV16 Immortalized keratinocytes – *four discrete time points* have been used, therefore a maximum of four phenotypes can be identified.

Another kind of comparison refers to *patients*. If we wish to compare effects on different patients then the relevant lambda coefficients, the "patient potentials", are patient dependent.

- *Selection and Number of extensive variables* – the common extensive variable in this work is *gene expression*. Researchers use Gene Profiling to select the suitable genes to describe the cancer process behavior for each phenotype.

The *Computational Surprisal Analysis* program has been designed, implemented and made available for *remote open* use for researchers, through the Web. The program offers documentation including a User's Guide and sample input and output, and a reasonable amount of initial support. The program and its documentation are accessible in a Web site (see the Methods section).

As an initial proof of concept, the *Computational Surprisal Analysis* tool has been used by investigators situated in a few locations, in Israel, Europe and the United States. The results reported in this paper were obtained by investigators in two of the mentioned locations. A definitive proof of concept will need much more extensive usage in terms of cancer types, investigator and patient numbers and time period durations.

From a speed-up point of view, *Computational Surprisal Analysis* can identify within several minutes transcription/translation patterns involved in the disease in hundreds and even thousands of cancer patients [9] and assign importance of these

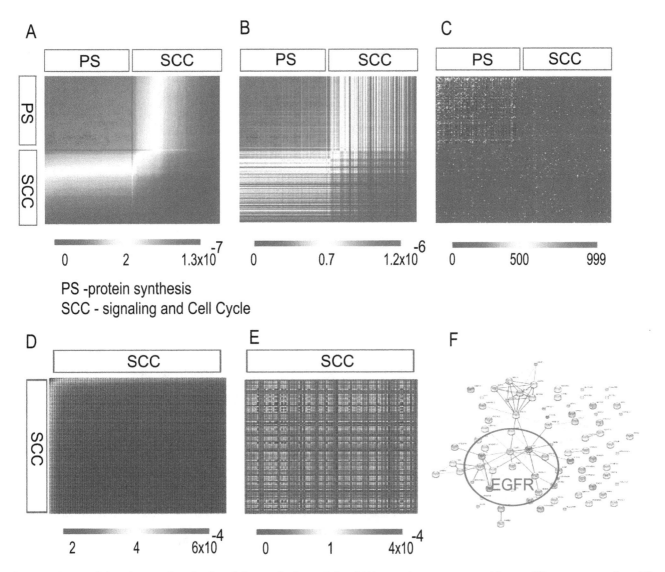

Figure 6. Connectivity of transcripts for Renal Cancer Patients. A list of 200 transcripts was generated for two different cancer patients (A) and (B): a heatmap of $G_{0i}G_{0j}$ values was obtained using the same list of the transcripts for the two patients. The 100 most stable transcripts (with the lowest values of G_{0i}) belong mostly to the protein synthesis category and have similar G_{0i} values in both patients. (PS-protein synthesis, SCC – Signaling and Cell Cycle). (C) A heatmap of the same list of the transcripts as in (A) and (B) was generated using STRING DB scores. A good correlation between (A) and (B) and (C) is observed. (D) and (E) Heatmaps of $G_{1i}G_{1j}$ values were obtained using 100 upregulated transcripts with the strongest contribution to the transcription pattern α_1 for the two different patients. A bigger heterogeneity was observed among these transcripts. (F) Connectivity map of the 100 transcripts most contributing to the main transcription pattern $\alpha = 1$ of the patient described in (A) and (D) was generated using STRING DB.

patterns to each patient [7–9], thereby accelerating the process of patient oriented analysis.

The *Computational Surprisal Analysis* tool has been built with an extensible software architecture and implementation having in mind our main goal to promote fast testing and heuristic thinking in the context of characterization of cancer processes' research. Thus we are open to concrete suggestions, and if necessary even consider partial redesign of the software architecture, while strictly keeping the synergistic integration directives, for additional softmodules such as:

- Complementary relevant algorithms;
- Data selection techniques;
- Access ways to diverse public databases;
- Different kinds of data display.

We are currently working on the development of essential quantitative additions to the *Computational Surprisal Analysis* tool. The following additions will be demonstrated in the next version of the CSA tool:

- new softmodules to make more precise the evaluation of the results obtained, such as: *a- Error estimates* for the results of the tool procedures; *b- Quantitative correlation criteria* for the correlations observed among related heatmaps.
- mobile client in a small dimension generic device, say a smartphone, eventually enabling performance of *Computational Surprisal Analysis* as a diagnosis tool, as discussed next.

Vision: *Computational Surprisal Analysis* as a Potential Cancer Diagnosis Tool

Gene Name	time1	time2	time3	time4
1FFX-BioB-5_at	4.067316	4.386599	4.436357	3.806662
1FFX-BioB-10_at	4.394038	4.681205	4.678421	4.009754
1FFX-BioB-3_at	3.942875	4.266429	4.26033	3.688879
1FFX-BioC-5_at	5.579981	5.675383	5.744818	5.255236
1FFX-BioC-3_at	5.701112	5.909622	5.993379	5.32577

Figure 7. Input file structure sample. It has unique names and expression levels per gene at four time points.

phenotype	time1	time2	time3	time4
0	-664	-659	-646	-648
1	-77	-42	50	72
2	39	-52	6	7
3	5	3	-47	39

Select phenotype to focus on: [0 ▾]

Figure 8. A sample matrix of Lagrange multipliers. Screen print of a particular case showing four phenotypes and four time points.

Our vision in the longer term is to enable *Computational Surprisal Analysis* as a cancer diagnosis tool in routine clinical practice (see e.g. [10]). This will demand a few intermediate goals to be achieved.

The first goal is to accumulate results, substantially increasing the confidence in the *Computational Surprisal Analysis* procedures. The results obtained for the renal cancer patients are very preliminary. These are reinforced by similar results obtained for colon and prostate cancer patients [6]. Together, they point out to the desired direction. But extensive use and corroboration of the *Computational Surprisal Analysis* tool is still necessary.

Conclusion

The main contributions of this work are summarized as follows:

1. *Genomic Characterization* – by contrast with stable gene networks, one can learn about specific groups of genes involved in transformations within cellular cancer processes;

2. *Computational Surprisal Analysis* – a fast and precise approach to genomic characterization. The obtained speed-up enables interactive heuristic thinking for research advancement of cellular cancer processes and opens doors for promising potential diagnostic tools in practice.

Materials and Methods

Data sets

Datasets used in the study include HPV-16 induced immortalized keratinocytes [11], WI-38 transformed fibroblasts [12], normal renal, tumor, and metastatic cells from three patients [13].

1. HF1 cells: cDNA was prepared from three independent HF1 cultures each of K, E, L and BP cells and hybridized to the Human Genome U133A Array (Affymetrix) as described [11], GEO accession number: GSE15156.

2. WI-38 System: cDNA was prepared using duplicates from 12 data points. cDNA was hybridized to GeneChip Human Genome Focus Array (Affymetrix) as described [12].

3. Renal carcinoma: cDNA was isolated from three clear renal cell carcinomas including autologous normal tissue and autologous metastasis and hybridized to the HG-U133_Plus2 Affymetrix Human Genome array as described [13], GEO accession number: GSE12606.

Analysis of mRNA expression data.

The gene expression data were analyzed using the Microarray Suite version 5.0 algorithm (Affymetrix). For each probe, a data analysis output file contained:

- a *signal quantitative metric*, which represents the relative level of expression of a transcript;

- a *detection* i.e. a qualitative classification of each signal as present, marginal, or absent;

- a *detection p-value*, indicating the significance of every detection call.

To compare data from different arrays, the signal of each array was scaled to the same target intensity value. For more details see [11–13].

After performance of Surprisal analysis the transcripts of interest were divided into biological categories using the DAVID DB [21] and their connectivity was examined by means of retrieved data from the StringDB [15]. We used confidence scores for functional connections that are derived by benchmarking the performance of the predictions against a common reference set of trusted, true associations [15]. The benchmarked confidence scores in StringDB correspond to the probability of finding the linked proteins within the same KEGG pathway [15].

Computational Methods

The *Computational Surprisal Analysis* program is Web-based, meaning that it can be accessed by a remote client located anywhere [22]. The program was designed and implemented by an object oriented approach [23]. The implementation technology consists of a server running on IIS (Internet Information Services) using C#.net.

Next we provide details (for further details see File S1) about the computation in each of the softmodules (see e.g. [24] for software modularity concepts).

In the 1st softmodule – *Surprisal Analysis* – the main task is to calculate for terms in equation (2), the values of the constraints $G_{\alpha i}$ the time-independent extent of participation of a gene transcript i

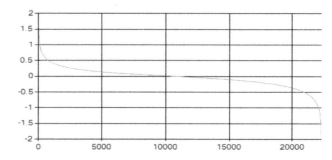

Figure 9. Eigenvector values $G_{\alpha i}$ for selected phenotype α. Values are sorted in decreasing order (vertical axis) against running index of genes (horizontal axis).

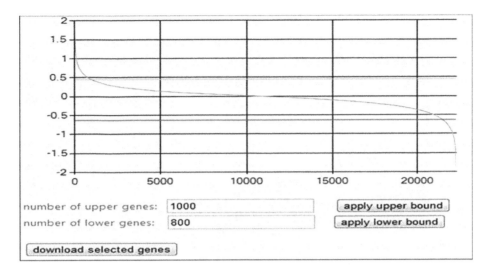

Figure 10. Selected genes with eigenvector values $G_{\alpha i}$ **for phenotype** α. This screen-print shows selected 1000 genes that are above an upper bound (yellow horizontal line) and 800 genes below a lower bound (red line).

in the transcription pattern α and λ_α the respective coefficient at time t – a Lagrange multiplier – of α (see e.g. [8]).

The input, with microarray data uploaded by the user, accepts a CSV (comma separated value) format file, a platform independent standard. All gene names and time names should be unique. Figure 7 shows a partial sample of the input file structure.

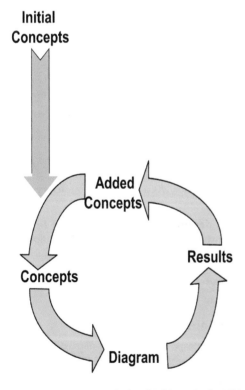

Figure 11. The Heuristic Thinking Cycle. With an initial set of concepts obtained from the surprisal analysis, one performs a computational experiment, whose outcome is a diagram. If one obtains interesting results, one may generalize by inserting this type of diagram in the 4th softmodule and by adding concepts to the subject domain. The cycle may be repeated as many times as desired.

The values of λ_α and the constraints $G_{\alpha i}$ are determined by singular value decomposition (SVD) (see e.g. [25] and references therein; see also e.g. [26] for a different application of SVD to genome data). This procedure extends the notion of matrix diagonalization to rectangular matrices. This is necessary since the number of input genes m may be very large – say of the order of tens of thousands, while the number of time points t, or another relevant intensive variable of equivalent size, is relatively small – say of the order of ten – thus the input matrix is certainly rectangular.

The output of the SVD procedure consists in two square symmetric matrices whose sizes are quite large – as the number of genes – and quite small – as the number of time points. The rank of these matrices is at most the number of time points. To get the eigenvectors and eigenvalues of these matrices, it is sufficient to solve for the small matrix.

The 1st softmodule output is as follows:

1. *List of genes* – of length m, extracted from the input file;
2. $\mathbf{G}_\alpha$ *vectors* – t vectors of length m, referred as eigenvectors;
3. *Lagrange multipliers* – a small matrix of size $t*t$ with values of Lagrange multipliers for each time point T and each phenotype α.

The small matrix of Lagrange multipliers is illustrated in Figure 8 showing a screen print of the *Computational Surprisal Analysis* tool. This case has 4 phenotypes and four time points. One can also select a phenotype to focus on.

In the 2nd softmodule – *Gene Profiling* – one interactively selects a sub-set of genes relevant to a certain phenotype. One starts by selecting a phenotype α to focus on. Once a phenotype is selected, a graph is displayed in the client screen in which the eigenvector values $G_{\alpha i}$ are given sorted in decreasing order (in the vertical axis) for the respective genes i (running index in the horizontal axis). As seen in Fig. 9, most of the values are around zero, thus not of interest.

The next interactive step is to select smaller sub-sets of genes of interest by applying an upper bound to obtain the desired higher values and a lower bound for the lower values. In the screen print of Figure 10 these bounds are seen as yellow and red horizontal

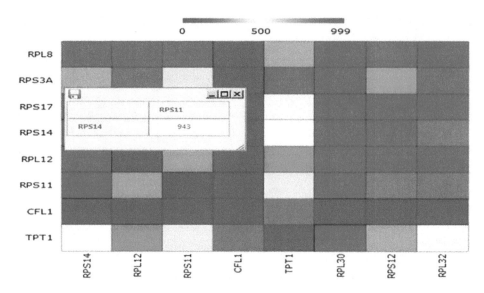

Figure 12. Zooming in on a Heatmap cell. This enables heatmap cell information online – the two crossing genes and the cell value information.

lines. One may then download a list of the selected genes to be used in the next softmodule.

In the 3rd softmodule – *Database Retrieval* – one uses the downloaded list of selected genes to retrieve data from public databases, such as STRING DB [15].

The first task of this softmodule is to enable selection of the desired database. The selection is done based upon a strategy design pattern [27], used to handle communication with different databases. Then it uses the correct unique naming of the relevant genes, making the eventually necessary naming and format conversions.

The 3rd softmodule output for the particular case of STRING DB uses a combined score. For this database various major sources of association data are benchmarked independently. A combined score is computed by STRING DB which indicates higher confidence when more than one type of information supports a given association.

Finally, the 4th softmodule enables infrastructures for heuristic thinking. The infrastructures of this softmodule may be expanded as needed.

We characterize heuristic thinking in the 4th softmodule to distinguish it from formal deduction. It is experimental, i.e. one performs computational experiments, which are approximate, rather than exact. We envisage heuristic thinking as a cyclic process whose main purpose is to discover new concepts, motivated by original types of visual diagrams. The heuristic cycle is schematically shown in Fig. 11.

The heuristic cycle is illustrated by the process leading to Fig. 2. The *initial concepts* are the $G_{\alpha i}$ terms from Surprisal Analysis. The *new type of diagram* in this computational experiment is a specific heatmap pair, seen in Fig. 2. The upper heatmap is obtained with the values obtained with Surprisal Analysis. The lower one is obtained from certain values retrieved from StringDB. The *interesting result* is the correlations between heatmaps with corresponding axes with the same transcript names, but totally independent data sources, even spanning different numerical scales. The *new concept* is the predictive power of pairs of $G_{\alpha i}$

values about transcriptional and protein network structures. *Results are not exact* since data is e.g. lacking in the values retrieved from StringDB.

In our tool a sub-softmodule allows drawing of heatmaps for comparison of Surprisal Analysis results with data retrieved from public databases. Each (non-zoomed in) heatmap has identical labels (genes) in both vertical and horizontal axes.

Specifically, Surprisal Analysis results are computed as products of pairs of the respective $G_{\alpha i}$ values that "meet" in the specific cell of the heatmap. Heatmaps of STRING DB values are obtained from combined gene connectivity scores.

The 4th softmodule output heatmatps that can be zoomed in on online to display heatmap cell information – the two crossing genes and the cell value – for heuristic analysis. This is illustrated in Fig. 12.

Supporting Information

Figure S1   CSV file structure sample. This sample has a title record followed by 5 data records. Each data record has a gene name and numerical expression levels per gene at four time points.

File S1   Additional detailed information needed for the usage of the Computational Surprisal Analysis program. This essentially consists of input and output file formats and explanatory material to facilitate understanding of computational features.

Author Contributions

Conceived and designed the experiments: NKB. Performed the experiments: NKB. Analyzed the data: NKB SS. Wrote the paper: IE NKB SS RDL FR. Conceived CSA Computational Surprisal Analysis: RDL IE. Applied surprisal analysis in biology: FR NKB. Designed the CSA Program: IE SS. Implemented and ran the CSA Program: SS. Checked the CSA Program and the data analysis: FR.

References

1. Levine RD (1978) Information Theory Approach to Molecular Reaction Dynamics. Ann Rev Phys Chem 29: 59.

2. Levine RD (1980) Information Theoretical Approach to Inversion Problems. Journal of Physics a-Mathematical and General 13: 91–108.

3. Levine RD (2005) Molecular Reaction Dynamics. Cambridge: The University Press.
4. Levine RD, Bernstein RB (1974) Energy disposal and energy consumption in elementary chemical reactions. Information theoretic approach. Accounts of Chemical Research 7: 393–400.
5. Gross A, Li CM, Remacle F, Levine RD (2013) Free energy rhythms in Saccharomyces cerevisiae: a dynamic perspective with implications for ribosomal biogenesis. Biochemistry 52: 1641–1648.
6. Kravchenko-Balasha N, Levitzki A, Goldstein A, Rotter V, Gross A, et al. (2012) On a fundamental structure of gene networks in living cells. Proc Natl Acad Sci U S A 109: 4702–4707.
7. Kravchenko-Balasha N, Remacle F, Gross A, Rotter V, Levitzki A, et al. (2011) Convergence of logic of cellular regulation in different premalignant cells by an information theoretic approach. BMC Syst Biol 5: 42.
8. Remacle F, Kravchenko-Balasha N, Levitzki A, Levine RD (2010) Information-theoretic analysis of phenotype changes in early stages of carcinogenesis. Proc Natl Acad Sci U S A 107: 10324–10329.
9. Zadran S, Remacle F, Levine RD (2013) miRNA and mRNA cancer signatures determined by analysis of expression levels in large cohorts of patients. Proc Natl Acad Sci U S A.
10. Faccioti MT (2013) Thermodynamically inspired classifier for molecular phenotypes of health and disease. Proc Natl Acad Sci USA Commentary, doi = 10.1073/pnas.1317876110
11. Kravchenko-Balasha N, Mizrachy-Schwartz S, Klein S, Levitzki A (2009) Shift from apoptotic to necrotic cell death during human papillomavirus-induced transformation of keratinocytes. J Biol Chem 284: 11717–11727.
12. Milyavsky M, Tabach Y, Shats I, Erez N, Cohen Y, et al. (2005) Transcriptional programs following genetic alterations in p53, INK4A, and H-Ras genes along defined stages of malignant transformation. Cancer Res 65: 4530–4543.
13. Stickel JS, Weinzierl AO, Hillen N, Drews O, Schuler MM, et al. (2009) HLA ligand profiles of primary renal cell carcinoma maintained in metastases. Cancer Immunol Immunother 58: 1407–1417.
14. Laidler K (1996) A glossary of terms used in chemical kinetics, including reaction dynamics (IUPAC Recommendations 1996). Pure & Appl Chem 68: 149–192.
15. Franceschini A, Szklarcsyk D, Frankild S, Kuhn M, Simonovic M, et al. (2013) STRING v9.1: protein-protein interaction networks, with increased coverage and integration. Nucleic Acids Res. 2013 Jan; 41 (Database issue): D808–15. doi:10.1093/nar/gks1094

16. Rajagopalan H, Lengauer C (2004) Aneuploidy and cancer. Nature 432: 338–341.
17. Kravchenko-Balasha N, Klein S, Safrai M, Levitzki A (2011) Contribution of gross chromosomal changes to HPV16-induced transformation. Mol Biosyst 7: 1501–1511.
18. Cohen N, Kravchenko-Balasha N, Klein S, Levitzki A (2013) Heterogeneity of gene expression in murine squamous cell carcinoma development-the same tumor by different means. PLoS One 8: e57748.
19. Minner S, Rump D, Tennstedt P, Simon R, Burandt E, et al. (2012) Epidermal growth factor receptor protein expression and genomic alterations in renal cell carcinoma. Cancer 118: 1268–1275.
20. Walther MM, Johnson B, Culley D, Shah R, Weber J, et al. (1998) Serum interleukin-6 levels in metastatic renal cell carcinoma before treatment with interleukin-2 correlates with paraneoplastic syndromes but not patient survival. J Urol 159: 718–722.
21. Dennis G, Jr., Sherman BT, Hosack DA, Yang J, Gao W, et al. (2003) DAVID: Database for Annotation, Visualization, and Integrated Discovery. Genome Biol 4: P3.
22. Exman I, Simon S (2012) Computational Surprisal Analysis Program and Documentation. The Jerusalem College of Engineering - Azrieli, Jerusalem, Israel. Accessible in the web site: http://www.jce.ac.il/. For detailed information please email to CompSurprisal@jce.ac.il.
23. Simon S(2012) Microarray Data Analysis System. B.Sc.Thesis, The Jerusalem College of Engineering - Azrieli., Jerusalem, Israel.
24. Exman I (2013) Linear Software Models Are Theoretical Standards of Modularity, in Cordeiro J, Hammoudi S, van Sinderen M (Eds.) ICSOFT 2012, Communications in Computer and Information Science, vol.411, pp.203–217, Springer-Verlag, Berlin, Germany.
25. Weisstein EW (2013) Singular Value Decomposition.From MathWorld-A Wolfram Web Resource. http://mathworld.wolfram.com/SingularValueDecomposition. html Last accessed October 2014.
26. Tomfohr J, Lu J, Kepler TB (2005) Pathway level analysis of gene expression using singular value decomposition. BMC Bioinformatics, 6: 225 doi:10.1186/1471-2105-6-225
27. Gamma E, Helm R, Johnson R, Vlissides J (1995) Design Patterns - Elements of Reusable Object-Oriented Software. Addison-Wesley, Boston, MA, USA.

17

RNA-Seq Analysis of *Quercus pubescens* Leaves: *De Novo* Transcriptome Assembly, Annotation and Functional Markers Development

Sara Torre[1], Massimiliano Tattini[1], Cecilia Brunetti[1,2], Silvia Fineschi[1], Alessio Fini[2], Francesco Ferrini[2], Federico Sebastiani[3]*

1 Institute for Plant Protection, Department of Biology, Agricultural and Food Sciences, The National Research Council of Italy (CNR), Sesto Fiorentino, Italy, **2** Department of Agri-Food and Environmental Sciences, University of Florence, Sesto Fiorentino, Italy, **3** Institute for Biosciences and BioResources, Department of Biology, Agricultural and Food Sciences, The National Research Council of Italy (CNR), Sesto Fiorentino, Italy

Abstract

Quercus pubescens Willd., a species distributed from Spain to southwest Asia, ranks high for drought tolerance among European oaks. *Q. pubescens* performs a role of outstanding significance in most Mediterranean forest ecosystems, but few mechanistic studies have been conducted to explore its response to environmental constrains, due to the lack of genomic resources. In our study, we performed a deep transcriptomic sequencing in *Q. pubescens* leaves, including de novo assembly, functional annotation and the identification of new molecular markers. Our results are a pre-requisite for undertaking molecular functional studies, and may give support in population and association genetic studies. 254,265,700 clean reads were generated by the Illumina HiSeq 2000 platform, with an average length of 98 bp. De novo assembly, using CLC Genomics, produced 96,006 contigs, having a mean length of 618 bp. Sequence similarity analyses against seven public databases (Uniprot, NR, RefSeq and KOGs at NCBI, Pfam, InterPro and KEGG) resulted in 83,065 transcripts annotated with gene descriptions, conserved protein domains, or gene ontology terms. These annotations and local BLAST allowed identify genes specifically associated with mechanisms of drought avoidance. Finally, 14,202 microsatellite markers and 18,425 single nucleotide polymorphisms (SNPs) were, *in silico*, discovered in assembled and annotated sequences. We completed a successful global analysis of the *Q. pubescens* leaf transcriptome using RNA-seq. The assembled and annotated sequences together with newly discovered molecular markers provide genomic information for functional genomic studies in *Q. pubescens*, with special emphasis to response mechanisms to severe constrain of the Mediterranean climate. Our tools enable comparative genomics studies on other *Quercus* species taking advantage of large intra-specific ecophysiological differences.

Editor: Zhong-Jian Liu, The National Orchid Conservation Center of China; The Orchid Conservation & Research Center of Shenzhen, China

Funding: This work was supported by the following Research Grants: Italian Ministry of University and Research (MIUR/PRIN-2012 TreeCity). The funders had no role in study design, data collection and analysis, decision to publish, or preparation of the manuscript.

Competing Interests: The authors have declared that no competing interests exist.

* Email: federico.sebastiani@ibbr.cnr.it

Introduction

The genus *Quercus* (oaks), a member of the Fagaceae family, comprises ~400 deciduous and evergreen trees and shrubs distributed from tropical to boreal regions, thus constituting significant components of forests in the northern hemisphere [1]. According to their widespread distribution, the genus differentiated into numerous species and populations, with different morphological and physiological traits, enabling their occurrence in areas with contrasting climates. *Quercus* species have been classified as drought-resistant [2], thus allowing their distribution in a wide range of soils [3]. In Central Europe, *Quercus robur* L., *Q. petraea* [Matt.] Libel. and *Q. pubescens* Willd. are most abundant white oak species, and inhabits areas with contrasting temperature and precipitation [4]. *Quercus pubescens* Willd. (pubescent or downy oak) is a thermophilous tree native to southern Europe, widely distributed from Spain to southwest Asia

and from European Mediterranean coastlines to central Europe. It is a xerophilous species and typically grows on dry, lime-rich soils in the sub-Mediterranean region, which is characterised by hot dry summers and mild dry winters [5].

Global climate change imposes to Mediterranean regions a general increase of temperatures and aridity, coupled with a higher frequency of extreme climatic events such as heat waves and late-winter frosts [6,7]. This represents a complex challenge for plants inhabiting Mediterranean-type ecosystems [8], in turn greatly affecting the composition, structure and functioning of forest ecosystems and, hence, the productivity of natural and managed forests [9–11]. Therefore, successful forest management practices in the future have to take into account a conversion from forests currently dominated by relatively drought-sensitive coniferous species (i.e., Norway spruce and Scots pine) and European beech (*Fagus sylvatica* L.) [12,13] to an admix of more drought- and temperature-tolerant trees, such as oak (*Quercus* spp.) [9,14].

Oaks are generally considered to be resistant to drought because of deep-penetrating roots, xeromorphic leaves and very effective control of stomata opening (thus reducing transpiration water loss) [2,15]. Nonetheless, drought tolerance may differ considerably among oak species and provenances, reflecting adaptation to environments with different water availability [16]. Therefore, the characterization of adaptive genetic variation is an issue of outstanding significance for managing natural resources (and gene conservation) as well as to predict their ability to cope with constrains imposed by the global climate change [17–19].

Recent advances in high-throughput sequencing technologies offer novel opportunities in functional genomics, as well as in discovering genes and developing molecular markers in non-model plants [20]. The massively parallel sequencing of RNA (RNA-Seq) represents a powerful tool for transcription profiling, providing a rapid access to a collection of expressed sequences (transcriptome), as compared with traditional expressed sequence tag (EST) sequencing. RNA-Seq technology has been successfully applied in different domains of life, ranging from animals to yeast up to a wide array of model and non-model plants [21–27].

A large number of sequenced transcripts, with approximately 2.5 million of ESTs deposited in databases, has been reported for Fagaceae family (*Quercus*, *Castanea*, *Fagus*, and *Castanopsis*, Fagaceae Genomics Web: http://www.fagaceae.org/) [28]. On the other hand, genomic resources for *Q. pubescens* are very limited at the present (no ESTs, just 178 nt sequences, mainly chloroplast fragments). Therefore, development of genomic resources for *Q. pubescens* is a timely issue to support molecular biology studies at different levels of scale (from evolutionary ecology to comparative and functional genomics).

In our study, we used Illumina RNA-seq technology to analyse the transcriptome of *Q. pubescens* leaves. We generated 254,265,700 clean reads containing a total of about 25 Gb of sequence data. *De novo* assembly was then applied followed by gene annotation and functional classification. Our RNA-seq analysis generated the first *Q. pubescens* consensus transcriptome and provides an unlimited set of molecular markers.

Material and Methods

Plant materials and RNA isolation

Juvenile and mature *Q. pubescens* leaves from 4 half-sib 4-years old plants were collected. These plants were cultivated in 3L pots and grew up in the greenhouse, under natural daylight condition. Five chloroplast (cp) and four nuclear (nu) microsatellites (SSRs) were used to test for parentage analysis (data not shown). Partially and fully expanded leaves at 2–6 internodes from apex were collected and immediately frozen in liquid nitrogen and stored at −80°C until processing. Seven cDNA libraries (one from each sampling) were prepared using pooled mRNA. Total RNA of each sample was extracted separately from 100 mg of leaves using Qiagen RNeasy Plant Mini Kit (Qiagen, Valencia, CA) following manufacturer's instructions with minor modifications: 10% v/v of N-lauroyl sarcosine 20% w/v was added to RLC buffer for each sample followed by incubation at 70°C for 10 min with vigorous shaking before proceeding with the standard protocol. The RNA samples were treated with 2 units of DNase I (Ambion, Life Technologies, Gaithersburg, MD) for 30 min at 37°C to remove contaminating genomic DNA.

The quality of each RNA sample was checked by means of agarose gel electrophoresis and quantified with Qubit fluorometer (Life Technologies). RNA integrity was confirmed using the Agilent 2100 Bioanalyzer (Agilent Technologies, Santa Clara, CA, USA), with a minimum RNA integrated number value of 7.5. Isolated RNAs from different samples were dissolved in RNase-free water and stored in −80°C freezer until subsequent analysis.

Transcriptome sequencing and assembly

Work flow of the present study is reported in the flow chart in Figure S1. The RNA samples were pooled equally to construct the cDNA libraries and processed as outlined in Illumina's "TruSeq RNA-seq Sample Prep kit" (Illumina, Inc., CA, USA).

The sample was loaded on Illumina flow cell and sequenced at ultra-high throughput on Illumina HiSeq2000 (Illumina Inc.). After sequencing of the cDNA library, base calling using Illumina pipeline software was used to transform the raw image data generated into sequence information. The CLC Genomics Workbench version 6.5.1 (CLC-Bio, Aarhus, Denmark) was selected for de novo transcriptome assembly in the present study because the CLC software has a faster computing pace with comparable or better assembly results than other bioinformatics programs [29]. The Illumina reads were trimmed at the ends by quality scores on the basis of the presence of ambiguous nucleotides (typically N) (maximum value set at 2) using a modified version of the Mott algorithm (the quality limit was set to 0.05), as implemented on CLC Genomics Workbench. Then, high-quality reads with overlaps were assembled to generate contigs using default parameters, obtaining 96006 contigs. RNA sequencing was performed at IGA Technology Services Srl Service Provider (Udine, Italy).

The raw reads produced in this study have been deposited at the Sequence Read Archive (SRA) of the National Centre of Biotechnology Information under the accession number SRP043444.

Functional Annotation and classification

All the transcripts were compared with the sequences of various databases to extract the maximum possible information based on sequence and functional similarity. For assignments of predicted gene descriptions, the BLASTX algorithm was used to search for homologous sequences (e-value cut off ≤1.0e-10) against the Viridiplantae, the UniProt (Swiss-Prot and TrEMBL) and NCBI RefSeq (collection of comprehensive, integrated, non-redundant, well-annotated set of proteins) protein databases. Based on the BLAST hits identified, GO (Gene Ontology, the Gene Ontology Consortium, 2000; www.geneontology.org) annotation (biological process, molecular functions and cellular components terms) was performed using BLAST2GO [30]: in particular, GO terms associated with each BLAST hit were retrieved (mapping step) and GO annotation assignment (annotation step) to the query sequences was carried out using the following annotation score parameters; e-value hit filter (default = 1.0e-6), annotation cut-off (default = 55), GO-weight (default = 5), hsp-hit coverage cut off (default = 0). Within the same routine an enzyme classification number (EC number) was assigned using a combination of similarity searches and statistical analysis terms.

In addition, conserved domains/motifs were further identified using Inter-ProScan, an on-line sequence search plug-in within the BLAST2GO program that combines different protein signature recognition methods, with the InterPro database (version 30.0,) and the resulting GO terms were merged with the GO term results from the annotation step of Blast2GO.

The Kyoto Encyclopedia of Genes and Genomes (KEGG) database is used extensively to reveal molecular interaction network and metabolic pathways [31]. KEGG pathways annotation was performed by mapping the sequences obtained from

Table 1. Summary of RNA-Seq and *de novo* sequence assembly for *Q. pubescens*.

Total raw reads	310,521,410
Total clean reads	254,265,700
Number of contigs	96,006
Mean lenght of contigs (bp)	618
N75	401
N50	910
N25	1,889

N75 length is defined as the length N for which 75% of all bases in the sequences are in a sequence of length L <N.
N50 length is defined as the length N for which 50% of all bases in the sequences are in a sequence of length L <N.
N25 length is defined as the length N for which 25% of all bases in the sequences are in a sequence of length L <N.

BLAST2GO to the contents of the KEGG metabolic pathway database.

Domain-based comparisons with KOG (EuKaryotic Orthologous Groups, a eukaryote-specific version of the Clusters of Orthologous Groups (COG) tool for identifying ortholog and paralog proteins) and Pfam (version 27.0) databases were performed using RPS-BLAST (Reverse PSI-BLAST) tool from locally installed NCBI BLAST+ v2.2.18 software.

Identification of putative candidate genes involved in drought avoidance

To uncover the potential candidate genes related to drought stress in *Q. pubescens*, 35 genes involved in epidermal development such as stomata, cuticle waxes, trichomes and root hairs [32] in *Arabidopsis* were selected to screen the potential orthologs from the contig dataset by Local BLASTN with E-value cutoff of 1e-5 (ftp://ftp.ncbi.nlm.nih.gov/blast/executables/LATEST-BLAST/).

RT-PCR validation of transcripts

Total RNA from *Q. pubescens* leaves was reverse-transcribed by using SuperScript III Reverse Transcriptase (Invitrogen) and oligo(dT)18. Twenty-one annotated transcripts were selected for RT-PCR validation. Forward (Fwd) and reverse (Rev) primers were designed using Primer3. The fragments were cloned in pGEM-T easy vector (Promega, Madison, WI) and transformed into JM109 cells. All recombinant plasmids were sequenced with the M13 universal primers using the Big Dye Terminator v.3.1 Cycle Sequencing Kit (Applied Biosystems, Foster City, CA) and run on an ABI 3730 DNA Analyzer (Applied Biosystems, Foster

City, CA) automatic sequencer. The plasmids with inserts longer than 1000 bp were treated with GPS-1 Genome Priming System (NEB, Beverly, MA) to generate and sequence random subclones.

SSR and SNP identification and validation

Mining of the simple sequence repeats (SSRs) present in the contigs of *Q. pubescens* was performed using MIcroSAtellite identification tool (MISA, http://pgrc.ipk-gatersleben.de/misa/), considering di-, tri-, tetra-, penta- and hexa-nucleotide motifs with a minimum of 5 contiguous repeat units [33]. The PRIMER3 software [34] was used to design forward and reverse primers flanking the SSR containing sequence [33]. For validation of SSR primers, total DNA was extracted from young leaves of eight *Q. pubescens* seedlings from two Italian populations (four for each one). For DNA extraction, the Dneasy Plant mini kit (Qiagen, Valencia, CA) was used following the manifacturer's instructions, and the amplification reactions were carried out as reported in Sebastiani et al. [35].

All the contigs from the transcriptome were used to mine SNPs and InDel markers. These markers were detected by the alignment of individual reads against contigs from the assembly using CLC Genomics Workbench ver. 6.5.1 that is based on the Neighborhood Quality Standard (NQS) algorithm of Altshuler et al. [36]. A minimum of two individual reads aligning with the references need to show the variant alleles in order to consider a sequence difference as a true polymorphism. From all variations, the high-confidence variations were screened based on the parameters that three or more non-duplicate reads confirm the same variations in both forward and reverse reads and single nucleotide-InDels should be found in at least 10% of total unique sequencing reads.

Table 2. Summary of annotations of assembled *Q. pubescens* contigs.

Database	Number of trascripts annotated	Percentage of trascripts annotated
Viridiplantae Nr	68,285	71.12%
RefSeq	77,623	80.85%
UniProt	73,148	76.19%
InterPro	48,622	50.27%
KOG	19,146	19.94%
Pfam	20,448	21.29%
GO	8,536	12.54%
KEGG	4,050	4.22%

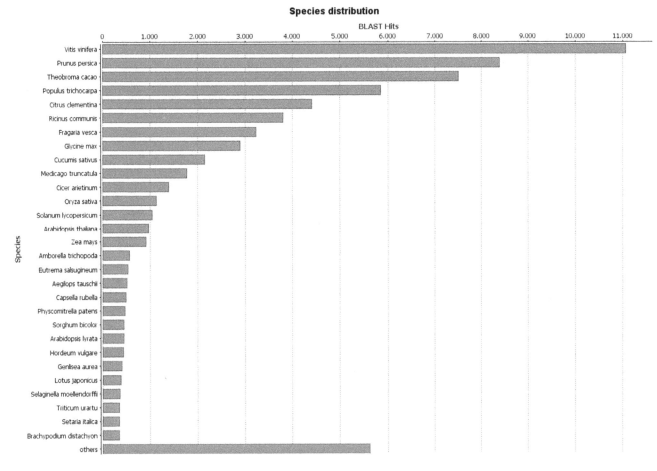

Figure 1. Hit species distribution of BLASTX matches of *Q. pubescens* **contigs.** Proportion of *Q. pubescens* contigs with similarity to sequences from Nr Viridiplantae protein database.

In order to validate the *in silico* SNPs from the transcripts assembly, 9 fragments carrying ten putative SNPs were amplified in the four genotypes used for the transcriptome assembly. Newly designed primer pairs and fragment sizes are listed in Figure S2. The amplified fragments were cloned into pGEM-T easy vector and transformed into JM109 cells. From two to eight randomly chosen clones for each genotype were sequenced in the forward direction with the M13 universal primer using the Big Dye Terminator v.3.1 Cycle Sequencing Kit (Applied Biosystems, Foster City, CA) and run on an ABI 3730 DNA Analyzer (Applied Biosystems) automatic sequencer.

Results and Discussion

Transcriptome Sequencing output and de novo Assembly

High-throughput sequencing technology has been extensively used to explore the transcriptome profile of non-model plant species. Our study depicts, for the first time, the fully expressed genome information of the downy-oak leaf. We performed RNA-Seq of leaf bulk sample of four different individuals to unveil *Q. pubescens* leaf transcriptome. The Illumina sequencing procedure generated 310,521,410 raw nucleotide paired reads 100 bp long. Removal of adapter sequences, ambiguous and low-quality reads, resulted in 254,265,700 clean reads of average read length

98.2 bp, corresponding to a complete dataset of about 25 Gb of sequence data (Table 1).

De-novo assembly of high quality reads was performed through CLC Genomics Workbench, and produced 96,006 contigs, thus creating a foundational reference transcriptome for *Q. pubescens* leaf expressed genome. N50 and N75 (parameters widely used for assessing the sequence quality) were 910 bp and 401 bp, respectively. Both indexes are higher than those previously reported for a wide range of plant transcriptome assemblies [25,37–39]. The mean length of these assembled contigs is 618 bp and the sequence length ranges from 129 bp to more than 10,000 bp. These values are comparable to those found in other non-model plants, which indeed range from 200 bp to 750 bp [24,32,40]. Our results are of particular interest, as transcriptome analysis was performed just on leaf tissue, and confirm the suitability of mRNA-Seq for extensive and accurate assembly of non-model plant transcriptomes.

Transcript Annotation

Functional annotation of novel plant transcriptome is great challenge for non-model plants for which references genome/gene sequences in databases are scarce. Here, annotation of the *Q. pubescens* transcriptome sequences was based on two levels of sequence similarity, namely sequence-based and domain-based alignments. Sequence-based alignments were performed against

The 30 most frequently occurring InterPro domains/families in *Q. pubescens* transcripts

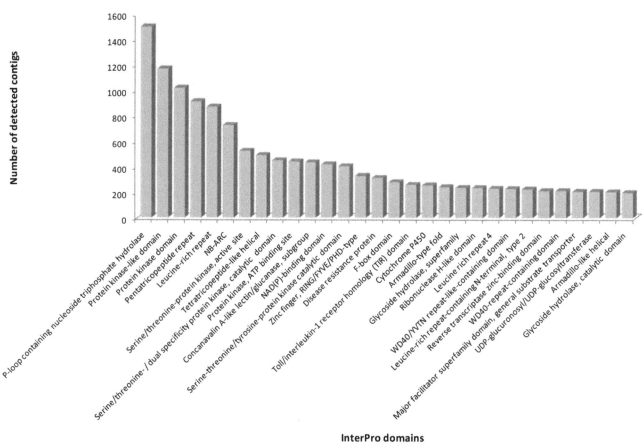

Figure 2. Histogram of the 30 most abundant InterPro domains revealed by the InterProScan annotation of the high quality *Quercus pubescens* transcript set.

four public databases, including the NCBI non-redundant protein (Nr) database, RefSeq protein (NP) at NCBI, UniProt (Swiss-Prot and TrEMBL), and the Kyoto Encyclopedia of Genes and Genomes (KEGG) using BLASTX algorithm with a significant E-value threshold of $1e^{-5}$. Domain/family searches contained Hidden Markov Model (HMM) domain/family searches in both the InterPro and Pfam databases and BLASTX alignments against the EuKaryotic Orthologous Groups (KOG) database at NCBI [25]. The E-value threshold was also set at $\leq 1e^{-5}$. Annotations statistics of BLASTX hits and domain hits are summarized in Table 2.

All assembled sequences were first aligned to the 2,935,608 protein sequences from a custom-made NCBI non-redundant database (Nr) filtered to give only Viridiplantae proteic sequences, which returned 68,285 significant BLAST hits (71.1%, see Table 2 and Table S1). The mapping rates of the *Quercus* contigs against the NP RefSeq and UniProt databases were 80.8% and 76.2%, respectively (Table 2 and significant hits in Table S1). Importantly, the high mapping rates of the contigs to the proteic databases suggest that most of the contigs can be translated into proteins. BLASTX hits and top hits in terms of the total hit numbers to all transcripts were mostly observed with *Vitis vinifera* (11,074 hits), *Prunus persica* (8,382 hits), *Theobroma cacao* (7,512 hits), *Populus trichocarpa* (5,853 hits) and *Citrus clementine* (4,416 hits) (Figure 1). Although *V. vinifera* shows highest correlation with *Q. pubescens*, only 10% of annotated transcripts in *Q. pubescens*

finds homology with protein sequences in *V. vinifera* (Figure 1). Indeed *Quercus* and *Vitis* belong to different orders, i.e. Fagales (Fagaceae,) and Vitales (Vitaceae), respectively.

Conserved domain annotation

To further exploit the potential function of the transcriptome sequences conserved domains in *Q. pubescens* were identified against the InterPro, Pfam and KOG databases. The aim of the annotation against this database is to identify similarity at domain level, where proteins have little similarity at sequence level but may share conserved structural domains. Searches against the InterPro database revealed 48266 top hits categorized into 5550 domain/families (Table 2). InterPro domains/families were therefore sorted according to the number of *Q. pubescens* contigs contained in each InterPro domain. The 30 most abundant InterPro domains/families have been reported in Figure 2. Most represented domain is IPR027417 (P-loop containing nucleoside triphosphate hydrolase) with 1505 annotated contigs, followed by IPR011009 (Protein kinase-like domain), IPR000719 (Protein kinase domain) and IPR002885 (Pentatricopeptide repeat). Among these protein domains/families, "Protein kinase" and its subcategories (such as Serine/threonine-protein kinase and Tyrosine-protein kinase), which are known to regulate the majority of cellular pathways, were highly represented indicating active signal transduction. Noteworthy, top ranked families are also

Table 3. KOG functional classification of all *Q. pubescens* transcripts.

KOG Classification	Sequences (n)	Percentage
Signal transduction mechanisms	3356	17.0
Multiple classes	2259	11.4
General function prediction only	1928	9.8
Posttranslational modification, protein turnover, chaperones	1776	9.0
Function unknown	1228	6.2
Translation, ribosomal structure and biogenesis	1065	5.4
Transcription	821	4.2
Carbohydrate transport and metabolism	753	3.8
Cytoskeleton	750	3.8
Intracellular trafficking, secretion, and vescicular transport	747	3.8
RNA processing and modification	723	3.7
Amino acid transport and metabolism	635	3.2
Secondary metabolites biosynthesis, transport and catabolism	604	3.1
Energy production and conversion	603	3.1
Lipid transport and metabolism	540	2.7
Inorganic ion transport and metabolism	445	2.3
Replication, recombination and repair	402	2.0
Coenzyme transport and metabolism	196	1.0
Cell cycle control, cell division, chromosome partitioning	192	1.0
Cell wall/membrane/envelope biogenesis	179	0.9
Defense mechanisms	175	0.9
Nucleotide transport and metabolism	167	0.8
Chromatin structure and dynamics	147	0.7
Extracellular structures	38	0.2
Nuclear structure	10	0.1

WD40-repeat domain and Cytochrome P450s which play key roles in signal transduction mechanisms, in particular regulating both trichome initiation and phenylpropanoid metabolism [41–43]. These findings conform to *Q. pubescens* being well equipped to cope with severe drought stress typical of Mediterranean climate. Pubescence has long been reported to increase reflectance in hairy leaves as compared with glabrous ones [44], and polyphenols, particularly tannins, linearly correlate with sclerophylly in Fagaceae [45]. These morphological and biochemical features, aimed at reducing water loss, decreasing leaf temperature and screening out solar irradiance are of crucial significance in the adaptive mechanisms of plants to the combined effect of water shortage and high solar irradiance [46].

Pfam analysis allowed to annotate 20,448 contigs (Table 2) which contained 3,337 kinds of Pfam domains, among which Protein kinases, WD domain and Cytochrome P450 were highly represented (2,198, 467 and 252 times, respectively). The top 10 most frequently detected domains were all in the above mentioned 30-most abundant InterPro domain list (Table S1).

The eukaryotic clusters (KOGs) present in the Cluster of Orthologous Groups (COG) database are made up of protein sequences from 7 eukaryotic genomes: three animals (the nematode *Caenorhabditis elegans*, the fruit fly *Drosophila melanogaster* and *Homo sapiens*), one plant, *Arabidopsis thaliana*, two fungi (*Saccharomyces cerevisiae* and *Schizosaccharomyces pombe*), and the intracellular microsporidian parasite *Encephalitozoon cuniculi*. Our assembled transcripts were searched against

KOG database for in-depth analysis of phylogenetically widespread domain families, in order to predict and classify their possible functions. Overall, 19.94% of contigs (19,146) were assigned into 25 KOG categories, with 3,505 KOG functional terms (Table 2 and Table 3). The three largest categories include 1) "Signal transduction mechanisms" (18.33%); 2) "General functions" (10.73%); and 3) "Post translational modification, protein turnover, chaperones" (9.51%) (Table 3). In the metabolism category, "Carbohydrate transport and metabolism" (5.17%) and "Secondary metabolites biosynthesis, transport and catabolism" (3.92%) were also highly represented. "Function unknown" represented 5.50%, which is quite expected since *Q. pubescens* is phylogenetically distant species compared to ones present in the eukaryotic KOG database.

GO classification

Gene Ontology (GO) terms and enzyme commission numbers (EC) for *Q. pubescens* transcripts were retrieved using Blast2GO [30]. Gene Ontology is an international classification system that provides a standardized vocabulary useful in describing functions of uncharacterized genes. Our results show that downy oak differs substantially from model plants. Indeed, just 19,178 (28.1%) retrieved the associated GO terms, and only 8,563 (12.5%) were annotated to a total of 32,844 GO term annotations, of the 68,285 most significant BLASTX hits against the NR plant species database (Table 2). All the extracted GO terms were summarized into the three main GO categories: 15,701 terms (47.8%) belong

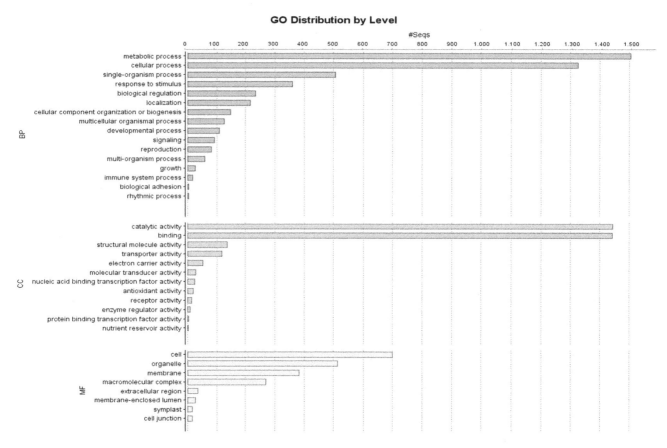

Figure 3. Histogram of GO classifications of assembled *Quercus pubescens* transcripts. Results are summarized for three main GO categories: biological process, cellular component and molecular function.

to the Biological Process class, 5,393 terms (16.4%) fit with the Molecular Function class and 11,750 terms (35.8%) belong to the Cellular Component class. Major sub-categories reported in Figure 3 come from GO level 2 classification. Two sub-categories "cell" (GO: 0005623) and "organelle" (GO: 0043226) occur in molecular function cluster; sub-categories "binding" (GO: 0005488) and "catalytic activity" (GO: 0003824) are clustered in cellular component; and five sub-categories "metabolic process" (GO: 0008152), "cellular process" (GO: 0009987), "single-organism process" (GO:0044699), "response to stimulus" (GO: 0050896) and "biological regulation" (GO: 0065007) were in the cluster of biological process. However, these results assigned only a small percentage of downy oak transcripts to GO terms, possibly due to large number of uninformative gene descriptions of protein hits. Of the 8,536 sequences annotated with GO terms, 2,805 were assigned to 114 EC numbers. In detail, transferase activity (40.6%), hydrolase activity (265%) and oxidoreductase activity (19.6%) were the most represented enzymes (Figure 4). The large number of annotated enzymes within these three groups suggest the presence of genes associated to pathways of secondary metabolite biosynthesis [47,48], as we detail below for KEGG pathway mapping.

KEGG pathway mapping

In order to identify the biological pathways active in *Q. pubescens*, the assembled contigs were annotated with corresponding EC numbers against the Kyoto Encyclopedia of Genes and Genomes (KEGG) Pathways database [31]. By mapping EC numbers to the reference canonical pathways, a total of 4,050

contigs (4,22%) were assigned to 138 KEGG biochemical pathways (Table 2). Figure 5 shows the 30 KEGG metabolic pathways mostly represented by unique sequences of *Q. pubescens*. These include "Purine metabolism" (548 members), a metabolic pathway of central significance in plant growth and development [49]. For instance, purine is involved in building blocks for nucleic acid synthesis and a well-known precursor for the synthesis of primary products and secondary products [50,51]. This is consistent with enzymes specifically involved in phenylpropanoid metabolism (total 485 seqs, 41 enzymes) detected in our analysis. These include both phenylalanine metabolism, the entry point in phenylpropanoid biosynthetic pathway, as well as downstream enzymes involved in general and branch pathways of phenylpropanoid biosynthesis, such as flavonoid biosynthesis. Additionally, others highly represented pathways are "Starch and sucrose metabolism" (427 members) "T cell receptor signalling pathway" (302 members) and "Glycolysis/Gluconeogenesis" (221 members).

Overall, 83,065 unique sequence-based or domain-based annotations using the seven selected database were assigned to *Q. pubescens* transcripts. These annotations provide a useful resource for investigating specific functions and pathways in downy oak.

Functional Genes Related to Drought Avoidance

To screen functional genes specifically related to drought stress, candidate genes from *Arabidopsis* [32,42] were local BLASTed against 96,006 transcripts in *Q. pubescens*. A total of 318 contigs homologous to 35 *Arabidopsis* candidate genes potentially involved in drought adaptation were identified in our transcrip-

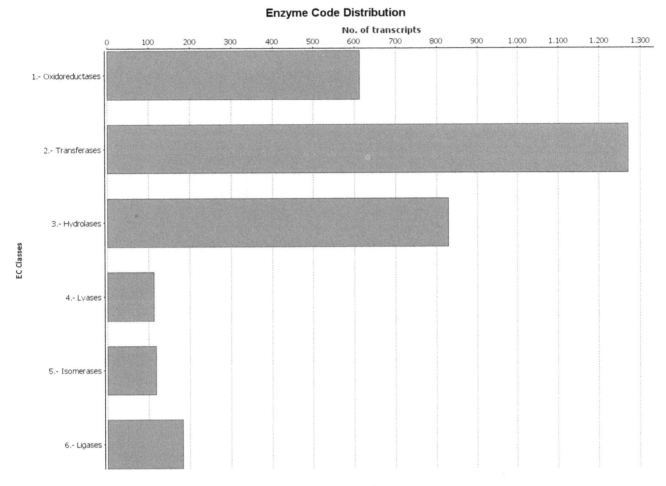

Figure 4. Catalytic activity distribution in annotated *Q.pubescens* transcripts.

tome dataset. Overall, 21 putative transcripts regulating the biogenesis and development of trichomes and root hairs have been identified as involved in drought avoidance (E-value, $1e^{-5}$), and succesfully validated by RT-PCR (Table 4). All amplified transcripts gave amplicons of expected sizes that were cloned and sequenced (Table S2). Programming of epidermal cell differentiation to form trichomes is a low-energy strategy to effectively cope with drought stress in species inhabiting dry and warm areas world-wide [52]. Secretory and non-secretory trichomes serve multiple functions in plants challenged against multiple stresses, as usually observed in Mediterranean areas, particularly during the summer season. As already mentioned, surface appendices are crucial to limit water loss [42,46] while screening out highly energetic solar wavelengths [53]. Molecular mechanisms of epidermal cell differentiation organs have been extensively studied in *Arabidopsis* [54]. A network of transcription factors, including TRANSPARENT TESTA GLABRA1 (TTG1), GLABRA3 (GL3), ENHANCER OF GLABRA3 (EGL3), which is a paralog of GL3, and GLABRA2 (GL2). GLABRA1 (GL1), which encodes an R2R3 MYB transcription factor, promotes trichome initiation, TTG1 encodes a WD40 protein, GL3/EGL3 encode basic helix-loop-helix (bHLH)-type transcription factors, and GL2 encodes a homeodomain/leucine zipper transcription factor [42,55]. MYB transcription factors have long reported to regulate differentiation in *Arabidopsis*, such as epidermal cell fate and seed coat development [56]. However, MYBs have been primarily (i.e. in

early land plants) involved in the regulation of flavonoid biosynthetic pathway, and following gene duplication and functional diversification (i.e., neo-functionalization) they acquired the new function of specifying multiple cell fates, such as the generation of trichomes formation [56,57]. As a consequence, our study identified a set of genes potentially involved in the biogenesis and development of leaf hairs and phenylpropanoid biosynthesis, thus facilitating disentangle mechanisms of drought resistance in pubescent oak at molecular level.

Simple sequence repeats (SSRs) and SNP detection

Simple Sequence Repeat (SSR) markers, also known as microsatellites, are short repeat DNA sequences of 2–6 base pairs, which are important for research involving population genetic structuring, demography, relatedness, and the genetic basis of adaptive traits [58,59]. In this study, a total of 14,202 putative SSRs were identified in 96,006 assembled transcripts, of which, 3,366 were compound SSRs. The SSRs included 7,011 (49.3%) dinucleotide motifs, 3,478 (24.5%) trinucleotide motifs, 212 (1.5%) tetranucleotide motifs, 65 (0.5%) pentanucleotide motifs and 72 (0.5%) hexanucleotide motifs (Figure 6). The most abundant repeat type was (AG/CT) for dinucleotide SSR and (GAA/TTC) for trinucleotide SSR. The observed frequency of SSR (14.8%) was slightly lower than that to that observed in related *Quercus* spp., (18.6% and 23.7% in [60] and [28], respectively). Surprisingly, di-nucleotide repeats were the most common SSRs

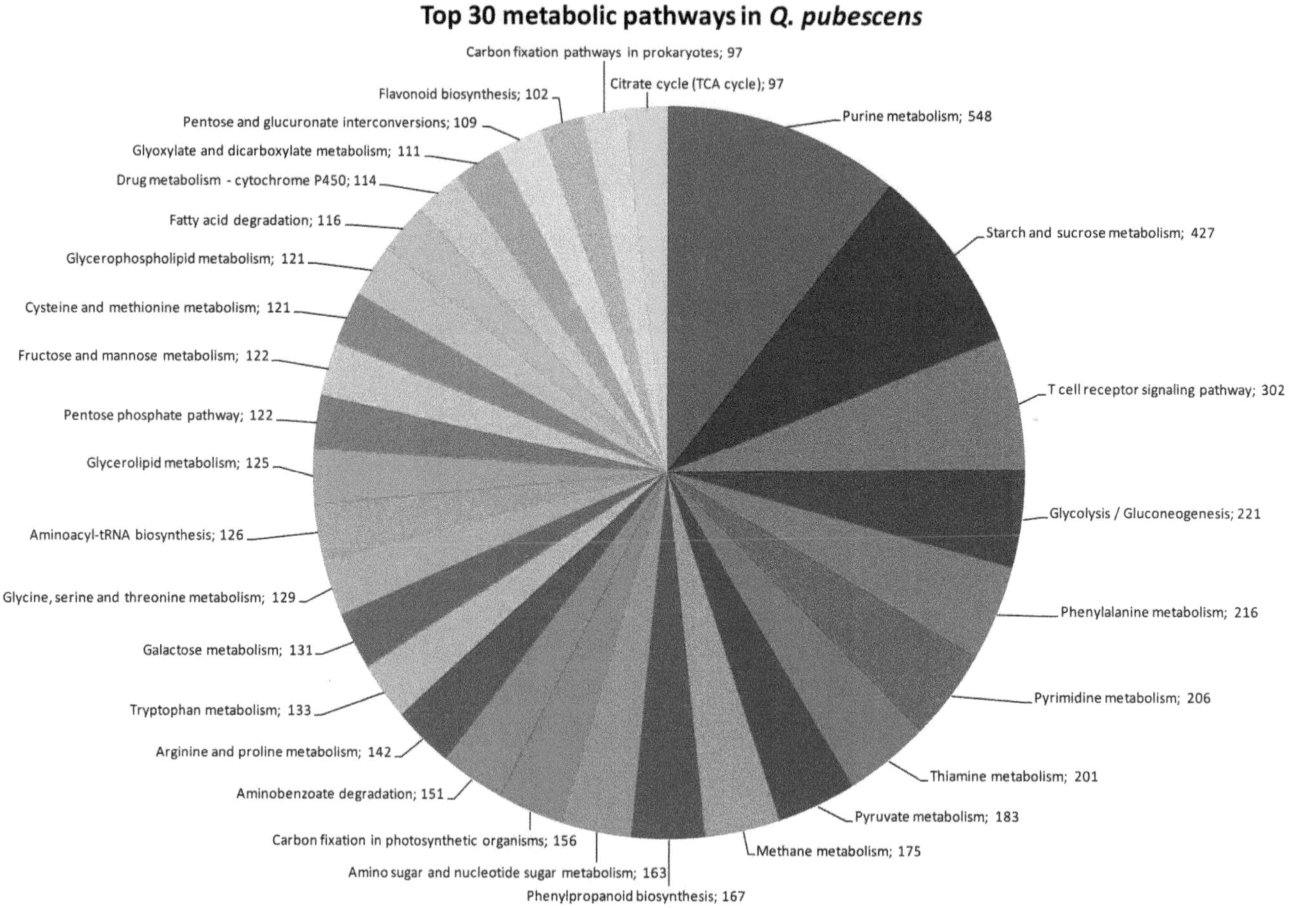

Top 30 metabolic pathways in *Q. pubescens*

Figure 5. Top 30 metabolic pathways in *Q. pubescens*. This table shows the KEGG metabolic pathways of plants that were well represented by unique sequences of *Quercus pubescens*. The number of sequences and enzymes involved are described

in our transcriptome (49.3%), with tri- and tetra-nucleotide repeats being present at much smaller frequencies, in contrast to the most frequent motif (tri-SSRs) found in *Q. robur* and *Q. petraea* [28,60] and in agreement with *P. contorta* [24]. Based on the 14,202 SSRs, 10,864 primer pairs were successfully designed using Primer3: information on the contig identification (ID), marker ID, repeat motive, repeat length, primer sequences, positions of forward and reverse primers, and expected fragment length are included in Table S3. Twenty microsatellites were randomly selected (15 dinucleotide and 5 trinucleotide SSRs) for PCR amplification in two individuals: 17 (85%) were effectively amplified producing fragments of the expected size, validating the quality of the assembly and the utility of the SSRs herein identified (validated primer pairs are highlighted in Table S3). To confirm marker usability and characterize the selected seventeen SSR markers for variation a total of 8 individuals from two Italian populations (four from Spello and four from Volterra) were analysed. All selected SSRs displayed consistent patterns, eleven loci were polymorphic and six monomorphic (the absence of polymorphism might be due to the small sample size). Primer sequences, repeat motifs and detected alleles are shown in Table S4. Similar research carried out using Illumina sequencing technology in sesame showed that about 90% primer pairs successfully amplified DNA fragments [39]. High-throughput transcriptome sequencing showed to be superior resources for the development of such markers not only because of the

enormous amount of sequence data in which markers can be identified, but also because discovered markers are gene-based. Such markers are advantageous because they facilitate the detection of functional variation and the signature of selection in genomic scans or association genetic studies [61,62]. Transcript-based SSRs are advantageous compared to SSRs in non-transcribed regions owing to their higher amplification rates and cross-species transferability [63]. Currently, although many SSR markers were identified in the Fagaceae family, only a few SSR markers were reported in *Q. pubescens* [64]. The predicted SSRs from the assembled transcriptome of *Q. pubescens*, will likely be of value for genetic analyses of *Q. pubescens* and other related non-model plants.

Single Nucleotide Polymorphisms (SNPs) were identified through the analysis of the multiple alignments produced during the assembly process by using CLC Genomics Workbench. The analysis of 96,006 contigs resulted in the in silico discovery of 19469 variants, including 18,425 (94.6%) SNPs, 858 In-Del, Insertion-Deletions (4.4%) and MNV, Multiple nucleotide variants, 182 (0.9%) (Table S5). The variants were distributed in 8652 contigs (9.0%) corresponding to 15,752,655 bp, 26.6% of the total *Q. pubescens* transcriptome. Ten SNPs, 8 from different contigs and 2 from the same contig (Figure S2) were confirmed by cloning and sequencing fragments ranging from 151 bp to 557 bp amplified in the four genotypes used for the transcriptome assembly. Newly designed primer pairs and fragment sizes are

Table 4. *Q. pubescens* contigs related to genes involved in drought avoidance in *Arabidopsis Thaliana*.

Gene name	Sequence similarity	Contig ID	Forward and Reverse Primers 5′-3′	Amplicon length (bp)
Auxin response factor 1 (ARF1)	Arabidopsis thaliana (AT1G59750)	Quercus_contig_413	F: TGGATAGAAGTCTCGCCCAC	706
			R: GCACATTTTCCGAGGGCAA	
Mitogen-activated protein kinase 6 (MPK6)	Arabidopsis thaliana (AT2G43790)	Quercus_contig_575	F: ACAATAGGTTCACTGGGATGGA	907
			R: TACAGTTGGTCCAAGGCCAA	
Rho GDP-dissociation inhibitor 1 (SCN1)	Arabidopsis thaliana (AT3G07880)	Quercus_contig_781	F: TGATGTCTTTGGCTGTTGGAG	749
			R: CTCTGCTCAAGTTGAAGCCC	
Glabra 2 (GL2)	Arabidopsis thaliana (AT1G79840)	Quercus_contig_1106	F: GATCAACCATCCTCACACTGC	2362
			R: TCTCTCTCTTTCTACGCACCT	
Phospholipase D deltaPLD delta	Arabidopsis thaliana (AT4G35790)	Quercus_contig_1195	F: TCTTGCACAGAGGCAGATGA	949
			R: ACACGAATGGAGTAATGGCA	
Can Of Wms1 (COW1)	Arabidopsis thaliana (AT4G34580)	Quercus_contig_1527	F: GGCAAAACATCTCACCAGCA	1888
			R: GGCCTTGCTTTGAAGGATCC	
GL2-Expression Modulator (GEM)	Arabidopsis thaliana (AT2G22475)	Quercus_contig_4979	F: TTCGTGGTTGTCAACAGAGA	474
			R: ACGGTGGATTCGGTGAAAGA	
Phospholipase D alpha 2 (PLD alpha2)	Arabidopsis thaliana (AT1G52570)	Quercus_contig_7695	F: TGTAGTCAGATTTGGCACCCA	2360
			R: CGTCTATGAGGTCGACAAGC	
Cyclin D 3;2 (CYCD3;2)	Arabidopsis thaliana (AT5G67260)	Quercus_contig_11597	F: GGGGACTTGGACTTGAGTGT	880
			R: GCACTTCCAAAACCACACCA	
Transparent Testa Glabra 1 (TTG1)	Arabidopsis thaliana (AT5G24520)	Quercus_contig_11685	F: GGACTTCGAGCATTGACACC	417
			R: GAGAATCATCCCCAGCCGTA	
Phospholipase D beta2 (PLD beta2)	Arabidopsis thaliana (AT4G00240)	Quercus_contig_15358	F: GCCACACGAGCTCATTCAAT	2523
			R: CCTGAATGGCAAGAAATGAACC	
Cyclin D 3;3 (CYCD3;3)	Arabidopsis thaliana (AT3G50070)	Quercus_contig_21908	F: GCACTTCAACAGACAGACGA	1085
			R: TCTGCAAGAAGAGGAAACCCA	
Cyclin D 3;1 (CYCD3;1)	Arabidopsis thaliana (AT4G34160)	Quercus_contig_22955	F: AGGTTCTGTTTAGCTTCCTCCT	1038
			R: TTGACTACGCGGTTTCAAGC	
Phospholipase D alpha1 (PLD alpha 1)	Arabidopsis thaliana (AT3G15730)	Quercus_contig_25616	F: GTCAGGCAAAGCAGAACCTC	1157
			R: TTGCAAGTGGTGGCTACAAG	
Enhancer of Glabra 3 (EGL3)	Arabidopsis thaliana (AT1G63650)	Quercus_contig_32077	F: CTGTGAGAAGCATTCAGTGGA	207
			R: CTTCACCAGCTGAGAGGGAC	
Werewolf (WER)	Arabidopsis thaliana (AT5G14750)	Quercus_contig_35143	F: GAAAAGGGCCTTGGACAGTG	332
			R: GGTTTTCCCTTTCTTGATCCCA	
Root Hair Defective 2 (RHD2)	Arabidopsis thaliana (AT5G51060)	Quercus_contig_39550	F: GTTGCGGTTCACAGTGTTCA	2451
			R: TCCGACTCGTGTTTCTGGAT	
Triptychon (TRY)	Arabidopsis thaliana (AT5G53200)	Quercus_contig_41116	F: GGAAACAAGCCAAGACCAGG	211
			R: GCAAATACCTCACCATGTCTCA	
Phospholipase D epsilon (PLD epsilon)	Arabidopsis thaliana (AT1G55180)	Quercus_contig_47871	F: CCCTAACACCTTCACTTGCC	186
			R: ATGAGCCCCACAGATGTTGG	
Glabra 1 (GL1)	Arabidopsis thaliana (AT3G27920)	Quercus_contig_56291	F: GATGGAGGAAGGGAACACGT	351
			R: TTTTGCTTCTTGAGGCCCAG	
Cyclin A2;3 (CYCA2;3)	Arabidopsis thaliana (AT1G15570)	Quercus_contig_72031	F: CAGGAGATTCATTCAAGCAGCA	248
			R: CAAGGACGGTGGTTTTCAGT	

listed in Figure S2. The polymorphisms were confirmed by detecting at least one variant for each SNP in the four genotypes (one chromatogram for each genotype is reported in Figure S2, labelled as sample 1 to sample 4). The frequency of the variants resulted equal to 1 variant per 6,854 nucleotides on average, lower than that observed in other forest tree species [24,48] that could be explained with the limited number of genotypes analyzed and the strict parentage relatedness that reduced the possibility of SNPs mining.

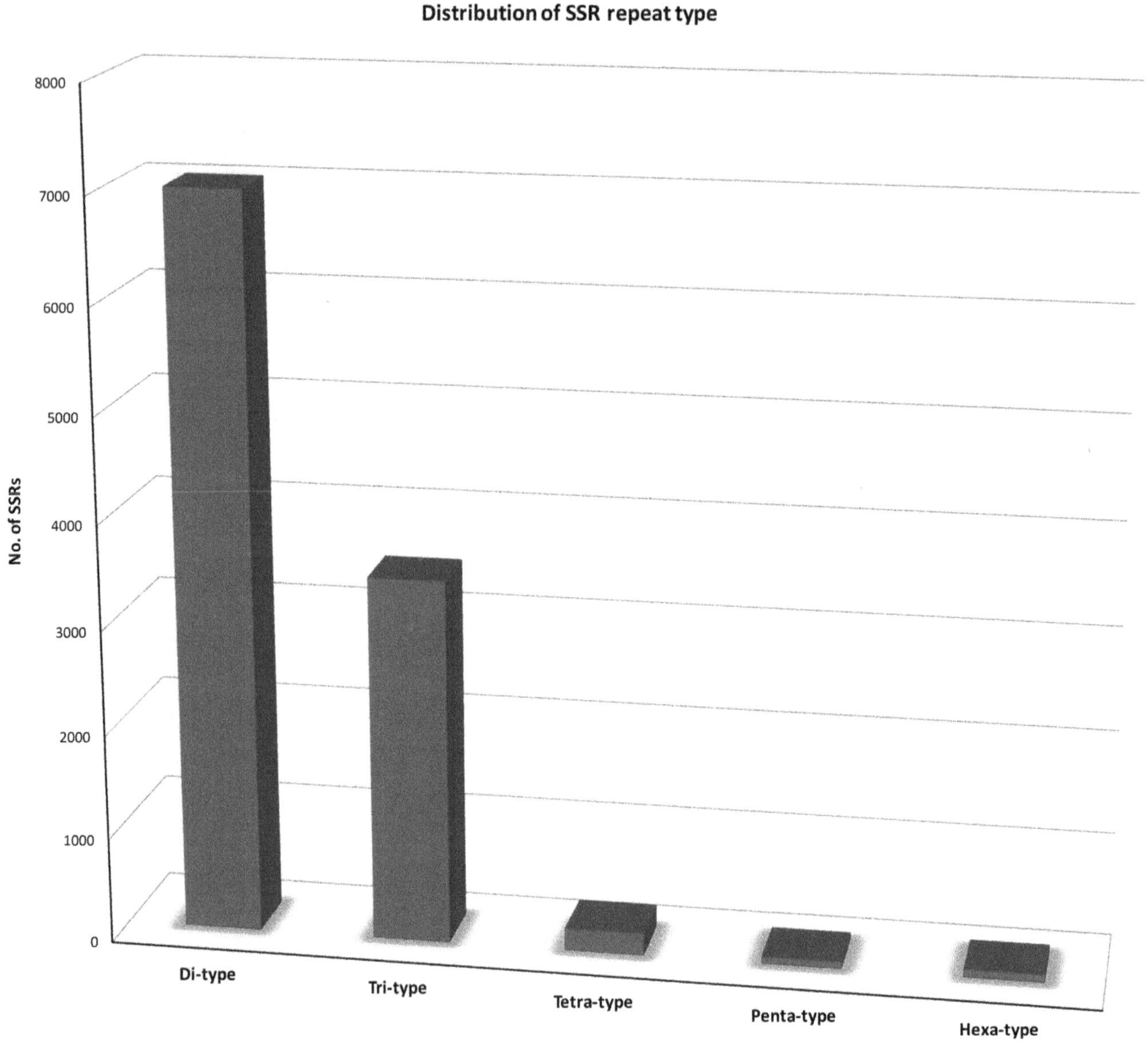

Distribution of SSR repeat type

Figure 6. SSRs distribution in the leaf transcriptome of *Q.pubescens*.

Conclusions

In the recent years, transcriptome sequencing became a most powerful and efficient approach to uncover genomic information in non-model organism [20]. The *de novo* assembly and annotation of the *Q. pubescens* transcriptome provided complete information concerning the expressed sequences of leaf tissue. Data of our study represent an important tool for discovering genes of interest and genetic markers, thus allowing investigation of the functional diversity in natural populations. Our study (i) generated 318 milion raw nucleotide paired-end reads, comprising 96,006 transcripts from *Q. pubescens*, (ii) identified putative function in 83,065 transcripts for the species and several genes related to numerous metabolic and biochemical pathways, (iii) discovered a large set of high quality marker motifs and variations (14,202 genomic SSRs with designed primers, and 18,425 higher confidence nuclear SNPs) which could be used for generation of polymorphism based analysis within species. Detection of func-

tional variations and the signature of selection in genome scans or association genetic studies are facilitated by these markers.

These tools will be crucial for future comparative genomics studies in other *Quercus* species, taking advantage of their remarkable ecophysiological differences. Our characterization of the leaf transcriptome in *Q. pubescens* has not only enriched the publicly available database of sequences for members of the *Quercus*, but will also facilitate genetic analysis of other non-model organisms. Furthermore, our data demostrate that Illumina paired-end sequencing can successfully be applied as a rapid and cost-effective method to non-model organisms, especially those with large genomes and without prior genome annotation.

Supporting Information

Figure S1   Flow diagram of whole transcriptome analysis for *Q. pubescens*. The steps and sets of sequences involved in Illumina sequencing, assembly of reads into contigs, annotation using protein databases, and genetic marker discovery and characterization.

Figure S2   Validation of ten predicted SNPs.

Table S1   BLAST hits from the NCBI Viridiplantae Nr database, NCBI NP RefSeQ database, UniProt database and KOG, Pfam and InterPro domain/families assigned to *Q. pubescens* contigs.

Table S2   Sequences of *Q. pubescens* genes related to drought avoidance.

Table S3   List of *in silico* SSR primer pairs derived from *Q. pubescens* transcriptome. Validated primer pairs are highlighted.

Table S4   Characteristics of the *Q. pubescens* microsatellites markers analyzed.

Table S5   List of single nucleotide variants derived from *Q. pubescens* transcriptome with sequence annotation (BLAST hit, GO and EC).

Acknowledgments

We appreciate the technical support for Illumina sequencing and initial data analysis from Institute of Applied Genomics at Udine, Italy.

Author Contributions

Conceived and designed the experiments: ST MT CB FF FS. Performed the experiments: ST CB FS AF. Analyzed the data: ST FS MT FF SF. Contributed reagents/materials/analysis tools: FF SF MT. Wrote the paper: ST MT FS.

References

1. Johnson PS, Shifley SR, Rogers R, editors (2002) The ecology and silviculture of oaks. Wallingford: Cabi.
2. Abrams MD (1990) Adaptations and responses to drought in Quercus species of North America. Tree Physiol 7: 227–238.
3. Struve D, Court F, Ferrini F, Bellasio C, Fini A (2010) Propagation of Quercus cerris, Q. petraea, and Q. pubescens Seedlings by Stem Cuttings. 45: 1729–1733.
4. Hu B, Simon J, Rennenberg H (2013) Drought and air warming affect the species-specific levels of stress-related foliar metabolites of three oak species on acidic and calcareous soil. Tree Physiol 33: 489–504.
5. Damesin C, Rambal S (1995) Field study of leaf photosynthetic performance by a Mediterranean deciduous oak tree (Quercus pubescens) during a severe summer drought. New Phytol: 159–167.
6. Diffenbaugh NS, Pal JS, Trapp RJ, Giorgi F (2005) Fine-scale processes regulate the response of extreme events to global climate change. Proc Natl Acad Sci U S A 102: 15774–15778.
7. Christensen JH, Christensen OB (2007) A summary of the PRUDENCE model projections of changes in European climate by the end of this century. Clim Change 81: 7–30.
8. Valladares F, Niinemets Ü (2008) Shade Tolerance, a Key Plant Feature of Complex Nature and Consequences. Annu Rev Ecol Evol Syst 39: 237–257.
9. Hanewinkel M, Cullmann D, Schelhaas M-J, Nabuurs G-J, Zimmermann NE (2012) Climate change may cause severe loss in the economic value of European forest land. Nat Clim Chang 3: 203–207.
10. Bréda N, Huc R, Granier A, Dreyer E (2006) Temperate forest trees and stands under severe drought: a review of ecophysiological responses, adaptation processes and long-term consequences. Ann For Sci 63: 625–644.
11. Ciais P, Reichstein M, Viovy N, Granier A, Ogée J, et al. (2005) Europe-wide reduction in primary productivity caused by the heat and drought in 2003. Nature 437: 529–533.
12. Ohlemuller R, Gritti ES, Sykes MT, Thomas CD (2006) Quantifying components of risk for European woody species under climate change. Glob Chang Biol 12: 1788–1799.
13. Petriţan AM, Lüpke B, Petriţan IC (2008) Influence of light availability on growth, leaf morphology and plant architecture of beech (Fagus sylvatica L.), maple (Acer pseudoplatanus L.) and ash (Fraxinus excelsior L.) saplings. Eur J For Res 128: 61–74.
14. Bussotti F, Ferrini F, Pollastrini M, Fini A (2013) The challenge of Mediterranean sclerophyllous vegetation under climate change: From acclimation to adaptation. Environ Exp Bot. 103: 80–98.
15. Kubiske M, Abrams M (1993) Stomatal and nonstomatal limitations of photosynthesis in 19 temperate tree species on contrasting sites during wet and dry years. Plant Cell Env 16: 1123–1129.
16. Dickson RE, Tomlinson PT (1996) Oak carbon metabolism in response to water stress. Ann For Sci 53: 181–196.
17. Grivet D, Sebastiani F, Alía R, Bataillon T, Torre S, et al. (2011) Molecular footprints of local adaptation in two mediterranean conifers. Mol Biol Evol 28: 101–116.
18. Giorgi F, Lionello P (2008) Climate change projections for the Mediterranean region. Glob Planet Change 63: 90–104.
19. Petit RJ, Hampe A, Cheddadi R (2005) Climate changes and tree phylogeography in the Mediterranean. Taxon 54: 877–885.
20. Wang Z, Gerstein M, Snyder M (2009) RNA-Seq: a revolutionary tool for transcriptomics. Nat Rev Genet 10: 57–63.
21. Mortazavi A, Williams BA, Mccue K, Schaeffer L, Wold B (2008) Mapping and quantifying mammalian transcriptomes by RNA-Seq. Nat Methods 5: 621–628.

22. Nagalakshmi U, Wang Z, Waern K, Shou C, Raha D, et al. (2008) The transcriptional landscape of the yeast genome defined by RNA sequencing. Science 320: 1344–1349.
23. Filichkin SA, Priest HD, Givan SA, Shen R, Bryant DW, et al. (2010) Genome-wide mapping of alternative splicing in Arabidopsis thaliana. 20: 45–58.
24. Parchman T, Geist K (2010) Transcriptome sequencing in an ecologically important tree species: assembly, annotation, and marker discovery. BMC Genomics 11: 180.
25. Shi C-Y, Yang H, Wei C-L, Yu O, Zhang Z-Z, et al. (2011) Deep sequencing of the Camellia sinensis transcriptome revealed candidate genes for major metabolic pathways of tea-specific compounds. BMC Genomics 12: 131. doi:10.1186/1471-2164-12-131.
26. Torales SL, Rivarola M, Pomponio MF, Fernández P, Acuña C V, et al. (2012) Transcriptome survey of Patagonian southern beech Nothofagus nervosa (= N. Alpina): assembly, annotation and molecular marker discovery. BMC Genomics 13: 291.
27. Wang Y, Pan Y, Liu Z, Zhu X, Zhai L, et al. (2013) De novo transcriptome sequencing of radish (Raphanus sativus L.) and analysis of major genes involved in glucosinolate metabolism. BMC Genomics 14: 836.
28. Ueno S, Le Provost G, Léger V, Klopp C, Noirot C, et al. (2010) Bioinformatic analysis of ESTs collected by Sanger and pyrosequencing methods for a keystone forest tree species: oak. BMC Genomics 11: 650.
29. Bräutigam A, Mullick T, Schliesky S, Weber APM (2011) Critical assessment of assembly strategies for non-model species mRNA-Seq data and application of next-generation sequencing to the comparison of C(3) and C(4) species. J Exp Bot 62: 3093–3102.
30. Conesa A, Götz S, García-Gómez JM, Terol J, Talón M, et al. (2005) Blast2GO: a universal tool for annotation, visualization and analysis in functional genomics research. Bioinformatics 21: 3674–3676.
31. Kanehisa M, Goto S, Kawashima S, Okuno Y, Hattori M (2004) The KEGG resource for deciphering the genome. Nucleic Acids Res 32: D277–80.
32. Shi Y, Yan X, Zhao P, Yin H, Zhao X, et al. (2013) Transcriptomic analysis of a tertiary relict plant, extreme xerophyte Reaumuria soongorica to identify genes related to drought adaptation. PLoS One 8: e63993.
33. Ashrafi H, Hill T, Stoffel K, Kozik A, Yao J, et al. (2012) De novo assembly of the pepper transcriptome (Capsicum annuum): a benchmark for in silico discovery of SNPs, SSRs and candidate genes. BMC Genomics 13: 571.
34. Rozen S, Skaletsky H (1999) Primer3 on the WWW for General Users and for Biologist Programmers. In: Misener S, Krawetz S, editors. Bioinformatics Methods and Protocols SE - 20. Methods in Molecular BiologyTM. Humana Press, Vol. 132. pp. 365–386.
35. Sebastiani F, Pinzauti F, Kujala ST, González-Martínez SC, Vendramin GG (2011) Novel polymorphic nuclear microsatellite markers for Pinus sylvestris L. Conserv Genet Resour 4: 231–234.
36. Altshuler D, Pollara VJ, Cowles CR, Van Etten WJ, Baldwin J, et al. (2000) An SNP map of the human genome generated by reduced representation shotgun sequencing. Nature 407: 513–516.
37. Wang Z, Fang B, Chen J, Zhang X, Luo Z, et al. (2010) De novo assembly and characterization of root transcriptome using Illumina paired-end sequencing and development of cSSR markers in sweet potato (Ipomoea batatas). BMC Genomics 11: 726.
38. Xia Z, Xu H, Zhai J, Li D, Luo H, et al. (2011) RNA-Seq analysis and de novo transcriptome assembly of Hevea brasiliensis. Plant Mol Biol 77: 299–308.
39. Wei W, Qi X, Wang L, Zhang Y, Hua W, et al. (2011) Characterization of the sesame (Sesamum indicum L.) global transcriptome using Illumina paired-end sequencing and development of EST-SSR markers. BMC Genomics 12: 451.

40. Torales SL, Rivarola M, Pomponio MF, Gonzalez S, Acuña C V, et al. (2013) De novo assembly and characterization of leaf transcriptome for the development of functional molecular markers of the extremophile multipurpose tree species Prosopis alba. BMC Genomics 14: 705.

41. Zhao L, Gao L, Wang H, Chen X, Wang Y, et al. (2013) The R2R3-MYB, bHLH, WD40, and related transcription factors in flavonoid biosynthesis. Funct Integr Genomics 13: 75–98.

42. Ishida T, Kurata T, Okada K, Wada T (2008) A genetic regulatory network in the development of trichomes and root hairs. Annu Rev Plant Biol 59: 365–386.

43. Hamberger B, Bak S (2013) Plant P450s as versatile drivers for evolution of species-specific chemical diversity. Philos Trans R Soc B19 368: 20120426.

44. Ehleringer JR (1984) Oecologia growth and reproduction in Encelia farinosa. Oecologia 63: 153–158.

45. Bussotti F, Gravano E, Grossoni P, Tani C (1998) Occurrence of tannins in leaves of beech trees (Fagus sylvatica) along an ecological gradient, detected by histochemical and ultrastructural analyses. New Phytol: 469–479.

46. Morales F, Abadía A, Abadía J, Montserrat G, Gil-Pelegrín E (2002) Trichomes and photosynthetic pigment composition changes: responses of Quercus ilex subsp. ballota (Desf.) Samp. and Quercus coccifera L. to Mediterranean stress conditions. Trees 16: 504–510.

47. Blanca J, Cañizares J, Roig C, Ziarsolo P, Nuez F, et al. (2011) Transcriptome characterization and high throughput SSRs and SNPs discovery in Cucurbita pepo (Cucurbitaceae). BMC Genomics 12: 104.

48. Torales SL, Rivarola M, Pomponio MF, Gonzalez S, Acuña C V, et al. (2013) De novo assembly and characterization of leaf transcriptome for the development of functional molecular markers of the extremophile multipurpose tree species Prosopis alba. BMC Genomics 14: 705.

49. Zrenner R, Stitt M, Sonnewald U, Boldt R (2006) Pyrimidine and Purine Biosynthesis and Degradation in Plants. Annu Rev Plant Biol 57: 805–836.

50. Stasolla C, Katahira R, Thorpe T, Ashihara H (2003) Purine and pyrimidine nucleotide metabolism in higher plants. J Plant Physiol 160: 1271–1295.

51. Boldt R, Zrenner R (2003) Purine and pyrimidine biosynthesis in higher plants. Physiol Plant 117: 297–304.

52. Tattini M, Guidi L, Morassi-Bonzi L, Pinelli P, Remorini D, et al. (2005) On the role of flavonoids in the integrated mechanisms of response of Ligustrum vulgare and Phillyrea latifolia to high solar radiation. New Phytol 167: 457–470.

53. Tattini M, Matteini P, Saracini E, Traversi ML, Giordano C, et al. (2007) Morphology and biochemistry of non-glandular trichomes in Cistus salvifolius L. leaves growing in extreme habitats of the Mediterranean basin. Plant Biol (Stuttg) 9: 411–419.

54. Schellmann S, Hülskamp M (2005) Epidermal differentiation: trichomes in Arabidopsis as a model system. Int J Dev Biol 49: 579–584.

55. Broun P (2005) Transcriptional control of flavonoid biosynthesis: a complex network of conserved regulators involved in multiple aspects of differentiation in Arabidopsis. Curr Opin Plant Biol 8: 272–279.

56. Serna L, Martin C (2006) Trichomes: different regulatory networks lead to convergent structures. Trends Plant Sci 11: 274–280.

57. Dubos C, Stracke R, Grotewold E, Weisshaar B, Martin C, et al. (2010) MYB transcription factors in Arabidopsis. Trends Plant Sci 15: 573–581.

58. Luikart G, England PR, Tallmon D, Jordan S, Taberlet P (2003) The power and promise of population genomics: from genotyping to genome typing. Nat Rev Genet 4: 981–994.

59. Avise J (2004) Molecular Markers, Natural History, and Evolution. Chapman & Hall, editor New York.

60. Durand J, Bodénès C, Chancerel E, Frigerio J-M, Vendramin G, et al. (2010) A fast and cost-effective approach to develop and map EST-SSR markers: oak as a case study. BMC Genomics 11: 570.

61. Bouck A, Vision T (2007) The molecular ecologist's guide to expressed sequence tags. Mol Ecol 16: 907–924.

62. Vasemägi A, Nilsson J, Primmer CR (2005) Expressed sequence tag-linked microsatellites as a source of gene-associated polymorphisms for detecting signatures of divergent selection in atlantic salmon (Salmo salar L.). Mol Biol Evol 22: 1067–1076.

63. Barbará T, Palma-Silva C, Paggi GM, Bered F, Fay MF, et al. (2007) Cross-species transfer of nuclear microsatellite markers: potential and limitations. Mol Ecol 16: 3759–3767.

64. Bruschi P (2003) Morphological and Molecular Diversity Among Italian Populations of Quercus petraea (Fagaceae). Ann Bot 91: 707–716.

18

Resequencing and Association Analysis of *PTPRA*, a Possible Susceptibility Gene for Schizophrenia and Autism Spectrum Disorders

Jingrui Xing[1], Chenyao Wang[1], Hiroki Kimura[1], Yuto Takasaki[1], Shohko Kunimoto[1], Akira Yoshimi[1], Yukako Nakamura[1], Takayoshi Koide[1], Masahiro Banno[1], Itaru Kushima[1], Yota Uno[1], Takashi Okada[1], Branko Aleksic[1]*, Masashi Ikeda[2], Nakao Iwata[2], Norio Ozaki[1]

1 Department of Psychiatry, Nagoya University Graduate School of Medicine, Nagoya, Japan, 2 Department of Psychiatry, School of Medicine, Fujita Health University, Toyoake, Aichi, Japan

Abstract

Background: The *PTPRA* gene, which encodes the protein RPTP-α, is critical to neurodevelopment. Previous linkage studies, genome-wide association studies, controlled expression analyses and animal models support an association with both schizophrenia and autism spectrum disorders, both of which share a substantial portion of genetic risks.

Methods: We sequenced the protein-encoding areas of the *PTPRA* gene for single nucleotide polymorphisms or small insertions/deletions (InDel) in 382 schizophrenia patients. To validate their association with the disorders, rare (minor allele frequency <1%), missense mutations as well as one InDel in the 3′UTR region were then genotyped in another independent sample set comprising 944 schizophrenia patients, 336 autism spectrum disorders patients, and 912 healthy controls.

Results: Eight rare mutations, including 3 novel variants, were identified during the mutation-screening phase. In the following association analysis, L59P, one of the two missense mutations, was only observed among patients of schizophrenia. Additionally, a novel duplication in the 3′UTR region, 174620_174623dupTGAT, was predicted to be located within a Musashi Binding Element.

Major Conclusions: No evidence was seen for the association of rare, missense mutations in the *PTPRA* gene with schizophrenia or autism spectrum disorders; however, we did find some rare variants with possibly damaging effects that may increase the susceptibility of carriers to the disorders.

Editor: Namik Kaya, King Faisal Specialist Hospital and Research center, Saudi Arabia

Funding: Funding for this study was provided by research grants from the Ministry of Education, Culture, Sports, Science and Technology of Japan; the Ministry of Health, Labor and Welfare of Japan; Grant-in-Aid for "Integrated research on neuropsychiatric disorders" carried out under the Strategic Research Program for Brain Sciences by the Ministry of Education, Culture, Sports, Science and Technology of Japan; Grant-in-Aid for Scientific Research on Innovative Areas, "Glial assembly: a new regulatory machinery of brain function and disorders"; and Grant-in-Aid for Scientific Research on Innovative Areas (Comprehensive Brain Science Network) from the Ministry of Education, Science, Sports and Culture of Japan. The funders had no role in study design, data collection and analysis, decision to publish, or preparation of the manuscript.

* Email: branko@med.nagoya-u.ac.jp

Introduction

Schizophrenia (SCZ) is a genetically heterogeneous disorder with heritability estimated at up to 80% [1]. In recent years, although research projects such as large-scale genome-wide association studies (GWAS) have focused on common variants, they have failed to explain the majority of the heritability of SCZ [2,3]. Subsequently, great interest has been drawn to rare (minor allele frequency, MAF <1%) missense mutations as potentially important contributing factors to the 'missing heritability' [4,5]. The concept of Autism Spectrum Disorders (ASD) has been

defined in the newly released Diagnostic and Statistical Manual of Mental Disorders version 5 (DSM-5) to include previous diagnoses of autistic disorder, Asperger's syndrome and PDD-NOS (pervasive developmental disorders not otherwise specified) [6]. Both SCZ and ASD are recognized as neurodevelopmental disorders, and are reported to have a major overlap of genetic risk, especially from *de novo*, deleterious mutations, [7–10]although further research concerning implicated loci and/or genetic risk factors (i.e., copy number variants [CNV], insertion/deletions, and single nucleotide variants) is required.

The human protein tyrosine phosphatase receptor type A (*PTPRA*) gene encodes the enzyme receptor-type tyrosine-protein phosphatase alpha (RPTP-α), a member of the protein tyrosine phosphatase (PTP) family that is involved in numerous neurodevelopmental processes related to the pathogenesis of SCZ and ASD such as myelination, radial neuronal migration, cortical cytoarchitecture formation and oligodendrocyte differentiation [11–14]. Moreover, RPTP-α is also functionally involved in the *neuregulin 1* (*NRG1*) signaling pathway, which regulates neurodevelopment as well as glutamatergic and gamma-aminobutyric acid–ergic neurotransmission [15–17]. The *NRG1* gene, together with two other genes in the same pathway—*ERBB4*, which encodes a downstream tyrosine kinase receptor[16–18], and *PTPRZ1*, which encodes an *ERBB4*-associated protein tyrosine phosphatase[19]—have been reported by some studies to be associated with SCZ [20–22].

Multiple lines of biological evidence implicate the *PTPRA* gene in the etiology of SCZ or ASD. Previous linkage studies conducted in 270 Irish high-density families (p = .0382) and an inbred, Arab Israeli pedigree of 24 members (LOD score = 2.56 at 9.53 cM) have pointed to the area that harbors the gene [23,24]. A GWAS comprising 575 cases and 564 controls of the Japanese ethnicity showed an association between polymorphisms within the *PTPRA* gene and SCZ (best uncorrected p = .002), albeit not at the level of genome-wide significance [25]. This result was followed by a replication study of 850 cases and 829 controls, which further confirmed the association (p = .04, p = .0008 for pooled analysis of first and second stages) [26]. Patients carrying copy number variations (CNVs) within the gene have been reported to suffer from autism, or have delayed language and speech development or stereotypical behaviors [27]. Reduced *PTPRA* expression levels have been observed in postmortem brains from patients with SCZ when compared to brains from healthy controls (13% decrease; p = .018). In the same study, a significant difference in the expression of mRNA levels of one alternative splicing variant within the gene (p = .024) was discovered in an expression analysis using lymphoblastoid cell lines (LCL) derived from 28 patients with SCZ and 20 healthy controls [26]. *Ptpra* knockout mice have been shown to exhibit neurodevelopmental deficiencies and schizophrenic-like behavioral patterns that are thought to model certain aspects of the disorder in humans. In addition, loss of *Ptpra* function in mice also leads to reduced expression of multiple myelination genes, [26] a phenomenon commonly associated with SCZ [28–32] and ASD [33–35] in human patients.

Given the aforementioned studies suggesting the association between *PTPRA* and SCZ/ASD, we decided to sequence the exonic areas of the gene in search for rare, protein-altering mutations that may further strengthen the evidence implicating *PTPRA* as a risk gene for these neurodevelopmental disorders.

Materials and Methods

Participants

Two independent sample sets were used in this study (Table 1). The first set, comprising 382 SCZ patients (mean age = 53.6 ± 14.2; male = 56.5%;), was sequenced for missense rare variants, including single nucleotide polymorphisms (SNPs), small InDels and splicing site variations. The second, larger set, comprising 944 SCZ patients (mean age = 50.4 ± 15.6, male = 58.7%), 336 ASD patients (mean age = 19.3 ± 10.0, male = 77.1%), and 912 controls (mean age = 39.1 ± 15.9, male = 44.5%), was used for association analysis of variants detected in the first phase.

All participants in this study were recruited in the Nagoya University Hospital and its associated institutes. Patients were included in the study if they (1) met DSM-5 criteria for SCZ or ASD and (2) were physically healthy. Controls were selected from the general population and had no personal or family history of psychiatric disorders (first-degree relatives only based on the subject's interview). The selection was based on the following: (1) questionnaire responses from the subjects themselves during the sample inclusion step; or (2) an unstructured diagnostic interview conducted by an experienced psychiatrist during the blood collection step. All subjects were unrelated, living in the central area of the Honshu island of Japan, and self-identified as members of the Japanese population. The Ethics Committees of the Nagoya University Graduate School of Medicine approved this study. Written informed consent was obtained from all participants. In addition, the patients' capacity to consent was confirmed by a family member when needed. Individuals with a legal measure of reduced capacity were excluded.

Resequencing and Data Analysis

The human *PTPRA* gene is located at Chromosome 20: 2,844,830–3,019,320 and has a total of 28 exons (Ensembl release 73; Genome assembly: GRCh37; Transcript: ENST00000380393) (Fig. 1). We included only coding regions and 3'UTR (exons 8–28) (Fig. 2). Genomic DNA was extracted from whole blood or saliva using QIAGEN QIAamp DNA blood kit or tissue kit (QIAGEN Ltd. Hilden, Germany). Primers for 10 amplicons ranging from lengths of 700 to 3000 bps covering all the target exons were designed with the Primer-BLAST tool by NCBI (http://www.ncbi.nlm.nih.gov/tools/primer-blast/) and tested for validity with UCSC In-Silico PCR (http://genome.ucsc.edu/cgi-bin/hgPcr). The Takara LA taq Kit (Takara Bio Inc. Shiga, Japan) was used for PCR amplification, and products were cleaned up with Illustra Exonuclease I and Alkaline Phosphatase (GE Healthcare & Life Science, Little Chalfont, United Kingdom). After that, Sanger sequencing was performed using the BigDye Terminator v3.1 Cycle Sequencing Kit (Applied Biosystems, Foster City, California, United States). Upon the initial discovery, for all variants, we used Sanger sequencing to confirm the detection.

Table 1. Profiles of participants in the resequencing and association sample sets.

| | Sequencing | Association Study | | | | Total |
	Schizophrenia	Schizophrenia	ASD	Control	Total	
Total	382	944	336	912	2192	2574
Male	216 (56.5%)	554 (58.7%)	259 (77.1%)	406 (44.5%)	1037 (47.3%)	1253 (48.7%)
Female	166 (43.5%)	369 (39.1%)	77 (22.9%)	503 (55.2%)	1131 (51.6%)	1297 (50.4%)
Mean Age (years)	53.6 ± 14.2	50.4 ± 15.6	19.3 ± 10.0	39.1 ± 15.9	44.9 ± 18.7	42.3 ± 18.7

Note: Some samples in the association study group were not identified by sex.

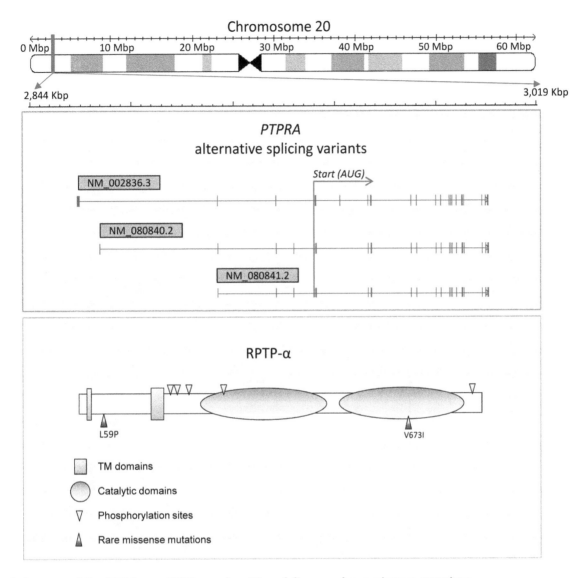

Figure 1. Structure of the *PTPRA* gene, RPTP-α, and position of discovered rare missense mutations.

Sequenced samples were read on an Applied Biosystems 3130xL Genetic Analyzer. Mutation detection was performed with Mutation Surveyor (Softgenetics, State College, PA, USA). The mutation calls were then revalidated for confidence.

Association Analysis

Missense and 3′UTR mutations with MAF<1% were picked up for the association stage. Due to the altering effects that splice site variants have on the structure of mRNAs, and consequently the production of the protein, [36,37] they were also included in the association analysis if they met the MAF criteria.

Custom TaqMan SNP genotyping assays were designed and ordered from Applied Biosystems. Allelic discrimination analysis was performed on an ABI PRISM 7900HT Sequence Detection System (Applied Biosystems, Foster City, California, United States). Differences in allele and genotype frequencies of the mutations were compared between SCZ patients/controls and ASD patients/

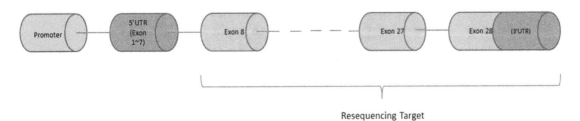

Figure 2. Targeted sequencing areas of the *PTPRA* Gene.

Table 2. Rare exonic mutations identified during the resequencing stage.

Genomic Position [a]	Exon	Base Pair Change [b]	AA Change [c]	Frequency	dbSNP Reference	1000 Genomes	ESP Variant Server
20:3016327	Exon 25	171999G>GA	673V>VI	1/382	rs61742029	Registered	Registered
20:2945609	Exon 9	107281T>TC	59L>LP	2/382	Not Registered	Not Registered	Not Registered
20:3018948	3'UTR	174620_174623 het_dupTGAT	—	1/382	Not Registered	Not Registered	Not Registered
20:3019013	3'UTR	174685A>AT	—	2/382	Not Registered	Not Registered	Not Registered
20:2945649	Exon 9	124753A>AG	Synonymous	4/382	rs138210276	Registered	Registered
20:3005207	Exon 21	160879G>GA	Synonymous	1/382	rs150908061	Registered	Registered
20:3017902	Exon 27	173574G>GT	Synonymous	2/382	rs375917163	Not Registered	Not Registered
20:3017903	Exon 27	173575C>CA	Synonymous	2/382	Not Registered	Not Registered	Not Registered

Notes:
[a]: Based on NCBI build 37.1.
[b]: Based on NCBI Reference Sequence NC_000020.10.
[c]: Based on NCBI Reference Sequence NP_001099043. AA: amino acid.
All mutations are heterozygous.

controls using Fisher's exact test (one-tail), with a threshold of significance set at $p < 0.05$.

Results

Mutation Screening Step

Eight rare mutations consisting of 2 missense SNPs, 4 synonymous SNPs and 2 variations located in the 3'UTR area were identified within the target exons (Table 2), 4 of which were not previously reported in dbSNP Build 139 (http://www.ncbi.nlm.nih.gov/projects/SNP/), the 1000 Genomes Project (http://www.1000genomes.org), or the NHLBI Exome Sequencing Project (ESP) Variant Server (http://evs.gs.washington.edu/EVS/). All detected mutations were heterozygous.

Association Analysis

Two missense mutations, rs61742029, which had been previously observed only in the Han Chinese population, L59P, a novel variant, as well as the 174620_174623dupTGAT mutation were validated for association with SCZ and/or ASD in stage 2 (Table 3). Although we were unable to detect significance with our sample sets, it is worth noting that L59P was only present in the SCZ patient group.

Evolutionary Conservation Analysis

Conservation status of rs61742029 and L59P in 11 common species was investigated using Mutation Taster (http://www.mutationtaster.org/). Results showed that the amino acids corresponding to the mutations in RPTP-α were highly conserved among different species (Table 4).

In Silico Functional Effects Prediction

Possible functional implications brought by amino acid changes due to the 2 missense mutations were analyzed with PolyPhen-2 (http://genetics.bwh.harvard.edu/pph2/), PMut (http://www.ngrl.org.uk/Manchester/page/pmut) and SIFT (http://sift.jcvi.org/). (Table 5) According to the results, the mutation L59P, which was only observed in schizophrenia patients, was predicted to be mostly benign, while rs61742029 showed a high probability of pathogenicity in PolyPhen-2.

3'UTR Motif Prediction

174620_174623dupTGAT, a small duplication discovered in the 3'UTR area, was predicted by RegRNA 2.0 (http://regrna2.mbc.nctu.edu.tw) to be located within a human Musashi Binding Element (MBE), an evolutionarily conserved region shown to affect neural cell differentiation through its mRNA translation regulator properties [38].

Clinical Information of the Carriers of Mutation L59P and 174620_174623dupTGAT

The patient carrying the *PTPRA* L59P mutation was a male diagnosed with SCZ at the age of 19. The patient was born in 1947 had a normal course of development during childhood. In early 1966, he started to suffer from auditory hallucinations, and soon withdrew into an indoor lifestyle. His family reported him being irritated when visited, as well as behaving improperly in public. He was promptly diagnosed and admitted to a psychiatry ward in the same year, and spent the rest of his life living in a hospital. A remarkable improvement was observed in his positive symptoms after admission and administration of antipsychotic drugs; however, he remained secluded, hardly communicating with people around him. At the time of his enrollment in the study, he was 162 cm tall

Table 3. Association analysis results of two rare missense mutations and one 3'UTR variant.

Mutation	Genotype Counts (Resequencing) [a]	Genotype Counts (Association)			P Value [b]	
		SZ	ASD	Ctrl	SZ	ASD
171999G>GA, 673V>VI	0/3/379	0/2/942	0/2/334	0/4/908	0.3276	0.2829
101281T>TC, 59L>L/P	0/2/380	0/0/944	0/0/336	0/0/912	1.0000	1.0000
174620_174623het_dupTGAT	0/1/381	0/0/944	0/0/336	0/1/911	0.4914	1.0000

Notes:
[a]: Homozygote of minor allele/heterozygote/homozygote of major allele.
[b]: Calculated using Fisher's exact test, one-tailed.
Ctrl: healthy controls.

and weighed 48 kg. No comorbid physical or mental illnesses were present. He had 3 children, among whom, one daughter had a history of mental disorder. The patient succumbed to pneumonia in the second half of 2013. In a computerized axial tomography (CAT) scan of the head taken a few weeks prior to patient's death, diffuse neocortical atrophy was observed.

The other patient carrying the L59P mutation was a female diagnosed with SCZ at the age of 34. No childhood development abnormalities were reported, but she was noted to have a history of irritability/aggressive tendencies in high school. Since onset, she had experienced auditory hallucinations and persecutory delusions, as well as continued irritability and aggression. Despite the efficacy of antipsychotic drugs on her positive symptoms, the patient suffered numerous relapses throughout her course of illness due to poor insight and lack of adherence to treatment. At the time of recruitment, she was 61 years old, with a chronic condition of diabetes and no comorbid mental conditions. She died in 2012 at the age of 62.

The patient carrying the *PTPRA* 174620_174623dupTGAT mutation was a male diagnosed with SCZ and comorbid intellectual disability at the age of 27, while he was enrolled in our study. He had a normal conception and birth, born to a 28-year-old father and 27-year-old mother. His father died when he was 3. Delayed intellectual development was observed since his childhood, with reports of illiteracy, hyperactivity, poor concentration and low performance at school. He subsequently dropped out of high school in his first year and started attending a technical school. After graduation, not being able maintain a steady position, he changed part-time jobs frequently. He presented at onset with hallucinations, persecutory delusions, and psychomotor excitement, and was subjected to involuntary commitment due to harmful behavior to others as a result of his delusions. At the time of admission, he was 168 cm tall and weighed 74 kg, with a Wechsler Adult Intelligence Scale (WAIS) score of 49 (Verbal IQ = 57, Performance IQ = 48); he also suffered from stuttering (anarthria literalis). After remission under antipsychotic treatment, he was discharged; however, lack of insight or compliance persisted. It was reported that his mother had a history of panic attacks, and one of his maternal relatives was also diagnosed with SCZ.

Discussion

To our knowledge, this is the first study that systematically screened all coding regions and 3'UTR of the *PTPRA* gene for rare variants in SCZ patients and assessed the association of identified mutations in such a study with SCZ/ASD.

Main Findings

In this study, we sequenced the encoding regions, splicing sites, and 3'UTR region of the *PTPRA* gene in 382 SCZ patients using the Sanger sequencing method, and discovered 8 rare variants. We then conducted association analysis in a much larger sample set for the 2 rare, missense mutations and one 3'UTR InDel identified during the mutation-screening phase in order to investigate their relationship with SCZ and/or ASD.

We were unable to detect a statistically significant association for any of the 3 mutations; this may be attributed partially to the low frequency of rare mutations in the population. However, according to our estimation using CaTS, the power calculator for two-stage association studies (http://www.sph.umich.edu/csg/abecasis/CaTS/), it would require a sample size of around 25,000 cases and controls for the study to obtain possible significance [39,40]. Also, L59P was only detected among SCZ patients in our sample, which infers possible connection of this mutation to the disorder. The evolutionary conservation status of the locus also indicates its biological importance.

Recent studies have discussed the limited impact of protein-coding variants detected in exome resequencing projects, attributing it partly to the fact that most associated variants alter gene expression rather than protein structure. These findings may help explain the lack of association for the 2 missense mutations we detected, while hinting that 174620_174623dupTGAT, predicted to be located within an expression-regulating element, may have a more significant effect. [10]

Additionally, an increasing amount of evidence suggests that genetic risks for SCZ and ASD may not be conferred by the effects of individual variants alone, but also the amplifying interactions between multiple susceptibility loci [41–44]. Thus it may be interesting to sequence the mutation carriers for additional related variants in future.

Limitations

Several limitations should be considered when interpreting the results of our study. The single candidate gene paradigm for a gene with less than robust ties to schizophrenia may have been one of the reasons leading to negative results. Besides, the Sanger method it employed predetermined its relatively small sample size and detection power in contrast with next generation resequencing. In addition, we did not have lymphoblastoid cell lines (LCLs) from the mutation carriers for expression analysis or blood samples from their family members for pedigree study. Therefore, we were unable to follow up the results with further biological evidence. Moreover, some potentially interesting regions of the *PTPRA* gene, such as the promoter, 5'UTR, and most of the intronic

Table 4. Evolutionary conservation information for rs61742029 and L59P

Mutation	Species	Match	Gene	AA	Alignment
L59P	Human	—	ENST0000380393	59	K T S N P T S S L T S **[L]** S V A P T F S P N I T L
	Mutant	Not conserved	—	59	K T S N P T S S L T S *P S V A P T F S P N I T
	P. Troglodytes	All identical	ENSPTRG00000033879	59	K T S N P T S S L T S **[L]** S V A P T F S P N I T
	M. Mulatta	All identical	ENSMMUG00000005878	59	K T S N P T S S L T S **[L]** S V A P T F S P N I T
	F. Catus	All identical	ENSFCAG00000019232	59	K T S S P A S S V T S **[L]** S V A P T F S P N L T
	M. Musculus	All identical	ENSMUSG00000027303	59	K T S N S T S S V I S **[L]** S V A P T F S P N L T
	G. Gallus	All identical	ENSGALG00000015995	56	N V S **[L]** N V S - S P M T T
	T. Rubripes	All identical	ENSTRUG00000014770	99	P T P S P A S D G T L **[L]** Q A D P N A T G R V L
	D.rerio	Not conserved	ENSDARG00000001769	101	P P V V P P A V P I *P T V V L P V P P T P T
	D. Melanogaster	No homologue	—	N/A	
	C. Elegans	No alignment	C09D8.1	N/A	
	X. Tropicalis	All conserved	ENSXETG00000017982	71	T T T R T A *V I L A P N V T D S I F
rs61742029	Human			664	L K K E E E C E S Y T *V R D L L V T N T R E E N
	mutated	all conserved		664	S Y T R D L L V T N T R E E N
	Ptroglodytes	all identical	ENSPTRG00000033879	673	L K K E E E C E S Y T ? R D L L V T N T R E E N
	Mmulatta	all identical	ENSMMUG00000005878	673	L K K E E E C E S Y T ? R D L L V T N T R E E N
	Fcatus	all identical	ENSFCAG00000019232	674	L K K E E E C E S Y T ? R D L L V T N T R E E N
	Mmusculus	all identical	ENSMUSG00000027303	700	L K K E E E C E S Y T ? R D L L V T N T R E E N
	Ggallus	all identical	ENSGALG00000015995	680	L K K E E E C E S Y T ? R D L L V T N T R E E N
	Trubripes	all identical	ENSTRUG00000014770	710	Y T R D L L V T N N R E N

*Marks the position of the amino acid change due to mutation.

Table 5. In silico functional effect prediction for rs61742029 and L59P.

Mutation	Prediction Tool		
	PolyPhen-2	Pmut	SIFT
rs61742029	Probably damaging	Neutral	Tolerated
L59P	Benign	Neutral	Tolerated

areas, were not sequenced (the rare intronic mutations we detected close to the exons can be viewed in Table S1).

Conclusion

In conclusion, our study did not detect any rare missense mutations within the *PTPRA* gene in our samples that showed statistical association with SCZ or ASD. Nonetheless, some potentially interesting variants were identified that might increase the susceptibility of their carriers to the disorders. Also, our results may help provide genetic clues for the involvement of the *PTPRA* gene in the pathogenesis of psychiatric disorders.

Supporting Information

Table S1 Rare intronic mutations identified during the resequencing stage. [a]: Based on NCBI build 37.1. [b]: Based on

NCBI Reference Sequence NC_000020.10. All mutations are heterozygous.

Acknowledgments

We sincerely thank the patients and healthy volunteers for their participation in this study. We would also like to express our gratitude to Ryoko Ishihara PhD, Mami Yoshida, and Hiromi Noma for their technical assistance and contributions to creating and managing the database.

Author Contributions

Conceived and designed the experiments: JX BA MI NI NO. Performed the experiments: JX CW HK YT. Analyzed the data: JX SK AY YN TK IK BA NO. Contributed reagents/materials/analysis tools: JX YU TO BA MI NI NO. Wrote the paper: JX SK AY YN TK MB IK YU TO BA NO.

References

1. Sullivan PF, Kendler KS, Neale MC (2003) Schizophrenia as a complex trait: evidence from a meta-analysis of twin studies. Arch Gen Psychiatry 60: 1187–1192.
2. Stefansson H, Ophoff RA, Steinberg S, Andreassen OA, Cichon S, et al. (2009) Common variants conferring risk of schizophrenia. Nature 460: 744–747.
3. International Schizophrenia C, Purcell SM, Wray NR, Stone JL, Visscher PM, et al. (2009) Common polygenic variation contributes to risk of schizophrenia and bipolar disorder. Nature 460: 748–752.
4. Manolio TA, Collins FS, Cox NJ, Goldstein DB, Hindorff LA, et al. (2009) Finding the missing heritability of complex diseases. Nature 461: 747–753.
5. Owen MJ, Craddock N, O'Donovan MC (2010) Suggestion of roles for both common and rare risk variants in genome-wide studies of schizophrenia. Arch Gen Psychiatry 67: 667–673.
6. Association AP (2013) Diagnostic and Statistical Manual of Mental Disorders (Fifth ed.): Arlington, VA: American Psychiatric Publishing.
7. Crespi BJ, Crofts HJ (2012) Association testing of copy number variants in schizophrenia and autism spectrum disorders. J Neurodev Disord 4: 15.
8. Sullivan PF, Daly MJ, O'Donovan M (2012) Genetic architectures of psychiatric disorders: the emerging picture and its implications. Nat Rev Genet 13: 537–551.
9. Ku CS, Polychronakos C, Tan EK, Naidoo N, Pawitan Y, et al. (2013) A new paradigm emerges from the study of de novo mutations in the context of neurodevelopmental disease. Mol Psychiatry 18: 141–153.
10. Schizophrenia Working Group of the Psychiatric Genomics C (2014) Biological insights from 108 schizophrenia-associated genetic loci. Nature 511: 421–427.
11. Bodrikov V, Leshchyns'ka I, Sytnyk V, Overvoorde J, den Hertog J, et al. (2005) RPTPalpha is essential for NCAM-mediated p59fyn activation and neurite elongation. J Cell Biol 168: 127–139.
12. Bodrikov V, Sytnyk V, Leshchyns'ka I, den Hertog J, Schachner M (2008) NCAM induces CaMKIIalpha-mediated RPTPalpha phosphorylation to enhance its catalytic activity and neurite outgrowth. J Cell Biol 182: 1185–1200.
13. Ye H, Tan YL, Ponniah S, Takeda Y, Wang SQ, et al. (2008) Neural recognition molecules CHL1 and NB-3 regulate apical dendrite orientation in the neocortex via PTP alpha. EMBO J 27: 188–200.
14. Wang PS, Wang J, Xiao ZC, Pallen CJ (2009) Protein-tyrosine phosphatase alpha acts as an upstream regulator of Fyn signaling to promote oligodendrocyte differentiation and myelination. J Biol Chem 284: 33692–33702.
15. Fischbach GD (2007) NRG1 and synaptic function in the CNS. Neuron 54: 495–497.
16. Fazzari P, Paternain AV, Valiente M, Pla R, Lujan R, et al. (2010) Control of cortical GABA circuitry development by Nrg1 and ErbB4 signalling. Nature 464: 1376–U1311.
17. Wen L, Lu YS, Zhu XH, Li XM, Woo RS, et al. (2010) Neuregulin 1 regulates pyramidal neuron activity via ErbB4 in parvalbumin-positive interneurons.

Proceedings of the National Academy of Sciences of the United States of America 107: 1211–1216.
18. Li B, Woo RS, Mei L, Malinow R (2007) The neuregulin-1 receptor ErbB4 controls Glutamatergic synapse maturation and plasticity. Neuron 54: 583–597.
19. Buxbaum JD, Georgieva L, Young JJ, Plescia C, Kajiwara Y, et al. (2008) Molecular dissection of NRG1-ERBB4 signaling implicates PTPRZ1 as a potential schizophrenia susceptibility gene. Molecular Psychiatry 13: 162–172.
20. Buonanno A (2010) The neuregulin signaling pathway and schizophrenia: from genes to synapses and neural circuits. Brain Res Bull 83: 122–131.
21. Mei L, Xiong WC (2008) Neuregulin 1 in neural development, synaptic plasticity and schizophrenia. Nature Reviews Neuroscience 9: 437–452.
22. Silberberg G, Darvasi A, Pinkas-Kramarski R, Navon R (2006) The involvement of ErbB4 with schizophrenia: Association and expression studies. American Journal of Medical Genetics Part B-Neuropsychiatric Genetics 141B: 142–148.
23. Fanous AH, Neale MC, Webb BT, Straub RE, O'Neill FA, et al. (2008) Novel linkage to chromosome 20p using latent classes of psychotic illness in 270 Irish high-density families. Biological Psychiatry 64: 121–127.
24. Teltsh O, Kanyas K, Karni O, Levi A, Korner M, et al. (2008) Genome-wide linkage scan, fine mapping, and haplotype analysis in a large, inbred, Arab Israeli pedigree suggest a schizophrenia susceptibility locus on chromosome 20p13. American Journal of Medical Genetics Part B-Neuropsychiatric Genetics 147B: 209–215.
25. Ikeda M, Aleksic B, Kinoshita Y, Okochi T, Kawashima K, et al. (2011) Genome-wide association study of schizophrenia in a Japanese population. Biol Psychiatry 69: 472–478.
26. Takahashi N, Nielsen KS, Aleksic B, Petersen S, Ikeda M, et al. (2011) Loss of function studies in mice and genetic association link receptor protein tyrosine phosphatase alpha to schizophrenia. Biol Psychiatry 70: 626–635.
27. Firth HVea (2009) Database of Chromosomal Imbalance and Phenotype in Humans using Ensembl Resources. Am J Hum Genet.
28. Hakak Y, Walker JR, Li C, Wong WH, Davis KL, et al. (2001) Genome-wide expression analysis reveals dysregulation of myelination-related genes in chronic schizophrenia. Proc Natl Acad Sci U S A 98: 4746–4751.
29. Hoistad M, Segal D, Takahashi N, Sakurai T, Buxbaum JD, et al. (2009) Linking white and grey matter in schizophrenia: oligodendrocyte and neuron pathology in the prefrontal cortex. Front Neuroanat 3: 9.
30. Mistry M, Gillis J, Pavlidis P (2013) Meta-analysis of gene coexpression networks in the post-mortem prefrontal cortex of patients with schizophrenia and unaffected controls. BMC Neurosci 14: 105.
31. Martins-de-Souza D (2010) Proteome and transcriptome analysis suggests oligodendrocyte dysfunction in schizophrenia. J Psychiatr Res 44: 149–156.
32. Takahashi N, Sakurai T, Davis KL, Buxbaum JD (2011) Linking oligodendrocyte and myelin dysfunction to neurocircuitry abnormalities in schizophrenia. Prog Neurobiol 93: 13–24.

33. Carmody DP, Lewis M (2010) Regional white matter development in children with autism spectrum disorders. Dev Psychobiol 52: 755–763.

34. Ginsberg MR, Rubin RA, Falcone T, Ting AH, Natowicz MR (2012) Brain transcriptional and epigenetic associations with autism. PLoS One 7: e44736.

35. Kleinhans NM, Pauley G, Richards T, Neuhaus E, Martin N, et al. (2012) Age-related abnormalities in white matter microstructure in autism spectrum disorders. Brain Res 1479: 1–16.

36. Roy SW, Gilbert W (2006) The evolution of spliceosomal introns: patterns, puzzles and progress. Nat Rev Genet 7: 211–221.

37. Ward AJ, Cooper TA (2010) The pathobiology of splicing. J Pathol 220: 152–163.

38. Okano H, Imai T, Okabe M (2002) Musashi: a translational regulator of cell fate. J Cell Sci 115: 1355–1359.

39. Hong EP, Park JW (2012) Sample size and statistical power calculation in genetic association studies. Genomics Inform 10: 117–122.

40. Liu L, Sabo A, Neale BM, Nagaswamy U, Stevens C, et al. (2013) Analysis of rare, exonic variation amongst subjects with autism spectrum disorders and population controls. PLoS Genet 9: e1003443.

41. Vawter MP, Mamdani F, Macciardi F (2011) An integrative functional genomics approach for discovering biomarkers in schizophrenia. Brief Funct Genomics 10: 387–399.

42. Lin Z, Su Y, Zhang C, Xing M, Ding W, et al. (2013) The interaction of BDNF and NTRK2 gene increases the susceptibility of paranoid schizophrenia. PLoS One 8: e74264.

43. Bartlett CW, Flax JF, Fermano Z, Hare A, Hou L, et al. (2012) Gene x gene interaction in shared etiology of autism and specific language impairment. Biol Psychiatry 72: 692–699.

44. Johnson NL, Giarelli E, Lewis C, Rice CE (2013) Genomics and autism spectrum disorder. J Nurs Scholarsh 45: 69–78.

19

Illuminating Choices for Library Prep: A Comparison of Library Preparation Methods for Whole Genome Sequencing of *Cryptococcus neoformans* Using Illumina HiSeq

Johanna Rhodes[1]*, **Mathew A. Beale**[1,2], **Matthew C. Fisher**[1]

1 Department of Infectious Disease Epidemiology, Imperial College London, London, United Kingdom, **2** Institute of Infection and Immunity, St. George's University of London, London, United Kingdom

Abstract

The industry of next-generation sequencing is constantly evolving, with novel library preparation methods and new sequencing machines being released by the major sequencing technology companies annually. The Illumina TruSeq v2 library preparation method was the most widely used kit and the market leader; however, it has now been discontinued, and in 2013 was replaced by the TruSeq Nano and TruSeq PCR-free methods, leaving a gap in knowledge regarding which is the most appropriate library preparation method to use. Here, we used isolates from the pathogenic fungi *Cryptococcus neoformans* var. *grubii* and sequenced them using the existing TruSeq DNA v2 kit (Illumina), along with two new kits: the TruSeq Nano DNA kit (Illumina) and the NEBNext Ultra DNA kit (New England Biolabs) to provide a comparison. Compared to the original TruSeq DNA v2 kit, both newer kits gave equivalent or better sequencing data, with increased coverage. When comparing the two newer kits, we found little difference in cost and workflow, with the NEBNext Ultra both slightly cheaper and faster than the TruSeq Nano. However, the quality of data generated using the TruSeq Nano DNA kit was superior due to higher coverage at regions of low GC content, and more SNPs identified. Researchers should therefore evaluate their resources and the type of application (and hence data quality) being considered when ultimately deciding on which library prep method to use.

Editor: Kirsten Nielsen, University of Minnesota, United States of America

Funding: Funding was provided by Medical Research Council grant (MRC MR/K000373/1) awarded to MCF. The funders had no role in study design, data collection and analysis, decision to publish, or preparation of the manuscript.

Competing Interests: NEBNext Ultra DNA kit were supplied free of charge, with no obligations, by New England Biolabs.

* Email: Johanna.Rhodes@Imperial.ac.uk

Introduction

For a newcomer into the field of high-throughput genomics, the plethora of available library preparation methods, with widely contrasting sample inputs, workflows, and potential biases can be bewildering. Sequencing by synthesis, as developed by Illumina, is currently the market leader in high-throughput next-generation sequencing (NGS) methods [1,2,3]. Illumina has progressively improved and enhanced on its early library preparation methods, with newer methods becoming simpler and quicker to perform, whilst also yielding more consistent results. This includes the different options for shearing genomic DNA; the standard method has been ultrasonication, but since the cost of the precision ultrasonicators recommended by Illumina is substantial, this has made library preparation prohibitive to many laboratories. A more recent alternative is the use of enzymatic cleavage with or without integrated transposome insertion of adaptor sequences, as used in the Nextera and Nextera XT protocols (Illumina) [4]. However, the use of enzymes to fragment genomic DNA has been shown to contain certain GC biases leading to unequal uneven sequence coverage [5].

Further considerations include the size selection of sheared DNA: both ultrasonic and enzymatic shearing can produce libraries with sheared DNA over a range of 600 bp or more, which is unsuitable for many sequencing projects that require a very specific sequence length. Size selection allows the refinement of the sheared DNA into a very specific size range. The earlier Illumina protocols were based on gel extraction, which was time consuming and technically challenging, whilst newer methods leverage the preference of paramagnetic SPRi beads (e.g. Ampure XP; Beckman-Coulter) for binding larger DNA fragments, allowing carefully controlled sequential binding steps to remove large then small fragments from a DNA library. These methods allow the size profile of DNA libraries to be refined to within 100–200 bp [6].

More recent kits have also been designed with the limitations of the technology in mind. One of the major considerations of genome sequencing is GC induced bias [4,7]. Theoretically, shearing by mechanical means such as ultrasonication should lead to random shearing. In contrast, cleavage by enzymatic means will be inherently biased by the location of restriction or insertion sites and by the GC content of the DNA [1]. Furthermore, protocols that incorporate PCR to enrich content, as included in most Illumina protocols, are introducing further GC-based bias as well as additional sequencing errors due to PCR amplification. This has led to the development of protocols that use polymerases less prone to GC bias and with increased amplification fidelity for PCR, or the elimination of PCR entirely (as seen in Illumina's PCR-free protocol).

The TruSeq DNA protocol has been the mainstay of genomics projects for a number of years. This method utilises a relatively high sample input concentration and, when following the manufacturer's instructions, produces useful libraries with a minimum input of 1 µg of genomic DNA (gDNA). By default, DNA is sheared by ultrasonicator and size selection is performed using gel extraction. Between 2011 and 2012, the Illumina sequencing platform was the clear market leader [8], and the TruSeq DNA method was the main method for library preparation supplied by Illumina for DNA sequencing. However, in May 2013 Illumina announced that the TruSeq DNA kits would be discontinued at the end of the year, with final shipping dates in March 2014. The withdrawal of such a well established and widely used kit may leave researchers uncertain as to which of the now wide variety of available kits that they should choose for their sequencing project. Our aim was to address this question both for ourselves and for other researchers in the field.

Here, we evaluate and compare two new library preparation methods, the TruSeq Nano DNA kit (Illumina) and the NEBNext Ultra DNA kit (New England Biolabs), against the original market leader, TruSeq DNA kit (Illumina). TruSeq Nano is marketed as having a basis in the original TruSeq DNA sample prep method, but requiring a lower input gDNA (100–200 ng). For this reason, we chose this over the TruSeq PCR-free method, which requires a similar or greater starting amount of gDNA (1–2 µg) to TruSeq DNA. NEBNext Ultra also boasts advantages such as low inputs of gDNA (5 ng), and creates indexed libraries suitable for the Illumina platform sequencing machines, and as such, is marketed as a cheaper alternative to Illumina.

The human-infecting pathogenic fungus *C. neoformans* var. *grubii* (*Cng* henceforth) is routinely sequenced in our laboratory, with DNA extraction methods optimised for whole-genome sequencing applications. As this fungus is the focus of several large-scale population genomics projects worldwide, there is a need to streamline sequencing protocols and the attendant bioinformatics pipelines in order to optimise the quality of data amongst projects. These needs are common to many laboratories aiming to sequence microbial eukaryotes with similar sized genomes to *Cng*; as such, this organism is an ideal model for reviewing library preparation methods.

Materials and Methods

DNA extraction

Glycerol stocks of stored *Cng* isolates were plated onto Saboroud Dextrose (SD) agar (Oxoid, Fisher Scientific) and grown at 30°C for 72 hours. Single colonies were selected and inoculated in 6 ml Yeast Peptone Digest (YPD) liquid media (Sigma-Aldrich) supplemented with 0.5 M NaCl, followed by inoculation at 37°C with agitation (165 rpm) for 40 hours. Fungal DNA was extracted using the MasterPure Yeast DNA Purification kit (Epicentre) according to the manufacturer's instructions, but with the addition of two cycles of rapid bead beating (45 seconds, 4.5 m/sec) using a RiboLyser Homogenizer (Hybaid, Middlesex, UK) and 1.0 mm

silica beads (Thistle Scientific, UK) prior to the heat inactivation step. Genomic DNA was resuspended in Buffer EB (Qiagen) to avoid EDTA in the final preparation.

Sample preparation and quality assessment

Purified DNA was quantified using the Qubit Broad Range double-stranded DNA assay (Life Technologies), and diluted in Buffer EB (Qiagen) to the concentration required for input into each library preparation protocol using a two-step, quantitation and dilution, then re-quantitation and re-dilution procedure to ensure accuracy of dilution. Selected DNA samples were assessed for quality by gel electrophoresis and Genomic DNA Screen Tapes using TapeStation 2200 (Agilent). The same genomic DNA purification was used as starting material for all three library preparation methods.

Library preparation

Library preparations were performed according to manufacturer's instructions, in 96-well MicroAmp Optical 96-Well Reaction Plates (Life Technologies) or Hard-Shell Low-Profile Thin-Wall 96-Well Skirted PCR plates (BioRad). Quality and band size of libraries were assessed using D1K and HS D1K Screen Tapes (Agilent) on a Tapestation 2200 (Agilent) at multiple steps during each protocol, typically after size selection and after PCR amplification. Libraries were quantified by qPCR using the Library Quantification Kit for Illumina sequencing platforms (KAPA Biosystems, Boston, USA), using a Prism 7300 Real Time PCR System (Life Technologies). Unless otherwise stated, libraries were normalised to a working concentration of 10 nM using the molarity calculated from qPCR adjusted for fragment size with the Tape Station median.

TruSeq DNA v2

Input genomic DNA (gDNA) was used at concentrations between 50 ng/µl and 150 ng/µl for the TruSeq DNA v2 protocol. Fifty-four microlitres of gDNA was transferred to an AFA fiber Snap-Cap microTUBE (Covaris) and sheared on an S2 Ultrasonicator (Covaris) with a Duty Cycle of 10%, Intensity set to 5.0, 200 cycles per burst, in frequency sweeping mode for 50 seconds. Library preparation was performed according to the manufacturer's instructions, with size selection performed using Tris-Borate-EDTA (TBE) agarose gel electrophoresis and MinElute Gel Extraction (Qiagen). Adaptor enrichment was performed using ten cycles of PCR according to the manufacturer's instructions.

TruSeq Nano DNA

Genomic DNA for input into the TruSeq Nano DNA protocol was quantified and diluted to 2 ng/µl. Fifty-four microlitres of gDNA was sheared using an S2 Ultrasonicator (Covaris) using the same settings as for the TruSeq DNA protocol. Library preparation was performed according to the manufacturer's instructions. Adaptor enrichment was performed using eight cycles of PCR according to the manufacturer's instructions.

NEBNext Ultra DNA

Genomic DNA for input into the NEBNext Ultra DNA protocol was quantified and diluted to 2 ng/µl. Fifty-four microlitres of gDNA was sheared using an S2 Ultrasonicator (Covaris) using the same settings as for the TruSeq DNA protocol. Library preparation was performed according to the manufacturer's instructions, with size selection performed using AMPure XP beads (45 µl beads for the initial step, and 25 µl for the second

Table 1. Cost comparison for library prep consumables, based on UK list prices (May 2014) where possible.

Consumables	TruSeq Nano		NEBNext Ultra	
	Per 24	**Per sample**	**Per 24**	**Per sample**
Core library prep kit	£812	£31.47	£640	£26.67
Additional oligos	£0	£0	£121	£5.04
Ampure XP beads	£0	£0	£44	£1.83
Covaris tubes	£110	£4.58	£110	£4.58
Quality control analysis	£200	£8.33	£200	£8.33
Filter tips (assuming £35/1000)	£71	£3.12	£48	£2.10
Total	£1193.40	£49.87	£1163.30	£48.56

Quality control analysis included quantification of all samples by Qubit Broad Range dsDNA assay (Life Technologies) prior to beginning, follow by final analysis using TapeStation 2200 D1K Screen Tapes (Agilent) and qPCR using the Kapa kit for Illumina libraries (Kapa Biosciences). Filter tip and Ampure XP bead costs are based on estimates of usage, with 'per sample' usage rounded up to the nearest tip.

step). Adaptor enrichment was performed using eight cycles of PCR, and using the NEBNext Multiplex oligos for Illumina (New England Biolabs).

Sequencing

TruSeq DNA v2 libraries were pooled in groups of ten per lane, whilst TruSeq Nano and NEBNext Ultra libraries were pooled in groups of eight per lane, and run with paired-end 100 bp reads on a HiSeq 2000 set to high yield mode at MRC Clinical Genomics Centre (Hammersmith, London, UK). Libraries prepared by the same method were sequenced on the same lane of a flow-cell, but the different methods were sequenced on different flow cells. All raw reads and information on lineages of isolates in this study have been submitted to the European Nucleotide Archive, under the project accession PRJEB7411.

Read alignment

All reads were mapped to the reference genome using an identical pipeline. Reads were mapped to the *Cng* reference genome, H99 [7] using BWA 0.75a [10] aln and quality threshold of 15. Samtools [11] version 0.1.18 was used to sort and index resulting BAM files, and generate information about the alignment output. Picard [12] version 1.72 was used to locate duplicate reads and assign correct read groups to BAM files. All resulting BAM files were recalibrated by locally realigning around INDELs using GATK RealignerTargetCreator and IndelRealigner [13].

SNP and INDEL detection

SNPs and INDELs were called from all alignments in the same way, using GATK UnifiedGenotyper [14,15] version 2.2-2 in haploid mode with a downsampling value of 10000. Both SNPs and INDELs were filtered according to mapping quality and read depth at each base. Any SNPs or INDELs not present in at least 80% of reads were also filtered out. SNPs were also called using bcftools [16] to confirm SNP numbers called using GATK.

Genome coverage

BAM files locally realigned around INDELs were used to determine the average (mean) coverage, using GATK [13] DepthOfCoverage package and default settings. The *Cng* H99 genome [9] was again used as the reference. IQR values were calculated using the MATLAB 'iqr()' function (release 2011b, The MathWorks Inc., Natick, MA). Coverage gaps were identified and counted using a custom MATLAB script.

GC-content analysis

The 'CollectGcBiasMetrics.jar' package, part of the Picard [12] software was used to collect information about GC bias in the reads of BAM file by counting the number of reads in each 100 bp window using default settings, and therefore providing a measure of coverage relating to GC content.

Results

The pathogenic fungus *Cng*, an organism with a genome of approximately 19 Mb in length, and a GC content of 48.23%, is routinely whole-genome sequenced and aligned to the reference strain in our laboratory. We randomly selected an isolate (VNI molecular type), which has been sequenced using various library prep methods, and sequenced this isolate using the TruSeq DNA v2 kit (Illumina), and two newer kits: the TruSeq Nano DNA kit (Illumina), and the NEBNext Ultra DNA kit (New England Biolabs). We expanded the range of isolates tested using the newer kits by randomly selecting a further four isolates (three of the VNI molecular type, one of VNII), which represent the span of known SNP diversity present in *Cng* genomes.

All samples were sequenced by HiSeq 2000, and the resulting reads and genome assemblies were compared. All resulting reads generated were mapped to the reference *Cng* genome, H99 [9] as described in Methods. Our aim was to determine firstly if the newer library preparation kits were equivalent or better than the existing TruSeq DNA v2 kit, and secondly which of the two newer kits performs better in terms of library quality and depth, but also cost, ease of use, and time.

Cost

Any comparison of cost is subject to both local variation and the constantly changing prices of competitive pricing strategies, and as such this information may be out dated very rapidly. In particular, at the time of writing, the Illumina TruSeq DNA v2 has been discontinued, so performing direct price comparisons is difficult. Never-the-less, certain comparisons may be made between the two current methods as the differences may not be obvious to the newcomer.

Whilst both kits contain most of the reagents required to perform library preparation, the difference between the kits is in the additional components that need to be purchased. For both methods, it is advisable to perform quantitation and dilution of genomic DNA prior to beginning, and both methods require

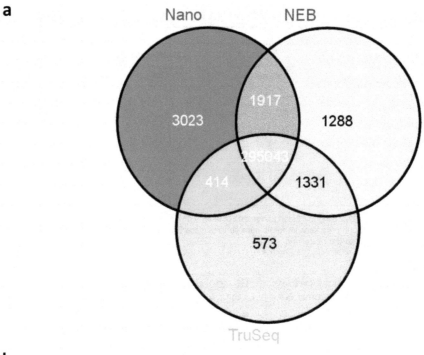

a

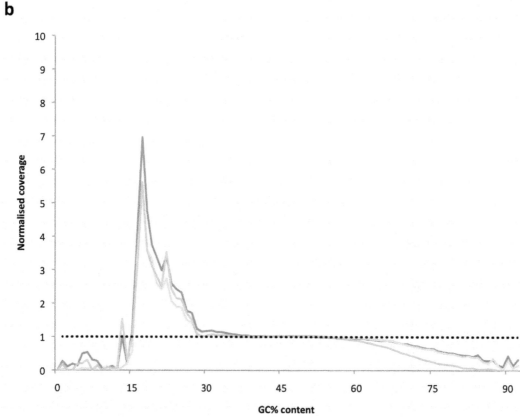

b

Figure 1. New library prep methods perform better than TruSeq DNA. a) Varying numbers of SNPs are found to be in common between the two newer library prep methods, and the original TruSeq DNA v2 kit. The majority of called SNPs were common to both of the newer library prep methods, and the original TruSeq DNA v2 kit; whilst both TruSeq Nano (blue) and NEBNext Ultra (yellow) performed better than the original TruSeq DNA v2 (green), with a larger number of SNPs called against a reference, a greater number of SNPs were uniquely called in the TruSeq Nano dataset along (blue). Venn diagrams were generated using the Venny software [17] of SNPs called using GATK [14,15]. b) Both NEBNext Ultra and TruSeq Nano exhibit higher coverage in GC-rich regions compared to the original TruSeq DNA v2 kit. Normalised coverage (binned into 100 bp windows) relating to GC content, where the blue line represents the TruSeq Nano-prepared isolates, the green line represents the TruSeq DNA v2-prepared isolate, and the yellow line represents the NEBNext Ultra-prepared isolate. The black dotted line at $x = 1$ is the expected normalised coverage showing no bias. Whilst all library preparation methods perform similarly, at GC-rich regions the newer library prep methods yield higher coverage than the original TruSeq DNA v2 method.

Table 2. SNP calls from two different pipelines and false positive rates associated with calling SNPs against the *Cng* reference [9].

Call platform	Call dataset	Called SNPs (GATK [13,14])	Called SNPs (bcftools [15])	Filtered SNPs (GATK [13,14])	False positive rate (%)
TruSeq DNA	CN-3	302435	283221	297361	1.68
	CN-1	52341	50033	49215	5.97
	CN-2	33378	31533	31483	5.67
TruSeq Nano	CN-3	306623	289467	300397	2.03
	CN-4	50556	48115	47599	5.85
	CN-5	11664	10938	10844	7.03
	CN-1	51837	49864	48804	5.85
	CN-2	33141	31322	31350	5.40
NEBNext Ultra	CN-3	305659	287502	299579	1.99
	CN-4	50134	47838	47425	5.40
	CN-5	11415	10042	10738	5.93

shearing by ultrasonication, necessitating the separate purchase of Covaris tubes (~£4.80 GBP/sample), and access to a Covaris Ultrasonicator. From this point on, the TruSeq Nano kit provides a near complete solution, including nearly all the reagents required to perform a complete library preparation up to final quality control and normalisation. In contrast, the NEBNext Ultra kit does not include all reagents, instead allowing users the flexibility to select the methods and reagents most appropriate to their investigation. This means that the quoted cost of the NEBNext Ultra kit is incomplete – additional purchases such as oligonucleotide primers with Illumina Index sequences for multiplexing and SPRi beads for library purification and size selection (Ampure XP beads), are required. Further considerations include the increased number of bead-based purification steps included in the TruSeq Nano kit (five, versus two in the NEBNext Ultra protocol) – during large library preps these extra steps significantly increase the usage of sterile, filtered pipette tips. Whilst following both protocols carefully, we estimated these additional clean-up steps (and other steps) accounted for an additional 29 tips per sample (or 660 per 24 sample kit). Overall, the cost of library prep is very similar between the two kits (Table 1); by our estimates, the NEBNext Ultra kit is marginally the cheaper of the two by approximately £1 per sample (or £30 per 24 samples).

Time and ease of use

Although Illumina publicise estimated time to complete a library preparation, these times are typically given for a very small numbers of samples. In our laboratory, we routinely prepare libraries in batches of 24 samples, and find it takes considerably longer. The original TruSeq DNA v2 protocol required gel extraction, including running samples on agarose gels for up to two hours – with 24 samples it may be necessary to run as many as four such gels. This labour intensive process could extend library preparation by a day or more. The replacement of gel extraction of libraries for size selection with SPRi bead selection in the two newer methods is a great time-saving improvement, and significantly streamlines workflow.

In our hands, 24-sample library prep takes approximately 2 days to complete using the newer protocols. Both TruSeq Nano and NEBNext Ultra methods have very similar work flows, and rely on SPRi bead-based size selection. Incubation times are similar for most steps. The Illumina protocol adds index sequences during adaptor ligation, whilst the NEBNext Ultra protocol adds

Table 3. False positive rates associated with called INDELs against the *Cng* reference [9].

Call platform	Call dataset	Called INDELs	Filtered INDELs	False positive rate (%)
TruSeq DNA	CN-3	28690	28676	0.05
	CN-1	5368	5354	0.26
	CN-2	3490	3476	0.40
TruSeq Nano	CN-3	26509	26495	0.05
	CN-4	5293	5279	0.26
	CN-5	1407	1393	1.00
	CN-1	5278	5264	0.27
	CN-2	3468	3454	0.40
NEBNext Ultra	CN-3	26233	26219	0.05
	CN-4	5225	5211	0.27
	CN-5	1391	1377	1.01

Table 4. IQR of read depths of TruSeq Nano and NEBNext Ultra prepared samples.

Call platform	Call dataset	Mean coverage	IQR	Bases at low coverage (<15×)	Bases at zero coverage
TruSeq DNA	CN-3	80	22	4.81%	2.12%
	CN-1	152	5	1.41%	0.79%
	CN-2	191	4	1.26%	0.83%
TruSeq Nano	CN-3	148	4	3.89%	1.46%
	CN-4	163	4	1.07%	0.59%
	CN-5	192	3	0.42%	0.22%
	CN-1	112	9	1.63%	0.93%
	CN-2	193	7	1.29%	0.86%
NEBNext Ultra	CN-3	158	6	4.06%	2.87%
	CN-4	159	4	1.15%	0.62%
	CN-5	146	7	0.49%	0.26%

indexes to adaptor tagged fragments during the PCR enrichment steps, but these differences do not significantly impact on workflow. The primary workflow difference between the two methods is the reduced number of SPRi purification steps with the NEBNext kit (including size selection, the TruSeq Nano protocol requires five bead purifications, whilst the NEBNext Ultra requires only two). Each of these steps takes approximately 30 mins for a 24-sample protocol, resulting in a time saving of at least 90 minutes for the NEBNext kit. Therefore, of the two kits NEBNext Ultra is faster, but only marginally so.

Data quality from the two newer methods is greater than that generated by the older TruSeq DNA v2 method

We first investigated the reads obtained from an isolate that was sequenced using all three library preparation methods. We assembled the reads and looked at read depth, SNP and INDEL calling, and genome coverage and GC bias.

Both TruSeq Nano and NEBNext Ultra yield more SNPs compared to TruSeq DNA v2. In population-based studies, the calling of SNPs and insertions and deletions (INDELs) are important for the discovery of genetic variation between individuals within a population. Over- or underestimating diversity can also influence the results of downstream analyses, such as recombination detection and population genetic structure. Therefore, there is a strong need for variant calling to be accurate. Errors in variant calling can lead to false positive SNPs being identified, or true positives being unaccounted for. High false positive rates would lead to extra validation being required, such as additional sequencing, which increases the amount of time and money spent to identify variants.

Variants were called against the *Cng* H99 reference genome [9] using the Genome Analysis Toolkit (GATK; The Broad Institute) UnifiedGenotyper, and filtered based on mapping quality and read depth, as described in Methods. Firstly, we investigated the reads from the isolates sequenced with the TruSeq DNA v2, TruSeq Nano (both Illumina) and NEBNext Ultra DNA kit (New England Biolabs). More true positive SNPs were called in isolates prepared with the two newer methods, compared to the original TruSeq DNA v2 method (Figure 1a). Comparison of the false positive rates for each library prep method (Table 2) indicate that SNPs are more likely to be incorrectly identified in the newer methods; however, the number of true positive SNPs identified (i.e. those that have fulfilled the filtering criteria) is ultimately higher in

the newer methods, compared to the original TruSeq DNA method.

The converse, however, is true for INDELs: whilst the false positive rate remained the same for all three library prep methods, more true positive INDELs were called in the same isolate prepared with TruSeq DNA, compared to those prepared with NEBNext Ultra and TruSeq Nano (Table 3).

Genome coverage and GC bias. Depth of coverage, as described in Methods, was found to be lower in the isolate prepared with TruSeq DNA v2, compared to the same isolate prepared with the two newer methods (Table 4). When analysing genome coverage statistics, low inter-quartile ranges (IQRs) are indicative of uniform coverage across the genome; a high IQR is indicative of non-uniform coverage. The isolate prepared using the TruSeq DNA kit was found to have a significantly higher IQR than the same isolate prepared with the newer kits (Table 4). Indeed, the TruSeq DNA v2-sequenced isolate was also found to have a greater number of bases at low and zero coverage (Table 4). Together, this indicates that the two newer library prep methods have not only improved the amount of coverage, but also the uniformity of coverage, and therefore, perform better than the original TruSeq DNA v2 kit.

This finding was supported by the GC bias on genome coverage exhibited by the TruSeq DNA v2 isolate: at GC-rich regions, the TruSeq DNA v2 isolate was seen to have less coverage, compared to the newer library prep methods (Figure 1b).

Both NEBNext Ultra and TruSeq Nano methods have advantages suitable for a replacement to TruSeq DNA v2

After investigating the efficacy of the new methods over the discontinued 'gold standard' method TruSeq DNA v2 method, we then proceeded to a more in depth comparison between the two new methods.

Both TruSeq Nano and NEBNext Ultra yield more SNPs compared to TruSeq DNA v2. The false positive rate for SNP calling is higher in genomes prepared with TruSeq Nano compared to NEBNext Ultra (Table 2); however, this is not the case when calling INDELs (Table 3). Despite this, more filtered, high confidence SNPs were identified in the isolates prepared with the TruSeq Nano DNA kit, compared to those prepared with the NEBNext Ultra kit. Further investigation revealed that more unique SNPs were called in the isolates prepared with the TruSeq

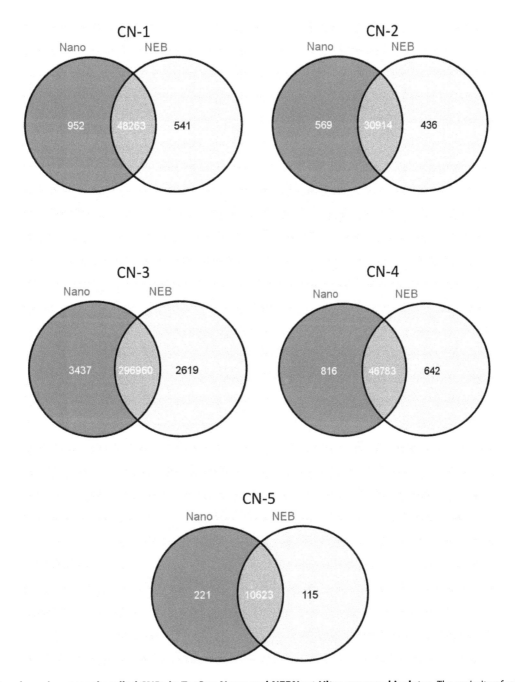

Figure 2. Uniquely and commonly called SNPs in TruSeq Nano and NEBNext Ultra-prepared isolates. The majority of called SNPs were common to both methods in each isolate. However, a greater number of SNPs were unique to the isolate prepared with the TruSeq Nano method (blue). Venn diagrams were generated using the Venny software [17] of SNPs called using GATK [14,15].

Nano kit (Figure 2) suggesting that not all SNPs are accurately called in isolates prepared with NEBNext Ultra.

Genome coverage and GC bias. To compare the uniformity of coverage across the genome in both TruSeq Nano and NEBNext Ultra library-prepared isolates, we measured the depth of coverage, as described in Methods.

In our data, both library preparation methods were capable of providing deep coverage (Table 4). However, higher inter-quartile ranges (IQRs) were observed in the coverage of NEBNext Ultra genomes, compared to the same genome prepared using TruSeq Nano (Table 4). A high IQR was observed for the NEBNext Ultra isolates, suggesting that this library prep method does not provide

a uniform coverage; a more uniform coverage is seen with the TruSeq Nano-prepared genomes. This was also evident when genome coverage was plotted against percentage GC content (Figure 3): coverage dropped more severely at high AT regions for isolates prepared with the NEBNext Ultra kit, however, both kits performed equally poorly at regions with high GC content.

Gaps in coverage, defined as any bases or regions of the genomes that are sequenced with less than 15% read depth, provide a meaningful way to look at non-uniform sequence coverage. Isolates prepared with the TruSeq Nano DNA kit again display statistically significant ($p<0.016$) more uniform coverage,

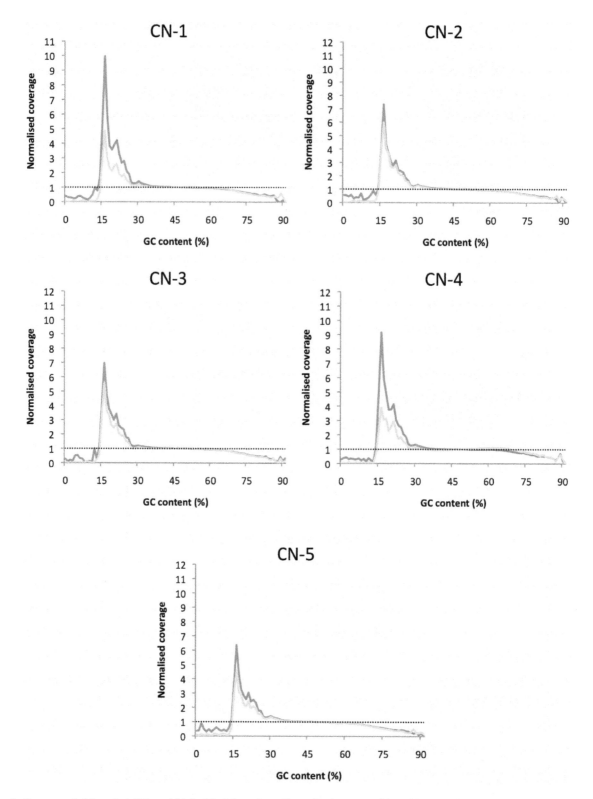

Figure 3. Coverage is biased at AT- and high GC-rich regions. Normalised coverage (binned into 100 bp windows) relating to GC content, where the blue line represents the TruSeq Nano-prepared isolate, and the yellow line represents the NEBNext Ultra-prepared isolate. The black dotted line at $x=1$ is the expected normalised coverage showing no bias. Whilst both library preparation methods perform similarly, the TruSeq Nano-prepared isolates generally provide more coverage at AT-rich regions.

with fewer gaps seen along the genome, compared to the isolates prepared with the NEBNext Ultra DNA kit (Table 4).

Discussion

With the discontinuation of the market leader for library preparation methods, Illumina's TruSeq DNA v2 kit, a gap has been created for a new method to become the most widely used kit. A fundamental feature of all library preparation methods for NGS is their speed, with decreasing laboratory and machine run time. The workflow for NEBNext proved to be quicker by approximately 90 minutes, but in the context of a two-day protocol, this is not a large difference. The cost comparison showed that for a 24-sample preparation, at current prices the NEBNext Ultra kit is also less expensive by £30.10, but again, in the context of an £1100 protocol, this is insubstantial. Therefore we cannot recommend one kit over another based solely on workflow and cost.

The ability to call SNPs is very similar for both the Illumina and NEB methods; however, detection of SNPs in isolates prepared using the NEBNext Ultra kits was not as accurate. This finding was confirmed when using a different SNP caller (bcftools [16]), suggesting there is an underlying difference in the data generated, not the bioinformatics pipeline used (Table 2). One would also desire high depth of coverage for stringent SNP detection: whilst one library preparation method did not outperform the other, the uniformity of coverage was more preferable in those isolates prepared using the Illumina TruSeq Nano DNA kit.

Sequencing of microbial genomes is subject to many caveats. Culturing the same colony for extraction on separate occasions may result in the generation of random mutations which lead to slightly altered consensus sequences. Library preparation may be subject to biases such as pipetting accuracy, extended incubation times, and PCR induced SNPs. Furthermore, variations in flow-cell clustering on HiSeq may lead to biases both between flow-cells and between lanes. For this study, we used the same genomic DNA purifications for each library preparation to minimize culture bias. The library preps and sequencing were only performed singly, but were performed by the same experienced person. Ideally, one would wish to repeat these library preparations and repeat the sequencing across multiple lanes of HiSeq in order to control for both library prep variability and lane bias. However, this was not possible due to cost and time constraints. Therefore we appreciate that some of the differences between methods may be the result of library prep and lane biases. However, in our laboratory we routinely include sample CN-5 with all 24-sample library preps, and therefore have a large number of replicates available using the TruSeq Nano protocol across many lanes and flow-cells of HiSeq. We have found the combined effects of library prep and lane bias to be low with this sample, with the Venn of 6 replicates containing 10,496 common SNPs and 142 unique SNPs (data not shown). Furthermore, we only performed sequencing of five isolates from a single organism of moderate GC content, and although interesting observations may be made, a larger sample size would be necessary to allow comprehensive comparisons between methods.

Coverage can be misleading and is more likely to be ambiguous for reads spanning repetitive regions of the genome, which includes regions of high AT and GC content. Ultimately, this can cause problems when aligning reads to a reference genome or for *de novo* assembly. Whilst steps are made to optimise the PCR amplification of the library, bias in coverage was still seen at regions with high GC content (Figure 3), with neither method preferable.

The uniformity of coverage, and reduced GC content bias seen in isolates prepared with the Illumina TruSeq Nano DNA kit suggest that in terms of data accuracy, this would be the ideal replacement for the resequencing of small microbial eukaryote genomes, and a potential market leader, to the now discontinued TruSeq DNA kit.

Author Contributions

Conceived and designed the experiments: MAB MCF. Performed the experiments: JR MAB. Analyzed the data: JR. Wrote the paper: JR MAB.

References

1. Quail MA, Smith M, Coupland P, Otto TD, Harris SR, et al. (2012) A tale of three next generation sequencing platforms: comparison of Ion Torrent, Pacific Biosciences and Illumina MiSeq sequencers. BMC Genomics 13(1): 341–354.

2. DeFrancesco L, Subbaraman N (2011) Sequencing firms eye pathology labs as next big market opportunity. Nat Biotechnol 29: 379–380.

3. Eisenstein M (2013) Companies 'going long' generate sequencing buzz at Marco Island. Nat Biotechnol 31: 265–266.

4. Adey A, Morrison HG, Xun X, Kitzman JO (2010) Rapid, low-input, low-bias construction of shotgun fragment libraries by high-density in vitro transposition. Genome Biol 11(12): R119.

5. Marine R, Polson SW, Ravel J, Hatfull G, Russell D, et al. (2011) Evaluation of a transposase protocol for rapid generation of shotgun high-throughput sequencing libraries from nanogram quantites of DNA. Appl Environ Microbiol 77(22): 8071–8079.

6. van Dijk EL, Jaszczyszyn Y, Thermes C (2014) Library preparation methods for next-generation sequencing: tone down the bias. Exp Cell Res 322(1): 12–20.

7. Dabney J, Meyer M (2012) Length and GC-biases during sequencing library amplification: a comparison of various polymerase-buffer systems with ancient and modern DNA sequencing libraries. BioTechniques. 52, 87–94

8. McPherson JD (2014) A defining decade in DNA sequencing. Nat Methods 11(10): 1003–1005.

9. Loftus BJ, Fung E, Roncaglia P, Rowley D, Amedeo P, et al. (2005) The genome of the basidiomycetous yeast and human pathogen *Cryptococcus neoformans*. Science 307: 1321–1324.

10. Li H, Durbin R (2009) Fast and accurate short read alignment with Burrows-Wheeler transform. Bioinformatics 25: 1754–1760.

11. Li H, Handsaker B, Wysoker A, Fennell T, Ruan J, et al. (2009) The Sequence Alignment/Map format and SAMtools. Bioinformatics 25(16): 2078–2079.

12. Picard. Available: http://picard.sourceforge.net. Accessed 2014 Aug 4.

13. McKenna A, Hanna M, Banks E, Sivachenko A, Cibulskis K, et al. (2010) The Genome Analysis Toolkit: a MapReduce framework for analyzing next-generation DNA sequencing data. Genome Res 20(9): 1297–1303.

14. Van der Auwera GA, Carneiro MO, Hartl C, Poplin R, del Angel G, et al. (2013) From fastq data to high-confidence variant calls: the Genome Analysis Toolkit best practices pipeline. Curr Protoc Bioinformatics 25: 1754–1760.

15. DePristo MA, Banks E, Poplin R, Garimella K, Maguire JR, et al. (2011) A framework for variation discovery and genotyping using next-generation DNA sequencing data. Nat Genet 43(5): 491–498.

16. Li H (2011) A statistical framework for SNP calling, mutation discovery, association mapping and population genetical parameter estimation from sequencing data. Bioinformatics 27(21): 2987–2993.

17. VENNY: An interactive tool for comparing lists with Venn diagrams. Available: http://bioinfogp.cnb.csic.es/tools/venny. Accessed 2014 Aug 4.

20

Whole-Genome Sequencing of the World's Oldest People

Hinco J. Gierman[1], Kristen Fortney[1], Jared C. Roach[2], Natalie S. Coles[3,4], Hong Li[2], Gustavo Glusman[2], Glenn J. Markov[1], Justin D. Smith[1], Leroy Hood[2], L. Stephen Coles[3,4], Stuart K. Kim[1]*

1 Depts. of Developmental Biology and Genetics, Stanford University, Stanford, CA, United States of America, **2** Institute for Systems Biology, Seattle, WA, United States of America, **3** Gerontology Research Group, Los Angeles, CA, United States of America, **4** David Geffen School of Medicine, University of California Los Angeles, Los Angeles, CA, United States of America

Abstract

Supercentenarians (110 years or older) are the world's oldest people. Seventy four are alive worldwide, with twenty two in the United States. We performed whole-genome sequencing on 17 supercentenarians to explore the genetic basis underlying extreme human longevity. We found no significant evidence of enrichment for a single rare protein-altering variant or for a gene harboring different rare protein altering variants in supercentenarian compared to control genomes. We followed up on the gene most enriched for rare protein-altering variants in our cohort of supercentenarians, TSHZ3, by sequencing it in a second cohort of 99 long-lived individuals but did not find a significant enrichment. The genome of one supercentenarian had a pathogenic mutation in DSC2, known to predispose to arrhythmogenic right ventricular cardiomyopathy, which is recommended to be reported to this individual as an incidental finding according to a recent position statement by the American College of Medical Genetics and Genomics. Even with this pathogenic mutation, the proband lived to over 110 years. The entire list of rare protein-altering variants and DNA sequence of all 17 supercentenarian genomes is available as a resource to assist the discovery of the genetic basis of extreme longevity in future studies.

Editor: Patrick Lewis, UCL Institute of Neurology, United Kingdom

Funding: This work was supported by the Ellison Medical Foundation/American Federation for Aging Research Fellowship, Stanford Dean's Fellowship, The Paul Glenn Foundation Biology of Aging Seed Grant, National Institute of General Medical Sciences Center for Systems Biology (P50 GM076547) and the University of Luxembourg – Institute for Systems Biology Program. The funders had no role in study design, data collection and analysis, decision to publish, or preparation of the manuscript.

Competing Interests: The authors have declared that no competing interests exist.

* Email: stuartkm@stanford.edu

Introduction

Supercentenarians are the world's oldest people, living beyond 110 years of age [1]. As would be expected for people that reach this age, supercentenarians have escaped many age-related diseases [2–5]. For example, there is a 19% lifetime incidence of cancer in centenarians compared to 49% in the normal population [6]. Similarly, supercentenarians have a lower incidence of cardiovascular disease and stroke than controls [5].

The genetic component of human lifespan based on twin studies has been estimated to be around 20–30 percent in the normal population [7], but higher in long-lived families [8–10]. Furthermore, siblings, parents, and offspring of centenarians also live well beyond average [11,12]. Lifestyle choices in terms of smoking, alcohol consumption, exercise, or diet does not appear to differ between centenarians and controls [13]. Taken together, these findings provide ample evidence that extreme longevity has a genetic component .

Several gene association studies have compared cohorts of long-lived subjects to controls. Analysis of candidate genes has shown that polymorphisms in the Insulin-like Growth Factor 1 Receptor gene (IGF1R) and the FOXO3 transcription factor gene are associated with extreme longevity [14,15]. Genome-wide association studies have shown that the ApoE4 haplotype is depleted in centenarians [16–18]. Sebastiani et al. compiled a list of 281 independent single-nucleotide polymorphisms (SNPs) that showed strong associations with extreme longevity (though none were genome-wide significant except for an ApoE SNP) [17]. They then showed that a genetic signature that combines information from these 281 SNPs is predictive for extreme longevity, indicating that at least some of these SNPs are truly associated with longevity. However, specific variants associated with longevity have not yet been identified [18,19].

More recently, studies have begun to use whole-exome sequencing and whole-genome sequencing (WGS) of centenarians to find variants associated with extreme longevity [19–21]. Ye et al. compared the genome sequence of a pair of 100-year-old twins to a pair of 40-year-old twins and found no evidence of accumulation of somatic mutations during aging [20]. By sequencing blood cells of a supercentenarian, Holstege et al. first identified somatic mutations and then used this information to infer clonal lineages in hematopoietic stem cells. They found that white blood cells in this individual were derived from only two clones of hematopoietic stem cells [21].

Here, we have sequenced the genomes of 17 supercentenarians. We limited the majority of our analyses to the thirteen genomes from Caucasian females. From this small sample size, we were unable to find rare protein-altering variants significantly associated with extreme longevity. However, we did find that one supercentenarian carries a pathogenic variant associated with arrhythmogenic right ventricular cardiomyopathy (ARVC), which had little or no effect on his/her health as this person lived over 110 years.

Materials and Methods

Ethics Statement, Supercentenarian Recruitment and Age Validation

Supercentenarian subjects, their family members, or their caretakers provided written informed consent. The study was approved by the Stanford University Institutional Review Board (IRB-19119) and by the Western Institutional Review Board (WIRB protocol #20101350). Supercentenarians were considered validated (i.e., 110 years or older) if they possessed each of the following documents: (1) A birth certificate, a baptismal certificate, or Census Record dating back to the original time of birth; (2) A marriage certificate in the case of married women not using their maiden names; (3) a current government-issued photo ID, such as a driver's license or passport. Supercentenarian health status and medical history for major age-related diseases were based on interviews conducted with subjects and/or their caretakers.

DNA Isolation, PCR and Sanger Sequencing

Whole-blood samples were drawn into PAXgene (Qiagen) blood tubes from which high molecular weight DNA was isolated. DNA samples were quantified using a dsDNA Broad-Range Assay on a Qubit Fluorometer (Life Technologies) and checked for size and degradation on an agarose gel. For Sanger sequencing, samples were amplified by nested PCR and variants were validated by forward and reverse reads. Primers were designed with Primer3 [22] and 10 ng was amplified with Phusion High-Fidelity Polymerase (Thermo Scientific). PCR bands were either column-purified or cut out from an agarose gel and purified with a Qiaquick Gel Extraction kit (Qiagen). PCR product was Sanger sequenced at Sequetech, Inc. Reads were trimmed by 10 bp at the 5' end and at a 0.01 error probability limit and then aligned to the human genome reference sequence build GRCh37 (hg19) using Geneious software. For sequencing of TSHZ3 in the Georgia Centenarian Study samples, all coding regions were sequenced except the first 13 amino acids (i.e., exon 1). None of the rare protein altering variants found in the 13 supercentenarians or the 4,300 NHBLI controls were located in exon 1. All experiments were performed according to manufacturer's protocol unless otherwise indicated.

Ancestry and Relatedness

Principal component analysis (PCA) of ancestry was done by analyzing the intersection of all genotyped SNPs from 1184 individuals from 12 different populations from HapMap Phase 3 [23] and the 17 supercentenarians. Only bi-allelic SNPs that had at least one non-reference allele in the 17 supercentenarians were used, resulting in a subset of 1.2 million SNPs. Genome-wide Complex Trait Analysis (GCTA) software was used to perform the PCA [24]. All pairs of 17 supercentenarians were tested for relatedness using Estimation of Recent Shared Ancestry (ERSA) [25,26].

Whole-Genome Sequencing and Analysis Pipelines

All DNA samples were submitted for WGS to 40x coverage by Complete Genomics, Inc. (CGI). Standard protocols were used to map reads and call variants using CGI pipeline 2.0.2 [27]. To analyze variants, we first produced a cross-reference matrix out of CGI variant files using custom Perl scripts [28] and the CGI command line tool CGAtools (listvar, testvar). To reduce platform errors and biases, we removed any variant with >50% double no-call rate in a control set of public genomes sequenced on the same CGI platform. We used 54 of the unrelated HapMap genomes (for variant analysis) or the 34 PGP genomes (for the RVT1 burden test). The 54 HapMap Genomes were obtained as part of the public CGI Diversity panel of 69 and the 34 PGP genomes were obtained from the Personal Genome Project [29]. The baseline characteristics of the 34 PGP genomes are listed in Table S1. Next, we used ANNOVAR and its build GRCh37 (hg19) database files [30] and custom scripts to annotate protein-altering variants: missense, frameshift, non-frameshift indels, stop-gain, stop-loss, and splice-site disruption. Splice-site variants were those disrupting the canonical splice-donor (GU) or splice-acceptor (AG) site of the RefSeq sequence. To test for enrichment of a rare protein-altering variant, we used the 379 European individuals from the 1000Genome (1000G EUR) Project Phase 1 (April 2012) build database as controls [31]. We included all protein-altering variants and did not require missense SNPs to be predicted as damaging by, e.g., SIFT or PolyPhen-2.

To filter out common variants, we used dbSNP version 131 [32]. This version was released on February 2010, and lacks most low-frequency variants deposited by large consortia like NHLBI and 1000G in later versions. Rare variants were tested for enrichment in cases (13 Caucasian female supercentenarians) vs. controls (379 European individuals from the 1000G Project) using Fisher's Exact Test. We repeated our analysis with reduced stringency by lowering the quality score threshold, but we did not see any significantly enriched variant or gene. Consistent with previous reports, Sanger sequencing of candidate rare protein-altering variants from WGS showed that 30 percent were likely sequencing errors [33,34].

Next, we applied a collapsing test to determine if any gene showed an enrichment of rare protein-altering variants in supercentenarian vs. control genomes. We started with the set of protein-altering variants in autosomal RefSeq genes observed in supercentenarians and controls (34 Caucasians from the PGP), and filtered to retain only rare variants with a minor allele frequency (MAF) <1.5% in 1000G EUR, and with an empirical MAF<10% in our samples. For each gene, we computed the RVT1 statistic [35] to determine whether the burden of mutations differed in supercentenarians and controls using R scripts [36]. RVT1 performs a logistic regression to model phenotype (case/control status) as a function of the proportion of rare variants seen in each genome. We repeated our burden test using a 5% instead of 1.5% as the 1000G EUR MAF cutoff, and again saw no significantly enriched gene. For the recessive model test, we compared all subjects having two or more variants per gene and scored significance using Fisher's Exact test.

Cohorts used to follow-up TSHZ3 variants

Samples from the Georgia Centenarian Study [37] were obtained from Coriell as DNA samples (Coriell ID: AGPLONG3). All Caucasian samples (n = 100) were analyzed and used for PCR and Sanger sequencing as described above. Two of our super-centenarians had previously participated in the Georgia Centenarian Study; their samples were identified by genotyping and removed from the cohort (NG18205, NG20051). In addition, we checked that none of the other supercentenarians with a protein-altering variant in TSHZ3 was present in the Georgia cohort by Sanger sequencing several loci in the Georgia cohort. We added a female Caucasian centenarian sample from our own study (age 100), bringing the total to 99. For controls, we used exome data for 4,300 Caucasians obtained from the NHLBI Exome Variant Server [38].

Table 1. Characteristics of supercentenarians.

Age	Age at Draw	Sex	Race	Major Age-related Diseases	Hearing	Vision	Dental	Communi-cation	Mobility
116	114	F	CAU	None	••	••	•••	•••	•
114	110	F	HIS	None	••	•	•	••	••
114	112	F	CAU	None	•	••	•	•	•
114	112	F	CAU	None	•	•	•	•	••
114	114	F	CAU	None	•	•	•	•	•
114	110	F	HIS	None	••	••	•••	••	•••
113	111	F	CAU	None	•••	•••	•••	••	••
113	112	F	CAU	None	•	•	•	••	••
113	113	F	AA	None	•••	•••	•••	•••	•••
112	110	F	CAU	None	••	••	•••	••	••
111	110	F	CAU	Alzheimer's	•	•	•	•	•
111	110	F	CAU	None	•	•••	•	••	••
111	110	F	CAU	None	•	•	•	••	••
111	110	F	CAU	None	••	•••	•••	•••	•••
111	110	M	CAU	Cancer	•••	•••	•••	••	•••
111	111	F	CAU	None	•	•	•	••	••
110	110	F	CAU	None	•	•	•	••	••

Age is age at death or last reported age alive. Age at (blood) draw was validated as described in methods. Sex is female (F) or male (M). Race (or ethnicity) is Caucasian (CAU), Hispanic (HIS) or African-American (AA). Major age-related diseases were known events of cancer, cardiovascular disease, stroke, Alzheimer's or type 2 diabetes at blood draw (i.e. enrollment). Functional status is indicated as: ••• (good), •• (moderate) or • (poor). Hearing: ••• good in both ears; •• impaired in one, good in other ear; • impaired in both ears. Vision: ••• could read newspaper; •• could watch television; • could do neither. Teeth: ••• had teeth of their own; •• no teeth of their own. Communication: ••• talked independently and coherently; •• slow speech, needed interpreter; • incoherent or no communication. Mobility: ••• could walk; •• uses wheelchair; • bed confined.

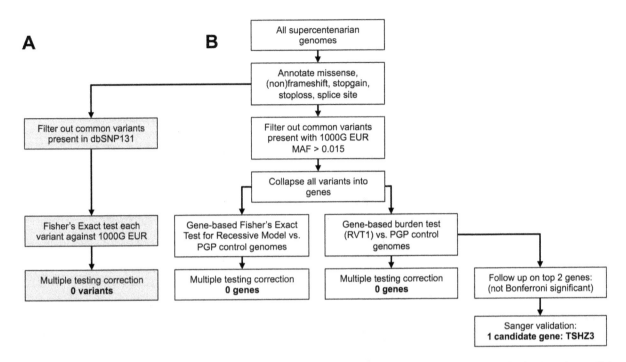

Figure 1. Pipeline to test supercentenarians for enrichment of rare protein-altering variants or genes harboring them. All female Caucasian supercentenarian genomes were annotated for protein-altering variants. (A) To test for enrichment of a single variant, we filtered against dbSNP131 and compared each remaining rare protein-altering variant against 1000G EUR. No single variant was significantly enriched. (B) To test for enrichment of a gene with rare protein-altering variants, we collapsed all variants in to their respective genes and filtered against 1000G EUR (MAF< 0.015). We tested for enrichment against 34 control genomes from PGP using the RVT1 burden test or a gene-based Fisher's Exact (for recessive model). No gene was significantly enriched for rare protein-altering variants in supercentenarians. We then Sanger validated TSHZ3 as the best candidate from our burden-test for follow-up.

Analysis of Pathogenic Variants

We used the recently published list from the American College of Medical Genetics and Genomics (ACMG) of potentially lethal pathogenic variants in 56 genes recommended for reporting to subjects [39]. All 17 supercentenarian genomes were annotated as described above, except without filtering for common variants. ClinVar and Human Gene Mutation Database (HGMD) were used to identify known pathogenic variants in the supercentenarian genomes in all 56 genes identified by the ACMG [40,41]. Besides the known pathogenic variants, new variants can be expected to be pathogenic in 45 of the 56 genes if the new variant clearly strongly reduces or eliminates protein function, such as frameshift, stop-gain, stop-loss, or splice-site mutations [42]. Any variant suggested to be benign based on annotation in ClinVar or HGMD was removed. The scoring of variants as either pathogenic or benign was also checked using Locus Specific Databases (LSDB). Pathogenic annotation of the c.631-2A>G mutation in DSC2 was confirmed in the Arrhythmogenic Right Ventricular Dysplasia/Cardiomyopathy (ARVD/C) database [43], which is part of the Leiden Open Variation Database [44].

Data Access

Upon acceptance for publication, the complete genome sequence for the 17 supercentenarians will be deposited in dbGAP and Google Genomics.

Results

The Supercentenarian Cohort

We recruited 17 supercentenarians and validated their age of 110 years or greater (see Methods). Their mean age at time of

death was 112 years and the subject that lived the longest died at the age of 116 years. At the time of her death, she was the world's oldest person and remains in the top ten of oldest people in recorded history [45]. We determined the medical history and health status of supercentenarians at the time of enrollment by interviewing them, their family, and caretakers. Many of the supercentenarians were cognitively and physically functional to a high degree well into old age. For example, one of our subjects worked as a pediatrician until the age of 103. Another subject drove a car until the age of 107. Table 1 gives an indication of some of the aspects of the supercentenarian health at the time of blood draw.

Among the 17 supercentenarians, at least one subject had a previous case of cancer and one was diagnosed with Alzheimer's disease. To the best of our knowledge, none of the supercentenarians were known to have cardiovascular disease, stroke or diabetes at the time of enrollment. In contrast, people in the US at age 85 often have had at least one major age-related disease. For example, 45 percent of 85-year olds have been diagnosed with cancer and 35 percent have had an incidence of cardiovascular disease [5]. The low rate of disease in our cohort of supercentenarians is consistent with previous reports showing that supercentenarians delay or escape most age-related diseases [5].

We isolated DNA from whole blood and sent the samples to Complete Genomics for WGS. Samples were sequenced to a read depth of 40x, and 94.1% of the genomes and 94.8% of the exomes had a read depth of at least 20x (Figure S1). To confirm the self-reported ancestry of all subjects, we performed a Principal Component Analysis (PCA) on the genomes of our 17 supercentenarians and that of 1184 HapMap individuals with known ancestry to serve as controls (Figure S2). This analysis confirmed

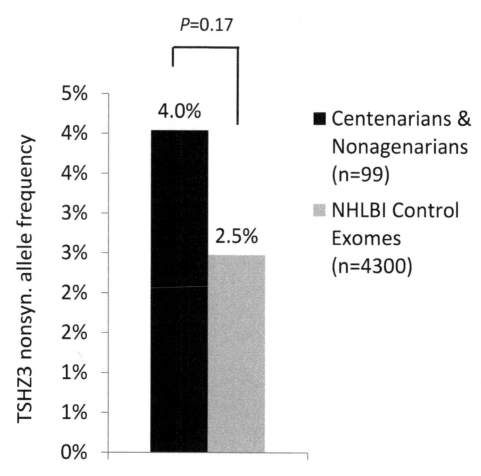

Figure 2. Rare protein-altering variants in TSHZ3 in the Georgia Centenarian cohort versus NHLBI cohort. To see if TSHZ3 is enriched for rare protein-altering variants in long-lived individuals, Sanger sequencing was performed on TSHZ3 in 99 Caucasians with extreme longevity (age 98–105). There was not a significant enrichment comparing the allele frequency of all rare protein-altering variants in the centenarians (4.0%; black bar) to 4300 Caucasian controls from the NHLBI exome project (2.5%; white bar). Both cohorts were annotated for protein-altering variants and filtered against 1000G EUR (MAF<0.015).

that 14 supercentenarians were of European ancestry, one was African American, and two were Hispanic. To prevent confounding our analyses due to differences in race or sex, we used only supercentenarian genomes that were both Caucasian and female for our main analyses. This left us 13 genomes for the main analysis with one male, two Hispanic, and one African-American genome reserved for follow-up analyses.

Next, we checked the genomes of our supercentenarians for unknown relatedness to each other, as any close relationship would confound analyses for enrichment of shared rare variants. We checked for shared regions of identity-by-descent using Maximum-likelihood Estimation of Recent Shared Ancestry [25,26]. The results indicated that none of the 17 supercentenarians were within five degrees of relationship of any other supercentenarian, which means that at least 97 percent of any of the supercentenarian genomes was not identical-by-descent to any of the other supercentenarian genomes.

Table 2. Baseline statistics of follow-up cohorts.

	Georgia Centenarian	NHLBI
	Study	Controls
Sample size, n	99	4300
Age, mean (range)	101 (98–105)	(≥18)
Females, n (%)	82 (83%)	2428 (56%)

Ages for Georgia Centenarian Study subjects were obtained from Corriell website. Number of females from NHLBI cohort was derived for X chromosome genotypes. Age information for NHLBI controls was obtained from www.nhlbi.nih.gov/recovery/media/NHLBI_DNA_cohort.htm.

Table 3. Protein-altering variants in TSHZ3 in Georgia Centenarian cohort.

Position on Chr19	Ref/Var	AA Pos	AA1/AA2	Supercent	Cent	Nona	1000G EUR MAF
31769738	G/A	321	R/W	0	1	0	novel
31769366	C/T	445	V/M	1	0	0	0.0013
31769293	T/C	469	E/G	1	2	1	0.01
31769021	T/C	560	M/V	0	1	0	novel
31768639	G/A	687	P/L	1	0	0	novel
31768594	A/C	702	L/W	0	0	1	novel
31768267	G/A	811	T/M	0	1	0	novel
31768178	C/T	841	E/K	1	0	0	novel
31767599	C/T	1034	E/K	0	1	0	novel

Position (bp) on chromosome 19 (Chr19) of variant, reference (Ref) and Variant (Var) allele, Amino Acid (AA) position, AA1 (ref), AA2 (var), Supercentenarian carriers (shown for reference), Centenarians carriers, Nonagenarians carriers, Minor allele frequency (MAF) in 1000G EUR.

Are Supercentenarians Enriched for a Rare Protein-Altering Variant?

For people born around 1900, the odds of living to 110 are estimated to be less than 10^{-5} per birth [46], hence we assume that any genetic variant that contributes strongly to extreme longevity would also be rare. One possibility is that a specific mutation could alter the protein-coding region in a gene and confer a significant increase in longevity. Such a mutation could act in a dominant or recessive fashion, and might be shared by a significant fraction of the supercentenarian genomes but not by control genomes. We created a computational pipeline to determine whether our supercentenarian genomes are enriched for such a variant compared to controls (Figure 1). We annotated the variants in all of the female Caucasian genomes and retained those predicted to alter a protein. The polymorphism could be a single nucleotide polymorphism (SNP) or an insertion/deletion (Indel). The polymorphism could change the protein-coding sequence by causing a missense, frameshift, non-frameshift indel, nonsense (i.e., stop-gain), stop-loss, or splice-site disruption (Table S2). To identify rare variants, we filtered out common variants by removing any variant present in the public database dbSNP build 131. We then compared the frequency of the rare protein-altering variants in the supercentenarian genomes with that in the 379 European individuals in the 1000Genomes Project (1000G EUR) using a Fisher's Exact Test. In total, there were 13,892 rare protein-altering variants screened in the supercentenarian genomes. To adjust for multiple hypothesis testing, we applied a Bonferroni correction using a threshold of $P<0.05/13,892 = 3.6\times10^{-6}$. A variant that was present in four supercentenarian genomes but absent in all genomes in 1000G EUR would have a P-value of 7.4×10^{-07} and would have been detected by our method. Using high quality sequence calls, preliminary analysis suggested that one novel variant was shared by three supercentenarian subjects but not by the control genomes; however, Sanger sequencing subsequently showed that this was a sequencing error in the supercentenarian data. To increase our sensitivity for finding a longevity variant, we repeated the analysis including low quality calls. This yielded three additional novel variants in the supercentenarian genomes. However, Sanger sequencing showed that each of the three variants was a sequencing error. Even though the overall error rates for SNPs in WGS data (>40x coverage) are under 1% [27], the process of screening for apparent rare protein-altering variants also enriches for sequencing errors [33]. Therefore, we conclude that we found no evidence for a statistically significant enrichment of a specific protein-altering variant in the female Caucasian supercentenarian genomes compared with controls. Table S2 contains a list of the rare coding variants found in our 17 supercentenarian and 34 PGP control genomes.

Are Supercentenarians Enriched for a Gene with Rare Protein-Altering Variants?

Another possibility is that there may be a gene that confers extreme longevity when it is altered by any one of a number of protein alterations. Many of the supercentenarians may carry variants in the same gene, but the variant in each supercentenarian may be different. The variants could act in a dominant fashion and affect only one of the two alleles. Or else they could act in a recessive fashion such that both alleles would be affected, either with the same variant (homozygous) or with different mutations in each allele (compound heterozygous). Therefore, we asked whether any of the genes in the female Caucasian supercentenarian genomes was enriched for harboring

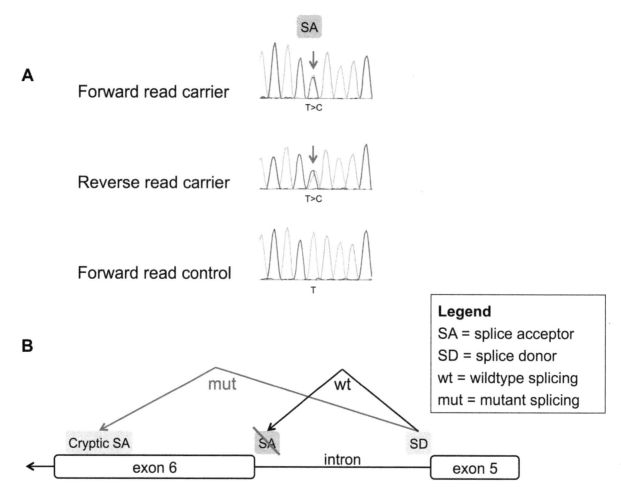

Figure 3. A supercentenarian with a known pathogenic mutation implicated in cardiomyopathy. (A) Sanger validation confirmed that one supercentenarian possessed a known pathogenic mutation in a splice acceptor site of Desmocollin-2 (DSC2), a component of the myocardial desmosome. (B) This rare mutation has been reported in 2 independent cases of Arrhythmogenic Right Ventricular Cardiomyopathy and has been shown to cause cryptic splicing and mRNA degradation [54,55].

rare protein-altering variants (either one or two copies) when compared to control genomes. Although the 1000G are a large group of controls, they cannot be used for a gene-based test as only the frequency of each variant is known, and not the individual genotypes. Therefore, as controls we used WGS of 34 Caucasian individuals (ages 21–79) from the Personal Genome Project (PGP) that were sequenced on the same platform as the supercentenarians [29].

We created a pipeline that used the annotated supercentenarian and PGP genomes from the previous analyses as input (see also Figure 1). Next, we filtered out common variants, which we defined as having a minor allele frequency of 1.5% or higher in the 1000G EUR (i.e., Caucasian populations in the 1000G). For each gene and each genome, we counted the number of rare protein-altering variants. We then computed the RVT1 statistic [35] to determine whether any gene showed a different burden of variants in supercentenarians vs. controls.

There were 10,508 genes with at least one rare, protein-altering variant in controls or supercentenarians. We used a Bonferroni threshold of $P<0.05/10,508 = 4.7\times10^{-06}$ to correct for multiple hypothesis testing. We were thus powered to detect genes altered in seven supercentenarians, if the gene harbored no alleles in any of the 34 controls. None of the genes showed a genome-wide significant enrichment using the Bonferroni threshold (Table S3).

Furthermore, we performed pathway analysis but failed to find a genetic pathway that showed a significant difference between supercentenarians and controls; specifically, we performed Gene Set Enrichment Analysis [47] using the results of the gene burden test, but no KEGG [48] pathway or Gene Ontology [49] category was significant at a false discovery rate <25%. To increase our sensitivity, we repeated our analyses including low-quality calls. This time, two genes initially appeared to be enriched for rare protein-altering alleles in the supercentenarian genomes, but Sanger sequencing showed that many of the variants were WGS errors.

We also specifically tested a recessive model for a gene conferring exceptional longevity, in which both alleles of a gene might harbor mutations. Supercentenarians would be enriched for carrying two or more different variants in such a gene (consistent with compound heterozygosity, if the mutations are out of phase), but controls would only carry zero or one mutation, but not two. The RVT1 test performs a logistic regression on the proportion of rare variants and hence might detect a bias in supercentenarians (two alleles in the gene) vs. the controls (one or zero alleles). But the RVT1 test was not specifically designed to compare the number of compound heterozygous cases and controls. We performed a gene-based test to compare the number of cases and controls carrying at least two variants in the same gene applying Fisher's

Exact Test to compute P values. We found that no gene was significantly enriched for two or more mutations after multiple testing correction (Table S4).

Although none of the genes showed a significant enrichment in the female Caucasian supercentenarian genomes, we nevertheless decided to follow up on the top three genes from the RVT1 burden test: TSHZ3, NAB2, and SCN11A (each with nominal $P = 4.3 \times 10^{-4}$). For SCN11A, three control genomes contained rare protein-altering variants with minor allele frequencies below 0.05 (but above 0.01). This result weakens the distinction between the supercentenarian genomes and the control genomes, and thus this gene was discarded from further analysis. NAB2 was discarded when Sanger sequencing showed that two out of four variants were sequencing errors. For TSHZ3, Sanger sequencing validated all four protein-altering variants, and this gene was chosen as a candidate for follow-up experiments.

To validate the result from the analysis of the supercentenarian genomes, we examined whether TSHZ3 is enriched for rare protein-altering variants in a cohort of 99 people aged 98–105 years from the Georgia Centenarian Study compared to 4,300 control exomes from the NHLBI Exome Variant Server [38] (Table 2). We obtained DNA samples of Caucasian nonagenarians and centenarians and performed Sanger sequencing of the TSHZ3 gene in all long-lived subjects. We used the same filter as for the genome-wide burden test of the supercentenarian genomes (MAF>0.01 in 1000G EUR.). We discovered a higher frequency of protein-altering alleles in the TSHZ3 sequence from 99 long-lived genomes (8 variants; 4%) than in the 4,300 Caucasian controls from the NHLBI cohort (213 variants; 2.5%), but this difference was not statistically significant ($P = 0.17$; Figure 2; Table 3). Analysis of a larger cohort of supercentenarians may show that the small difference in variants in TSHZ3 compared to controls is statistically significant.

In summary, the results from all three analyses do not show a statistical enrichment for a gene harboring rare protein-altering variants in female Caucasian supercentenarians compared to controls.

Do Supercentenarians Carry Pathogenic Alleles?

WGS has revealed that seemingly healthy individuals can carry pathogenic mutations that are potentially fatal [50]. Based on their extreme longevity, supercentenarians can be viewed as extremely healthy individuals. We asked whether these extremely healthy individuals might also carry pathogenic mutations. To do this, we analyzed all 17 supercentenarian genomes for the presence of pathogenic alleles as defined by the recent publication of the American College of Medical Genetics and Genomics (ACMG) [39]. The ACMG recommends that these mutations be reported to the patient, even if they are incidental findings. Their paper was a concerted and systematic effort resulting in a list of 56 genes, which are known to harbor strongly pathogenic mutations known to be fatal.

Two supercentenarians possessed a variant that was annotated as being pathogenic by the Human Gene Mutation Database (HGMD) or ClinVar. The first supercentenarian carried a missense SNP (L1564P) in the Breast Cancer Associated 1 (BRCA1) gene. Although null mutations in BRCA1 are pathogenic, the pathogenicity of L1564P is unclear. The L1564P variant appeared in the breast cancer of a 33-year old female along with another missense SNP (Q1785H) [51]. Using an *in vitro* assay, it was found that both missense SNPs in this breast cancer were mild alleles that partially reduced, but did not eliminate, BRCA1 protein function [52]. The L1564P mutation, the Q1785H mutation or both together may have caused breast cancer in this

one individual. Hence, the pathogenicity of the L1564P mutation in our supercentenarian remains unclear.

The second supercentenarian possessed a known pathogenic SNP (rs397514042) that disrupts a splice-site in Desmocollin-2 (DSC2). Desmocollin-2 is part of the myocardial desmosome structure in the heart. Loss-of-function mutations in DSC2 and other genes of the desmosome are associated with Arrhythmogenic Right Ventricular Cardiomyopathy (ARVC) [53]. rs397514042 causes an A -> G change in the splice acceptor site of exon 6 of DSC2. Sanger sequencing validated the presence of this SNP in the supercentenarian genome (Figure 3). The variant is annotated as a pathogenic mutation in HGMD, ClinVar, and the Locus Specific Database (LSDB) ARVD/C, which is part of the Leiden Open Variation Database (LOVD).

The rs397514042 SNP has been observed in two patients with ARVC [54,55]. Heuser et al. further showed that the mutant allele (rs397514042) leads to a decrease in DSC2 mRNA and protein in the patient compared to the reference allele. In zebrafish lacking DSC2, expression of the wild-type human allele rescued the mutant phenotype and led to normal desmosomes, but expression of the mutant human allele corresponding to rs397514042 did not fully rescue the mutant phenotype and resulted in malformed desmosomes. Although the evidence suggests that this SNP can be highly pathogenic, its penetrance is unknown. The supercentenarian subject carrying rs397514042 was asymptomatic to the best of our knowledge and died from a cause unrelated to cardiomyopathy. We conclude that at least 1 out of 17 supercentenarians possessed a known pathogenic SNP.

Discussion

We have sequenced the genomes of 17 supercentenarians (over 110 years of age) to see if we could uncover the genetic basis for their extreme longevity. We analyzed rare protein-altering variants, but found no strong evidence for enrichment of either a single variant or a single gene harboring different variants in female Caucasian supercentenarians compared to controls. From our gene-based analysis, the gene showing the most enrichment for protein-altering variants in supercentenarians compared to controls was the TSHZ3 transcription-factor gene. Because it was the top hit, we pursued this gene further in a study consisting of 99 genomes from subjects aged 98–105 years old. We found that TSHZ3 carried protein-altering variants in more of the long-lived subjects than the controls, although this difference was not statistically significant ($P = 0.17$).

A larger sample size would be required to establish whether the difference in frequency of protein-altering variants in TSHZ3 between subjects with extreme longevity compared to controls is statistically significant. We did not analyze single nucleotide variants in non-coding DNA in the supercentenarians because of the large number of non-coding variants compared to coding variants. Our analysis of putative rare protein-altering variants in the whole genome sequencing data led us to test a number of candidates, of which 30% were subsequently determined to be false positive variant calls in WGS data. This high false discovery rate is consistent with previous reports [34] and is largely due to a selection bias as sequencing errors often appear as rare protein-altering variants [33].

Our analyses show that it is extremely unlikely that there is a single gene harboring rare protein-altering variants shared by all supercentenarians but no controls. It is not surprising that a highly complex trait such as longevity is not explained by a single Mendelian gene.

To our surprise, we discovered that one of our supercentenarians carried a known pathogenic allele in the DSC2 gene associated with arrhythmogenic right ventricular cardiomyopathy (ARVC). This is a potentially fatal condition, causing affected individuals to die of sudden cardiac death. This example points out an important aspect about policy regarding the reporting of pathogenic mutations found in genomic sequences. The American College of Medical Genetics and Genomics identified a set of genes that can cause pathology when disrupted. But what is often not known is how frequently people with the variant have pathology (i.e., the penetrance). Our example shows that the DSC2 pathogenic mutation rs397514042 did not cause a fatal cardiomyopathy during the proband's over 110 years of life. Thus, the presence of this mutation in the DNA sequence of a young person today should be reported to him/her and their families with caution, as it may or may not result in arrhythmogenic right ventricular cardiomyopathy. Generally, variants that are annotated as pathogenic are of unknown penetrance [56].

The full set of protein-coding variants are given in Table S2 and the full-genome sequence from this paper are publicly available via dbGAP and Google Genomics. By making our data available as a public resource, we hope it can be included in future meta-analyses of supercentenarian genomes. Supercentenarians are extremely rare and their genomes could hold secrets for the genetic basis of extreme longevity.

Supporting Information

Figure S1 Genome coverage for supercentenarians. Average genome coverage is shown for the whole genome (dark grey) and exome (light grey) of all 17 supercentenarians. Coverage is shown for ≥1x and ≥20x coverage.

Figure S2 Principal Component Analysis of supercentenarian ancestry. PCA was performed on all 17 supercentenarians (black dots) and HapMap genotypes. All Caucasian supercentenarians (CAU) clustered with Caucasian HapMap

individuals, while the two supercentenarians of Hispanic ethnicity clustered with Mexican HapMap individuals and the African-American supercentenarian (AA) clustered with African HapMap individuals. HapMap populations are ASW (African ancestry in Southwest USA), CEU (Utah residents with Northern and Western European ancestry from the CEPH collection), CHB (Han Chinese in Beijing, China), CHD (Chinese in Metropolitan Denver, Colorado), GIH (Gujarati Indians in Houston, Texas), JPT (Japanese in Tokyo, Japan), LWK (Luhya in Webuye, Kenya), MXL (Mexican ancestry in Los Angeles, California), MKK (Maasai in Kinyawa, Kenya), TSI (Toscani in Italy) and YRI (Yoruba in Ibadan, Nigeria). See insert for color codes.

Table S1 Baseline statistics for 34 Caucasian PGP genomes.

Table S2 All variants in protein coding regions with genotypes for all 17 supercentenarian and 34 PGP control genomes.

Table S3 Burden of rare protein-altering variants per gene in supercentenarians and controls.

Table S4 Gene-based Fisher's Exact test for recessive model of rare protein-altering variants in supercentenarians and controls.

Author Contributions

Conceived and designed the experiments: SKK LSC LH HJG KF. Performed the experiments: HJG KF JCR HL GG GJM JDS. Analyzed the data: HJG KF JCR HL GG GJM JDS. Contributed reagents/materials/analysis tools: NSC LSC. Contributed to the writing of the manuscript: HJG KF JCR NSC HL GG GJM JDS LH LSC SKK.

References

1. Coles LS, Muir ME, Young RD (2014) Validated worldwide supercentenarians, living and recently deceased. Rejuvenation Res 17: 80–83. doi:10.1089/rej.2014.1553
2. Evert J, Lawler E, Bogan H, Perls T (2003) Morbidity profiles of centenarians: survivors, delayers, and escapers. J Gerontol A Biol Sci Med Sci 58: 232–237.
3. Terry DF, Wilcox MA, McCormick MA, Perls TT (2004) Cardiovascular disease delay in centenarian offspring. J Gerontol A Biol Sci Med Sci 59: 385–389.
4. Willcox DC, Willcox BJ, Wang N-C, He Q, Rosenbaum M, et al. (2008) Life at the extreme limit: phenotypic characteristics of supercentenarians in Okinawa. J Gerontol A Biol Sci Med Sci 63: 1201–1208.
5. Andersen SL, Sebastiani P, Dworkis DA, Feldman L, Perls TT (2012) Health span approximates life span among many supercentenarians: compression of morbidity at the approximate limit of life span. J Gerontol A Biol Sci Med Sci 67: 395–405. doi:10.1093/gerona/glr223.
6. Pavlidis N, Stanta G, Audisio RA (2012) Cancer prevalence and mortality in centenarians: a systematic review. Crit Rev Oncol Hematol 83: 145–152. doi:10.1016/j.critrevonc.2011.09.007.
7. Herskind AM, McGue M, Holm NV, Sørensen TI, Harvald B, et al. (1996) The heritability of human lifespan: a population-based study of 2872 Danish twin pairs born 1870–1900. Hum Genet 97: 319–323.
8. Schoenmaker M, de Craen AJM, de Meijer PHEM, Beekman M, Blauw GJ, et al. (2006) Evidence of genetic enrichment for exceptional survival using a family approach: the Leiden Longevity Study. Eur J Hum Genet EJHG 14: 79–84. doi:10.1038/sj.ejhg.5201508.
9. vB Hjelmborg J, Iachine I, Skytthe A, Vaupel JW, McGue M, et al. (2006) Genetic influence on human lifespan and longevity. Hum Genet 119: 312–321. doi:10.1007/s00439-006-0144-y.
10. Sebastiani P, Perls TT (2012) The genetics of extreme longevity: lessons from the new England centenarian study. Front Genet 3: 277. doi:10.3389/fgene.2012.00277.

11. Perls TT, Wilmoth J, Levenson R, Drinkwater M, Cohen M, et al. (2002) Life-long sustained mortality advantage of siblings of centenarians. Proc Natl Acad Sci U S A 99: 8442–8447. doi:10.1073/pnas.122587599.
12. Perls T, Kohler IV, Andersen S, Schoenhofen E, Pennington J, et al. (2007) Survival of parents and siblings of supercentenarians. J Gerontol A Biol Sci Med Sci 62: 1028–1034.
13. Rajpathak SN, Liu Y, Ben-David O, Reddy S, Atzmon G, et al. (2011) Lifestyle factors of people with exceptional longevity. J Am Geriatr Soc 59: 1509–1512. doi:10.1111/j.1532-5415.2011.03498.x.
14. Suh Y, Atzmon G, Cho M-O, Hwang D, Liu B, et al. (2008) Functionally significant insulin-like growth factor I receptor mutations in centenarians. Proc Natl Acad Sci U S A 105: 3438–3442. doi:10.1073/pnas.0705467105.
15. Willcox BJ, Donlon TA, He Q, Chen R, Grove JS, et al. (2008) FOXO3A genotype is strongly associated with human longevity. Proc Natl Acad Sci U S A 105: 13987–13992. doi:10.1073/pnas.0801030105.
16. Nebel A, Kleindorp R, Caliebe A, Nothnagel M, Blanché H, et al. (2011) A genome-wide association study confirms APOE as the major gene influencing survival in long-lived individuals. Mech Ageing Dev 132: 324–330. doi:10.1016/j.mad.2011.06.008.
17. Deelen J, Beekman M, Uh H-W, Helmer Q, Kuningas M, et al. (2011) Genome-wide association study identifies a single major locus contributing to survival into old age; the APOE locus revisited. Aging Cell 10: 686–698. doi:10.1111/j.1474-9726.2011.00705.x.
18. Sebastiani P, Solovieff N, Dewan AT, Walsh KM, Puca A, et al. (2012) Genetic signatures of exceptional longevity in humans. PloS One 7: e29848. doi:10.1371/journal.pone.0029848.
19. Sebastiani P, Riva A, Montano M, Pham P, Torkamani A, et al. (2012) Whole genome sequences of a male and female supercentenarian, ages greater than 114 years. Front Genet 2: 90. doi:10.3389/fgene.2011.00090.
20. Ye K, Beekman M, Lameijer E-W, Zhang Y, Moed MH, et al. (2013) Aging as accelerated accumulation of somatic variants: whole-genome sequencing of

centenarian and middle-aged monozygotic twin pairs. Twin Res Hum Genet Off J Int Soc Twin Stud 16: 1026–1032. doi:10.1017/thg.2013.73.

21. Holstege H, Pfeiffer W, Sie D, Hulsman M, Nicholas TJ, et al. (2014) Somatic mutations found in the healthy blood compartment of a 115-yr-old woman demonstrate oligoclonal hematopoiesis. Genome Res 24: 733–742. doi:10.1101/gr.162131.113.

22. Untergasser A, Cutcutache I, Koressaar T, Ye J, Faircloth BC, et al. (2012) Primer3–new capabilities and interfaces. Nucleic Acids Res 40: e115. doi:10.1093/nar/gks596.

23. International HapMap 3 Consortium, Altshuler DM, Gibbs RA, Peltonen L, Altshuler DM, et al. (2010) Integrating common and rare genetic variation in diverse human populations. Nature 467: 52–58. doi:10.1038/nature09298.

24. Yang J, Lee SH, Goddard ME, Visscher PM (2011) GCTA: a tool for genome-wide complex trait analysis. Am J Hum Genet 88: 76–82. doi:10.1016/j.ajhg.2010.11.011.

25. Huff CD, Witherspoon DJ, Simonson TS, Xing J, Watkins WS, et al. (2011) Maximum-likelihood estimation of recent shared ancestry (ERSA). Genome Res 21: 768–774. doi:10.1101/gr.115972.110.

26. Li H, Glusman G, Hu H, Shankaracharya, Caballero J, et al. (2014) Relationship estimation from whole-genome sequence data. PLoS Genet 10: e1004144. doi:10.1371/journal.pgen.1004144.

27. Drmanac R, Sparks AB, Callow MJ, Halpern AL, Burns NL, et al. (2010) Human genome sequencing using unchained base reads on self-assembling DNA nanoarrays. Science 327: 78–81. doi:10.1126/science.1181498.

28. Perl Development Team (2013) The Perl Programming Language. Available: http://www.perl.org/. Accessed 27 February 2014.

29. Ball MP, Thakuria JV, Zaranek AW, Clegg T, Rosenbaum AM, et al. (2012) A public resource facilitating clinical use of genomes. Proc Natl Acad Sci 109: 11920–11927. doi:10.1073/pnas.1201904109.

30. Wang K, Li M, Hakonarson H (2010) ANNOVAR: functional annotation of genetic variants from high-throughput sequencing data. Nucleic Acids Res 38: e164–e164. doi:10.1093/nar/gkq603.

31. Consortium T 1000 GP (2012) An integrated map of genetic variation from 1,092 human genomes. Nature 491: 56–65. doi:10.1038/nature11632.

32. Sherry ST, Ward M-H, Kholodov M, Baker J, Phan L, et al. (2001) dbSNP: the NCBI database of genetic variation. Nucleic Acids Res 29: 308–311. doi:10.1093/nar/29.1.308.

33. MacArthur DG, Balasubramanian S, Frankish A, Huang N, Morris J, et al. (2012) A systematic survey of loss-of-function variants in human protein-coding genes. Science 335: 823–828. doi:10.1126/science.1215040.

34. Han J, Ryu S, Moskowitz DM, Rothenberg D, Leahy DJ, et al. (2013) Discovery of novel non-synonymous SNP variants in 988 candidate genes from 6 centenarians by target capture and next-generation sequencing. Mech Ageing Dev. doi:10.1016/j.mad.2013.01.005.

35. Morris AP, Zeggini E (2010) An evaluation of statistical approaches to rare variant analysis in genetic association studies. Genet Epidemiol 34: 188–193. doi:10.1002/gepi.20450.

36. R Core Team (2013) R: A Language and Environment for Statistical Computing. Available: http://www.r-project.org/. Accessed 27 February 2014.

37. Poon LW, Clayton GM, Martin P, Johnson MA, Courtenay BC, et al. (1992) The Georgia Centenarian Study. Int J Aging Hum Dev 34: 1–17. doi:10.2190/8M7H-CJL7-6K5T-UMFV.

38. Tennessen JA, Bigham AW, O'Connor TD, Fu W, Kenny EE, et al. (2012) Evolution and functional impact of rare coding variation from deep sequencing of human exomes. Science 337: 64–69. doi:10.1126/science.1219240.

39. Green RC, Berg JS, Grody WW, Kalia SS, Korf BR, et al. (2013) ACMG recommendations for reporting of incidental findings in clinical exome and genome sequencing. Genet Med Off J Am Coll Med Genet 15: 565–574. doi:10.1038/gim.2013.73.

40. Landrum MJ, Lee JM, Riley GR, Jang W, Rubinstein WS, et al. (2014) ClinVar: public archive of relationships among sequence variation and human phenotype. Nucleic Acids Res 42: D980–985. doi:10.1093/nar/gkt1113.

41. Cooper DN, Krawczak M (1996) Human Gene Mutation Database. Hum Genet 98: 629.

42. Richards CS, Bale S, Bellissimo DB, Das S, Grody WW, et al. (2008) ACMG recommendations for standards for interpretation and reporting of sequence variations: Revisions 2007. Genet Med Off J Am Coll Med Genet 10: 294–300. doi:10.1097/GIM.0b013e31816b5cae.

43. Van der Zwaag PA, Jongbloed JDH, van den Berg MP, van der Smagt JJ, Jongbloed R, et al. (2009) A genetic variants database for arrhythmogenic right ventricular dysplasia/cardiomyopathy. Hum Mutat 30: 1278–1283. doi:10.1002/humu.21064.

44. Fokkema IFAC, Taschner PEM, Schaafsma GCP, Celli J, Laros JFJ, et al. (2011) LOVD v.2.0: the next generation in gene variant databases. Hum Mutat 32: 557–563. doi:10.1002/humu.21438.

45. Gerontology Research Group (2014) Table A - Verified Supercentenarians. Available: http://grg.org/Adams/A.HTM. Accessed 21 July 2014.

46. Schoenhofen EA, Wyszynski DF, Andersen S, Pennington J, Young R, et al. (2006) Characteristics of 32 supercentenarians. J Am Geriatr Soc 54: 1237–1240. doi:10.1111/j.1532-5415.2006.00826.x.

47. Subramanian A, Tamayo P, Mootha VK, Mukherjee S, Ebert BL, et al. (2005) Gene set enrichment analysis: A knowledge-based approach for interpreting genome-wide expression profiles. Proc Natl Acad Sci U S A 102: 15545–15550. doi:10.1073/pnas.0506580102.

48. Kanehisa M, Goto S, Sato Y, Furumichi M, Tanabe M (2012) KEGG for integration and interpretation of large-scale molecular data sets. Nucleic Acids Res 40: D109–D114. doi:10.1093/nar/gkr988.

49. Gene Ontology Consortium (2013) Gene Ontology annotations and resources. Nucleic Acids Res 41: D530–535. doi:10.1093/nar/gks1050.

50. Dewey FE, Grove ME, Pan C, Goldstein BA, Bernstein JA, et al. (2014) Clinical interpretation and implications of whole-genome sequencing. JAMA J Am Med Assoc 311: 1035–1045. doi:10.1001/jama.2014.1717.

51. Panguluri RC, Brody LC, Modali R, Utley K, Adams-Campbell L, et al. (1999) BRCA1 mutations in African Americans. Hum Genet 105: 28–31.

52. Carvalho MA, Marsillac SM, Karchin R, Manoukian S, Grist S, et al. (2007) Determination of cancer risk associated with germ line BRCA1 missense variants by functional analysis. Cancer Res 67: 1494–1501. doi:10.1158/0008-5472.CAN-06-3297.

53. Van Tintelen JP, Hofstra RM, Wiesfeld AC, van den Berg MP, Hauer RN, et al. (2007) Molecular genetics of arrhythmogenic right ventricular cardiomyopathy: emerging horizon? Curr Opin Cardiol 22: 185–192. doi:10.1097/HCO.0-b013e3280d942c4.

54. Heuser A, Plovie ER, Ellinor PT, Grossmann KS, Shin JT, et al. (2006) Mutant Desmocollin-2 Causes Arrhythmogenic Right Ventricular Cardiomyopathy. Am J Hum Genet 79: 1081–1088. doi:10.1086/509044.

55. Baskin B, Skinner JR, Sanatani S, Terespolsky D, Krahn AD, et al. (2013) TMEM43 mutations associated with arrhythmogenic right ventricular cardio-myopathy in non-Newfoundland populations. Hum Genet 132: 1245–1252. doi:10.1007/s00439-013-1323-2.

56. Bick AG, Flannick J, Ito K, Cheng S, Vasan RS, et al. (2012) Burden of Rare Sarcomere Gene Variants in the Framingham and Jackson Heart Study Cohorts. Am J Hum Genet 91: 513–519. doi:10.1016/j.ajhg.2012.07.017.

21

Genome-Wide and Gene-Based Association Studies of Anxiety Disorders in European and African American Samples

Takeshi Otowa[1,2], **Brion S. Maher**[3], **Steven H. Aggen**[1], **Joseph L. McClay**[4], **Edwin J. van den Oord**[4], **John M. Hettema**[1]*

1 Department of Psychiatry, Virginia Institute for Psychiatric and Behavioral Genetics, Virginia Commonwealth University, Richmond, Virginia, United States of America, **2** Department of Neuropsychiatry, Graduate School of Medicine, University of Tokyo, Tokyo, Japan, **3** Department of Mental Health, Johns Hopkins Bloomberg School of Public Health, Baltimore, Maryland, United States of America, **4** Department of Pharmacy, Center for Biomarker Research and Personalized Medicine, Virginia Commonwealth University, Richmond, Virginia, United States of America

Abstract

Anxiety disorders (ADs) are common mental disorders caused by a combination of genetic and environmental factors. Since ADs are highly comorbid with each other, partially due to shared genetic basis, studying AD phenotypes in a coordinated manner may be a powerful strategy for identifying potential genetic loci for ADs. To detect these loci, we performed genome-wide association studies (GWAS) of ADs. In addition, as a complementary approach to single-locus analysis, we also conducted gene- and pathway-based analyses. GWAS data were derived from the control sample of the Molecular Genetics of Schizophrenia (MGS) project (2,540 European American and 849 African American subjects) genotyped on the Affymetrix GeneChip 6.0 array. We applied two phenotypic approaches: (1) categorical case-control comparisons (CC) based upon psychiatric diagnoses, and (2) quantitative phenotypic factor scores (FS) derived from a multivariate analysis combining information across the clinical phenotypes. Linear and logistic models were used to analyse the association with ADs using FS and CC traits, respectively. At the single locus level, no genome-wide significant association was found. A transpopulation gene-based meta-analysis across both ethnic subsamples using FS identified three genes (*MFAP3L* on 4q32.3, *NDUFAB1* and *PALB2* on 16p12) with genome-wide significance (false discovery rate (FDR] <5%). At the pathway level, several terms such as transcription regulation, cytokine binding, and developmental process were significantly enriched in ADs (FDR <5%). Our approaches studying ADs as quantitative traits and utilizing the full GWAS data may be useful in identifying susceptibility genes and pathways for ADs.

Editor: Sonia Brucki, University Of São Paulo, Brazil

Funding: This research was supported by NIH grant R01MH087646 (JMH). Samples and associated phenotype data for the MGS study were collected under the following grants: NIMH Schizophrenia Genetics Initiative U01s: MH046276 (CR Cloninger), MH46289 (C Kaufmann), and MH46318 (MT Tsuang); and MGS Part 1 (MGS1) and Part 2 (MGS2) R01s: MH67257 (NG Buccola), MH59588 (BJ Mowry), MH59571 (PV Gejman), MH59565 (Robert Freedman), MH59587 (F Amin), MH60870 (WF Byerley), MH59566 (DW Black), MH59586 (JM Silverman), MH61675 (DF Levinson), and MH60879 (CR Cloninger). TO was supported by a research fellowship from the Japan Society for the Promotion of Science (no. 21–8373). The funders had no role in study design, data collection and analysis, decision to publish, or preparation of the manuscript.

* Email: jhettema@vcu.edu

Introduction

Anxiety disorders (ADs) are common mental disorders characterized by excessive, prolonged, and debilitating levels of anxiety, with substantial lifetime prevalence [1]. They are subdivided into clinical diagnostic categories such as generalized anxiety disorder (GAD), panic disorder (PD), posttraumatic stress disorder (PTSD), obsessive-compulsive disorder (OCD) and phobias, based on their onset, symptoms, and course. ADs are complex diseases that are caused by a combination of genetic and environmental factors. Family and twin studies have demonstrated that ADs have significant familial aggregation, and their heritability estimates range from 30 to 50% [2,3].

Numerous genetic studies of ADs have been conducted targeting candidate genes. The most intensively studied candidate genes are related to neurotransmitter systems involved in the regulation of anxiety, neuropeptides, and stress response [3]. However, most of these studies have produced inconsistent or negative results. One of the reasons for inconsistency between studies may be due to Type I error from poorly-chosen candidates or Type II error due to small sample size underpowered to detect individual susceptibility variants of small effect.

Genome-wide association studies (GWAS) have proven to be a successful method for the identification of common genetic variants that increase susceptibility to complex diseases or traits. Recently, several GWAS of ADs such as PD [4,5], PTSD [6,7,8],

OCD [9], and phobias [10] have been published. However, the top findings in these studies have not overlapped with previous candidates and explained only small proportions of the total genetic variance. The failure to replicate the same single nucleotide polymorphisms (SNP) between studies may be attributable to poor power with small sample sizes and allelic and/or phenotypic heterogeneity across populations.

GWAS usually focus on the most significant individual variants without considering the global evidence of the gene tested. Unlike genetic variants that have different allele frequencies, linkage disequilibrium (LD) structure, and heterogeneity across diverse human populations, the gene itself is highly consistent across populations [11]. Gene-based analysis might produce more consistent results and improve power with a smaller number of statistical tests. Furthermore, with the gene as the unit of analysis, biological pathway analysis using available functional information might facilitate the identification of the pathogenic mechanisms of complex diseases such as ADs. Therefore, both gene- and pathway-based analyses could have better statistical power for detecting susceptibility loci and provide a complementary approach to single-locus analysis.

Most genetic association studies focus on categorical traits comparing allele frequencies for diagnosed cases versus controls. However, if GWAS indicate that multiple genes affect these disorders, this implies that their genetic liability is distributed quantitatively rather than qualitatively [12]. For common disorders like ADs, disease states can be interpreted as being the extremes of continuous liability dimensions. Therefore, statistical power can be enhanced by studying the broader distribution than by dichotomizing the same distribution into cases and controls [12,13]. Furthermore, previous studies suggest that ADs exhibit strong lifetime comorbidity, partially due to shared genetic risk factors between them and with anxious personality traits like neuroticism [14,15,16]. Therefore, studying AD phenotypes in a coordinated manner is an alternative approach to increase the statistical power for identifying susceptibility genes for ADs, as demonstrated by prior reports from our group [17].

The aim of this study is to conduct GWAS of ADs as quantitative traits as well as categorical traits in unselected population samples from the United States consisting of 2540 European American (EA) and 849 African American (AA) subjects. To optimally utilize the GWAS data sets, we examined our results at 3 levels: (i) SNP-based analyses (ii) gene-based analyses and meta-analyses combining these results, and (iii) gene-set based analyses.

Materials and Methods

Subjects

Data for the analyses came from the "control" sample originally part of a large schizophrenia study (Molecular Genetics of Schizophrenia (MGS)). The full MGS control sample is described in detail elsewhere [18]. Briefly, the available sample consisted of unrelated subjects selected during 2004–2007 by random digit dialing from approximately 60,000 US households. Institutional review board approval was obtained at NorthShore University HealthSystem. Participants first consented online to use of their DNA and phenotypic information for the study of any illness or trait and then signed an identical hard-copy consent at the time of venipuncture. They were screened and excluded for psychotic and bipolar disorders for use as a comparison group for genetic association studies of these more severe psychiatric phenotypes but were not excluded for other common psychiatric disorders such as depression and anxiety. Self-reported ancestry [19] was confirmed

by genotypic data with ancestry-informative markers [18]. The data were obtained with permission from dbGaP (Database of Genotypes and Phenotypes, http://www.ncbi.nlm.nih.gov/gap, Study Accessions: phs000021.v3.p2 ("Genetic Association Information Network (GAIN)") and phs000167.v1.p1 "nonGAIN"). Data for the EA subjects were combined from both the GAIN (n = 1442) and nonGAIN (n = 1367) datasets. These derived from the same original sample but had been separately deposited into dbGaP. Data for the AA subjects were obtained from the GAIN subsample (n = 979).

Diagnostic measures

All MGS control subjects completed an online psychiatric screening interview that included the lifetime version of the Composite International Diagnostic Interview, Short Form (CIDI-SF) [20]. The CIDI-SF is accurate compared with the full CIDI [20] and has been used for self-report. Because of its brevity and cost effectiveness, the CIDI-SF is suitable for an online interview to screen common psychiatric disorders in the general population [18]. For those subjects with requisite response data, we applied DSM-based algorithms to the CIDI-SF responses to obtain the following six lifetime clinical phenotypes: major depression (lifetime prevalence of total sample, 30.0%), GAD (18.4%), panic attacks (2.1%), agoraphobia (6.5%), social phobia (14.3%), and specific phobia (11.7%). We note that only panic attacks, and not panic disorder, could be identified due to limitations in the items included in that section of the CIDI-SF. In the present study, we used the latter five AD phenotypes for the analyses. Besides attempting to identify subjects meeting full symptomatic criteria ("cases", score = 2), we also sought to differentiate subjects who were highly symptomatic but did not meet full criteria ("subsyndromal", score = 1) versus those with few or no reported symptoms ("unaffecteds", score = 0). This was operationalized by either (i) keeping the full symptomatic criteria and removing the diagnostic requirements of distress/impairment or (ii) reducing the symptomatic severity or duration. This strategy produced ordered, rather than classification variables that served as input indicators for the factor analyses described below. It also identifies more extreme comparison groups for use in case-control (CC) analyses, since diagnostic thresholds are defined for clinical purposes and may not sufficiently differentiate subjects by the risk alleles they carry.

Given prior evidence supporting shared genetic liability across these AD phenotypes [14,15,16], we performed factor analyses to estimate an overall score (factor score; FS) for each subject. Due to substantial correlation between phenotypic and genetic factor structure of ADs, this approach should provide FS that represent shared genetic risk. We conducted the analyses as reported in our previous paper [17]. Briefly, we entered scores for the five AD clinical phenotypes into factor analyses in Mplus (version 4) [21]. Exploratory factor analyses with one versus two latent factors each produced reasonable solutions that adequately fit the data, so, we chose to use the former solution representing a single common factor. The overall factor structure was similar across the AA and EA subjects although their thresholds somewhat differed, indicating differences in frequency of phenotypic scores (prevalence) between populations. We constrained factor loadings to be equal across these two samples in order to score all subjects in a manner that was consistent across populations. A confirmatory factor analysis was carried out in Mplus to estimate a single FS for each subject for use as quantitative phenotype in association analyses.

Statistical analyses

To correct for multiple testing, false discovery rate (FDR, q-value) was calculated, which is an estimate of the proportion of false discoveries among all significant markers when the corresponding p-value is used as the threshold for declaring significance [22]. This approach provides a good way to find true effects controlling false discoveries and is much less affected by number of tests, which is an arbitrary factor [23]. Q-values less than 5% and 25%, respectively, were taken as significant and suggestively significant for SNP-, gene-, and pathway-based analyses.

SNP-based analysis. As previously described in detail [24], DNA samples were genotyped at the Broad Institute using the Affymetrix 6.0 array. Quality control procedures excluded about 5% of all subjects due to low genotype call rates (<0.95), heterozygosity outliers, sample duplicates, sex typing discrepancies, or genetic relatedness. SNPs were excluded if a SNP call rate <0.95, Hardy-Weinberg equilibrium p-value $<1 \times 10^{-5}$, and minor allele frequency (MAF) <0.05 for both cases and controls. A total of 626,833 (EA) and 730,090 (AA) autosomal SNPs were available for further analyses.

We performed regression analyses assuming additive genetic effects in PLINK [25] to test the main effects of SNPs on the outcome phenotypes. These included gender and age as covariates, given their strong association with ADs. To account for the genetic substructure of human populations, multidimensional scaling (MDS) was used. MDS produced eight components, none of which were correlated with FS or CC status. Therefore, no MDS dimensions were included as covariates in the analyses. In the present study, two phenotypic strategies were compared. First, linear regression analyses including all subjects were conducted using FS as a quantitative outcome variable. These scores incorporate all of the phenotypic information in a statistically coordinated fashion from the factor analyses. Second, logistic regression was applied in a CC approach, designating subjects scoring a "2" for any of the clinical phenotypes as a "case" versus those scoring "0" on all as "hyper-normal" controls (no full or subsyndromal AD or major depression).

Quantile-quantile (QQ) plots were used to evaluate overall significance of the GWA analyses and the potential impact of population stratification. The inflation factor λ was calculated on the basis of the median chi-square. Haploview 4.2 [26] was used to create Manhattan plots of p-values from the GWA analyses and to examine LD between markers. Power calculations were performed using the program Quanto v1.2.4 (http://hydra.usc.edu/gxe).

Gene-based analysis. Gene-based association analysis in each population was performed using the versatile gene-based test for genome-wide association studies (VEGAS) [27]. In brief, VEGAS tests for association on a per-gene basis, by considering the p-value of all SNPs within genes (including +/−50 kb from the 5′ and 3′ UTR), accounting for LD and number of SNPs per gene. For a given gene with n SNPs, association p-values were first converted to upper tail chi-squared statistics with 1 degree of freedom (df). The observed gene-based test statistic was then the sum of all of the chi-squared 1 df statistics within the gene. Using the Monte Carlo simulation, the empirical gene-based p-value was calculated as the proportion of simulated test statistics that exceeded the observed gene-based test statistic.

Previous studies have found consistent genetic effects on common diseases across different racial groups even if LD patterns and allele frequencies differ considerably across populations [11,28–30]. Therefore, to increase statistical power, trans-population meta-analysis of gene-based GWA analyses using FS or CC was conducted. To test overall significance, Stouffer's Z-score

method [31] implemented in METAL [32] was used. Z-scores for each gene were combined across samples in a weighted sum, with weights proportional to the square-root of the sample size for each study [31]. Given unequal numbers of cases and controls, the effective sample sizes were calculated as $N_{eff} = 4/(1/N_{cases}+1/N_{controls})$ for the CC analyses.

Gene-set enrichment analysis. Gene-set enrichment analysis was carried out to complement the results from gene-based GWA analyses and to determine which potential biological pathways could play a role in ADs. For the analysis, we included all genes from the gene-based meta-analysis test with a p-value < 0.01 using the public domain tool provided by the Database for Annotation, Visualization and Integrated Discovery (DAVID) bioinformatics platform [33]. We used gene ontology (GO) to create gene-sets because it provided the largest amount of information and is well structured. Considering the redundant nature of annotations, groups of similar annotations were combined using 'Functional Annotation Clustering' (kappa value>0.5). We selected the best significantly enriched terms of individual groups. By performing these enrichment analyses, we attempted to identify whether the genes most associated with ADs were more prevalent in any known GO terms than would be expected by chance.

Results

SNP-based analysis

After application of QC parameters, 2540 EA and 849 AA subjects had FS values available for analyses. Of these, samples for case-control analysis consisted of 1697 EA subjects (757 cases and 940 controls) and 597 AA subjects (324 cases and 273 controls), respectively (Table 1). The genomic inflation factors λ for the FS and CC analyses, respectively, were 1.004 and 1.005 in EA and 1.004 and 1.008 in AA, suggesting no significant inflation (Figure S1 in File S1). The QQ and Manhattan plots for theses SNP-based GWA analyses are displayed in Figures S1 and S2 in File S1.

Overall, no SNP reached genome-wide significance or suggestive significance for any GWA analyses in either the EA or AA samples (Table 2 and Figure S2 in File S1). The most significant signal was observed at SNP rs4692589 located in *MFAP3L* on 4q32.3 from the results using the FS traits in the EA sample ($p = 8.63 \times 10^{-7}$, $q = 0.37$; Table 2). Of note, among top findings in the same analysis was SNP rs2170820, located in *TMEM132D* (12q24.3), a gene which has been reported to be associated with PD in a European Caucasian sample [4].

Gene-based analysis

Using VEGAS, SNPs in each GWA analysis were mapped to approximately 17,700 genes (FS-EA: 17,660, FS-AA: 17,678, CC-EA: 17,655, CC-AA: 17,669). No deviations from the expected distribution of p-values were observed in the QQ plots of each gene-based analysis (Figure S3 in File S1). Using FS, a gene reached a significant q-value (*MFAP3L*, $q = 0.035$; Table 3) and another 11 genes reached suggestive significance ($q<0.25$) in the EA sample, whereas none reached suggestive significance in the AA sample. Using CC, three genes reached suggestive significance (*PF4V1*, *CXCL1*, and *CXCL6*) in the EA sample, whereas none reached suggestive significance in the AA sample.

Although there was no full overlap of top associated genes between the two populations, several genes showed evidence of association in both. Therefore, we conducted trans-population meta-analyses of gene-based studies using FS or CC. Top findings from the gene-based meta-analysis using FS and CC are shown in Table 3. Three genes met the criteria for genome-wide signifi-

Table 1. Demographic characteristics of European and African American samples.

Sample	European American		African American	
	case	control	case	control
Factor score	2540		849	
Gender ratio (female/male)	1.07		1.60	
Age (s.d.)	50.8 (16.4)		45.6 (13.3)	
Case control	757	940	324	273
Gender ratio (female/male)	1.72	0.67	2.34	1.05
Age (s.d.)	48.3 (14.6)	52.1 (17.2)	44.4 (12.6)	46.2 (13.3)

s.d., standard deviation.

cance according to the threshold that allows for 5% false discovery rate (*NDUFAB1*, *PALB2*, and *MFAP3L*; all q-values $= 0.028$). Ten other genes in five loci reached a suggestively significant level using FS (4q32, 11p15, 16p12, 20p13, and 20q11), while three genes reached the genome-wide suggestive level using CC (*PF4V1*, *CXCL1*, and *CXCL6*; Table 3).

Gene-set enrichment analysis

We next examined all genes with $p < 0.01$ in the gene-based meta-analysis to see whether they were enriched with known GO terms, using DAVID with the whole genome background as a base set. The numbers of genes included in the analyses were 296 (FS) and 322 (CC). GO enrichment analysis showed that two terms using FS ("pattern specification process" and "cytokine binding") and two terms using CC ("nucleoplasm" and "transcription regulator activity") were significantly enriched in ADs ($q < 0.05$) (Table 4).

Discussion

We report here the results from the GWAS of ADs in two populations using quantitative and categorical phenotypes at SNP, gene, and pathway levels. We included 2540 EA and 849 AA subjects from the MGS control sample and conducted association analyses using two phenotypic approaches that sought to combine information across these disorders based upon prior research that suggests that they possess shared genetic risk factors. The first utilized factor analysis to extract a single phenotypic score for each subject for use as a quantitative trait. The second approach focused on categorical diagnoses that compared allele frequencies for clinical cases versus hyper-normal controls.

There were notable differences between results obtained using the two phenotypic methods. Most of the top SNPs were not the same, although many that were nominally significant in one were also in the other. The overall significance of SNPs (p- and q-values) was greater using FS than CC in the EA sample. This is not surprising, as the factor analytic phenotypes should provide more powerful targets for genetic association than the categorical phenotypes for several reasons: quantitative traits generally have greater information content, and there were more subjects with useable quantitative traits than categorical traits [34]. However, this was not the case with the AA sample where the significance of top findings was similar between the FS and CC analyses (Tables 2). In the AA sample, the difference in the sample sizes between the FS and CC analyses was not as large as for the EA sample, which may result in the smaller differences in power.

At the SNP level, none of the SNP results reached genome-wide significance. The most likely reasons for the modest p-values seen in each GWA analysis may be insufficient power to detect very small genetic effects. In the FS analyses, the power of our samples were 35% in EA (n = 2540) and 0.6% in AA (n = 849) with an additive model, a type I error rate of 5×10^{-8}, and an effect size explaining of 1% total variance. In the CC analyses, the power of the samples were 0.09% in EA (757 cases vs. 940 controls) and 0.01% (324 cases vs. 273 controls) with the log-additive model, a type I error rate of 5×10^{-8}, a frequency of 0.25 and an effect size of 1.2. Therefore, it was not surprising that we could not detect any locus of genome-wide significance.

While SNP-based GWA analysis focuses on the most significant individual variants, the gene-based approach tests the global null hypothesis about the SNPs located per gene. Gene-based tests allowed us to explore the impact of multiple variants in a gene even if the gene did not contain any SNP reaching genome-wide significance. Therefore, we performed gene-based GWA analyses in the present study. Only when using FS in the trans-population gene-based meta-analysis did we detect significant association signals in three genes (*MFAP3L* on 4q32.3 and *NDUFAB1* and *PALB2* on 16p12). We will review these genes in turn.

NDUFAB1 is a subunit of NADH dehydrogenase, a nuclear encoded subunit of mitochondrial Complex I, which regulates the redox status of nicotinamide adenine dinucleotide/nicotinamide adenine dinucleotide hydride (NAD/NADH), and could be observed in both the cytoplasm and nucleus. NDUFAB1 may be involved in the regulation of NAD and NADH which influence fundamental cellular processes such as cellular metabolism, gene expression, and ion channel regulation, although the function of NDUFAB1 in ADs remains to be established [35,36].

PALB2 encodes for the protein PALB2, which co-localizes with BRCA2 in the cell nucleus and promotes its localization and stability in cellular structure like chromatin and nuclear matrix [37]. SNP rs420256 in *PALB2* has been reported to be associated with bipolar disorder in Caucasians in previous studies [38,39]. In our study, rs420259 did not show any significant association with ADs in either the EA or AA samples (FS-EA $p = 0.11$; FS-AA $p = 0.37$). Rs8062954 on the same LD block ($r^2 = 0.12$, D' = 1.00) with rs420259 was nominally associated with ADs using FS in the AA sample (FS-AA $p = 4.88 \times 10^{-5}$).

MFAP3L encodes a transmembrane protein, microfibrillar-associated protein 3-like. The intracellular region of this protein reportedly contains a cluster of phosphorylation sites and phosphatidylinositol-3 kinase (PI3K) regulatory subunit, which suggests the involvement of MFAP3L in the signal transduction of PI3K/AKT pathway [40]. The PI3K/AKT pathways are known

Table 2. Top findings of SNP-based GWAS in the European (EA) and African American (AA) samples.

Sample	SNP	Chr	Position (bp)	A1	Beta (OR)*	p	q	Gene
EA								
FS								
	rs4692589	4	171,171,820	C	−0.067	8.63E-07	0.37	MFAP3L
	rs10893268	11	123,943,822	T	−0.069	1.18E-06	0.37	OR8A1
	rs12153327	5	100,729,499	C	−0.064	2.02E-06	0.42	
	rs7657455	4	171,195,418	G	−0.064	2.90E-06	0.45	MFAP3L
	rs10016872	4	171,116,951	C	−0.061	3.97E-06	0.48	
	rs2170820	12	128,588,656	C	−0.063	4.63E-06	0.48	TMEM132D
	rs1551277	7	47,795,842	A	0.068	6.88E-06	0.53	PKD1L1
	rs12703441	7	141,539,176	C	−0.062	6.97E-06	0.53	
	rs6463447	7	47,797,795	A	0.068	7.60E-06	0.53	PKD1L1
	rs4736192	8	140,049,007	A	0.073	9.24E-06	0.53	
CC								
	rs2115691	4	74,962,555	G	0.67	4.45E-06	0.90	CXCL1
	rs3097411	4	74,957,318	C	0.68	6.58E-06	0.90	CXCL1
AA								
FS								
	rs7141336	14	90,355,981	C	0.19	5.83E-06	1.00	TTC7B
	rs17548918	3	21,355,095	C	0.26	8.75E-06	1.00	
	rs241257	1	4,514,682	A	0.17	9.09E-06	1.00	
CC								
	rs12120353	1	4,520,856	A	2.13	3.08E-06	0.99	
	rs10762651	10	76,492,123	T	0.54	6.06E-06	0.99	DUPD1
	rs17105932	11	106,048,675	T	0.45	6.91E-06	0.99	GUCY1A2
	rs6799682	3	178,659,210	A	1.79	7.53E-06	0.99	
	rs17105964	11	106,074,793	G	0.46	8.74E-06	0.99	GUCY1A2

GWAS, genome-wide association study; SNP, single nucleotide polymorphism.
Chr, chromosome; bp, base position; OR, odds ratio; FS, factor score analysis; CC, case-control analysis.
A1, minor allele based on whole sample.
*Beta was calculated with FS and OR was calculated with CC.
Genes with SNPs located up to 20 kb down- or upstream were shown.
SNPs with p-values <10^{-5} were shown.

Table 3. Meta-analysis of gene-based GWA analyses in European-American (EA) and African-American (AA) samples.

Gene	Chr	Start (bp)	Stop (bp)	Meta-analysis		EA			AA		
				p	q	nSNPs	p	q	nSNPs	p	q
FS											
NDUFAB1	16	23,499,835	23,515,140	4.04E-06	0.028	14	9.00E-06	0.053	16	1.26E-01	0.98
PALB2	16	23,521,983	23,560,179	4.37E-06	0.028	17	6.00E-06	0.053	23	1.78E-01	0.98
MFAP3L	4	171,144,322	171,184,004	4.78E-06	0.028	40	2.00E-06	0.035	43	3.59E-01	0.98
AADAT	4	171,217,947	171,247,947	1.64E-05	0.072	27	3.40E-05	0.12	27	1.50E-01	0.98
UBFD1	16	23,476,362	23,493,211	3.66E-05	0.13	17	2.00E-05	0.09	18	3.84E-01	0.98
EARS2	16	23,440,834	23,476,197	4.41E-05	0.13	22	4.10E-05	0.12	25	2.86E-01	0.98
DCTN5	16	23,560,307	23,588,683	5.71E-05	0.14	17	1.13E-04	0.20	22	1.73E-01	0.98
CTNNBL1	20	35,755,847	35,933,934	6.80E-05	0.15	76	1.05E-03	0.68	83	2.21E-02	0.98
VSTM2L	20	35,964,912	36,007,161	9.20E-05	0.16	39	6.07E-04	0.54	40	5.97E-02	0.98
GGA2	16	23,383,143	23,429,309	9.89E-05	0.16	19	9.60E-05	0.19	22	3.02E-01	0.98
C11orf40	11	4,549,228	4,555,626	1.03E-04	0.16	54	8.30E-05	0.18	59	3.41E-01	0.98
COG7	16	23,307,316	23,372,004	1.32E-04	0.19	29	7.10E-05	0.18	32	4.44E-01	0.98
SRXN1	20	575,267	581,890	1.60E-04	0.22	42	4.79E-03	0.83	47	7.76E-03	0.98
TARS	5	33,476,654	33,503,953	2.27E-04	0.29	17	1.63E-04	0.25	25	3.98E-01	0.98
OR52I2	11	4,564,618	4,565,671	2.49E-04	0.29	51	1.68E-04	0.25	56	4.17E-01	0.98
CC											
PF4V1	4	74,937,876	74,939,062	6.64E-05	0.37	29	4.00E-06	0.059	44	9.61E-01	0.99
CXCL1	4	74,953,972	74,955,817	8.51E-05	0.37	32	7.00E-06	0.059	48	8.96E-01	0.98
CXCL6	4	74,921,276	74,923,341	1.27E-04	0.37	19	1.00E-05	0.059	30	9.45E-01	0.99

Genes with q-values <5% or <25% in either EA, AA, or meta-analysis of the two populations were shown.
GWA, genome-wide association; Chr, chromosome; bp, base position; nSNPs, number of SNPs located within the gene.
FS, factor score analysis; CC, case-control analysis.

Table 4. GO term enrichment analysis based on the results from the meta-analysis of gene-based GWAS in European and African American samples.

GO term		Count	%	Fold Enrichment	p	q
FS						
GO: 0007389	B: pattern specification process	14	5.0	3.6	0.0002	0.0025
GO: 0019955	M: cytokine binding	9	3.2	5.5	0.0002	0.0030
GO: 0000793	C: condensed chromosome	7	2.5	3.6	0.0132	0.16
GO: 0030155	B: regulation of cell adhesion	7	2.5	3.5	0.0154	0.23
GO: 0016563	M: transcription activator activity	13	4.6	2.1	0.0196	0.24
CC						
GO: 0005654	C: nucleoplasm	26	9.2	2.0	0.0015	0.019
GO: 0030528	M: transcription regulator activity	40	14.1	1.6	0.0017	0.024
GO: 0009952	B: anterior/posterior pattern formation	8	2.8	3.8	0.0049	0.078

GWAS, genome-wide association study; FS, factor score analysis; CC, case-control analysis.
B, biological process; M, molecular function; C, cellular component.

for regulating metabolism, cell growth, and cell survival [41]. Recent studies have indicated that both dopamine and serotonin partially exert their actions by modulating the activity of AKT [42,43]. Furthermore, chromosome 4q32 region was suggested to be associated with ADs (PD, SAD, and phobia) in a previous linkage study [44], although this region was not confirmed in a recent meta-analysis of linkage data for ADs [45].

To further explore the GWAS data, we took a pathway-based approach, providing complementary information to single-marker and gene-based methods. In the GO term enrichment analyses, we found two terms ("pattern specification process" and "cytokine binding") using FS and two terms ("nucleoplasm" and "transcription regulator activity") using CC to be significantly enriched in ADs, based on the results from the trans-population gene-based meta-analysis. As observed in the SNP- and gene-based analyses, the significance of the top pathways was greater using FS than CC (Table 4). Among these significant pathways, one intriguing pathway is "cytokine binding", proteins of which function to control the survival, growth and differentiation of tissues and cells via interaction with cytokines. Recent studies have suggested that inflammation of neurons and inflammatory cytokine production contribute to the pathophysiology of depression and anxiety [46]. Actually, cytokines and their signaling pathways have significant effects on the metabolism of multiple neurotransmitters such as serotonin, dopamine, and glutamate and on synaptic plasticity [47]. An increase in inflammatory markers such as IL-1, IL-6, TNF-alpha, and IFN-gamma have been documented in ADs including PTSD, PD, and OCD as well as anxiety-related personality traits such as neuroticism [46]. The genes in the significant pathways are worthy of follow-up in the future research.

Several limitations in this study should be addressed. First, in the present study, we did not perform replication analyses of the top findings identified in the SNP-, gene-, pathway-based analyses. However, to increase the statistical power, we conducted the meta-analyses of the gene-based analyses by combining the two populations. In future research, further replication studies are needed to confirm our findings. Second, the distribution of FS used for the GWA analyses was not normally distributed. Like most psychiatric phenotypes, the distribution was quite skewed, with many of the unaffected subjects falling under a peak at the lower end of the score. Therefore, p-values for some markers in the

GWAS might have been biased by this feature of the FS distribution. We tested this for SNPs on different chromosomes by comparing normal-theory regression with permutation testing and did not detect major differences. Third, the gender ratio differs significantly between cases and controls in both EA and AA samples, which may affect results. Therefore, we conducted the analyses controlling for gender and age instead of conducting gender-specific analyses because it reduce the statistical power. Fourth, the gene- and pathway-based analyses assumed that the local SNPs only modify the function of the local gene. Thus, both *cis* and *trans* regulation of the genes should be considered in the future analyses [48]. Fifth, since the sample size of the EA sample was much larger than the AA sample, most of the top findings in the gene-based meta-analysis were found in the EA sample. Therefore, caution is needed to interpret the results given genetic heterogeneity between the two populations.

In conclusion, our results demonstrate the potential advantage of studying AD phenotypes as quantitative traits for identifying shared susceptibility genes. In addition, our study provides a strategy to utilize the full information of GWAS to find new genes and pathways that would be missed in a single SNP analysis. Further studies are necessary to confirm our findings and clarify the underlying mechanisms of ADs.

Supporting Information

File S1   Figure S1 in File S1 Quantile-quantile (QQ) plots of each SNP-based genome-wide association analysis. (a) FS-EA, (b) FS-AA, (c) CC-EA, (d) CC-AA. FS, factor score analysis; CC, case-control analysis; EA, European Americans; AA, African Americans. **Figure S2 in File S1 Manhattan plots of each genome-wide association analysis.** (a) FS-EA, (b) FS-AA, (c) CC-EA, (d) CC-AA. FS, factor score analysis; CC, case-control analysis; EA, European Americans; AA, African Americans. **Figure S3 in File S1 Quantile-quantile (QQ) plots of gene-based genome-wide association analysis.** (a) FS-EA, (b) FS-AA, (c) CC-EA, (d) CC-AA. FS, factor score analysis; CC, case-control analysis; EA, European Americans; AA, African Americans.

Author Contributions

Conceived and designed the experiments: TO BSM EJV JMH. Analyzed the data: TO BSM SHA JLM. Wrote the paper: TO BSM SHA JLM EJV JMH.

References

1. Kessler RC, Berglund P, Demler O, Jin R, Merikangas KR, et al. (2005) Lifetime prevalence and age-of-onset distributions of DSM-IV disorders in the National Comorbidity Survey Replication. Arch Gen Psychiatry 62: 593–602.

2. Hettema JM, Neale MC, Kendler KS (2001) A review and meta-analysis of the genetic epidemiology of anxiety disorders. Am J Psychiatry 158: 1568–1578.

3. Smoller JW, Block SR, Young MM (2009) Genetics of anxiety disorders: the complex road from DSM to DNA. Depress Anxiety 26: 965–975.

4. Erhardt A et al. (2011) TMEM132D, a new candidate for anxiety phenotypes: evidence from human and mouse studies. Mol Psychiatry 16: 647–663.

5. Otowa T, Kawamura Y, Nishida N, Sugaya N, Koike A, et al. (2012) Meta-analysis of genome-wide association studies for panic disorder in the Japanese population. Transl Psychiatry 2: e186.

6. Logue MW, Baldwin C, Guffanti G, Melista E, Wolf EJ, et al. (2013) A genome-wide association study of post-traumatic stress disorder identifies the retinoid-related orphan receptor alpha (RORA) gene as a significant risk locus. Mol Psychiatry 18: 937–942.

7. Xie P, Kranzler HR, Yang C, Zhao H, Farrer LA, et al. (2013). Genome-wide Association Study Identifies New Susceptibility Loci for Posttraumatic Stress Disorder. Biol Psychiatry 74: 656–663.

8. Guffanti G, Galea S, Yan L, Roberts AL, Solovieff N, et al. (2013). Genome-wide association study implicates a novel RNA gene, the lincRNA AC068718.1, as a risk factor for post-traumatic stress disorder in women. Psychoneuroendocrinology. E-pub ahead of print Sep 8 2013. doi: 10.1016/j.psyneuen. 2013.08.014.

9. Stewart SE et al. (2013) Genome-wide association study of obsessive-compulsive disorder. Mol Psychiatry 18: 788–798.

10. Walter S, Glymour MM, Koenen K, Liang L, Tchetgen Tchetgen EJ, et al. (2013) Performance of polygenic scores for predicting phobic anxiety. PLoS One 8: e80326.

11. Neale BM, Sham PC (2004) The future of association studies: gene-based analysis and replication. Am J Hum Genet 75: 353–362.

12. Plomin R, Haworth CM, Davis OS (2009) Common disorders are quantitative traits. Nat Rev Genet 10: 872–878.

13. Cohen J (1983) The cost of dichotomization. Appl Psychol Meas 7: 249–253.

14. Jardine R, Martin NG, Henderson AS (1984) Genetic covariation between neuroticism and the symptoms of anxiety and depression. Genet Epidemiol 1: 89–107.

15. Hettema JM, Neale MC, Myers JM, Prescott CA, Kendler KS (2006) A population-based twin study of the relationship between neuroticism and internalizing disorders. Am J Psychiatry 163: 857–864.

16. Kendler KS, Gardner CO, Gatz M, Pedersen NL (2007) The sources of co-morbidity between major depression and generalized anxiety disorder in a Swedish national twin sample. Psychol Med 37: 453–462.

17. Hettema JM, Webb BT, Guo AY, Zhao Z, Maher BS, et al. (2011) Prioritization and association analysis of murine-derived candidate genes in anxiety-spectrum disorders. Biol Psychiatry 70: 888–896.

18. Sanders AR, Levinson DF, Duan J, Dennis JM, Li R, et al. (2010) The Internet-based MGS2 control sample: self report of mental illness. Am J Psychiatry 167: 854–865.

19. Nurnberger JI Jr, Blehar MC, Kaufmann CA, York-Cooler C, Simpson SG, et al. (1994) Diagnostic interview for genetic studies. Rationale, unique features, and training. NIMH Genetics Initiative. Arch Gen Psychiatry 51: 849–859.

20. Kessler RC, Andrews G, Mroczek DK, Ustun B, Wittchen H-U (1998) The World Health Organization Composite International Diagnostic Interview Short Form (CIDI-SF). International Journal of Methods in Psych Res 7: 171–185.

21. Muthén LK, Muthén BO (2006) Mplus User's Guide. Fourth Edition. Los Angeles, CA.

22. Benjamini Y, Hochberg Y (1995) Controlling the false discovery rate: a practical and powerful approach to multiple testing. J Roy Stat Soc B 57: 289–300.

23. van den Oord EJ, Kuo PH, Hartmann AM, Webb BT, Möller HJ, et al. (2008) Genomewide association analysis followed by a replication study implicates a novel candidate gene for neuroticism. Arch Gen Psychiatry 65: 1062–1071.

24. Shi J et al. (2011) Genome-wide association study of recurrent early-onset major depressive disorder. Mol Psychiatry 16: 193–201.

25. Purcell S, Neale B, Todd-Brown K, Thomas L, Ferreira MA, et al. (2007) PLINK: a tool set for whole-genome association and population-based linkage analyses. Am J Hum Genet 81: 559–575.

26. Barrett JC, Fry B, Maller J, Daly MJ (2005) Haploview: analysis and visualization of LD and haplotype maps. Bioinformatics 21: 263–265.

27. Liu JZ, McRae AF, Nyholt DR, Medland SE, Wray NR, et al. (2010) A versatile gene-based test for genome-wide association studies. Am J Hum Genet 87: 139–145.

28. Ioannidis JP, Ntzani EE, Trikalinos TA (2004) 'Racial' differences in genetic effects for complex diseases. Nat Genet. 36: 1312–1318.

29. Wang X, Liu X, Sim X, Xu H, Khor CC, et al. (2012) A statistical method for region-based meta-analysis of genome-wide association studies in genetically diverse populations. Eur J Hum Genet 20: 469–75.

30. Cheung CL, Sham PC, Xiao SM, Bow CH, Kung AW. (2012) Meta-analysis of gene-based genome-wide association studies of bone mineral density in Chinese and European subjects. Osteoporos Int 23: 131–42.

31. Stouffer SA, Suchman EA, DeVinney LC, Star SA, Williams RM Jr. (1949) The American Soldier: adjustment during army life, Vol. 1. Princeton: Princeton University Press.

32. Willer CJ, Li Y, Abecasis GR (2010) METAL: fast and efficient meta-analysis of genomewide association scans. Bioinformatics 26: 2190–2191.

33. Huang da W, Sherman BT, Lempicki RA (2009) Systematic and integrative analysis of large gene lists using DAVID bioinformatics resources. Nat Protoc 4: 44–57.

34. Yang J, Wray NR, Visscher PM (2010) Comparing apples and oranges: equating the power of case-control and quantitative trait association studies. Genet Epidemiol 34: 254–257.

35. Zhang Q, Piston DW, Goodman RH (2002) Regulation of corepressor function by nuclear NADH. Science 295: 1895–1897.

36. Lin SJ, Guarente L (2003) Nicotinamide adenine dinucleotide, a metabolic regulator of transcription, longevity and disease. Curr Opin Cell Biol 15: 241–246.

37. Xia B, Sheng Q, Nakanishi K, Ohashi A, Wu J, et al. (2006) Control of BRCA2 cellular and clinical functions by a nuclear partner, PALB2. Mol Cell 22: 719–729.

38. The Wellcome Trust Case Control Consortium (2007) Genome-wide association study of 14,000 cases of seven common diseases and 3,000 shared controls. Nature. 447: 661–678.

39. Tesli M, Athanasiu L, Mattingsdal M, Kahler AK, Gustafsson O, et al. (2010) Association analysis of PALB2 and BRCA2 in bipolar disorder and schizophrenia in a scandinavian case-control sample. Am J Med Genet B Neuropsychiatr Genet 153B: 1276–1282.

40. Kang B, Hao C, Wang H, Zhang J, Xing R, et al. (2008) Evaluation of hepatic-metastasis risk of colorectal cancer upon the protein signature of PI3K/AKT pathway. J Proteome Res 7: 3507–3515.

41. Sheppard K, Kinross KM, Solomon B, Pearson RB, Phillips WA (2012) Targeting PI3 kinase/AKT/mTOR signaling in cancer. Crit Rev Oncog 17: 69–95.

42. Cowen DS (2007) Serotonin and neuronal growth factors - a convergence of signaling pathways. J Neurochem 101: 1161–1171.

43. Beaulieu JM, Gainetdinov RR, Caron MG (2009) Akt/GSK3 signaling in the action of psychotropic drugs. Annu Rev Pharmacol Toxicol 49: 327–347.

44. Kaabi B, Gelernter J, Woods SW, Goddard A, Page GP, et al. (2006) Genome scan for loci predisposing to anxiety disorders using a novel multivariate approach: strong evidence for a chromosome 4 risk locus. Am J Hum Genet 78: 543–553.

45. Webb BT, Guo AY, Maher BS, Zhao Z, van den Oord EJ, et al. (2012) Meta-analyses of genome-wide linkage scans of anxiety-related phenotypes. Eur - J Hum Genet 20: 1078–84.

46. Miller AH, Haroon E, Raison CL, Felger JC (2013) Cytokine targets in the brain: impact on neurotransmitters and neurocircuits. Depress Anxiety 30: 297–306.

47. Kitagishi Y, Kobayashi M, Yamashina Y, Matsuda S (2012) Elucidating the regulation of T cell subsets (review). Int J Mol Med 30: 1255–1260.

48. Becker J, Wendland JR, Haenisch B, Nöthen MM, Schumacher J (2012) A systematic eQTL study of cis-trans epistasis in 210 HapMap individuals. Eur J Hum Genet 20: 97–101.

22

Protein Interaction Networks Reveal Novel Autism Risk Genes within GWAS Statistical Noise

Catarina Correia[1,2,3], **Guiomar Oliveira**[4,5,6], **Astrid M. Vicente**[1,2,3]*

1 Departamento de Promoção da Saúde e Doenças não Transmissíveis, Instituto Nacional de Saúde Doutor Ricardo Jorge, 1649-016 Lisboa, Portugal, **2** Center for Biodiversity, Functional & Integrative Genomics, Faculty of Sciences, University of Lisbon, 1749-016 Lisboa, Portugal, **3** Instituto Gulbenkian de Ciência, 2780-156 Oeiras, Portugal, **4** Unidade Neurodesenvolvimento e Autismo, Centro de Desenvolvimento, Hospital Pediátrico (HP) do Centro Hospitalar e Universitário de Coimbra (CHUC), 3000-602 Coimbra, Portugal, **5** Centro de Investigação e Formação Clinica do HP-CHUC, 3000-602 Coimbra, Portugal, **6** Faculdade de Medicina da Universidade de Coimbra, 3000-548 Coimbra, Portugal

Abstract

Genome-wide association studies (GWAS) for Autism Spectrum Disorder (ASD) thus far met limited success in the identification of common risk variants, consistent with the notion that variants with small individual effects cannot be detected individually in single SNP analysis. To further capture disease risk gene information from ASD association studies, we applied a network-based strategy to the Autism Genome Project (AGP) and the Autism Genetics Resource Exchange GWAS datasets, combining family-based association data with Human Protein-Protein interaction (PPI) data. Our analysis showed that autism-associated proteins at higher than conventional levels of significance ($P<0.1$) directly interact more than random expectation and are involved in a limited number of interconnected biological processes, indicating that they are functionally related. The functionally coherent networks generated by this approach contain ASD-relevant disease biology, as demonstrated by an improved positive predictive value and sensitivity in retrieving known ASD candidate genes relative to the top associated genes from either GWAS, as well as a higher gene overlap between the two ASD datasets. Analysis of the intersection between the networks obtained from the two ASD GWAS and six unrelated disease datasets identified fourteen genes exclusively present in the ASD networks. These are mostly novel genes involved in abnormal nervous system phenotypes in animal models, and in fundamental biological processes previously implicated in ASD, such as axon guidance, cell adhesion or cytoskeleton organization. Overall, our results highlighted novel susceptibility genes previously hidden within GWAS statistical "noise" that warrant further analysis for causal variants.

Editor: Branko Aleksic, Nagoya University Graduate School of Medicine, Japan

Funding: The AGP study was funded by Autism Speaks (USA), the Health Research Board (HRB, Ireland; AUT/2006/1, AUT/2006/2, PD/2006/48), The Medical Research Council (MRC, UK), Genome Canada/Ontario Genomics Institute and the Hilibrand Foundation (USA). Additional support for individual groups was provided by the US National Institutes of Health (NIH Grants: HD055751, HD055782, HD055784, MH52708, MH55284, MH061009, MH06359, MH066673, MH080647, MH081754, MH66766, NS026630, NS042165, NS049261), the Canadian Institutes for Health Research (CIHR), Assistance Publique - Hôpitaux de Paris (France), Autism Speaks UK, Canada Foundation for Innovation/Ontario Innovation Trust, Deutsche Forschungsgemeinschaft (Grant: Po 255/17-4) (Germany), EC Sixth FP AUTISM MOLGEN, Fundação Calouste Gulbenkian (Portugal), Fondation de France, Fondation FondaMental (France), Fondation Orange (France), Fondation pour la Recherche Médicale (France), Fundação para a Ciência e Tecnologia (Portugal), the Hospital for Sick Children Foundation and University of Toronto (Canada), INSERM (France), Institut Pasteur (France), the Italian Ministry of Health (convention 181 of 19 October 2001), the John P. Hussman Foundation (USA), McLaughlin Centre (Canada), Ontario Ministry of Research and Innovation (Canada), the Seaver Foundation (USA), the Swedish Science Council, The Centre for Applied Genomics (Canada), the Utah Autism Foundation (USA) and the Wellcome Trust core award 075491/Z/04 (UK). The Autism Genetic Resource Exchange is a program of Autism Speaks and is supported, in part, by grant 1U24MH081810 from the National Institute of Mental Health to Clara M. Lajonchere (PI). Catarina Correia is supported by grant SFRH/BPD/64281/2009 from the Fundação para a Ciência e Tecnologia. The funders had no role in study design, data collection and analysis, decision to publish, or preparation of the manuscript.

Competing Interests: The authors have declared that no competing interests exist.

* Email: astrid.vicente@insa.min-saude.pt

Introduction

Autism Spectrum Disorder (ASD) is a complex neurodevelopmental illness with significant clinical and genetic heterogeneity. Family and twin studies demonstrated that ASD is one of the most heritable neuropsychiatric disorders, but there is yet no consensus on the underlying genetic architecture [1,2]: while single-gene disorders, metabolic disorders and Copy Number Variants (CNVs) account for approximately 30% of the etiology of ASD [1,3–7], the contribution of common risk variants to the remaining heritability is still unclear. Thus far, each large genome-wide association study (GWAS) carried out for ASD highlighted a single, non-overlapping locus [8–11], which frequently was not replicated by subsequent independent replication studies [12].

Devlin et al. (2011) have recently predicted that common variants having an odds ratio of 1.5 or more are very unlikely to exist; few, if any, common variants with an impact on risk exceeding 1.2 may still await discovery, but require much larger sample sizes, while variants with modest impact may range from zero to many thousands [13]. The small effect of common risk variants for ASD represents a challenge for their individual detection using conventional single-marker association analysis, which likely allows many true *loci* to remain hidden within the GWAS statistical "noise". Evidence from classical quantitative genetic analysis further suggests that most of the heritability missing in complex diseases is rather hidden below the threshold for genome-wide significant associations [14,15].

New strategies are therefore needed to increase the power of GWAS analysis. The use of molecular networks, which is not limited by *a priori* sorting the genes into incompletely annotated predefined gene sets, is emerging as an appealing unbiased alternative to pathway analysis. Network-based approaches have been widely applied in the analysis of high-throughput expression data from a wide range of diseases [16] and have proven successful in the identification of subnetwork markers more reproducible and with a higher prediction performance than individual markers [17]. More recent studies incorporated protein networks into the analysis of genome-wide association data, using networks to search for interacting *loci* in human GWAS data [18,19] or to identify genome wide-enriched pathways [20–24]. However, an unsupervised global network analysis of ASD GWAS data that includes all signals without arbitrary significance thresholds has not been performed, and may lead to the identification of many risk variants of small effect below the accepted threshold for statistical significance.

Based on the premise that disease-causing genes are likely to be functionally related, in the present study we applied a network-based approach to two ASD GWAS datasets, the AGP consortium GWAS and the GWAS carried out in the Autism Genetic Resource Exchange (AGRE) dataset [10]. For this purpose we integrated genome wide association data with Human Protein-Protein interaction data and examined topological network properties indicative of connectivity at various levels of association, confirming our hypothesis that genes associated to ASD at a "statistical noise" level are functionally connected beyond random expectation. We compared the enrichment in known ASD candidates of network genes versus top GWAS genes, and the overlap of network genes vs the overlap at gene or SNP level between the two ASD datasets. The network obtained was further tested for ASD specificity using networks derived from six unrelated diseases GWAS, and explored for biological processes associated with ASD.

Materials and Methods

A workflow of the strategy for network definition, validation and identification of the most relevant candidate genes is shown in Figure 1.

Ethics statement

All the data used is previously published and publicly available. Written informed consent has been previously obtained from all families and procedures had approval from institutional review boards from all the institutions involved in recruitment and research, following national and international ethical and legal regulations and the principles of the Declaration of Helsinki.

Datasets

The AGP dataset included 2818 trios consisting of autistic patients and both parents collected as part of the AGP Consortium. Patients were diagnosed and genotyped as previously reported [8]. Written informed consent was obtained from all families and procedures had approval from institutional review boards [8]. A total of 723 423 SNPs meeting the QC criteria [9], genotyped in 8491 individuals, were tested for association using the Transmissions Disequilibrium Test (TDT) implemented in PLINK v1.07 [25].

The GWAS replication dataset from the Autism Genetic Resource Exchange (AGRE) included 943 ASD families (4,444 subjects) from the AGRE cohort [10]. SNP genotyping data was obtained from AGRE [10]. Analysis in this study was limited to

SNPs in common with the AGP GWAS and meeting the same QC criteria (425 587 SNPs).

Summary SNP association results were obtained from the database of Genotype and Phenotype (dbGAP) repository for 6 case-control GWAS for other pathologies, including Parkinson's Disease (PD) [26], Systemic Lupus Erythematosus (SLE) [27], Multiple Sclerosis (MS) [28], Type 1 Diabetes (T1D) [29], Breast Cancer (BC) [30] and Neuroblastoma (NB) [31] (Table S1). All individuals included were of European ancestry and the sample size was as similar as possible to the replication ASD dataset (AGRE).

Integration of gene association data with Protein-Protein interaction data

Genotyped SNPs from the AGP and AGRE GWAS were assigned to specific genes if they were located within or up to 10 kb from the gene, using the GRCh37/hg19 genome build (Step 1). Each gene was assigned a gene score using MAGENTA (Meta-analysis Gene-set Enrichment of variant associations) [32], which allocates to each gene the most significant *P*-value among the TDT *P*-values of all individual SNPs mapped to that gene. MAGENTA then uses step-wise multivariate linear regression analysis to regress out of this *P*-value the confounding effects of gene size, number of SNPs per kilobase (kb), number of independent SNPs, number of recombination hotspots and the number of linkage disequilibrium units per kb.

Genes selected at various gene-wise *P*-value cutoffs ($0.5<$ -LogP<5) were superimposed onto their corresponding protein on a large human protein-protein interaction (PPI) network, converting Entrez gene IDs to Uniprot IDs (release 2010_04) (Step 2). This PPI network, covering 12372 proteins and 58365 interactions, was previously built compacting data from six public PPI databases: BIND, BioGRID, HPRD, IntAct, MINT and MPPI [33–40].

PPI network analysis

Topological properties from the resulting network were analyzed to select the gene-wise *P*-value for which corresponding proteins were functionally connected beyond random expectation, thus the lowest gene-wise *P*-value for which there is still relevant biological data in the GWAS that can be captured through network analysis (step 3). Three metrics indicative of this functional coherence were estimated for various association gene-wise *P*-value thresholds, for the two ASD datasets, and compared with those determined for 1000 equal size sets of randomly selected proteins from the human PPI network. The metrics evaluated were 1) the percentage of proteins directly interacting; 2) the percentage of isolated nodes, which represents the fraction of selected proteins with no interactions with any other selected protein; and 3) the size of the largest connected component (LCC), the largest group of selected proteins that are reachable from each other in the network. An empirical *P*-value was obtained computing the fraction of random samples where the value of the network metric is greater (or smaller in the case of isolates) than the observed one. Network analysis was performed using python module Network X.

Performance against a candidate gene list and overlap between datasets

To evaluate the performance of the proteins included in the LCC in retrieving known ASD candidate genes, the precision and recall against a curated list of ASD candidate genes were calculated (step 4). This list was obtained from SFARIGene and

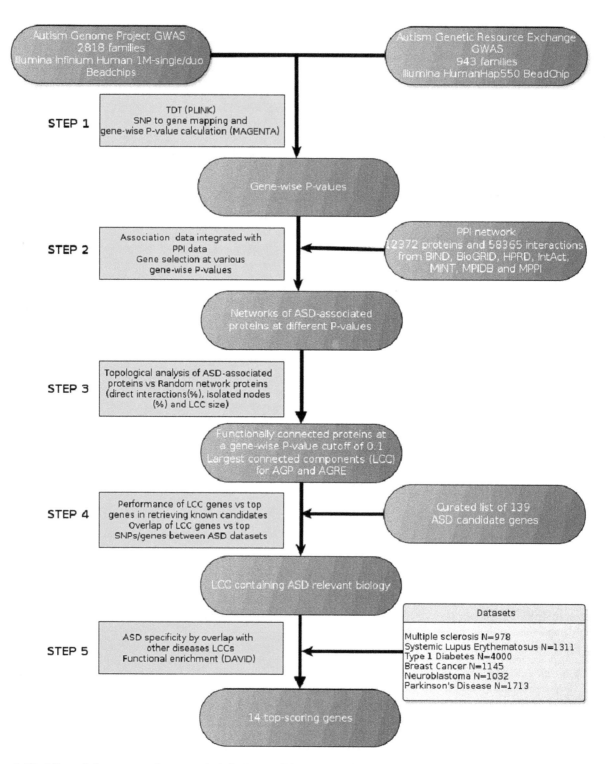

Figure 1. Workflow of the strategy for network definition, validation and identification of most relevant candidate genes.

includes 236 genes having at least minimal evidence of association with ASD (categories 1 to 4) or categorized as syndromic (https://gene.sfari.org/autdb/Welcome.do).

Precision (Positive Predictive value) is the proportion of known candidate genes among the selected genes, while recall (Sensitivity) is the proportion of known candidate genes retrieved by the selection. The precision and recall calculated for the genes encoding LCC proteins were compared to those determined using two other gene selection criteria: a) all genes selected at the same gene *P*-value cutoff used to derive LCC; b) the same number of top genes (ranked according to gene-wise *P*-values) as those included in the LCC.

Overlap between the AGP and AGRE datasets at SNP, gene and LCC levels was determined using the Jaccard index, defined as the size of the intersection divided by the size of the union of the datasets. For comparison purposes the size of each dataset LCC was used to select from each GWAS dataset an equal number of top SNPs (ranked by their TDT *P*-value) and top genes (ranked by their gene-wise *P*-value).

Gene ranking and functional enrichment

To rank ASD-associated proteins included in the AGP LCC by ASD specificity and reproducibility, a prioritization system was created, assigning a score to each protein based on their presence in the LCC derived from the AGRE ASD replication dataset and from each of the six unrelated disease datasets (step 5). Each protein included in the AGP LCC had an initial score of 0.5. If the protein was present in the AGRE ASD dataset LCC, 0.5 was added to the initial protein score, whereas for each unrelated disease dataset LCC where the protein was present, one sixth of 0.5 was subtracted from the score. Therefore, protein scores vary between 0 and 1, with zero representing a protein present in the LCCs of the AGP dataset and the 6 unrelated diseases, while a score of 1 is attributed to a protein present only in the LCCs of both ASD datasets.

Functional enrichment was tested by DAVID (The Database for Annotation, Visualization and Integrated Discovery 2008_version6[th]; http://david.abcc.ncifcrf.gov) [41,42], a publicly available bioinformatics tool that identifies functionally related groups of genes. Overrepresentation of mouse-mutant phenotypes was evaluated using the web tool MamPhea [43]. The complete list of the genes in the PPI network was used as background and *P*-values were corrected by the Benjamini correction. Top-scoring genes were further investigated using NextBio platform (Cupertino, CA, USA), a curated and correlated repository of experimental data derived from an extensive set of public resources (eg. ArrayExpress and GEO) [44]. Protein-protein networks were visualized in Cytoscape [45].

Results

Genes associated to ASD at *P*<0.1 are functionally related

Transmission Disequilibrium Tests were initially carried out in parallel for the AGP and AGRE datasets to identify small effect risk variants. In the sample of 2818 AGP families, single SNP transmission disequilibrium tests of the 723423 SNPs meeting the QC criteria showed no SNPs reaching the threshold for genome-wide significance. Two SNPs showed association signals at $P < 1 \times 10^{-6}$ and very few exceeded $P < 1 \times 10^{-5}$. In the AGRE dataset, after a similar quality control protocol and using only SNPs common to both datasets, three SNPs located in regions with no overlap with the AGP top findings showed association at $P < 1 \times 10^{-6}$. Given the dearth of meaningful results from these two GWAS efforts, we proceeded with a network analysis strategy.

The first step involved calculating gene-wise association *P*-values corrected for gene size and linkage disequilibrium, taking into account only the SNPs mapping within 10kb from each gene (403360 SNPs), followed by the integration of GWAS data onto protein interaction data. Then, we determined the lowest gene-

wise *P*-value threshold for which genes encoding the network proteins were functionally related, inferred by their proximity in the network. Statistical noise is expected to have random connections in the network, while disease proteins are more likely to establish direct interactions between them and more rarely be isolated in the network, translating into a larger group of proteins that are all interconnected. For both ASD datasets, proteins encoded by genes selected at a gene-wise $-\text{Log}_{10}P$ cutoff between 0.5 and 1.5 were found to establish significantly more direct interactions than equal sized sets of randomly selected proteins (Empirical *P* values $0.001 < P < 0.043$), with the significance maintained up to $-\text{Log}_{10}P = -2.0$ in the case of AGRE dataset (Figure S1, Figure 2A). The number of isolated nodes was found to be significantly smaller in sets of ASD-associated proteins at the same range of gene-wise $-\text{Log}_{10}P$-values than in random sets (Empirical *P* values $0.001 < P < 0.038$), again with significant differences maintained for lower gene-wise *P*-values in the AGRE dataset (Figure S1, Figure 2A). When compared to the same number of random proteins from the network, proteins encoded by genes selected at a gene-wise $-\text{Log}_{10}P < 1$ from either ASD dataset are interconnected in a significantly larger LCC (Empirical P values $0.001 < P < 0.007$) (Figure S1, Figure 2B). The large size of the largest connected components, 416 and 367 proteins for the AGP and AGRE datasets, respectively, indicates the existence of several small effect risk genes reinforcing the high genetic heterogeneity in ASD.

Based on the lowest gene-wise *P*-value for which the percentage of direct interactions was significantly higher, the percentage of isolated nodes significantly smaller and the size of the LCC significantly larger than random expectation (Figure 2A and B), we established gene-wise $-\text{Log}_{10}P = 1$ as the cutoff value to infer functional coherence from the two ASD datasets.

The overall results indicate that, as hypothesized, genes associated with ASD at the range of GWAS statistical noise encode proteins that are functionally related and preferentially directly interact, confirming our expectation that there is indeed unexplored relevant biology at this statistical level.

Functionally coherent sub networks associated with ASD contain relevant ASD biology

To test whether the identified groups of functionally connected proteins captured by the largest connected components indeed contain ASD-relevant biology, we compared the performance of the genes selected through the LCC against a list of known candidates, [5] with the performance of all genes selected from the GWAS at the same gene-wise *P*-value cutoff or the performance of a number of GWAS top genes equal to the number of genes encoding LCC proteins. Genes implicated in ASD are largely unknown, thus low precision values are expectable given the incompleteness and noise in the available knowledge in the field.

Table 1 shows that, for both datasets, genes encoding proteins included in the LCC presented a 2 to 2.5 fold higher precision against the list of known genes than all the GWAS genes selected at the same statistical level cutoff. In other words, genes included in the LCC, and thus encoding functionally related proteins, are enriched in known candidates compared with the set of genes selected from the GWAS at the same statistical level, demonstrating that our filtering approach of association results based on PPIs more specifically captures ASD-relevant genes. A 1.3 to 3.3 fold increase is observed when comparing LCC genes with the same number of GWAS top genes, showing that a protein interaction-based selection was more accurate than selecting only the most strongly associated genes.

A.

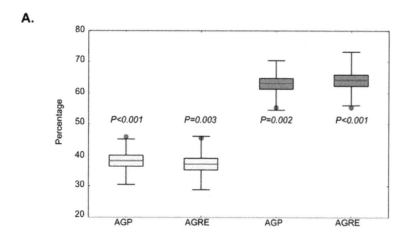

B.

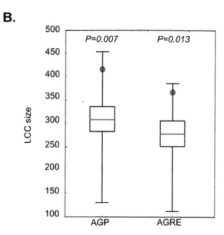

Figure 2. Network properties of proteins selected at gene-wise *P*<0.1 in each ASD. a) Comparison of percentage of direct interactions and isolated nodes between proteins selected at gene-wise *P*<0.1 in each GWAS dataset (red circles) vs 1000 random samples of network proteins (represented by light gray and dark gray box plots, for direct interactions and isolated nodes, respectively). The bottom and top of the box represent the 25th and 75th percentile and the extremity of the whiskers the maximum and minimum of the random samples data. **b**) Same comparison for the largest connected component (LCC) size.

Concerning the proportion of known genes that are retrieved by our selection, or recall, LCC encoding genes had a lower recall compared with all genes selected at the same cutoff, as expected since LCC genes are a subset of this selection (Table 1). However, compared with the top-gene selection, the 1.4 to 3 fold increase in the recall achieved by LCC encoding genes, indicates that additional relevant low effect genes are being captured. Further inspection of the known genes present in the top gene set and the LCC encoding genes confirmed that LCCs capture not only larger effect genes overlapping with top genes, such as *MET* (Uniprot P08581)(in AGP dataset), but additionally capture low effect genes, such as *TSC2* (Uniprot <u>P49815</u>), which single gene association analysis alone does not have the power to detect.

One of the major problems in ASD GWAS and GWAS in general is the low reproducibility of results between different datasets. Indeed, we found only one SNP (rs11837890 in *TBK1* gene) and 10 genes in common between the two datasets, when comparing the same number of SNPs or genes (ranked by *P*-values) than genes included in the LCCs from each dataset. Remarkably, we observed a 25 and 2.5-fold increase in the overlap between the two ASD datasets (AGP and AGRE) at PPI network level when compared to SNP or gene level, respectively (Figure S2).

Taken together, these results showed that our selection of functionally connected genes based on the largest connected component is an effective approach to capture ASD-relevant

disease candidate genes, which might escape detection in an analysis based only on association evidence, even at gene-level.

Functionally connected genes in ASD suggest novel susceptibility genes

Given the observation that the largest connected component contains ASD-relevant proteins, we further explored this network for biological processes implicated in ASD (step 5). The largest connected components generated by genes selected at -Log$_{10}$*P*<1 from the AGP and AGRE datasets comprised 416 and 367 proteins, respectively. A first look into the biological processes represented in these networks, using functional enrichment analysis, revealed an enrichment in pathways related to regulation of apoptosis and cell cycle. Additionally, intersection of the protein network data with knockout mice phenotypes from the Mouse Genome Informatics Database, showed that these proteins are primarily involved in aberrant embryogenic and developmental processes and anomalous immune system phenotypes.

A closer inspection of these LCCs at the gene level showed that around 30 (7–8%) of the encoding genes were implicated in neuropsychiatric or neurodegenerative disorders (Table S2). More interestingly, 20 (5–6%) of the LCC encoding genes were found to carry *de novo* mutations in ASD described in at least one of the three whole exome sequencing studies recently published [4,7,46], with 3 genes overlapping between the two datasets (*CSDE1* (Uniprot <u>O75534</u>), *PGD* (Uniprot <u>P52209</u>), *TSC2*). In addition, 80

Table 1. Precision and recall were consistently higher for LCC genes relative to top GWAS genes or genes selected at *P*<0.1.

Gene subset	Precision (%)		Recall (%)	
	AGP dataset	**AGRE dataset**	**AGP dataset**	**AGRE dataset**
LCC genes	2.16	2.74	3.81	4.24
GWAS Top genes	1.68	0.82	1.27	2.97
Genes selected at *P*<0.1	0.96	1,11	8.47	9.43

Precision and Recall (Percentage), by ASD dataset, of three sets of genes (genes selected at a gene wise *P*-value cutoff of 0.1, genes included in the LCC and the same number of GWAS top genes) against a list of known disease candidates.

(~19%) of the AGP LCC-encoding genes were deleted or duplicated by CNVs identified by the AGP whole genome analysis as potentially pathogenic (with less than 50% of length overlap with control datasets) (Table S2).

To further examine the specificity of the proteins in the AGP LCC for ASD, this network was compared with LCCs generated from six unrelated diseases GWAS (MS, SLE, T1D, BC, NB, PD). Based on the presence of each protein in the LCC of each unrelated disease and in the AGRE LCC, we derived a highly stringent ASD-specificity protein score, allowing the prioritization of encoding genes for follow-up. Low scoring proteins were not replicated in the AGRE dataset, and were present in one or more unrelated diseases, whereas the highest scoring proteins were present in both ASD LCCs, but in none of the LCCs generated from the unrelated diseases. This analysis revealed that the majority of proteins (~63%) were present only in the AGP network, while 31% of the proteins were present in at least one additional non-ASD network, and thus were not specific. From the 25 proteins identified in both ASD networks, the majority (56%) was not present in any ASD-unrelated network and 28% were present in one of the ASD-unrelated networks.

Using this gene scoring system, based on gene reproducibility and specificity for ASD, we built a network with the 14 top scoring genes and their first neighbors in the LCC network (Figure 3). The largest component of this network, although approximately 7 times smaller than the original LCCs, showed a similar overlap (~5%) with genes reported to have *de novo* mutations in ASD (*PGD*, *SYNE1* (Uniprot Q8NF91), *TSC2*) and an increased overlap with known candidate genes (*SYNE1*, *TSC2* and *SHANK3* (Uniprot Q9BYB0)) and with genes contained in potentially relevant CNVs identified by the AGP analysis (~26%). Enrichment in mouse phenotypes was also similar but, in addition, an enrichment in abnormal nervous system phenotype became significant, and in abnormal behavior/neurological phenotype borderline significant.

The genes encoding the 14 top scoring proteins were considered the best candidates for harboring common variants associated with ASD risk (Table 2). These genes are involved in various biological processes, such as NGF signaling, axon guidance, cell adhesion and migration, cytoskeleton regulation, apoptosis and DNA repair. A *de novo* mutation in the phosphogluconate dehydrogenase gene (*PGD*) has recently been reported in ASD [4], while potentially pathogenic CNVs deleting or duplicating the *ABL1* (Uniprot P00519), *RPS6KA1* (Uniprot Q15418) and *PPP1CB* (Uniprot P62140) genes were identified in ASD patients from the AGP study. A query of our genes in the NEXTBIO platform, a data mining framework that integrates and correlates global public datasets with several normal and disease phenotypes, revealed correlations of six genes with ASD. For instance, deletions within the *NASP* (Uniprot P49321) gene were identified in ASD patients from the Simons Simplex Collection (SSC) [47]. An altered expression of this gene, as well as of the *NR4A1* (Uniprot P22736), *ABI1* (Uniprot Q8IZP0), *BBS4* (Uniprot Q96RK4), *LMNA* (Uniprot P02545) and *ABL1* genes, was found in postmortem brain tissue [48] or lymphoblastoid cells [49] of ASD patients. Some of the 14 top-scoring genes, namely the *CTSB* (Uniprot P07858), *BBS4, LMNA* and *ABL1* genes, were associated with abnormal nervous system phenotypes in animal models. The most strongly associated genes to ASD, using the AGP data, were the peroxiredoxin 1 gene (*PRDX1* (Uniprot Q06830)) and cathepsin B gene (*CTSB*).

Discussion

In this study we have conducted a network-based analysis of two ASD GWAS datasets, hypothesizing that small effect ASD risk variants hidden at the level of GWAS statistical noise can be discovered from networks of genes with related biological functions. Mapping of association data to a PPI network indeed revealed that, in both datasets, ASD-associated genes at $P<0.1$ encoded proteins that directly interact beyond random expectation, are more rarely found isolated in the network and are connected in significantly larger LCCs than expected by chance, suggesting a functional connection. These results support recent findings from the AGP consortium, showing that stronger association of allele scores with case status was generally achieved when those scores were based on markers associated at significance thresholds higher than 0.2 [8]. The International Schizophrenia GWAS consortium had similar results of optimal discrimination between cases and controls only after the inclusion of markers with P-values as high as 0.2, [14] using this allele scoring approach.

The relevance to ASD of these networks was further illustrated by their higher performance in retrieving known ASD candidates compared to top GWAS genes, and the increased similarity between the two ASD datasets, when compared to SNP or gene level overlap. Remarkably, the AGP and AGRE LCCs included 20 genes, respectively, in which *de novo* mutations have been described in whole-exome sequencing studies of nearly a thousand ASD patients [4,7,50]. A large overlap of our results with the published data of these sequencing studies was not expected, because the LCCs encoding genes are likely to harbor variants transmitted by unaffected parents, whereas these sequencing studies mainly focused, and reported only, *de novo* variants which do not explain the heritability of the disorder, but support recent observations that common and rare variants associated with ASD disturb common neuronal networks [51]. Moreover, around 20% of the AGP LCC encoding genes were deleted or duplicated by potentially pathogenic CNVs detected in the AGP whole genome CNV screening of 2446 ASD patients.

As an additional filter for meaningful ASD biology, we derived an ASD candidate gene prioritization system ranking the genes encoding proteins included in the AGP LCC for ASD reproducibility and specificity. The scoring system used was very stringent, in particular since some of the control disorders are neurological (Parkinson's, multiple sclerosis or neuroblastoma) and may share susceptibility genes and pathways with autism [52–56]. While we may have discarded relevant autism risk genes that are ubiquitous and common to these disorders, we believe that we enriched our list of genes in true positive results with a higher chance of experimental validation. In fact, the enrichment analysis performed with the top-scoring genes and their first neighbors showed a high content in mouse genes associated with nervous system or neurological phenotypes and a similar or higher overlap with candidate genes or genes reported with *de novo* mutations or potentially pathogenic CNVs in ASD.

This approach generated a list of 14 top-scoring genes, present in the two ASD networks and none of the other disorders, which were considered strong candidates to harbor common variants associated with ASD risk. These genes are mostly novel candidates for ASD, and are involved in nervous system pathways or other more fundamental biological processes which have been widely associated to ASD, such as ubiquitination [4,9,57,58], cytoskeleton organization and regulation [5,47,59] and cell adhesion [10,60]. For instance, the *CTSB, BBS4, LMNA* and *ABL1* genes have been associated with neurobiological phenotypes identified in an enrichment analysis of mouse neurobiological phenotypes from a list of 112 ASD candidate genes [61], with *CTSB* and *ABL1* associated with cerebellum morphological and development abnormalities. The AGP genome-wide analysis identified potentially pathogenic CNVs spanning *ABL1, RPS6KA1* and

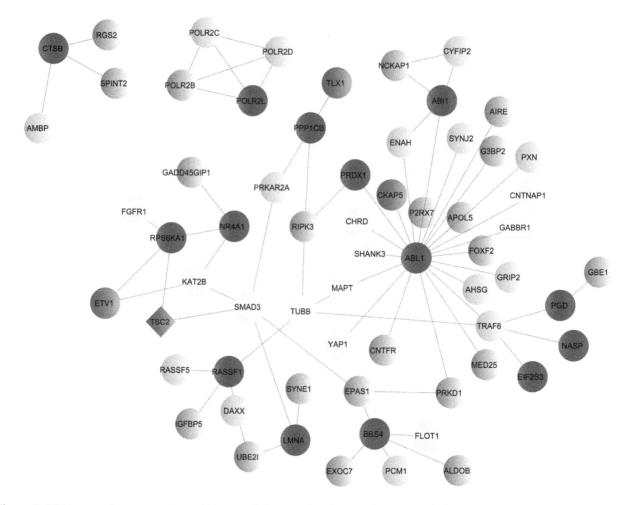

Figure 3. ASD top scoring gene network. This network illustrates the 14 top scoring genes included in the ASD LCC and their first neighbors. Nodes are colored based on a score reflecting their presence in the second ASD dataset and in the 6 unrelated diseases LCCs. A darker color represents a higher score, which means a higher specificity for ASD.

PPP1CB, whose relevance needs to be further established. Likewise, in the phosphogluconate dehydrogenase gene (PGD), a *de novo* mutation has recently been reported in a patient with ASD [4], although with an uncertain deleterious effect. This gene plays a critical role in protecting cells from oxidative stress [62] and, together with *PRDX1*, which also has an important antioxidant protective role in cells [63,64] and shows the strongest association with ASD, supports emerging evidence for a role of oxidative stress in ASD pathophysiology [65,66].

Thus far the use of protein networks to address common risk variants in ASD was limited to enrichment analysis of GWAS top hit genes in co-expressed or differentially expressed networks [51,67]. In contrast, this study incorporated protein interaction data into GWAS analysis, without *a priori* assumptions of association thresholds. The present results have shown that autism-associated genes at higher than conventional levels of significance are functionally related, and were used to extract relevant disease biology and uncover small effect variants contributing to the disorder. The study highlighted a group of novel susceptibility genes relevant for CNS function with a high probability of bearing common variants associated with autism, which have been elusive thus far, and warranting further analysis for identification of causal variants.

Supporting Information

Figure S1   Network properties per gene-wise *P*-value for each ASD dataset. For each $-Log_{10}$ gene wise association *P*-value cutoff in the x-axis, the percentage of direct interactions (A) and isolated nodes (B) and the logarithm of the LCC size (C) were plotted for proteins encoded by disease-associated genes (red line) and for the mean of 1000 equal sized random samples of proteins (blue line). Dark grey areas represent the range between the 25th and 75th quartiles and light gray areas indicate the range between the minimum and maximum values of the random data. Empirical *P*-values are indicated for each gene wise association *P*-value comparison. Values are plotted until the $-Log_{10}$ for which the percentage of direct interactions and isolated nodes reaches 0 and 100%, respectively.

Figure S2   Overlap between the two ASD datasets at SNP, gene or network level. Venn diagrams showing the overlap between the two ASD datasets (AGP and AGRE) at SNP, gene or network level.

Table S1   GWAS datasets used in the analysis and genotyping platforms.

Table 2. Top scoring ASD network genes.

Gene (Uniprot ID)	Description	Location	Relevant biological processes	Gene-wise association P-value (MAGENTA)	Published studies in autism	Neurological and behavioral features in mouse models
NASP(P49321)	nuclear autoantigenic sperm protein (histone-binding)	1p34.1	blastocyst development, cell proliferation, cell cycle	$1.470e^{-02}$	NEXTBIO: deletion in idiopathic females(Sakai et al. 2011), significantly downregulated in brain samples (Chow et al.2011)	NA
PRDX1(Q06830)	peroxiredoxin 1	1p34.1	redox regulation, cell proliferation	$1.760e^{-04}$	-	NA
RPS6KA1(Q15418)	ribosomal protein S6 kinase, 90kDa, polypeptide 1	1p36.11	protein kinase, synaptic transmission, axon guidance, long-term potentiation, toll-like and NGF receptor signaling pathway	$2.422e^{-02}$	-	NNP
PGD(P52209)	phosphogluconate dehydrogenase	1p36.22	cell redox regulation	$7.851e^{-02}$	De novo mutation in autistic patient (O'Roak et al. 2012)	NNP
LMNA(P02545)	lamin A/C	1q22	regulation of cell migration, regulation of apoptotic process, spermatogenesis	$8.226e^{-02}$	Nextbio altered expression in Lymphoblastoid cells from males with autism (15q11–13 duplication) and brain samples (Chow et al. 2011; Nishimura et al. 2007)	abnormal axon morphology, abnormal myelination
PPP1CB(P62140)	protein phosphatase 1, catalytic subunit, beta isozyme	2p23	regulation of cell cycle, focal-adhesion, long-term potentiation, regulation of actin cytoskeleton	$3.749e^{-02}$	-	NA
RASSF1(Q9NS23)	Ras association (RalGDS/AF-6) domain family member 1	3p21.3	Cell cycle, response to DNA damage stimulus, positive regulation of protein ubiquitination	$1.949e^{-02}$	-	NA
CTSB(P07858)	cathepsin B	8p23.1	regulation of apoptotic process, cellular response to thyroid hormone stimulus	$2.343e^{-03}$	-	Purkinje cell degeneration, abnormal neuron apoptosis (details) neuron degeneration
ABL1(P00519)	c-abl oncogene 1, non-receptor tyrosine kinase	9q34.1	axon guidance, regulation of cell adhesion, motility, cycle, actin cytoskeleton organization, response to DNA damage stimulus	$9.560e^{-02}$	NextBio:altered expression in autistic brain samples (Chow et al. 2011)	abnormal cerebellum morphology, small cerebellum, abnormal cerebellum development, abnormal cerebellar foliation, ectopic Purkinje cell, abnormal cerebellar lobule formation, absent cerebellar lobules, abnormal neuron differentiation
ABI1(Q8IZP0)	Abl-interactor 1 previously known as spectrin SH3 domain binding protein 1	10p12.1	transmembrane receptor protein tyrosine kinase signaling pathway, negative regulation of cell proliferation	$7.352e^{-02}$	NextBio:downregulation in autistic brain samples (Chow et al. 2011)	NA
POLR2L(P62875)	polymerase (RNA) II (DNA directed) polypeptide L, 7.6kDa	11p15.5	DNA repair, regulation of transcription	$7.821e^{-02}$	-	NNP

Table 2. Cont.

Gene (Uniprot ID)	Description	Location	Relevant biological processes	Gene-wise association P-value (MAGENTA)	Published studies in autism	Neurological and behavioral features in mouse models
NR4A1(P22736)	nuclear receptor subfamily 4, group A, member 1 also known as nerve Growth factor IB (NGFIB)	12q13.13	nuclear transcription factor, epidermal and fibroblast growth factor receptor signaling pathway, nerve growth factor receptor signaling pathway	$4.783e^{-02}$	NextBio:downregulation in autistic brain samples (Chow et al. 2011)	NA
BBS4(Q96RK4)	Bardet-Biedl syndrome 4	15q22.3–q23	centrosome organization, microtubule cytoskeleton organization, neural tube closure, dendrite, striatum, hippocampus, cerebral cortex development	$7.511e^{-02}$	Nextbio:altered expression in lymphoblasts and brain samples (Chow et al. 2011; Nishimura et al. 2007)	abnormal neural tubemorphology/ development, thincerebral cortex, abnormal basal ganglion morphologyabnormal olfactory neuron morphology, small hippocampusenlarged lateral ventriclesenlarged third ventricle
EIF2S3(P41091)	eukaryotic translation initiation factor 2, subunit 3 gamma, 52kDa	Xp22.11	cellular protein metabolic process	$7.322e^{-02}$	-	NNP

List of the 14 top scoring ASD network genes, present in both ASD networks and in none of the other disorders (ASD specificity score = 1), with information on gene-wise association P-value and biological processes relevant for ASD.

NNP - No neurological phenotypes|; NA - No mouse model available.

Table S2 AGP LCC network genes. List of the 416 genes included in the AGP LCC with information on gene-wise association *P*-value, specificity score for ASD and previous findings regarding implication in ASD and other neurological disorders.

Acknowledgments

We gratefully acknowledge the children with ASD and their families enrolling at the AGP and AGRE participating study sites. We are thankful to José Pereira Leal, Yoan Dieckmann and the remaining members of the Computational Genomics group at Instituto Gulbenkian de Ciência for helpful discussions and data sharing. We are grateful to all the AGP investigators, and particularly to Richard Anney, for sharing data, resources and scientific discussions. We gratefully acknowledge the resources provided by the Autism Genetic Resource Exchange (AGRE) Consortium and the participating AGRE families.

We acknowledge the NIH GWAS repository. Public available analysis data for Multiple Sclerosis, Systemic Lupus Erythematosus, Type 1 diabetes, Breast Cancer, Neuroblastoma and Parkinson's Disease were obtained from dbGaP at http://www.ncbi.nlm.nih.gov/gap through dbGaP accession numbers pha002861, pha002848, pha002862, pha002853, pha002845, pha002868, respectively.

Author Contributions

Conceived and designed the experiments: CC AMV. Performed the experiments: CC. Analyzed the data: CC AMV. Contributed reagents/materials/analysis tools: CC GO AMV. Wrote the paper: CC AMV.

References

1. Devlin B, Scherer SW (2012) Genetic architecture in autism spectrum disorder. Curr Opin Genet Dev 22: 229–237.
2. Geschwind DH (2011) Genetics of autism spectrum disorders. Trends Cogn Sci 15: 409–416.
3. Betancur C (2010) Etiological heterogeneity in autism spectrum disorders: more than 100 genetic and genomic disorders and still counting. Brain Res 1380: 42–77.
4. O'Roak BJ, Deriziotis P, Lee C, Vives L, Schwartz JJ, et al. (2012) Exome sequencing in sporadic autism spectrum disorders identifies severe de novo mutations. Nat Genet 44: 471.
5. Pinto D, Pagnamenta AT, Klei L, Anney R, Merico D, et al. (2010) Functional impact of global rare copy number variation in autism spectrum disorders. Nature 466: 368–372.
6. Sanders SJ, Ercan-Sencicek AG, Hus V, Luo R, Murtha MT, et al. (2011) Multiple recurrent de novo CNVs, including duplications of the 7q11.23 Williams syndrome region, are strongly associated with autism. Neuron 70: 863–885.
7. Sanders SJ, Murtha MT, Gupta AR, Murdoch JD, Raubeson MJ, et al. (2012) De novo mutations revealed by whole-exome sequencing are strongly associated with autism. Nature 485: 237–241.
8. Anney R, Klei L, Pinto D, Almeida J, Bacchelli E, et al. (2012) Individual common variants exert weak effects on the risk for autism spectrum disorderspi. Hum Mol Genet 21: 4781–4792.
9. Anney R, Klei L, Pinto D, Regan R, Conroy J, et al. (2010) A genome-wide scan for common alleles affecting risk for autism. Hum Mol Genet 19: 4072–4082.
10. Wang K, Zhang H, Ma D, Bucan M, Glessner JT, et al. (2009) Common genetic variants on 5p14.1 associate with autism spectrum disorders. Nature 459: 528–533.
11. Weiss LA, Arking DE, Daly MJ, Chakravarti A (2009) A genome-wide linkage and association scan reveals novel loci for autism. Nature 461: 802–808.
12. Curran S, Bolton P, Rozsnyai K, Chiocchetti A, Klauck SM, et al. (2011) No association between a common single nucleotide polymorphism, rs4141463, in the MACROD2 gene and autism spectrum disorder. Am J Med Genet B Neuropsychiatr Genet 156B: 633–639.
13. Devlin B, Melhem N, Roeder K (2011) Do common variants play a role in risk for autism? Evidence and theoretical musings. Brain Res 1380: 78–84.
14. Purcell SM, Wray NR, Stone JL, Visscher PM, O'Donovan MC, et al. (2009) Common polygenic variation contributes to risk of schizophrenia and bipolar disorder. Nature 460: 748–752.
15. Yang J, Benyamin B, McEvoy BP, Gordon S, Henders AK, et al. (2010) Common SNPs explain a large proportion of the heritability for human height. Nat Genet 42: 565–569.
16. Barabasi AL, Gulbahce N, Loscalzo J (2011) Network medicine: a network-based approach to human disease. Nat Rev Genet 12: 56–68.
17. Chuang HY, Lee E, Liu YT, Lee D, Ideker T (2007) Network-based classification of breast cancer metastasis. Mol Syst Biol 3: 140.
18. Emily M, Mailund T, Hein J, Schauser L, Schierup MH (2009) Using biological networks to search for interacting loci in genome-wide association studies. Eur J Hum Genet 17: 1231–1240.
19. Pan W (2008) Network-based model weighting to detect multiple loci influencing complex diseases. Hum Genet 124: 225–234.
20. Akula N, Baranova A, Seto D, Solka J, Nalls MA, et al. (2011) A network-based approach to prioritize results from genome-wide association studies. PLoS One 6: e24220.
21. Baranzini SE, Galwey NW, Wang J, Khankhanian P, Lindberg R, et al. (2009) Pathway and network-based analysis of genome-wide association studies in multiple sclerosis. Hum Mol Genet 18: 2078–2090.
22. Jensen MK, Pers TH, Dworzynski P, Girman CJ, Brunak S, et al. (2011) Protein interaction-based genome-wide analysis of incident coronary heart disease. Circ Cardiovasc Genet 4: 549–556.
23. Jia P, Zheng S, Long J, Zheng W, Zhao Z (2011) dmGWAS: dense module searching for genome-wide association studies in protein-protein interaction networks. Bioinformatics 27: 95–102.
24. Lee I, Blom UM, Wang PI, Shim JE, Marcotte EM (2011) Prioritizing candidate disease genes by network-based boosting of genome-wide association data. Genome Res 21: 1109–1121.
25. Purcell S, Neale B, Todd-Brown K, Thomas L, Ferreira MA, et al. (2007) PLINK: a tool set for whole-genome association and population-based linkage analyses. Am J Hum Genet 81: 559–575.
26. Simon-Sanchez J, Schulte C, Bras JM, Sharma M, Gibbs JR, et al. (2009) Genome-wide association study reveals genetic risk underlying Parkinson's disease. Nat Genet 41: 1308–1312.
27. Hom G, Graham RR, Modrek B, Taylor KE, Ortmann W, et al. (2008) Association of systemic lupus erythematosus with C8orf13-BLK and ITGAM-ITGAX. N Engl J Med 358: 900–909.
28. Baranzini SE, Wang J, Gibson RA, Galwey N, Naegelin Y, et al. (2009) Genome-wide association analysis of susceptibility and clinical phenotype in multiple sclerosis. Hum Mol Genet 18: 767–778.
29. Barrett JC, Clayton DG, Concannon P, Akolkar B, Cooper JD, et al. (2009) Genome-wide association study and meta-analysis find that over 40 loci affect risk of type 1 diabetes. Nat Genet 41: 703–707.
30. Hunter DJ, Kraft P, Jacobs KB, Cox DG, Yeager M, et al. (2007) A genome-wide association study identifies alleles in FGFR2 associated with risk of sporadic postmenopausal breast cancer. Nat Genet 39: 870–874.
31. Maris JM, Mosse YP, Bradfield JP, Hou C, Monni S, et al. (2008) Chromosome 6p22 locus associated with clinically aggressive neuroblastoma. N Engl J Med 358: 2585–2593.
32. Segre AV, Groop L, Mootha VK, Daly MJ, Altshuler D (2010) Common inherited variation in mitochondrial genes is not enriched for associations with type 2 diabetes or related glycemic traits. PLoS Genet 6: e1001058.
33. Bader GD, Betel D, Hogue CWV (2003) BIND: the Biomolecular Interaction Network Database. Nucleic Acids Research 31: 248–250.
34. Ceol A, Chatr Aryamontri A, Licata L, Peluso D, Briganti L, et al. (2010) MINT, the molecular interaction database: 2009 update. Nucleic acids research 38: D532–539.
35. Kerrien S, Aranda B, Breuza L, Bridge A, Broackes-Carter F, et al. (2011) The IntAct molecular interaction database in 2012. Nucleic Acids Research 40: D841–D846.
36. Keshava Prasad TS, Goel R, Kandasamy K, Keerthikumar S, Kumar S, et al. (2009) Human Protein Reference Database—2009 update. Nucleic acids research 37: D767–772.
37. Mishra GR, Suresh M, Kumaran K, Kannabiran N, Suresh S, et al. (2006) Human protein reference database—2006 update. Nucleic acids research 34: D411–414.
38. Pagel P, Kovac S, Oesterheld M, Brauner B, Dunger-Kaltenbach I, et al. (2005) The MIPS mammalian protein–protein interaction database. Bioinformatics 21: 832–834.
39. Peri S, Navarro JD, Amanchy R, Kristiansen TZ, Jonnalagadda CK, et al. (2003) Development of human protein reference database as an initial platform for approaching systems biology in humans. Genome Res 13: 2363–2371.
40. Stark C (2006) BioGRID: a general repository for interaction datasets. Nucleic Acids Research 34: D535–D539.
41. Huang DW, Sherman BT, Lempicki RA (2009) Systematic and integrative analysis of large gene lists using DAVID bioinformatics resources. Nat Protoc 4: 44–57.
42. Huang DW, Sherman BT, Lempicki RA (2009) Bioinformatics enrichment tools: paths toward the comprehensive functional analysis of large gene lists. Nucleic Acids Res 37: 1–13.
43. Weng MP, Liao BY (2010) MamPhEA: a web tool for mammalian phenotype enrichment analysis. Bioinformatics 26: 2212–2213.

44. Kupershmidt I, Su QJ, Grewal A, Sundaresh S, Halperin I, et al. (2010) Ontology-based meta-analysis of global collections of high-throughput public data. PLoS One 5.

45. Shannon P, Markiel A, Ozier O, Baliga NS, Wang JT, et al. (2003) Cytoscape: a software environment for integrated models of biomolecular interaction networks. Genome Res 13: 2498–2504.

46. Neale BM, Kou Y, Liu L, Ma'ayan A, Samocha KE, et al. (2012) Patterns and rates of exonic de novo mutations in autism spectrum disorders. Nature 485: 242–245.

47. Sakai Y, Shaw CA, Dawson BC, Dugas DV, Al-Mohtaseb Z, et al. (2011) Protein interactome reveals converging molecular pathways among autism disorders. Sci Transl Med 3: 86ra49.

48. Chow ML, Li HR, Winn ME, April C, Barnes CC, et al. (2011) Genome-wide expression assay comparison across frozen and fixed postmortem brain tissue samples. BMC Genomics 12: 449.

49. Nishimura Y, Martin CL, Vazquez-Lopez A, Spence SJ, Alvarez-Retuerto AI, et al. (2007) Genome-wide expression profiling of lymphoblastoid cell lines distinguishes different forms of autism and reveals shared pathways. Hum Mol Genet 16: 1682–1698.

50. Neale BM, Kou Y, Liu L, Ma'ayan A, Samocha KE, et al. (2012) Patterns and rates of exonic de novo mutations in autism spectrum disorders. Nature 485: 242–245.

51. Ben-David E, Shifman S (2012) Networks of neuronal genes affected by common and rare variants in autism spectrum disorders. PLoS Genet 8: e1002556.

52. Diskin SJ, Hou C, Glessner JT, Attiyeh EF, Laudenslager M, et al. (2009) Copy number variation at 1q21.1 associated with neuroblastoma. Nature 459: 987–991.

53. Eijkelkamp N, Linley JE, Baker MD, Minett MS, Cregg R, et al. (2012) Neurological perspectives on voltage-gated sodium channels. Brain 135: 2585–2612.

54. Hollander E, Wang AT, Braun A, Marsh L (2009) Neurological considerations: autism and Parkinson's disease. Psychiatry Res 170: 43–51.

55. Scheuerle A, Wilson K (2011) PARK2 copy number aberrations in two children presenting with autism spectrum disorder: further support of an association and possible evidence for a new microdeletion/microduplication syndrome. Am J Med Genet B Neuropsychiatr Genet 156B: 413–420.

56. Crespi B (2011) Autism and cancer risk. Autism Res 4: 302–310.

57. Glessner JT, Wang K, Cai G, Korvatska O, Kim CE, et al. (2009) Autism genome-wide copy number variation reveals ubiquitin and neuronal genes. Nature 459: 569–573.

58. Yaspan BL, Bush WS, Torstenson ES, Ma D, Pericak-Vance MA, et al. (2011) Genetic analysis of biological pathway data through genomic randomization. Hum Genet 129: 563–571.

59. Gilman SR, Iossifov I, Levy D, Ronemus M, Wigler M, et al. (2011) Rare de novo variants associated with autism implicate a large functional network of genes involved in formation and function of synapses. Neuron 70: 898–907.

60. Hussman JP, Chung RH, Griswold AJ, Jaworski JM, Salyakina D, et al. (2011) A noise-reduction GWAS analysis implicates altered regulation of neurite outgrowth and guidance in autism. Mol Autism 2: 1.

61. Buxbaum JD, Betancur C, Bozdagi O, Dorr NP, Elder GA, et al. (2012) Optimizing the phenotyping of rodent ASD models: enrichment analysis of mouse and human neurobiological phenotypes associated with high-risk autism genes identifies morphological, electrophysiological, neurological, and behavioral features. Mol Autism 3: 1.

62. He W, Wang Y, Liu W, Zhou CZ (2007) Crystal structure of Saccharomyces cerevisiae 6-phosphogluconate dehydrogenase Gnd1. BMC Struct Biol 7: 38.

63. Hofmann B, Hecht HJ, Flohe L (2002) Peroxiredoxins. Biol Chem 383: 347–364.

64. Immenschuh S, Baumgart-Vogt E (2005) Peroxiredoxins, oxidative stress, and cell proliferation. Antioxid Redox Signal 7: 768–777.

65. Frustaci A, Neri M, Cesario A, Adams JB, Domenici E, et al. (2012) Oxidative stress-related biomarkers in autism: systematic review and meta-analyses. Free Radic Biol Med 52: 2128–2141.

66. Ghanizadeh A, Akhondzadeh S, Hormozi M, Makarem A, Abotorabi-Zarchi M, et al. (2012) Glutathione-related factors and oxidative stress in autism, a review. Curr Med Chem 19: 4000–4005.

67. Voineagu I, Wang X, Johnston P, Lowe JK, Tian Y, et al. (2011) Transcriptomic analysis of autistic brain reveals convergent molecular pathology. Nature 474: 380–384.

Permissions

All chapters in this book were first published in PLOS ONE, by The Public Library of Science; hereby published with permission under the Creative Commons Attribution License or equivalent. Every chapter published in this book has been scrutinized by our experts. Their significance has been extensively debated. The topics covered herein carry significant findings which will fuel the growth of the discipline. They may even be implemented as practical applications or may be referred to as a beginning point for another development.

The contributors of this book come from diverse backgrounds, making this book a truly international effort. This book will bring forth new frontiers with its revolutionizing research information and detailed analysis of the nascent developments around the world.

We would like to thank all the contributing authors for lending their expertise to make the book truly unique. They have played a crucial role in the development of this book. Without their invaluable contributions this book wouldn't have been possible. They have made vital efforts to compile up to date information on the varied aspects of this subject to make this book a valuable addition to the collection of many professionals and students.

This book was conceptualized with the vision of imparting up-to-date information and advanced data in this field. To ensure the same, a matchless editorial board was set up. Every individual on the board went through rigorous rounds of assessment to prove their worth. After which they invested a large part of their time researching and compiling the most relevant data for our readers.

The editorial board has been involved in producing this book since its inception. They have spent rigorous hours researching and exploring the diverse topics which have resulted in the successful publishing of this book. They have passed on their knowledge of decades through this book. To expedite this challenging task, the publisher supported the team at every step. A small team of assistant editors was also appointed to further simplify the editing procedure and attain best results for the readers.

Apart from the editorial board, the designing team has also invested a significant amount of their time in understanding the subject and creating the most relevant covers. They scrutinized every image to scout for the most suitable representation of the subject and create an appropriate cover for the book.

The publishing team has been an ardent support to the editorial, designing and production team. Their endless efforts to recruit the best for this project, has resulted in the accomplishment of this book. They are a veteran in the field of academics and their pool of knowledge is as vast as their experience in printing. Their expertise and guidance has proved useful at every step. Their uncompromising quality standards have made this book an exceptional effort. Their encouragement from time to time has been an inspiration for everyone.

The publisher and the editorial board hope that this book will prove to be a valuable piece of knowledge for researchers, students, practitioners and scholars across the globe.

List of Contributors

Rui Zhong and Guanghua Xiao
Quantitative Biomedical Research Center, Department of Clinical Sciences, University of Texas Southwestern Medical Center, Dallas, Texas, United States of America

Jeffrey D. Allen and Yang Xie
Quantitative Biomedical Research Center, Department of Clinical Sciences, University of Texas Southwestern Medical Center, Dallas, Texas, United States of America Harold C. Simmons Comprehensive Cancer Center, University of Texas Southwestern Medical Center, Dallas, Texas, United States of America

Zalman Vaksman, Natalie C. Fonville and Hongseok Tae
Virginia Bioinformatics Institute, Virginia Tech, Blacksburg, Virginia, 24061, United States of America

Harold R. Garner
Virginia Bioinformatics Institute, Virginia Tech, Blacksburg, Virginia, 24061, United States of America Genomeon LLC, Floyd, Virginia, 24091, United States of America

Gersende Maugars and Sylvie Dufour
Muséum National d'Histoire Naturelle, Sorbonne Université s, Biology of Aquatic Organisms and Ecosystems (BOREA), Paris, France, Université Pierre et Marie Curie, Paris, France, Université Caen Basse Normandie, Caen, France, Unité Mixte de Recherche (UMR) 7208 Centre National de la Recherche Scientifique (CNRS), Paris, France, Institut de Recherche pour le Développement (IRD) 207, Paris, France

Joëlle Cohen-Tannoudji and Bruno Quérat
Université Paris Diderot, Sorbonne Paris Cité , Biologie Fonctionnelle et Adaptative (BFA), Paris, France UMR CNRS 8251, Paris, France, INSERM U1133 Physiologie de l'axe gonadotrope, Paris, France

Liming Lai and Steven X. Ge
Department of Mathematics and Statistics, South Dakota State University, Brookings, South Dakota, United States of America

Tara Wahab, Marika Hjertqvist, Ingela Hedenström and Sven Löfdahl
Public Health Agency of Sweden, Department of Microbiology, Stockholm, Sweden

Dawn N. Birdsell, Cedar L. Mitchell, David M. Wagner and Paul S. Keim
Northern Arizona University, Center for Microbial Genetics and Genomics, Flagstaff, AZ, United States of America

Eric S. Ho
Department of Biology, Lafayette College, Easton, Pennsylvania, United States of America

Joan Kuchie
New Jersey City University, Jersey City, New Jersey, United States of America

Siobain Duffy
Department of Ecology, Evolution and Natural Resources, Rutgers University, New Brunswick, New Jersey, United States of America

Jiang Bian and Mathias Brochhausen
Division of Biomedical Informatics, University of Arkansas for Medical Sciences, Little Rock, AR 72205, United States of America

Mengjun Xie
Department of Computer Science, University of Arkansas at Little Rock, Little Rock, AR 72204, United States of America

Teresa J. Hudson
Department of Psychiatry and Behavioral Sciences, University of Arkansas for Medical Sciences, Little Rock, AR 72205, United States of America Department of Veterans Affairs HSR&D Center for Mental Healthcare and Outcomes Research, Central Arkansas Veterans Healthcare System, Little Rock, AR 722205, United States of America

Hari Eswaran
Division of Biomedical Informatics, University of Arkansas for Medical Sciences, Little Rock, AR 72205, United States of America Department of Obstetrics & Gynecology Research, University of Arkansas for Medical Sciences, Little Rock, AR 72205, United States of America

Josh Hanna
Clinical and Translational Science Informatics and Technology, University of Florida, Gainesville, FL 32610, United States of America

William R. Hogan
Department of Health Outcomes & Policy, University of Florida, Gainesville, FL 32610, United States of America
Clinical and Translational Science Institute, University of Florida, Gainesville, FL 32610, United States of America

Yin Qi
Chengdu Institute of Biology, Chinese Academy of Sciences, Chengdu, China

Michael E. Sparks, Daniel Kuhar and Dawn E. Gundersen-Rindal
USDA-ARS Invasive Insect Biocontrol and Behavior Laboratory, Beltsville, Maryland, United States of America

Kent S. Shelby
USDA-ARS Biological Control of Insects Research Laboratory, Columbia, Missouri, United States of America

Weizhao Yang
Chengdu Institute of Biology, Chinese Academy of Sciences, Chengdu, China
University of Chinese Academy of Sciences, Beijing, China

Jinzhong Fu
Chengdu Institute of Biology, Chinese Academy of Sciences, Chengdu, China
Department of Integrative Biology, University of Guelph, Guelph, Ontario, Canada

Xiangkai Zhu Ge, Zihao Pan, Lin Hu, Haojin Wang, Jianjun Dai and Hongjie Fan
College of Veterinary Medicine, Nanjing Agricultural University, Nanjing, China

Jingwei Jiang and Frederick C. Leung
Bioinformatics Center, Nanjing Agricultural University, Nanjing, China
School of Biological Sciences, University of Hong Kong, Hong Kong SAR, China

Shaohui Wang
Shanghai Veterinary Research Institute, Chinese Academy of Agricultural Sciences, Shanghai, China

Matthew McKnight Croken
Department of Microbiology and Immunology, Albert Einstein College of Medicine, Bronx, New York, United States of America

Yanfen Ma
Department of Pathology, Albert Einstein College of Medicine, Bronx, New York, United States of America

Lye Meng Markillie and Galya Orr
Environmental Molecular Sciences Laboratory, Pacific Northwest National Laboratory, Richland, Washington, United States of America

Ronald C. Taylor
Computational Biology and Bioinformatics Group, Biological Sciences Division, Pacific Northwest National Laboratory, Richland, Washington, United States of America

Louis M. Weiss
Department of Pathology, Albert Einstein College of Medicine, Bronx, New York, United States of America
Department of Medicine, Albert Einstein College of Medicine, Bronx, New York, United States of America

Kami Kim
Department of Microbiology and Immunology, Albert Einstein College of Medicine, Bronx, New York, United States of America
Department of Pathology, Albert Einstein College of Medicine, Bronx, New York, United States of America
Department of Medicine, Albert Einstein College of Medicine, Bronx, New York, United States of America

Robert M. Kirkpatrick, Matt McGue, William G. Iacono and Michael B. Miller
University of Minnesota, Department of Psychology, Minneapolis, Minnesota, United States of America

Saonli Basu
University of Minnesota, School of Public Health, Division of Biostatistics, Minneapolis, Minnesota, United States of America

Alexander E. Lipka and Fei Lu
Institute for Genomic Diversity, Cornell University, Ithaca, New York, United States of America

Jerome H. Cherney
Department of Crop and Soil Sciences, Cornell University, Ithaca, New York, United States of America

Edward S. Buckler
Institute for Genomic Diversity, Cornell University, Ithaca, New York, United States of America
Agricultural Research Service, United States Department of Agriculture, Ithaca, New York, United States of America

Department of Plant Breeding and Genetics, Cornell University, Ithaca, New York, United States of America

Denise E. Costich
Institute for Genomic Diversity, Cornell University, Ithaca, New York, United States of America,

Agricultural Research Service, United States Department of Agriculture, Ithaca, New York, United States of America

Mario Tello
Centro de Biotecnología Acuícola, Departamento de Biología, Facultad de Química y Biología, Universidad de Santiago de Chile, Santiago, Chile

Michael D. Casler
Agricultural Research Service, United States Department of Agriculture, Madison, Wisconsin, United States of America
Department of Agronomy, University of Wisconsin-Madison, Madison, Wisconsin, United States of America

Paula Bustamante and Omar Orellana
Programa de Biología Celular y Molecular, ICBM, Facultad de Medicina, Universidad de Chile, Santiago, Chile

Guang Guo
Department of Sociology, the University of North Carolina at Chapel Hill, Chapel Hill, North Carolina, the United States of America
Carolina Population Center, the University of North Carolina at Chapel Hill, Chapel Hill, North Carolina, the United States of America
Carolina Center for Genome Sciences, the University of North Carolina at Chapel Hill, Chapel Hill, North Carolina, the United States of America

Lin Wang
Center for Child and Family Policy, Duke University, Durham, North Carolina, the United States of America

Hexuan Liu
Department of Sociology, the University of North Carolina at Chapel Hill, Chapel Hill, North Carolina, the United States of America
Carolina Population Center, the University of North Carolina at Chapel Hill, Chapel Hill, North Carolina, the United States of America

Thomas Randall
National Institute of Environmental Health Sciences, Research Triangle Park, North Carolina, the United States of America

Nataly Kravchenko-Balasha
NanoSystems Biology Cancer Center, Division of Chemistry, Caltech, Pasadena, California, United States of America

Simcha Simon and Iaakov Exman
Software Engineering Department, The Jerusalem College of Engineering, Azrieli, Jerusalem, Israel

F. Remacle
The Institute of Chemistry, The Hebrew University, Jerusalem, Israel
Département de Chimie, Université de Liége, Liége, Belgium

R. D. Levine
The Institute of Chemistry, The Hebrew University, Jerusalem, Israel
Department of Molecular and Medical Pharmacology, David Geffen School of Medicine, University of California Los Angeles, Los Angeles, California, United States of America

Sara Torre, Massimiliano Tattini and Silvia Fineschi
Institute for Plant Protection, Department of Biology, Agricultural and Food Sciences, The National Research Council of Italy (CNR), Sesto Fiorentino, Italy

Cecilia Brunetti
Institute for Plant Protection, Department of Biology, Agricultural and Food Sciences, The National Research Council of Italy (CNR), Sesto Fiorentino, Italy

Alessio Fini and Francesco Ferrini
Department of Agri-Food and Environmental Sciences, University of Florence, Sesto Fiorentino, Italy

Federico Sebastiani
Institute for Biosciences and BioResources, Department of Biology, Agricultural and Food Sciences, The National Research Council of Italy (CNR), Sesto Fiorentino, Italy

Jingrui Xing, Chenyao Wang, Hiroki Kimura, Yuto Takasaki, Shohko Kunimoto, Akira Yoshimi, Yukako Nakamura, Takayoshi Koide, Masahiro Banno, Itaru Kushima, Yota Uno, Takashi Okada, Branko Aleksic and Norio Ozaki
Department of Psychiatry, Nagoya University Graduate School of Medicine, Nagoya, Japan

Masashi Ikeda and Nakao Iwata
Department of Psychiatry, School of Medicine, Fujita Health University, Toyoake, Aichi, Japan

Johanna Rhodes and Matthew C. Fisher
Department of Infectious Disease Epidemiology, Imperial College London, London, United Kingdom

Mathew A. Beale
Department of Infectious Disease Epidemiology, Imperial College London, London, United Kingdom
Institute of Infection and Immunity, St. George's University of London, London, United Kingdom

Hong Li, Gustavo Glusman, Leroy Hood and Jared C. Roach
Institute for Systems Biology, Seattle, WA, United States of America

Natalie S. Coles and L. Stephen Coles
Gerontology Research Group, Los Angeles, CA, United States of America
David Geffen School of Medicine, University of California Los Angeles, Los Angeles, CA, United States of America

Glenn J. Markov, Justin D. Smith, Stuart K. Kim, Hinco J. Gierman and Kristen Fortney
Depts. of Developmental Biology and Genetics, Stanford University, Stanford, CA, United States of America

Takeshi Otowa
Department of Psychiatry, Virginia Institute for Psychiatric and Behavioral Genetics, Virginia Commonwealth University, Richmond, Virginia, United States of America
Department of Neuropsychiatry, Graduate School of Medicine, University of Tokyo, Tokyo, Japan

Brion S. Maher
Department of Mental Health, Johns Hopkins Bloomberg School of Public Health, Baltimore, Maryland, United States of America

Steven H. Aggen and John M. Hettema
Department of Psychiatry, Virginia Institute for Psychiatric and Behavioral Genetics, Virginia Commonwealth University, Richmond, Virginia, United States of America

Joseph L. McClay and Edwin J. van den Oord
Department of Pharmacy, Center for Biomarker Research and Personalized Medicine, Virginia Commonwealth University, Richmond, Virginia, United States of America

Catarina Correia and Astrid M. Vicente
Departamento de Promoção da Saúde e Doenças não Transmissíveis, Instituto Nacional de Saúde Doutor Ricardo Jorge, 1649-016 Lisboa, Portugal
Center for Biodiversity, Functional & Integrative Genomics, Faculty of Sciences, University of Lisbon, 1749-016 Lisbon, Portugal
Instituto Gulbenkian de Ciência, 2780-156 Oeiras, Portugal

Guiomar Oliveira
Unidade Neurodesenvolvimento e Autismo, Centro de Desenvolvimento, Hospital Pediátrico (HP) do Centro Hospitalar e Universitário de Coimbra (CHUC), 3000-602 Coimbra, Portugal
Centro de Investigação e Formação Clinica do HP-CHUC, 3000-602 Coimbra, Portugal
Faculdade de Medicina da Universidade de Coimbra, 3000-548 Coimbra, Portugal

Index

Printed in the USA
CPSIA information can be obtained
at www.ICGtesting.com
JSHW051431221024
72173JS00006B/1437